Lecture Notes in Artificial Intelligence 822

Subseries of Lecture Notes in Computer Science
Edited by J. G. Carbonell and J. Siekmann

Lecture Notes in Computer Science

Edited by G. Goos and J. Hartmanis

Frank Pfenning (Ed.)

Logic Programming and Automated Reasoning

5th International Conference, LPAR '94
Kiev, Ukraine, July 16-22, 1994
Proceedings

Springer-Verlag
Berlin Heidelberg New York
London Paris Tokyo
Hong Kong Barcelona
Budapest

Series Editors

Jaime G. Carbonell
School of Computer Science, Carnegie Mellon University
Schenley Park, Pittsburgh, PA 15213-3890, USA

Jörg Siekmann
University of Saarland
German Research Center for Artificial Intelligence (DFKI)
Stuhlsatzenhausweg 3, D-66123 Saarbrücken, Germany

Volume Editor

Frank Pfenning
Department of Computer Science, Carnegie Mellon University
Pittsburgh, PA 15213-3891, USA

CR Subject Classification (1991):I.2.3, F.4.1, D.1.6

ISBN 3-540-58216-9 Springer-Verlag Berlin Heidelberg New York
ISBN 0-387-58216-9 Springer-Verlag New York Berlin Heidelberg

CIP data applied for.

Printed in Germany

Typesetting: Camera ready by author
SPIN: 10130483 45/3140-543210 - Printed on acid-free paper

Preface

This volume contains the papers presented at the Fifth International Conference on Logic Programming and Automated Reasoning (LPAR'94) held from July 16–22 aboard the "Marshal Koshevoi" on the Dnieper near Kiev, Ukraine. The LPAR conference is held annually in the former Soviet Union. It brings together researchers of the closely related fields of logic programming and automated reasoning, covering all subareas of those fields. Proceedings of previous conferences are available as Spinger-Verlag Lecture Notes in Artificial Intelligence volumes 592, 624, and 698.

Forty-seven papers from all continents were submitted, among which the program committee selected twenty-four for presentation at the conference. Each paper was reviewed by at least three referees. I would like to thank the members of the program committee and the additional referees for their excellent work in reviewing the submissions and ensuring a program of the highest quality. Besides the 24 contributed papers, the scientific program of LPAR'94 included 3 invited talks and 4 advanced tutorials. I would like to thank Manuel Hermenegildo, Michel Parigot, and Andrei Voronkov for their invited talks and Christine Paulin-Mohring, Hoon Hong, Kryzstof Apt & Roland Bol, and Michael Gelfond for their advanced tutorials.

Many people were involved in the organization of LPAR'94. First and foremost, I wish to thank Andrei Voronkov, the local arrangements chair, for his untiring efforts on behalf of the conference and also his personal financial support. Carnegie Mellon University has also contributed financially; other applications for sponsorship are pending at this time. I would also like to acknowledge the crucial help of Eugene Dantsin, Anatoli Degtyarev, Igor Romanenko, Konstantin Vershinin, and Alexander Zhezherun in organizing the conference.

Pittsburgh, Pennsylvania
April 1994

Frank Pfenning
Program Chair, LPAR'94

Program Committee

David Basin, MPI Saarbrücken
Antonio Brogi, University of Pisa
Philippe Codognet, INRIA Rocquencourt
Saumya Debray, University of Arizona
Melvin Fitting, Lehmann College
Steffen Hölldobler, TU Dresden
Masami Hagiya, University of Tokyo
Michael Hanus, MPI Saarbrücken
Claude Kirchner, INRIA Lorraine
Jack Minker, University of Maryland
Grigori Mints, Stanford
Tobias Nipkow, TU Munich
Christine Paulin-Mohring, ENS Lyon
Frank Pfenning, Carnegie Mellon University
Lutz Plümer, University of Bonn
Vladimir Sazonov, PSI Pereslavl-Zalesski, Russia
Danny de Schreye, Catholic University Leuven
Dana Scott, Carnegie Mellon University
Gert Smolka, DFKI Saarbrücken
Sergei Soloviev, Aarhus University
Konstantin Vershinin, Institute of Cybernetics, Kiev
Andrei Voronkov, University of Uppsala
Mark Wallace, ECRC Munich
Lincoln Wallen, Oxford University

Local Arangements

Andrei Voronkov, University of Uppsala

Organizing Committee

Eugene Dantsin (co-chair)
Konstantin Vershinin (co-chair)
Anatoli Degtyarev
Igor Romanenko
Andrei Voronkov
Alexander Zhezherun

Reviewers

Alexander Andreev
Egon Börger
Jonas Barklund
Antje Beringer
Peter Bigot
A. Bockmayr
S. Brüning
Paola Bruscoli
Christoph Brzoska
Bart Demoen
Daniel Diaz
Uwe Egly
Thom Fruehwirth
Carmen Gervet
Parke Godfrey
Gerd Gröeger
U. Hans
A. Herold
Claus Hintermeier
G. Janssens
Patricia Johann
Nils Klarlund
Stefan Lüttringhaus-Kappel
Evelina Lamma
Michael Leuschel
A. P. Lisitsa
Yuan Liu
Peter Madden
S. Martini
Micha Meier
Paola Mello
Eric Monfroy
Anne Mulkers
Giuseppe Nardiello
Shinya Nishizaki
D. Pedreschi
Martin Protzen
Christophe Ringeissen
Igor Romanenko
Vladimir Rudenko
Carolina Ruiz
Yozo Toda
Franco Turini
Jörg Würtz
Joerg Zimmermann

Contents

Generalization and Reuse of Tactic Proofs

Amy Felty and Douglas Howe

AT&T Bell Laboratories, 600 Mountain Ave., Murray Hill, NJ 07974, USA.

Abstract. A *tactic proof* is a tree-structured sequent proof where steps may be justified by tactic programs. We describe a prototype of a generic interactive theorem-proving system that supports the construction and manipulation of tactic proofs containing metavariables. The emphasis is on *proof reuse*. Examples of proof reuse are proof by analogy and reconstruction of partial proofs as part of recovering from errors in definitions or in proof strategies. Our reuse operations involve solving higher-order unification problems, and their effectiveness relies on a proof-generalization step that is done after a tactic is applied. The prototype is implemented in λProlog.

1 Introduction

Most interactive theorem proving systems support some notion of "high-level" proof, although this is usually informal. Often it is a textual transcript of the commands that were used to direct the prover. It can also be a composite tactic program formed by combining all the individual tactics used to prove a theorem. Informal or not, in practice such objects serve as explanations of formal proofs and as the basis for useful proof-manipulating operations.

One general way to directly support high-level proof objects is to extend tree-structured sequent proofs so that a step in a sequent proof can be justified either by an inference rule of the implemented logic, or by a program e whose execution produces a partial proof that justifies the inference, providing steps that lead from the antecedent sequents of the inference to the concluding sequent.

Because most interactive proofs are conducted top-down, we restrict the program e to consist of a program e', called a *tactic*, together with an input goal g. We call proofs where steps may be justified by tactics *tactic proofs*. If we also require that g be identical to the conclusion g' of the inference justified by a tactic, then this proof structure is the same as that of Nuprl [1]. We do not make this restriction because it is incompatible with the use of metavariables in proofs.

The focus of this paper is the reuse of tactic proofs. One obvious example of proof reuse is proof by analogy, where an existing proof is adapted to a new theorem. A more common application in interactive systems is in error recovery. During the course of a proof it is often necessary to make a change that affects the part of the proof that has already been built. Such a change might be to the statement of the goal, to a definition the proof depends on, to an induction hypothesis or to a previous step in the proof. The problem is to recover as much of the existing (partial) proof as possible after such a change.

One way to reuse proof steps after a change is to *replay* them. In the setting of tactic proofs, this can be done by reconstructing the proof tree by successively reapplying all the tactics in a top-down fashion.

There are two problems with this approach. First, it can be time consuming. Second, it is not a robust procedure for many of the kinds of local changes typical in error recovery. As a simple example, suppose a step in the proof used a tactic that just repeatedly applied &-introduction until no conjunctions remained in the succedent of the goal sequent. In particular, suppose the tactic refined the goal $\vdash \phi_1 \,\&\, \phi_2 \,\&\, \phi_3$ to the three subgoals $\vdash \phi_1$, $\vdash \phi_2$, and $\vdash \phi_3$.

Now suppose that ϕ_1 has been changed to $\phi_4 \,\&\, \phi_5$. When the replay of the steps in the original proof gets to the above tactic step, the goal is now $\vdash (\phi_4 \,\&\, \phi_5) \,\&\, \phi_2 \,\&\, \phi_3$. Rerunning the tactic produces subgoals $\vdash \phi_4$, $\vdash \phi_5$, $\vdash \phi_2$, and $\vdash \phi_3$. In order to continue replay, we need to know that the subproofs for the last two of the original three subgoals should be used for the last two of the new subgoals. In this simple case it is obvious how to make this association, but in general, when there can be other changes, it is not.

The basic idea underlying our solution to this problem is simple, and involves relaxing the requirement on how a tactic relates to the step it justifies. In the above example, the step is determined by the execution of the tactic: the tactic, when applied to the goal, produces a proof tree whose concluding sequent, or *conclusion*, is the goal, and whose non-axiomatic leaf sequents, or *premises*, are the subgoals. However, the proof produced by the tactic may justify many more inferences than the one that is determined this way. For example, if the proof is the obvious one involving just &-introduction rules, then the identity of the formulas ϕ_i is irrelevant.

We capture this kind of generality by performing proof generalization, making use of metavariables in proofs. Inference rules of the logic are implemented as schemas with metavariables in a manner very similar to what is found in Isabelle [10]. A rule schema justifies any inference which can be obtained by instantiating metavariables in the schema. When a tactic produces a proof using these rule schemas, we can generalize to find a "minimal" proof using these schemas. We then allow this tactic to justify any step corresponding to an instance of this minimal proof.

Consider again the &-introduction example. The generalization of the proof produced by the tactic has conclusion $H \vdash A \,\&\, B \,\&\, C$ and premises $H \vdash A$, $H \vdash B$, and $H \vdash C$. Instantiating H to the empty hypothesis list and A, B, C to ϕ_1, ϕ_2, ϕ_3 yields the original inference. When a conjunct is added as above, the same tactic step can be used by taking A to be $\phi_4 \,\&\, \phi_5$. The number of subgoals remains the same.

This example also shows a tradeoff we have made between generality and intelligibility. After the conjunction is added, in the step where repeated &-introduction is applied, there will be a subgoal where another &-introduction could be applied. In other words, it may appear as though the tactic did not progress as far as it might have, since if we reran the tactic on the new goal there would be four subgoals instead of three. The situation is worse when tactics explicitly refer to components of the sequent. For example, if the tactic is `Elim 1`, which applies &-elimination to the first hypothesis, then the generalized step is simply the &-elimination rule. This means that the proof could be modified so that the eliminated hypothesis is the second one. However, explicit references to hypothesis numbers is typically regarded as bad style since it makes proof replay much less robust. We believe that the &-introduction example is more typical. In any case, the original input goal for the tactic is retained, so when reading a proof it is still possible to precisely understand the connection between a tactic and the step it justifies.

We have implemented a prototype of an interactive theorem proving system based on these ideas. The system includes a command interface for building and viewing tactic proofs. We have also implemented a reuse command that attempts to reuse a proof when the statement of the root goal is changed.

λProlog [9] is both the implementation language and the tactic programming language in our system. Using ML as an implementation language would give us a greater degree of control over unification and metavariable instantiation, but a substantial amount of work would be required to implement λProlog's built-in support for metavariables, variable-binding and backtracking.

The design of our system is generic, in the sense that it can easily accommodate most logics that can be specified in the general style of LF [5]. The exact style of encoding of logics in our system is very similar to [3], except that we have made a commitment to sequent-calculus presentations.

The next section describes the structure of proofs in our system and gives a somewhat abstract account of proof generalization and reuse. This is followed by an example session with our prover, a section giving some implementation details and, finally, a conclusion discussing some extensions and giving a few further comparisons with related work.

2 Proofs

This section gives a simplified account of the proof data-structure. A few of the more important differences between this account and the implementation are given at the end of the section.

Two of the principle constituents of proofs are *goals* and *tactics*. Goals are intended to be sequents in the logic being implemented (the "object logic"), and tactics are programs from some programming language. To make the presentation simple, and to keep the description here close to what has been implemented, we assume that both goals and tactics are represented as terms in the simply-typed λ-calculus. In our implementation, object logics are encoded using λ-terms and tactics are programs in λProlog, a language whose programs are all λ-terms.

Let Λ be the set of terms of the typed λ-calculus over some set of base types and some set of constants. We identify $\alpha\beta\eta$-equal terms. Thus, if there is a substitution σ such that $\sigma(e) = \sigma(e')$, then e and e' have a higher-order unifier. We distinguish a base type and define the set of *goals* to be the set of all terms in Λ of this type.

Metavariables in this setting are simply the free variables of a goal. We will use capital letters to stand for metavariables. Ordinary variables in our representation are bound by λ-abstractions. See the implementation section for details on this representation.

A *proof* is a tree of goals where each node has associated with it a *justification.* The justification says how the goal can be inferred from its children. We will describe the kinds of justifications below. For now, assume that for any justification j there is an associated pair $s(j) = (g, \overline{g})$, called a *step*, where g is a goal and $\overline{g}$ is a sequence $g_1, \ldots, g_n$ $(n \geq 0)$ of goals. g is the *conclusion* of the step $(g, \overline{g})$, and g_i, $1 \leq i \leq n$, is the ith *premise* of the step. Define $concl(s(j)) = g$ and $prem_i(s(j)) = g_i$, $1 \leq i \leq n$. We place the following restriction on proofs. Let g be a node in the tree, let j be its associated justification, and let $\overline{g}$ be the sequence of children of g (in left-to-right order). Write $s(j) = (g', \overline{g}')$. We require that there be a substitution σ such that $\sigma(g') = g$ and $\sigma(\overline{g}') = \overline{g}$ (using the obvious extension of substitution to sequences of goals).

Thus $s(j)$ can be thought of as a rule schema, with premises $\overline{g}'$ and conclusion g', and the valid instances of the schema are obtained by substituting for metavariables. For example, one of the allowed justifications in our implementation of first-order logic is the constant *and_i* (for &-introduction), and

$$s(and\_i) \quad = \quad (H \vdash A \,\&\, B, \;\; (H \vdash A, \; H \vdash B)),$$

which corresponds to the rule schema

$$\frac{H \vdash A \quad H \vdash B}{H \vdash A \,\&\, B.}$$

Note that proof trees are preserved under *instantiation:* if σ is a substitution, p is a proof, and $\sigma(p)$ is obtained by replacing every goal g in p by $\sigma(g)$ (and keeping the same associated justifications), then $\sigma(p)$ is a proof.

There are three kinds of justifications. One corresponds to primitive rules of the object logic and one to tactics. There is also a justification j_{prem}, where $s(j_{prem})$ is $(G, ())$. This corresponds to a trivial "rule" which infers any goal from no premises. Goals in a proof tree that have j_{prem} as their justification are called *premises* of the proof. Thus proof trees represent incomplete proofs in the object logic. The root goal of a proof is called its *conclusion.*

Justifications corresponding to inference rules of the object logic are represented as a set $R \subset \Lambda$ of constants called *rule names.* For each $r \in R$ there is an associated step $s(r)$.

The third form of justification is the *tactic justification.* Tactics are represented as a subset T of Λ. A tactic is a program that takes a goal as argument and, if it produces an output, returns a proof and a substitution. For each goal g and tactic $e \in T$ such that e produces an output on input g, there is a justification $j_{e,g}$.

Let p be the proof returned by e on input g. One possibility for $s(j_{e,g})$ is to take the conclusion and premises of p [4]. Since proofs are closed under instantiation, any instance of this step is sound. However, this is restrictive. If there is a proof p' of which p is an instance, then the step derived from p' is also sound and is more general. So, we define $s(j_{e,g})$ to be a "minimal" p' having p as an instance. We call p' a *generalization* of p.

We can cast the problem of finding this generalization p' as a unification problem. For each node u in p, let j^u be its associated justification. Without loss of generality, we may assume that $s(j^u)$ and $s(j^v)$ have no metavariables in common when $u \neq v$. To find a minimal p', we find a minimal unifier σ such that

$$\sigma(prem_i(s(j^u)) = \sigma(concl(s(j^v))$$

for all nodes u and v of p such that v is the ith child of u. We then obtain p' from p by replacing the goal at each node u by $\sigma(concl(s(j^u)))$.

In general, most-general higher-order unifiers do not exist, and so the definition of $s(j_{e,g})$ is under-specified. The implementation computes generalizations by solving the above unification problems. The exact choice of σ is implementation dependent.

The generalization step in the definition of $s(j_{e,g})$ is exploited in the procedure for proof reuse. This procedure reuses the existing justifications in a proof tree to justify a tree with different goals. The particular reuse procedure we have implemented is almost identical to the generalization procedure. The only substantial difference is that we also require that

$$\sigma(g) = \sigma(concl(s(j^r)))$$

where r is the root of the (sub-) proof we wish to reuse and g is the new root goal we want to reuse the proof for.

Proof trees are typically extended by *refining* a premise with a tactic. Tactic refinement works as follows. Let g be a premise of a proof p, and suppose that the tactic e with argument g returns a proof p' and a substitution σ. Let g' be the conclusion of p' and let $\overline{g}'$ be the sequence of premises of p'. If $g' = \sigma(g)$, then the *refinement of* p *at* g *using* e is obtained from $\sigma(p)$ by replacing the premise justification of $\sigma(g)$ by $j_{e,g}$, and adding, as children of $\sigma(g)$, nodes $g'_1, \ldots, g'_n$ each with j_{prem} as its justification.

For example, if g is $\vdash X = 0$ and if e is a tactic that instantiates X with 0, we might have $\sigma(X) = 0$, $\vdash 0 = 0$ for g', and $(\vdash 0 = 0)$ for $\overline{g}'$. The act of refining will replace X by 0 in the entire proof, and produce a new premise $\vdash 0 = 0$ as a child of the old premise.

The most important difference between the implementation and the above account of tactics in proofs is that in the implementation, the logic variables of λProlog are used for metavariables. This means that tactics do not need to explicitly return a substitution; instantiation of metavariables is part of the execution of a tactic.

The justifications associated with the nodes of a proof are stored along with the goals in the implemented proof data structure. A tactic justification $j_{e,g}$ is implemented as a tuple containing the text of the program e along with the goal g. Also, to avoid having to recompute the application of e on g every time $s(j_{e,g})$ is needed, we also put into the tuple the *justification tree* that results from erasing the goals from the proof produced by e on input g. The justification tree is all that is needed to perform the generalization step for $s(j_{e,g})$. The tactic and its argument are retained in addition to the justification tree because they are informative to a user.

3 An Example Session

The following session illustrates interaction with our system, including refinement commands, navigation within a proof, as well as the **reuse** command. We attempt to prove the simple formula $(pb \vee qa) \& (pa \supset ra) \& (ra \supset qb) \supset \exists x\, qx$ from first-order logic. The example is contrived, though it illustrates the main operations. The tactics used here implement the basic inference rules of a sequent calculus. The lines beginning with "!:" are for user input. All metavariables are printed as capital letters.

We begin the session by entering the following query to λProlog.

```
prove ((p b or q a) and (p a imp r a) and (r a imp q b)
       imp (exists X\ (q X))).
```

This results in a prompt for input. The user supplies the commands to run the `intro` tactic and then `and_e*_tac` to eliminate the conjunctions in the hypothesis, using the `next` command in between to go to the next premise in the tree.

```
!: tactic intro.
Address:
|- (p b or q a) and (p a imp r a) and (r a imp q b)
    imp exists X\ (q X)
By tactic intro
(p b or q a) and (p a imp r a) and (r a imp q b) |- exists X\ (q X)

!: next.
Address: 1
(p b or q a) and (p a imp r a) and (r a imp q b) |- exists X\ (q X)
By ?

!: tactic and_e*_tac.
Address: 1
(p b or q a) and (p a imp r a) and (r a imp q b) |- exists X\ (q X)
By tactic and_e*_tac
(p b or q a) and (p a imp r a) and (r a imp q b), p b or q a,
(p a imp r a) and (r a imp q b), p a imp r a, r a imp q b
|- exists X\ (q X)
```

After running each tactic, the node of the proof is redisplayed. The output above shows the address of the node of the proof being displayed (a list of integers, empty in the first case), followed by the goal at the node, its justification, following the word By and the subgoals of the node.

In displaying the remainder of the session, we leave off the hypotheses that are not important, and sometimes leave out the output of navigation commands. Continuing the proof, the user applies a tactic that applies several inference rules.

```
!: next.
Address: 1 1
p b or q a, p a imp r a, r a imp q b |- exists X\ (q X)
By ?

!: tactic (then or_e_tac (then intro (try close_tac))).
Address: 1 1
p b or q a, p a imp r a, r a imp q b |- exists X\ (q X)
By tactic then or_e_tac (then intro (try close_tac))
p b, p a imp r a, r a imp q b |- q T
```

Here the proof was split into two branches by eliminating the disjunction and the second was completed. Note that introducing an existential quantifier introduces a metavariable T which can be filled in later.

At this point, the user realizes that the original goal had an error. The b in (p b) should have been an a. Our command language includes a **transform** command to transform one proof to another. It takes as an argument the transformation predicate. The **reuse** predicate copies the structure of the current proof to build a proof of the new formula.

```
!: root.
!: transform
    (reuse ((p a or q a) and (p a imp r a) and (r a imp q b))
           imp (exists X\ (q X)).
!: next.
Address: 1 1 1
p a, p a imp r a, r a imp q b |- q T
By ?
```

The operation succeeds and one subgoal remains. The proof is completed with the (repeat backchain) tactic.

```
!: tactic backchain.
Address: 1 1 1
p a, p a imp r a, r a imp q b |- q T
By tactic backchain
!: next.
No next premise: Proof Complete!
```

The application of **reuse** in this example works as follows. Let ϕ be the argument given to **reuse**. At the point **reuse** is applied, the current proof has four nodes, u_1, u_2, u_3 and u_4, with u_i the parent of u_{i+1}, $1 \leq i \leq 3$. Call the corresponding justifications j_i. j_1, j_2 and j_3 are tactic justifications, and u_4 is a premise. Let $s(j_i) = (g_i, (h_i))$, $1 \leq i \leq 3$. The reuse procedure uses λProlog's built-in unification to compute a unifier σ solving the equations

$$\phi = g_1, \;\; h_1 = g_2, \;\; h_2 = g_3, \;\; h_3 = G.$$

The new proof has the same justifications, but its goals are, from root to leaf, $\sigma(g_1)$, $\sigma(g_2)$, $\sigma(g_3)$, and $\sigma(G)$.

Reuse employs proof generalization in computing the steps $s(j_i)$. For example, consider j_2. This corresponds to the tactic **and_e*_tac**. The justification tree stored in j_2 consists of a three node tree with rule name *and_e* as the justification at the root and at the only child of the root, followed by j_{prem} at the leaf. This justification will justify any inference using exactly two consecutive applications of the &-elimination rule. The steps for the two rule justifications are $(g_1, (h_1))$ and $(g_2, (h_2))$, where

$$\begin{aligned} g_i &= H_i, A_i \mathbin{\&} B_i, H_i' \vdash C_i \\ h_i &= H_i, A_i \mathbin{\&} B_i, A_i, B_i, H_i' \vdash C_i, \end{aligned}$$

$i = 1, 2$. The generalization procedure attempts to compute a unifier σ for the equation $h_1 = g_2$ (the equation involving the premise is trivial). The result of computing $s(j_2)$ is then $(\sigma(g_1), \sigma(h_2))$.

A complication here is that this unification problem gives rise to unification constraints. λProlog will compute a substitution that is not a unifier, and leave some equations as constraints on further instantiation of metavariables. The main cause of constraints is our representation of hypothesis lists using function composition (as is done in Isabelle) so that higher-order unification can be used to handle metavariables standing for subsequences of hypothesis lists. For example, H_i and H_i' above are of functional type and range over hypothesis lists. These constraints are not a major problem for us because we always immediately use the result of generalization in some more specific context, as in the reuse example above where unification involves the goal ϕ. See Section 4 for the precise form of the step associated with the &-elimination rule.

4 Implementation

This section describes the implementation of our system. It starts with a brief account of the implementation language.

4.1 λProlog

λProlog is a partial implementation of higher-order hereditary Harrop (hohh) formulas [9] which extend positive Horn clauses in essentially two ways. First, they allow implication and universal quantification in the bodies of clauses, in addition to conjunctions, disjunctions, and existentially quantified formulas. In this paper, we only consider the extension to universal quantification. Second, they replace first-order terms with the more expressive simply typed λ-terms and allow quantification over predicate and function symbols. The application of λ-terms is handled by β-conversion, while the unification of λ-terms is handled by higher-order unification.

The terms of the language are the terms of Λ where the set of base types includes at least the type symbol o, which denotes the type of logic programming propositions. In this section, we adopt the syntax of λProlog. Free variables are represented by tokens with an upper case initial letter and constants are represented by tokens with a lower case initial letter. Bound variables can begin with either an upper or lower case letter. λ-abstraction is represented using backslash as an infix symbol.

Logical connectives and quantifiers are introduced into λ-terms by introducing suitable constants with their types. In particular, we introduce constants for conjunction (`,`), disjunctions (`;`), and (reverse) implication (`:-`) having type `o -> o -> o`. The constant for universal quantification (`pi`) is given type `(A -> o) -> o` for each type replacing the "type variable" `A`. A function symbol whose target type is `o`, other than a logical constant, will be considered a *predicate*. A λ-term of type `o` such that the head of its $\beta\eta$-long form is not a logical constant will be called an *atomic formula*. A *goal* is a formula that does not contain implication. A *clause* is a closed formula of the form (`pi` x_1\...(`pi` x_n\(A:- G))) where G is a goal formula and A is an atomic formula with a constant as its head. In presenting clauses, we leave off outermost universal quantifiers, and write (A:- G).

Search in λProlog is similar to that in Prolog. Universal quantification in goals (`pi x`\G) is implemented by introducing a new parameter `c` and trying to prove [`c`/`x`]G. Unification is restricted so that if G contains logic variables, the new constant `c` will not appear in the terms eventually instantiated for those logic variables.

λProlog permits a degree of polymorphism by allowing type declarations to contain type variables (written as capital letters). It is also possible to build new types using type constructors. Two examples used in our implementation are `list` and `pair`, along with the standard constructors `nil` and `::` for lists and `p` for pairs. The map function on lists, for example, is defined as followed.

```
type    map             (A -> B -> o) -> list A -> list B -> o.
map F nil nil.
map F (A::L) (B::M) :- F A B, map F L M.
```

Several non-logical features of λProlog are used in our implementation. We use the cut (`!`) operator to eliminate backtracking points. For example, we implement `var` and `notvar` predicates for variable tests using `!` and `fail`. In addition, we use a primitive `make_abs` described in [4] which takes any term and replaces all logic variables with λ-bindings at the top-level. It has type `A -> abs A -> list mvar -> o` where `abs` is a type constructor introduced for this purpose and the third argument is a list containing all of the logic variables in the order they occurred in the term. We use this operation to "freeze" the degree of instantiation of a term as well as to implement a `match` procedure. In order to correctly freeze a term, this operation also freezes a record of any unification constraints on the logic variables occurring in the term. In our `match` procedure the pattern may contain variables with constraints, however the instance may not. An explicit check is included in the implementation, causing `match` to fail when this requirement is not met. To avoid any problems in our implementation, we make the restriction that logic variables in proofs cannot contain constraints.

This is not a severe restriction since, in practice, any constraints that arise get solved before calling the primitive proof construction operations.

4.2 Encoding Logics

As in [3], an object logic is encoded by giving a set of constants with their types to specify the syntax and a set of clauses specifying the inference rules. Similar encodings are also given in [10, 5]. We introduce the types **form**, **seq**, and **prule_name** for formulas, sequents, and primitive rule names, respectively. To represent hypothesis lists of sequents we introduce a type `lform` and an an element constructor **e** of type `form -> (lform -> lform)`. Lists of formulas have type `(lform -> lform)`. The following constants are provided for the specification of object logics.

```
type   |-          (lform -> lform) -> form -> seq.
type   aseq        (A -> seq) -> seq.
type   prule_def   prule_name -> seq -> list seq -> o.
```

The predicate **prule_def** associates a (sequent version of a) step with each rule name. λ-abstracted sequents are also sequents: the constructor **aseq** converts a term `x\(S x)` into a sequent. In a sequent, **aseq** `x\(S x)`, the bound variable `x` represents a new object level variable whose scope is the sequent `(S x)`.

To specify first-order logic, we introduce the type `tm` for first-order terms, constants **and**, `or`, and **imp** of type `form -> form -> form`, and constants **forall** and **exists** of type `(tm -> form) -> form`. The following **prule_def** clauses specify some of the rules of a sequent calculus for intuitionistic logic.

```
prule_def close (|- (u\ (H1 (e A (H2 u)))) A) nil.
prule_def and_i (|- H (A and B)) ((|- H A)::(|- H B)::nil).
prule_def imp_i (|- H (A imp B)) ((|- (u\ (e A (H u))) B)::nil).
prule_def forall_i (|- H (forall A)) ((aseq (x\ (|- H (A x))))::nil).
prule_def exists_i (|- H (exists A)) ((|- H (A T))::nil).
prule_def and_e (|- (u\ (H1 (e (A and B) (H2 u)))) C)
          ((|- (u\ (H1 (e (A and B) (e A (e B (H2 u)))))) C)::nil).
```

Note the use of λ-abstraction and the **aseq** constructor to represent the eigenvariable condition on the all-introduction rule. In contrast, the exists-introduction rule introduces a new logic variable `T` for the substitution term.

4.3 Proofs and Tactics

Below are the basic types and operations for our implementation of proofs.

```
kind  goal        type.
type  bgoal       (l seq -> l seq) -> seq -> goal.
type  agoal       (A -> goal) -> goal.
kind  step        type.
type  step        goal -> list goal -> step.
kind  proof       type.
```

```
kind  just            type.
type  just_step       just -> step -> o.
type  aproof          (A -> proof) -> proof.
type  one_step_proof  step -> just -> proof -> o.
type  compose_proofs  proof -> list proof -> proof -> o.
type  prem_just       just -> o.
type  prule_just      prule_name -> just -> o.
type  tactic_to_just  (goal -> proof -> o)
                        -> goal -> proof -> just -> o.
```

These are intended to form abstract data types and an abstract interface for justifications and proofs. All of our operations for building and modifying proofs do so via the above operations.

The |-, **aseq**, and **prule_def** constants defined earlier are also part of the abstract data types. The type **goal** is the type of goals. Goals are essentially sequents. They also have an additional argument, a list of sequents, which provides more flexibility in using derived rules as is done in Isabelle. We do not use this feature here, so we omit operations which use it. λ-abstracted goals are also goals. The type **step** and the constructor **step** implement the steps of Section 2.

The predicate **just_step** translates a justification to a step. It is defined by case analysis on the three kinds of justifications discussed in Section 2. There is one constructor for each kind of justification. In addition, the type **jtree** and two constructors are introduced for building justification trees, which form a part of tactic justifications.

```
type  prem    just.
type  prule   prule_name -> just.
type  trule   abs (pair (goal -> proof -> o) goal) -> jtree -> just.
kind  jtree   type.
type  jtree   just -> list jtree -> jtree.
type  ajtree  (A -> jtree) -> jtree.
```

Tactic justifications have three parts. The first is a tactic, which is a predicate of type `goal -> proof -> o`, and the second is the tactic argument. These two form an "abstracted" pair. Since the logic variables of λProlog are used for metavariables, we cannot simply directly store the tactic argument in the justification because subsequent instantiations of metavariables in the proof might change it. So, when a tactic justification is created, the components have their logic variables "abstracted out", *i.e.*, bound by λ-abstractions, to prevent them from being instantiated by further proof operations. The **make_abs** operation described earlier is used for this purpose. The third component of a tactic justification is the justification tree. A justification tree is either a pair of a justification and a list of justification trees, or it is a λ-abstracted justification tree where, as in sequents and goals, λ-abstracted variables represent object level variables. In the current implementation, because primitive rules do not take arguments, there can be no metavariables in justification trees.

The implementation of **just_step**, along with its auxiliary predicates is as follows.

```
just_step prem (step G nil).
just_step (prule N) S :- prule_step N S.
just_step (trule TacAp JT) S :- tactic_step JT S.
prule_step N (step G Gs) :-
   prule_def N S Ss, seq_goal S G, map seq_goal Ss Gs.
type  alist    (A -> list B) -> list B.
tactic_step JT (step G Gs) :- jtree_prems G JT AGs, map_lam AGs Gs.
jtree_prems (agoal G) (ajtree JT) (alist Gs) :-
   pi x\ (jtree_prems (G x) (JT x) (Gs x)).
jtree_prems G (jtree J JTs) (G::nil) :- J = prem, !.
jtree_prems G (jtree J JTs) Prems :-
   just_step J (step G Gs), map3 jtree_prems Gs JTs Gss,
   map map_lam Gss Gss1, flatten Gss1 Prems.
```

The predicate seq_goal is used by prule_step to translate a sequent to a goal. The predicate jtree_prems is used by tactic_step and performs the generalization step described in Section 2 on the input justification tree, but instead of building the proof, retains only the final conclusion and premise goals. Since there may be more than one way to unify the premise of one step with the conclusion of the next, the first solution found by λProlog will be the one chosen, and subsequent unifiers will be enumerated upon backtracking. However, for our example object logic, there will always be a single unifier at each step, though it will have possibly many constraints on it. Subsequent unification or matching with a specific step generally solves these constraints. An alist constructor and two list operations map_lam and flatten are used in these predicates. Abstraction over goals and justification trees is mapped to abstraction over a list of goals. The abstractions are pushed inward to each goal in the list by the map_lam predicate. The flatten predicate is the usual list operation to flatten a list of lists to a single list.

The definition of proofs as well as the one_step_proof predicate and its auxiliary operation goal_prem are defined below.

```
type  proof           goal -> just -> list proof -> proof.
one_step_proof (step G Gs) J (proof G J Ps) :-
   just_step J S, match S (step G Gs), map goal_prem Gs Ps.
goal_prem (bgoal L S) (proof (bgoal L S) prem nil).
goal_prem (agoal G) (aproof P) :- pi x\ (goal_prem (G x) (P x)).
```

Proofs are built using the proof constructor whose arguments are a goal, a justification, and the subproofs at the child nodes. This constructor is hidden. Three ways of building proofs are provided to the user. One is to use aproof to turn an abstracted proof into a proof. The second way to build proofs is to construct a one-step proof from a step and a justification. The query (one_step_proof S J P) computes the step corresponding to the justification J, checks that the step S=(step G Gs) is an instance, then produces a proof whose root has goal G and justification J, and whose children are premises with goals from the list Gs. The premises may use the aproof constructor. This would be the case if, for example, J were the justification for the rule forall_i. For instance, the query:

```
one_step_proof (step (bgoal (|- (u\ u) (forall x\ (q x))))
   ((agoal x\ (bgoal (|- (u\ u) (q x)))))::nil)) (prule forall_i) P
```

returns the following value for P:

```
(proof (bgoal (|- (u\ u) (forall x\ (q x)))) (prule forall_i)
  ((aproof x\ (proof (bgoal (|- (u\ u) (q x))) prem nil))::nil)).
```

The final way to construct proofs is with compose_proofs which attaches the members of a list of proofs at the premises of another proof. We do not show its implementation here. It is used in the implementation of then, a combinator for sequencing tactics. Some care was taken with this operation in order to make tactics efficient. In particular, it produces a variant representation of a proof that delays actual computation of the composition. Often the actual composition never needs to be performed, and when it does, it will usually be in the context of other delayed compositions, and grouped compositions can be handled much more efficiently.

There is one predicate for constructing each of the three kinds of justifications.

```
prem_just prem.
prule_just R (prule R).
tactic_to_just T G P (trule TacAp JT) :-
   var JT, !, make_abs (p T G) TacAp MVars, T G P, proof_jtree P JT.
proof_jtree (aproof P) (ajtree JT) :- !,
   pi x\ (proof_jtree (P x) (JT x)).
proof_jtree (proof G J Ps) (jtree J JTs) :- map proof_jtree Ps JTs.
```

The tactic_to_just operation first uses make_abs to freeze the metavariables in the tactic and goal. Then, the tactic is run on the the goal, returning the tactic's proof from which the corresponding justification tree is extracted using the proof_jtree operation.

This completes the description of the implementation of the operations defined by the abstract interface. These operations are used to implement tactics and tacticals for refinement. The first two below are the operations for both tactic and primitive rule operations. Their implementations are fairly simple. We omit the definition of prems which computes the premises of a proof.

```
type  tactic_refine  (goal -> proof -> o) -> goal -> proof -> o.
type  prule_refine   prule_name -> goal -> proof -> o.
tactic_refine T G P :- tactic_to_just T G TPf J,
  prems TPf Gs, one_step_proof (step G Gs) J P.
prule_refine R G P :- prule_just R J,
  just_step J (step G Gs), one_step_proof (step G Gs) J P.
```

Tacticals are implemented similarly to those in [3]. The main difference is the use of compose_proofs in the implementation of then to provide a way to compose our proof structures via the operations in the abstract interface.

```
maptac T (agoal G) (aproof P) :- !, pi x\ (maptac T (G x) (P x)).
```

```
maptac T G P :- T G P.
then T1 T2 G P :- T1 G P1, prems P1 Gs,
  map (maptac T2) Gs Ps, compose_proofs P1 Ps P.
```

Tactics are secure in the sense that proofs are built and checked only via the primitive operations of the abstract interface. A simple example is the implementation of `close_tac`.

```
close_tac G P :- prule_refine close G P.
```

The `reuse` operation illustrated in Section 3 has the following simple implementation, whose core is the use of the `jtree_proof` operation.

```
reuse A P NewP :- proof_jtree P JT,
   jtree_proof (bgoal (u\ u) (|- (u\ u) A)) JT NewP.
jtree_proof (agoal G) (ajtree JT) (aproof P) :- !,
   pi x\ (jtree_proof (G x) (JT x) (P x)).
jtree_proof G (jtree J JTs) P :- prem_just J, !, goal_prem G P.
jtree_proof G (jtree J JTs) P :-
   just_step J (step G Gs), one_step_proof (step G Gs) J TopP,
   map3 jtree_proof Gs JTs Ps, compose_proofs TopP Ps P.
```

The implementation of `jtree_proof` is similar to `jtree_prems` above except that it takes an input goal and builds a proof instead of simply computing a list of premises. The input goal is necessary in order to avoid unification constraints that might otherwise be generated by `just_step` in the third clause above. This operation can be viewed as simultaneously performing generalization (via `just_step`) and specialization of the conclusion of each step to a given input goal.

5 Discussion

Although the programs in this paper make extensive use of many of the higher-order features of λProlog, such features are used in a fairly limited way. For example, quantification over both functions and predicates is at most second-order. Operationally, the unification problems that arise in executing these programs are similar in nature to those encountered in [3] and are all fairly simple. The most significant departure is the `just_step` operation which results in unifiers with possibly many constraints. However, as mentioned, these constraints generally are immediately solved by subsequent unifications.

The reuse operation was illustrated on an example that involved a minor change in the original sequent, allowing us to reuse the entire proof. Several other useful operations can be implemented directly using proof generalization via the `jtree_proof` operation and minor modifications. For example, proof generalization provides a simple operation to backup or undo proofs during refinement. In particular, a user can designate a subproof to be deleted, and `jtree_proof` with the original root goal as input can be used to construct a new proof. Any instantiations done by steps in the deleted subtree will not be present in the new proof. More complicated operations can be defined by combining generalization with replay.

Our implementation generalizes a system we described in [4]. That system supported a variety of undo procedures provided that proofs were constructed by a given collection of operations including refinement by tactics, pruning, and instantiation and reinstantiation of metavariables in proofs. By a simple modification, our **reuse** operation can be added to this collection. To do so, additional data must be stored in tactic justifications and **reuse** must be modified to update this data as it builds a new proof.

Isabelle [10] and Coq [2] have metavariables and support tactic-style theorem-proving, but refinement trees are implicit, and operations on these trees are limited. This also applies to KIV [6], even though it explicitly supports a form of refinement trees. In contrast to ALF [8] and Coq, our system only supports simple types for metavariables. If the object logic has a richer type system, then types must be represented explicitly, for example as predicates in the object logic.

References

1. R. L. Constable, et al. *Implementing Mathematics with the Nuprl Proof Development System.* Prentice-Hall, Englewood Cliffs, New Jersey, 1986.
2. G. Dowek, A. Felty, H. Herbelin, G. Huet, C. Murthy, C. Parent, C. Paulin-Mohring, and B. Werner. The coq proof assistant user's guide. Technical Report 154, INRIA, 1993.
3. A. Felty. Implementing tactics and tacticals in a higher-order logic programming language. *Journal of Automated Reasoning*, 11(1):43–81, August 1993.
4. A. Felty and D. Howe. Tactic theorem proving with refinement-tree proofs and metavariables. In *Twelfth International Conference on Automated Deduction.* Springer-Verlag Lecture Notes in Computer Science, June 1994.
5. R. Harper, F. Honsell, and G. Plotkin. A framework for defining logics. *Journal of the ACM*, 40(1):143–184, January 1993.
6. M. Heisel, W. Reif, and W. Stephan. Tactical theorem proving in program verification. In M. Stickel, editor, *Tenth Conference on Automated Deduction*, volume 449 of *Lecture Notes in Computer Science*, pages 117–131. Springer-Verlag, 1990.
7. C. Horn. *The Oyster Proof Development System.* University of Edinburgh, 1988.
8. L. Magnussan. Refinement and local undo in the interactive proof editor ALF. In *Informal Proceedings of the 1993 Workshop on Types for Proofs and Programs*, 1993.
9. D. Miller, G. Nadathur, F. Pfenning, and A. Scedrov. Uniform proofs as a foundation for logic programming. *Annals of Pure and Applied Logic*, 51:125–157, 1991.
10. L. Paulson. Isabelle: The next 700 theorem provers. In P. Odifreddi, editor, *Logic and Computer Science*, pages 361–385. Academic Press, 1990.

Program Tactics and Logic Tactics

Fausto Giunchiglia[1,2] and Paolo Traverso[1]
Mechanized Reasoning Group
[1]IRST - Istituto per la Ricerca Scientifica e Tecnologica
38050 Povo, Trento, Italy
[2]University of Trento, Via Inama 5, 38100 Trento, Italy
fausto@irst.it leaf@irst.it

Abstract. In the past, tactics have been mostly implemented as programs written in some programming language, e.g. ML. We call the tactics of this kind, *Program Tactics*. In this paper we present a first order classical metatheory, called MT, with the following properties: (1) tactics are terms of the language of MT. We call these tactics, *Logic Tactics*; (2) there exists a mapping between Logic Tactics and the Program Tactics implemented within the GETFOL theorem prover. Property (1) allows us to use GETFOL to prove properties of and to build new Logic Tactics. Property (2) can be exploited to perform a bidirectional translation between Logic Tactics and Program Tactics.

1 Introduction

GETFOL [8] [1] is a tactic-based interactive theorem prover which allows for both "backward tactics" and "forward tactics". Roughly speaking, backward tactics are functions from goals to lists of subgoals, while forward tactics are functions from lists of theorems to theorems. In GETFOL, tactics can be developed as programs of the programming language GET. These kinds of tactics are conceptually similar to the tactics developed in ML [17] and used in LCF and its descendants [16, 20, 21, 5]. We call these tactics, **Program Tactics**.

This paper describes a first order classical metatheory, called MT, with the following properties:

1. Tactics are terms of the language of MT. We call these tactics, **Logic Tactics**.
2. There exists a precise correspondence between Logic Tactics and GET Program Tactics.

Having Program and Logic Tactics plus properties 1. and 2. gives important advantages. First, first order theorem proving can be used to prove properties of and build new Logic Tactics. Second, the link between Logic and Program Tactics allows us to use logical deduction to automatically and safely synthesize/optimize Program Tactics. This ability can be used to reason about and extend/modify the GETFOL system code. Finally, this seems a first step towards the development of a methodology for the implementation of provably correct theorem provers.

[1] GETFOL has been developed on top of a reimplementation of the FOL system [24].

The idea is to use GETFOL to proof check correctness statements about its own code.

The paper is structured as follows. In Section 2 we define Logic Tactics. In Section 3 we construct a model of MT, thus proving its consistency. We also discuss some of the requirements that this model imposes on Program Tactics. In Section 4 we prove some interesting properties of Logic Tactics, namely that deduction in MT can be used to prove when a tactic succeeds and when it fails. In Section 5 we discuss the related work. In Section 6 we discuss current work and future developments. In this paper, we do not formally describe GET Program Tactics. They are similar to the ML Program Tactics developed in other theorem provers [16, 20, 21, 5]. Moreover, we do not discuss how expressions in MT can be translated into GET Programs Tactics and vice versa. This non-trivial issue is addressed in other papers, in particular in [10, 9].

2 Logic Tactics

Let OT be a first order object theory, defined as a triple $< \mathcal{L}, \mathcal{A}, \mathcal{R} >$, $\mathcal{L}$ being the language, $\mathcal{A}$ the set of axioms and $\mathcal{R}$ the set of inference rules of OT. We assume that inference rules $\rho \in \mathcal{R}$ apply to pairs $< \Gamma, A >$, written $\Gamma \longrightarrow A$, where A is a formula and Γ a finite set of formulas. We call $\Gamma \longrightarrow A$, a sequent. We also call sequents of the form $A \longrightarrow A$, assumptions. We assume that $\mathcal{R}$ contains rules which are a sequent version of the Natural Deduction (ND) rules [23, 11, 12]. (ND is the logic of GETFOL.) Nevertheless, the work described in this paper is largely independent of the specific inference rules considered. We take the notion of deduction defined in [23]. We call a deduction of a formula A depending on the possibly empty set Γ of formulas, a proof of the sequent $\Gamma \longrightarrow A$. We say that $\Gamma \longrightarrow A$ is a theorem of OT, or that $\Gamma \longrightarrow A$ is provable in OT, iff there exists a proof in OT of $\Gamma \longrightarrow A$.

We define the distinct first order logical theory MT $= < \mathcal{ML}, \mathcal{MA}, \mathcal{MR} >$ to be the metatheory of OT. The set of rules of MT, $\mathcal{MR}$ includes ND rules and rules for equality. We fix a naming relation between MT and the objects of OT, i.e. $\mathcal{ML}$ contains names of sequents, wffs and terms of OT. For instance, the constants "$\Gamma \longrightarrow \forall x A(x)$", "$\forall x A(x)$" and "$x$" are the names of the sequent $\Gamma \longrightarrow \forall x A(x)$, of the wff $\forall x A(x)$ and of the variable x, respectively. For each object level n-ary inference rule ρ, $\mathcal{ML}$ has a n-ary function symbol (that we write as f_ρ), and a n-ary predicate symbol (that we write as P_ρ). (For simplicity, in the following, we consider unary inference rules only. The extension for n-ary rules possibly with parameters is trivial.) For each $\rho \in \mathcal{R}$, $\mathcal{MA}$ has the following axiom:

$$(A1)\ \forall x((T(x) \wedge P_\rho(x)) \supset T(f_\rho(x)))$$

T is the provability predicate. We have an axiom $T(\text{"}s\text{"})$, for any sequent s which is an object level axiom or an assumption. MT has axioms about f_ρ and P_ρ. For instance, if ρ is (a form of) universal specialization that replaces the outermost universally quantified variable with a free variable, we have that

$f_\rho(``\Gamma \longrightarrow \forall x A(x)") = ``\Gamma \longrightarrow A(x)"$, $P_\rho(``\Gamma \longrightarrow \forall x A(x)")$ and $\neg P_\rho(``\Gamma \longrightarrow A(x)")$ are theorems of MT. This intuitively means that the rule whose premise is $\Gamma \longrightarrow \forall x A(x)$ has conclusion $\Gamma \longrightarrow A(x)$, that the rule is applicable to $\Gamma \longrightarrow \forall x A(x)$, and not to $\Gamma \longrightarrow A(x)$. P_ρ may express object level rule restrictions. For instance, if ρ is the universal introduction rule, then we have that $\neg P_\rho(``A(x) \longrightarrow A(x)")$ is provable in MT. Therefore, $(A1)$ states that, if the rule ρ is applicable $[P_\rho(x)]$ to a provable sequent $[T(x)]$, then the conclusion of the rule $[f_\rho(x)]$ is a provable sequent $[T(f_\rho(x))]$. Finally, MT has axioms about the syntactic categories of OT, e.g. $Seq(``s")$ for any sequent s of OT, and about the relations between sequents and theorems, i.e. $\forall x\ (T(x) \supset Seq(x))$. A detailed description of the metatheory described so far and of its relation with the GETFOL code can be found in [11, 12].

In the following we extend MT to be expressive enough to represent Logic Tactics which can be put in correspondence with Program Tactics. Program Tactics make extensive use of conditional constructs. We therefore extend MT's language with conditional term constructors *if* A *then* t_1 *else* t_2, where A is a wff and t_1, t_2 are terms, and its deductive machinery with the relevant elimination and introduction rules (reported in figure 1). Rule *if E* [*if* $E_\neg$] states

$$\dfrac{\begin{array}{cc}[A] & [\neg A] \\ \vdots & \vdots \\ B(t_1) & B(t_2)\end{array}}{B(\mathit{if}\ A\ \mathit{then}\ t_1\ \mathit{else}\ t_2)}\ \mathit{if}\ I \qquad \dfrac{A \quad B(\mathit{if}\ A\ \mathit{then}\ t_1\ \mathit{else}\ t_2)}{B(t_1)}\ \mathit{if}\ E \qquad \dfrac{\neg A \quad B(\mathit{if}\ A\ \mathit{then}\ t_1\ \mathit{else}\ t_2)}{B(t_2)}\ \mathit{if}\ E_\neg$$

Fig. 1. Conditional inference rules

that from $P(\mathit{if}\ A\ \mathit{then}\ t_1\ \mathit{else}\ t_2)$ and A $[\neg A]$, we can derive $P(t_1)$ $[P(t_2)]$. Rule *if I* states that, given a deduction of $P(t_1)$ from A and a deduction of $P(t_2)$ from $\neg A$, we can prove $P(\mathit{if}\ A\ \mathit{then}\ t_1\ \mathit{else}\ t_2)$ ($[A]$ denotes the fact that A is discharged). The resulting theory is a conservative extension of MT.

Program Tactics may encode proof strategies that are not guaranteed to succeed, i.e. they may attempt to apply a rule that is not applicable. If this is the case, the Program Tactic fails. The ability of handling failure is an essential feature of programming languages (like GET and ML) that are used to encode Program Tactics. In ML, for instance, the user can specify that, under certain conditions, a program fails and that, when a program fails, an alternative program can be tried. This is achieved in ML with the construct `?`. The value of the expression `e1 ? e2` is the value of `e1` if `e1` does not fail, otherwise it is the value of `e2`. MT must have the same capability. To obtain this, we add to the language a predicate *Fail* which holds of failures in the application of object level inference rules. This predicate symbol corresponds to a GET boolean function which returns TRUE when its argument computes a data structure that encodes failure.

We therefore extend the language of MT with a constant, *fail* that corresponds to the data structure for failure, and define the predicate *Fail* in terms of *fail* as follows:

$$(D1) \quad \forall x \; (Fail(x) \leftrightarrow x = fail)$$

For simplicity, we suppose that we have only one constant for failure. (Program Tactics distinguish different failures depending on the tactic which fails. In ML this is achieved by means of a "failure token" passed as argument to the expression that generates failure, i.e. **failwith**. In the actual GET code different data structures are generated depending on the tactic that fails. MT can be easily extended with a set of constants each denoting a different failure.) We can now define a function symbol ?

$$(D3) \; \forall x_1 x_2 \quad ?(x_1, x_2) = \begin{array}{l} if \; (x_1 = fail) \\ then \; x_2 \\ else \; x_1 \end{array}$$

which has a behaviour analogous to the ML construct ?. Indeed, if $\vdash_{MT} x_1 \neq fail$, then $\vdash_{MT} ?(x_1, x_2) = x_1$ (where $\vdash_{MT}$ stands for provability in MT). If $\vdash_{MT} x_1 = fail$, then $\vdash_{MT} ?(x_1, x_2) = x_2$.

In the following, we consider only "forward tactics". (The results presented can be generalized to "backward tactics".) GET forward Program Tactics either construct a theorem or fail. In the former case, they construct a data structure that memorizes a sequent. In the latter, they construct a data structure for failure. The basic assumption underlying GET computations is that these data structures cannot be confused, i.e. GET Program Tactics are always able to distinguish between (a data structure memorizing) failure and (a data structure memorizing) a sequent. This fact is asserted in MT by the following axiom:

$$(A2) \quad \forall x \; \neg(Seq(x) \wedge Fail(x))$$

Moreover, a GET Program Tactic never asserts failure as a theorem. Analogously, in MT, from axiom (A2) and the axiom stating $\forall x(T(x) \supset Seq(x))$ we can prove

$$\neg \; T(fail) \tag{1}$$

Since Program Tactics construct either theorems or failures, they accept as arguments both theorems and failures. This allows us to compose them. Being a well sorted argument for a tactic is expressed by the predicate *Tac*.

$$(D2) \quad \forall x \; (Tac(x) \leftrightarrow T(x) \vee Fail(x))$$

Let us consider Program Tactics that apply a single inference rule ρ. If ρ is applicable, the Program Tactic succeeds and constructs a theorem, i.e. the conclusion of the application of ρ. If ρ is not applicable, then the Program Tactic fails. If a failure is given in input, the Program Tactic that applies ρ fails, i.e. it "propagates" failure. For each $\rho \in \mathcal{R}$, we extend MT with the function symbol t_ρ and the following axiom

$$(A3)\ \forall x\ (Tac(x) \supset t_\rho(x) = \mathit{if}\ (\neg Fail(x) \wedge P_\rho(x))\ \mathit{then}\ f_\rho(x)\ \mathit{else}\ \mathit{fail}\ )$$

Notice that the function symbol t_ρ corresponds intuitively to a Program Tactic that applies a single inference rule ρ. If ρ is applicable to a given premise s which is a theorem of OT, then $\vdash_{\mathrm{MT}} Tac(\text{“}s\text{”})$, $\vdash_{\mathrm{MT}} \neg Fail(\text{“}s\text{”})$ and $\vdash_{\mathrm{MT}} P_\rho(\text{“}s\text{”})$. Hence, we have $\vdash_{\mathrm{MT}} t_\rho(\text{“}s\text{”}) = f_\rho(\text{“}s\text{”})$ (rule $\mathit{if}\ E$), where $f_\rho(\text{“}s\text{”})$ denotes the conclusion of the application of ρ. If ρ is not applicable to s, then we have $\vdash_{\mathrm{MT}} \neg P_\rho(\text{“}s\text{”})$, and therefore $\vdash_{\mathrm{MT}} t_\rho(\text{“}s\text{”}) = \mathit{fail}$ (rule $\mathit{if}\ E_\neg$). Finally, we have failure propagation, i.e. $\vdash_{\mathrm{MT}} t_\rho(\mathit{fail}) = \mathit{fail}$.

Let us now consider Program Tactics that are built as compositions of simpler Program Tactics. GETFOL, like most tactic-based theorem provers [16, 20, 21, 5], provides the ability to combine Program Tactics by means of *tacticals*. Tacticals are implemented by control constructs that compose tactics in a principled manner. For instance, tacticals are used to control sequential and repeated applications of tactics and to handle failure in the application of tactics. Tacticals compose tactics by taking tactics as arguments and returning tactics as results. In ML, this is achieved by using a higher order syntax where tactics are passed as arguments to programs. In MT (which is first order) we obtain a similar result by adding to $\mathcal{ML}$ the constants "t_ρ", i.e. for each function symbol $t_\rho \in \mathcal{ML}$ we have a constant "t_ρ" $\in \mathcal{ML}$. We say that "t_ρ" is the name of t_ρ. For each "t_ρ", we have in MT an axiom stating the relation between the function symbol and its name.

$$(A4)\ \forall x\ (Tac(x) \supset apply(\text{“}t_\rho\text{”}, x) = t_\rho(x))$$

where, *apply* is a function symbol. Notice that "t_ρ" is a name of an object of MT rather than of OT. We have constants ("*idtac*" and "*failtac*") and function symbols (*idtac* and *failtac*) for trivial tacticals that return the argument unchanged and that generate failure, respectively. We also have the following axioms:

$$(A5)\ \forall x\ (Tac(x) \supset idtac(x) = x)$$
$$(A6)\ \forall x\ (Tac(x) \supset failtac(x) = fail)$$

In MT, tacticals are function symbols. We call these function symbols, **Logic Tacticals**. The Logic Tacticals considered in this paper are *then*, *orelse*, *try*, *progress* and *repeat*. They correspond to tacticals implemented in LCF and NuPRL [5]. Their axiomatization is given in figure 2. Intuitively, *LTac* holds over terms that are Logic Tactics (as defined formally below). *then* is used to apply tactics sequentially. It applies its first argument; if it succeeds, it applies the second, it fails otherwise. *orelse* captures failure. It applies the first tactic; if it fails, it applies the second. An alternative proof strategy can thus be applied when the first strategy fails. Notice that, in LCF, ORELSE is defined by means of

$(A7)$ **idtac** : $\forall x\ (Tac(x) \supset apply(\text{“}idtac\text{”}, x) = idtac(x))$
$(A8)$ **failtac** : $\forall x\ (Tac(x) \supset apply(\text{“}failtac\text{”}, x) = failtac(x))$
$(A9)$ **then** : $\forall x \forall t_i \forall t_j\ (Tac(x) \wedge LTac(t_i) \wedge LTac(t_j) \supset$
$apply(then(t_i, t_j), x) = if\ (apply(t_i, x) = fail)$
$then\ fail$
$else\ apply(t_j, apply(t_i, x)))$
$(A10)$ **orelse** : $\forall x \forall t_i \forall t_j\ (Tac(x) \wedge LTac(t_i) \wedge LTac(t_j) \supset$
$apply(orelse(t_i, t_j), x) = ?(apply(t_i, x), apply(t_j, x)))$
$(A11)$ **try** : $\forall x \forall t_i\ (Tac(x) \wedge LTac(t_i) \supset$
$apply(try(t_i), x) = apply(orelse(t_i, \text{“}idtac\text{”}), x))$
$(A12)$ **progress** : $\forall x \forall t_i\ (Tac(x) \wedge LTac(t_i) \supset$
$apply(progress(t_i), x) = if\ (apply(t_i, x) = x)$
$then\ fail$
$else\ apply(t_i, x))$
$(A13)$ **repeat** : $\forall x \forall t_i\ (Tac(x) \wedge LTac(t_i) \supset$
$apply(repeat(t_i), x) = if\ (apply(t_i, x) = fail)$
$then\ x$
$else\ apply(repeat(t_i), apply(t_i, x)))$

where x, t_i and t_j are variables of MT.

Fig. 2. Axiomatization of tacticals

?, i.e. `let (T1 ORELSE T2)g = T1(g) ? T2(g)` [17]. Analogously, axiom (A10) states the relation between *orelse* and ?. *try* applies the tactic to the argument. If it fails, it returns the argument. *try* is used to apply proof strategies without having failure. *progress* applies the tactic to the argument. If the result is equal to the argument (no progress in the proof has been obtained) then it fails. *repeat* applies the tactic until the tactic fails. *repeat* can be used to express repeated applications of tactics.

Logic Tactics can be formally defined as follows. They are a subset of the terms of MT. This set is based upon the set of constants “t_ρ”: $\mathcal{T}_0 = \{\text{“}t_\rho\text{”} : \rho \in \mathcal{R}\}$. From $\mathcal{T}_0$, we inductively construct the **set of Logic Tactics** $\mathcal{T}$.

1. “*idtac*” $\in \mathcal{T}$, “*failtac*” $\in \mathcal{T}$, $\mathcal{T}_0 \subseteq \mathcal{T}$.
2. If $t_1, t_2 \in \mathcal{T}$, then $then(t_1, t_2) \in \mathcal{T}$, $orelse(t_1, t_2) \in \mathcal{T}$, $repeat(t_1) \in \mathcal{T}$, $try(t_1) \in \mathcal{T}$, and $progress(t_1) \in \mathcal{T}$.

We have an axiom in MT for each term in the set of Logic Tactics, i.e.

$$(A14)\quad LTac(t), \quad \text{if } t \in \mathcal{T}$$

3 A model of MT

We define an interpretation $\mathcal{M} = \langle \mathcal{D}, g \rangle$ of $\mathcal{ML}$, where $\mathcal{D}$ is the domain of interpretation and g is the interpretation function.

The domain of interpretation $\mathcal{D}$ includes a set (called $\mathcal{D}_o$) of objects of the object theory OT, e.g. the sequent $\Gamma \longrightarrow \forall x A(x)$. These objects are denoted by terms of MT, e.g. the constant "$\Gamma \longrightarrow \forall x A(x)$". The domain contains the two special elements E and F. E intuitively means "undefined" and is used to handle partialness. F is used to interpret failure, i.e. the constant *fail* of MT. The domain includes a further subset, called $\mathcal{D}_f$, which is used to interpret Logic Tactics. Tacticals are interpreted as functions defined over elements of $\mathcal{D}_f$.

Definition 1 (Domain $\mathcal{D}$ of $\mathcal{M}$). Let OT $= \langle \mathcal{L}, \mathcal{A}, \mathcal{R} \rangle$ be a first order theory and let MT $= \langle \mathcal{ML}, \mathcal{MA}, \mathcal{MR} \rangle$ be its metatheory. Let $\mathcal{M}$ be an interpretation with domain $\mathcal{D}$ of $\mathcal{ML}$. $\mathcal{D} = \mathcal{D}_o \cup \{\mathtt{E}\} \cup \{\mathtt{F}\} \cup \mathcal{D}_f$. $\mathcal{D}_o$ is the set of terms, wffs and sequents of OT. E and F are distinct from any other element of $\mathcal{D}$.

$\mathcal{D}_f$ is the smallest set satisfying the following inductive rules.

1. $F_{id} \in \mathcal{D}_f$, $\quad F_F \in \mathcal{D}_f$, $\quad \{F_\rho : \rho \in \mathcal{R}\} \subseteq \mathcal{D}_f$.
2. If d_1 and d_2 $\in \mathcal{D}_f$, then $F_{then}[d_1, d_2] \in \mathcal{D}_f$, $F_{orelse}[d_1, d_2] \in \mathcal{D}_f$, $F_{repeat}[d_1] \in \mathcal{D}_f$, $F_{try}[d_1] \in \mathcal{D}_f$ and $F_{progress}[d_1] \in \mathcal{D}_f$.

where we have an element F_ρ for each $\rho \in \mathcal{R}$. The members of $\mathcal{D}_f$ are functions over the set of theorems of OT union the element F, i.e. functions from $T_{OT} \cup \{\mathtt{F}\}$ to $T_{OT} \cup \{\mathtt{F}\}$, where T_{OT} is the set of theorems of OT. They are defined as follows.

Let $x \in T_{OT} \cup \{\mathtt{F}\}$:

1. $F_{id}(x) = x$
2. $F_F(x) = \mathtt{F}$
3. $F_\rho(x) = \begin{cases} y & \text{if } x \neq \mathtt{F},\ \rho \text{ is applicable to } x \text{ and} \\ & y \text{ is the conclusion of the application of } \rho \text{ to } x \\ \mathtt{F} & \text{otherwise} \end{cases}$
4. $F_{then}[d_1, d_2](x) = \begin{cases} d_2(d_1(x)) & \text{if } d_1(x) \neq \mathtt{F} \\ \mathtt{F} & \text{otherwise} \end{cases}$
5. $F_{orelse}[d_1, d_2](x) = \begin{cases} d_1(x) & \text{if } d_1(x) \neq \mathtt{F} \\ d_2(x) & \text{otherwise} \end{cases}$
6. $F_{repeat}[d](x) = \begin{cases} F_{repeat}[d](d(x)) & \text{if } d(x) \neq \mathtt{F} \\ x & \text{otherwise} \end{cases}$
7. $F_{try}[d](x) = \begin{cases} d(x) & \text{if } d(x) \neq \mathtt{F} \\ x & \text{otherwise} \end{cases}$
8. $F_{progress}[d](x) = \begin{cases} d(x) & \text{if } d(x) \neq x \\ \mathtt{F} & \text{otherwise} \end{cases}$

Some explanations are in order. We use the notation $f[\ ]$ to denote elements of $\mathcal{D}_f$. For each $d_1, d_2 \in \mathcal{D}_f$, we have an element $F_{then}[d_1, d_2]$, $F_{orelse}[d_1, d_2]$, $F_{repeat}[d_1]$, $F_{try}[d_1]$ and $F_{progress}[d_1]$ in $\mathcal{D}_f$. We use the notation $f(\ )$ to denote function application. If $d_1, d_2 \in \mathcal{D}_f$ and $x \in T_{OT} \cup \{\mathtt{F}\}$, then $d_1(x)$ stands for "the function d_1 applied to the argument x", and $d_2(d_1(x))$ stands for the composition $d_2 \circ d_1$ applied to x.

Notice that, for any $d \in \mathcal{D}_f$, $F_{repeat}[d]$ is recursively defined. $F_{repeat}[d]$ is the least fixed point of the functional Φ_d over $[T_{OT} \cup \{\mathtt{F}\} \rightarrow T_{OT} \cup \{\mathtt{F}\}]$, defined as

$$\Phi_d(\varphi)(x) = \begin{cases} \varphi(d(x)) & \text{if } d(x) \neq \mathtt{F} \\ x & \text{otherwise} \end{cases}$$

where φ is a function variable. It can be proved that Φ_d is monotonic for the partial ordering $f_1(x) \sqsubseteq f_2(x)$ (where $f_1, f_2 \in \mathcal{D}_f$) for all $x \in T_{OT} \cup \{\mathtt{F}\}$ such that

$$\mathtt{F} \sqsubseteq x \text{ and } x \sqsubseteq x \text{ for all } x \in T_{OT} \cup \{\mathtt{F}\}$$

The next step is to define the interpretation function g.

Definition 2 (Interpretation function g of $\mathcal{M}$). Let OT $= \langle \mathcal{L}, \mathcal{A}, \mathcal{R} \rangle$ be a first order theory and let MT $= \langle \mathcal{ML}, \mathcal{MA}, \mathcal{MR} \rangle$ be its metatheory. Let $\mathcal{M}$ be an interpretation of $\mathcal{ML}$. The interpretation function g of $\mathcal{M}$ is defined as follows.

1. $g(\text{“}s\text{”}) = s$, $g(\text{“}w\text{”}) = w$ and $g(\text{“}t\text{”}) = t$, where s, w and t are any sequent, wff and term of OT, respectively.
2. $g(fail) = \mathtt{F}$.
3. $g(Seq)$ is the set of sequents of OT.
4. $g(T) = T_{OT}$, where T_{OT} is the set of theorems of OT.
5. $g(=)$ is the identity relation over $\mathcal{D}$.
6. $g(LTac) = \mathcal{D}_f$.
7. g assigns to each predicate symbol $P_\rho \in \mathcal{ML}$ the subset of sequents ρ is applicable to.
8. g assigns to each function symbol $f_\rho \in \mathcal{ML}$ a function over $\mathcal{D}$ that, if ρ is applicable to $d \in \mathcal{D}$, returns the conclusion of ρ and returns $\mathtt{E}$, otherwise. Let ρ_p be the partial function, defined only over $g(P_\rho)$, that returns the conclusion of ρ. Then
$$g(f_\rho)(d) = \begin{cases} \rho_p(d) & \text{if } d \in g(P_\rho) \\ \mathtt{E} & \text{otherwise} \end{cases}$$
9. $g(t_\rho)$ is the function over $\mathcal{D}$ such that,
$$g(t_\rho)(d) = \begin{cases} \rho_p(d) & \text{if } d \in T_{OT} \cap g(P_\rho) \\ \mathtt{F} & \text{if } d \in (T_{OT} - g(P_\rho)) \cup \{\mathtt{F}\} \\ \mathtt{E} & \text{otherwise} \end{cases}$$
10. $g(idtac)$ is the function over $\mathcal{D}$ such that
$$g(idtac)(d) = \begin{cases} d \text{ if } d \in T_{OT} \cup \{\ \mathtt{F}\ \} \\ \mathtt{E} \text{ otherwise} \end{cases}$$
11. $g(failtac)$ is the function over $\mathcal{D}$ such that
$$g(failtac)(d) = \begin{cases} \mathtt{F} \text{ if } d \in T_{OT} \cup \{\ \mathtt{F}\ \} \\ \mathtt{E} \text{ otherwise} \end{cases}$$
12. $g(\text{“}idtac\text{”}) = F_{id}$, $g(\text{“}failtac\text{”}) = F_F$ and $g(\text{“}t_\rho\text{”}) = F_\rho$, for all $\rho \in \mathcal{R}$.
13. $g(then)$ is a function over $\mathcal{D} \times \mathcal{D}$ such that
$$g(then)(d_1, d_2) = \begin{cases} F_{then}[d_1, d_2] & \text{if } d_1, d_2 \in \mathcal{D}_f \\ \mathtt{E} & \text{otherwise} \end{cases}$$

14. $g(orelse)$ is a function over $\mathcal{D} \times \mathcal{D}$ such that
$$g(orelse)(d_1, d_2) = \begin{cases} F_{orelse}[d_1, d_2] & \text{if } d_1, d_2 \in \mathcal{D}_f \\ \mathbf{E} & \text{otherwise} \end{cases}$$
15. $g(repeat)$ is a function over $\mathcal{D}$ such that
$$g(repeat)(d) = \begin{cases} F_{repeat}[d] & \text{if } d \in \mathcal{D}_f \\ \mathbf{E} & \text{otherwise} \end{cases}$$
16. $g(try)$ is a function over $\mathcal{D}$ such that
$$g(try)(d) = \begin{cases} F_{try}[d] & \text{if } d \in \mathcal{D}_f \\ \mathbf{E} & \text{otherwise} \end{cases}$$
17. $g(progress)$ is a function over $\mathcal{D}$ such that
$$g(progress)(d) = \begin{cases} F_{progress}[d] & \text{if } d \in \mathcal{D}_f \\ \mathbf{E} & \text{otherwise} \end{cases}$$
18. $g(apply)$ is a function over $\mathcal{D} \times \mathcal{D}$ such that
$$g(apply)(d_1, d_2) = \begin{cases} d_1(d_2) & \text{if } d_1 \in \mathcal{D}_f \text{ and } d_2 \in \mathcal{T}_{OT} \cup \{\mathtt{F}\} \\ \mathbf{E} & \text{otherwise} \end{cases}$$

Wffs and terms get interpreted according to the usual standard tarskian semantics. The semantics of conditional terms is as follows. Let A be a wff of MT. If A is true, then the value of *if* A *then* t_1 *else* t_2 is the value of t_1. Otherwise it is the value of t_2.

Theorem 3. *MT is consistent.*

We prove the consistency of MT by showing that $\mathcal{M} =< \mathcal{D}, g >$ is a model of MT.

$\mathcal{M}$ has been built to identify some requirements that the code implementing Program Tactics must satisfy in order to allow for a relation with Logic Tactics. E has been introduced to totalize function symbols (e.g. f_ρ) that otherwise would be partially defined. f_ρ corresponds to a function in the GETFOL code that is undefined for some inputs. For instance, universal specialization is implemented by means of a function that, given a (data structure corresponding to) a universally quantified wff, returns (a data structure corresponding to) its matrix. This function is partial since it is undefined for (data structures corresponding to) wffs that are not universally quantified. Partialness is a general characteristic of a large amount of the code of GETFOL (and of any running system). For instance, this is the case also for tacticals, which are defined only over tactics, and for *apply*, which is defined only over pairs of tactics and theorems or failures. Partialness allows us to achieve efficiency (the code does not have to test and decide for all the possible inputs). Extending the domain with E to handle partial functions is a well known standard technique (see, for instance, [4, 19]). One essential difference between the standard approaches and the approach undertaken here is that we have two distinct special elements, E and F. From a theoretical point of view, we could construct a model where E and F are collapsed in a unique element. Nevertheless, the distinction between E and F is important in order to define a correspondence between Logic and Program Tactics. E is not denoted by any symbol in the language of MT and is not implemented by any data structure in the GETFOL code. It is used to capture in the model "defined on paper" the fact that some programs must be partial. On the contrary, F is denoted by *fail* in MT and is implemented by a data structure in the GETFOL code. This data structure is a witness of observable failures. It is returned by and passed as argument to Program Tactics. F_F, F_ρ, $F_{then}[d_1, d_2]$, $F_{orelse}[d_1, d_2]$, $F_{repeat}[d_1]$, $F_{try}[d_1]$ and $F_{progress}[d_1]$ specify how Program Tactics and tacticals must deal with this data structure.

Logic Tacticals are assigned to functions (e.g. $g(then)$, $g(orelse)$ and $g(repeat)$) that, given elements of $\mathcal{D}_f$ (denoted by Logic Tactics), return an element of the same set $\mathcal{D}_f$. Therefore, intuitively, tacticals are interpreted according to their original intended meaning, i.e. as functions that given tactics return tactics. Moreover, notice that elements of $\mathcal{D}_f \subseteq \mathcal{D}$ are functions over $(T_{OT} \cup \{\mathtt{F}\}) \subseteq \mathcal{D}$. $g(apply)$ allows us to apply these functions to their arguments. This fact, plus the fact that Logic Tactics denote elements of $\mathcal{D}_f$, allows us to interpret Logic Tactics in a first order setting.

4 Reasoning in MT

In this section we prove some general properties of Logic Tactics. A Logic Tactic, when applied to some arguments, is provably equal to the name of a theorem of OT iff it corresponds to a proof of the theorem in OT. It is provably equal to failure iff it corresponds to a tree of rule applications that is not a proof. Finally, (non) termination is captured formally in MT by the (un)provability of certain statements.

Program Tactics, when executed, build trees of inference rule applications where either all the rules are applicable (the tactic succeeds) or there is a rule which is not applicable (the tactic fails). A *sequent tree* Π is defined formally as a tree of sequents, each labeled by an inference rule. We associate to every object level sequent tree Π a *sequential (logic) tactic* t_π in MT. Sequential logic tactics of object level sequent trees are defined inductively over the structure of sequent trees. In the base case, a sequent tree is a single sequent. If the sequent is either an axiom or an assumption, then the sequent tree is a proof. If it is neither an axiom nor an assumption, then the sequent tree is not a proof. In both cases, its sequential tactic is "*idtac*". In the step case, if t_{π_1} is the sequential tactic of Π_1, and Π is built from Π_1 by applying ρ to the end sequent of Π_1, then $then(t_{\pi_1}, \text{“}t_\rho\text{”})$ is the sequential tactic of Π. For instance, if a sequent tree is built by applying first the rule ρ_1 to an axiom or an assumption, and then ρ_2 and ρ_3 are applied in the sequent tree in the given order, then the corresponding sequential tactic is $then(then(then(\text{“}idtac\text{”}, \text{“}t_{\rho_1}\text{”}), \text{“}t_{\rho_2}\text{”}), \text{“}t_{\rho_3})$.

Program Tactics, when executed, are applied to given arguments. Similarly, in MT, we define a *sequential (logic) tactic application* τ_π of Π. Let s be the leaf of Π. Let t_π is the sequential tactic of Π. τ_π is $apply(t_\pi, \text{“}s\text{”})$, if s is an axiom or an assumption. τ_π is $apply(t_\pi, fail)$, if s is neither an axiom nor an assumption. A *(logic) tactic application* τ is a term of the form $apply(t, \text{“}s\text{”})$, where $t \in T$

and s is a sequent. We say that Π is a sequent tree of s if s is the end sequent of Π. We prove that sequential tactic applications have the right behaviour.

Theorem 4 (Failure and success for sequential logic tactics). *Let Π be a sequent tree of s. Let τ_π be the sequential tactic application of Π. Then*

$$\begin{array}{lllll} (1) & \vdash_{MT} \tau_\pi = \text{“}s\text{”} & \Longleftrightarrow_{(a)} \Pi \textit{ is a proof of } s. & \Longleftrightarrow_{(b)} & \vdash_{MT} T(\tau_\pi) \\ (2) & \vdash_{MT} \tau_\pi = fail & \Longleftrightarrow_{(a)} \Pi \textit{ is not a proof.} & \Longleftrightarrow_{(b)} & \vdash_{MT} \neg T(\tau_\pi) \end{array}$$

Proof. (Hinted) We first prove (by induction over the structure of Π) that “Π proof of s implies $\vdash_{MT} \tau_\pi$ = “s” and $\vdash_{MT} T(\text{“}s\text{”})$”. If Π is built from Π_1 by applying ρ to the end sequent s_1 of Π_1, we have that $\vdash_{MT} \tau_\pi = f_\rho(\text{“}s_1\text{”})$. But $\vdash_{MT} f_\rho(\text{“}s_1\text{”}) = \text{“}s\text{”}$ and $\vdash_{MT} T(f_\rho(\text{“}s_1\text{”}))$. We then prove (again by induction) that “Π not proof implies $\vdash_{MT} \tau_\pi = fail$”. Here we have two cases. If Π_1 is not a proof, we use the induction hypotheses and axiom (A9). If Π_1 is a proof, we use theorem “(1)(a) $\Leftarrow$ ” applied to Π_1 and the fact that ρ is not applicable. Theorem “(2)(b) $\Rightarrow$ ” is a consequence of theorem “(2)(a) $\Leftarrow$ ” and axiom (A2). Theorems “(1)(a) $\Rightarrow$ ” and “(1)(b) $\Leftarrow$ ” are proved by contradiction. Suppose that Π is not a proof. From theorems “(2)(a) $\Leftarrow$ ” and “(2)(b) $\Rightarrow$ ” we would have $\vdash_{MT} \tau_\pi = fail$ and $\vdash_{MT} \neg T(\tau_\pi)$, respectively. Then MT would be inconsistent (against theorem 3). Theorems “(2)(a) $\Rightarrow$ ” and “(2)(b) $\Leftarrow$ ” are proved in a similar way.

Part (1) of theorem 4 states that a successful tactic corresponding to a proof can be proved equal to the name of a sequent (part (1)(a)) that is a theorem of OT (part (1)(b)). ($\vdash_{MT} T(\text{“}s\text{”}) \Longleftrightarrow \vdash_{OT} s$, where $\vdash_{OT}$ stands for provability in OT, is a corollary of theorems 3 and 4). Part (2) states that a tactic that does not correspond to a proof can be proved equal to failure (part (2)(a)) and it does not denote an object level theorem (part (2)(b)). Notice that the fact that a Program Tactic fails to prove a sequent does not imply that the sequent is not provable. Analogously, part (2) states that the tactic does not denote a theorem ($\neg T(\tau_\pi)$), but *does not state* the much stronger fact that s is not a theorem ($\neg T(\text{“}s\text{”})$). Theorem 4 can be generalized to Logic Tactics.

Corollary 5 (Failure and success for Logic Tactics). *Let Π be a sequent tree of s. Let τ_π be the sequential tactic application of Π. Let τ be a tactic application. If $\vdash_{MT} \tau = \tau_\pi$, then*

$$\begin{array}{lllll} \vdash_{MT} \tau = \text{“}s\text{”} & \Longleftrightarrow & \Pi \textit{ is a proof of } s. & \Longleftrightarrow & \vdash_{MT} T(\tau) \\ \vdash_{MT} \tau = fail & \Longleftrightarrow & \Pi \textit{ is not a proof.} & \Longleftrightarrow & \vdash_{MT} \neg T(\tau) \end{array}$$

A Program Tactic succeeds iff it builds a proof (Π) of a theorem (s). A Logic Tactic application (τ) is provably equal to the constant denoting the theorem (“s”) iff it corresponds to a proof Π of s. A Program Tactic fails when it tries to apply some inference rule that is not applicable, i.e. when it tries to build a sequent tree Π that is not a proof. A Logic Tactic application is provably equal to failure ($fail$) iff it corresponds to a sequent tree Π which is not a proof.

Notice that, under the hypotheses of corollary 5, we can prove that $\vdash_{MT} T(\tau) \vee Fail(\tau)$, i.e. $\vdash_{MT} Tac(\tau)$, that is that τ either succeeds or fails. This is actually what happens with Program Tactics that terminate. However, this may not be the case. Consider, for instance, the Logic Tactic *repeat*("*idtac*"). Since "*idtac*" applied to a given sequent always succeeds, the corresponding Program Tactic applies "*idtac*" an infinite number of times. Any sequential tactic application τ_π corresponds to a finite number of applications of inference rules. Therefore, a τ_π such that $\vdash_{MT} apply(repeat(\text{"}idtac\text{"}), \text{"}s\text{"}) = \tau_\pi$ does not exist and corollary 5 cannot be applied. The condition $\vdash_{MT} \tau = \tau_\pi$ of corollary 5 captures the fact that the Program Tactic corresponding to τ terminates. An interesting problem is to find some general conditions under which we have $\vdash_{MT} \tau = \tau_\pi$. A lot of work has been done on providing conditions for and on proving the termination of recursive programs (e.g. see [1]). This issue is not discussed here. An obvious sufficient condition for $\vdash_{MT} \tau = \tau_\pi$ is that τ does not contain occurrences of the tactical *repeat* which cannot be rewritten into terms without *repeat*.

5 Related work

Program Tactics have been mostly implemented in ML [17] and used successfully in several theorem provers, like LCF [16, 20], Isabelle [21] and NuPRL [5]. Logic Tactics have been encoded in higher order logical theories and logic programming languages. In [18], the higher order NuPRL type theory is used as a language for constructing theorem proving procedures. In [7, 6], tactics and tacticals are implemented in λProlog, an extended higher-order logic programming language. There are two main differences with our work. First, MT is first order. Reasoning about tactics can be done entirely in a first order logic. We do not discuss here the advantages of working in a first order setting, see for instance [13, 4]. Second, neither [18] nor [7, 6] provide a relation between Logic Tactics and programs that implement the theorem prover. NuPRL and λProlog cannot reason about and extend/modify their own system code. Beside these main facts, there are also technical (but important) differences between Logic Tactics in MT and tactics in λProlog. Tactics in λProlog specify proof search strategies by providing an interpreter on top of λProlog which is itself interpreted under the fixed λProlog search strategy. As a consequence of this and of the fact that tactics are relational, failure is treated as falsity (the tactical `orelse` is defined as disjunction) and failure handling is performed by backchaining using a depth first search paradigm. Similarly, `then` is defined as conjunction. In MT, the axiomatization of *then* and *orelse* is fully declarative and independent of any system underlying search strategy.

Some work closely related to ours (but which seems at an earlier stage) is the work on 2OBJ [14]. 2OBJ is a tactic-based theorem prover built upon OBJ3 [15], a term rewriting implementation of equational logic. Like MT, 2OBJ supports a first order treatment of tactics. In 2OBJ, tactics are programmed in its equational logic. However, there is no relation between tactics in 2OBJ and the implementation of OBJ3. Moreover the metatheory of 2OBJ has no explicit notion of failure.

The idea of reasoning about tactics to guide the theorem proving search has been strongly influenced by the work on proof planning [3]. The work on proof planning has developed sophisticated techniques for proofs by induction and has been successful in proving automatically many interesting theorems. Further work is needed in MT to exploit the possibility of reasoning about tactics. On the other hand, MT allows us to express tactics as terms of the logic. Our goal is to exploit this fact to perform proof planning as (interactive) metalevel theorem proving.

As stated in the introduction, our ultimate goal (still far from being achieved) is to prove the correctness of the theorem prover within the theorem prover itself. We share this goal with the work in progress on Acl2 [2]. There are various differences between the two approaches. One difference, which is relevant to this paper, is that in Acl2 the logic language and the implementation language are the same. Keeping Logic Tactics and Program Tactics distinct, as we do, seems to provide some advantages, for instance for what concerns how to deal with state. For example, it is possible for us to store in a global variable the set of proven theorems and to reason declaratively about it. The idea is to see state (e.g. the current proof) as storing partial computations relative to a function or predicate (e.g. the provability predicate T). This allows us to lift the code that updates and reads state into axioms which formalize the function and predicate whose computations are approximately represented by the state itself. Some of the details about this issue are in [10, 9]. Another advantage is that we may have Program Tactics which are not translated into Logic Tactics or vice versa. This is a necessary feature in the presence of non-terminating Program Tactics (see discussion in the next section), a problem that has to be taken into consideration in GETFOL.

6 Conclusion

We have described a first order metatheory, called MT, which is expressive enough to represent tactics and tacticals. Tactics are terms of MT (called Logic Tactics) and tacticals are function symbols of MT. MT has been constructed so that it is possible to define a relation between Logic Tactics and GET Program Tactics. The next step, currently under development, is to embed in MT all the constructs used in the development of Program Tactics, e.g. in ML. For instance, conditionals can be included in Logic Tactics by means of conditional terms, i.e. the set $\mathcal{T}$ of Logic Tactics can be inductively extended with terms of the form *if* A *then* t_1 *else* t_2, where A is a wff and t_1 and $t_2 \in \mathcal{T}$. $\mathcal{T}$ can also be extended with a *let* environment term constructor, *let* $x = t_1$ *in* t_2, where x is a variable of MT. Inference rules can be added to eliminate and introduce *let*. Logic Tactics can include selective failure trapping (e.g. the construct ?? of ML), loops and failure trap with re-iteration (e.g. the constructs ! and !! of ML) and so on. We can prove that these extensions are conservative. Finally, Program Tactics can also be defined recursively. However, introducing rules which allow for the construction of recursive Logic Tactics may not preserve consistency. For instance, if the following wff

$$\begin{aligned} \forall x\ t(x) = & \ \textit{if}\ (t(x) = \textit{apply}(\text{“}\textit{idtac}\text{”}, x)) \\ & \ \textit{then apply}(\text{“}\textit{failtac}\text{”}, x) \\ & \ \textit{else apply}(\text{“}\textit{idtac}\text{”}, x) \end{aligned}$$

is provable, then MT is inconsistent. Notice that the wff above defines a recursive tactic t which corresponds to a Program Tactic that does not terminate. Intuitively, it states that if the tactic t succeeds, then it fails, and if it fails, it succeeds. As discussed in section 3, one form of recursion which is safely represented in MT and which permits adding non terminating tactics is obtained by using the tactical *repeat*. *repeat* is the standard tactical used to write strategies with recursive applications of tactics and it covers a lot of interesting cases. However, in general, it is not powerful enough. At the moment we are studying some more general sufficient conditions for a characterization of recursive (possibly "not terminating") Logic Tactics which preserve consistency.

Finally, a major future goal is to study the possibility for MT to construct powerful proof strategies as Logic Tactics. We have started to develop the family of rewriting functions implemented in Cambridge LCF and described in [22].

References

1. R.S. Boyer and J.S. Moore. *A Computational Logic.* Academic Press, 1979. ACM monograph series.
2. R.S. Boyer and J.S. More. A theorem prover for a computational logic. In *Proceedings of the 10th Conference on Automated Deduction, Lecture Notes in Computer Science 449, Springer-Verlag,* pages 1–15, 1990.
3. A. Bundy. The Use of Explicit Plans to Guide Inductive Proofs. In R. Luck and R. Overbeek, editors, *Proc. of the 9th Conference on Automated Deduction,* pages 111–120. Springer-Verlag, 1988. Longer version available as DAI Research Paper No. 349, Dept. of Artificial Intelligence, Edinburgh.
4. R. Cartwright and J. McCarthy. Recursive Programs as Functions in a First Order Theory, March 1979. SAIL MEMO AIM-324. Also available as CS Dept. Report No. STAN-CS-79-17.
5. R.L. Constable, S.F. Allen, H.M. Bromley, et al. *Implementing Mathematics with the NuPRL Proof Development System.* Prentice Hall, 1986.
6. A. Felty. Implementing Tactics and Tacticals in a Higher-Order Logic Programming Language. *To appear in: Journal of Automated Reasoning,* 1993.
7. A. Felty and D. Miller. Specifying Theorem Provers in a Higher-Order Logic Programming Language. In R. Luck and R. Overbeek, editors, *Proc. of the 9th Conference on Automated Deduction,* pages 61–80. Springer-Verlag, 1988.
8. F. Giunchiglia. The GETFOL Manual - GETFOL version 1. Technical Report 92-0010, DIST - University of Genova, Genoa, Italy, 1992.
9. F. Giunchiglia and A. Armando. A Conceptual Architecture for Introspective Systems. Forthcoming IRST-Technical Report, 1993.

10. F. Giunchiglia and A. Cimatti. Introspective Metatheoretic Reasoning. In *Proc. of META-94, Workshop on Metaprogramming in Logic*, Pisa, Italy, June 19-21, 1994. Also IRST-Technical Report 9211-21, IRST, Trento, Italy.
11. F. Giunchiglia and P. Traverso. Reflective reasoning with and between a declarative metatheory and the implementation code. In *Proc. of the 12th International Joint Conference on Artificial Intelligence*, pages 111–117, Sydney, 1991. Also IRST-Technical Report 9012-03, IRST, Trento, Italy.
12. F. Giunchiglia and P. Traverso. A Metatheory of a Mechanized Object Theory. Technical Report 9211-24, IRST, Trento, Italy, 1992. Submitted for publication to: Journal of Artificial Intelligence.
13. J. Goguen. Higher-order functions considered unnecessary for higher-order programming. In D. A. Turner, editor, *Research Topics in Functional Programming*, pages 309–351. Addison Wesley, 1990.
14. J. Goguen, A. Stevens, H. Hilbrdink, and K. Hobley. 2OBJ: a metalogical framework theorem prover based on equational logic. *Phil. Trans. R. Soc. Lond.*, 339:69–86, 1992.
15. J. Goguen, T. Winkler, J. Meseguer, K. Futatsugi, and J. Jouannaud. Introducing OBJ. In J. Goguen, D. Coleman, and R.Gallimore, editors, *Applications of algebraic specification using OBJ.* Cambridge, 1992.
16. M.J. Gordon, A.J. Milner, and C.P. Wadsworth. *Edinburgh LCF - A mechanized logic of computation*, volume 78 of *Lecture Notes in Computer Science.* Springer Verlag, 1979.
17. M.J. Gordon, R. Milner, L. Morris, and C. Wadsworth. A Metalanguage for Interactive Proof in LCF. CSR report series CSR-16-77, Department of Artificial Intelligence, Dept. of Computer Science, University of Edinburgh, 1977.
18. D. J. Howe. Computational metatheory in Nuprl. In R. Lusk and R. Overbeek, editors, *CADE9*, 1988.
19. Z. Manna. *Mathematical Theory of Computation.* McGraw-Hill, New York, 1974.
20. L. Paulson. Tactics and Tacticals in Cambridge LCF. Technical Report 39, Computer Laboratory, University of Cambridge, 1979.
21. L. Paulson. The Foundation of a Generic Theorem Prover. *Journal of Automated Reasoning*, 5:363–396, 1989.
22. Lawrence C. Paulson. A Higher-Order Implementation of Rewriting. *Science of Computer Programming*, 3:119–149, 1983.
23. D. Prawitz. *Natural Deduction - A proof theoretical study.* Almquist and Wiksell, Stockholm, 1965.
24. R.W. Weyhrauch. Prolegomena to a Theory of Mechanized Formal Reasoning. *Artif. Intell.*, 13(1):133–176, 1980.

On the Relation between the $\lambda\mu$-Calculus and the Syntactic Theory of Sequential Control

Philippe de Groote

INRIA-Lorraine - CRIN - CNRS
Campus Scientifique - B.P. 239
54506 Vandœuvre-lès-Nancy Cedex - FRANCE
e-mail: degroote@loria.fr

Abstract. We construct a translation of first order $\lambda\mu$-calculus [15] into a subtheory of Felleisen's λ_c-calculus [5, 6]. This translation preserves typing and reduction. Then, by constructing the inverse translation, we show that the two calculi are actually isomorphic.

1 Introduction

For a long time it has been widely thought that a classical proof, as opposed to an intuitionistic one, did not carry any computational content (see, for instance, [8, App. B, §B.1] and [12, p. 67, Proposition 8.3]). In 1990, however, T. Griffin opened a new research area by introducing a classical formulae-as-types notion of control based on Felleisen's $\mathcal{C}$ operator [9]. Since then, various authors have defined different systems that enlighten the constructive content of classical logic [1, 2, 7, 13, 14, 15, 16, 17].

Despite its originality, Griffin's work has been criticized by some logicians. In [15], for instance, M. Parigot writes that *the system he* (Griffin) *obtains is not satisfactory from the logical point of view: the reduction is in fact a reduction strategy and the type assigned to $\mathcal{C}$ doesn't fit in general the reduction rule for $\mathcal{C}$.* Such criticisms are based on a misunderstanding of Griffin's motivations. His goal was not to define a new calculus but to type an existing one, namely Felleisen's syntactic theory of sequential control (λC, for short).

The possible defects of Griffin's proposal are only due to the fact that the computation rule of a sequential control operator such as $\mathcal{C}$ is inherently context sensitive. In order to push out this context sensitiveness as far as possible, M. Felleisen defines a large part of his calculus by means of usual notions of reduction, i.e., notions of reduction that are compatible with the term formation rules. Therefore, if one consider only the subtheory defined by these congruent notions of reduction, Griffin's typing amounts to a system that satisfies interesting properties such as confluence and subject reduction.

Moreover, from a computational point of view, Griffin-Felleisen system is at least as powerful as first order $\lambda\mu$-calculus since the latter is isomorphic to a subtheory of the former. This is the central result of this paper that we establish by constructing a translation of the $\lambda\mu$-calculus into the λ_c-calculus. This result also demonstrates that Griffin's and Parigot's approaches are not as different as one could think at first sight.

The remainder of this paper is organized as follows. The two next sections introduce briefly Felleisen's λ_c-calculus and Parigot's $\lambda\mu$-calculus ($\lambda\mu$, for short). In Section 4, we define the translation of $\lambda\mu$ into λC, and we study its properties. In Section 5, we construct the inverse translation. Finally, we present our conclusions in Section 6.

All through the paper, we assume that the reader has an elementary knowledge of λ-calculus and natural deduction. We also adopt Barendregt's variable convention, which protects one from clashes between free and bound variables. This background material may be found in standard books such as [3, 8, 10, 18, 19].

2 Felleisen's λ_c-Calculus

Felleisen's calculus is a call-by-value λ-calculus including a control operator $\mathcal{C}$ akin to Scheme `call/cc` [5, 6]. The core syntax of the language is given by the following grammar:

$$T ::= x \mid (\lambda x. T) \mid (T\,T) \mid (\mathcal{C}\,T),$$

where a λ_c-term of the form $\mathcal{C}\,T$ is called a *$\mathcal{C}$-application.*

The operational semantics of the language may be easily defined by rewriting rules expressed in terms of *applicative contexts.* Let a *value* be defined to be a variable or a λ-abstraction, and let V range over values. Applicative contexts are defined by the following grammar:

$$\mathbf{C} ::= [\,] \mid V\,\mathbf{C} \mid \mathbf{C}\,T.$$

As usual, $[\,]$ represents a hole, and the expression $\mathbf{C}[M]$ denotes the λ_c-term obtained by putting the λ_c-term M into the hole of the applicative context $\mathbf{C}$.

The rewriting rules defining the operational semantics of the language are the following:

$$\mathbf{C}[(\lambda x. M)\,V] \rightarrow \mathbf{C}[M[V/x]], \tag{C1}$$

$$\mathbf{C}[\mathcal{C}\,M] \rightarrow M\,(\lambda x. \mathcal{A}\,(\mathbf{C}[x])). \tag{C2}$$

In Rule C1, V stands for a value, and $M[V/x]$ denotes the usual capture-avoiding substitution. In Rule C2, $\mathcal{A}$ is the *abort* operator that can be defined as

$$\mathcal{A}\,M \stackrel{\text{def}}{=} \mathcal{C}\,(\lambda x. M),$$

where x is a dummy variable that does not occur free in M.

It is easy to show that any closed λ_c-term is either a value or can be written in a unique way as $\mathbf{C}[M]$, where M is either a β_v-redex or a $\mathcal{C}$-application. Therefore, Rules C1 and C2 defines a totally deterministic strategy of evaluation, and the applicative context $\mathbf{C}$ that is uniquely determined by each rewriting step may be interpreted as being the *current continuation.* This interpretation allows one to explain intuitively the behavior of the operator $\mathcal{C}$. When evaluated within an applicative context $\mathbf{C}$, a $\mathcal{C}$-application gives complete control to its argument by applying it to a procedural abstraction of the current continuation $\mathbf{C}$. In the sequel, if this procedural abstraction is invoked with a value V, the new current applicative context is abandoned, and control is given to the term $\mathbf{C}[V]$.

While Rules C1 and C2 are useful to define the operational semantics of the language, there are not convenient to reason about programs. For this reason, Felleisen has developed a calculus in which a large part of the operational semantics of his language is expressed by means of proper notions of reduction, that is notions of reduction that are compatible with the term formation rules. These notions of reduction are the following:

$$(\lambda x.\, M)\, V \rightarrow M[V/x] \qquad (\beta_v)$$

$$(\mathcal{C}\, M)\, N \rightarrow \mathcal{C}\, (\lambda k.\, M\, (\lambda f.\, \mathcal{A}\, (k\, (f\, N)))) \qquad (\mathcal{C}_{\mathrm{L}})$$

$$V\, (\mathcal{C}\, M) \rightarrow \mathcal{C}\, (\lambda k.\, M\, (\lambda f.\, \mathcal{A}\, (k\, (V\, f)))) \qquad (\mathcal{C}_{\mathrm{R}})$$

$$\mathcal{C}\, M \rightarrow \mathcal{C}\, (\lambda k.\, M\, (\lambda f.\, \mathcal{A}\, (k\, f))) \qquad (\mathcal{C}_{\mathrm{top}})$$

$$\mathcal{C}\, (\lambda k. \mathcal{C}\, M) \rightarrow \mathcal{C}\, (\lambda k.\, M\, (\lambda f.\, \mathcal{A}\, f)) \qquad (\mathcal{C}_{\mathrm{idem}})$$

The resulting calculus satisfies the Church-Rosser property and a form of the standardization theorem [6]. It also captures a large part of the original operational semantics. In order to get equivalence, only one additional computation rule is needed:

$$\mathcal{C}\, M \;\rhd M\, (\lambda f.\, \mathcal{A}\, f) \qquad (\mathcal{C}_{\mathrm{T}})$$

Moreover, the application of this computation rule, which is not a proper notion of reduction, may be delayed.

In [9], T. Griffin analyses the rewriting rule C2, and proposes to give the operator $\mathcal{C}$ the type $\neg\neg A \rightarrow A$. As stressed by M. Parigot, this type assignment is not preserved by evaluation[1]. The only type violation, however, is due to the computation rule $\mathcal{C}_{\mathrm{T}}$. Therefore, if one considers only the proper notions of reduction, Griffin's type assignment satisfies the subject reduction property.

For the purpose of this paper, we will slightly modify Felleisen's calculus. First of all, Parigot's $\lambda\mu$-calculus is not a call-by-value calculus. Hence, in order to establish our equivalence result, we must abandon Felleisen's call-by-value strategy. In other words, we must replace the notion of reduction β_v by the usual notion of reduction β. By doing this, one destroys the confluence of the calculus because a term of the form

$$(\lambda x.\, M)\, (\mathcal{C}\, N)$$

[1] Griffin, of course, mentions the problem, and solves it by encapsulating each program M into the expression $\mathcal{C}\, (\lambda k.\, k\, M)$.

may now be reduced in two different ways. Therefore, in order to conserve the Church-Rosser property, we will drop the notion of reduction $\mathcal{C}_{\mathrm{R}}$. We will also drop the notion of reduction $\mathcal{C}_{\mathrm{idem}}$, simply because it is not needed.

Another modification concerns the presence of the abort operators in Felleisen's reduction rules. As far as control is concerned, these abort operators are useful. However, from a proof-theoretic point of view, there are irrelevant. In general, the type scheme assigned to the abort operator is $\bot \to A$. In Felleisen's rules, however, the abort operators must all be assigned the trivial type $\bot \to \bot$. Take for instance the notion of reduction $\mathcal{C}_L$. It corresponds to the following proof-reduction step:

$$\dfrac{\dfrac{\neg\neg(A \to B)}{A \to B} \qquad A}{B} \quad \to \quad \dfrac{\dfrac{\dfrac{\neg\neg(A \to B) \qquad \dfrac{\dfrac{\dfrac{[\neg B] \qquad \dfrac{[A \to B] \quad A}{B}}{\bot}}{\bot}}{\neg(A \to B)}}{\bot}}{\neg\neg B}}{B}$$

Clearly, the inference $\frac{\bot}{\bot}$ is useless.

To summarize, the calculus that we will consider is the one induced by the modified notions of reduction that follows:

$$(\lambda x.\, M)\, N \to M[N/x] \tag{β}$$

$$(\mathcal{C}\, M)\, N \to \mathcal{C}\,(\lambda k.\, M\,(\lambda f.\, k\,(f\, N))) \tag{$\mathcal{C}_{\mathrm{L}}$}$$

$$\mathcal{C}\, M \to \mathcal{C}\,(\lambda k.\, M\,(\lambda f.\, k\, f)) \tag{$\mathcal{C}_{\mathrm{top}}$}$$

From now on, when we will speak of Felleisen's calculus (λC), we will mean the subtheory resulting from the three modified notions of reduction β, $\mathcal{C}_{\mathrm{L}}$, and $\mathcal{C}_{\mathrm{top}}$. This calculus satisfies the Church-Rosser property; this can be established by replaying Felleisen's proof because it is based on the Hindley-Rossen lemma. The symbol $\to_c$ will denote the one-step reduction relation of λC; and the symbols $\twoheadrightarrow_c$ and $=_c$ will stand, respectively, for the reflexive, transitive closure and the reflexive, transitive, symmetric closure of the one-step reduction. Finally, when a λ_c-term M is typable with type A according to Griffin's system, we will write $\vdash_C M : A$.

3 Parigot's $\lambda\mu$-Calculus

Parigot's $\lambda\mu$-calculus is a classical extension of Krivine's AF_2 [11]. It is therefore a second-order system. In this paper, we will focus on first-order $\lambda\mu$-calculus.

This restriction affects neither the syntax of the language, nor the reduction rules. Simply, it allows fewer terms to be typable.

$\lambda\mu$-Terms are built from two distinct alphabets of variables: the set of λ-variables, and the set of so-called μ-variables. The core syntax of the language is given by the following grammar:

$$T \ ::= \ x \mid (\lambda x. T) \mid (T T) \mid (\mu\alpha. T) \mid [\alpha]T,$$

where x ranges over λ-variables, and α ranges over μ-variables. A $\lambda\mu$-term of the form $\mu\alpha. T$ is called a μ-abstraction, and a $\lambda\mu$-term of the form $[\alpha]T$ is called a named term. As λ, μ is binding operator: the free occurrences of a μ-variable α in T become bound in $\mu\alpha. T$.

The typing rules are given by means of a classical sequent calculus. The sequents are either of the form $\Gamma \vdash \Delta$ or of the form $\Gamma \vdash A, \Delta$, where the antecedent Γ is a set of formulas indexed by λ-variables, the succedent Δ is a set of formulas indexed by μ-variables, and A is a distinguished formula. The typing rules are the following:

Logical rules

$$x : A^x \vdash A$$

$$\frac{M : \Gamma, A^x \vdash B, \Delta}{\lambda x. M : \Gamma \vdash A \rightarrow B, \Delta} \qquad \frac{M : \Gamma \vdash A \rightarrow B, \Delta \qquad N : \Pi \vdash A, \Sigma}{M N : \Gamma, \Pi \vdash B, \Delta, \Sigma}$$

Naming rules

$$\frac{M : \Gamma \vdash A, \Delta}{[\alpha]M : \Gamma \vdash A^\alpha, \Delta} \qquad \frac{M : \Gamma \vdash A^\alpha, \Delta}{\mu\alpha. M : \Gamma \vdash A, \Delta}$$

In addition to the usual notion of reduction β, there is a *structural* notion of reduction, which is related to μ-abstraction. The intuition behind the operations of naming and μ-abstraction may be explained as follows: in a $\lambda\mu$-term $\mu\alpha. M$ of type $A \rightarrow B$, only the subterms named by α are *really* of type $A \rightarrow B$; therefore, when such a term is applied to an argument, this argument must be passed over to the subterms named by α. The structural reduction rule formalizes this intuition:

$$(\mu\alpha. M)\, N \rightarrow M[N/\!*\, \alpha],$$

where the structural substitution is inductively defined as follows:

(i) $x[N/\!*\, \alpha] \ = \ x;$

(ii) $(\lambda x. M)[N/\!*\, \alpha] \ = \ \lambda x. M[N/\!*\, \alpha];$

(iii) $(M\, O)[N/\!*\, \alpha] \ = \ M[N/\!*\, \alpha]\, O[N/\!*\, \alpha];$

(iv) $(\mu\beta. M)[N/\!*\, \alpha] \ = \ \mu\beta. M[N/\!*\, \alpha];$

(v) $([\alpha]M)[N/\!*\, \alpha] \ = \ [\alpha](M[N/\!*\, \alpha]\, N);$

(vi) $(\lbrack\beta\rbrack M)[N/{*}\,\alpha] \;=\; \lbrack\beta\rbrack M[N/{*}\,\alpha] \quad \text{if } \alpha \neq \beta.$

There are some other notions of reduction, among which *renaming*:

$$[\alpha](\mu\beta.\, M) \rightarrow M[\alpha/\beta]$$

According to M. Parigot himself, such notions of reduction *are essentially trivial from a computational viewpoint* [16]. Moreover, like the η-reduction steps in λ-calculus, they can be postponed with respect to the structural and the β-reduction steps. We will not allow for them.

In [15], M. Parigot proposes the two following rules to handle the negation:

$$\frac{M \,:\, \Gamma,\, A^{x} \vdash \Delta}{\lambda x.\, \mu\alpha.\, M \,:\, \Gamma \vdash \neg A,\, \Delta} \qquad \frac{M \,:\, \Gamma \vdash \neg A,\, \Delta \qquad N \,:\, \Pi \vdash A,\, \Sigma}{[\beta](M\,N) \,:\, \Gamma,\, \Pi \vdash \Delta,\, \Sigma},$$

where the μ-variable α is fresh. These rules, which are based on an explicit treatment of *falsum* ($\bot$), present some peculiarities.

On the one hand, the occurrence of the μ-variable β introduced by the elimination rule will desperately remain free. Therefore judgment such as the following are derivable:

$$\lambda y.\, \mu\alpha.\, [\phi](y\,(\lambda x.\, \mu\delta.\, [\alpha]\, x)) \;:\, \vdash \neg\neg A \rightarrow A$$

This is quite surprising: while the above $\lambda\mu$-term stands for a completed proof, it contains a free μ-variable (something like a useless hypothesis that has not been discarded).

On the other hand, unlike the other logical rules, the rules for the negation do not correspond to the intuitionistic ones.

For these reasons, we will substitute the following alternative rules for the original ones:

$$\frac{M \,:\, \Gamma,\, A^{x} \vdash \Delta}{\lambda x.\, M \,:\, \Gamma \vdash \neg A,\, \Delta} \qquad \frac{M \,:\, \Gamma \vdash \neg A,\, \Delta}{M\, x \,:\, \Gamma,\, A^{x} \vdash \Delta}.$$

These rules are based on an implicit treatment of *falsum* that amounts to identify any sequent of the form $\Gamma \vdash \Delta$ with the sequent $\Gamma \vdash \bot,\, \Delta$.

From now on, when we will speak of the $\lambda\mu$-calculus ($\lambda\mu$), we will mean first-order $\lambda\mu$-calculus, with the structural notion of reduction and the usual notion of reduction β, and with the alternative rules for negation. The symbol $\rightarrow_{\mu}$ will denote the one-step reduction relation of $\lambda\mu$; and the symbols $\twoheadrightarrow_{\mu}$ and $=_{\mu}$ will stand for the reflexive, transitive closure and the reflexive, transitive, symmetric closure of the one-step reduction respectively. Finally, when a judgement of the form $M \,:\, \vdash A$ is derivable according to the typing rules of $\lambda\mu$, we will write $\vdash_{\mu} M : A$.

4 Translation of $\lambda\mu$ into λC

In this section we give a homomorphic translation of $\lambda\mu$ into λC that preserves typing and reduction.

For the purpose of this translation, we consider that all the variables (i.e., the μ-variables and the λ-variables) belong to the same alphabet.

Definition 4.1 (C-transform) *The C-transform $\langle M\rangle$ of a $\lambda\mu$-term M is inductively defined as follows:*

(i) $\langle x\rangle = x$;

(ii) $\langle \lambda x.\, M\rangle = \lambda x.\, \langle M\rangle$;

(iii) $\langle M\, N\rangle = \langle M\rangle\, \langle N\rangle$;

(iv) $\langle \mu\alpha.\, M\rangle = \mathcal{C}\, (\lambda\alpha.\, \langle M\rangle)$;

(v) $\langle [\alpha] M\rangle = \alpha\, \langle M\rangle$.

The two next propositions establish that the C-transform preserves typing and reduction.

Proposition 4.2 *If M is a $\lambda\mu$-term and A is a simple type such that $\vdash_\mu M : A$ then $\vdash_C \langle M\rangle : A$.*

Proof. We interpret any sequent

$$M : \Gamma \vdash A, \Delta$$

of the $\lambda\mu$-calculus by the following intuitionistic sequent:

$$\Gamma, \neg\Delta \vdash M : A,$$

where the context $\neg\Delta$ corresponds to the context Δ in which each type has been negated.

Then, using Felleisen's operator $\mathcal{C}$, we may simulate μ-abstraction and naming as follows:

$$\cfrac{\cfrac{\Gamma, \neg\Delta, \neg A^\alpha \vdash M : \bot}{\Gamma, \neg\Delta \vdash \lambda\alpha.\, M : \neg\neg A}}{\Gamma, \neg\Delta \vdash \mathcal{C}\, (\lambda\alpha.\, M) : A}$$

$$\frac{\neg A^\alpha \vdash \alpha : \neg A \qquad \Gamma, \neg\Delta \vdash M : A}{\Gamma, \neg\Delta, \neg A^\alpha \vdash \alpha\, M : \bot}$$

□

Proposition 4.3 *Let M and N be $\lambda\mu$-terms. If $M \twoheadrightarrow_\mu N$, then $\langle M \rangle \twoheadrightarrow_c \langle N \rangle$.*

Proof. The property is obvious for the β-reduction steps. For the structural reduction steps, we have that:

$$\begin{aligned}
\langle (\mu\alpha.\, M)\, N \rangle &= \mathcal{C}\,(\lambda\alpha.\, \langle M \rangle)\, \langle N \rangle \\
&\rightarrow_c \mathcal{C}\,(\lambda k.\, (\lambda\alpha.\, \langle M \rangle)\, (\lambda f.\, k\, (f\, \langle N \rangle))) \\
&\rightarrow_c \mathcal{C}\,(\lambda k.\, \langle M \rangle[\lambda f.\, k\, (f\, \langle N \rangle)/\alpha])
\end{aligned}$$

Then, to establish that

$$\mathcal{C}\,(\lambda k.\, \langle M \rangle[\lambda f.\, k\, (f\, \langle N \rangle)/\alpha]) \twoheadrightarrow_c \langle \mu\alpha.\, M[N/\!*\, \alpha] \rangle,$$

it remains to establish that

$$\langle M \rangle[\lambda f.\, k\, (f\, \langle N \rangle)/\alpha] \twoheadrightarrow_c \langle M[N/\!*\, \alpha] \rangle[k/\alpha].$$

This last property may be established by induction on the definition of the structural substitution. The only intersting case is when M is of the form $[\alpha]\,O$:

$$\begin{aligned}
\langle [\alpha]O \rangle[\lambda f.\, k\, (f\, \langle N \rangle)/\alpha] &= (\alpha\, \langle O \rangle)[\lambda f.\, k\, (f\, \langle N \rangle)/\alpha] \\
&= (\lambda f.\, k\, (f\, \langle N \rangle))\, \langle O \rangle[(\lambda f.\, k\, (f\, \langle N \rangle))/\alpha] \\
&\rightarrow_c k\, (\langle O \rangle[(\lambda f.\, k\, (f\, \langle N \rangle))/\alpha]\, \langle N \rangle) \\
&\twoheadrightarrow_c k\, (\langle O[N/\!*\, \alpha] \rangle[k/\alpha]\, \langle N \rangle) \\
&\qquad \text{by induction hypothesis} \\
&= \alpha\, (\langle O[N/\!*\, \alpha] \rangle\, \langle N \rangle)[k/\alpha] \\
&\qquad \alpha \notin FV(\langle N \rangle) \\
&= \langle [\alpha](O[N/\!*\, \alpha]\, N) \rangle[k/\alpha] \\
&= \langle ([\alpha]O)[N/\!*\, \alpha] \rangle[k/\alpha]
\end{aligned}$$

□

Notice that the notion of reduction $\mathcal{C}_{\text{top}}$ does not play any role in the above proof. This notion of reduction is necessary only for the results of the next section.

5 The Inverse Translation

We have shown that $\lambda\mu$ may be injected into $\lambda\mathcal{C}$. In this section, we show that the two calculi are actually isomorphic. To this end, we construct the inverse translation.

The key of this inverse translation is the following $\lambda\mu$-derivation that corresponds to the double negation rule[2]:

$$\dfrac{M : \vdash \neg\neg A \qquad \dfrac{\dfrac{f : A^f \vdash A}{[\alpha]f : A^f \vdash A^\alpha}}{\lambda f.[\alpha]f : \vdash \neg A, A^\alpha}}{\dfrac{M(\lambda f.[\alpha]f) : \vdash A^\alpha}{\mu\alpha.M(\lambda f.[\alpha]f) : \vdash A}}$$

This derivation motivates the definition that follows.

Definition 5.1 (μ-transform) *The μ-transform $\overline{M}$ of a $\lambda\mu$-term M is inductively defined as follows:*

(i) $\overline{x} = x$;

(ii) $\overline{\lambda x.M} = \lambda x.\overline{M}$;

(iii) $\overline{MN} = \overline{M}\,\overline{N}$;

(iv) $\overline{CM} = \mu\alpha.\overline{M}(\lambda f.[\alpha]f)$.

By construction, we have that the μ-transform preserves typing.

Proposition 5.2 *If M is a λ_c-term and A is a simple type such that $\vdash_C M : A$ then $\vdash_\mu \overline{M} : A$.*

Proof. A straightforward induction on the derivation of $\vdash_C M : A$. □

The μ-transform does not preserve reduction. This is due to the fact that the elementary reduction steps of λC are more basic than the notion of structural reduction of $\lambda\mu$. Nevertheless, the equality is preserved.

Proposition 5.3 *Let M and N be λ_c-terms. If $M =_c N$, then $\overline{M} =_\mu \overline{N}$.*

Proof. The property is obvious for the β-reduction steps. For the notions of reduction C_L and C_{top} we proceed, respectively, as follows.

$$\begin{aligned}
\overline{(CM)N} &= (\mu\alpha.\overline{M}(\lambda f.[\alpha]f))\overline{N} \\
&=_\mu \mu\alpha.\overline{M}(\lambda f.[\alpha](f\,\overline{N})) \\
&=_\mu \mu\alpha.\overline{M}(\lambda f.(\lambda x.[\alpha]x)(f\,\overline{N})) \\
&=_\mu \mu\alpha.(\lambda k.\overline{M}(\lambda f.k\,(f\,\overline{N})))(\lambda x.[\alpha]x) \\
&= \overline{C(\lambda k.M(\lambda f.k\,(f\,N)))}
\end{aligned}$$

[2] Remark that the resulting $\lambda\mu$-term is not the one given by M. Parigot in [15]. The difference, which is necessary for our purpose, is due to the rules that we have given to handle the negation

$$\begin{aligned}\overline{\mathcal{C}\,M} &= \mu\alpha.\,\overline{M}\,(\lambda f.[\alpha]f)\\ &=_\mu \mu\alpha.\,\overline{M}\,(\lambda f.(\lambda x.[\alpha]x)\,f)\\ &=_\mu \mu\alpha.\,(\lambda k.\,\overline{M}\,(\lambda f.\,k\,f))\,(\lambda x.[\alpha]x)\\ &= \overline{\mathcal{C}\,(\lambda k.\,M\,(\lambda f.\,k\,f))}\end{aligned}$$

□

It remains to establish that the two transforms are inverse of each other. This is where the notion of reduction $\mathcal{C}_{\text{top}}$ is needed.

Proposition 5.4 *Let M be a closed $\lambda\mu$-term and N be a λ_c-term. The $\mathcal{C}$- and the μ-transforms are such that:*

$$\overline{\langle M\rangle} =_\mu M \qquad \text{(a)}$$

$$\langle\overline{N}\rangle =_c N \qquad \text{(b)}$$

Proof. (a) The proof is by induction on the structure of M. We prove that for any $\lambda\mu$-term M

$$\overline{\langle M\rangle} =_\mu M^*,$$

where M^* is obtained by replacing each free μ-variable α occurring in a subterm $[\alpha]O$ of M, by the application $\alpha\,O$.

The only non-trivial case is when M is a μ-abstraction:

$$\begin{aligned}\overline{\langle\mu\alpha.\,O\rangle} &= \overline{\mathcal{C}\,(\lambda\alpha.\,\langle O\rangle)}\\ &= \mu\beta.\,(\lambda\alpha.\,\overline{\langle O\rangle})\,(\lambda f.[\beta]f)\\ &=_\mu \mu\beta.\,(\lambda\alpha.\,O^*)\,(\lambda f.[\beta]f)\\ &=_\mu \mu\beta.\,O^*[\lambda f.[\beta]f/\alpha]\\ &=_\mu (\mu\beta.\,O[\beta/\alpha])^*\end{aligned}$$

(b) The proof is by induction on the structure of N. The only interesting case is the one of a $\mathcal{C}$-application:

$$\begin{aligned}\langle\overline{\mathcal{C}\,O}\rangle &= \langle\mu\alpha.\,\overline{O}\,(\lambda f.[\alpha]f)\rangle\\ &= \mathcal{C}\,(\lambda\alpha.\,\langle\overline{O}\rangle\,(\lambda f.\,\alpha\,f))\\ &=_c \mathcal{C}\,(\lambda\alpha.\,O\,(\lambda f.\,\alpha\,f))\\ &=_c \mathcal{C}\,O\end{aligned}$$

□

We are now in the position of establishing that the two calculi are isomorphic.

Proposition 5.5 *If M and M' are closed $\lambda\mu$-terms, if N and N' are λ_c-terms, then*

$$M =_\mu M' \quad \text{iff} \quad \langle M\rangle =_c \langle M'\rangle \qquad \text{(a)}$$

$$N =_c N' \quad \text{iff} \quad \overline{N} =_\mu \overline{N'} \qquad \text{(b)}$$

Proof. From Propositions 4.3, 5.3, and 5.4. □

6 Conclusions

The isomorphism that we have presented in this paper clarifies the relation existing between two different calculi that both extend the formulae-as-types principle to classical logic. Surprisingly enough, we have shown that the main differences between the two approaches are primarily syntactic and that first-order $\lambda\mu$-calculus may be seen as a subtheory of a call-by-name variant of Felleisen's syntactic theory of sequential control.

It could be argued, however that our result is only partial because we did not take into account some features of the original $\lambda\mu$ and λC, respectively renaming and the use of the abort operator. As we said, from a proof-theoretic point of view, these two features are merely trivial. Nevertheless, it is interesting to see how we could allow for them.

As for the abort operator, we can modify the definition of the C-transform as follows:

(iv) $\langle [\alpha] M \rangle \;=\; \mathcal{A}(\alpha \langle M \rangle)$,

the other clauses being unchanged. Then, in order to preserve Proposition 4.3, we need the following reduction rule:

$$\mathcal{A}(\mathcal{A}\, M) \rightarrow_c \mathcal{A}\, M,$$

which is a particular case of Felleisen's notion of reduction $\mathcal{C}_{\text{idem}}$. On the other hand, the definition of the μ-transform may be kept unchanged but, in order to preserve Proposition 5.3, we would need to allow for the following notion of reduction:

$$\mu\alpha.\, M \rightarrow_\mu M$$

where $\mu\alpha.\, M$ and M are both of type $\bot$, and where α does not occur free in M. This notion of reduction, which is not included in Parigot's theory, is related to our treatment of negation.

As for renaming, it can be simulated in Felleisen's calculus by using the notion of reduction that follows:

$$M\,(\mathcal{C}\, N) \rightarrow_c N\,(\lambda x.\, M\, x),$$

where the type of M is of the form $\neg A$. This notion of reduction, which is absent from Felleisen's theory, is used by F. Barbanera and S. Berardi in [1].

In establishing our isomorphism, we did not use Felleisen's notion of reduction $\mathcal{C}_{\text{R}}$:

$$M\,(\mathcal{C}\, N) \rightarrow_c \mathcal{C}\,(\lambda k.\, N\,(\lambda v.\, \mathcal{A}\,(k\,(M\, v)))).$$

This notion of reduction corresponds, at the level of the $\lambda\mu$-calculus, to the following reduction rule:

$$M\,(\mu\alpha.\, N) \rightarrow_\mu \mu\alpha.\, N[M\, */\alpha],$$

where $N[M\, */\alpha]$ is obtained by replacing inductively each subterm of N of the form $[\alpha] O$ by $[\alpha](M\, O)$. This rule is symmetrical to the structural reduction rule. As observed by M. Parigot in [15], to add this rule to his theory destroys the confluence of the calculus. Nevertheless the addition of such rules allows the calculus to have a stronger notion of normal form, and the confluence can be restore by defining an appropriate call-by-value strategy. The resulting calculus provides an alternative solution to the problem of the *uniqueness of the representation of data.* This problem is solved by M. Parigot in [16] by using Krivine's storage operators, which is actually a way of enforcing a call-by-value mechanism.

References

[1] F. Barbanera and S. Berardi. Continuations and simple types: a strong normalization result. In *Proceedings of the ACM SIGPLAN Workshop on Continuations.* Report STAN-CS-92-1426, Stanford University, 1992.

[2] F. Barbanera and S. Berardi. Extracting constructive content from classical logic via control-like reductions. In M. Bezem and J.F. Groote, editors, *Proceedings of the International Conference on on Typed Lambda Calculi and Applications*, pages 45–59. Lecture Notes in Computer Science, 664, Springer Verlag, 1993.

[3] H.P. Barendregt. *The lambda calculus, its syntax and semantics.* North-Holland, revised edition, 1984.

[4] Ph. de Groote. A CPS-translation of the $\lambda\mu$-calculus. In *Proceedings of the Colloquium on Trees in Algebra and Programming (CAAP'94).* Lecture Notes in Computer Science, Springer Verlag, 1994.

[5] M. Felleisen, D.P. Friedman, E. Kohlbecker, and B. Duba. A syntactic theory of sequential control. *Theoretical Computer Science*, 52:205–237, 1987.

[6] M. Felleisen and R. Hieb. The revised report on the syntactic theory of sequential control and state. *Theoretical Computer Science*, 102:235–271, 1992.

[7] J.-Y. Girard. A new constructive logic: Classical logic. *Mathematical Structures in Computer Science*, 1:255–296, 1991.

[8] J.-Y. Girard, Y. Lafont, and P. Taylor. *Proofs and Types*, volume 7 of *Cambridge Tracts in Theoretical Computer Science.* Cambridge University Press, 1989.

[9] T. G. Griffin. A formulae-as-types notion of control. In *Conference record of the seventeenth annual ACM symposium on Principles of Programming Languages*, pages 47–58, 1990.

[10] J.R. Hindley and J.P. Seldin. *Introduction to combinators and λ-calculus.* London Mathematical Society Student Texts. Cambridge University Press, 1986.

[11] J.-L. Krivine. *Lambda-calcul, types et modèles.* Masson, 1990.

[12] J. Lambek and P.J. Scott. *An introduction to higher order categorical logic.* Cambridge University Press, 1986.

[13] C. R. Murthy. An evaluation semantics for classical proofs. In *Proceedings of the sixth annual IEEE symposium on logic in computer science*, pages 96–107, 1991.

[14] C. R. Murthy. A computational analysis of Girard's translation and LC. In *Proceedings of the seventh annual IEEE symposium on logic in computer science*, pages 90–101, 1992.

[15] M. Parigot. $\lambda\mu$-Calculus: an algorithmic interpretation of classical natural deduction. In A. Voronkov, editor, *Proceedings of the International Conference on Logic Programming and Automated Reasoning*, pages 190–201. Lecture Notes in Artificial Intelligence, 624, Springer Verlag, 1992.

[16] M. Parigot. Classical proofs as programs. In G. Gottlod, A. Leitsch, and D. Mundici, editors, *Proceedings of the third Kurt Gödel colloquium - KGC'93*, pages 263–276. Lecture Notes in Computer Science, 713, Springer Verlag, 1993.

[17] M. Parigot. Strong normalization for second order classical natural deduction. In *Proceedings of the eighth annual IEEE symposium on logic in computer science*, pages 39–46, 1993.

[18] D. Prawitz. *Natural Deduction, A Proof-Theoretical Study.* Almqvist & Wiksell, Stockholm, 1965.

[19] S. Stenlund. *Combinators λ-terms and proof theory.* D. Reidel Publishing Company, 1972.

On a Proof-Theoretical Analysis of $\Sigma_1^1 - \mathbf{AC}$, $\Sigma_1^1 - \mathbf{DC}$ and $\Delta_1^1 - \mathbf{CA}$

Sergei Tupailo

Department of Mathematics, Stanford University
Stanford, CA 94305-2125, sergei@csli.stanford.edu

Abstract. We present a simple method of embedding of $\Delta_1^1 - \mathbf{CA}$, $\Sigma_1^1 - \mathbf{AC}$ and $\Sigma_1^1 - \mathbf{DC}$ into $\mathbf{RA}_{\epsilon_0}$, $(\mathbf{RA}+\mathbf{PAC})_{\epsilon_0}$ and $(\mathbf{RA}+\mathbf{PDC})_{\epsilon_0}$ respectively, where PAC is Predicative Axiom of Choice and PDC is Predicative Axiom of Dependent Choice. These ramified systems are known to have proof-theoretic ordinals $\phi\varepsilon_0 0$, which in the case of PAC and PDC can be proved by normalization of Ramified Analysis with Hilbert's epsilon-symbol. In all cases (particularly, of $\Delta_1^1 - \mathbf{CA}$) our embedding is straightforward and avoids any intermediate steps (like Σ_1^1-Reflection), which was always the case before.

1 Initial Systems $\Sigma 0$ and $\Sigma 0\omega$

As a basic system we take the Second Order Arithmetic with Arithmetical Comprehension Axiom $\Pi_0^1 - \mathbf{CA}$. To fix notations, we choose the following Gentzen-type formulation $\Sigma 0$ of $\Pi_0^1 - \mathbf{CA}$:

- rules for first order quantifiers are ordinary;
- rules for second order quantifiers are as follows:

$$\frac{F[A], \Gamma \longrightarrow \Theta}{\exists X F[X], \Gamma \longrightarrow \Theta}\ \exists^2 \rightarrow \qquad \frac{\Gamma \longrightarrow \Theta, F[A]}{\Gamma \longrightarrow \Theta, \forall X F[X]}\ \rightarrow \forall^2$$

(A does not occur in the conclusion),

$$\frac{\Gamma \longrightarrow \Theta, F[\lambda x G[x]]}{\Gamma \longrightarrow \Theta, \exists X F[X]}\ \rightarrow \exists^2 \qquad \frac{F[\lambda x G[x]], \Gamma \longrightarrow \Theta}{\forall X F[X], \Gamma \longrightarrow \Theta}\ \forall^2 \rightarrow$$

where formula $G[a]$ does not contain bound predicate variables;
- Induction Axiom is taken in the form:

$$F[0], \forall x(F[x] \rightarrow F[x']) \longrightarrow \forall x F[x] \qquad (Ind)$$

where F is an arbitrary formula.

By $\Sigma 0\omega$ we mean the correspondent system with ω-rule for the first order quantifiers, without Induction and free individual variables. By a *realization* of a sequent we mean the result of substituting numerals for all its free individual variables.

We call an expression *arithmetical* iff it does not contain bound predicate variables. A cut is called *arithmetical* iff its cut formula is arithmetical.

Σ^1_1*-formula (sequent)* is defined in a standard way: all occurrences of $\exists^2$ are required to be positive, and all occurrences of $\forall^2$ are required to be negative. Π^1_1*-formula (sequent)* is defined similarly.

2 Ramified Analysis

By $\mathbf{RA}_{\varepsilon_0}$ we mean a standard Gentzen-type formulation of Ramified Analysis up to level ε_0. Predicative Axiom of Choice **PAC** is an axiom scheme

$$\forall x \exists Y^\alpha F[x, Y^\alpha] \longrightarrow \exists Y^\beta \forall x F[x, Y^\beta_x] \qquad (PAC)$$

where $\alpha < \beta$. Predicative Axiom of Dependent Choice is an axiom scheme

$$\forall x \forall X^\alpha \exists Y^\alpha F[x, X^\alpha, Y^\alpha] \longrightarrow \forall X^\alpha \exists Y^\beta (Y^\beta_0 \doteq X^\alpha \wedge \forall x F[x, Y^\beta_x, Y^\beta_{x'}]) \qquad (PDC)$$

where $\alpha < \beta$. In the above notations P_t is $\lambda y P(< t, y >)$ and $P \doteq Q$ is $\forall x (P(x) \leftrightarrow Q(x))$.

It is well-known that $|\mathbf{RA}_{\varepsilon_0}| = \phi\varepsilon_0 0$. As it shown in [3],[4] by normalization of Ramified Analysis with Hilbert's epsilon axiom $F[T^\alpha] \longrightarrow F[\epsilon X^\beta F[X^\beta]]$ ($\alpha < \beta$) and Extensionality $\forall X^\alpha (F[X^\alpha] \leftrightarrow G[X^\alpha]) \longrightarrow \epsilon X^\alpha F[X^\alpha] \doteq \epsilon X^\alpha G[X^\alpha]$, the systems $(\mathbf{RA}+\mathbf{PAC})_{\varepsilon_0}$ and $(\mathbf{RA}+\mathbf{PDC})_{\varepsilon_0}$ have the same proof-theoretic ordinal.

Let σ be an ordinal, $0 < \sigma < \varepsilon_0$, and F be a formula in the language of $\Sigma 0\omega$. By σ*-interpretation* F^σ of F we mean the result of superscribing bound predicate variables of F by σ, and substituting predicators of levels $< \sigma$ for free predicate variables of F. σ*-interpretation* of a sequent is defined similarly.

The result of this paper is the following **Theorem:**

If a Σ^1_1-sequent S is derivable in $\Delta^1_1 - \mathrm{CA}$, $\Sigma^1_1 - \mathrm{AC}$ or $\Sigma^1_1 - \mathrm{DC}$ then there exists $\sigma < \varepsilon_0$ such that for any its realization S' and for any σ-interpretation S^σ of S', S^σ is derivable in $\mathbf{RA}_{\varepsilon_0}$, $(\mathbf{RA}+\mathbf{PAC})_{\varepsilon_0}$ or $(\mathbf{RA}+\mathbf{PDC})_{\varepsilon_0}$ respectively.

From this the same statement for Π^1_2-sequents will follow immediately.

The method of the proof is cutelimination plus direct embedding and is very much the same for all three systems.

We will need the following simple **Fact 1** for **RA**:

if $\sigma < \tau$ and a formula F^τ is obtained from F^σ by replacing positive occurrences of $\exists X^\sigma$ by $\exists X^\tau$ and negative occurrences of $\forall X^\sigma$ by $\forall X^\tau$ then $F^\sigma \longrightarrow F^\tau$ is derivable in $\mathbf{RA}_{\varepsilon_0}$.

3 $\Pi^1_0 - \mathbf{AC}$

By Π^1_0 – **AC** we mean the system obtained from Π^1_0 – **CA** by adding the Arithmetical Axiom of Choice:

$$\forall x \exists Y F[x, Y] \longrightarrow \exists Y \forall x F[x, Y_x]$$

where $F[a, B]$ is arithmetical. In this section we embed Π^1_0 – **AC** into $(\mathbf{RA} + \mathbf{PAC})_{\varepsilon_0}$. This embedding will be used repeatedly in subsequent sections.

We choose the following system $\Sigma\mathbf{1}$ for Π^1_0 – **AC**. It is obtained from $\Sigma 0$ by adding the following rule of inference:

$$\frac{\Gamma \longrightarrow \Theta, \forall x \exists Y F[x, Y]}{\Gamma \longrightarrow \Theta, \exists Y \forall x F[x, Y_x]} \quad AC$$

where formula $F[a, B]$ is arithmetical.

By $\Sigma\mathbf{1}\omega$ we mean the correspondent ω-version of $\Sigma\mathbf{1}$.

Step 1. Embedding into ω-system.

Lemma. *If S is derivable in $\Sigma\mathbf{1}$ then every realization of S is derivable in $\Sigma\mathbf{1}\omega$ by a derivation of the height $< \omega * 2$.*

The **proof** is standard. □

Step 2. Elimination of complex cuts.

Lemma. *If S is derivable in $\Sigma\mathbf{1}\omega$ by a derivation of the height $< \varepsilon_0$ then S is derivable in $\Sigma\mathbf{1}\omega$ by a derivation of the height $< \varepsilon_0$ possessing the following property:*

> the only cuts in it are arithmetical and cuts with cut formulas of the kind $\exists Y \forall x F[x, Y_x]$, where $F[a, A]$ is arithmetical. (*)

The **proof** is standard. □

Step 3. Embedding into $(\mathbf{RA} + \mathbf{PAC})_{\varepsilon_0}$.

Lemma. *If a Σ^1_1-sequent S is derivable in $\Sigma\mathbf{1}\omega$ by a derivation of the height α possessing the property (*), then for every $\sigma = \omega^\alpha * \beta > 0$ and every interpretation S^σ of S, S^σ is derivable in $(\mathbf{RA} + \mathbf{PAC})_\sigma$.*

The **proof** is by induction on α. The only two interesting cases to be considered are when the lowermost rule of inference is a cut or AC.

1. Case of a cut.

(a) cut on $\exists Y \forall x F[x, Y_x]$

$$\frac{d_0 : \Gamma \longrightarrow \Theta, \exists Y \forall x F[x, Y_x] \qquad d_1 : \exists Y \forall x F[x, Y_x], \Gamma \longrightarrow \Theta}{\Gamma \longrightarrow \Theta} \quad cut$$

$\Gamma^\sigma \longrightarrow \Theta^\sigma$ is derived by a cut on $\exists Y^\sigma \forall x F^\sigma[x, Y^\sigma_x]$. Right premise of this cut

$$\exists Y^\sigma \forall x F^\sigma[x, Y^\sigma_x], \Gamma^\sigma \longrightarrow \Theta^\sigma \tag{1}$$

is derived from

$$\forall x F^{\sigma}[x, P^{\delta}_{x}], \Gamma^{\sigma} \longrightarrow \Theta^{\sigma} \qquad (2)$$

for all predicators P^{δ} of levels $\delta < \sigma$. The latter sequent 2 is derivable by induction hypothesis, since $\forall x F[x, A_x], \Gamma \longrightarrow \Theta$ is a Σ^1_1-sequent derivable by a derivation with the property (*) of the height $\alpha_1 < \alpha$ (rule AC is formulated in such a way that inversions hold in $\Sigma 1\omega$). We used the equality $\omega^{\alpha} * \beta = \omega^{\alpha_1} * \omega^{\alpha-\alpha_1} * \beta$.

Left premise

$$\Gamma^{\sigma} \longrightarrow \Theta^{\sigma}, \exists Y^{\sigma} \forall x F^{\sigma}[x, Y^{\sigma}_{x}] \qquad (3)$$

is obtained from d_0 by induction hypothesis, since $\Gamma \longrightarrow \Theta, \exists Y \forall x F[x, Y_x]$ is a Σ^1_1-sequent.

(b) arithmetical cut

This case is managed with in the same way as previous one, with the simplification that premises are Σ^1_1-sequents automatically.

2. Case of AC.

$$\frac{d_0 : \Gamma \longrightarrow \Theta, \forall x \exists Y F[x, Y]}{\Gamma \longrightarrow \Theta, \exists Y \forall x F[x, Y_x]} \; AC$$

σ-interpretation

$$\Gamma^{\sigma} \longrightarrow \Theta^{\sigma}, \exists Y^{\sigma} \forall x F^{\sigma}[x, Y^{\sigma}_{x}] \qquad (4)$$

of the conclusion is derived in the following way. Let $\gamma < \sigma$ be the maximum level of predicators substituted for free predicate variables of the conclusion of the AC-rule in the current σ-interpretation. Let δ be of the kind $\omega^{\alpha_0} * \beta_0$, where $\alpha_0 < \alpha$ is the height of d_0, such that $\gamma < \delta < \sigma$ (such δ always exists - cf. [1], Th.14.12). Note that under this choice of δ F^{σ} is simultaneously F^{δ} (we shall write simply F for brevity). By induction hypothesis we can derive

$$\Gamma^{\delta} \longrightarrow \Theta^{\delta}, \forall x \exists Y^{\delta} F[x, Y^{\delta}] \qquad (5)$$

From this by *Fact 1* from section 2 we obtain

$$\Gamma^{\sigma} \longrightarrow \Theta^{\sigma}, \forall x \exists Y^{\delta} F[x, Y^{\delta}] \qquad (6)$$

which derives 4 together with PAC

$$\forall x \exists X^{\delta} F[x, X^{\delta}] \longrightarrow \exists X^{\sigma} \forall x F[x, X^{\sigma}_{x}] \qquad (7)$$

□

4 $\Sigma^1_1 - \mathbf{AC}$

By $\Sigma^1_1 - \mathbf{AC}$ we mean the system obtained from $\Pi^1_0 - \mathbf{CA}$ by adding the Σ^1_1 Axiom of Choice:

$$\forall x \exists Y F[x, Y] \longrightarrow \exists Y \forall x F[x, Y_x]$$

where $F[a, B]$ is a Σ^1_1-formula. In this section we show how $\Sigma^1_1 - AC$ is reduced to $\Pi^1_0 - AC$.

Lemma. *In $\Pi^1_0 - \mathbf{AC}$ every Σ^1_1-formula is equivalent to a formula of the form $\exists X F[X]$ and every Π^1_1-formula is equivalent to a formula of the form $\forall X F[X]$ where $F[A]$ is arithmetical.*

Proof. Given a Σ^1_1-formula, after reduction to the prenex form only existential second order quantifiers will remain. The rest of the proof is by induction on the number of quantifiers in the prenex form. Starting from inside, we apply the following transformations:

in the case $\exists x \exists X$ quantifiers are permuted to $\exists X \exists x$;

in the case $\exists X \exists Y$ quantifiers are compressed to $\exists X$ (Arithmetical Comprehension Axiom $\Pi^1_0 - CA$ is used);

in the case $\forall x \exists Y$ quantifiers are permuted to $\exists Y \forall x$ using $\Pi^1_0 - AC$ and $\Pi^1_0 - CA$.

For a Π^1_1-formula G the assertion follows from the fact that $\neg G$ is Σ^1_1. □

Lemma. *$\Sigma^1_1 - AC$ is derivable in $\Sigma 0$ from $\Pi^1_0 - AC$.*

Proof. By the previos Lemma we can consider only $\Sigma^1_1 - AC$ of the form

$$\forall x \exists X \exists Y F[x, X, Y] \longrightarrow \exists X \forall x \exists Y F[x, X_x, Y]$$

where $F[a, A, B]$ is arithmetical. Suppose $\forall x \exists X \exists Y F[x, X, Y]$. By Arithmetical Comprehension Axiom we obtain $\forall x \exists Z F[x, Z_0, Z_1]$ (Z is to be taken $\lambda z(l(z) = 0 \wedge X(r(z)) \vee l(z) = 1 \wedge Y(r(z))))$. By $\Pi^1_0 - \mathbf{AC}$ we have $\exists Z \forall x F[x, Z_{x0}, Z_{x1}]$. From this by Arithmetical Comprehension again we obtain $\exists X \forall x \exists Y F[x, X_x, Y]$ (X is to be taken $\lambda z Z(< l(z), < 0, r(z) >>)$). □

Hence, we have an embedding of $\Sigma^1_1 - \mathbf{AC}$ into $(\mathbf{RA} + \mathbf{PAC})_{\epsilon_0}$.

5 $\Sigma^1_1 - \mathbf{DC}$

By $\Sigma^1_1 - \mathbf{DC}$ we mean the system obtained from $\Pi^1_0 - \mathbf{AC}$ by adding the Σ^1_1 Axiom of Dependent Choice:

$$\forall x \forall X \exists Y F[x, X, Y] \longrightarrow \forall X \exists Y (Y_0 \doteq X \wedge \forall x F[x, Y_x, Y_{x'}])$$

where $F[a, A, B]$ is a Σ^1_1-formula. In this section we embed $\Sigma^1_1 - \mathbf{DC}$ into $(\mathbf{RA} + \mathbf{PDC})_{\epsilon_0}$. Since we have $\Pi^1_0 - AC$, we can restrict $\Sigma^1_1 - DC$ to the form

$$\forall x \forall X \exists Y \exists Z F[x, X, Y, Z] \longrightarrow \forall X \exists Y \exists Z (Y_0 \doteq X \wedge \forall x F[x, Y_x, Y_{x'}, Z_x])$$

where $F[a, A, B, C]$ is arithmetical.

We choose the following system $\Sigma\mathbf{2}$ for $\Sigma^1_1 - \mathbf{DC}$. It is obtained from $\Sigma\mathbf{1}$ by adding the following rule of inference:

$$\frac{\Gamma \longrightarrow \Theta, \forall x \forall X \exists Y \exists Z F[x, X, Y, Z]}{\Gamma \longrightarrow \Theta, \exists Y \exists Z (Y_0 \doteq R \wedge \forall x F[x, Y_x, Y_{x'}, Z_x])} \; DC$$

where formula $F[a, A, B, C]$ and predicator R are arithmetical.

By $\Sigma\mathbf{2}\omega$ we mean the correspondent ω-version of $\Sigma\mathbf{2}$.

Step 1. Embedding into ω-system.

Lemma. *If S is derivable in $\Sigma 2$ then every realization of S is derivable in $\Sigma 2\omega$ by a derivation of the height $< \omega * 2$.*

The **proof** is standard. □

Step 2. Elimination of complex cuts.

Lemma. *If S is derivable in $\Sigma 2\omega$ by a derivation of the height $< \varepsilon_0$ then S is derivable in $\Sigma 2\omega$ by a derivation of the height $< \varepsilon_0$ possessing the following property:*

> the only cuts in it are arithmetical and cuts with cut formulas of the kind $\exists Y \forall x F[x, Y_x]$ and $\exists Y \exists Z (Y_0 \doteq R \wedge \forall x F[x, Y_x, Y_{x'}, Z_x])$, where $F[a, A]$, $F[a, A, B, C]$ and R are arithmetical. (*)

The **proof** is standard. □

Step 3. Embedding into $(\mathbf{RA} + \mathbf{PDC})_{\varepsilon_0}$.

Lemma. *If a Σ^1_1-sequent S is derivable in $\Sigma 2\omega$ by a derivation of the height α possessing the property (*), then for every $\sigma = \omega^\alpha * \beta > 0$ and every interpretation S^σ of S, S^σ is derivable in* $(\mathbf{RA} + \mathbf{PDC})_\sigma$.

The **proof** is by induction on α. The only three interesting cases to be considered are when the lowermost rule of inference is a cut, AC or DC.

Note that $PDC(\alpha, \beta)$ derives $PAC(\alpha, \beta)$ in $\mathbf{RA}$. Hence cases of an arithmetical cut, cut on $\exists Y \forall x F[x, Y_x]$ and AC can be treated exactly as in the section 3. Consider remaining cases.

3. Case of a cut on $\exists Y \exists Z (Y_0 \doteq R \wedge \forall x F[x, Y_x, Y_{x'}, Z_x])$.

This case is treated exactly as Case 1 in 3. σ-interpretation of the left premise is obtained directly by the induction hypothesis since it is Σ^1_1; the right premise is reduced to Σ^1_1-form by two inversion¡s of the exterior $\exists^2$ (rules AC and DC are formulated in such a way that inversions hold in $\Sigma 2\omega$) and the induction hypothesis and two $\exists^2$-introductions are applied.

4. Case of DC.

$$\frac{d_0 : \Gamma \longrightarrow \Theta, \forall x \forall X \exists Y \exists Z F[x, X, Y, Z]}{\Gamma \longrightarrow \Theta, \exists Y \exists Z (Y_0 \doteq R \wedge \forall x F[x, Y_x, Y_{x'}, Z_x])} \; DC$$

σ-interpretation

$$\Gamma^\sigma \longrightarrow \Theta^\sigma, \exists Y^\sigma \exists Z^\sigma (Y^\sigma_0 \doteq R^\sigma \wedge \forall x F[x, Y^\sigma_x, Y^\sigma_{x'}, Z^\sigma_x]) \tag{1}$$

of the conclusion is derived in the following way. Let $\gamma < \sigma$ be the maximum level of predicators substituted for free predicate variables of the conclusion of the DC-rule in the current σ-interpretation. Let δ be of the kind $\omega^{\alpha_0} * \beta_0$, where $\alpha_0 < \alpha$ is the height of d_0, such that $\gamma < \delta < \sigma$ (such δ always exists - cf. [1], Th.14.12). Note that under this choice of δ F^σ is simultaneously F^δ (we shall write simply F for brevity) and R^σ is simultaneously R^δ. By induction hypothesis we can derive

$$\Gamma^\delta \longrightarrow \Theta^\delta, \exists Y^\delta \exists Z^\delta F[n, P^\zeta, Y^\delta, Z^\delta] \tag{2}$$

for each n and each predicator P^ζ of level $\zeta < \delta$. From this by $\forall^2$-introduction and an omega-rule we obtain

$$\Gamma^\delta \longrightarrow \Theta^\delta, \forall x \forall X^\delta \exists Y^\delta \exists Z^\delta F[x, X^\delta, Y^\delta, Z^\delta] \tag{3}$$

From this by *Fact 1* we obtain

$$\Gamma^\sigma \longrightarrow \Theta^\sigma, \forall x \forall X^\delta \exists Y^\delta \exists Z^\delta F[x, X^\delta, Y^\delta, Z^\delta] \tag{4}$$

which derives 1 together with PDC

$$\forall x \forall X^\delta \exists Y^\delta \exists Z^\delta F[x, X^\delta, Y^\delta, Z^\delta] \longrightarrow \forall X^\delta \exists Y^\sigma (Y^\sigma_0 \doteq X^\delta \wedge \forall x \exists Z^\delta F[x, Y^\sigma_x, Y^\sigma_{x'}, Z^\delta]) \tag{5}$$

and PAC

$$\forall X^\sigma \forall Y^\sigma \forall x \exists Z^\delta F[x, X^\sigma, Y^\sigma, Z^\delta] \longrightarrow \forall X^\sigma \forall Y^\sigma \exists Z^\sigma \forall x F[x, X^\sigma, Y^\sigma, Z^\sigma_x]) \tag{6}$$

□

6 Δ^1_1 – CA

By Δ^1_1 **– CA** we mean the system obtained from Π^1_0 **– AC** (Π^1_0 **– CA**) by adding the Δ^1_1-Comprehension Axiom

$$\forall x(G[x] \leftrightarrow H[x]) \longrightarrow \exists X \forall x(X(x) \leftrightarrow G[x])$$

where $G[a]$ is a Σ^1_1-formula and $H[a]$ is a Π^1_1-formula. If we have $\Pi^1_0 - AC$, we can restrict Δ^1_1-Comprehension Axiom to the form

$$\forall x(\exists Y G[x, Y] \leftrightarrow \forall Z H[x, Z]) \longrightarrow \exists X \forall x(X(x) \leftrightarrow \exists Y G[x, Y])$$

where $G[a, B]$ and $H[a, C]$ are arithmetical, which under presence of $\Pi^1_0 - AC$ is obviously equivalent to the form above. In this section we embed Δ^1_1 **– CA** with Δ^1_1-Comprehension in the second form into $(\mathbf{RA} + \mathbf{PAC})_{\varepsilon_0}$. However, if we work over $\Pi^1_0 - CA$, not $\Pi^1_0 - AC$, the whole construction will be carried over $\Pi^1_0 - CA$, PAC will not be used, and the resulting embedding will be into $\mathbf{RA}_{\varepsilon_0}$, not $(\mathbf{RA} + \mathbf{PAC})_{\varepsilon_0}$.

We choose the following systems $\Sigma\mathbf{3}$ and $\Sigma'\mathbf{3}$ for $\Delta^{\mathbf{1}}_{\mathbf{1}}-\mathbf{CA}$. They are obtained respectively from $\Sigma\mathbf{0}$ and $\Sigma\mathbf{1}$ by adding the following rule of inference:

$$\frac{\Gamma \longrightarrow \Theta, \forall x(\exists Y G[x,Y] \leftrightarrow \forall Z H[x,Z])}{\Gamma \longrightarrow \Theta, \exists X \forall x(\exists Y G[x,Y] \rightarrow X(x) \wedge X(x) \rightarrow \forall Z H[x,Z])}\ \Delta$$

where formulas $G[a,B]$ and $H[a,C]$ are arithmetical.

It is easy to see that this Δ-rule implies $\Delta^1_1 - CA$ as formulated above.

By $\Sigma\mathbf{3}\omega$ ($\Sigma'\mathbf{3}\omega$) we mean the correspondent ω-version of $\Sigma\mathbf{3}$ ($\Sigma'\mathbf{3}$).

Step 1. Embedding into ω-system.

Lemma. *If S is derivable in $\Sigma\mathbf{3}$ ($\Sigma'\mathbf{3}$) then every realization of S is derivable in $\Sigma3\omega$ ($\Sigma'3\omega$) by a derivation of the height $< \omega * 2$.*

The **proof** is standard. □

Step 2. Elimination of complex cuts.

Lemma. *If S is derivable in $\Sigma3\omega$ ($\Sigma'3\omega$) by a derivation of the height $< \varepsilon_0$ then S is derivable in $\Sigma3\omega$ ($\Sigma'3\omega$) by a derivation of the height $< \varepsilon_0$ possessing the following property:*

> the only cuts in it are arithmetical, cuts with cut formulas of the kind $\exists X \forall x(\exists Y G[x,Y] \rightarrow X(x) \wedge X(x) \rightarrow \forall Z H[x,Z])$ adjacent to Δ-rules introducing these formulas, and (in the case of $\Sigma'3\omega$ only) cuts with cut formulas of the kind $\exists Y \forall x F[x,Y_x]$ where $F[a,B]$ is arithmetical. (*)

The **proof** is standard. □

Step 3. Embedding into $(\mathbf{RA}(+\mathbf{PAC}))_{\varepsilon_0}$.

Lemma. *If a Σ^1_1-sequent S is derivable in $\Sigma3\omega$ ($\Sigma'3\omega$) by a derivation of the height α possessing the property (*), then for every $\sigma = \omega^\alpha * \beta > 0$ and every interpretation S^σ of S, S^σ is derivable in $\mathbf{RA}_\sigma$ ($(\mathbf{RA}+\mathbf{PAC})_\sigma$).*

The **proof** is by induction on α. The only interesting case(s) to be considered is when the lowermost rule of inference is a cut (and AC if applicable). Furthermore, cases of AC, arithmetical cut and cut on $\exists Y \forall x F[x,Y_x]$ are treated exactly as in sections 3 and 5. So, we have to consider only the case of a cut on $\exists X \forall x(\exists Y G[x,Y] \rightarrow X(x) \wedge X(x) \rightarrow \forall Z H[x,Z])$.

Let

$$d_1 : \exists X \forall x(\exists Y G[x,Y] \rightarrow X(x) \wedge X(x) \rightarrow \forall Z H[x,Z]), \Gamma \longrightarrow \Theta$$

be a derivation of its right premise and

$$d_0 : \Gamma \longrightarrow \Theta, \forall x(\exists Y G[x,Y] \leftrightarrow \forall Z H[x,Z])$$

be a derivation of the premise of the adjacent Δ-rule and let $\alpha_0, \alpha_1 < \alpha$ be the heights of d_0, d_1.

$\Gamma^\sigma \longrightarrow \Theta^\sigma$ is derived by a cut on $\exists X^\sigma \forall x(\exists Y^\sigma G^\sigma[x,Y^\sigma] \rightarrow X^\sigma(x) \wedge X^\sigma(x) \rightarrow \forall Z^\sigma H^\sigma[x,Z^\sigma])$. Right premise of this cut

$$\exists X^\sigma \forall x(\exists Y^\sigma G^\sigma[x,Y^\sigma] \rightarrow X^\sigma(x) \wedge X^\sigma(x) \rightarrow \forall Z^\sigma H^\sigma[x,Z^\sigma]), \Gamma^\sigma \longrightarrow \Theta^\sigma \quad (1)$$

is derived by ω-rule from

$$\forall x(\exists Y^\sigma G^\sigma[x,Y^\sigma] \to P^\delta(x) \wedge P^\delta(x) \to \forall Z^\sigma H^\sigma[x,Z^\sigma]), \Gamma^\sigma_\cdot \longrightarrow \Theta^\sigma \tag{2}$$

for all predicators P^δ of levels $\delta < \sigma$. The latter sequent 2 is derivable by induction hypothesis, since $\forall x(\exists Y G[x,Y] \to A(x) \wedge A(x) \to \forall Z H[x,Z]), \Gamma \longrightarrow \Theta$ is a Σ^1_1-sequent derivable by a derivation with the property (*) of the height $\alpha_1 < \alpha$ (rule Δ (and AC) is formulated in such a way that inversions hold in $\Sigma 3\omega$ ($\Sigma' 3\omega$)). We used the equality $\omega^\alpha * \beta = \omega^{\alpha_1} * \omega^{\alpha - \alpha_1} * \beta$.

Left premise

$$\Gamma^\sigma \longrightarrow \Theta^\sigma, \exists X^\sigma \forall x(\exists Y^\sigma G^\sigma[x,Y^\sigma] \to X^\sigma(x) \wedge X^\sigma(x) \to \forall Z^\sigma H^\sigma[x,Z^\sigma]) \tag{3}$$

of this cut is derived in the following way. Let $\gamma < \sigma$ be the maximum level of predicators substituted for free predicate variables of the conclusion of the Δ-rule in the current σ-interpretation. Let δ be of the kind $\omega^{\alpha_0} * \beta_0$, such that $\gamma < \delta < \sigma$ (such δ always exists - cf. [1], Th.14.12). Note that under this choice of δ G^σ is simultaneously G^δ, and H^σ is simultaneously H^δ (we shall write simply G and H for brevity). Now 3 is derived from

$$\longrightarrow \exists X^\sigma \forall x(\exists Y^\delta G[x,Y^\delta] \leftrightarrow X^\sigma(x)) \tag{4}$$

which is simply derived by Predicative Comprehension,

$$\Gamma^\sigma \longrightarrow \Theta^\sigma, \forall x(\exists Y^\delta G[x,Y^\delta] \leftrightarrow \exists Y^\sigma G[x,Y^\sigma]) \tag{5}$$

and

$$\Gamma^\sigma \longrightarrow \Theta^\sigma, \forall x(\exists Y^\sigma G[x,Y^\sigma] \to \forall Z^\sigma H[x,Z^\sigma]) \tag{6}$$

Direction $\to$ of 5 is derived from Predicative Comprehension. Direction $\leftarrow$ is derived from Predicative Comprehension and sequents 6 and

$$\Gamma^\sigma \longrightarrow \Theta^\sigma, \forall x(\forall Z^\delta H[x,Z^\delta] \to \exists Y^\delta G[x,Y^\delta]) \tag{7}$$

Sequents 6 and 7 are derived in the following way. By inversions we have that sequents

$$\Gamma \longrightarrow \Theta, \forall Z H[n,Z] \to \exists Y G[n,Y] \tag{8}$$

and

$$G[n,B], \Gamma \longrightarrow \Theta, H[n,C] \tag{9}$$

are derivable in $\Sigma 3\omega$ ($\Sigma' 3\omega$) for each n by derivations of the height α_0. Both these sequents are Σ^1_1. From 9 by induction hypothesis we obtain

$$G[n,P^{\delta_1}], \Gamma^\sigma \longrightarrow \Theta^\sigma, H[n,Q^{\delta_2}] \tag{10}$$

for each P, Q of levels $\delta_1, \delta_2 < \sigma$, which derives 6. From 8 by induction hypothesis we obtain

$$\Gamma^\delta \longrightarrow \Theta^\delta, \forall Z^\delta H[n, Z^\delta] \rightarrow \exists Y^\delta G[n, Y^\delta] \tag{11}$$

which together with *Fact 1* derives 7.
This concludes the derivation. □

7 About Π_2^1-Sequents

By a *Π_2^1-formula* we mean a formula of the kind $\forall X_1 \ldots \forall X_n F$ where F is a Σ_1^1-formula. By a *Σ_2^1-formula* we mean a formula of the kind $\exists X_1 \ldots \exists X_n F$ where F is a Π_1^1-formula. A *Π_2^1-sequent* is a sequent $G_1 \ldots G_m \longrightarrow H_1 \ldots H_n$ where all G's are Σ_2^1 and all H's are Π_2^1. We can formulate the following **Theorem:**

If a Π_2^1-sequent S is derivable in $\Delta_1^1 - \mathbf{CA}$, $\Sigma_1^1 - \mathbf{AC}$ or $\Sigma_1^1 - \mathbf{DC}$ then there exists $\sigma < \varepsilon_0$ such that for any its realization S' and for any σ-interpretation S^σ of S', S^σ is derivable in $\mathbf{RA}_{\varepsilon_0}$, $(\mathbf{RA} + \mathbf{PAC})_{\varepsilon_0}$ or $(\mathbf{RA} + \mathbf{PDC})_{\varepsilon_0}$ respectively.

The **proof** follows from the same theorem for Σ_1^1-sequents proved in the previous sections and the fact that inversion is admissible in all four systems $\Sigma\mathbf{1}\omega$, $\Sigma\mathbf{2}\omega$, $\Sigma\mathbf{3}\omega$ and $\Sigma'\mathbf{3}\omega$.

Acknowledgement

Thanks to Grigori Mints for a number of useful suggestions.

References

1. K. Schütte: Proof Theory. Springer, 1977
2. G. Jäger, K. Schütte: Eine syntaktische Abrenzung der $(\Delta_1^1 - CA)$-Analysis. In: Bayerische Akademie der Wissenschaften, Sitzungsberichte, Munich, J. 1979, 15-34.
3. S.Tupailo: Normalization for Arithmetical Comprehension with Restricted Occurrences of Hilbert's Epsilon Symbol, Eesti TA Toimetised, Füüsika-Matemaatika, kd. 42, nr.4, 1993, lk. 289-299.
4. S. Tupailo: Normalization for Ramified Analysis with Hilbert's Epsilon-Symbol, to be published.

Proof Plans for the Correction of False Conjectures *

Raul Monroy, Alan Bundy, & Andrew Ireland

Department of Artificial Intelligence
The University of Edinburgh
80 South Bridge, EH1 1HN
Scotland, U.K
raulm, bundy, & air@aisb.ed.ac.uk

Abstract. Theorem proving is the systematic derivation of a mathematical proof from a set of axioms by the use of rules of inference. We are interested in a related but far less explored problem: the analysis and correction of false conjectures, especially where that correction involves finding a collection of antecedents that, together with a set of axioms, transform non-theorems into theorems. Most failed search trees are huge, and special care is to be taken in order to tackle the combinatorial explosion phenomenon. Fortunately, the planning search space generated by proof plans, see [1], are moderately small. We have explored the possibility of using this technique in the implementation of an abduction mechanism to correct non-theorems.

1 Introduction

The problem of building an artificial mathematician to find a mathematical proof has been a topic of much interest in Artificial Intelligence. We are interested in a related but far less explored problem: the analysis and correction of false conjectures, especially where that correction involves finding a collection of antecedents that, together with a set of axioms, transform non-theorems into theorems. More formally, and following [5]:

Given a set of axioms $\mathcal{A}$ and a false conjecture G, i.e. $\mathcal{A} \rightarrow G$ does not hold, our aim is to identify C such that:

1. $\mathcal{A} \wedge C \rightarrow G$ is a theorem, i.e. the addition of C turns the non-theorem into a theorem;
2. $\mathcal{A} \wedge C$ is satisfiable, i.e. C is *consistent* with the set of axioms;
3. $C \rightarrow G$ does not hold, i.e. C is *nontrivial*; and
4. C is *minimal* in that it does not contain any redundant literals.

* We are grateful to Jane Hesketh and the anonymous referees for their useful comments on an earlier draft of this paper. The research reported here was supported by SERC grant GR/H/23610 to the second and third author, and ITESM & CONACyT studentship 64745 to the first author.

By way of motivation, consider the following non-theorem [2]

$$\forall N : \text{nat. double}(\text{half}(N)) = N \tag{1}$$

where the functions double and half have their natural interpretation returning twice and half their inputs, respectively. Clearly, a condition like $N < 0$ does not meet our requirements because it is inconsistent with sort/type information. In addition, the formula

$$\forall N : \text{nat. } (\text{double}(\text{half}(N)) = N) \rightarrow (\text{double}(\text{half}(N)) = N)$$

is not a useful solution since the condition is trivial. The abduction mechanism we present in this paper is capable of finding the condition even(N), which is clearly consistent, nontrivial, and minimal. Note that a condition of the form even(N) $\wedge N \neq \text{s}(0)$ would not be minimal because the second conjunct follows from the definition of the predicate even.

2 Proof Plans

Reasoning and searching are necessary for the solution to the problem of correcting a false conjecture. *Abduction* seems to be a candidate mechanism for the former. Abduction, as proposed by C.S. Peirce [13], is a fundamental form of logical inference that allows us to find hypotheses that account for some observed facts. Its simplest form is:

From A → B, and B
Infer A as a possible justification of B

Most of the mechanisms for driving the generation of abductive hypotheses are based on resolution (see [12] or [11] for a survey on abduction mechanisms). However, most failed proof search spaces are huge and these mechanisms are severely affected by the combinatorial explosion phenomenon, see [16].

Fortunately, the planning search spaces generated by *proof plans* are moderately small, see [1]. This technique guides the search for a proof in the context of tactical style reasoning [8]. Tactic specifications called *methods* express the preconditions under which a tactic is applicable and the effects of applying such a tactic. The proof plan technique has been implemented in a system called CLAM [3] and successfully applied to the domain of inductive proofs [2]. In this paper, we show how to implement an abduction mechanism using plans for inductive proofs. The mechanism relies on the meta-level reasoning used for forming a proof plan, since it provides a basis for analysing failed proof attempts.

[2] Following the Prolog convention, we denote variables with symbols that start with an upper-case letter.

2.1 Rippling

The key idea behind inductive proofs is the use of induction hypotheses in completing step-case proof obligations. The search control heuristic called *rippling* [4] was designed for this task. It works by applying a special syntactic class of rewrite rules called *wave-rules*. The simplest form of such a wave-rule gives rise to the following schema:

$$F(\boxed{S(\underline{U})}^{\uparrow}) \Rightarrow \boxed{T(\underline{F(U)})}^{\uparrow} \tag{2}$$

where F, S, and T are functors. Note that T may be empty while S and F may not. F and $\boxed{S(\underline{U})}^{\uparrow}$ are called *wave-function* and *wave-term*, respectively. Wave-terms are composed of a *wave-front* and one or more *wave-holes*. Wave-holes are the underlined sub-terms of wave-terms. Sub-expressions of the induction conclusion that also appear in the hypothesis are either underlined or not enclosed by boxes. For our current wave-rule example, F and U would match such sub-expressions. Note how the application of (2) has the effect of moving the S through the F. Also, note that the arrow indicates the direction in which wave-fronts are moved within the term structure.

By marking these wave-terms and tracking their movements, we can ensure that our rewriting makes progress towards the desired effect: the removal of the obstructive wave-fronts so that *fertilization* can be applied. Fertilization, according to Boyer and Moore, is the process of applying an induction hypothesis.

2.2 Proof Critics

Experience has shown that a failed proof attempt may hold the key for discovering a complete proof. In [9], the author proposes the use of *planning critics* as a mechanism to provide the means of exploiting failure and partial success in the search for a proof. Planning critics are aimed at capturing our intuition as to how a partial proof can be completed. For this reason, proof critics are associated with proof methods. Any time the application of a particular proof method fails, a collection (possibly empty) of planning critics is invoked. Their application often results in a modification of either the current plan structure, the given conjecture, or the theory in which we are working.

3 Correcting Faulty Conjectures

Our abduction mechanism to correct faulty theorems is built upon CLAM. It consists of a collection of proof critics that define heuristics to detect, isolate, and correct some kinds of faults. Generally speaking, the mechanism works as follows. Let us assume we are given a conjecture, say G. We first let CLAM attempt to find an inductive proof plan for G. If the conjecture is faulty, this process will fail and terminate pointing at an unprovable sub-goal that arose from one case of the inductive proof. According to the point at which failure occurred (c.f. proof methods), a particular collection of critics is then invoked to perform a syntactic analysis on the unprovable sub-goal. From such an analysis, we build the condition that is to be added to the current conjecture. Often, these unprovable sub-goals represent contradictions to either the current set of axioms or sort/type information.

False conjectures that exhibit faults in boundary values were successfully corrected using the information provided by the base case proof obligation. We worked by refinement when a suggested condition from a previous patching attempt turned out to be necessary but not sufficient. We also corrected false conjectures in which the fault exhibited arguments in wrong positions within the conjecture structure; this sort of fault can be found in attempts at proving commutativity of operators that are not Abelian. In the following sections, we introduce the definition of some proof critics of the abduction mechanism by example.

3.1 Exploiting Contradictory Blocked Goals

Consider the non-theorem:

$$\forall A, B : \mathrm{list}(DataType).\ \mathrm{length}(A <> B) > \mathrm{length}(A) \tag{3}$$

The recursive definitions of <>, >, and length give rise to the rewrite rules[3]:

$$\boxed{X :: \underline{U}}^{\uparrow} <> V \Rightarrow \boxed{X :: \underline{U <> V}}^{\uparrow} \tag{4}$$

$$\mathrm{nil} <> U \Rightarrow U$$

$$\boxed{\mathrm{s}(\underline{X})}^{\uparrow} > \boxed{\mathrm{s}(\underline{Y})}^{\uparrow} \Rightarrow X > Y \tag{5}$$

$$X > 0 \Rightarrow X \neq 0$$

$$0 > X \Rightarrow \mathrm{false}$$

$$\mathrm{length}(\boxed{X :: \underline{U}}^{\uparrow}) \Rightarrow \boxed{\mathrm{s}(\underline{\mathrm{length}(U)})}^{\uparrow} \tag{6}$$

$$\mathrm{length}(\mathrm{nil}) \Rightarrow 0$$

We attempt to prove (3) using the primitive induction on lists selecting A as the induction variable[4]. The base case ($A = \mathrm{nil}$) leads to the following sub-goal

$$\forall B : \mathrm{list}(DataType).\ \mathrm{length}(B) \neq 0 \tag{7}$$

With (7), a nested induction is suggested, $v_n :: B$. This time the base case ($B = \mathrm{nil}$) gives rise to a contradictory blocked goal:

$$\mathrm{length}(\mathrm{nil}) \neq 0$$

$$0 \neq 0$$

---

[3] The operators ::, <>, and s() represent the infix list constructor function, the lists concatenation function, and the successor constructor function, respectively.

[4] This will be abbreviated as $IndScheme[IndVar]$; where $IndVar$ is the induction variable, and $IndScheme$ is the suggested induction rule of inference.

Definition 1 Contradictory Blocked Goals. A goal G is said to be *contradictory blocked* if it cannot be further rewritten, all its variables are instantiated, and it is false in the domain of the theory in which we are working.

This contradiction suggests our first patch, namely, to introduce $B \neq \text{nil}$, i.e. the negation of the base case for the most recent induction, as a condition to the original conjecture. Note that by omitting this case condition, our method guarantees that the contradictory blocked goal will not be experienced again. Hence, we have a new conjecture of the form:

$$\forall A, B : \text{list}(DataType).\ B \neq \text{nil} \rightarrow \text{length}(A <> B) > \text{length}(A) \tag{8}$$

With the revised conjecture (8), a $v_n :: A$ induction schema is again suggested. This time the base case proof obligation goes through and so does the step case. In the step case we have an induction hypothesis of the form:

$$\forall B : \text{list}(DataType).\ B \neq \text{nil} \rightarrow \text{length}(a <> B) > \text{length}(a) \tag{9}$$

and an initial induction conclusion of the form:

$$b \neq \text{nil} \rightarrow \text{length}(\boxed{v_0 :: \underline{a}}^{\uparrow} <> b) > \text{length}(\boxed{v_0 :: \underline{a}}^{\uparrow}) \tag{10}$$

Rippling-out (10) with (4) results in:

$$b \neq \text{nil} \rightarrow \text{length}(\boxed{v_0 :: \underline{a <> b}}^{\uparrow}) > \text{length}(\boxed{v_0 :: \underline{a}}^{\uparrow})$$

By wave-rule (6) this rewrites both, the right-hand side (RHS), and the left-hand side (LHS) of the above formula to give us:

$$b \neq \text{nil} \rightarrow \boxed{s(\underline{\text{length}(a <> b)})}^{\uparrow} > \boxed{s(\underline{\text{length}(a)})}^{\uparrow}$$

and finally, wave-rule (5) gives us:

$$b \neq \text{nil} \rightarrow \text{length}(a <> b) > \text{length}(a)$$

Note that this expression matches the induction hypothesis (9). We can appeal therefore directly to the hypothesis to complete the proof. This process is called *strong fertilization.*

The critic definition depicted in Fig. 1 provides a general explanation of the mechanism.

CRITIC induction

Input:	*Plan*,	; If current goal G is
	node(*Plan*, [], [] $\vdash$ *Goal*),	; contradictory blocked,
	current_node(*Plan*, *Address*, $H \vdash G$)	; negate the condition
Precondition:	contradictory_blocked_goal(G)	; for the most recent
Patch:	failed_at(*Plan*, *Address*, *Case*),	; induction and add it
	insert_condition($\neg$*Case*, *Goal*, *NewGoal*),	; as a condition to the
	resume_plan(*Plan*, [], [] $\vdash$ *NewGoal*)	; original goal *Goal*

Meanings of the meta-logic terms:

- node(*Plan*, *Address*, *Sequent*) is used to access the sequent recorded at node *Address*. [] denotes the root node.
- current_node(*Plan*, *Address*, *Seq*) is used to get the address of the current node, and to access the sequent recorded at that node.
- failed_at(*Plan*, *Address*, *Case*) means that *Case* is the case at which failure occurred in the most recent induction.
- insert_condition(*Cond*, *F*, *NewF*) means *NewF* is the result of inserting condition *Cond* in conjecture *F*.
- resume_plan(*Plan*, *Address*, *Sequent*) resumes the proof plan formation of *Plan*.

Fig. 1. Exploiting contradictory blocked goals

3.2 On Fixing Non-Theorems by Refinement

As the reader may now suspect, it is possible to have a false conjecture in which the patch suggested by the above heuristic is not sufficient to transform the non-theorem into a theorem. This situation is likely to occur whenever the condition consists of either a predicate other than equality or a combination of predicates.

As a solution to this problem, we have defined a strategy which supports the refinement of a previous patch. As will become clear later, our strategy exploits both syntactic (rippling) and semantic information. Consider again (1), the example conjecture introduced in Sect. 1. The recursive definitions of double and half give rise to the following rewrites:

$$\mathrm{double}(0) \Rightarrow 0$$

$$\mathrm{double}(\boxed{\mathrm{s}(\underline{X})}^{\uparrow}) \Rightarrow \boxed{\mathrm{s}(\mathrm{s}(\underline{\mathrm{double}(X)}))}^{\uparrow} \tag{11}$$

$$\mathrm{half}(0) \Rightarrow 0$$

$$\mathrm{half}(\mathrm{s}(0)) \Rightarrow 0$$

$$\mathrm{half}(\boxed{\mathrm{s}(\mathrm{s}(\underline{X}))}^{\uparrow}) \Rightarrow \boxed{\mathrm{s}(\underline{\mathrm{half}(X)})}^{\uparrow} \tag{12}$$

In addition, we assume that our theory of natural numbers includes the predicates even and odd[5]:

$$\text{even}(0) \Rightarrow \text{true}$$
$$\text{even}(\text{s}(0)) \Rightarrow \text{false} \qquad (13)$$
$$\text{even}(\boxed{\text{s}(\text{s}(\underline{X}))}^{\uparrow}) \Rightarrow \text{even}(X) \qquad (14)$$
$$\text{odd}(0) \Rightarrow \text{false}$$
$$\text{odd}(\text{s}(0)) \Rightarrow \text{true} \qquad (15)$$
$$\text{odd}(\boxed{\text{s}(\text{s}(\underline{X}))}^{\uparrow}) \Rightarrow \text{odd}(X) \qquad (16)$$

Furthermore, we assume the wave-rule for the cancellation of the successor function:

$$\boxed{\text{s}(\underline{X})}^{\uparrow} = \boxed{\text{s}(\underline{Y})}^{\uparrow} \Rightarrow X = Y \qquad (17)$$

We attempt to prove (1) using s(s(n)) induction. The first base case ($N = 0$) is trivial. It is the second base case ($N = \text{s}(0)$) which is interesting since it gives rise to a contradiction, as shown below.

$$\text{double}(\text{half}(\text{s}(0))) = \text{s}(0)$$
$$\text{double}(0) = \text{s}(0)$$
$$0 = \text{s}(0)$$

This suggests our first patch attempt of introducing the condition $N \neq \text{s}(0)$ using the strategy defined in the previous section. This gives a new conjecture of the form:

$$\forall N : \text{nat}.\ N \neq \text{s}(0) \rightarrow \text{double}(\text{half}(N)) = N \qquad (18)$$

With the revised conjecture, (18), a two step induction is again suggested. This time both base cases go through. In the step case our induction hypothesis is:

$$n \neq \text{s}(0) \rightarrow \text{double}(\text{half}(n)) = n \qquad (19)$$

and the initial induction conclusion takes the form:

$$\boxed{\text{s}(\text{s}(\underline{n}))}^{\uparrow} \neq \text{s}(0) \rightarrow \text{double}(\text{half}(\boxed{\text{s}(\text{s}(\underline{n}))}^{\uparrow})) = \boxed{\text{s}(\text{s}(\underline{n}))}^{\uparrow}$$

Rippling-out this formula with (12), (11), and (17) results in:

$$\boxed{\text{s}(\text{s}(\underline{n}))}^{\uparrow} \neq \text{s}(0) \rightarrow \text{double}(\text{half}(n)) = n$$

At this point, any further rippling is blocked. Note how this formula matches the induction hypothesis (19) *modulo* the antecedent. Although strong fertilization is not possible we are *potentially* in a position to perform what is defined as *conditional fertilization.* Conditional fertilization extends strong fertilization

[5] The predicate odd is not needed, but is included to show that the technique does not fail in the presence of irrelevant information.

METHOD conditional_fertilize

Input:	$H \vdash C_{IC} \rightarrow G_{IC}$,	; Current Sequent.
	$\text{hyp}(H, C_{IH} \rightarrow G_{IH})$	; Induction hypothesis.
Preconditions:	$\text{exp\_at}(G_{IC}, Posn) = G_{IH}$,	; Matching modulo antecedent.
	$\text{tautology}(H <> C_{IC} \vdash C_{IH})$	; The condition of the hypothesis
		; is provable given what is known.

Meanings of the meta-logic terms:

- $\text{hyp}(H, Hyp)$ means Hyp is in hypothesis list H.
- $\text{exp\_at}(Exp, Posn)$ is the subexpression in Exp at position $Posn$.
- $\text{tautology}(H \vdash C)$ is true when the condition C is provable given the hypothesis list H.

Fig. 2. Preconditions of the conditional fertilization method

with conditional equations. The preconditions to apply conditional fertilization are shown in Fig. 2.

For our example the first precondition holds while the second is obviously false. The failure of the fertilize method suggests that our initial condition, $N \neq \text{s}(0)$, was *necessary* but not *sufficient* in order to make (1) into a theorem.

Our second attempt at patching (1) is syntactically driven and represents a refinement of our first patch. We analyse the second failure with the aim of finding a wave-function which will not lead to the blockage experienced in the second proof attempt, i.e.

$$\underbrace{\boxed{\text{s}(\text{s}(\underline{n}))}^{\uparrow} \neq \text{s}(0)}_{\textbf{blockage}} \rightarrow \ldots$$

We are looking for a wave-rule of the form $F(\boxed{\text{s}(\text{s}(\underline{X}))}^{\uparrow}) \Rightarrow \ldots$, since it allows further rippling. In addition, we know that F must be of type nat→bool. Taking these constraints into consideration there are two[6] candidate wave-rules within our theory: (14) and (16). For our current example therefore F may be $\lambda x.\text{even}(x)$ or $\lambda x.\text{odd}(x)$.

Now we exploit our semantic knowledge. From the first patch attempt we know that[7] $F(\text{s}(0))$ must evaluate to false. Looking at rewrites (13) and (15) we see that even is the correct instantiation for F. The corrected conjecture becomes:

$$\forall N : \text{nat}.\ \text{even}(N) \rightarrow \text{double}(\text{half}(N)) = N$$

[6] Note that wave-rule (12) is ruled-out for type reasons.

[7] This ensures that the second attempt at patching (1) subsumes the first one.

which is actually provable.

This strategy is captured in the critic definition given in Fig. 3.

CRITIC conditional_fertilize

Input:	*Plan*,	; Current plan,
	node(*Plan*, [], [] $\vdash$ *Goal*),	; node, and sequent.
	current_node(*Plan*, *Address*, $H \vdash C_{IC} \rightarrow G_{IC}$),	
	hyp(H, $C_{IH} \rightarrow G_{IH}$),	
Preconditions:	exp_at(G_{IC}, *Posn*) $= G_{IH}$,	; Syntacticly and
	context(*Plan*, *Address*, *IndVar*, *CondList*),	; semanticly-guided
	exp_at(C_{IC}, *Blockage*),	; partial wave-rule
	match_wave_rule(*Blockage*, *CondList*, F),	; matching.
Patch:	subsumption_checking(F(*IndVar*), *CondList*, *NewCondList*),	
	insert_condList(*NewCondList*, *Goal*, *NewGoal*),	
	resume_plan(*Plan*, [], [] $\vdash$ *NewGoal*)	

Meaning of the meta-logical terms:

- context(*Plan*, *Address*, *IndVar*, *CondList*) is used to access the variable which is being inducted upon, and the current set of abducted conditions.
- match_wave_rule(*Blockage*, *Conditions*, F) means F is the main functor of a wave-rule whose LHS matches *Blockage* and the definition of F is consistent with *Conditions*.
  subsumption_checking(P, *CondList*, *NewCL*) means *NewCL* is as *CondList* except that the conditions subsumed by the definition of P have been removed.
- insert_condList(*List*, G, *NewG*) inserts each condition of *List* in G.

Fig. 3. Refining previous patching attempts

3.3 Lochs and Dykes

Consider the following faulty conjecture:

$$\forall A, B : \text{list}(T).\ \text{rev}(\text{rev}(A <> B)) = \text{rev}(\text{rev}(B)) <> \text{rev}(\text{rev}(A)) \tag{20}$$

This formula is false in that the RHS has two arguments in wrong positions. We assume the rewrite rules derived from the definition of $<>$ and the following rewrite rules:

$$\text{rev}(\boxed{X :: \underline{U}}^{\uparrow}) \Rightarrow \boxed{\underline{\text{rev}(U)} <> X :: \text{nil}}^{\uparrow} \tag{21}$$

$$\text{rev}(\text{nil}) \Rightarrow \text{nil}$$

$$\text{rev}(\boxed{\underline{U} <> X :: \text{nil}}^{\uparrow}) \Rightarrow \boxed{X :: \underline{\text{rev}(U)}}^{\uparrow} \tag{22}$$

$$\boxed{X :: \underline{U}}^{\uparrow} = \boxed{X :: \underline{V}}^{\uparrow} \Rightarrow U = V \tag{23}$$

We attempt to prove (20) using a $v_n :: A$ induction. The base case is trivial. The step case proceeds as follows. Our induction hypothesis is the following:

$$\forall B : \text{list}(T).\ \text{rev}(\text{rev}(a <> B)) = \text{rev}(\text{rev}(B)) <> \text{rev}(\text{rev}(a)) \tag{24}$$

and the initial induction conclusion is:

$$\text{rev}(\text{rev}(\boxed{v_1 :: \underline{a}}^{\uparrow} <> b)) = \text{rev}(\text{rev}(b)) <> \text{rev}(\text{rev}(\boxed{v_1 :: \underline{a}}^{\uparrow}))$$

By applying wave-rules (4), (21), and (22), we get

$$\boxed{v_1 :: \underline{\text{rev}(\text{rev}(a <> b))}}^{\uparrow} = \text{rev}(\text{rev}(b)) <> \boxed{v_1 :: \underline{\text{rev}(\text{rev}(a))}}^{\uparrow} \tag{25}$$

At this point, no further rewriting is possible but *weak fertilization* is applicable. The use of the induction hypothesis as a rewrite rule is called weak fertilization. Having fertilized (25), the resulting formula is considered as a sub-goal to be proved using (a nested) induction. However, any proof attempt will be fruitless because the conjecture is false. The problem is that we cannot assume this in advance. As a partial solution we have implemented a simple counter-example finder that evaluates a few standard instantiations to check whether a given formula is trivially unprovable. The counter-example finder provides us with the means of detecting a faulty occurrence.

It is clear that the LHS of (25) is fully rippled, whereas its RHS is blocked. According to the rippling paradigm, we say that the wave-fronts on the RHS cannot ripple-out all the way up to the very top of that side. We may think that there is a *dyke*, i.e. a barrier, in the middle of the loch such that it is not possible for the waves to raise up in the conjecture structure.

Our failure location process is guided by the partial use of the induction hypothesis. This process is called *lemma calculation* [10] and is simply the implementation of weak fertilization as a proof critic. It is invoked whenever rippling gets blocked and there exists the opportunity to partially exploit the induction hypothesis.

For our example, the lemma calculation technique would first apply the induction hypothesis to get:

$$v_1 :: (\text{rev}(\text{rev}(b)) <> \text{rev}(\text{rev}(a))) = \text{rev}(\text{rev}(b)) <> v_1 :: \text{rev}(\text{rev}(a))$$

which generalises to the following lemma:

$$\forall X : T,\ \forall U, V : \text{list}(T).\ X :: (U <> V) = U <> X :: V \tag{26}$$

If an induction proof is able to establish this conjectured formula, the following wave-rule would be available:

$$U <> \boxed{X :: \underline{V}}^{\uparrow} \Rightarrow \boxed{X :: \underline{U <> V}}^{\uparrow}$$

Note how this wave-rule would allow further rewriting and completing the proof. As the reader may now notice, (26) is not a valid lemma. But even if it is not valid we can still exploit the information that it provides. If we look carefully at it, we will notice that the wave-front term, i.e. $X :: \ldots$, introduced by the step case proof obligation has to move outwards past both <> and U. This observation enables to deduce that correcting (20) can be achieved by performing one of the following actions:

- Emptying one of the lochs, i.e. to force $A = nil$ or $B = nil$.
- Eliminating the dyke, i.e. to force $A = B$.

From the above actions, we prefer the latter. This strategy has been implemented by switching the positions of these variables in one side of the expression, looking for a pattern of the form:

$$F1(A, F2(X, B)) = F2(X, F1(A, B))$$

or any possible combination, e.g. $F2(X, F1(A, B)) = F1(A, F2(X, B))$.

The critic definition depicted in Fig. 4 shows the general mechanism.

CRITIC wave

Input:	*Plan*,	; Current plan, node,
	node(*Plan*, [], *Goal*),	; and sequent.
	current_node(*Plan*, *Address*, $H \vdash G$)	
Preconditions:	disprove($H \vdash G$),	; Current goal is faulty.
	lemma_calculation_applicable($H \vdash G$, *BlockedSide*, *RippledSide*),	
	calculated_lemma($H \vdash G$, *BlockedSide*, *Lemma*),	
	lochs_dykes(*Lemma*, X, Y),	; The suggested lemma
	switch(X, Y, *Goal*, *Side*, *NewGoal*),	; follows the lochs and
	not disprove([] $\vdash$ *NewGoal*)	; dykes patterns.
Patch:	resume_plan(*Plan*, [], [] $\vdash$ *NewGoal*)	

Meanings of the meta-logical terms:

- disprove(*Seq*) means that it is possible to find a counter-example for *Seq*.
- lemma_calculation_applicable(*Seq*, B, R) means that lemma calculation technique is applicable. B and R are the blocked and the rippled side, respectively.
- calculated_lemma(*Seq*, B, *Lemma*) calculates *Lemma* to complete a proof.
- lochs_dykes(*Lemma*, X, Y) means that *Lemma* matches the lochs and dykes patterns and that X and Y are in wrong position within the term structure.
- switch(Exp_1, Exp_2, F, *Side*, *NewF*) is used to exchange the positions of subexpressions Exp_1 and Exp_2 in side *Side* of F.

Fig. 4. Exploiting lochs and dykes

4 Implementation Aspects

Correcting faulty conjectures by adding conditions gives rise to the problem of finding a proof for conditional equations. Generally speaking, we now have goals of the form:

$$C[N] \rightarrow P[N] \vdash C[\![\boxed{S(\underline{N})}]\!] \rightarrow P[\![\boxed{S(\underline{N})}]\!]$$

where C, P, and S are terms with a distinguished argument, C is the antecedent, and S any constructor function.

These kinds of goals introduce technical problems in proofs by induction. This is because the antecedents get in the way in an actual proof. We have extended the capabilities of the proof planner to cope in such situations. We use two different strategies. In the first one, we allow fertilization once we have proved that the condition of the induction hypothesis holds, we called this *conditional weak fertilization.* In the second one, we split a proof into cases using the condition of the induction hypothesis and its negation. These strategies have also been implemented as proof critics, thus preserving the core of the system.

5 Comparison to Related Work

5.1 Resolution-Based Abduction Mechanisms

As we have previously mentioned, most of the mechanisms for driving the generation of abductive hypotheses are based on resolution. [15, 14, 5, 6] have independently proposed a mechanism which, roughly speaking, works as follows:

1. Convert the set of axioms and the given conjecture into clausal form;
2. Perform, let us say, SLD-resolution, using the set of support strategy. If the conjecture is false, this deduction process either does not terminate or results in a finitely failed AND/OR proof search tree with the leaves labelled as unprovable goals. If sufficient of these goals were true then the conjecture would be provable.
3. Perform an analysis on the unprovable goals and build from it (often more than) one condition that logically implies the goal.

As the reader may now suspect, the search space generated by this procedure normally is huge, and so is the number of dead end goals. The latter fact is of much importance, since it causes a combinatorial explosion in the process of building a consistent, nontrivial, and minimal condition. On the other hand, our mechanism avoids the combinatorial explosion because the proof plans technique carefully guides the search for an inductive proof and assists the detection, isolation, and analysis of faults.

5.2 PreS

In [7], the authors propose a technique, they call PreS, to correct faulty conjectures. PreS works as a separate module of an inductive theorem prover. When given faulty conjecture G, PreS is aimed at synthesising P such that $P \rightarrow G$ holds. P's definition is built according to the success or failure at establishing base and step cases of inductive proofs. We illustrate this by example.

Consider again non-theorem (1). From Sect. 3.2, we know that a proof attempt, using two step induction, results in

- success in the first base case ($N = 0$);
- failure, in the second base case ($N = \mathrm{s}(0)$); and
- success in the step case if we take $\mathrm{double}(\mathrm{half}(n)) = n$ as the induction hypothesis, and $\mathrm{double}(\mathrm{half}(\mathrm{s}(\mathrm{s}(n)))) = \mathrm{s}(\mathrm{s}(n))$ as the conclusion.

PreS records the following observations:

$$P(0) \text{ is true}, \quad P(\mathrm{s}(0)) \text{ is false}, \quad P(\mathrm{s}(\mathrm{s}(N))) \text{ if } P(N)$$

which actually is the recursive definition of the predicate even.

This approach is interesting in that the definition of P is built using synthesis techniques of the proofs as programs paradigm. Regrettably, PreS is explained only by example, no general mechanism is defined, and no characterisation of failure is provided. For instance, it is not clear how PreS manages, if it does, faulty conjectures in which base cases go through and nested inductions (with possibly generalisations) are required to complete a proof; which is a common situation when proving properties about lists or trees. Our mechanism, on the other hand, captures the restricted way in which the proof of a conjecture that exhibits a particular kind of fault can fail, and provides a general mechanism to patch such failures.

6 Results and Further Work

The strategies presented in this paper have been built upon CLAM v3.1 [17] as a collection of critics. CLAM v3.1 was especially designed to realise the proof critics technique, see [9], described in Sect. 2.2.

We tested our mechanism by making it correct a set of 45 faulty conjectures that included the sorts of faults mentioned in Sect. 3. It proved to be capable of correcting 80% of them. It corrected 72.3% of false conjectures with wrong definitions in boundary values; 72.3% of faulty conjectures with wrong definitions beyond boundary values; and 91.67% of non-theorems in which the fault consisted of wrong definitions in the properties of operators. Table 1 shows some example non-theorems that were successfully corrected.

Our approach only finds one among several possible corrections to a non-theorem. Such a correction is

- consistent if a successful proof plan is found; and

- non-trivial because it consists of either the negation of case conditions provided by a well-founded rule of inference (mathematical induction), or well-defined predicates.

Minimality, however, requires a non-trivial subsumption checking algorithm. We are currently working on this.

Table 1. Example non-theorems successfully corrected. The predicate oddl returns true whenever its input, a list of objects, is of length odd. qrev is the tail reverse function. x, y, a, b, and c in this table represent universally quantified variables and range over either the Peano natural numbers or lists

Critic	Non-Theorems	Theorems
Fig. 1	$\mathrm{length}(a <> b) > \mathrm{length}(a)$	$b \neq \mathrm{nil} \rightarrow \mathrm{length}(a <> b) > \mathrm{length}(a)$
	$\mathrm{length}(a) < \mathrm{length}(a <> b)$	$b \neq \mathrm{nil} \rightarrow \mathrm{length}(a) < \mathrm{length}(a <> b)$
	$\mathrm{half}(x) < \mathrm{double}(x)$	$x \neq 0 \rightarrow \mathrm{half}(x) < \mathrm{double}(x)$
	$\mathrm{half}(x) < x$	$x \neq 0 \rightarrow \mathrm{half}(x) < x$
	$x < \mathrm{double}(x)$	$x \neq 0 \rightarrow x < \mathrm{double}(x)$
	$x + y > x$	$y \neq 0 \rightarrow x + y > x$
	$x + y > \mathrm{s}(x)$	$y > \mathrm{s}(0) \rightarrow x + y > \mathrm{s}(x)$
Fig. 1 and Fig. 3	$\neg\mathrm{even}(x)$	$\mathrm{odd}(x) \rightarrow \neg\mathrm{even}(x)$
	$\neg\mathrm{odd}(x)$	$\mathrm{even}(x) \rightarrow \neg\mathrm{odd}(x)$
	$\mathrm{double}(\mathrm{half}(x)) = x$	$\mathrm{even}(x) \rightarrow \mathrm{double}(\mathrm{half}(x)) = x$
	$\mathrm{double}(\mathrm{half}(x)) \neq x$	$\mathrm{odd}(x) \rightarrow \mathrm{double}(\mathrm{half}(x)) \neq x$
	$\mathrm{even}(x) \rightarrow \mathrm{even}(x + y)$	$\mathrm{even}(y) \rightarrow (\mathrm{even}(x) \rightarrow \mathrm{even}(x + y))$
	$\neg\mathrm{even}(\mathrm{length}(a))$	$\mathrm{oddl}(a) \rightarrow \neg\mathrm{even}(\mathrm{length}(a))$
	$\mathrm{odd}(\mathrm{length}(a))$	$\mathrm{oddl}(a) \rightarrow \mathrm{odd}(\mathrm{length}(a))$
Fig. 4	$a <> (b <> c) = (a <> c) <> b$	$a <> (c <> b) = (a <> c) <> b$
	$\mathrm{rev}(\mathrm{rev}(a <> b)) = b <> a$	$\mathrm{rev}(\mathrm{rev}(b <> a)) = b <> a$
	$\mathrm{rev}(a <> b) = \mathrm{rev}(a) <> \mathrm{rev}(b)$	$\mathrm{rev}(a <> b) = \mathrm{rev}(b) <> \mathrm{rev}(a)$
	$a <> \mathrm{rev}(b) = \mathrm{qrev}(b, a)$	$rev(b) <> a = \mathrm{qrev}(b, a)$
	$a <> b = b <> a$	$b <> a = b <> a$
	$\mathrm{rev}(a <> x :: \mathrm{nil}) = \mathrm{rev}(a) <> x :: \mathrm{nil}$	$\mathrm{rev}(a <> x :: \mathrm{nil}) = x :: \mathrm{nil} <> \mathrm{rev}(a)$

OYSTER has been especially designed to be applied in the problem of computer program synthesis. We would like to apply the strategies outlined in this paper in the correction of faulty computer program specifications. This process may involve the creation of guards to constrain the input domain of the synthesised code. Note the similarity between these guards and the conditions that transform non-theorems into theorems.

References

1. Bundy, A.: The Use of Explicit Plans to Guide Inductive Proofs. In 9th Conference on Automated Deduction. Lusk, R. and Overbeek, R.(Eds.). (1988) 111–120. Longer version available from Edinburgh as DAI Research Paper No. 349.
2. Bundy, A. and van Harmelen, F. and Hesketh, J. and Smaill, A.: Experiments with Proof Plans for Induction. Journal of Automated Reasoning **7** (1991) 303–324.
3. Bundy, A. and van Harmelen, F. and Horn, C. and Smaill, A.: The Oyster-Clam system. In Proceedings of the 10th International Conference on Automated Deduction. Springer-Verlag. Stickel, M.E. (Ed.). (1990) 647–648.
4. Bundy, A. and Stevens, A. and van Harmelen, F. and Ireland, A. and Smaill, A.: Rippling: A Heuristic for Guiding Inductive Proofs. Artificial Intelligence **62** (1993) 182–253.
5. Cox, P.T. and Pietrzykowski, T.: Causes for Events: Their Computation and Applications. Lecture Notes in Computer Science: Proceedings of the 8th International Conference on Automated Deduction. Siekmann, J. (Ed.) Springer-Verlag. (1986) 608–621.
6. Finger, J.J.:RESIDUE: A deductive approach to design synthesis. Research Report STAN-CS-85-1035. Stanford University (1985).
7. Franova, M. and Kodratoff, Y.: Predicate Synthesis from Formal Specifications. Proceedings of ECAI-92. (1992) 87–91.
8. Gordon, M.J. and Milner, A.J. and Wadsworth, C.P.: Edinburgh LCF - A mechanised logic of computation. Lecture Notes in Computer Science **78** (1979).
9. Ireland, A.: The Use of Planning Critics in Mechanizing Inductive Proofs. International Conference on Logic Programming and Automated Reasoning – LPAR 92, St. Petersburg. Lecture Notes in Artificial Intelligence **624**. Voronkov A. (Ed.). Springer-Verlag. (1992) 178–189.
10. Ireland, A. and Bundy, A.: Using Failure to Guide Inductive Proof. Technical Report, Department of Artificial Intelligence (1992). Available from Edinburgh as DAI Research Paper 613.
11. Monroy, R.: Abduction Mechanisms. Working Paper No. 254, Department of Artificial Intelligence, Edinburgh Univerisity (1994).
12. Paul, G.: Approaches to Abductive Reasoning: an Overview. Artificial Intelligence Review, vol. 7, 109–152. Kluwer Academic Publisher (1993).
13. Peirce, C.S.: Collected papers of Charles Sanders Peirce. Vol. 2, 193. Harston, C. and Weiss, P. (Eds.) Harvard University Press. (1959).
14. Poole, G. and Goebel, R. and Aleliunas, R.: Theorist: a logical reasoning system for defaults and diagnosis. The Knowledge Frontier: Essays in Representation of Knowledge. Cercone, N. and McCalla, G. (Eds.), Springer-Verlag (1987) 331–352.
15. Pople, H.E.: On the Mechanization of Abductive Logic. Proceedings of the third IJCAI. Nilsson, N. (Ed.). (1972) 147–152.
16. Selman, B. and Levesque, H.L.: Abductive and Default Reasoning: A Computational Core. In Proccedings of the 8th National Conference on Artificial Intelligence. (1989) 343–348.
17. van Harmelen, F.: The CLAM Proof Planner, User Manual and Programmer Manual. Technical Paper 4. Department of Artificial Intelligence, Edinburgh University. 1989.

On the Value of Antiprenexing

Uwe Egly

FG Intellektik, TH Darmstadt
Alexanderstraße 10, D–64283 Darmstadt
e-mail: uwe@intellektik.informatik.th-darmstadt.de

Abstract. In this paper, we examine the effect of antiprenexing on the proof length if resolution deduction concepts are applied. Roughly speaking, our version of antiprenexing moves $\forall$-quantifiers downward in the formula tree whereas $\exists$-quantifiers are moved upward. We show that two different Skolemization techniques result in two clause sets with rather different resolution refutations. The lower bounds on the length of both refutations differ exponentially. Furthermore, we demonstrate that both techniques can be improved if antiprenexing is applied before Skolemization. Finally, we examine the influence of antiprenexing if extended resolution deduction concepts are used.

1 Introduction

Transforming an arbitrary first order formula into a corresponding clausal normal form is a widely used technique in automated theorem proving. Such a transformation to clausal normal form requires Skolemization as one of a number of subtasks. There are only a few methods optimizing the result of Skolemization, namely the introduction of new Skolem terms of minimal arity. Such a technique called antiprenexing was used by Bibel in [4] in order to obtain formulae in miniscope form. Although he observed that there may be less complex proofs in case antiprenexing is applied, he did not quantify the decrease of proof complexity. If Bibel's approach is used in the context of R-deduction (resolution deduction), a shortest R-refutation of a miniscope formula may be exponentially longer[1] than an R-refutation of an equivalent formula which is not in miniscope. A similar effect may occur if the optional step 3 of the normal form algorithm in [12, p.34] is performed.

In this paper, we examine the effect of introducing Skolem terms with arity greater than necessary. We distinguish two different kinds of Skolemization (both without moving quantifiers), namely structural Skolemization (cf [12]) denoted by SK_s and Skolemization obeying free and bound variables (cf [1]) denoted by SK_f. In what follows, we illustrate both, SK_s and SK_f. We assume that two different quantifiers do not bind the same variable. Take the formula

$$\mathcal{F} = \forall x_1 \forall x_2 \exists y (A(x_1, y) \wedge (\exists z B(x_1, z) \vee C(x_1, x_2, y)))$$

[1] The length of a refutation is the number of distinct clauses in the refutation.

as an example. We eliminate $\exists$ by SK_s and get

$$\forall x_1 \forall x_2 (A(x_1, g(x_1, x_2)) \wedge (B(x_1, h(x_1, x_2)) \vee C(x_1, x_2, g(x_1, x_2)))).$$

Namely, we replace an existential variable by a Skolem term depending on all universal variables which occur in the path starting from the $\exists$-quantifier of the variable under consideration to the root of the formula tree. Hence, both Skolem terms depend on x_1 as well as on x_2. If SK_f is applied, the Skolem terms depend on all free variables in the quantified subformula. If the first $\exists$-quantifier (from left to right) in $\exists x D(x, y_1, \ldots, y_n)$ has to be Skolemized, then the result is $D(g(y_1, \ldots, y_n), y_1, \ldots, y_n)$ if $y_1, \ldots, y_n$ are the free variables in $\exists x D(x, y_1, \ldots, y_n)$ and g is a globally new Skolem function symbol. For $\mathcal{F}$, we obtain

$$\forall x_1 \forall x_2 (A(x_1, g(x_1, x_2)) \wedge (B(x_1, l(x_1)) \vee C(x_1, x_2, g(x_1, x_2)))).$$

Obviously, the Skolem term $l(x_1)$ introduced into B depends on less variables than the corresponding Skolem term $h(x_1, x_2)$. Skolem terms of the latter kind may result in at least exponentially longer refutations if R-deduction is applied.

In some cases, the result of both kinds of Skolemization can be optimized by antiprenexing. Roughly speaking, our version of antiprenexing moves $\forall$-quantifiers downward in the formula tree whereas $\exists$-quantifiers are moved upward. In contrast to [4], we do not get a formula which is completely in miniscope form. The reason for avoiding full miniscope form is the need for $\exists$-quantifier duplication if a miniscope form is required. As a consequence, different Skolem terms are introduced. These different Skolem terms may cause an exponential increase of proof length in case R-deduction is applied.

Antiprenexing is also applied if extended resolution calculi like FR-deduction [2], restricted FR-deduction, QR-deduction [7], or QER-deduction [8] are used. These deduction concepts extend R-deduction by function introduction rules, which enable the introduction of new Skolem terms. As a result, lemmata are obtained which cannot be derived by R-deduction. Although resolution is often seen as a restricted form of a cut rule, it neither introduces new function symbols nor new predicate symbols into the resolvent. Each term in a resolvent is an instance of a term inherited from the parent clauses. In contrast to pure R-deduction, R-deduction concepts extended by such function introduction rules are non-analytic, i.e., new Skolem function symbols may be introduced. Let C be a clause, and let $F(C)$ be the formula corresponding to C. Take the following formula as an example.

$$F(C_2) = \forall x \forall y (\neg P(x, y) \vee P(f(x), y) \vee P(f(x), g(x, y)))$$

Replace the quantifier $\forall y$ by $\forall y \exists z$ and replace y by z in the last literal of C_2. We may obtain the following intermediate formula

$$A = \forall x \forall y \exists z (\neg P(x, y) \vee P(f(x), y) \vee P(f(x), g(x, z)))$$

where y is replaced by z in the last literal. If we skolemize A using structural Skolemization, then we get a new clause of the form

$$D_1 = \neg P(x,y) \vee P(f(x),y) \vee P(f(x),g(x,h(x,y)))$$

with a new Skolem term $h(x,y)$. If we apply antiprenexing to A and Skolemize the resulting formula, then

$$D_2 = \neg P(x,y) \vee P(f(x),y) \vee P(f(x),g(x,l(x)))$$

is obtained with a new Skolem term $l(x)$. Using D_2 instead of D_1 may result in an exponential decrease of refutation length if R-deduction is applied. Although SK_f yields a clause similar to D_2 even without antiprenexing, this is not possible in general. We will discuss this in Section 4.

The rest of the paper is organized as follows. In Section 2, basic definitions and notations are introduced. In Section 3, we first examine how the different Skolemization techniques affect the length of R-refutations. A second topic is how antiprenexing can enable short refutations. In Section 4, two extended R-deduction concepts are examined w.r.t. refutation length. In Section 5, we conclude.

2 Preliminaries

In this section, we introduce some concepts needed later. As usual in the context of resolution-based theorem proving, we adopt the refutational approach,i.e., instead of proving a formula F, we refute $\neg F$. Observe that $\exists$-quantifiers are removed by Skolemization. First, we define antiprenexing.

Definition 2.1
Apply the rules shown in Table 1 until no more rule is applicable. The process of shifting quantifiers defined by $R_1 \dots R_6$ is called antiprenexing[2].

R_1	$\exists x(A(x) \vee B)$	$\Longrightarrow \exists x A(x) \vee B$	x does not occur in B
R_2	$\forall x(A(x) \wedge B)$	$\Longrightarrow \forall x A(x) \wedge B$	x does not occur in B
R_3	$\exists x(A(x) \wedge B)$	$\Longrightarrow \exists x A(x) \wedge B$	x does not occur in B
R_4	$\forall x(A(x) \vee B)$	$\Longrightarrow \forall x A(x) \vee B$	x does not occur in B
R_5	$\exists x A(x) \vee \exists y B(y)$	$\Longrightarrow \exists x(A(x) \vee B(y)\{y \leftarrow x\})$	
R_6	$\forall x(A(x) \wedge B(x))$	$\Longrightarrow \forall x A(x) \wedge \forall y B(x)\{x \leftarrow y\}$	y is a new variable

Table 1. Six rules defining antiprenexing.

[2] Although antiprenexing is misleading in case of R_5, we adopt this name due to historical reasons.

As already noted in [5], the antiprenexed form of a formula is not unique in general. Observe that in our definition here, $\exists$-quantifiers are prenexed by R_5 in order to generate the same Skolem function for both, x in A and y in B.

A *clause* is a disjunction of literals. The *empty clause* is denoted by $\Box$. For all clauses, $A \vee \Box \vee B = A \vee B$. Since we want to estimate and compare the length of R-refutations, we need a definition of clauses avoiding implicit factorization. By defining a clause as a disjunction of literals instead of definining it as a set of literals, the contraction of literals has to be performed explicitly.

The *clause form* of a clause C is a closed formula

$$F(C) = (\forall x_1) \dots (\forall x_n)\, C,$$

where $\{x_1, \dots, x_n\}$ are the variables occurring in clause C.

The *literal set* of a clause $C = L_1 \vee \dots \vee L_n$ is defined as the set of all literals occurring in the clause C. Here, $LS(C) = \{L_1, \dots, L_m\}$ $(m \leq n)$. Let C be a clause, $C_1, C_2 \neq \Box$, and $LS(C) = LS(C_1 \vee C_2)$. The variables occurring in both subclauses C_1, C_2 are $\{x_1, \dots, x_k\}$, whereas the variables in $\{y_1, \dots, y_l\}$ ($\{z_1, \dots, z_m\}$) only occur in C_1 (C_2). Then the formula

$$(\forall x_1) \dots (\forall x_k)[(\forall y_1) \dots (\forall y_l)\, C_1 \vee (\forall z_1) \dots (\forall z_m)\, C_2]$$

is a *reduced clause form* of C. Obviously, the reduced clause form is obtained from the corresponding clause form by applying rule R4 of Table 1.

Although there are more rules introducing new function symbols (e.g. Q-extension [7] or quantorial extension [6, 8], we restrict our attention to F-extension [2] and restricted F-extension. Let q denote a quantifier. Then $\{q^d\} = \{\forall, \exists\} \setminus \{q\}$.

Definition 2.2
Let $A = (\forall x_1) \dots (\forall x_m)[(\forall u_1) \dots (\forall u_a)\, C_1 \vee (\forall v_1) \dots (\forall v_b)\, C_2]$ *be the reduced clause form of a clause* $C \in \mathcal{C}$. *Let* $\{y_1, \dots, y_k\} \subseteq \{x_1, \dots, x_m\}$, $\{z_1, \dots, z_l\} = \{x_1, \dots, x_m\} \setminus \{y_1, \dots, y_k\}$. *The Skolemized form of*

$$F(C) \wedge (\forall z_1) \dots (\forall z_l)[(q_1 y_1) \dots (q_k y_k)(\forall \mathbf{u})\, C_1 \vee (q_1^d y_1) \dots (q_k^d y_k)(\forall \mathbf{v})\, C_2]$$

is called an F-extension *of* $\mathcal{C}$. *If* $k = 1$, *we have a* 1-F-extension.

Definition 2.3
Let $A = (\forall x_1) \dots (\forall x_m)[C_1 \vee C_2]$ *be the clause form of a clause* $C \in \mathcal{C}$. *The Skolemized form of*

$$\begin{aligned} F(C) \wedge (\forall x_1) \dots (\forall x_{m-k})(q_{m-k+1} u_{m-k+1})(q^d_{m-k+1} u^d_{m-k+1}) \dots \\ \dots (q_m u_m)(q^d_m u^d_m)[C_1 \mu_1 \vee C_2 \mu_2] \end{aligned}$$

is called a restricted F-extension *of* $\mathcal{C}$. μ_1 (μ_2) *is a variable-pure substitution renaming* x_i $(m - k + 1 \leq i \leq m)$ *to* y_i (z_i), $u_i \in \{y_i, z_i\}$, *and* $\{u_i^d\} = \{y_i, z_i\} \setminus \{u_i\}$. *If* $k = 1$, *we have a* restricted 1-F-extension.

In both definitions, it is necessary to consider $F(\mathcal{C})$ in the conjunction in order to guarantee that globally new Skolem function symbols are introduced.

Definition 2.4
Let $\mathcal{C}$ be a set of clauses. The elements of this clause set are called input clauses. A sequence $C_1, \ldots, C_n$ is called FR-deduction *(resolution deduction with function introduction) of a clause C from $\mathcal{C}$ if the following conditions hold.*

1. $C_n = C$
2. *for all* $i = 1, \ldots, n$
   a. *C_i is a variant of an input clause, or*
   b. *C_i is a variant of a C_j for $j < i$, or*
   c. *C_i is a factor of a C_j for $j < i$, or*
   d. *C_i is a resolvent of a C_j, C_k for $j, k < i$.*
   e. *$\{C_i\} \cup \bigcup_{j<i}\{C_j\} \cup \mathcal{C}$ is an F-extension of $\{C_1, \ldots, C_{i-1}\} \cup \mathcal{C}$.*

The sequence is called restricted FR-deduction *if F-extension in 2.e. is replaced by restricted F-extension.* 1-FR-deduction *is obtained by replacing F-extension in 2.e. by 1-F-extension.*

FR-deduction is sound as well as complete [2]. The soundness and completeness of restricted FR-deduction follows immediately from the equivalence of the prenex form and the antiprenexed form. Omitting condition *2.e.* in Definition 2.4 yields a definition of an *R-deduction* (resolution deduction) of clause C from $\mathcal{C}$.

3 Antiprenexing and Resolution Proof Complexity

In this section, we examine the effect of two different Skolemization techniques on the length of refutations. We demonstrate that antiprenexing is advantageous in combination with both techniques. In what follows, we assume that each variable is uniquely bounded by one quantifier, i.e., two different quantifiers do not bind the same variable.

We distinguish two different kinds of Skolemization. The first one is the usual (structural) Skolemization algorithm (see for instance [12]). Let F be a formula and let F' be the negation normal form of F. Let $\exists x A(x, v_1, \ldots, v_l)$ be a subformula of F' with the quantifier to be eliminated in the next Skolemization step. Let $\mathcal{V}$ denote the set of all universal variables occurring in the path from the current $\exists$-quantifier to the root of the formula tree for F'. Each occurrence of an existential variable x in $A(x, v_1, \ldots, v_l)$ is replaced by a Skolem term depending on all variables of $\mathcal{V}$ and the quantification $\exists x$ is omitted. We denote this Skolemization by SK_s.

A second kind of Skolemization is used in [1][3]. The $\exists$-quantifiers in F' are replaced from left to right. Let $\exists x A(x, v_1, \ldots, v_l)$ be the left most $\exists$-quantifier and let $\mathcal{V} = \{v_1, \ldots, v_l\}$ denote the set of all free variables occurring in the quantified formula $\exists x A(x, v_1, \ldots, v_l)$. Then each occurrence of x in $A(x, v_1, \ldots, v_l)$

[3] We discuss further techniques in Section 5

is replaced by a Skolem term depending on all free variables $v_1, \ldots, v_l$ and the quantification $\exists x$ is omitted. We denote this Skolemization by SK_f.

3.1 On Different Forms of Skolemization

In this subsection, we demonstrate that SK_s and SK_f may behave quite different when applied to the same formula. We first define the notion of projection. Roughly speaking, we omit argument positions by applying projection to a clause set $\mathcal{C}$ in order to simplify the proof of lower bounds for the length of each R-refutation of $\mathcal{C}$. In the sequel, we use different clause sets for the presentation. However, these different clause sets will result in the same clause set for which the proof is performed.

Definition 3.1
Let q be an m-ary predicate symbol. Let $\mathcal{I}$ be a non-empty set of indices such that $\mathcal{I} \subseteq \{1, 2, \ldots, m\}$ and let $\mathcal{M} = \{(Q, Q')\}$ be a (set of) pairs of predicate symbols. A projection *of a positive literal $L = q(t_1, \ldots, t_m)$ w.r.t. $\mathcal{M}$ and $\mathcal{I}$, denoted by $P^{\mathcal{I}}_{\mathcal{M}}(L)$, is defined as follows.*

$$P^{\mathcal{I}}_{\mathcal{M}}(L) = \begin{cases} L & \text{if the predicate symbol of } L \text{ in not equal to } Q \\ Q'(t_{i_1}, \ldots, t_{i_l}) & \text{if } L = Q(t_1, \ldots, t_m),\ \mathcal{I} = \{i_1, \ldots, i_l\}, \\ & \text{and } i_j < i_k \text{ whenever } j < k, \end{cases}$$

The definition of a projection is extended to negative literals, to clauses $C = L_1 \vee \ldots \vee L_m$ and to clause sets $\mathcal{C} = \{C_1, \ldots, C_n\}$.

$$\begin{aligned} P^{\mathcal{I}}_{\mathcal{M}}(\neg L) &= \neg P^{\mathcal{I}}_{\mathcal{M}}(L) \\ P^{\mathcal{I}}_{\mathcal{M}}(C) &= P^{\mathcal{I}}_{\mathcal{M}}(L_1) \vee \ldots \vee P^{\mathcal{I}}_{\mathcal{M}}(L_m) \\ P^{\mathcal{I}}_{\mathcal{M}}(\mathcal{C}) &= P^{\mathcal{I}}_{\mathcal{M}}(C_1), \ldots, P^{\mathcal{I}}_{\mathcal{M}}(C_n) \end{aligned}$$

In general, Q' has to be a new predicate symbol not occurring elsewhere. The projection operation is performed by using clauses obtained from the universal closure of the equivalence

$$Q'(t_{i_1}, \ldots, t_{i_l}) \equiv Q(t_1, \ldots, t_m).$$

If $\mathcal{M}_n$ is of the from $\{(P_1, Q_1), \ldots, (P_n, Q_n)\}$ $(n > 1)$ then

$$P^{\mathcal{I}}_{\mathcal{M}_n}(L) = P^{\mathcal{I}}_{\mathcal{N}_n}(\ldots(P^{\mathcal{I}}_{\mathcal{N}_1}(L))\ldots)$$

with $\mathcal{N}_i = \{(p_i, q_i)\}$.

The requirement that q' is a new predicate symbol is necessary if q occurs with different arities in a clause or in a clause set.

Proposition 3.1
$P^{\mathcal{I}}_{\mathcal{M}}(\mathcal{C})$ does not preserve satisfiability in general.

Proof. Take $p(a,b)$ and $\neg p(a,c)$ as the only clauses in $\mathcal{C}$. Then, $\mathcal{C} \not\vdash_R \Box$. Let $\mathcal{C}' = P^{\mathcal{I}}_{\mathcal{M}}(\mathcal{C})$ with $\mathcal{I} = \{1\}$ and $\mathcal{M} = \{(p,q)\}$. Then, $\mathcal{C}' = \{q(a), \neg q(a)\}$ and $\mathcal{C} \vdash_R \Box$. By the soundness and completeness of R-deduction, we conlude that $\mathcal{C}$ is satisfiable but $\mathcal{C}'$ is unsatisfiable. ∎

Observe that a refutation of $P^{\mathcal{I}}_{\mathcal{M}}(\mathcal{C})$ is a necessary condition for a refutation of $\mathcal{C}$. Furthermore, the length of $\mathcal{C}' \vdash_R \Box$ is a lower bound for the length of $\mathcal{C} \vdash_R \Box$ if both R-refutations exist.

Proposition 3.2
Let Γ be an R-refutation of $\mathcal{C}_n = \{C_1, C_2, C_3\}$[4] with

$$\begin{aligned} C_1 &= P(a,b) \\ C_2 &= \neg P(x,y_2) \vee P(f(x), g(x,y_2)) \vee P(f(x), h(x,y_2)) \\ C_3 &= \neg P(f^{2^n}(a), z_2) \end{aligned}$$

Then the length of Γ is greater than 2^n.

Proof. Due to lack of space, we cannot present the proof in full detail but we sketch the proof. A proof with all details can be found in [9]. The proof is divided into two main steps.

1. Let C be a clause R-derivable from $\mathcal{C}_n$. Then, no clause in this derivation has a factor. The main part of the proof consists of the transformation of an R-deduction of a clause E from $\{C_2\}$ to a linear input R-deduction of E from $\{C_2\}$ via a tree R-deduction of the same kind. This transformation is possible because a set of Horn clauses can be obtained from $\mathcal{C}_n$ by consistently changing signs [11]. It is then shown that there is no factor in every linear input R-deduction of E from $\{C_2\}$.
2. We define the degree of a literal L and the degree of a clause C. For a negative literal L, the degree is the number of nested function symbols f in the first argument of L. If L is positive, then the degree is 2^n minus this number. If the number of nested function symbols f is greater than 2^n, then the degree of L is 2^{n-1}. The degree of a clause is the sum of the degrees of its literals. The degree of each input clause as well as the degree of each clause R-derivable from $\{C_2\}$ is greater than 2^n. Now it is proved that, for a clause C, the sum of the degree D and the length of an R-derivation of C from $\mathcal{C}_n$ is greater than 2^n. It is necessary for this part that the R-refutation is factor-free. Then the length of each R-refutation is greater than 2^n, because the degree of $\Box$ is zero.

∎

[4] By a construction in [6, p.66], no deeply nested terms are necessary. The effect of the deep terms is simulated by a permutation of variables, where the order is exponential but the number of variables is polynomial in the length of the input clause set. Hence, the results also hold if we use as our length measure the number of letters in the word representation of a proof.

In the following, we show that SK_s and SK_f may behave quite different when applied to the same formula.

Let $\mathcal{G}_n$ be the following formula.

$$\mathcal{G}_n = \forall x \forall y_2 [Q(a,a,b) \wedge (\forall v \neg Q(v,x,y_2) \vee \exists u_1 Q(a,f(x),u_1) \vee \exists u_2 Q(b,f(x),u_2)) \wedge \forall z_1 \forall z_2 \neg Q(z_1 f^{2^n}(a), z_2)]$$

If SK_s is applied, introducing $g(x,y_2)$ for u_1 and $h(x,y_2)$ for u_2, repectively, we get a clause set $\mathcal{C}'_n$. Proposition 3.2 implies an exponential lower bound on the length of each R-refutation of $\mathcal{C}'_n$, because $\mathcal{C}_n = P^{\mathcal{I}}_{\mathcal{M}}(\mathcal{C}'_n)$ with $\mathcal{I} = \{2,3\}$ and $\mathcal{M} = \{(Q,P)\}$. If we apply SK_f, $\mathcal{D}_n$ is obtained consisting of the following clauses.

$$D_1 = Q(a,a,b)$$
$$D_2 = \neg Q(v,x,y) \vee Q(a,f(x),g(x)) \vee Q(b,f(x),h(x))$$
$$D_3 = \neg Q(z_1, f^{2^n}(a), z_2)$$

For $\mathcal{D}_n$, there exists short R-refutations. This is demonstrated in the proof of the following proposition.

Proposition 3.3
There is an R-refutation of $\mathcal{D}_n$ of linear length.

Proof. Resolving two variants of D_2 yields the resolvent

$$\neg Q(v,x,y) \vee Q(b,f(x),h(x)) \vee Q(a,f^2(x),g(f(x))) \vee Q(b,f^2(x),h(f(x))).$$

A further resolution of this clause and D_2 yields

$$R_1 = \neg Q(v,x,y) \vee Q(a,f^2(x),g(f(x))) \vee Q(b,f^2(x),h(f(x))) \vee Q(a,f^2(x),g(f(x))) \vee Q(b,f^2(x),h(f(x))).$$

There is a factor F_1 of R_1, namely

$$\neg Q(v,x,y) \vee Q(a,f^2(x),g(f(x))) \vee Q(b,f^2(x),h(f(x))).$$

Using the newly derived factor instead of D_2 in the next resolutions yields F_2, which is as follows.

$$\neg Q(v,x,y) \vee Q(a,f^4(x),g(f^3(x))) \vee Q(b,f^4(x),h(f^3(x))).$$

Iterating this procedure with the newly derived factors yields

$$\neg Q(v,x,y) \vee Q(a,f^{2^n}(x),g(f^{2^n-1}(x))) \vee Q(b,f^{2^n}(x),h(f^{2^n-1}(x))).$$

By three final resolution steps we get $\Box$. The length of the refutation is less than $5n+8$. ∎

Different forms of Skolemization applied to the same formula yield rather different R-refutations. Observe the possibility to simulate the effect of antiprenexing by SK_f in this example. In the next subsection we show that both Skolemization methods benefit from antiprenexing.

3.2 Different Forms of Skolemization and Antiprenexing

Consider the following formula

$$\mathcal{F}_n = \forall x \forall y \exists z_1 \forall z \exists z_2 [P(a,b) \wedge (\neg P(x,y) \vee P(f(x),z_1) \vee P(f(x),z_2) \wedge \neg P(f^{2^n}(a),z)]$$

The clause set $\mathcal{C}_n = \{C_1, C_2, C_3\}$ is obtained by Skolemizing $\mathcal{F}_n$ regardless which Skolemization is applied. The clauses are as follows.

$$C_1 = P(a,b)$$
$$C_2 = \neg P(x,y) \vee P(f(x),g(x,y)) \vee P(f(x),h(x,y,z))$$
$$C_3 = \neg P(f^{2^n}(a),z)$$

Proposition 3.2 implies that the length of each R-refutation of $\mathcal{C}_n$ is exponential in n. If we apply antiprenexing to $\mathcal{F}_n$, we obtain $\mathcal{G}_n$.

$$\mathcal{G}_n = P(a,b) \wedge \forall x(\forall y \neg P(x,y) \vee \exists z_1(P(f(x),z_1) \vee P(f(x),z_1)) \wedge \forall z \neg P(f^{2^n}(a),z)$$

Let $\mathcal{E}_n$ be obtained by transforming the formula $\neg\mathcal{G}_n$ into clausal form.

$$E_1 = P(a,b)$$
$$E_2 = \neg P(x,y) \vee P(f(x),g(x)) \vee P(f(x),h(x))$$
$$E_3 = \neg P(f^{2^n}(a),z)$$

It is easy to verify that there is an R-refutation of $\mathcal{E}_n$ of length linear in n.

In contrast to the clause E_2, C_2 has Skolem terms $g(x,y)$ and $h(x,y,z)$ of arity greater than one. Different logically equivalent formulae may yield refutations of different length. The reason is the prevention of factorization steps in an R-refutation due to Skolem terms which depend on more variables than necessary. The introduction of such Skolem terms may be avoided by antiprenexing. Therefore, we get the following theorem.

Theorem 3.1
Applying antiprenexing may yield exponentially shorter resolution refutations regardless whether SK_s or SK_f is applied.

The main difference between our approach of antiprenexing and the approach in [4] is the possibility to move $\exists$-quantifier upward in the formula tree. In the sequel, we demonstrate why such a movement can be advantageous. Let $\mathcal{H}_n$ be defined as follows.

$$\mathcal{H}_n = Q(a,b,c,d) \wedge \forall x \forall y(\forall z \forall u \neg Q(x,y,z,u) \vee \exists z_1 \forall z_3 Q(f(x),z_1,y,z_3) \vee \exists z_2 Q(f(x),z_2,y,z_2)) \wedge \forall v_1 \forall v_2 \forall v_3 \neg Q(f^{2^n}(a),v_1,v_2,v_3)$$

If we Skolemize $\mathcal{H}_n$, we get C'_n regardless which Skolemization technique is used. The clauses are as follows.

$$\begin{aligned} C'_1 &= Q(a,b,c,d) \\ C'_2 &= \neg Q(x,y,z,u) \vee Q(f(x),g(x,y),y,z_3) \vee Q(f(x),h(x,y),y,h(x,y)) \\ C'_3 &= \neg Q(f^{2^n}(a),v_1,v_2,v_3) \end{aligned}$$

Let $C_n = P^{\mathcal{I}}_{\mathcal{M}}(C'_n)$ with $\mathcal{I} = \{1,2\}$ and $\mathcal{M} = \{(Q,P))\}$. By Proposition 3.2, the length of each R-refutation of C_n is exponential in n. Therefore, the length of each R-refutation of C'_n is exponential in n, because the lower bound on the length of an R-refutation of C_n is also a lower bound on the length of an R-refutation of C'_n. If we Skolemize the antiprenexed form of $\mathcal{H}_n$, denoted by

$$\begin{aligned} \mathcal{H}'_n = Q(a,b,c,d) \wedge \forall x \forall y(\forall z \forall u \neg Q(x,y,z,u) \vee \exists z_1(\forall z_3 Q(f(x),z_1,y,z_3) \vee \\ Q(f(x),z_1,y,z_1))) \wedge \forall v_1 \forall v_2 \forall v_3 \neg Q(f^{2^n}(a),v_1,v_2,v_3) \end{aligned}$$

we obtain a clause of the form

$$\neg P(x,y,z,u) \vee P(f(x),g(x,y),y,z_3) \vee P(f(x),g(x,y),y,g(x,y))$$

instead of C'_2 in the resulting clause set. There is an R-refutation of length linear in n, mainly because the possibility to get a factor of this clause. Let us remark that the word representation of the refutation remains exponential in this example.

4 Antiprenexing and Skolem Term Introduction

If Skolem term introduction rules are applied, a reduced clause form (obtained by antiprenexing) is advantageous. The reason is that, if only the clause form is used, a separation of the clause into different independent subclauses may be avoided. Furthermore, the introduction of Skolem terms with more arguments than necessary can avoid factorization. Since factorization steps may cause an exponential decrease of proof length, this avoidance of factorization sometimes yields exponentially longer refutations. Another reason is the possibility to derive clauses which behave like tautologies instead of essential lemmata which may be used to shorten a refutation.

Let C_n be a clause set consisting of the following clauses.

$$\begin{aligned} C_1 &= P(g(a,b),h(a,b),h(a,b)) \\ C_2 &= \neg P(x,y,y) \vee P(f(x),g(x,y),u_1) \vee P(f(x),h(x,y),u_2) \\ C_3 &= \neg P(f^{2^n}(g(a,b)),z,z) \end{aligned}$$

Observe that neither g nor h is a Skolem function symbol. By a projection to the first two arguments, Proposition 3.2 implies that each R-refutation of C_n has length exponential in n.

Proposition 4.1
There is an FR-refutation of C_n of length linear in n.

Proof. 1-F-extension applied to C_n yields the clause

$$C_4 = \neg p(x,y,y) \vee p(f(x), g(x,l(x)), u_1) \vee p(f(x), h(x,l(x)), u_2).$$

For simplicity, we replace $g(x,l(x))$ by $m_1(x)$ and $h(x,l(x))$ by $m_2(x)$. Although such replacements are not possible by FR-deduction, they are performed here for presentational reason. Since the new terms depend on the same variables than the old ones, refutation length is not affected. Thus, we obtain the following clause.

$$C_5 = \neg p(x,y,y) \vee p(f(x), m_1(x), u_1) \vee p(f(x), m_2(x), u_2).$$

Resolving two variants of C_5 yields a clause of the form

$$\begin{aligned} C_6 = \neg p(x,y,y) &\vee p(f(f(x)), m_1(f(x), u) \vee \\ &p(f(f(x)), m_2(f(x)), v) \vee p(f(x), m_1(x), w). \end{aligned}$$

Resolving C_6 with a variant of C_5 yields

$$\begin{aligned} C_7 = \neg p(x,y,y) &\vee p(f(f(x)), m_1(f(x)), u) \vee \\ &p(f(f(x)), m_2(f(x)), v) \vee p(f(f(x)), m_1(f(x)), w) \vee \\ &p(f(f(x)), m_2(f(x)), z)). \end{aligned}$$

There is a factor C_8 of C_7, where the corresponding substitution is $\{z \leftarrow v, w \leftarrow u\}$.

$$C_8 = \neg p(x,y,y) \vee p(f(f(x)), m_1(f(x)), u) \vee p(f(f(x)), m_2(f(x)), v)$$

Iterating this deduction but with the newly derived factors instead of C_5 yields a clause of the form

$$D = \neg p(x,y,y) \vee p(f^{2^n}(x), m_1(f^{2^n-1}(x)), u) \vee p(f^{2^n}(x), m_2(f^{2^n-1}(x)), v).$$

Three final resolutions conclude the FR-refutation of C_n. By a simple calculation, a bound linear in n is computed for the length of the FR-refutation. ∎

If restricted F-extension is used instead of F-extension (i.e. antiprenexing is not applied) then there is no possibility to obtain a short refutation of C_n. We consider only refutations without superfluous clauses. Let Γ be a refutation of a clause set C of the form Γ_1, C, Γ_2 such that no variant of C occurs in Γ_2. Clause $C \neq \Box$ is superfluous in Γ if it is not the parent clause of an inference step in Γ_2. We can get a refutation without superfluous clauses by deleting all superfluous clauses C. In the following, we show that each clause derivable by restricted F-extension from C_n is superfluous in all refutations of C_n.

Lemma 4.1
Each clause obtained by applying restricted F-extension to C_n is superfluous.

Proof. Deriving clauses by restricted F-extension using clause C_1 is impossible because $V(C_1) = \emptyset$. Introducing new Skolem terms into C_3^n yields a superfluous clause because a clause of the form $\neg p(f^{2^n}(a), m_1, m_1)$ (m_1 is a globally new function symbol) is neither resolvable with C_1 nor with clauses derived from $\{C_2\}$. The only possibility is to introduce new terms into C_2. In what follows, we discuss the possibilities to introduce terms for different variables.

If we introduce a new Skolem term for the variable x then the clause is superfluous. Let $C_2^{\{x\}}$ denote the clause C_2 but with a new Skolem term introduced for some occurrences of x. The literal in which variable x is replaced is only resolvable with a literal from C_2 or with literals from $C_2^{\{x\}}$ since C_1 as well as C_3^n have ground terms as first argument. Furthermore, the Skolem term is distributed in other literals of clauses derived from $C_n \cup \{C_2^{\{x\}}\}$. But finally, all the literals of a non-superfluous clause have to be resolved upon or the literals have to be factorized. Even if a factor is possible, instances of the newly introduced Skolem terms are retained. Since the only possibility to reduce the length of a clause without a factor is a resolution against C_1 or C_3^n, a clause with a new Skolem term introduced for one or more occurrences of x cannot occur in a refutation. Hence, $C_2^{\{x\}}$ and all clauses derived using $C_2^{\{x\}}$ are superfluous.

Let $V(t)$ denote the set of variables occurring in a term t. If we introduce new Skolem terms for the variables u_1 or u_2 then the clauses are superfluous. The reason is the impossibility to resolve a literal $p(f^i(x), g(f(^{i-1}(x), t), l(x, y, u_1, u_2))$ $(i \geq 1)$ where $y \in V(t)$ and $l(x, y, u_1, u_2)$ is the newly introduced Skolem term with any other negative literal occurring in C_n. If occurrences of the variable y are replaced then the clause is superfluous, since either the negative literal is not resolvable with any other positive literal in the clause set or a term of the form $l(x, u_1, u_2)$ is introduced in a positive literal preventing a resolution step with any negative literal.

Observe that, if more than one variable is replaced, the corresponding Skolem terms are different. As a consequence, each clause obtained by restricted F-extension applied to C_n is superfluous. ■

Corollary 4.1
Let C be a clause R-derivable from $\{C_2\}$. Then each clause obtained by restricted F-extension from C is superfluous.

Proof. By similar arguments like in the case of C_2 in the proof of Lemma 4.1. ■

Lemma 4.2
Let C be a clause R-derivable from C_n. Then each clause obtained by restricted F-extension from C is superfluous.

Proof. Due to Corollary 4.1, it is sufficient to consider clauses whose first argument is a ground term. The reason is that each non-superfluous clause with a non-ground term is R-derivable from $\{C_2\}$. There are two kinds of clauses to distinguish.

1. $D_1 = D_{1,1} \lor \neg p(t, y, y) \lor D_{1,2}$

2. $D_2 = D_{2,1} \lor p(f^i(t), g(f^{i-1}(t), s), u_1) \lor D_{2,2}$

Resolvents of 1. and 2. have the form of D_1 or D_2. The terms s and t are ground terms. $D_{1,1}$, $D_{1,2}$, $D_{2,1}$, and $D_{2,2}$ are possibly empty positive subclauses of D_1 and D_2, respectively. For $D_{1,i}$ and $D_{2,i}$ ($i \in \{1,2\}$), the following equations hold.

$$V(D_{1,i}) = \{y, u_1, \ldots, u_m\}$$
$$V(D_{2,i}) = \{u_1, \ldots, u_n\}$$

where $V(D)$ denotes the set of all variables occurring in D, and $m+1$ and n are the number of literal of D_1 and D_2, respectively. If we replace occurrences of y or u_i either in D_1 or in D_2, we get superfluous clauses. The reason is that Skolem terms introduced for variables $\{z_1, \ldots, z_l\}$ in D depend at least on all variables in $V(C)\setminus\{z_1, \ldots, z_l\}$. Furthermore, l new Skolem function symbols are introduced. As in the case of clauses derived from $\{C_2\}$, each clause obtained by restricted F-extension is superfluous. ∎

Each restricted FR-refutation of C_n degenerates to an R-refutation of C_n. As a consequence, the length of each restricted FR-refutation of C_n is exponential in n. We get the following theorem.

Theorem 4.1
Restricted FR-deduction cannot polynomially simulate FR-deduction.

5 Conclusion

We examined different effects which influence the result of Skolemization. First, we demonstrated that the Skolemization procedure may influence the length of R-refutations of the resulting clause set. Then we showed that both versions of Skolemization can benefit from the application of antiprenexing. In particular, an exponential decrease of refutation length was enabled by applying antiprenexing. Our version of antiprenexing moves ∀-quantifiers downward in the formula tree whereas ∃-quantifiers are moved upward. In contrast to [4], we do not get a formula which is completely in miniscope form. The reason for avoiding full miniscope form is the need for ∃-quantifier duplication if a miniscope form is required. As a consequence, different Skolem terms are introduced. These different Skolem terms may cause an exponential increase of proof length in case R-deduction is applied. We showed that applying restricted FR-deduction may yield an exponential increase of proof length compared to FR-deduction. This increase cannot be avoided since we do not allow antiprenexing which decreases the arity of Skolem terms in this case.

The idea of introducing function symbols depending on the free variables of the quantified subformula has been rediscovered. In [10], a run-time Skolemization procedure for tableaux calculi is presented which introduces Skolem terms of the same arity and depending on the same variables as the Skolem terms introduced by SK_f. In [6] as well as in [13], SK_f is integrated into the structure-preserving transformation of a formula to clause form.

In [3], the proof of a formula given in [14] is examined. The Herbrand complexity of Statman's formula is non-elementary in the length of the formula. Although there is a short proof, for instance in LK with cut, the cut-free proof is non-elementariely longer than the proof with cut. In [3], however, there is a short cut-free proof in an LK calculus extended by T-extension. A T-extension is a sequent of the form

$$A_1 \rightarrow A_1, \ldots, A_n \rightarrow A_n, B_1, \ldots, B_l \vdash C_1, \ldots, C_m$$

where $B_1, \ldots, B_l \vdash C_1, \ldots, C_m$ is a sequent and A_i $(1 \leq i \leq n)$ is a first order formula. Now, if the different $A_i \rightarrow A_i$ are required to be in a specific prenex normal form, then these implications degenerate to tautologies which cannot shorten the proof. As a consequence, there is no short proof. Hence, the difference between the length of the two proofs cannot be bounded by an elementary function. Although such an increase of proof length may perhaps be avoided by choosing the "right" prenex normal form, antiprenexing yields a non-elementary decrease of proof length for a specific prenex form in this example.

Acknowledgement: The author would like to thank Wolfgang Bibel and Stefan Brüning for their constructive criticism and for their useful comments on an earlier draft of this paper.

References

1. P. B. Andrews. Theorem Proving via General Matings. *Journal of the Association for Computing Machinery*, 28, No.2:193–214, 1981.
2. M. Baaz and A. Leitsch. Complexity of Resolution Proofs and Function Introduction. *Annals of Pure and Applied Logic*, 57:181–215, 1992.
3. M. Baaz and A. Leitsch. On Skolemization and Proof Complexity. *Fundamenta Informaticae*, 1994.
4. W. Bibel. An Approach to a Systematic Theorem Proving Procedure in First-Order Logic. *Computing*, 12:43–55, 1974.
5. W. Bibel. *Automated Theorem Proving.* Vieweg, Braunschweig, second edition, 1987.
6. E. Eder. *Relative Complexities of First Order Calculi.* Vieweg, Braunschweig, 1992.
7. U. Egly. Shortening Proofs by Quantifier Introduction. In A. Voronkov, editor, *Proceedings of the International Conference on Logic Programming and Automated Reasoning*, pages 148–159. Springer Verlag, 1992.
8. U. Egly. On Different Concepts of Function Introduction. In G. Gottlob, A. Leitsch, and D. Mundici, editors, *Proceedings of the Kurt Gödel Colloquium*, pages 172–183. Springer Verlag, 1993.
9. U. Egly. *Function Introduction and the Complexity of Proofs.* PhD thesis, TH Darmstadt, Alexanderstr. 10, D–64283 Darmstadt, 1994. Forthcoming.
10. R. Hähnle and P. H. Schmitt. The Liberalized δ-Rule in Free Variable Semantic Tableaux. *Journal of Automated Reasoning.* To appear.

11. H. R. Lewis. Renaming a Set of Clauses as a Horn Set. *Journal of the ACM*, 25(1):134–135, 1978.
12. D. W. Loveland. *Automated Theorem Proving: A Logical Basis*, volume 6 of *Fundamental Studies in Computer Science*. North–Holland Publishing Company, Amsterdam, New York, Oxford, 1978.
13. D. A. Plaisted and S. Greenbaum. A Structure-Preserving Clause Form Translation. *Journal of Symbolic Computation*, 2:293–304, 1986.
14. R. Statman. Lower Bounds on Herbrand's Theorem. In *Proc. AMS 75*, pages 104–107, 1979.

Implementing a Finite-domain CLP-language on Top of Prolog: a Transformational Approach

Henk Vandecasteele and Danny De Schreye

Department of Computer Science, K. U. Leuven, Celestijnenlaan 200A, B-3001 Heverlee, Belgium, henk.vandecasteele@cs.kuleuven.ac.be

Keywords: program transformation, Constraint Logic Programming, finite domains.

1 Introduction

We present an implementation of a finite domain CLP language in Prolog. In Logic Programming, it is standard practice to implement *enhanced* Logic Programming languages in Prolog through meta-interpretation. The advantage of such an approach is that those features of the *enhanced* language that coincide with corresponding features of Prolog can be implemented through downward reflection. Only features of the language that require a treatment different from that in Prolog are reificated in the meta-interpreter. However, it is well-known that this type of implementation may produce significant overhead. One of the main motivations of LP-work on partial evaluation has been to remove this overhead through transformation. We refer to [4] for a more extensive discussion on these issues.

It has frequently been observed (e.g. A. Mariën at [3], that an alternative solution, avoiding the need for partial evaluation, is to implement the enhanced language by means of a transformer from the enhanced language to Prolog. Denoting a meta-interpreter for the enhanced language as M and a partial evaluator for prolog as PE, conceptually such a transformer can be defined as a program T, such that for every program P in the enhanced language T(P) $\equiv$ PE(M(P)). The point raised by Mariën is that writing T from scratch is not considerably more difficult than writing M and should therefore be considered as a valid (and more economic) approach to implementing the enhanced language.

In this paper we describe such a transformation for a specific enhanced language, which is a finite domain CLP-language. A related transformation is described in [5]. There however, 1) the considered language is much more trivial than the language dealt with in the current paper, 2) the target language is a prolog-variant with a delay-mechanism. Due to these differences, the transformation are only barely comparable.

Since we are developing the implementation for a very expressive CLP-language, the transformation is performed in two steps. First, the CLP program is transformed to an equivalent program in a more low-level language. The latter language is similar to the cc(FD)-language proposed in [10]. The importance of this step is that the low-level language allows for more efficient constraint checking. In a second step, the low-level CLP-program is transformed to a Prolog implementation.

Our high level CLP-language has as its most specific feature that it takes a 'glass-box' approach to Constraint Programming. This mean that the programmer is offered a limited form of access to the constraint-solver, allowing him to specify the type of pruning the solver should perform, the enumeration strategy it should use and even the backtracking variant that is should evoke. Most other Constraint Logic Programming systems use 'black-box' constraint solvers. Typical examples are PrologIII [14], with among others the simplex-algorithm, and BNR-prolog [1], with interval-arithmetic. An advantage of the latter approach is that the user has not to be concerned with how the solver works. A disadvantage is that a different representation of a problem can give totally different performance results. When the user aims to develop an efficient program, deep knowledge of the solver is required. Our approach is similar to the CHIP-approach [8], where the user can influence the solving method with for instance forward and lookahead directives. However in languages such as CHIP, support for this type of user influence is still limited. We developed a fast algorithm which has some properties in common with interval-arithmetic, but which can still be highly influenced by the user: it provides an extension of forward and lookahead primitives and powerful enumeration primitives which, among others, use techniques like dynamic rearrangement (firstfail) and different backtrack-strategies.

The papers is organised as follows. In section 2 we introduce the considered finite-domain CLP-language. Section 3 contains a brief description of the lower-level CLP-language and of the transformation of the first to the latter. In section 4 we present a high-level description of the transformation to Prolog in a more general context (not restricted to the enhanced language at hand). Section 5 specialises this transformation to the context of our CLP-language and provides details on the required library predicates defining the finite domain solver. Some performance results are provided in Section 6. We end with a discussion.

2 The finite domain language

2.1 Introduction

In [13] B. Nadel presents a generic algorithm which brings together several of the pruning algorithms for finite domain programs known at that time. The algorithm has a parameter which indicates which pruning technique to use. The level of checking ranges from backward checking, forward checking, look-ahead to several versions of arc-consistency checking. In his work he pointed out that an algorithm with a high level of constraint checking is often not the best algorithm to solve constraint satisfaction problems. This can be explained by the fact that the higher the level of constraint-checking, the more checking is done at each node of the search tree. In many cases, this is not compensated by the decrease of nodes in the search tree.

In the BNR-approach [1] with interval-arithmetic another approach is taken. The algorithm always achieves arc-consistency but the computation time to check a constraint is minimised, by approximating the constraints to constraints which only use the (lower- and upper-) bounds of the domains. In fact by doing this, arc-consistency is not really reached with respect to the original constraints, there is only arc-consistency between the variables with respect to the approximated constraints.

Another subject in this field of research, is enumeration. We propose a general parameterised enumeration-technique with non-standard backtracking.

In our approach we want to combine the generic formulation of Nadel allowing various forms of pruning and - in our extension - backtracking, with the interval-arithmetic approach.

2.2 Specifying the pruning technique.

As pointed out above, there are three methods for decreasing the computation time for finding a solution to a finite domain problem:

- Varying the number of constraint checks at each node of the search.
- Minimising the time-consumption for one constraint check.
- Varying the enumeration and backtrack-strategy.

In the finite domain CLP-language, ROPE, developed in the context of the Esprit project PRINCE, the main aim was to integrate these three methods as well as possible. In [13] varying the number of constraint checks at each node is done by specifying a pruning strategy (forward checking, ...). One strategy is specified for all the constraints in the problem. In our approach we want to be able to express a pruning technique for each of the constraints in the problem. As some constraints do more pruning and are more important than others they can be given a higher level constraint checking technique. Minimising the time-consumption in the BNR-approach is done by checking the constraints only on the bounds of the domains. This also entails that the constraints only need to be activated if the bounds of the domain of the concerned variable change. In the BNR-approach this is done for all the constraints in the problem. In our approach we want this to be specified for each constraint in detail. Thus for some constraints one can specify a full domain checking approach, for others only checking on bounds. Both these techniques allow the user to tailor the pruning technique to the problem at hand. To specify the pruning behaviour we allow declarations:

Definition 1 The prune declaration.
<constraint> prune(X_1 <r>, ..., X_n <r>)
where <r> ::= g | a | p | p<list> | ad | pd | pd<list>
and <list> = (Y_1, ... Y_k)

For every variable X_i of an expression the user is allowed to specify one of the directives: g, a, p, p<list>, ad, pd or pd<list>. Directive 'g' means that this variable must be ground before any pruning is performed. Directive 'a' and 'ad' mean that on this variable no pruning is required. Directive 'p' and 'pd' mean that this variable must be pruned. If there is a list of variables connected to the 'p' or 'pd' directive, then the pruning of that variable must be delayed until all the variables in the list are ground. Variables which do not appear in the prune structure are supposed to have the directive 'a'.

As explained above one can use the bounds of the domain of a variable for pruning the domain of another variable with a constraint, or one can prune on the basis of the full domain. This difference is expressed in the declaration by selecting either the 'p' directive or the 'pd' directive (and similar, the 'a' directive or the 'ad' directive). So, for a variable with a directive without a 'd' only the bounds of the variable are used to prune the domains of other variables in the constraint. In case the directive ends with a 'd' (from 'd'omain) the full domain is taken into account for the pruning of the other variables. Remark that the forward and lookahead directives of CHIP [8] are special cases of this prune declaration. If the meaning of the previous declarations is not yet clear the following examples, explaining different forms of pruning for X = Y + 1, may help.

Example 1. **X = Y + 1 prune(X : pd, Y : pd)**

Procedurally this will result in the following behaviour: whenever the domain of the variable X or Y changes, the new domain of the other variable is computed corresponding to the changes. In this case the full domain of both variables is taken into account. If the domain of Y is restricted to the three values 2, 6 and 120 then the domain of X will be restricted to the set {3, 7, 121}.

Example 2. **X = Y + 1 prune(X : p, Y : p(X))**

results in the behaviour: whenever the bounds of the domain of Y change, the new domain of X is computed. With this prune-construction only the bounds of the domain of Y is taken into account. So if the domain of Y is restricted to the three values 2, 6 and 120 then the domain of X will be restricted to the set {3,4,5, ... 121}. On the other hand the variable Y is pruned only after the variable X has become ground. For this variable we get forward checking behaviour.

Example 3. **X = Y + 1 prune(X : a, Y : p).**

Here we have: the variable Y will be pruned whenever the bounds of the variable X change, but X will not be pruned if the variable Y changes.

The techniques we use for enumeration and the backtracking behaviour attached to them have no large impact on the transformations we propose here, and will be left out.

2.3 Two examples.

We can now introduce the two examples we will later on use for explaining the transformations and the executing mechanism of the solver. First we have what we call 'the rabbit program'. There are rabbits and pheasants playing on the grass. We can see 9 animals in total. We can also notice 24 feet. How many pheasants and how many rabbits are playing?

Example 4. **rabbit(P, R):-**
P + R = 9 prune(P:p, R:p),
2*P + 4*R = 24 prune(P:p, R:p).

For both constraints in the program we want lookahead pruning, but not checking on the full domain, only on the bounds.

We also use the queens-problem. This is the well-known problem of placing n queens on a board of size n x n such that no queen attacks another.

Example 5. **Queens**

```
queens(Q,N):-
        generate(Q,N,N), safe(Q), enum(Q).
        /* enum/1 is a special enumeration-predicate */
generate([],0,_).
generate([X|T],M,N):- M > 0 , X in 1..N, M1 is M - 1, generate(T,M1,N).
safe([]).
safe([X|T]):-noAttack(X,1,T),safe(T).
noAttack(_,_,[]).
noAttack(X,N,[Y|Z]):- X <> Y + N prune(X:p(Y), Y:p(X)),
        X<>Y prune(X:p(Y),Y:p(X)), Y<>X+N prune(X:p(Y),Y:p(X)),
        S is N + 1, noAttack(X,S,Z).
```

In this program there are 4 finite domain primitives: in the predicate definition of *generate/2* there is the primitive *X in 1.. N* which restricts the domain of X to the set of values from 1 to N. Then there are three difference constraints in the predicate definition of *noAttack/3* for which we want forward checking.

3 Transforming to a lower-level language

As we have to test the constraints as efficiently as possible, in a first transformation, we transform them to more low-level and easy to test constraints. Such easy to test constraints must have the following properties:

- the constraint can be checked very fast,
- the constraint can be propagated with little overhead.

Therefore we propose to transform the finite domain primitives to a low-level language with the following syntax, which is inspired by [10]:

3.1 Syntax

<low-constr> ::= X in <range>
| ask(ground(X),<low-constr>) | ask(X in <range>,<low-constr>)
| [<low-constr>, ... ,<low-constr>]
(The conjunction of <low-constr>, ... and <low-constr>)

Here, <range> is defined as:
<range> ::= <term> .. <term> (an interval)

| <term>	(one value)
| dom(X)	(The domain of a variable)
| int(X)	(The interval made of the bounds of the domain of the variable)
| <range>:<range>	(union)
| <range>&<range>	(intersection)
| compl(<range>)	(complementation)
| (<range>)	(to avoid ambiguities)
| <range> <op> <range>	(pointwise domain computation)
| <range><op> Y |<nat>	(translate and scale a domain)

where <term> is an expression of integers, ground finite domain variables and bounds of finite domain variables.

<term> ::= Y | <nat> | infinity | <term><op><term> | lb(X) | ub(X)
| (< term >) with lb(X) the lowerbound of the domain and ub(X) the upperbound.

<op> ::= + | − | * | *mod* | *div*

3.2 An initial Transformation.

We sketch the transformation from the high-level language by transforming the examples of the previous section.

Example 6. **X = Y + 1 prune(X : pd, Y : pd)** is transformed to:

X in dom(Y) + 1, (1)
Y in dom(X) - 1. (2)

When for example the first constraint (1) must be checked, the domain of Y is shifted by one unit and the intersection with the current domain of X is made. The constraints (1) and (2) need to be propagated as follows: (1) must be activated whenever the domain of Y changes and (2) must be activated whenever the domain of X changes. This behaviour matches exactly with the behaviour described for this constraint in the previous section.

Example 7. **X = Y + 1 prune(X : p, Y : p(X))** is transformed to:

X in int(Y) + 1, (3)
ask(ground(X), Y in X - 1). (4)

Constraint (3) will compute the lower-bound and the upperbound of Y and then translate this interval with one unit. Then the intersection of this new interval with the domain of X is made. Constraint (3) only needs to be activated as soon as the bounds of the domain of Y changes. Constraint (4) is only activated once after the variable X has become ground.

Example 8. **X = Y + 1 prune(X : a, Y : p)** to:

Y in int(X) - 1. (will be activated as soon as the bounds of X change)

We end the section with some further examples including the rabbit and the queens-example.

Example 9. **X < Y / Z prune(X:p, Y:p(X, Z), Z:p(X)).** is transformed to:

Z in 1 .., (1) X in 0 .. ub(Y) / lb(Z), (2)
ask(ground(X), ask(ground(Z), Y in Z * X .. infinity)), (3)
ask(ground(Y), Z in 0 .. ub(Y)/X). (4)

The first constraint(1) removes the chance oin divide by 0. The second constraint will be activated whenever the upperbound on the domain of Y changes, or the lowerbound on the domain of Z changes. Then the domain of X will be intersected with the interval [0, ub(Y) / lb(Z)], with ub(R) the largest value in the domain of R. The constraints (3) and (4) will be delayed until some variables becomes ground. After that constraint (3) will be checked once. Constraint(4) will pop up in case the smallest value in the domain of X is removed from the domain.

The constraint part of the rabbit problem and the queens program:

Example 10. **Rabbit**

P in 9 - int(R), R in 9 - int(P) ,
P in (24 - 4*int(R)) div 2, R in (24 - 2*int(P)) div 4 .

Example 11. **Queens**

ask(ground(Y), X in compl(Y+N)) , ask(ground(X), Y in compl(X-N)) ,
ask(ground(Y), X in compl(Y)) , ask(ground(X), Y in compl(X)) ,
ask(ground(Y), X in compl(Y-N)) , ask(ground(X), Y in compl(X+N)) .

4 Meta-interpretation versus transformation.

4.1 Using meta-interpretation.

The meta-program filters out the non-standard features of the enhanced language and treats them as specified in its semantics. A simplified version of such a meta-interpreter (without *cut* and *or*) in Prolog could look like:

Algorithm 2.

```
meta((Goal1, Goal2)):- !, meta(Goal1), meta(Goal2).
meta(Goal):- isFeature(Goal), !, takeCareOfFeature(Goal).
meta(Goal):- builtin(Goal), !, call(Goal).
meta(Goal):- clause(Goal, Body), meta(Body).
```

In general one will also need extra parameters in the interpreter for passing information from one call of *takeCareOfFeature* to another. Such extra parameters could be compacted to two parameters, an in- and out-parameter. This results in the following scheme of the interpreter:

Algorithm 3.

meta((Goal1, Goal2), ParamIn, ParamOut):- !,
meta(Goal1, ParamIn, Param), meta(Goal2, Param, ParamOut).
meta(Goal, ParamIn, ParamOut):- isFeature(Goal, ParamIn), !,
takeCareOfFeature(Goal, ParamIn, ParamOut).
meta(Goal, Param, Param):- builtin(Goal), !, call(Goal).
meta(Goal, ParamIn, ParamOut):-
clause(Goal, Body), meta(Body, ParamIn, ParamOut).

4.2 Using transformation.

To avoid the overhead of the parsing, a compilation of the enhanced program through transformations is more useful. In case there is no extra information to be passes around this transformation is quite simple: wrapping the special features of the enhanced language in calls to predefined library predicates will do the job. Given the program:

Example 12.

```
a(X, Y):- r(X), c(X, Y).
a(X, Y):- s(X, Y, Z), a(Y, Z).
```

with r/1 and s/3 special calls. Then this would be transformed to:

```
a(X, Y):- takeCareOfFeature(r(X)), c(X, Y).
a(X, Y):- takeCareOfFeature(s(X, Y, Z)), a(Y, Z).
```

If there is need for extra information to be passed around from one call to takeCareOfFeature to another then every clause of the program needs an extra parameter, and the clause must be renamed. For every predicate definition in the program a new clause is added with the original name of the clause which calls the transformed clause with the initialised extra parameters. Applying this technique to the example results in:

Example 13.

```
a(X, Y):- initialise(ParameterIn),
        a_1(X, Y, ParameterIn, ParameterOut), results(ParameterOut).
a_1(X, Y, ParamIn, ParamOut):-
        takeCareOfFeature(r(X), ParamIn, Param1),
        c(X, Y, Param1, ParamOut).
a_1(X, Y, ParamIn, ParamOut):-
        takeCareOfFeature(s(X, Y, Z), ParamIn, Param1),
        a_1(Y, Z, Param1, ParamOut).
```

In some cases such parameter passing can be avoided by instantiating the variables where the special features of the language act on, with the information to be passed. This technique is not general but is applicable in our case. Then we also have to rename the predicates, as we have to intercept the output of the program and reconstruct the output that the original program was supposed to produce. The compiled program then looks like:

Example 14.

```
a(X, Y):- getFreeVariables(a(X, Y), Free), a_1(X, Y),
        printResults(Free), fail.
a_1(X, Y):- takeCareOfFeature(r(X)), c_1(X, Y).
a_1(X, Y):- takeCareOfFeature(s(X, Y, Z)), a_1(Y, Z).
```

First the free variables are extracted from the query. After successful completion of the program we print the results of the original program and we fail (as we do not want Prolog to print out the internal representation of X and Y).

Of course with this kind of technique special care must be taken: normal prolog-unification of the special variables must be prevented while transforming the program. Also the use of builtin's on these special variables must be taken care of. Also one can not allow queries like ?- a,b. A definition c:- a,b. must be added to the input program and then we must call ?- c. More details on this approach in the context of our finite domain language are given in the next section. First we give the two compiled example-programs.

Example 15. **Compiled rabbit program**

```
rabbit(P, R):-
        getFreeVariables(rabbit(P, R), Free), % Getting the free variables
        rabbit_1(P, R), % executing the program
        showSolution(Free), fail. % print the results
rabbit_1(P, R):-
        constraint__( P in 9 - int(R) ), % The two transformed constraints
        constraint__( R in 9 - int(P) ),
        constraint__( P in (24 - 4*int(R)) div 2 ),
        constraint__( R in (24 - 2*int(P)) div 4 ).
```

Example 16. **Compiled queens program**

```
queens( Q , N ) :-
        getFreeVariables(queens( Q , N ), Free ),
        queens_1( Q , N ), showSolution( Free ), fail .
queens_1( Q , N ) :-
        generate_1( Q , N , N ), safe_1( Q ), constraint__(enum( Q )) .
generate_1([],0, _ ) .
generate_1([ X | T ], M , N ) :-
        M > 0, constraint__( X in 1 .. N ),
        M1 is M - 1, generate_1( T , M1 , N ) .
safe_1([]) .
safe_1([ X | T ]) :- noAttack_1( X ,1, T ), safe_1( T ) .
noAttack_1( _ , _ ,[]) .
noAttack_1( X , N ,[ Y | Z ]) :-
        constraint__(ask(ground(Y), X in compl(Y + N)) ),
        constraint__(ask(ground(X), Y in compl(X - N)) ),
        constraint__(ask(ground(Y), X in compl(Y)) ),
        constraint__(ask(ground(X), Y in compl(X)) ),
        constraint__(ask(ground(Y), X in compl(Y - N)) ),
```

```
constraint__(ask(ground(X), Y in compl(X + N)) ).
S is N + 1, noAttack_1( X , S , Z ) .
```

5 The finite domain library

As one can notice, there are three predicates in the finite domain library:

- getFreeVariables/2. This predicates searches for the free variables in first arguments and stores them in a list in the second argument.
- showSolution/1 prints out the list of prolog-expressions while substituting the finite domain variable with their semantic value.
- constraint__/1 is far the most interesting predicate of the finite domain library. This predicate instantiates domain variables to a specific structure, fulfilling the purpose of passing on relevant information for the solver, adds the constraint to the constraint store and activates the solver for checking the constraint.

In the next subsections we first explain how the constraint-store and the domains of the finite domain variables are represented.

5.1 Representation of the constraint store

As stated before, specific information needed by the constraint solver is not represented by extra arguments of the transformed predicates, but by instantiating domain variables to a specific structure. The information needed by the solver in our case is: the current domain of a domain variable and the current constraint store. Passing on this information through the domain variable itself is particularly interesting for our application, since we need to propagate constraints as soon as some type of changes occurs to the domain of a variable. Thus, by instantiating a domain variable to a structure *finiteVar(Domain, Constraints)*, where *Domain* is a representation of the domain of the variable and *Constraints* of all constraints in the store that contain the variable, easy access for propagation is guaranteed. Actually, as one can notice from the different possible forms of pruning, for each constraint, there can only be four conditions under which the constraint needs to be activated. The constraint needs to be activated

- after every change to the domain of this variable,
- if this variable becomes ground,
- if the lowerbound of this variable's domain changes,
- if the upperbound of this variable's domain changes.

Note that for some pruning directives more than one of these conditions may be applicable. The structure for the constraint-store is then easily chosen: *store(Always, Ground, LowerBound, UpperBound)*. With *Always* the constraints that need to be checked whenever the domain of the associated domain changes, *Ground* the constraints that need to be checked as soon as the finite domain variable becomes ground and *Lowerbound* and *UpperBound* whenever the lowerbound (resp the upperbound) of the domain changes.

If we handle a new constraint we check for the operators used in the expression. An expression int(X), lb(X) will lead to storing the constraint in the LowerBound-constraint-list of the variable X. dom(Y) tells the system to put the constraint in the Always constraint-list of Y. ask(ground(Z), constraint) will put the constraint in the Ground list of the variable Z.

As an example, after treating the 4 low-level constraints of the rabbit program we obtain the following instantiation of the finite domain variables P and R:

Example 17.

P=finiteVar(Domain1,store([],[],[Constr2,Constr4],[Constr2,Constr4])),
R=finiteVar(Domain2,store([],[],[Constr1,Constr3],[Constr1,Constr3])),
with
Constr1=P in 9 - int(R), Constr2=R in 9 - int(P),
Constr3=P in (24 - 4*int(R)) div 2, Constr4=R in (24 - 2*int(P)) div 4.
(the values for the domains will be discussed in the next subsection)

Note that the representation we choose here for the list of constraints is too simplistic. As constraints can be added at any time of the execution we have to use open-ended lists. Also, for some optimisations in the finite domain library, there is need for removing constraints from the constraint-store. This was solved by adding a free variable to every constraint. A constraint can be deactivated by instantiating this free variable to the atom 'old'.

5.2 Representation of the domains

As we are going to reason on the bounds of the domains, add and subtract domains we need a representation which is convenient for this kind of computations. Therefore we choose a conjunction of intervals. For example a domain with the values 1, 2, 3, 4, 8, 10, 11, 12 will be represented as 1..4 : 8..8 : 10..12 using the same operators as defined in the low-level language. A fresh finite domain variable is initialised with the domain 0..infinity. As we have to update the domains of the finite domain variables we also need a structure which we can update by further instantiating. Here an open-ended structure is again the solution to our problem. Every finite domain variable then starts with the domain-representation: [0..infinity| _]

For the rabbit-problem: after adding the two constraints *constraint1* and *constraint2* both finite domain variables are instantiated as

finiteVar([0..infinity, 0..9 | _], store).

after adding the two other constraints *constraint3* and *constraint4* the data-structure is

P = finiteVar([0..infinity, 0..9, 3..7, 5..6, 6..6| _], Store1)
R = finiteVar([0..infinity, 0..9, 2..6, 3..4, 3..3| _], Store2)

As a result of adding the two constraints to the constraint store and letting them propagate the two variables become ground. How this result is achieved is explained in the next subsection.

5.3 The fixpoint computation

The library call constraint__/1 actually does three things: It adds the new constraint to the constraint-store. While doing so, new finite domain variables are instantiated to the structure *finiteVar(Domain, Store)*. As we argued above, adding a constraint is done by adding the constraint to the constraint-store of every variable which appears in the constraint. Another function of the library call constraint__/1 is starting the propagation mechanism. This is the process of checking constraints until we are sure that no constraint would further prune the domains of the finite domain variables, as the user specified in the prune-declarations.

The algorithm used for this is a variant of the AC3 algorithm of Mackworth [12]. There is a queue of constraints to be tested. Whenever a domain of a variable changes, the corresponding constraints to be checked in the constraint-store of the variable are added to the end of the queue (if they are not already there). The algorithms stops as the queue is empty.

Algorithm 4.

```
fixpoint(emptyQueue):- !.
fixpoint(Queue):-
        firstFromQueue(Queue, Constraint, Queue1),
        testConstconstraint(Constraint, NewConstraints),
        addToQueue(Queue1, NewConstraints, NewQueue),
        fixpoint(NewQueue).
constraint_(NewConstraint):-
        addToConstraintStore(NewConstraint),
        fixpoint([NewConstraint]).
```

As the reader can see, the predicate *addToConstraintStore/1* does not need any extra parameters as the constraint-store is represented by the finite domain variables the new constraint *NewConstraint* acts on.

6 Testing the language

Some initial experiments have been performed with the system. The transformation does not cause any problem and the transformed programs are quite efficient. The examples indicate that in some examples the gained flexibility in directing the solver can be relevant. The efficiency is estimated in the number of constraint checks.

Send + more = money. It is the classical problem of assigning a value from 0 to 9 to each letter of the set {m,o,n,e,y,s,d,r} such that the addition holds, every letter has a different value, and s and m are not 0. The constraints can easily be expressed by 4 linear equations which can be executed with different pruning models. As extreme cases, we can execute them with forward checking or lookahead. Forward checking yields a solution after 3952 constraint-checks, lookahead finds a solution after 260 constraint checks. But a program annotated with the following prune-directives:

Y+10*O1 = D+E prune(Y:p(D,E), D:p(Y,E), E:p(Y, D), O1:p),
E+10*O2 = N+R+O1 prune(E:p(N,R), N:p(E,R), R:p(E, N), O1:p, O2:p),
N+10*O3 = E+O+O2 prune(N:p(E,O), E:p(N,O), O:p(N, E), O2:p, O3:p),
O+9 *M = S +O3 prune(O:p, M:p, S:p, O3:p),

finds a solution after only 158 constraint checks. The problem was not further studied, maybe a better pruning variant can be found.

The queens example. This example illustrates the importance of enumeration techniques. The program is essentially the one in subsection 4.3.2. However, although not discussed in this paper, our 'glass-box' finite domain language provides further features, allowing a user to select an appropriate enumeration (and even backtrack-variant) strategy. The heuristic for selecting the next variable for enumeration and the heuristic for selecting the next value from the domain of that variable are parameters of the algorithm. This is in general a good technique for optimising the heuristics. They can be tested on smaller problems and afterwards, the full scale problem with the selected combination of heuristics. We tested with different heuristics for selecting domain variables and for selecting values from the domains. With naive selection-methods, from queens13 on, the number of constraint checks rapidly grows (> 15000). Among the different techniques for selecting the next domain variable the firstfail technique is certainly the best heuristic. For selecting the value from a domain there are some alternatives. Selecting the values in the middle of the domain first gives satisfactory results, although randomly selecting the value in the domain of the variable seems to be able to compete with that. A combination of the two, a random selection following a Gauss distribution (giving the middle values more chance) gives the best results: the queens problem up to 32 queens can be solved in less than 1500 constraint checks.

The bridge problem. The subject of the problem is building a 5-segment bridge [8]. The process of building the bridge is split in different tasks with precedence constraints and resource constraints. The precedence constraints are straightforward. For the resource constraints there are essentially two approaches: set up the disjunctive constraints with the cardinality operator [9] (Also implemented in our solver) : *card(1,* $S1 + D1 \leq S2$*,* $S2 + D2 \leq S1$*)* and then try to minimise the end-date by enumerating the start-dates of the tasks. This results in an enormous search-space of which a lot of states actually represent the same solution. Another approach is creating a choice-point for every disjunction.

disjunctive(S1, D1, S2, D2):- $S1 + D1 \leq S2$.
disjunctive(S1, D1, S2, D2):- $S2 + D2 \leq S1$.

We can also combine these two methods: first express the resource constraints with the cardinality constraint, and then creating choicepoints for every disjunction. This approach is a lot more effective as some disjunctive constraints can already prune the search-space before a choice is made. Running the program without the disjunctive constraints yields and proves the optimality in 75288 constraint-checks, while the approach with the disjunctions in the constraint store finds and proves the solution in 56188 constraint-checks (while there are still redundant checks).

Some profiling results indicate that the prolog-machine spends very few time in the compiled finite domain program. Most time is used in the finite domain solver. This means that our attempt to remove the overhead-level between the finite domain program and prolog succeeded. It also indicates that further optimisations will be located in the solver. Actually the efficiency of the implementation still suffers from the fact that domain and constraint management is implemented through list traversal. In [2] a related implementation was carried out in prolog2 [11], using backtrackable destructive assignment to implement these features. The resulting efficiency (for forward checking and lookahead pruning directives) is comparable to that of CHIP.

In fact for a more efficient implementation (not in Prolog) of the low-level language we refer the reader to [6]. The aim of our solver was not implementing a fast machinery for these low-level primitives but the development of some useful primitives for the user with an automatic transformation to these low-level primitives. Another alternative is implementing this low-level language with attributed variables as has been done in ECL^iPS^e [7].

7 Conclusion

The goal of the work reported on in this paper has been to implement an enhanced logic language (a finite domain language) on top of prolog. Usually this is done by writing a meta-interpreter which filters out the non-standard features of the language. We succeeded to replace such a meta-interpreter by a transformation a priori. In addition to removing the meta-level of the finite domain program we also perform transformations of the finite domain primitives to more efficient primitives.

This fits in the more general framework of designing, implementing and studying the properties (both on the theoretical and practical level) of a new finite domain CLP language that provides a more extensive range of constraint algorithms obtainable from the various choices for pruning and enumeration, as discussed above. In this language, a user may select a promising algorithm through parametrised declarations. Simple resetting of the parameters may yield a completely different solver, which invites a trial-and-error approach to the problem of tuning the solver to the problem at hand.

One might worry about the degree in which the declarative nature of constraint logic programming could be violated by such an approach. We believe that the opposite is the case. In existing systems, involving only one or very few different solvers, programming an efficient solution to a given problem often requires a deep understanding of the solver(s) and the selection of an appropriate representation of the problem tuned to the solver(s). This is strongly related to the problem of CLP programming methodology. We hope that our system will prove to provide an alternative solution to this problem. Instead of adapting the problem representation to the solver, our system should allow for a more declarative representation of the problem and require a tuning of the underlying solver through the selection of a limited number of parameters to obtain a satisfactory efficiency. Through further experiments with our prototype, we hope to be able to produce a set of heuristics to guide this selection.

Acknowledgement

Henk Vandecasteele is supported by the Esprit project PRINCE, contract n° 5246. Danny De Schreye is senior research asssociate of the Belgian NFWO. We thank anonymous referees for useful comments.

References

1. Frédéric Benhamou and William Older. Applying Interval Arithmetic to Integer and Boolean Constraints. Technical report, Bell Northern Research, 1992.
2. Bart Van Den Bosch. Implementation of a clp library and an application in nurse scheduling. Master's thesis, Katholieke Universiteit Leuven, 1993.
3. Maurice Bruynooghe. Second International Workshop on Meta-programming in Logic, 1990. Leuven, Belgium.
4. Maurice Bruynooghe and Danny De Schreye. Meta-interpretation. In S. C. Shapiro, editor, *Encyclopedia of Artificial Intelligence*, pages 939–940. John Wiley & Sons, Inc, 1992.
5. Danny De Schreye, D. Pollet, J. Ronsyn, and Maurice Bruynooghe. Implementing finite-domain constraint logic programming on top of a prolog-system with a delay mechanism. In N. Jones, editor, *proceedings of ESOP90*, LNCS 432, pages 106–117. Springer-Verlag, 1990.
6. Daniel Diaz and Philippe Codognet. A minimal extention of the WAM for clp(fd). In Davis S. Warren, editor, *Proceedings of the Tenth International Conference on Logic Programming.*, pages 774–790, 1993.
7. ECRC. *ECLIPSE 3.4, Extensions User Manual.*, 1994.
8. Pascal Van Hentenryck. *Constraint Satisfaction in Logic Programming.* The MIT press, 1989.
9. Pascal Van Hentenryck and Yves Deville. The cardinality operator: A new logical connective for constraint logic programming. In *proceedings of ICLP*, 1991.
10. Pascal Van Hentenryck, Vijay Saraswat, and Yves Deville. Constraint processing in cc(FD). Brown University, 1992.
11. IBM. *IBM SAA AD/Cycle Prolog/2 Language Reference, Release 1*, 1992.
12. Alan K. Mackworth. Consistency in networks of relations. *Artificial Intelligence*, 8:99–118, 1977.
13. Bernard A. Nadel. Constraint satisfaction algorithms. *Computational Intelligence*, 5(4):188–224, November 1989.
14. PrologIA. *Prolog III Reference Manual*, December 1991.

RISC-CLP(CF) Constraint Logic Programming over Complex Functions *

Hoon Hong

Research Institute for Symbolic Computation
Johannes Kepler University
A-4040 Linz, Austria
e-mail: hhong@risc.uni-linz.ac.at

Abstract. A constraint logic programming system for the domain of complex functions is described. The intended users of the language are scientist and engineers who often reason/compute with constraints over complex functions, such as functional equalities, differential equations, etc. Constraints are solved by iterating several solving methods such as Laplace transformation, non-linear equation solving, etc. A prototype has been built and is illustrated in the paper.

1 Introduction

The constraint logic programming (CLP) framework [16, 7] provides a natural and general way to combine deduction and constraint solving, for the goal of reasoning with or solving non-trivial problems in a declarative way.

During last years, several important CLP systems have been developed such as (only to mention a few) Prolog III [7], CLP($\mathcal{R}$) [15], CHIP [8], CAL [19], CLP(BNR) [18, 1], RISC-CLP(Real) [9, 11] (See also [4] for an extension). The computation domain provided by these systems are trees, finite sets (domains), booleans, real numbers, and various combinations.

In this paper, we describe a new CLP system for the domain of complex functions. A complex function is a function of the type $\mathbf{C} \rightarrow \mathbf{C}$ where $\mathbf{C}$ is the set of all complex numbers. Thus a constant in the language denotes a complex function, and in the same way a variable ranges over the set of complex functions.

This particular domain was chosen because the system is intended to be used by scientist and engineer such as physicists, chemists, economists, electrical engineers, mechanical engineers etc. Scientist and engineers model their systems using "laws" which are very often differential equations or functional equalities, which are particular kinds of constraints over functions. As a simple example, the well known Newton's second law of the classical mechanics

$$f = m\frac{d^2x}{dt^2}$$

* This research was done in the framework of ACCLAIM, a research project of the basic research action in ESPRIT sponsored by the European Community.

is a constraint on the force f, the mass m, and the displacement x. Note that the variable x is *not* a number, but a *function* of time. If it were a number, the differentiation would be meaningless. There are numerous such examples, as can be found in any standard books on mathematical physics or advanced engineering mathematics.

Constraints are solved by the cooperation of several specialized sub-solvers such as non-linear equation solver, differential equation solver, etc. This design was crucial for the success of the RISC-CLP(CF) system because many interesting and important real life problems could not be solved by a single method.

The structure of the subsequent sections is as follows: In Section 2, we describe the syntax and the semantics of the language RISC-CLP(CF). In Section 3, we describe the inference engine which interprets the logical symbols in the language. In Section 4, we describe the constraint solver which handles the non-logical symbols in the language. In Section 5, we give several examples from scientific and engineering applications.

2 Language

In this section, we describe the language of RISC-CLP(CF), that is, the syntax and the semantics. The presentation will be intentionally informal and intuitive because we believe that it is better for human communication. Once one gets a grasp of the underlying idea, its formalization becomes easier.

Let us begin by recalling that any constraint logic programming language consists of two parts: logical part and constraint part. The logical part is already given by the general framework of CLP. Thus, a program consists of clauses, a clause consists of a head and a body, a head is an atomic formula, and a body consists of constraints and/or atomic formulas. (For a precise description, see the top part of Figure 1.)

One will notice that we introduced the construct called "guarded clause" which is indicated by the connective '`:?`'. We postpone the explanation of this until the next section since it is a construct for specifying "control", not logic.

Now we turn our attention to the constraint part of the language. For the syntax, we would like to provide sufficiently many symbols for expressing (possibly differential) constraints over complex numbers, rational functions, radicals, Dirac delta function, Heaviside step function, and all the elementary transcendental functions such as exponential, logarithm, trigonometric, hyperbolic, and their inverses. For instance, we will provide symbols such as

```
2  K  y  t  sin  exp  +  '  =
```

For the complete set of symbols and the precise syntax, see the middle part of Figure 1.

In order to discuss the semantics of these symbols, let us consider the following simple constraint:

```
y' = 2 * K * sin(t)
```

```
<program>      : <clause>...<clause>
<clause>       : <unguarded>
               | <guarded>
<unguarded>    : <atom>  :-  <literal>,...,<literal>
<guarded>      : <atom>  :?  <literal>,...,<literal>
<query>        : <literal>,...,<literal>.
<literal>      : <atom>
               | <constraint>
<atom>         : <id> [ <term>,...,<term> ]

<constraint>   : <term> = <term>
<term>         : <number>
               | <id>
               | exp | ln   | delta  | step
               | sin | sinh | arcsin | arcsinh
               | cos | cosh | arccos | arccosh
               | tan | tanh | arctan | arctanh
               | csc | csch | arccsc | arccsch
               | sec | sech | arcsec | arcsech
               | cot | coth | arccot | arccoth
               | <term>'
               | <term> + <term>
               | <term> - <term>
               | <term> * <term>
               | <term> / <term>
               | <term> ^ <term>
               | <term> ( <term> )
               | ( <term> )

<id>           : a string of letters, numbers, or '_', starting with a letter.
<number>       : an integer.
               | Pi | E | I       for π, e, i respectively.
```

Fig. 1. Syntax of RISC-CLP(CF)

where `t` is the so called "independent variable", `y` is the "dependent variable", and `K` is a "parameter" which does not depend on `t`.

In order to talk about the meaning of this expression, we first need to fix the intended domain. One might consider having two domains: the set of complex numbers (for the fixed number `2` and the variable number `K`) and the set of complex functions (for the fixed function `sin` and the variable function `y`). But this introduces the unnecessary trouble of type checking and coercion. Thus we will use only one domain: the set of all complex functions. This choice of the domain naturally leads to the following semantic decisions:

`y` a variable symbol ranging over the set of all complex functions.

`'` a function symbol denoting the differentiation operation on complex functions.

`=` a predicate symbol denoting the functional equality.

`2` a constant symbol denoting the complex function whose value is always the complex number 2.

`*` a function symbol denoting the multiplication operation of two complex functions.

`K` a variable symbol ranging over the set of all complex functions, with the additional property that its derivative is zero.

`sin` a constant symbol denoting the sine function.

Next, we pay attention to the symbol: `t`. What is this? It is called an "independent variable", but this notion is very difficult to reconcile with the basic notions of the first order language. Fortunately there is a simple solution. We only need to interpret it as follows:

`t` a constant symbol denoting the identity complex function $\lambda t.t$.

In fact, this interpretation is consistent with the following often used expression:

```
t' = 1
```

Here `t` is clearly meant to be the identity function.

Finally we are at the last remaining symbol: `()`. This symbol is usually interpreted as "evaluation" of a function on a number. But this collides with our choice of the domain. Again, there is a simple solution. We only need to relax the notion of evaluation to that of composition:

`()` a function symbol denoting the composition operation of two complex functions.

Thus, `sin(t)` is interpreted as the composition of two complex functions sin and $\lambda t.t$. This has a side-benefit that `y` and `y(t)` denote the same complex function, justifying the usual practice of interchangeably using these two "at random".

All the remaining symbols such as "`cos tan arccos +`" can be interpreted in the exactly same way as above, and we will not describe them (tedious). On top of these, one can easily build all other semantic notions such as *interpretation of terms, solvability, model*, etc. We will not describe how they are defined since they are done in the usual standard way. See [19] for a succinct and elegant description of how this can be done.

Finally, note that the choice of the particular symbol `t` as the identity function is arbitrary. The language allows the user to choose any symbol for the identity function. In fact, the user can also specify which variables are parameters (function variables whose derivatives are zero) and which are function variables.

$t \leftarrow$ **Engine** $(\bar{C}, C, A, s)$

Inputs	$\bar{C}$	:	a set of sets of constraints.	
	C	:	a set of constraints.	
	A	:	a set of atomic formulas.	
	s	:	'**`guarded`**'	if the current clause is guarded.
			'**`unguarded`**'	else
Outputs	t	:	'**`stop_search`**'	if the user asked to stop,
			'**`cont_search`**'	otherwise.
Globals	P	:	a program.	

(1) [Check.]
If $A = \emptyset$ or $s =$ **`guarded`**,
  (a) $\bar{C}^* \leftarrow$ **Solver** $(\bar{C}, C)$. *(see Figure 3.)*
  (b) Set $\bar{C} \leftarrow \bar{C}^*$ and $C \leftarrow \emptyset$.
  (c) If $\bar{C}$ is empty, return **`cont_search`**.

(2) [Answer.]
If $A = \emptyset$,
  (a) Output $\bar{C}$ to the user.
  (b) Ask the user whether to continue searching.
  (c) If yes, return **`cont_search`**, else return **`stop_search`**.

(3) [Expand.]
Remove the first atomic formula A_1 from A.
For each matching clause R do
  (a) Expand the atomic formula A_1 by using the clause R, obtaining a set C' of new constraints, and a set A' of new atomic formulas.
  (b) If R is guarded, then $s' \leftarrow$ **`guarded`**, else $s' \leftarrow$ **`unguarded`**.
  (c) If **Engine** $(\bar{C},\ C' \cup C,\ A' \cup A,\ s')$ is **`stop_search`**, then return **`stop_search`**.
Return **`cont_search`**. □

Fig. 2. Algorithm: **Engine**

For the examples shown in this paper, we used the following convention: the identity is t, the parameters are the identifiers starting with an uppercase letter, and the function variables are the ones starting with a lowercase letter.

3 Inference Engine

The inference engine interprets the logical symbols: the implication '`:-`', the conjunction '`,`', and the predicate symbols. Its operation is as usual. It maintains a list of constraints and atomic formulas and repeatedly expands atomic formulas by matching clauses in the program. When all atomic formulas disappear, the remaining constraints are reported to be an answer. It also follows the usual "depth first" strategy, namely first expanding the left-most atomic formula by the top-most matching clause.

However, there is one difference. By default, the engine does *not* call the solver at any internal node of the search tree. It calls the solver only when it is at a leaf node (that is when there is no atomic formula to expand). The decision is based on the observation that for numerous examples from science and engineering, the calls of the solver at internal nodes almost always succeed, and thus it seldom causes search space pruning. It only causes overhead.

In fact, this can be explained. When a scientist writes a program, he/she uses constrains in order to describe the relationships between physical quantities. The relationships are usually either physical laws or definitions of derived quantities. Thus they are meant to be consistent! Scientists are not interested in inconsistent systems. If inconsistency happens, it is a sign that something is wrong with their modeling process.

However, there might be times when the user does want to do some search space pruning. In such case, the user can override override this default behavior by annotating some clause to be "guarded". (For a concrete syntax of guarded clause, see the grammar in Figure 1.)

Figure 2 gives an algorithmic description of the inference engine incorporating the ideas explained above. The input $\bar{C}$ (a set of sets of constraints) represents a disjunction of conjunctions of constraints which have been computed by the previous call of the constraint solver. The reason for having *disjunction* of conjunctions is that sometimes constraints have "multiple" solutions. The input C (a set of constraints) represents a conjunction of constraints that have not yet been sent to the constraint solver. The flag s tells the type (guarded/unguarded) of the clause that has been just used to expand an atomic formula in the goal.

It is a recursive algorithm, and should be initially called with $\bar{C}, C, A, s$ where $\bar{C} = \{\{\}\}$, C is the set of constraints in a query, A is the set of atomic formulas in the query, and s is **unguarded**.

4 Constraint Solver

To motivate the discussion of the solver used in the RISC-CLP(CF) system, let us consider the following simple constraint solving problem:

```
y' = K * y,  y(0) = 1, y(2) = 3, y(T) = 5.
```

Let us observe how a human solver would tackle this problem.

1. Solve '`y' = K * y`' obtaining '`y = C * exp(K * t)`'.
2. Substitute this into '`y(0) = 1`', obtaining '`C * exp (K * 0) = 1`'.
3. Solve this, obtaining '`C  = 1`'.

$$\bar{C}^* \leftarrow \textbf{Solver}\,(\bar{C}, C)$$

Inputs $\bar{C}$: a set of sets of constraints,
(representing a disjunction of conjunctions of constraints).
C : a set of constraints,
(representing a conjunction of constrains).

Outputs $\bar{C}^*$: a set of sets of constraints,
(representing a disjunction of conjunctions of constraints),
such that $\bar{C}^*$ is equivalent to but "simpler" than $\bar{C} \wedge C$.

Globals M^*: the ordered set of all method identifiers.

Locals W : a set $\{\ldots, < C_i', M_i >, \ldots\}$ where
C_i' is a set of constraints and
M_i is the ordered set of the identifiers of the methods
which have *not* been applied on C_i'.

(1) [Normalize.]
Carry out basic normalization on C, such as cancellation of equal terms, symbolic differentiation, etc.

(2) [Setup.]
Let $\bar{C} = \{\bar{C}_1, \ldots, \bar{C}_n\}$.
Set $W \leftarrow \{W_1, \ldots, W_n\}$ where $W_i =< \bar{C}_i \cup C, M^* >$.
Set $\bar{C}^* \leftarrow \emptyset$.

(3) [Simplify.]
While W is not empty do
 Remove the first $< C', M >$ from W.
 If M is empty,
  Insert C' to $\bar{C}^*$.
 Else
  Let **method** be the first identifier in M.
  $\bar{C}' \leftarrow$ **method** (C'). *(see Figure 4.)*
  If $\bar{C}' = \{C'\}$,
   Insert $< C', M - \{\textbf{method}\} >$ to W,
  Else,
   For each set $\bar{C}_i'$ in $\bar{C}'$,
    Insert $< \bar{C}_i', M^* - \{\textbf{method}\} >$ to W. □

Fig. 3. Algorithm: **Solver**

Various Constraint Solving Methods

Inputs C : a set of constraints,
Outputs $\bar{C}$: a set of sets of constraints equivalent to C.

`Numerical_Substitution`

(a) While there is a constraint such as "`T = term`" where `T` is a parameter which does not appear in `term`, substitute `term` into everywhere `T` appears. Do the same for `y(0)`, `y(K)`, etc.

`Functional_Substitution`

(a) While there is a constraint such as "`y = term`" where `y` is a functional variable which does not appear in `term`, substitute `term` into everywhere `y` appears.

`Numerical_Equations`

(a) Let $C' \subseteq C$ be the set of the constraints involving only numeric unknowns such as parameters or $y(0)$.
(b) Solve C' numerically for the numerical unknowns.

`Functional_Equations`

(a) Let $C' \subseteq C$ be the set of the constraints involving function variables but not involving differentiation operator.
(b) Solve C' symbolically for the function variables.

`Numerical_Equalities`

(a) Let $C' \subseteq C$ be the set of the constraints involving no variables.
(b) Evaluate both sides of each constraints and compare for equality.
(d) If both sides of each constraint are the same, then return $\{\{\}\}$, else return $\{\}$.

`Functional_Equalities`

(a) Let $C' \subseteq C$ be the set of the constraints involving the identity function symbol but not any function variables.
(b) Carry out the Laplace transform on C'.
(c) Infer a system of equations on parameters from the Laplace transformed constraints.
(d) Solve the system of equations for the parameters.

`Differential_Equations`

(a) Let $C' \subseteq C$ be the set of constraints involving differentiation operator.
(b) Solve C' by using various techniques such as Laplace transformation, integrating factors, etc.

Fig. 4. Algorithms: **Methods**

4. Substitute this into '`y = C * exp(K* t)`' obtaining '`y = exp(K * t)`'.
5. Substitute this into '`y(2) = 3`', obtaining '`exp(K * 2) = 3`'.
6. Solve this, obtaining '`K = 1/2 * ln(3)`'.
7. Substitute this into '`y = exp(K*t)`', obtaining '`y = exp(1/2*ln(3)*t)`'.
8. Substitute this into '`y(T) = 5`', obtaining '`5 = exp(1/2 * ln(3) * T)`'.
9. Solve this, obtaining '`T = 2 * ln(5) / ln(3)`'.
10. We are done. The solution is:

```
T = 2 * ln(5)/ln(3)          = 2.929947040
K = 1/2 * ln(3)              = 0.549306145
y = exp(1/2 * ln(3) * t)     = exp(0.5493061445 * t)
```

We notice that the human solver applies several different solving methods repeatedly until the constraints cannot be changed anymore. In fact, it is the only way to solve deeply nested constrains such as `y(y(T)) = y(T)`.

Thus, we will use the same scheme in designing our solver. However, here one should be careful to ensure that

- the iteration eventually terminates,
- all methods are applied in a fair frequency, and
- no method is applied more than once consecutively.

It is a scheduling problem. This can be done by maintaining a list of the methods that still need to be applied. Initially this list contains all the methods. When a method is applied, it is removed from the list. If the resulting constraints are different from the input constraints, then we include all other methods into the list. We repeat this process until the list becomes empty.

Sometimes, applying a method on a set of constraints, we get multiple solutions, that is, a set of sets of constraints, which represents a disjunction of conjunctions of constraints. However, it does not cause much trouble; we only need to keep a stack of sets of constraints, and deal with one set of constraints at a time.

The algorithm **Solver** in Figure 3 systematically incorporates these ideas. One important remark. The list M^* is an ordered set of all methods (identifiers). In case there are two methods that still need to applied, then the one appearing first in M^* will be chosen. The correctness of the algorithm does not depend on the order of the methods in M^*. But the efficiency of the algorithm heavily depends on the order. Thus, one needs to be careful in ordering the methods in M^*.

Finally we turn our attention to individual constraint solving methods. See Figure 4 where we give a quick summary of the methods that are currently used by the solver. Recall that the solver is designed in such a way that we can always plug in a new method without changing any other parts.

Below we give simple (trivial) examples in order to illustrate the functionalities of the methods.

Numerical Substitution:

In: `{ T = 3,  y = T * t^2 }`

```
    Out:  {{ T = 3,  y = 3 * t^2  }}
Functional Substitution:
    In:   { y = K * t^2,  y(1) = 2 }
    Out:  {{ y = K * t^2,  K * 1^2 = 2 }}
Numerical Equations:
    In:   { X^2 + Y^2  = 2,  X = Y}
    Out:  {{ X = 1, Y = 1},  { X = -1, Y = -1 }}
Functional Equations:
    In:   { t^2 * sin(y) = sin(t) }
    Out:  {{ y = arcsin(sin(t)/t^2) }}
Numerical Equalities:
    In:   { exp(Pi * I) = -1 }
    Out:  {{ }}
Functional Equalities:
    In:   { K * t = 0,  sin(L + t) = K + cos(t) }
    Out:  {{ K = 0,  L = 1/2 * Pi }}
Differential Equations:
    In:   { y' = 2 * y }
    Out:  {{ y = C * exp(2 * t) }}
```

The substitution can be handled easily by careful syntactic operations. The other problems look also easy for the simple examples above. But they are actually quite non-trivial for real life examples which usually involve systems of several equations in many variables. These problems require sophisticated algorithms from computer algebra and numerical analysis. In fact, all these problems are currently hotly pursued research topics in those communities. We will not attempt to give any descriptions of these here since it is clearly beyond the scope of this paper and the conference, and also it will require too much space.

We only mention that the current implementation solves numerical equations by a combination of Gröbner basis method [2] and an interval method [14, 13], functional equations and numerical equalities by a certain set of rewrite rules [5], functional equalities by carrying out Laplace transform and applying quantifier elimation [10, 6], differential equations by Laplace transform and several other techniques such as integral factors [17].

5 Examples

A prototype system has been implemented in the C language using two computer algebra libraries SACLIB [3] and MAPLE [5]. In this section, we illustrate the system on a few examples taken from several application areas [17]. Each of the examples took less than 1 second on a SGI workstation.

5.1 Newton's Law of Cooling

Put a hot object (such as heated copper ball) into a cool medium (such as water). The hot object slowly cools down. Newton's law of cooling states that the time rate of change of the temperature T of the object is proportional to the difference between T and the temperature of the surrounding medium. The following clause captures this fact.

```
NewtonCoolingLaw [temp_obj, temp_med] :-
        temp_obj' = - K * (temp_obj - temp_med).
```

where

`temp_obj`	is the temperature of the object as a function of time.
`temp_med`	is the temperature of the medium as a function of time.
`K`	is an unknown physical constant.

Suppose that a copper ball is heated to a temperature of 100 degrees (C). Then at time $t = 0$, it is placed in water that is maintained at a temperature of 30 degrees. At the end of 3 minutes the temperature of the ball is reduced to 70 degrees. Find the time at which the temperature of the ball is reduced to 31 degrees.

One could directly compose a query for this problem. But assuming that similar questions will be asked often, it will be worthwhile to write an "access" clause that simplifies such kind of querying.

```
Cooling [Temp_med,Temp_obj, Time1,Temp1_obj, Time2,Temp2_obj] :-
        temp_med(0)     = Temp_med,
        temp_obj(0)     = Temp_obj,
        temp_obj(Time1) = Temp1_obj,
        temp_obj(Time2) = Temp2_obj,
        temp_med' = 0,
        NewtonCoolingLaw [temp_obj, temp_med].
```

where

`Temp_med`	is the initial temperature of the medium.
`Temp_obj`	is the initial temperature of the object.
`Time1`	is a time.
`Temp1_obj`	is the temperature of the object at time `Time1`.
`Time2`	is a time.
`Temp2_obj`	is the temperature of the object at time `Time2`.

Using this program, now we ask the question posed above to the RISC-CLP(CF) system.

```
?- Cooling [30, 100, 3, 70, Time, 31].
```

Then the system responds:

```
        Time = -3*ln(70)/ln(4/7)
             = 22.77542199
```

Now one might be interested in finding the relationship between the temperature of the copper ball and the time. Here is a query for this.

```
?- Cooling [30, 100, 3, 70, Time, Temp].
```

Then the system responds:

```
Temp = 30+70*exp(1/3*Time*ln(4/7))
     = 30.+70.*exp(-.1865385960*Time)
```

Now we ask what should be the initial temperature of the copper ball so that its temperature drops by 40 degrees at the first minute and 10 more degrees at the second minute.

```
?- Cooling [30, Temp, 1, Temp - 40, 2, Temp - 50].
```

Then the system responds:

```
Temp = 250/3
       83.33333333
```

One could go on asking various different questions such as these.

5.2 Radioactive Carbon Dating

In the atmosphere, the ratio of radioactive carbon ${}_6C^{14}$ and ordinary carbon ${}_6C^{12}$ does not change, and it is the same as the ratio of the two in living organisms. But when an organism dies, the absorption of ${}_6C^{14}$ by breathing and eating terminates. Then the ${}_6C^{14}$ in the dead organism decays at the rate proportional to its amount. The half life of ${}_6C^{14}$ is 5730 years. But the ordinary carbon does not decay.

Utilizing these facts, one can estimate the age of a fossil. This is W. Libby's idea of radiocarbon dating (Nobel Prize for chemistry 1960). The following program translates the facts described above in almost one-to-one manner.

```
CarbonDating [ Ratio_Air, Ratio_Fossil, Age_Fossil ] :-
   ratio_air'     = 0,
   ratio_air(0)   = c14_fossil(0) / c12_fossil(0),
   c14_fossil'    = K * c14_fossil',
   c14_fossil(5730) / c14_fossil(0) = 1/2.
   c12_fossil'  = 0,
   ratio_air(Age_Fossil) = Ratio_Air,
   c14_fossil(Age_Fossil) / c12_fossil(Age_Fossil) = Ratio_Fossil.
```

where

`Ratio_Air`	is the present ratio of ${}_6C^{14}$ and ${}_6C^{12}$ in the air.
`Ratio_Fossil`	is the present ratio of ${}_6C^{14}$ and ${}_6C^{12}$ in the fossil..
`Age_Fossil`	is the age of the fossil.
`ratio_air`	is the ratio of ${}_6C^{14}$ and ${}_6C^{12}$ in the air as a function of time.
`c14_fossil`	is the amount of ${}_6C^{14}$ in the fossil as a function of time.
`c12_fossil`	is the amount of ${}_6C^{12}$ in the fossil as a function of time.
`K`	is a physical constant of ${}_6C^{14}$.

Suppose that an experimentalist tells me the ratio of the two carbons in a fossil is 1/4 of that in the air, but without telling me the values of the two ratios. Now I ask: What is the age of the fossil?

```
?- CarbonDating[ Ratio_Air, 1/4 * Ratio_Air, Age_Fossil ].
```

Then the RISC-CLP(CF) system responds as follows:

```
        Age_Fossil = 5730*ln(4)/ln(2),
                   = 11460.00000,
        Ratio_Air = _C2
OR
        Ratio_Air = 0
```

Note that it found two mathematically correct solutions, though the second one is a degenerate case which is meaningless from the physical point of view. Note also that in the first solution, the value of **Ratio_Air** is set to some new variable called **_C2** generated by the system. This basically says that it can take any value. In this particular case, it would have been better not to produce this line at all. But currently we do not know how to do this in general.

Next, suppose that we want to obtain a general formula which relates the age of the fossil with the ratios.

```
?- CarbonDating [ Ratio_Air, Ratio * Ratio_Air, Age_Fossil].
```

The systems gives you:

```
        Ratio = exp(-1/5730*ln(2)*Age_Fossil),
              = exp(-1209680943.0E-13*Age_Fossil),
        Ratio_Air = _C2
OR
        Ratio_Air = 0
```

So it tells me, if I ignore the degenerate case, that the **Ratio** decreases exponentially in **Age_Fossil** with the decay constant $1/5730\ln(2)$.

5.3 RLC circuit

Finally, we consider an example from electrical circuits involving resistors, inductors, and capacitors. We will just give a program without explaining the underlying electronic laws since it should be easy to read them off from the program directly.

```
Resistor [ R, v, i ] :-
        v = R * i.
Inductor [ L, v, i ] :-
        v = L * i'.
Capacitor [ C, v, i ] :-
        i = C * v'.
```

```
Serial_RLC_circuit [R, L, C, v, i] :-
        Resistor  [ R, v1, i ],
        Inductor  [ L, v2, i ],
        Capacitor [ C, v3, i ],
        v = v1 + v2 + v3.
```

Consider a serial RLC circuit with $R = 2$, $L = 1$, $C = 1/2$ with a 50 volt battery and a switch. Suppose the current was 0 at time 0. We turn on the switch at time 0. What will happen to the current?

```
?- Serial_RLC_circuit [2, 1, 1/2, 50, i ], i(0) = 0.
```

The system answers:

```
i(t) = -_C2*exp(-t)*sin(t)
```

Note that a new constant _C2 has been introduced, which indicates that we did not supply enough information pato uniquely determine the current as a function of time. So we supply one more condition.

```
?- Serial_RLC_circuit [2, 1, 1/2, 50, i ], i(0) = 0, i(1) = 1/2.
```

Now the system responds:

```
i(t) = 1/2/exp(-1)/sin(1)*exp(-t)*sin(t)
     = 1.615196411*exp(-1.*t)*sin(t)
```

We see that the current is a damped oscillation.

6 Conclusion

We have described the constraint logic programming system RISC-CLP(CF) where constraints over functions are solved by iterating several specialized solving methods. Various experiments indicate that this approach is quite powerful and useful, in particular when the constraints are intricately related with each other. But it also raises new questions such as: How do we ensure termination/confluency of such a solver in general? Some work has been done in this direction [12], but it is still a wide open area of research.

I would like to thank Andreas Neubacher and Kurt Siegl for implementing some parts of the constraint solver and the communication routines between Maple and the RISC-CLP(CF) system.

References

1. F. Behhamou and W. Older. Applying interval arithmetic to real, integer, and boolean constraints. *Journal of Logic Programming*, 1993. Submitted.

2. B. Buchberger. Applications of Gröbner bases in non-linear computational geometry. In *Proc. Workshop on Scientific Software (invited lecture)*, pages 59–88. Springer Verlag, 1987.
3. B. Buchberger, G. Collins, M. Encarnación, H. Hong, J. Johnson, W. Krandick, R. Loos, and A. Neubacher. *A SACLIB Primer*. Tech. Rep. 92-34, RISC-Linz, Johannes Kepler University, Linz, Austria.
4. Olga Caprotti. Extending risc-clp(real) to handle symbolic functions. In A. Miola, editor, *DISCO '93: International Symposium on Design and Implementation of Symbolic Computation Systems*. Springer Verlag, September 1993.
5. B. W. Char, K. O. Geddes, G. H. Gonnet, and S. M. Watt. *Maple User's Guide*. WATCOM Publications Limited, 4th edition, 1985.
6. G. E. Collins and H. Hong. Partial cylindrical algebraic decomposition for quantifier elimination. *Journal of Symbolic Computation*, 12(3):299–328, September 1991.
7. A. Colmerauer. An Introduction to Prolog III. *Communications of the ACM*, 33(7):69–90, July 1990.
8. M. Dincbas, P. Van Hentenryck, H. Simonis, A. Aggoun, T. Graf, and F. Berthier. The Constraint Logic Programming Language CHIP. In *Proceedings on the International Conference on Fifth Generation Computer Systems FGCS-88*, Tokyo, Japan, December 1988.
9. H. Hong. Non-linear real constraints in constraint logic programming. In *International Conference on Algebraic and Logic Programming*, pages 201–212, 1992.
10. H. Hong, editor. *Computational Quantifier Elimination*. Oxford University press, 1993. Special issue of the Computer Journal: Volume 36, number 5.
11. H. Hong. RISC-CLP(Real): Constraint logic programming over real numbers. In F. Benhamou and A. Colmerauer, editors, *Constraint Logic Programming: Selected Research*. MIT Press, 1993.
12. H. Hong. Confluency of Cooperative Constraint Solvers. Technical Report 94-08, Research Institute for Symbolic Computation, Johannes Kepler University A-4040 Linz, Austria, 1994.
13. H. Hong and V. Stahl. Safe start region by fixed points and tightening. *Journal of Computing, (Archives for Informatics and Numerical Computation)*. Accepted, to appear in 1994.
14. H. Hong and V. Stahl. Safe start region by fixed points and tightening. In *The proceedings of Scientific Computing, Computer Arithmetic and Validated Numerics*, September 1993.
15. J. Jaffar and S. Michaylov. Methodology and implementation of a CLP system. In J.-L. Lassez, editor, Proceedings 4th ICLP, pages 196–218, Cambridge, MA, May 1987. The MIT Press.
16. Joxan Jaffar and Jean-Louis Lassez. Constraint logic programming. In *Proceedings of the 14th ACM Symposium on Principles of Programming Languages, Munich, Germany*, pages 111–119. ACM, January 1987.
17. E. Kreyszig. *Advanced Engineering Mathematics*. John Wiley & Sons, Inc., 1993.
18. W. Older and A. Vellino. Constraint arithmetic on real intervals. In F. Benhamou and A. Colmerauer, editors, *Constraint Logic Programming: Selected Research*. MIT Press, 1993.
19. K. Sakai and A. Aiba. CAL: A Theoretical Background of Constraint Logic Programming and its Applications. *Journal of Symbolic Computation*, 8:589–603, 1989.

Logical Closures

Dominic Duggan*

Department of Computer Science
University of Waterloo
Waterloo, Ontario
Canada N2L 3G1.
dduggan@uwaterloo.ca

Abstract. Uniform proof procedures for hereditary Harrop formulae have been proposed as a foundation for logic programming. A non-standard approach to defining hereditary Harrop formula is given, allowing quantification over predicate variables but distinguishing the forms of predicate quantification. The benefits of this approach include a treatment of higher order procedures which avoids some scoping problems with languages such as λ-Prolog, and the possibility of extending the language straightforwardly with a module system such as that developed for Standard ML. To enable a style of programming found in existing logic programming languages, a form of implementation inheritance is introduced into the language. Combining this with explicit type quantification provides a form of dynamic dispatching similar to CLOS generic procedures in a statically typed language.

1 Introduction

Uniform proof procedures for hereditary Harrop formulae have been proposed as a foundation for logic programming [17], extending the operational semantics of SLD-resolution with new constructs for hypothetical implication and local constant introduction. An attractive aspect of this theory is its extension to higher-order logic, as exemplified by Nadathur, Miller and Pfenning's λ-Prolog [18, 19]. Allowing logical formulae as data objects and explicit variable binding based on λ-abstraction introduces some of the higher order capabilities of functional languages such as ML into the logic programming paradigm[1].

Traditionally procedure definitions in logic programming are very different from thoese in functional programming. In the latter, procedures are (possibly recursive) λ-expressions, while in the former procedures are defined by a collection of clauses with a particular predicate constant at the head. Despite the fact that it is higher-order, λ-Prolog chooses the former notion of procedure definition. We propose a new approach

* Supported by NSERC Operating Grant 0105568.

[1] Another example of a logic programming language based on hereditary Harrop formulae is Pfenning's Elf language [21]. However this language is based on a first-order type theory of general product types, and its extension to higher-order remains problematic because of the restriction of higher-order hereditary Harrop formulae which disallows implication in the Herbrand universe [17]. The work presented here originated in attempts to extend Pfenning's proposal to higher-order.

to defining procedures in (possibly higher-order) logic programming. The basis for this is a non-standard approach to defining hereditary Harrop formulae, allowing quantification over predicates variables but distinguishing the forms of predicate quantification. A benefit of this is that we weaken the restriction of hereditary Harrop formulae that prevents implications in the Herbrand universe, while maintaining the uniform proof property of hereditary Harrop formulae. Hypothetical implication and universal quantification over predicate variables form an integral role in our introduction of *logical closures* for higher-order logic programming. This notion of logical closures corrects scoping problems which have been encountered in practice with languages such as λ-Prolog, and also has further implications for coercive interface matching in SML-like module languages for logic programming.

A justification for our approach is that we view logic programs as inductive definitions rather than as logical theories. It is possible to justify this intuition by giving an extensional semantics for our language [5], giving a functorial version of Wadge's extensional semantics for higher-order Horn logic programming [25]. Although the view of logic programs as inductive definitions has been advocated by others, it can sometimes be overly restrictive to require logic program definitions to be "closed up". To enable a style of programming found in existing logic programming languages, we introduce a form of implementation inheritance into the language which, combined with explicit type quantification, gives our language a form of generic procedure definition.

The language presented here is polymorphic. However in contrast to any existing logical languages and most functional languages, the language is based on explicit type quantification. Besides allowing some fundamental example programs to be effectively typed [3], explicit type quantification also provides the basis for a form of generic procedure definition (in the CLOS sense [11]), based on dynamic type discrimination. As a somewhat incestuous example of this, we show how Miller's reduction of higher-order unification in λ-Prolog to a program in L_λ [16] can be defined as a generic procedure in our language, where only simple L_λ-like unification is required [15].

2 Procedures for Logic Programming

In this section we introduce a new semantics for procedures in logic programming, based on the ideas discussed in the introduction, and illustrate its usefulness via some examples. Although we present a specific concrete syntax, our concern is with the underlying constructs of the language rather than with the details of the syntax.

The base types for our language are `Prop` and `Type`, with `Prop:Type`. The underlying type theory distinguishes several different forms of proposition types. Goal represents the kind of propositions which may actually be executed as logic programs (invoked as goal clauses) while Rule represents the kind of propositions which may be used as program clauses in defining a procedure. Prop itself is used in the introduction of new predicate variables. In the absence of further qualification, occurrences of `Prop` refer to the type Goal of goal clauses.

We assume the following constructs for the kernel language:

Abstract Syntax			Concrete Syntax
Term	Type	Use	
$\lambda x : A \cdot M$	$A \to B$	$(M\ N)$	{x:A}→B
(M, N)	$A \times B$	$\pi_i M$	{x:A,y:B}
$\Lambda t : K \cdot M$	$\Delta t : K \cdot A$	$M[A]$	[t:K]A

Traditionally logic programming languages are procedural in nature, with a flat syntax where intermediate values are explicitly named [2], and where semantically procedures are viewed as logical theories[3]. We take a non-standard approach to logic programming language design in this paper, regarding logic programs as *inductive definitions*. Internalizing this notion of inductive definition using higher-order predicate quantification[4] provides the basis for introducing a form of implementation inheritance into the language. As an indication of our departure from the more usual operational and denotational semantics for logic programming, we assume that our language has a let construct for defining local procedures:

$$\texttt{let } x = M \texttt{ in } N \quad \beta\text{-reduces to} \quad \{M/x\}N$$

Such a construct is more usually found in functional languages such as ML and Haskell, and is for example a difference from the approach to lexical scoping for logic programming suggested by Miller [14].

In basing a logic programming language on type theory, we concentrate on the issue of how to syntactically restrict formulae so that they are executable as logic programs by an abstract interpreter which satisfies some logical completeness property. We do not consider the provision of a unification algorithm, for reasons of space; the algorithm provided in [6] supports the examples in this paper, including the combination of products and polymorphism. This algorithm supports the simple form of higher-order unification discovered by Miller [15], which captures the variable-binding aspects of higher-order

---

[2] Appel [1] makes the following observation about high-level languages:

> The beauty of Fortran - and the reason it was an improvement over assembly language - is that it relieves the programmer of the obligation to make up names for intermediate results... The λ-calculus gives us these same advantages for functional values as well.

We consider this as grounds for criticizing the flat syntax which almost all logic languages have adopted to date, only partially ameliorated in constraint logic languages.

[3] Again Paulson and Smith [20] have given a convincing critique of this aspect of logic programming language design:

> Hogger writes at length about pure logic programs, typically to reverse a list or test for list membership. By comparison, the pure functional programs in Bird and Wadler perform $\alpha - \beta$ search, construct Huffman coding trees, and print calendars... We suggest [that] an inductive definition is a logic program's intrinsic declarative content. Clauses should not be viewed as assertions in first-order logic, but as rules generating a set.

We consider this as grounds for criticizing the view of logic programs as logical theories.

[4] The use of predicate quantification to control the scope of predicate constants was originally suggested by Miller [14].

unification[5]. This aspect is useful for metaprogramming with "higher-order abstract syntax" [22], from which our main example will be drawn.

Logic programs are defined as procedures using the form:

```
closed procedure P : [t:K]{x:A}→Prop with C1 ... Ck
```

where each clause C_i C_i is of the form $P[B_i]\,(M_i) \longleftarrow G_i$ for some goal formula G_i, type B_i of kind K and term M_i of type A. This defines a predicate P of type $\Delta t : K \cdot A \rightarrow \mathsf{Goal}$ (or `[t:K]{x:A}→Prop` in the concrete syntax). After this definition we have:

$$\mathtt{P} = \Lambda t : K \cdot \lambda x : A \cdot \forall P : (\Delta t : K \cdot A \rightarrow \mathsf{Prop}) \cdot (C_1 \& \ldots \& C_k) \supset (P\ [t]\ x)$$

According to the operational semantics of the language, and also the proof-theoretic interpretation of the connectives, the resulting goal is executed (proven) by introducing a new constant for the eigenvariable P, assuming the clauses for P as new clauses (axioms) and executing (proving) the goal $(P\ [t]\ x)$ in the extended context.

Consider now another form of procedure definition:

```
open procedure P : {x:A}→Prop with C1 ... Ck
```

Our intention is that such a definition eventually expand into the inductive closure of a predicate defined by the specified clauses. However we want such procedure definitions to be incremental over future extensions of clauses, so we parameterize the procedure abstraction by future extensions. To this purpose we introduce *open types* and *closed types*:

$$\begin{aligned} \mathtt{open}\ \{\mathtt{x{:}A}\} &= ((A \rightarrow \mathsf{Prop}) \rightarrow \mathsf{Rule}) \rightarrow (A \rightarrow \mathsf{Prop}) \rightarrow \mathsf{Rule} \\ \mathtt{closed}\ \{\mathtt{x{:}A}\} &= A \rightarrow \mathsf{Goal} \end{aligned}$$

After the above definition we have:

$$\begin{aligned} &\mathtt{P} \in \mathtt{open}\ \{\mathtt{x{:}A}\} \\ &\mathtt{P} = \lambda E : (A \rightarrow \mathsf{Prop}) \rightarrow \mathsf{Rule} \cdot \lambda P : A \rightarrow \mathsf{Prop} \cdot C_1 \& \ldots \& C_m \& (E\ P) \end{aligned}$$

Have defined P in this way we may then consider extending it using a second construct for defining procedures:

```
open procedure Q extends P with C'1 ... C'l
```

where each C'_j is of the form $Q\,(M'_j) \longleftarrow G'_j$. Intuitively this defines the new procedure Q (whose definition may shadow P if they have the same name) to "inherit" the clauses of P along with the n new clauses specified. More precisely after this definition we have:

$$\begin{aligned} \mathtt{Q} = \lambda E : (A \rightarrow \mathsf{Prop}) \rightarrow \mathsf{Rule} \cdot \lambda Q : (A \rightarrow \mathsf{Prop}) \cdot \\ (P\ (\lambda Q : A \rightarrow \mathsf{Prop} \cdot C'_1 \& \ldots \& C'_l \& (E\ Q))\ Q) \end{aligned}$$

[5] Although higher-order unification might be considered necessary, as in λ-Prolog, to enable the application of procedure variables, we consider this an unsatisfactory way of treating procedure variables. Since this topic is somewhat beyond the scope of the current paper, we do not consider it further.

where P is bound to the definition above. The clauses in a procedure are the accumulation of all the clauses in the procedures it extends or inherits from.

To use such a procedure we must "close it up". We define a closure operator which converts from an open to a closed procedure abstraction:

$$\texttt{close P} = \lambda x : A \cdot \forall R : A \to \mathsf{Prop} \cdot (P\ (\lambda R : A \to \mathsf{Prop} \cdot \mathsf{True})\ R) \supset (R\ x)$$
$$\texttt{close P} \in \texttt{closed}\ \{\texttt{x:A}\}$$

where P is bound to the definition above.

Sometimes providing the incremental definition of a single procedure is not enough; such a procedure may depend on the definitions of several other procedures in some mutual recursive fashion. We generalize the above mechanism for procedure definition and extension to a mechanism for defining *clusters* of procedures. A cluster contains the definition of several procedures, with mutual recursion allowed in the definitions. In fact since such a definition may be extended incrementally, these clusters are more akin to *classes* in Smalltalk (with the `self` pseudo-variable left implicit). The general form of a cluster definition is:

$$\texttt{open cluster M defines } \texttt{P}_1\texttt{:}\{\texttt{x}_1\texttt{:A}_1\} \to \texttt{Prop}, \ldots, \texttt{P}_n\texttt{:}\{\texttt{x}_n\texttt{:A}_n\} \to \texttt{Prop}$$
$$\texttt{with } \texttt{C}_1, \ldots, \texttt{C}_k$$

After such a definition we have:

$$\begin{aligned}\texttt{M} = \lambda E : (A_1 \to \mathsf{Prop}) \to \cdots \to (A_n \to \mathsf{Prop}) \to \mathsf{Rule} \cdot \\ \lambda P_1 : A_1 \to \mathsf{Prop} \cdots \lambda P_n : A_n \to \mathsf{Prop} \cdot C_1 \& \ldots C_k \& (E\ P_1 \ldots P_n)\end{aligned}$$

It is straightforward to define an incremental version of this which moreover allows new procedures to be defined in the extension. We also generalize the construct for closing a procedure definition to closing a cluster definition. Let:

$$\begin{aligned}\mathcal{P} &\stackrel{\text{def}}{=} \forall P_1 : A_1 \to \mathsf{Prop} \cdots \forall P_n : A_n \to \mathsf{Prop} \cdot \\ &\qquad (M\ (\lambda Q_1 : A_1 \to \mathsf{Prop} \cdots \lambda Q_n : A_n \to \mathsf{Prop} \cdot \mathsf{True})\ P_1 \ldots P_n) \\ \mathcal{G}_i &\stackrel{\text{def}}{=} \lambda x_i : A_i \cdot \mathcal{P} \supset (P_i\ x_i)\end{aligned}$$

Then the closure of such a cluster is defined to be:

$$\texttt{close M} = (\mathcal{G}_1, \ldots, \mathcal{G}_n)$$

The closure of a cluster is a record of closed procedures, accessed using the syntax $\texttt{M.P}_i\texttt{(t')}$ in the concrete language ($(\pi_i(M)\ t')$ in the kernel language).

As an example of our mechanisms, we give a cluster for implementing higher-order unification. The approach we use is originally due to Miller [16]. In Miller's L_λ language this procedure must be specified as a family of predicates indexed by the type of the terms being unified. We repeat Miller's definition using a single procedure definition, which is sufficient because of our richer type system.

```
open cluster HOU defines equal:[A:Type]{x,y:A}→Prop,
      subst:[A,B:Type]{t:(A→B);s:A;ts:B}→Prop with
  equal[A→B](t,s)    ←
      (∀u:A)(∀v:A) equal[A](u,v) ⊃ equal[B](t(u),s(v))
  subst[A→B](m,s,ms)    ←
      (∀x:A) equal[A](x,s) ⊃ equal[B](m(x),ms)
  ...
```

These clauses respectively define equality for λ-abstractions, and the result of substituting a term (s) for the free variable in another term (m). These operations can provide a basis for operations on higher-order abstract syntax, where object-language variable binding is represented using metalanguage λ-abstraction. For example the following signature gives a representation for a simple language with abstraction and application:

```
Term:Type,   Abs:(Term→Term)→Term,   App:Term→(Term→Term)
```

To provide a constraint solver for equality constraints between terms in this representation, we can specialize the above cluster for higher-order unification to this signature by specifying the base cases for equality:

```
closed cluster Term_HOU extends HOU with
  equal[Term](Abs(t), Abs(s)) ← equal[Term→Term](t, s)
  equal[Term](App(ta,sa), App(tb,sb)) ←
      equal[Term](ta,tb) & equal[Term](sa,sb)
```

So far our example has assumed only second-order representations. At higher types the definition of equality for λ-terms should contain a case for applications, defined in terms of substituting the argument:

```
equal[B](t(s),ts) ← subst[A,B](t,s,ts)
```

However this violates Miller's restriction on patterns [15]; the higher-order unification required to backchain on such a clause would defeat the purpose of the exercise. Instead the original definition of HOU should define a clause for `subst` which explicitly handles the case of substituting a λ-abstraction into a term and reducing any resulting β-redexes:

```
subst [A→B, C] (m,s,ms) ←
  (∀f:A→B)
  equal[A→B](f,s) ⊃
  ((∀n:A)(∀ns:B) subst[A,B](f,n,ns) ⊃ equal[B](f(n),ns)) ⊃
 equal[C](m(f),ms)
```

This clause will be executed by introducing a new constant for the eigenvariable `f` (used to denote the variable being substituted for) and a new clause which defines the operation of reducing a β-redex resulting from substituting a λ-abstraction for `f`. In some sense one can consider this procedure as performing a form of dynamic type discrimination, "dispatching" to a particular version of `subst` based on the types of its arguments. The key to the definition of this "generic procedure" is the type discrimination which is possible once types are allowed as terms.

Finally we consider the language's support for higher-order programming. Although quantification over predicate variables is used crucially in the definitions above of procedures and clusters, the quantification is used in such a way that such predicate variables are only introduced as eigenvariables during execution, and so can be treated as locally defined constants. Procedure clauses are formulae of type Rule; syntactic restrictions in the language ensure that predicate variables of type Rule (and Prop) are only used in this way. On the other hand no such restrictions apply to predicate variables of type Goal, the type of goal clauses. This allows *closed* procedure parameters in the language.

It is interesting to compare how procedure values are formed here compared with for example λ-Prolog. In the latter a procedure value is basically a closure containing calls on procedures defined in the environment where that closure was formed, for example:

```
compose (P, Q, (λx,z:A.(∃y:A)P(x,y)& Q(y,z)))
```

The difficulty with this definition is that once such a closure is formed its semantics may be changed if further clauses are added to the definitions of the composed procedures, for example during module composition or at run-time via hypothetical implication. Our approach instead is to "close up" the definition of a procedure which may be bound in a closure, while still allowing the incremental definition of open procedures. An equivalent definition of `compose` in our language is:

```
compose (P, Q,
(λx,y:A.
   ((∀R:{u,v:A}→Prop) ((∀u,v,w:A) P(u,v) & Q(v,w) ⊃ R(u,w))
      ⊃ R(x,y))
```

The "output" argument in this definition uses universal quantification (and hypothetical implication) in an essential way to properly scope the definition of the procedure being returned. We may consider this output argument as a form of *logical closure*. To statically ensure uniformity of proofs, λ-Prolog does not allow implications in its "Herbrand universe," which plays a crucial role in the closure of a procedure here [17]. On the other hand λ-Prolog has a stronger completeness property (discussed in Section 4) and a more straightforward implementation.

3 The Type System

In this section we present the type theory underlying our calculus. We use judgements of the form Γ **env** and $\Gamma \rhd \mathcal{F}$, where Γ is a typing environment and $\mathcal{F}$ a formula of the meta-logic. Formulae of the meta-logic and terms of the language are organized into the following categories:

$$
\begin{array}{rll}
\mathcal{F} \in \text{Formulae} & ::= & K\ \mathbf{kind} \mid A \in K \mid M \in A \mid A \preceq B \mid \\
 & & A = B \mid M = N \\
\Gamma \in \text{Envs} & ::= & \mathsf{nil} \mid \Gamma, t : K \mid \Gamma, x : A \\
K \in \text{Kinds} & ::= & \mathbf{1} \mid \mathsf{Type} \mid K_1 \times K_2 \mid K_1 \to K_2 \\
A, B \in \text{Types} & ::= & \mathsf{tc} \mid t \mid \mathbf{1} \mid A \times B \mid A \to B \mid \Delta t : K \cdot A \mid \\
 & & () \mid (A, B) \mid \pi_i(A) \mid \lambda t : K \cdot A \mid (A\ B) \\
M, N \in \text{Terms} & ::= & \mathsf{c} \mid x \mid () \mid (M, N) \mid \pi_i(M) \mid \\
 & & \lambda x : A \cdot M \mid (M\ N) \mid \Lambda t : K \cdot M \mid M[A]
\end{array}
$$

We omit the details of the type rules for lack of space. Further details are provided in [4]. Essentially the types constitute a simply typed λ-calculus with products. Our calculus is basically Harper and Mitchell's Core-XML [10], corresponding to the first two type universe levels in (an intensional version of) Martin-Löf's predicative type theory [13]. The formation rules for terms (given in [4]) include higher-order Λ-abstraction over types and type operators. As in Martin-Löf's type system [13] and Luo's ECC [12], types are stratified into levels, in this case the level of simple types and the level of polymorphic types. This predicative stratification in the type system is necessary because impredicativity in the underlying logic plays a crucial role in our language constructs [2].

In order to allow polymorphic functions of arbitrary arity (rather than relying on currying throughout), we extend this core calculus with *bindings* and *signatures*. We base the formation rules for bindings and signatures on the rules for structures and signatures, respectively, of Harper, Mitchell and Moggi [9]. The syntax for the extension is given by:

$$
\begin{array}{lll}
S \in \text{Signatures} & ::= [t : K, A] & \\
B \in \text{Bindings} & ::= s \mid [A, M] & \\
A \in \text{Types} & ::= \ldots \mid \textbf{fst}\ B \mid \Delta s : S \cdot A & \\
M \in \text{Terms} & ::= \ldots \mid \textbf{snd}\ B \mid \Lambda s : S \cdot M \mid M[B] &
\end{array}
$$

The type rules for bindings and signatures are standard [9], and are provided in [4]. For the description of the interpreter in Section 5 we omit bindings and signatures from the syntax of terms, reasoning that a term containing bindings may be converted to one without bindings [4]. Signatures and bindings are necessary for the description of the μ form in the next section.

A notational complication here is how to denote an arbitrary term in normal form (for the simply typed subset of this calculus, $\lambda\overline{x_m} : \overline{A_m} \cdot M\ \overline{N_n}$ would suffice). We use $\Lambda\overline{t_{m_1}} : \overline{K_{m_1}} \cdot \lambda\overline{x_{m_2}} : \overline{A_{m_2}} \cdot y\ [\overline{B_{n_1}}]\ \overline{M_{n_2}}$ to denote a term in normal form with an initial prefix of λ and Λ abstractions binding $t_1, \ldots, t_{m_1}, x_1, \ldots, x_{m_2}$, and with head variable y applied to $B_1, \ldots, B_{n_1}, M_1, \ldots, M_{n_2}$. We will denote the type of such a term by $\Delta\overline{t_{m_1}} : \overline{K_{m_1}} \cdot \overline{A_{m_2}} \to B$. Products introduce other complications:

Definition 1 Locators. The original term calculus is extended by the following rules:

$$L ::= \mathbf{1} \mid \pi_1 \mid \pi_2 \mid L_1 \circ L_2$$

where L is the syntactic class of *locators*. Locators are equal under the reflexive symmetric transitive closure of the following rules:

$$\mathbf{1} \circ L = L \qquad L \circ \mathbf{1} = L \qquad L_1 \circ (L_2 \circ L_3) = (L_1 \circ L_2) \circ L_3$$

Definition 2 Product Normal Form. Define the syntax for the locator calculus by replacing the rules for projectors $\pi_i A$ and $\pi_i M$ with the following:

$$A ::= L\ A \qquad M ::= L\ M$$

For convenience we identify terms M and located terms $\mathbf{1}\ M$, similarly for types. The types and terms in *product normal form* are described by the following grammar (where $\to$, $\times$ and Δ are treated as type constants tc):

$$
\begin{array}{l}
A ::= (L\ \mathsf{tc}\ \overline{A_m}) \mid (L\ t\ \overline{A_m}) \mid \lambda t : K \cdot A \mid (A, A') \\
M ::= (L\ \mathsf{c}\ [\overline{A_m}]\ \overline{M_n}) \mid (L\ x\ [\overline{A_m}]\ \overline{M_n}) \mid \lambda x : A \cdot M \mid \Lambda t : K \cdot M \mid (M_1, M_2)
\end{array}
$$

Further details of the typing and conversion relations for the locator calculus, and the conversion to product normal form, may be found in [6].

4 Hereditary Harrop Formulae

In this section we introduce a logic into the preceding type system which serves as a logic programming language. Our approach is based on the framework of uniform proof procedures developed by Miller, Nadathur, Pfenning and Scedrov [17]. Unlike λ-Prolog and Elf, we use the type system to place context-sensitive restrictions on the formation of propositions.

$$\textsc{Prop}\quad \frac{\Gamma\ \mathbf{env}}{\Gamma \rhd \mathsf{Prop} \in \mathsf{Type}} \quad \frac{\Gamma\ \mathbf{env}}{\Gamma \rhd \mathsf{Goal} \in \mathsf{Type}} \quad \frac{\Gamma\ \mathbf{env}}{\Gamma \rhd \mathsf{Rule} \in \mathsf{Type}}$$

$$\textsc{Atom}\quad \frac{\Gamma\ \mathbf{env}}{\Gamma \rhd \mathsf{Prop} \preceq \mathsf{Goal}} \quad \frac{\Gamma\ \mathbf{env}}{\Gamma \rhd \mathsf{Prop} \preceq \mathsf{Rule}}$$

$$\top F, \bot F\quad \frac{\Gamma\ \mathbf{env}}{\Gamma \rhd \mathsf{true} \in \mathsf{Prop}} \quad \frac{\Gamma\ \mathbf{env}}{\Gamma \rhd \mathsf{false} \in \mathsf{Goal}}$$

$$\&F\quad \frac{\Gamma \rhd P \in \kappa \quad \Gamma \rhd Q \in \kappa \quad \kappa \in \mathcal{K}}{\Gamma \rhd P \& Q \in \kappa}$$

$$\forall F\quad \frac{\Gamma, x : A \rhd P \in \kappa \quad \kappa \in \mathcal{K}}{\Gamma \rhd \forall x : A \cdot P \in \kappa} \quad \frac{\Gamma, t : K \rhd P \in \kappa \quad \kappa \in \mathcal{K}}{\Gamma \rhd \forall t : K \cdot P \in \kappa}$$

$$\supset F\quad \frac{\Gamma \rhd P \in \mathsf{Rule} \quad \Gamma \rhd Q \in \mathsf{Goal}}{\Gamma \rhd P \supset Q \in \mathsf{Goal}} \quad \frac{\Gamma \rhd P \in \mathsf{Goal} \quad \Gamma \rhd Q \in \mathsf{Rule}}{\Gamma \rhd P \supset Q \in \mathsf{Rule}}$$

$$\frac{\Gamma \rhd P \in \mathsf{Prop} \quad \Gamma \rhd Q \in \mathsf{Prop}}{\Gamma \rhd P \supset Q \in \mathsf{Prop}}$$

$$\mu F\quad \frac{\Gamma, \overline{x_m} : \overline{S_m \rightarrow \mathsf{Prop}} \rhd P \in \mathsf{Rule} \quad \Gamma \rhd B \in S_i}{\Gamma \rhd (\mu \overline{x_m} : \overline{S_m} \cdot P) @_i B \in \mathsf{Goal}}$$

Fig. 1. Formation Rules for Propositions

We refine the type Prop of propositions into the types Prop, Rule and Goal for, respectively, "rigid" atoms, definite clauses (rules) and goal clauses. The syntax of terms is extended with syntax for propositions:

$$\begin{array}{rll}
\mathcal{F} \in \text{Formulae} & ::= \ldots & \mid\ \Phi\ \mathbf{context} \ \mid\ \Phi \longrightarrow P \\
\Phi \in \text{Contexts} & ::= \{\} & \mid\ \Phi, P \\
A, B \in \text{Types} & ::= \ldots & \mid\ \mathsf{Prop} \ \mid\ \mathsf{Rule} \ \mid\ \mathsf{Goal} \\
M, N, P, Q \in \text{Terms} & ::= \ldots & \mid\ \mathsf{true} \ \mid\ \mathsf{false} \ \mid\ P \& Q \ \mid\ P \supset Q \ \mid \\
& & \forall x : A \cdot P \ \mid\ \forall t : K \cdot P \ \mid\ (\mu \overline{x_m} : \overline{S_m} \cdot P) @_i B
\end{array}$$

CONTEXT	$\dfrac{\Gamma\ \mathbf{env}}{\Gamma \rhd \{\}\ \mathbf{context}} \quad \dfrac{\Gamma \rhd \Phi\ \mathbf{context} \quad \Gamma \rhd P \in \kappa \quad \kappa \in \mathcal{K}}{\Gamma \rhd \Phi, P\ \mathbf{context}}$
HYP, CUT	$\dfrac{\Gamma \rhd \Phi\ \mathbf{context} \quad P \in \Phi}{\Gamma \rhd \Phi \longrightarrow P} \quad \dfrac{\Gamma \rhd \Phi \longrightarrow P \quad \Gamma \rhd \Phi, P \longrightarrow Q}{\Gamma \rhd \Phi \longrightarrow Q}$
$\top R$	$\dfrac{\Gamma \rhd \Phi\ \mathbf{context}}{\Gamma \rhd \Phi \longrightarrow \mathsf{true}}$
$\&L, \&R$	$\dfrac{\Gamma \rhd \Phi, P_i \longrightarrow Q}{\Gamma \rhd \Phi, P_1 \& P_2 \longrightarrow Q} \quad \dfrac{\Gamma \rhd \Phi \longrightarrow P \quad \Gamma \rhd \Phi \longrightarrow Q}{\Gamma \rhd \Phi \longrightarrow P \& Q}$
$\supset L, \supset R$	$\dfrac{\Gamma \rhd \Phi, Q \longrightarrow R \quad \Gamma \rhd \Phi \longrightarrow P}{\Gamma \rhd \Phi, P \supset Q \longrightarrow R} \quad \dfrac{\Gamma \rhd \Phi, P \longrightarrow Q}{\Gamma \rhd \Phi \longrightarrow P \supset Q}$
$\forall L$	$\dfrac{\Gamma \rhd \Phi, \{M/x\}P \longrightarrow Q \quad \Gamma \rhd M \in A}{\Gamma \rhd \Phi, \forall x : A \cdot P \longrightarrow Q} \quad \dfrac{\Gamma \rhd \Phi, \{A/t\}P \longrightarrow Q \quad \Gamma \rhd A \in K}{\Gamma \rhd \Phi, \forall t : K \cdot P \longrightarrow Q}$
$\forall R$	$\dfrac{\Gamma, x : A \rhd \Phi \longrightarrow P}{\Gamma \rhd \Phi \longrightarrow \forall x : A \cdot P} \quad \dfrac{\Gamma, t : K \rhd \Phi \longrightarrow P}{\Gamma \rhd \Phi \longrightarrow \forall t : K \cdot P}$
μL	$\dfrac{\begin{array}{c}\Gamma \rhd Q_1 \in \Delta s_1 : S_1 \cdot \mathsf{Prop} \ \ldots\ \Gamma \rhd Q_m \in \Delta s_m : S_m \cdot \mathsf{Prop} \\ \Gamma \rhd \Phi \longrightarrow \{\overline{Q_m}/\overline{x_m}\}P \quad \Gamma \rhd \Phi, Q_i B \longrightarrow Q\end{array}}{\Gamma \rhd \Phi, (\mu \overline{x_m} : \overline{S_m} \cdot P)@_i B \longrightarrow Q}$
μR	$\dfrac{\Gamma, \overline{x_m} : \overline{S_m \rightarrow \mathsf{Prop}} \rhd \Phi, P \longrightarrow x_i\ B \quad \Gamma \rhd B \in S_i}{\Gamma \rhd \Phi \longrightarrow (\mu \overline{x_m} : \overline{S_m} \cdot P)@_i B}$

Fig. 2. Proof Rules for Propositions

For reasoning about provability with respect to a set of hypotheses we also introduce a new judgement form $\Gamma \rhd \Phi \longrightarrow P$. The sequent formula $\Phi \longrightarrow P$ denotes provability of the formula P with respect to the hypotheses Φ. Note that whereas an environment Γ is a list of variable bindings, a context Φ is a set of propositions. Fig. 1 gives the formation rules for propositions, while Fig. 2 gives the proof rules. In these rules, $\mathcal{K}$ denotes the set {Prop, Goal, Rule}. The subtyping rules (ATOM) allow rigid atoms to be treated as either definite or goal clauses. We have formation rules for conjunction &, implication $\supset$ and universal quantification $\forall$ for both rules and goals. The interesting rules are those for implication; these reflect the standard restrictions for first order hereditary Harrop formulae. In a system without quantification over predicates, this logic is essentially that for L_λ [15]. In allowing quantification over predicates we place the following restriction on the formation of programs:

> **Restriction on Well-Formed Programs:** A valid (closed) program is a well-typed program which is $\beta\eta$-convertible to a term does not contain any occurrences of the type constants Prop or Rule.

Prop and Rule are now used for typing purposes only. Any predicate variables introduced by the universal quantifier must have type Goal and so may only be used in the formation of atomic goals; the typing rules for goals and rules ensure that such an atom cannot appear in the "head" of a rule. We still need some way to introduce new predicate constants which are not so restricted. This motivates the addition of the μ constructor for introducing new predicate names (intuitively this constructor forms the fixed point of a collection of mutually recursively defined procedures). This constructor allows the use of the Prop type constructor in a controlled way.

We omit μ forms from consideration in the operational semantics by "macro-expanding" such forms into their intended interpretation:

$$(\mu \overline{x_m} : \overline{S_m} \cdot P)@_i B \Longrightarrow \forall x_1 : S_1 \to \mathsf{Prop} \cdots \forall x_m : S_m \to \mathsf{Prop} \cdot P \supset (x_i\ B)$$

Bindings and binding variables may then be removed by the transformation mentioned in the previous section. The proof of the following is therefore standard [8]:

Lemma 3 Cut Elimination. *Suppose* $\Gamma \vdash P \in \mathsf{Goal}$ *and* $\Gamma \vdash \Phi$ **context**, *and* $\Gamma \vdash \Phi \longrightarrow P$. *Then there exists a derivation for* $\Gamma \rhd \Phi \longrightarrow P$ *which does not involve any use of the* CUT *rule.*

The standard proof involves permuting applications of Cut below applications of the other rules until applications of Cut have been moved to the leaves, then replacing Cut with Hyp. Since the logic is a restriction of higher-order logic with type universes, termination of this process is a consequence of Luo's Strong Normalization theorem for ECC [12]. Let $\Gamma \vdash \Phi \in \mathsf{Rule}$ denote that $\Gamma \vdash P \in \mathsf{Rule}$ for every $P \in \Phi$. The following is verified by a straightforward induction on cut-free derivations:

Lemma 4. *Suppose* $\Gamma \vdash \Phi \in \mathsf{Rule}$, $\Gamma \vdash P \in \mathsf{Goal}$ *and* $\Gamma \vdash \Phi \longrightarrow P$. *Then for any sequent* $\Gamma' \rhd \Phi' \longrightarrow P'$ *in a cut-free derivation tree,* $\Gamma' \vdash \Phi' \in \mathsf{Rule}$ *and* $\Gamma' \vdash P' \in \mathsf{Goal}$.

Note that as a consequence, the logic in Table 2 is essentially "positive" in nature. Because of the typing of falsity (false), it is not possible to introduce negative propositions into the set of hypotheses in a cut-free derivation. This aspect of the logic is inherited from hereditary Harrop formulae. In addition the restrictions on typing of predicate variables ensures that the predicate variable at the head of any clause in the hypotheses is rigid.

5 A Uniform Proof Procedure

In this section we develop an operational semantics for our language, by specifying an abstract interpreter which satisfies the uniform proof procedure property of Miller, Nadathur, Pfenning and Scedrov [17]. A *configuration* of the abstract interpreter is a tuple $(\Gamma;\ \mathcal{G};\ \mathcal{P};\ \mathcal{C})$ where Γ is a global type environment, $\mathcal{G}$ a multiset of type membership judgements, $\mathcal{P}$ a multiset of goal propositions, and $\mathcal{C}$ a multiset of equality judgements:

$$\begin{array}{lll} \Gamma \in \text{Environments} & ::= \mathsf{nil} & \mid \Gamma, x : A \mid \Gamma, t : K \\ \mathcal{G} \in \text{Type Judgements} & ::= \top & \mid \Gamma \rhd A \in K \mid \Gamma \rhd M \in A \mid \mathcal{G}_1, \mathcal{G}_2 \\ \mathcal{P} \in \text{Goal Propositions} & ::= \top & \mid \Gamma \rhd \Phi \longrightarrow P \mid \Gamma \rhd \Phi; P \longrightarrow Q \mid \mathcal{P}_1, \mathcal{P}_2 \\ \mathcal{C} \in \text{Constraints} & ::= \top & \mid \Gamma \rhd M = N \mid \Gamma \rhd A = B \mid \mathcal{C}_1, \mathcal{C}_2 \end{array}$$

The new judgement form $\Gamma \rhd \Phi; P \longrightarrow Q$ is used to describe intermediate states during a backchaining transition of the interpreter (beginning with **Backchain**).

Backchain: $(\Gamma;\ \mathcal{G};\ \mathcal{P}, (\Gamma' \rhd \Phi \longrightarrow (L\ x\ \overline{[A_m]}\ \overline{N_n}));\ \mathcal{C}) \implies$

$(\Gamma;\ \mathcal{G};\ \mathcal{P}, (\Gamma' \rhd \Phi; P \longrightarrow (L\ x\ \overline{[A_m]}\ \overline{N_n}));\ \mathcal{C})$ where $P \in \Phi$, $(L\ x) \in \mathtt{heads}(P)$

TermWit: $(\Gamma;\ \mathcal{G};\ \mathcal{P}, (\Gamma' \rhd \Phi; \forall x : A \cdot P \longrightarrow Q);\ \mathcal{C}) \implies$

$(\Gamma;\ \mathcal{G}, (\Gamma' \rhd M \in A);\ \mathcal{P}, (\Gamma' \rhd \Phi; \{M/x\}P \longrightarrow Q);\ \mathcal{C})$

Select: $(\Gamma;\ \mathcal{G};\ \mathcal{P}, (\Gamma' \rhd \Phi; P_1 \& P_2 \longrightarrow Q);\ \mathcal{C}) \implies$

$(\Gamma;\ \mathcal{G};\ \mathcal{P}, (\Gamma' \rhd \Phi; P_i \longrightarrow Q);\ \mathcal{C})$ where $\mathtt{head}(Q) \in \mathtt{heads}(P_i)$

Subgoal: $(\Gamma;\ \mathcal{G};\ \mathcal{P}, (\Gamma' \rhd \Phi; P_1 \supset P_2 \longrightarrow Q);\ \mathcal{C}) \implies$

$(\Gamma;\ \mathcal{G};\ \mathcal{P}, (\Gamma' \rhd \Phi; P_2 \longrightarrow Q), (\Gamma' \rhd \Phi \longrightarrow P_1);\ \mathcal{C})$

Atom: $(\Gamma;\ \mathcal{G};\ \mathcal{P}, (\Gamma' \rhd \Phi; (L\ x\ \overline{[A_m]}\ \overline{N_n}) \longrightarrow P);\ \mathcal{C}) \implies$

$(\Gamma;\ \mathcal{G};\ \mathcal{P};\ \mathcal{C}, (\Gamma' \rhd (L\ x\ \overline{[A_m]}\ \overline{N_n}) = P))$

Fig. 3. Backchaining Transitions for Uniform Proof Procedure

As usual in logic programming, the backchaining transitions are constrained by the head of the atom on which we are backchaining. Define the auxiliary functions $\mathtt{head}(P)$ and $\mathtt{heads}(P)$ as follows (where $\mathtt{head}(P)$ is only defined for atomic P):

$$\mathtt{head}((L\ x\ \overline{[A_m]}\ \overline{M_n})) \stackrel{\text{def}}{=} (L\ x)$$
$$\mathtt{heads}(P) \stackrel{\text{def}}{=} Q \text{ where } (V, Q) = \mathtt{heads}(\{\}, P)$$
$$\mathtt{heads}(V, (L\ x\ \overline{[A_m]}\ \overline{M_n})) \stackrel{\text{def}}{=} \{(V, (L\ x))\}$$
$$\mathtt{heads}(V, \forall x : A \cdot P) \stackrel{\text{def}}{=} \mathtt{heads}(V \cup \{x\}, P)$$
$$\mathtt{heads}(V, \forall t : K \cdot P) \stackrel{\text{def}}{=} \mathtt{heads}(V, P)$$
$$\mathtt{heads}(V, P \supset Q) \stackrel{\text{def}}{=} \mathtt{heads}(V, Q)$$
$$\mathtt{heads}(V, P \& Q) \stackrel{\text{def}}{=} \mathtt{heads}(V, P) \cup \mathtt{heads}(V, Q)$$
$$\mathtt{heads}(V, \{\}) \stackrel{\text{def}}{=} \{\}$$
$$\mathtt{heads}(V, (\Phi, P)) \stackrel{\text{def}}{=} \mathtt{heads}(V, \Phi) \cup \mathtt{heads}(V, P)$$

Our interest in the proof procedure is primarily to verify that with the restrictions we have placed on goal formulae, the backchaining step in the procedure is sufficient for analysing propositional types. This justifies the backchaining interpreter for the language given in Fig. 3.

Lemma 5. *Suppose* $\Gamma \Vdash P \in \mathsf{Goal}$ *and*

$$(\Gamma;\ \top;\ \rhd \{\} \longrightarrow P;\ \top) \stackrel{*}{\Longrightarrow} (\Gamma;\ \mathcal{G};\ \mathcal{P}, (\Gamma' \rhd \Phi \longrightarrow Q);\ \mathcal{C})$$

then $\Gamma, \Gamma' \Vdash \Phi \in \mathsf{Rule}$ *and* $\Gamma, \Gamma' \Vdash Q \in \mathsf{Goal}$.

Corollary 6. *Suppose* $\Gamma \Vdash A \in \mathsf{Goal}$ *and*

$$(\Gamma;\ \top;\ \rhd \{\} \longrightarrow P;\ \top) \stackrel{*}{\Longrightarrow} (\Gamma;\ \mathcal{G};\ \mathcal{P}, (\Gamma' \rhd \Phi \longrightarrow Q);\ \mathcal{C})$$

then for all $(V, x) \in \texttt{heads}(\{\}, \Phi)$, $x \notin V$.

This corollary is crucial; it allows us to verify the sufficiency of backchaining alone for analysing goal clauses in an abstract interpreter for the language. The following is verified by a by-now-standard argument based on permuting left and right rules until all left rules are applied above the application of right rules:

Theorem 7 Completeness of the Proof Procedure. *Suppose* $\Gamma \Vdash P \in \mathsf{Goal}$ *and* $\Gamma \vdash \{\} \longrightarrow P$. *Then:*

$$(\Gamma;\ \top;\ (\rhd \{\} \longrightarrow P);\ \top) \stackrel{*}{\Longrightarrow} (\Gamma;\ \top;\ \top;\ \top)$$

Corollary 8. $\Gamma \nvdash \{\} \longrightarrow \mathsf{false}$.

6 Conclusions

We have presented an approach to procedure definition which corrects scoping problems with current higher order logic programming languages. Our treatment of procedures incorporates a notion of "logical closures" to provide the correct notion of procedural abstraction; we also introduce a related notion of "implementation inheritance" to support a style of programming found in logic programming. The operational semantics for the language is based on the provision of a uniform proof procedure, and the identification of a class of "hereditary Harrop formulae" for which this interpreter is logically complete (based on the framework of [17]).

The decision to base procedural abstraction on inductive closures (internalized using the universal quantifier) is an important one. For higher order programming it appears essential, as well as for coercive interface matching in a SML-like module language. Consider the following SML code:

```
signature S = sig type t;  val x:t end ;
functor F (X : S) = ...
structure S' = struct type t=int;  val x=3;  val y=5 end;
structure S'' = F (S');
```

The crucial concept here is using *field names* to decide how to match a module with an interface; for example, in `S''`, the `t` and `x` fields of `X` are bound to the corresponding fields in `S`. The difficulty with applying this concept to logic programming is the absence of a single "definition site" for a procedure definition (since a procedure is considered to be the collection of its defining clauses), so it is not clear how to apply this idea of coercive interface matching. Our approach to procedure definition solves this problem by using universal predicate quantification and hypothetical implication to "close up" the definition of a procedure into a single expression, bound to a single name in a module.

We conjecture that consideration of procedure definitions as inductive definitions may also provide a framework for incorporating more powerful control constructs in higher-order logic programming (in particular negation-by-failure). Paulson and Smith have considered monotone inductive definitions as a framework for unifying logic and functional programming [20]. Schroeder-Heister and Hallnas have developed the theory of partial inductive definitions as a foundation for logic programming incorporating embedded implications in goals. However their language is first-order without polymorphism, while they have a notion of *definitional reflection*, based on ω-induction, which we do not consider [24].

Saraswat [23] has developed an approach to higher-order constraint programming wherein procedures are defined as transducer expressions operating over a global store. However his approach does not extend to languages with hypothetical implication, nor would it extend to a polymorphic language with dynamic type discrimination (he only considers a simple type system). Miller *et al* [17] do not allow free variables at the heads of clauses, or implication in the Herbrand base, in their theory of higher-order hereditary Harrop formulae. The latter restriction in particular is necessary to ensure the uniformity of proofs in their system. Felty [7] considers a version of simple type theory, without $\vee$ or $\exists$, but also without the restrictions of [17], in the context of encoding Coquand-Huet constructions in higher-order logic. Although she verifies uniformity for the resulting proof system, simple backchaining is no longer sufficient for a complete proof procedure; a complete interpreter would need to "guess" lemmata at certain stages during the computation. Whereas Felty's approach is useful for interactive proof search, our approach is more appropriate for the operational semantics of a programming language.

In basing a logic programming language on a type system with polymorphism, several design alternatives arise [2]. Some of these alternatives, and the advantages of the framework just presented, are discussed in [4].

References

1. Andrew Appel. *Compiling with Continuations*. Cambridge University Press, 1992.
2. Thierry Coquand. An analysis of Girard's paradox. In *Proceedings of IEEE Symposium on Logic in Computer Science*, 1986.
3. Dominic Duggan. Higher-order substitutions. Technical Report CS-93-44, University of Waterloo, 1993. 34 pages. Submitted for publication. An earlier version of this paper was presented at the *λ-Prolog Workshop*, Philadelphia PA, July 1992.
4. Dominic Duggan. Logical closures. Technical Report UW CS-94-20, Department of Computer Science, University of Waterloo, 1994.

5. Dominic Duggan. Possible worlds semantics for higher-order, explicitly polymorphic logic programming. In preparation, 1994.
6. Dominic Duggan. Unification with extended patterns. Technical Report CS-93-37, University of Waterloo, 1994. 57 pages. Revised March 1994. Submitted for publication.
7. Amy Felty. Encoding the calculus of constructions in a higher-order logic. In *Proceedings of IEEE Symposium on Logic in Computer Science*, 1993.
8. Jean-Yves Girard, Yves Lafont, and Paul Taylor. *Proofs and Types*. Cambridge University Press, 1989.
9. Robert Harper, John Mitchell, and Eugenio Moggi. Higher-order modules and the phase distinction. In *Proceedings of ACM Symposium on Principles of Programming Languages*, pages 341–354. Association for Computing Machinery, 1990.
10. Robert Harper and John C. Mitchell. On the type structure of Standard ML. *ACM Transactions on Programming Languages and Systems*, 15(2):211–252, 1993.
11. S. C. Keene. *Object Oriented Programming in Common Lisp: A Programming Guide in CLOS*. Addison-Wesley, 1989.
12. Zhaohui Luo. ECC, an extended calculus of constructions. In *Proceedings of IEEE Symposium on Logic in Computer Science*, pages 385–395. IEEE, 1989.
13. P. Martin-Löf. An intuitionistic theory of types: Predicative part. In H. E. Rose and J. C. Shepherdson, editors, *Logic Colloquium '73*, pages 73–118. North-Holland, 1973.
14. Dale Miller. Abstractions in logic programming. In Peirgiorgio Odifreddi, editor, *Logic and Computer Science*, pages 329–359. Academic Press, 1990.
15. Dale Miller. A logic programming language with lambda-abstraction, function variables and simple unification. *Journal of Logic and Computation*, 1(4):497–536, 1991.
16. Dale Miller. Unification of simply typed λ-terms as logic programming. In *Proceedings of the International Conference on Logic Programming*, pages 255–269. MIT Press, 1991.
17. Dale Miller, Gopalan Nadathur, Frank Pfenning, and Andre Scedrov. Uniform proofs as a foundation for logic programming. *Annals of Pure and Applied Logic*, 51:125–157, 1991.
18. Gopalan Nadathur and Dale Miller. An overview of λ-Prolog. In *Proceedings of the International Conference on Logic Programming*, pages 810–827. MIT Press, 1988.
19. Gopalan Nadathur and Dale Miller. Higher-order Horn clauses. *Journal of the ACM*, 37(4):777–814, October 1990.
20. Lawrence C. Paulson and Andrew W. Smith. Logic programming, functional programming and inductive definitions. In Peter Schroeder-Heister, editor, *Extensions of Logic Programming*. Springer-Verlag, 1990.
21. Frank Pfenning. Logic programming in the LF logical framework. In Gerard Huet and Gordon Plotkin, editors, *Logical Frameworks*, pages 149–181. Cambridge University Press, 1990.
22. Frank Pfenning and Conal Elliott. Higher-order abstract syntax. In *Proceedings of ACM SIGPLAN Conference on Programming Language Design and Implementation*, pages 199–208. Association for Computing Machinery, 1988.
23. Vijay Saraswat. The category of constraint systems is Cartesian closed. In *Proceedings of IEEE Symposium on Logic in Computer Science*, pages 341–345, 1992.
24. Peter Schroeder-Heister. Hypothetical reasoning and definitional reflection in logic programming. In Peter Schroeder-Heister, editor, *Extensions of Logic Programming*. Springer-Verlag Lecture Notes in Computer Science, 1990.
25. William Wadge. Higher order Horn logic programming. In *Proceedings of the IEEE International Logic Programming Symposium*, 1991.

Higher-Order Rigid E-Unification

Jean Goubault

Bull Corporate Research Center, rue Jean Jaurès, Les Clayes sous Bois, France
(Jean.Goubault@frcl.bull.fr)

Abstract. Higher-order E-unification, i.e. the problem of finding substitutions that make two simply typed λ-terms equal modulo β or $\beta\eta$-equivalence and a given equational theory, is undecidable. We propose to *rigidify* it, to get a resource-bounded decidable unification problem (with arbitrary high bounds), providing a complete higher-order E-unification procedure. The techniques are inspired from Gallier's rigid E-unification and from Dougherty and Johann's use of combinatory logic to solve higher-order E-unification problems. We improve their results by using general equational theories, and by defining optimizations such as higher-order rigid E-preunification, where flexible terms are used, gaining much efficiency, as in the non-equational case due to Huet..

1 Introduction

Higher-order E-unification is the problem of finding complete sets of unifiers of two simply typed λ-terms modulo β or $\beta\eta$-equivalence, and modulo an equational theory $\mathcal{E}$. This problem has applications in higher-order automated theorem proving, in logic programming extended to higher orders, and in machine learning among other fields. A promising approach was pioneered in 1992 by Dougherty and Johann [10], who proposed to use combinatory logic instead of λ-calculus: this approach eliminates the complexities due to the presence of bound variables, eases the inclusion of first-order equational theories, and in fact allows to reuse work done for first-order equational unification, since combinatory logic is a first-order equational theory itself. It also deals naturally with the extension of the typing scheme to include type variables, which classical approaches have not managed to solve completely.

Dougherty and Johann's work has a few nagging restrictions, notably that $\mathcal{E}$ must be a first-order theory admitting a confluent and terminating rewriting system, and deals only with $\beta\eta$-equivalence. Moreover, they notice that Huet's [25] notion of preunification should be used rather than full unification, meaning that notions of flexible terms should be identified and used.

To lift these restrictions, we formulate higher-order E-unification, both modulo β and $\beta\eta$-equivalence, as a first-order E-unification problem, using Curry's equations to make combinatory equality identical to β (resp. $\beta\eta$) equivalence. A nice way to solve such problems is to make them rigid, yielding what Gallier et al. call *rigid E-unification* [12]. Using Goubault's congruence closure-based algorithm [19] to solve this problem allows us to identify flexible terms during unification and to perform various other optimizations.

The plan of the paper is as follows: Section 2 gives a short overview of related work in the field, so as to place our ideas in proper perspective. Section 3 defines our notations, and Section 4 shows how we can deal with λ-calculus through combinatory logic by using Curry's equations, which we derive for Curry's CBWK system, which better simulates λ-calculus than the usual SK basis. In Section 5, we recall what rigid E-unification is, and how we can solve it. This enables us to formulate higher-order rigid E-unification in Section 6, and to define optimizations in the form of rigid E-preunification first, then by using normalization properties of the λ-calculus. We conclude in Section 7.

2 Related Works and Intuitions

Higher-order unification was pioneered by Darlington [8] and was used first to extend resolution to second-order [31] and higher-order logic [32]. It was also used in the method of matings [2], and in higher-order logic programming [27] for instance. A more complete survey can be found in [14].

It consists in, given two simply-typed λ-terms t and t' of the same type, finding complete sets of substitutions σ such that $t\sigma =_\beta t'\sigma$ (resp. $t\sigma =_{\beta\eta} t'\sigma$), where $=_\beta$ is β-equivalence, and $=_{\beta\eta}$ is $\beta\eta$-equivalence.

It was made practical by Huet, who invented a much more efficient algorithm [25] for *preunification*, where flexible-flexible pairs are never reduced, since they are always satisfiable. Gallier and Snyder [15] have reformulated Huet's algorithm as a set of transformations of systems, and Snyder [34] has extended it to deal with higher-order E-unification, i.e. the problem of finding σ such that $(\forall \mathbf{x} \cdot \mathcal{E}) \vdash_= t\sigma =_\beta t'\sigma$ (resp. $(\forall \mathbf{x} \cdot \mathcal{E}) \vdash_= t\sigma =_{\beta\eta} t'\sigma$), where $\forall \mathbf{x} \cdot \mathcal{E}$ is a (well-typed) equational theory, that is, a finite set $\mathcal{E}$ of universally quantified equations, and $\vdash_=$ is the consequence relation in higher-order logic with equality. Nipkow and Qian [30] then refined Snyder's rules to allow for modular higher-order E-unification.

On the other hand, Dougherty and Johann [10] have proposed to use combinatory logic to solve the same problem. Although they deal only with first-order equational theories $\mathcal{E}$, their approach offers a simpler alternative to Snyder's rules in dealing with λ-bound variables, as there are no such variables in combinatory logic. Moreover, it integrates equational theories more smoothly inside the unification procedure, since dealing with equations in $\mathcal{E}$ or with combinatory axioms is of the same nature. Finally, their approach is the first that solves higher-order unification in the presence of type variables, for which Huet's procedure (due to the Projection rule) would require unbounded non-determinism.

The main objection to using combinatory logic instead of λ-calculus is that combinatory equality $=_w$ is weaker than β or $\beta\eta$-equivalence. Dougherty and Johann solve this problem by considering only *first-order* equational theories $\mathcal{E}$, and by using transformations, not of systems of equations, but of sets of systems. However, Curry has shown that we could add to the system of equations $Kxy \doteq x$, $Sxyz \doteq xz(yz)$ defining $=_w$, a finite number of ground equations, thus defining a theory $\mathcal{C}$ such that equality modulo $\mathcal{C}$ is exactly equality in the

λ-calculus (see [3], corollary 7.3.15, p.161). In short, higher-order E-unification, for any general $\mathcal{E}$, is just first-order E-unification modulo the theory $\mathcal{E} \wedge \mathcal{C}$.

On the other hand, although E-unification is undecidable in general, *rigid* E-unification is decidable and NP-complete [16]. Rigid E-unification [12] is the problem of finding substitutions σ such that $\mathcal{E}\sigma \Rightarrow t\sigma \doteq t'\sigma$ holds in the quantifier-free theory of equality, what we write $\mathcal{E}\sigma \vdash_{0,=} t\sigma \doteq t'\sigma$ ($\vdash_{0,=}$ being the consequence relation in this theory, defined as propositional calculus plus all the rules of equality; equivalently, $\vdash_{0,=}$ is the deduction relation with free variables considered as constants). Checking the latter can be done in polynomial time by the congruence closure algorithm [11, 29], and this stimulated Goubault [19] in finding a new algorithm for rigid E-unification based on congruence closure.

The link between general and rigid E-unification comes from Herbrand-Gallier's theorem [12], saying that an existential formula in first-order logic with equality (as $(\forall \mathbf{x} \cdot \mathcal{E} \wedge A) \Rightarrow t \doteq t'$ in our case) is valid if and only if some finite disjunction of closed instances of it holds in the quantifier-free theory of equality. So, to find σ such that $\mathcal{E} \wedge A$ entails $t\sigma \doteq t'\sigma$ means finding an integer k, and $k+1$ substitutions $\sigma, \sigma_1, \ldots, \sigma_k$ such that $(\mathcal{E} \wedge A)\sigma_1 \wedge \ldots \wedge (\mathcal{E} \wedge A)\sigma_k \vdash_{0,=} t\sigma \doteq t'\sigma$, or equivalently to find k and a rigid E-unifier of $\mathcal{E}_1 \wedge A_1 \wedge \ldots \wedge \mathcal{E}_k \wedge A_k \vdash_{0,=} t \doteq t'$, where $\mathcal{E}_i$ and A_i are copies of $\mathcal{E}$ and A respectively, i.e. these formulas with their free variables replaced by fresh ones.

Solving an E-unification problem by rigidifying it reminds of Prawitz's ideas [33] to prove in first-order logic, which led to the development of the connection method [4], a.k.a. the method of matings [1], and with equality to Gallier's equational matings [13, 12]. Our approach therefore inherits the strong points of these methods, and notably provides a good control on the amount of resources used by the procedure, by controlling the growth of k. Moreover, using rigid E-unification enables us to use more relaxed notions of completess for sets of unifiers, like that presented by Gallier or Goubault, thus providing more concise representations of complete sets of unifiers.

Finally, this approach can also be seen as a generalization of Gallier et al.'s rigid E-unification to higher-order logic. As such, it may provide a path to new proof methods for higher-order logic.

3 Notations

First-order terms $s, t, \ldots$ are either *variables* $x, y, \ldots$ or *applications* $f(t_1, \ldots, t_m)$ of m-ary *function symbols* f. *Types* τ are terms built on type variables that we write α, β, and functions, including the binary arrow $\rightarrow$; we write $\tau \rightarrow \tau'$ for $\rightarrow(\tau, \tau')$, and assume that $\rightarrow$ is right-associative.

We denote by $\text{fv}(t)$ the set of *free variables* in a term t. A *substitution* σ is a partial map from variable to terms, of finite domain. The *application* $t\sigma$ of σ to t is defined as usual, as well as the *composition* $\sigma\sigma'$ such that $t(\sigma\sigma') = (t\sigma)\sigma'$ for every t. The *instances* of t are the $t\sigma$'s, for any σ.

Equations $s \doteq t$ are (unoriented) pairs of terms, and *systems* E, F, of equations are finite sets of equations, viewed as conjunctions. Substitution application naturally extends to equations and systems. $ST(o)$ denotes the set of subterms of any term, equation or system o.

Simply-typed *λ-terms* t, t', ..., are either: typed variables x_τ (of type τ and any of its instance; we assume there are countably infinitely many variables of each type), which we write x when the type is clear from the context, knowing that all occurrences of a same variable in the same scope have the same type; or *constants* c of types that we assume known in advance; or *applications* tt' (application being left-associative) of t of type $\tau \to \tau'$ to t' of type τ, the application having type τ'; or *abstractions* $\lambda x_\tau \cdot t$ of type $\tau \to \tau'$ if t has type τ'. Every term t has a principal type [21, 28] τ such that the set of instances of τ is the set of types of t. We write $t : \tau$ for "t has type τ". Finally, we consider two λ-terms to be equal modulo renamings of their bound variables (α-renaming).

The set of *free variables* $\text{fv}(t)$ of a λ-term t is defined in the usual way. We shall always assume that our λ-terms are rectified, i.e. no variable is bound twice in the same term.

β-equivalence is the finest congruence $=_\beta$ on λ-terms such that $(\lambda x \cdot t)t' =_\beta t[t'/x]$, where $x[t'/x] = t'$, $y[t'/x] = y$ if y is a variable other than x or a constant, $(t''t''')[t'/x] = t''[t'/x]t'''[t'/x]$ and $(\lambda y \cdot t'')[t'/x] = \lambda y \cdot t''[t'/x]$, with $y \neq x$. *βη-equivalence* is the finest congruence $=_{\beta\eta}$ containing $=_\beta$ such that $\lambda x \cdot tx =_{\beta\eta} t$ if $x \notin \text{fv}(t)$. *Reducing* means using these definitions as rewrite rules from left to right, and *normalizing* means reducing until we cannot progress (which happens eventually in the simply-typed case), in which case the final term is said to be in normal form. From now on, $=_\lambda$ is any of these two relations.

4 Higher-Order Logic and Combinatory Terms

Combinatory logic is usually presented as a first-order equational theory of two constants S and K, of arity 0, and one binary function symbol @, meant to represent application, so that we shall write tt' instead of $@(t, t')$. The axioms of the SK system are $\forall x, y \cdot Kxy \doteq x$ and $\forall x, y, z \cdot Sxyz \doteq xz(yz)$.

Any λ-term t can be translated into an SK-term $(t)_{\text{SK}}$, and conversely any SK-term t can be translated into a λ-term $(t)_\lambda$ [22]. These translations preserve types, provided we let S have type $(\tau \to \tau' \to \tau'') \to (\tau \to \tau') \to \tau \to \tau''$, K have type $\tau \to \tau' \to \tau$ for every types τ, τ', τ'', and tt' have type τ' when t has type $\tau \to \tau'$ and t' has type τ. Moreover, SK augmented with Curry's equations $\mathcal{C}$ [3] defines an equality $=_{\text{SK}}$ by $t =_{\text{SK}} t'$ iff $\text{SK} \wedge \mathcal{C} \vdash_= t \doteq t'$, such that $t =_\lambda t' \Leftrightarrow (t)_{\text{SK}} =_{\text{SK}} (t')_{\text{SK}}$ and $t =_{\text{SK}} t' \Leftrightarrow (t)_\lambda =_\lambda (t')_\lambda$. These equations encode the rule (ξ), which is not a consequence of SK: for all SK-terms t and t', $t =_{\text{SK}} t' \Rightarrow (\lambda x \cdot t)_{\text{SK}} =_{\text{SK}} (\lambda x \cdot t')_{\text{SK}}$ holds.

The problem with SK, however, is that, although there are translations from λ-terms to SK-terms that produce polynomial-sized SK-terms (even linear-sized [6]) in polynomial time, no such translation can produce normalized SK-terms. In fact, SK-normal forms for translations of λ-terms need an exponential amount of space (precisely, it is exponential in the number of nested λ-abstractions). Although the procedure we shall present can deal quite easily with non-normalized terms, normalization is a quite practical simplification algorithm for which we should not need exponential space. The problem has already been dealt with in the area of compilation of functional languages (see [9]), where alternative combinatory bases have been used. One of the simplest basis to correct this problem is Curry's CBWK basis:

- $Cxyz \doteq xzy$, $C : (\alpha \to \beta \to \gamma) \to \beta \to \alpha \to \gamma$
- $Bxyz \doteq x(yz)$, $B : (\beta \to \gamma) \to (\alpha \to \beta) \to \alpha \to \gamma$
- $Wxy \doteq xyy$, $W : (\alpha \to \alpha \to \beta) \to \alpha \to \beta$
- $Kxy \doteq x$, $K : \alpha \to \beta \to \alpha$

Again, there are translations $(.)_{\mathrm{CBWK}}$ from λ-terms to CBWK-terms and $(.)_\lambda$ in the converse direction. Here are the definitions, following those of similar operations for SK in [22], section 9C, p.99. If x is a variable, then $(x)_{\mathrm{CBWK}} = x$; $(\lambda x \cdot t)_{\mathrm{CBWK}} = \lambda^* x \cdot (t)_{\mathrm{CBWK}}$; and $(tt')_{\mathrm{CBWK}} = (t)_{\mathrm{CBWK}}(t')_{\mathrm{CBWK}}$, where λ^* is either λ^β (preserving β-equivalence) or λ^η (preserving $\beta\eta$-equivalence):

- $\lambda^\eta x \cdot x = WK$, • $\lambda^\eta x \cdot t = Kt$ if $x \notin \mathrm{fv}(t)$, • $\lambda^\eta x \cdot tx = t$ if $x \notin \mathrm{fv}(t)$,
- $\lambda^\eta x \cdot tt' = Bt(\lambda^\eta x \cdot t')$ if $x \notin \mathrm{fv}(t)$, $x \in \mathrm{fv}(t')$ and $x \neq t'$,
- $\lambda^\eta x \cdot tt' = C(\lambda^\eta x \cdot t)t'$ if $x \in \mathrm{fv}(t)$, $x \notin \mathrm{fv}(t')$,
- $\lambda^\eta x \cdot tt' = W(\lambda^\eta x_1 \cdot \lambda^\eta x_2 \cdot t[x_1/x]t'[x_2/x])$ if $x \in \mathrm{fv}(t)$, $x \in \mathrm{fv}(t')$, with x_1 and x_2 two new variables.

and:

- $\lambda^\beta x \cdot x = WK$, • $\lambda^\beta x \cdot t = Kt$ if $x \notin \mathrm{fv}(t)$,
- $\lambda^\beta x \cdot tt' = Bt(\lambda^\eta x \cdot t')$ if $x \notin \mathrm{fv}(t)$, $x \in \mathrm{fv}(t')$,
- $\lambda^\beta x \cdot tt' = C(\lambda^\eta x \cdot t)t'$ if $x \in \mathrm{fv}(t)$, $x \notin \mathrm{fv}(t')$,
- $\lambda^\beta x \cdot tt' = W(\lambda^\eta x_1 \cdot \lambda^\eta x_2 \cdot t[x_1/x]t'[x_1/x])$ if $x \in \mathrm{fv}(t)$, $x \in \mathrm{fv}(t')$, with x_1 et x_2 two new variables,

and where the last three λ^η are not typos. $(.)_\lambda$ is defined in the obvious way. These translations have the properties that $(.)_{\mathrm{CBWK}} \circ (.)_\lambda$ is the identity, and are doable in polynomial time.

To give an idea of the conciseness of CBWK terms, we take some examples from Huet's work on higher-order resolution [24]. The term $\lambda x_\iota \cdot \neg Fxx$, arising as solution for Cantor's theorem, is $S(K\neg)(SF(SKK))$ in SK, and $B\neg(WF)$ in CBWK. The term $\bigcap(\lambda x_\iota \cdot Fz \leq z)$ (Knaster-Tarski's least fixed point) is $\bigcap(S(S(K(\leq))F)(SKK))$ in SK and $\bigcap(W(B(\leq)F))$ in CBWK. Finally, $\lambda z \cdot F(Gz)$ and $G(Z(\lambda z \cdot F(Gz))E)$ (pigeonhole problem) are $S(KF)G$ and $G(Z(S(KF)G)E)$ in SK, and BFG and $G(Z(BFGE))$ in CBWK.

We need to define Curry's equations $\mathcal{C}$ ensuring that equality in CBWK $\wedge\, \mathcal{C}$ corresponds to equality in λ-calculus. Finding them follows the same pattern as for SK (see [3], section 7.3); we give them here without proof (see [18]):

Definition 1 *Define the following abbreviations:* $B' = BB$, $I = WK$, $J = BK$, $J' = BJ$, $I_1 = CBI$, $C_2 = BC$, $C_3 = BC_2$, $W_2 = BW$, $W_3 = BW_2$, $W_4 = BW_3$, $B_2 = B'B$, $B_{2,1} = BB'$, $B_{1,2} = B_{2,1}B'$, $B_{3,1} = BB_{2,1}$, $S = BW_2(C_2B')$.

Curry's equations C_β for β-equivalence are axioms 1 and 3–10 below, and axioms $C_{\beta\eta}$ for $\beta\eta$-equivalence are 2–7 and 11-13 below:

1. $W_3(C_2(B_{2,1}J)) \doteq JI_1$ 2. $W_3(C_2(B_{2,1}J)) \doteq K$

3. $W_4(C_3(B_{3,1}(W_3(C_2B_{1,2})))) \doteq W_4(C(B'(B'(C_2B')))S)$

4. $W_4(C_3(B_{3,1}(W_3(C_2(B_{2,1}C_2))))) \doteq W_4(C_2(C_3(B_{3,1}S)))$

5. $W_3(C_2(B_{2,1}W_2)) \doteq W_3(W_2(C_3(B_{3,1}S)))$ 6. $J \doteq CB_2K$ 7. $J \doteq C_2K$

8. $J \doteq W_3(J'J)$ 9. $C \doteq W_3(BJ'C)$ 10. $B \doteq W_3(J'B)$

11. $I \doteq W_2J$ 12. $I \doteq W_2K$ 13. $I \doteq I_1$

Finally, notice that these equations are well-typed.

5 Rigid E-Unification and Congruence Closure

We recap some of the most important points of Goubault's approach to rigid E-unification [19]. Recall that the problem is that of finding a substitution σ such that $E\sigma \vdash_{0,=} s\sigma \doteq t\sigma$. Goubault extends this to finding σ such that $E\sigma \vdash_{0,=} F\sigma$ for general systems of equations E and F, and notices that this is equivalent to finding an idempotent σ such that $E \wedge E(\sigma) \vdash_{0,=} F$, where $E(\sigma)$ is the conjunction of equations $x \doteq x\sigma$ for all variables x in the domain of σ.

Goubault's algorithm works by propagating non-deterministically a 4-tuple (E, F, B, μ), where E and F are as above, B is the set of variables that become bound by unification, and μ is a set of already considered equations, ensuring termination. E is represented by a Union-Find structure, as in the congruence closure algorithm [11].

A Union-Find structure is a collection of inverted trees represented finite equivalence classes of terms; given a term t, a canonical representant of the class of t is given by following links upward to the root $find(t)$ of the tree, which is a canonical representative of the class of t; we call roots *colors*. Merging classes of different colors c and c' can be done by adding a link from, say, c to c', considering c' as the new root; this is the *union* procedure. Congruence closure is built on this mechanism by propagating mergings upward in the term structure. We give here Nelson and Oppen's version [29]. We assume that *list* maps every color to the list of applications having at least one argument of this color. The following procedure *merge* updates the Union-Find structure so as to represent the finest congruence coarser than the current one that makes equal its arguments. To compute $merge(u, v)$:

1. if $find(u) = find(v)$, return;
2. call $union(u, v)$;
3. for all $s \in list(u)$, $t \in list(v)$, if $find(s) \neq find(t)$ and $congruent(s, t)$, then call $merge(s, t)$.

where $congruent(s, t)$ is true iff $s = t$, or $s = f(s_1, \ldots, s_m)$, $t = f(t_1, \ldots, t_m)$ and, for all i, $find(s_i) = find(t_i)$. To make this propagation as fast possible, auxiliary structures are used to represent sets of applications that have at least one argument of any given color: the function *list* and a *signature table* in [11].

$$\textbf{(Norm)}\ (E, F \cup \{s \doteq t\}, B, \mu) \mapsto (E, F \cup \{color_E(s) \doteq color_E(t)\}, B, \mu)$$
$$\text{if } color_E(s) \neq s \text{ or } color_E(t) \neq t$$

(1) Normalization

(Delete) $(E, F \cup \{c \doteq c'\}, B, \mu) \mapsto (E, F, B, \mu)$ if $c = c'$

(Decomp) $(E, F \cup \{c \doteq c'\}, B, \mu) \mapsto (E, F \cup \{t_1 \doteq t'_1, \ldots, t_m \doteq t'_m\}, B, \mu \cup \{c \doteq c'\})$
if $c \neq c'$, $(c \doteq c') \notin \mu$ and
for $f(t_1, \ldots, t_m) \in EqApp_E(c)$, $f'(t'_1, \ldots, t'_{m'}) \in EqApp_E(c')$,
with $f = f'$, $m = m'$ and $f \not\sim^+_{E,B} f$

(Mutate) $(E, F \cup \{c \doteq c'\}, B, \mu) \mapsto (E, F, \{s_1 \doteq t_1, \ldots, s_m \doteq t_m,$
$s'_1 \doteq t'_1, \ldots, s'_{m'} \doteq t'_{m'}, f(s_1, \ldots, s_m) \doteq f'(s'_1, \ldots, s'_{m'})\}, B, \mu \cup \{c \doteq c'\})$
if $c \neq c'$, $(c \doteq c') \notin \mu$ and
for $f(t_1, \ldots, t_m) \in EqApp_E(c)$, $f'(t'_1, \ldots, t'_{m'}) \in EqApp_E(c')$,
$f(s_1, \ldots, s_m) \in ST(E \cup F \cup \{c, c'\})$,
$f'(s'_1, \ldots, s'_{m'}) \in ST(E \cup F \cup \{c, c'\})$ with $f \sim^+_{E,B} f'$

(Bind) $(E, F \cup \{c \doteq c'\}, B, \mu) \mapsto (E \cup \{x \doteq c'\}, F \cup \{c \doteq c'\}, B \cup \{x\}, \emptyset)$
if $c \neq c'$ and $x \in (SVar_E \cup EqVar_E(c)) \setminus (B \cup EssVar_E(c'))$

(Guess) $(E, F \cup \{c \doteq c'\}, B, \mu) \mapsto (E \cup \{x \doteq f(t_1, \ldots, t_m)\},$
$F \cup \{f(t_1, \ldots, t_m) \doteq c'\}, B \cup \{x\}, \emptyset)$
if $c \neq c'$, $f(t_1, \ldots, t_m) \in ST(E \cup F \cup \{c, c'\})$
and $x \in EqVar_E(c) \setminus (B \cup EssVar_E(f(t_1, \ldots, t_m)))$

(2) Rules on colors

Fig. 1. Rules for rigid E-unification

The latter is a map from terms of the form $f(c_1, \ldots, c_m)$, where the c_i are colors, to the common color of all terms $f(t_1, \ldots, t_m)$ such that t_i has color c_i, for all i.

In the roots of Union-Find trees, we can store all sorts of information on colors. Goubault uses this to provide functions $color_E$ ($c = color_E(t)$ returns the color c of t modulo E after possibly adding t and its subterms as nodes to the Union-Find trees), $EssVar_E$ (mapping colors c to the set of variables *essentially free* in c, i.e. occurring free in all terms of color c), $EqApp_E$ (mapping colors c to the set of non-variable terms of color c), $EqVar_E$ (mapping c to the set of variables of color c), and the set $SVar_E$ of variables that are sides of equations in E. He also defines a partial equivalence relation $\sim^+_E$ between function symbols, transitive closure of $\sim_E$ such that $f \sim_E f'$ iff there are two distinct applications of f and f' with the same colors; and $\sim^+_{E,B}$ such that $f \sim^+_{E,B} f'$ iff $f \sim^+_E f'$ or $SVar_E \setminus B \neq \emptyset$. The non-deterministic transformation rules are given in Fig. 1.

To find σ such that $E_0\sigma \vdash_{0,=} F_0\sigma$, we start the procedure with $(E_0, F_0, \emptyset, \emptyset)$. The fundamental result is that the procedure terminates in polynomial time on each computation path, and the set of outcomes (E, F, B, μ) such that $F = \emptyset$ is a complete set of implicit representations of rigid E-unifiers, in the sense that, if $s(E, B)$ is the restriction of $color_E$ to B and $\equiv_E$ is the relation defined by $\sigma_1 \equiv_E \sigma_2$ iff $E \cup E(\sigma_1) \vdash_{0,=} E(\sigma_2)$ and $E \cup E(\sigma_2) \vdash_{0,=} E(\sigma_1)$ (i.e, $E(\sigma_1)$ and $E(\sigma_2)$ define the same equational theories modulo E), then: for every outcome

$(E, \emptyset, B, \mu)$, there is an idempotent σ such that $E(\sigma) \equiv_{E_0} E(s(E, B))$; and for every rigid E-unifier σ of F_0 modulo E_0, there is a substitution σ' and an outcome of the procedure such that $E(s(E, B)) \cup E(\sigma') \equiv_{E_0} E(\sigma)$[1]. In short, the $s(E, B)$'s are concise forms for rigid E-unifiers; we get all rigid E-unifiers by instantiating them (adding the equations of $E(\sigma')$) and replacing equals by equals modulo E_0. Any $s(E, B)$ therefore represents many different rigid E-unifiers, enough so that we need only a finite number of them to represent all rigid E-unifiers.

In the case where terms are simply typed (with type variables), as they are in our typed combinatory logic framework, we use the following trick, due to Dahl [7], allowing us to encode types in the terms themselves: create a new binary function symbol $\mathbf{T}$, and replace any first-order term t of type τ that is not already an application of $\mathbf{T}$ or a type, by $\mathbf{T}(t, \tau)$ (recall that we have defined types as terms). This translates the typed case into the untyped case. In practice, however, we dispense with this encoding: as all equal terms always have the same type, it is enough to restrict all rules of Fig. 1 so that they generate only well-typed equations by (syntactically) unifying the types of their sides and propagating bindings of type variables together with other bindings in E and B.

6 Higher-Order Rigid E-unification

Let $\mathcal{C}$ be the set of Curry equations of Section 4 for β or $\beta\eta$-equivalence, CBWK be the axioms for C, B, W and K. Let $\forall \mathbf{x} \cdot \text{CBWK} \wedge \mathcal{C}$ be the universal quantification closure of CBWK$\wedge\mathcal{C}$. Notice that, although $\mathcal{C}$ is ground in the untyped case, Dahl's translation introduces free type variables, which are universally quantified, and so are part of the $\mathbf{x}$ variables. A more careful examination of how closed combinators are typed would show that we do not need to consider Curry's equations as non-closed, by changing slightly the way we unify types of terms; we won't develop this here, as it would uselessly complicate the exposition. Let also $\mathcal{E}$ be a system of well-typed equations among simply-typed λ-terms.

Then, for any two well-typed λ-terms s and t of the same type τ, $\mathcal{E} \vdash_= s\sigma \doteq_\lambda t\sigma$ if and only if $\forall \boldsymbol{\alpha} \cdot (\forall \mathbf{x} \cdot \text{CBWK} \wedge \mathcal{C} \wedge (\mathcal{E})_{\text{CBWK}}) \vdash_= (s)_{\text{CBWK}} \doteq (t)_{\text{CBWK}}$, where $\boldsymbol{\alpha}$ is the list of type variables in τ, and $\mathbf{x}$ is that of all term and type variables in CBWK, $\mathcal{C}$ and $(\mathcal{E})_{\text{CBWK}}$ (the latter being the system of equations whose sides are translated by $(.)_{\text{CBWK}}$). This amounts to $(\forall \mathbf{x} \cdot \text{CBWK} \wedge \mathcal{C} \wedge (\mathcal{E})_{\text{CBWK}}) \vdash_= (s)_{\text{CBWK}} \doteq (t)_{\text{CBWK}}$, where all type variables in $\boldsymbol{\alpha}$ are replaced by new type constants (this is skolemization in positive form). And, finally, by Herbrand-Gallier's theorem, the latter is equivalent to finding integers i, j, k such that CBWK copied i times, $\mathcal{C}$ copied j times and $\mathcal{E}$ copied k times entails $(s)_{\text{CBWK}} \doteq (t)_{\text{CBWK}}$ by the $\vdash_{0,=}$ relation. Notice that, to do this, we need to rigidify types as well, i.e. to rename not only term variables, but also type variables into fresh ones in each copy.

In an implementation, we won't actually fix i, j and k and solve the resulting decidable rigid E-unification problem, but interleave rigid E-unification steps

[1] The completeness theorem in [19] is erroneous; this is the correct formulation, as in the errata sheet of [20].

with so-called *amplification* steps, as in Gallier et al.'s method [12], which increment them as needed by adding new copies of the original equations. Standard techniques [4, 18] in automated theorem proving can then be used to control the search for rigid and non-rigid higher-order E-unifiers.

6.1 Flexible Terms and Rigid Preunification

The specificity of λ-calculus is hidden by the encoding into combinatory terms, but can be recovered by suitable auxiliary algorithmic tricks. One of the most important particularities of λ-calculus is that, in some sense, the role of free variables in first-order unification is really played by flexible terms in λ-calculus. This observation was made by Huet, and leads to his notion of preunification [25]. In the same vein, we define higher-order rigid E-preunification.

Flexible terms t are defined by Huet as terms in normal form, of the form $\lambda x_1 \dots x_m \cdot x t_1 \dots t_n$, where x is free. We then say that t is *flexible* in x. If the type of t is $\tau_1 \to \dots \to \tau_m \to \tau_{m+1} \to \dots \to \tau_{m+p} \to \tau$, with τ not of the form $\tau' \to \tau''$, and t_i has type τ_i', then x can be replaced by $\lambda y'_{1\ \tau'_1} \dots y'_{n\ \tau'_n} y_{1\ \tau_{m+1}} \dots y_{p\ \tau_{m+p}} \cdot v(\tau)$, where v is a fixed function symbol not in the original problem with $v(\tau) : \tau$. Therefore, systems of flexible terms are always unifiable (in the non-rigid sense); moreover, with $\beta\eta$-equivalence, any flexible term in x is always unifiable with any term t' such that $x \notin \mathrm{fv}(t')$, by binding x to $\lambda y'_{1\ \tau'_1} \dots y'_{n\ \tau'_n} \cdot t' x_1 \dots x_m$.

The key to the efficiency of Huet's procedure is mainly due to these remarks, and we wish to incorporate them in our procedure. We therefore modify the procedure of Fig. 1 so that it stops when all equations $c \doteq c'$ between colors in F are such that both c and c' are colors of flexible terms. In the $\beta\eta$-equivalence case, we can moreover stop when $F = \{c_1 \doteq c'_1, \dots, c_m \doteq c'_m, \dots, c_n \doteq c'_n\}$ where c_i is flexible in some variable x_i not essentially free in c'_i or $c_j \doteq c'_j$, $i < j \leq m$, and c_j and c'_j, $m < j \leq n$, are flexible in variables other than the x_i's, $1 \leq i \leq m$. We call the resulting couple (E, F) a *triangular presolved form* for the initial problem.

Such a presolved form is a concise representation of many solved forms for the higher-order rigid E-unification problem with i copies of equations in $\mathcal{E}$, j' copies of CBWK and k' copies of $\mathcal{C}$, with $j' \geq j$, $k' \geq k$. Notice that in general we cannot guarantee $j' = j'$ and $k' = k$, but this is of no harm when we really want to solve higher-order E-unification problems.

The only remaining problem is to recognize colors of flexible terms. To do this, we first have to recognize flexible terms in combinatory logic. Let's write $f^n x$ for $\underbrace{f(\dots(f\,x)\dots)}_{n \text{ times}}$, and $=$ for provable equality in CBWK $\wedge\ \mathcal{C}$. We then translate our syntactic criterion for flexibility above into a semantic one:

Definition 2 *Let t be a term of* CBWK, *$x : \tau_1 \to \dots \to \tau_m \to \tau$ be free in t, with τ not a function type (we say that τ is x's* kind, *up to variable renaming, and that m is its* arity*).*

t is flexible *in x if and only if $t[K^m y/x] = K^n y$, where y is a new variable of type τ, and n is the arity of t.*

This is needed as colors do not necessarily represent λ-terms in normal form. Notice also that in higher-order E-unification, a term may be flexible in several different variables (consider $\lambda x \cdot y$ in the context of equation $y \doteq z$).

To recognize most flexible terms syntactically, we now define the following family of closed terms (closed except for type variables):

Definition 3 *The set of* K-terms *is the smallest set such that* B, C, K *and* W *are* K*-terms; if* t *is a* K*-term, then* Wt, Bt *and* $C(Kt)$*, when typable, are* K*-terms; if* t *and* t' *are* K*-terms, then* Btt' *and* Ctt'*, when typable, are* K*-terms.*

Lemma 1. *Let* t *be a* K*-term. For every* y *of non-function type, for every* $m \geq 0$*, if* $t(K^m y)$ *is typable, then for some* $n \geq 0$, $t(K^m y) = K^n y$.

Proof: By structural induction on K-terms:

- $B(K^m y) = \lambda zz' \cdot K^m y(zz')$, which is typable only if $m \geq 1$, and then $B(K^m y) = \lambda zz' \cdot K^{m-1} y = K^{m+1} y$, so that $n = m + 1$.
- $C(K^m y) = \lambda zz' \cdot K^m yz'z$, which is typable only if $m \geq 2$, and then $C(K^m y) = \lambda zz' \cdot K^{m-2} y = K^m y$, so that $n = m$.
- $K(K^m y) = K^{m+1} y$, so that $n = m + 1$;
- $W(K^m y) = \lambda x \cdot K^m yxx$, which is typable only if $m \geq 2$, and which is then $\lambda x \cdot K^{m-2} y = K^{m-1} y$;
- $Wt(K^m y) = t(K^m y)(K^m y) = K^{m'} y(K^m y)$ for some $m' \geq 1$, i.e. $n = m' - 1$.
- $Bt(K^m y) = \lambda z \cdot t(K^m yz)$, which is typable only if $m \geq 1$, and then $Bt(K^m y) = \lambda z \cdot t(K^{m-1} y) = \lambda z \cdot K^{m'} y$ for some $m' \geq 0$, so $n = m' + 1$.
- $C(Kt)(K^m y) = \lambda z \cdot Ktz(K^m y) = \lambda z \cdot t(K^m y) = \lambda z \cdot K^{m'} y$ for some $m' \geq 0$, which is equal to $K^{m'+1} y$.
- $Btt'(K^m y) = t(t'(K^m y)) = t(K^{m'} y)$ for some $m' \geq 0$, which is equal to $K^{m''} y$, for some $m'' \geq 0$.
- $Ctt'(K^m y) = t(K^m y)t' = K^{m'} yt'$ for some $m' \geq 1$, so $n = m' - 1$.

□

Let's call *unbound* variables the free variables that are outside the set B in the 4-tuple (E, F, B, μ) of the procedure in Fig. 1. Then:

Definition 4 *The set of* strongly flexible terms *in the unbound variable* x *is the smallest set containing* x*, and such that if* t *is strongly flexible in* x*, then* $t't$ *and* tt'' *are strongly flexible in* x*, for every* K*-term* t' *and every term* t'' *such that these expressions type-check.*

Lemma 2. *Every strongly flexible term in* x *is flexible in* x

Proof: By induction on the formation rules of strongly flexible terms.

Call a term t (m, n)*-flexible* in x iff $t[K^m y/x] = K^n y$. We shall assume that the kind is always a non-variable type: if it was a variable α, we could always replace α by some type of arbitrary large arity and of constant kind, which would reduce this case to the previous one, since then a (m, n)-flexible term is $(m + k, n + k)$-flexible for every $k \geq 0$.

First, variables x are (m,m)-flexible.

Second, let t be (m,n)-flexible. Then $t[K^m y/x] = K^n y$. If tt' is typable, then $n \geq 1$, so $(tt')[K^m y/x] = K^n y(t'[K^m y/x]) = K(K^{n-1}y)(t'[K^m y/x]) = K^{n-1}y$, and tt' is $(m, n-1)$-flexible.

Third, let t be (m,n)-flexible, and t' be a K-term. Then $(t't)[K^m y/x] = (t'[K^m y/x])(t[K^m y/x]) = (t'[K^m y/x])(K^n y) = t'(K^n y)$ since t' is closed, and this is $K^{n'} y$ for some $n' \geq 0$ by Lemma 1. So $t't$ is (m,n')-flexible. □

Moreover, the strongly flexible terms correspond to Huet's flexible terms:

Lemma 3. *For any unbound variable x other than the x_i's, $(\lambda x_1 \ldots x_n \cdot x t_1 \ldots t_m)_{\text{CBWK}}$ is strongly flexible.*

Proof: By induction on n. If $n = 0$, the lemma is proved. Then, if t is a strongly flexible term in x, we show that $\lambda^* y \cdot t$, with $y \neq x$, is strongly flexible in x by induction on the number of steps we used to build $\lambda^* y \cdot t$ from t.

If $t = x$, then $\lambda^* y \cdot t = Kx$, which is strongly flexible.

If $t = t't''$, with t' strongly flexible, then $\lambda^* y \cdot t = Kt$ if $y \notin \text{fv}(t)$, $\lambda^* y \cdot t = C(\lambda^* y \cdot t')t''$ if $y \notin \text{fv}(t'')$ and $y \in \text{fv}(t')$, $\lambda^* y \cdot t = Bt'(\lambda^* y \cdot t'')$ if $y \in \text{fv}(t'')$ and $y \notin \text{fv}(t')$, except possibly $\lambda^* y \cdot t = t'$ if $t'' = y$ and λ^* is λ^η, at last $\lambda^* y \cdot t = W(\lambda^* y_1 y_2 \cdot (\lambda^* y \cdot t')y_1((\lambda^* y \cdot t')y_2))$, where all these terms are strongly flexible by induction hypothesis.

If $t = t''t'$, with t'' a K-term (hence closed), and t' a strongly flexible term, then $\lambda^* y \cdot t = Kt$ if $y \notin \text{fv}(t')$, or $\lambda^* y \cdot t = Bt''(\lambda^* y \cdot t')$ otherwise, and all these terms are strongly flexible by induction hypothesis. □

We now want to identify colors of flexible terms. But we can encode this in the roots c of the Union-Find trees, by adding a field `flex` for the set of all variables in which some t such that $color_E(t) = c$ is strongly flexible.

We also make room for a `Kflags` field to determine K-termness. This field is a set of flags among `K`, and auxiliary flags `BK`, `CK`, and `KK`. A term is a K-term if and only if the `Kflags` field of its color contains `K`.

Maintaining these fields is performed by modifying the *union* procedure. We ensure that these sets are the smallest such that the following rules are satisfied, where `flex`(c) is the `flex` field of the color c and `Kflags`(c) is its `Kflags` field (we have written cc' for the common color of any application of a term of color c to a term of color c', if they are in the Union-Find structure):

$$\texttt{K} \in \texttt{Kflags}(find(t)), \text{ where } t \text{ is } C, B, W \text{ or } K$$

$$\frac{c = find(W) \quad \texttt{K} \in \texttt{Kflags}(c')}{\texttt{K} \in \texttt{Kflags}(cc')}$$

$$\frac{c = find(B) \quad \texttt{K} \in \texttt{Kflags}(c')}{\texttt{K}, \texttt{BK} \in \texttt{Kflags}(cc')} \qquad \frac{\texttt{BK} \in \texttt{Kflags}(c) \quad \texttt{K} \in \texttt{Kflags}(c')}{\texttt{K} \in \texttt{Kflags}(cc')}$$

$$\frac{c = find(C) \quad \texttt{K} \in \texttt{Kflags}(c')}{\texttt{CK} \in \texttt{Kflags}(cc')} \qquad \frac{\texttt{CK} \in \texttt{Kflags}(c) \quad \texttt{K} \in \texttt{Kflags}(c')}{\texttt{K} \in \texttt{Kflags}(cc')}$$

$$\frac{c = find(K) \quad \texttt{K} \in \texttt{Kflags}(c')}{\texttt{KK} \in \texttt{Kflags}(cc')} \qquad \frac{c = find(C) \quad \texttt{KK} \in \texttt{Kflags}(c')}{\texttt{K} \in \texttt{Kflags}(cc')}$$

$$x \in \texttt{flex}(find(x)) \quad \frac{x \in \texttt{flex}(c)}{x \in \texttt{flex}(cc')} \quad \frac{\texttt{K} \in \texttt{Kflags}(c) \; x \in \texttt{flex}(c')}{x \in \texttt{flex}(cc')}$$

The $union(u, v)$ procedure is then modified so that it does in addition: compute the set $Kflags_1$ of the flags of u with respect to the **Kflags** fields of the colors of its subterms (found by composing $find$ with $list$), and the set $flex_1$ of flex-variables of u as a function of the **flex** and **Kflags** fields of the colors of its subterms. Do the same with v, getting $Kflags_2$ and $flex_2$; then set the **Kflags**(u) to $Kflags_1 \cup Kflags_2$, and **flex**(u) to $flex_1 \cup flex_2$, where u is the new root of the Union-Find tree after $union$. The **Kflags** sets can be represented as bit-vectors in a machine word, and **flags** can be coded as multiple-word bit-vectors, provided variables are given short indexes; then all operations are polynomial-time computable.

6.2 Colored Normalization

At each step of the rigid E-unification algorithm, where the problem has the form $(E, F \cup \{c \doteq c'\}, B, \mu)$, we can also reduce the equation $c \doteq c'$ by the known properties of λ-calculus. For example, if c has the form Ktt', we can add the equation $Ktt' \doteq t$ to E, enabling **(Delete)** to take place more rapidly.

To do this, we need to identify redexes modulo colors. As in the previous section, we can recognize them by propagating flags associated with colors upwards (sets of flags will again be stored in a new field **labels** in the roots of Union-Find trees). For example, to recognize redexes of the form Ktt', we create flags **K1**, **K2** and **Kredex** such that only the color of K has flag **K1**, any color of an application $@(u, v)$ where u has the **K1** flag has the **K2** flag, and any color of an application uv where u has the **K2** flag has the **Kredex** flag, so that colors of K-redexes are precisely those having the **Kredex** flag.

Then, knowing that c is the color of a redex Ktt', we can find the colors of all possible such t's by going down the term structure: they can be found thanks to the $EqApp_E$ map, which precisely retrieves all possible argument lists (and head function symbols) from a given color.

To maintain these fields, we modify the $merge$ procedure of the congruence closure algorithm, which is responsible for identifying two colors c and c' and propagating the new equational consequences upward in the term structure. We have it take a third argument l, which is a set of flags to add to the new $union(c, c')$, then $merge(u, v, l)$ is:

1. if $find(u) = find(v)$ and $l \subseteq$ **labels**($find(u)$), return;
2. let l' be the set of labels of $find(u)$ or $find(v)$, union l;
3. call $union(u, v)$ and set the **labels** fields of $find(u)$ and $find(v)$ to l';
4. compute $list(u)$ and $list(v)$, and $l'' = \bigcup_{k \in l'} up(k)$;
5. for every $s \in list(u)$, $t \in list(v)$, if $congruent(s, t)$, then call $merge(s, t, l'')$.

where up(**K1**) $= \{$**K2**$\}$, up(**K2**) $= \{$**Kredex**$\}$. This procedure is sound, terminates since the number of labels times the number of colors is finite. The addition of new equations $Ktt' = t$ to E must also terminate, since simply-typed λ-calculus is strongly normalizing.

Of course, we can encode any redex in this way, and not only CBWK-redexes, but also λ-redexes that are not CBWK-redexes, which would otherwise need

Curry's equations to be recognized. Notice that this may also ease the recognition of flexible terms, by equating terms with strongly flexible terms.

7 Conclusion

We have presented a complete method for solving higher-order E-unification problems by rigidifying them, using combinatory systems and rigid E-unification, improved by using specificities of the λ-calculus like flexible terms and termination of normalization. We have improved Dougherty and Johann's approach to higher-order unification by using a better combinatory basis, by identifying flexible terms and defining presolved forms, and by providing some optimizations of the basic procedure. Alternatively, we can see our work as a generalization of Gallier et al.'s work on rigid E-unification to the higher-order case.

For the moment, we feel that this method is not really practical, because little work has yet been done on rigid E-unification, and current algorithms are still costly; and because, although CBWK is more usable than SK, it is still rather basic and needs many instances of its axioms to prove even simple equalities.

However, first, rigid E-unification is a rather recent invention, so we hope for drastic improvements on the current algorithms; second, we always have the choice to change our combinatory basis. In this respect, the experience gained in the 1980's in compilation of functional languages [9] should profitably be used to design more expressive computational paradigms based on combinators. Actually, because of Turner's remark that combinators and graph reduction techniques are of the same nature, it might be possible to benefit from work on optimal reduction of λ-calculus, as originated by Lévy [26]. As the number of reduction steps needed to prove equality of two λ-terms is somehow related to the number of instances of reduction axioms needed to prove it, the more efficient the computational paradigm, the more efficient the higher-order rigid E-unification procedure based on it should be.

On the other hand, using combinators and rigid E-unification shows great potential. First, this approach translates higher-order problems into first-order ones, for which many optimization techniques and heuristics have been designed over the years; and it does not preclude the use of higher-order specific optimizations, as we have done. Second, in this approach, we do not need to normalize terms before unification, as in other approaches; as normalization can take quite a long time [35], this may accelerate the discovery of unifiers in some cases; moreover, when several unifications have to be done in sequence, this dispenses us from normalizing (although we can always partially normalize, as we have done). Third, our method shows a great degree of sharing, or reuse, of facts: common subterms are shared in a Union-Find structure, partial proofs of equality of terms are shared as equations stored in this very structure (so that our procedure *memoizes* partial proofs), and we have noticed that our representation for rigid E-unifiers is quite concise, so that it represents many rigid E-unifiers at once. Fourth, this approach is not tied to Church's simple type system (constant-only types), and provides type variables and ML-like datatypes (since we never restricted $\rightarrow$ to be the only function symbol for constructing types; for example, we can introduce a unary function symbol l such that $l(\tau)$ is the type of lists of objects of type τ). Finally, this approach is easily extended to other combinatory-based or λ-based theories, like Scott–Milner's LCF [17] (which is basically typed λ-calculus enriched with Gödel recursors and fixpoint operators in each type[2]), even untyped ones like Bunder's formulation of naive set theory [5] or Holmes' systems TRC (resp. TRCU) [23] that is strongly related to Quine's NF set theory (resp. with urelements).

Acknowledgements

I wish to thank Jean Gallier and Gérard Huet for their encouraging support.

References

1. P. B. Andrews. Theorem proving via general matings. *J.ACM*, 28(2):193–214, 1981.
2. P. B. Andrews, D. Miller, E. Cohen, and F. Pfenning. Automating higher-order logic. *Contemporary Mathematics*, 29:169–192, 1984.
3. H. Barendregt. *The Lambda Calculus, Its Syntax and Semantics*, volume 103. North-Holland, 1984.
4. W. Bibel. *Automated Theorem Proving.* Vieweg, 2nd edition, 1987.
5. M. W. Bunder. Predicate calculus and naive set theory in pure combinatory logic. *Archiv für Mathematische Logik und Grundlagenforschung*, 21:169–177, 1981.
6. F. W. Burton. A linear space translation of functional programs to Turner combinators. *Information Processing Letters*, 14(5):201–204, 1982.
7. V. Dahl. Translating Spanish into logic through logic. *American Journal of Computational Linguistics*, 7:149–164, 1981.
8. J. Darlington. A partial mechanization of second-order logic. *Machine Intelligence*, 6:91–100, 1971.
9. A. Diller. *Compiling Functional Languages.* John Wiley and Sons, 1988.
10. D. J. Dougherty and P. Johann. A combinatory logic approach to higher-order E-unification. In *11th CADE*, LNAI 607, pages 79–93. Springer, 1992.
11. P. K. Downey, R. Sethi, and R. E. Tarjan. Variations on the common subexpression problem. *J.ACM*, 27(4):758–771, 1980.
12. J. Gallier, P. Narendran, S. Raatz, and W. Snyder. Theorem proving using equational matings and rigid E-unification. *J.ACM*, 39(2):377–429, 1992.
13. J. Gallier, S. Raatz, and W. Snyder. Theorem proving using rigid E-unification equational matings. In *2nd LICS*, pages 338–346, 1987.
14. J. Gallier and W. Snyder. Designing unification procedures using transformations: A survey. In I. Moschovakis, editor, *Workshop on Logic From Computer Science*, MSRI, Berkeley, CA, USA, 1989.
15. J. Gallier and W. Snyder. Higher-order unification revisited: Complete sets of transformations. *J.Symb.Comp.*, 8:101–140, 1989.

[2] Notice then that we can still use colored normalization, except we must now explicitly limit the number of fixpoint redexes we reduce.

16. J. Gallier, W. Snyder, P. Narendran, and D. Plaisted. Rigid E-unification is NP-complete. In *3rd LICS*, pages 218–227, 1988.
17. M. J. C. Gordon, R. Milner, and C. Wadsworth. *Edinburgh LCF, A Mechanical Logic of Computation*. LNCS 78. Springer, 1979.
18. J. Goubault. *Démonstration automatique en logique classique : complexité et méthodes*. PhD thesis, École Polytechnique, Palaiseau, France, 1993.
19. J. Goubault. A rule-based algorithm for rigid E-unification. In A. Leitsch, editor, *Third Kurt Gödel Colloquium*, LNCS 713. Springer Verlag, 1993.
20. J. Goubault. A rule-based algorithm for rigid E-unification. Technical Report 93024, Bull S.A., 1993.
21. J. R. Hindley. The principal type scheme of an object in combinatory logic. *Trans.AMS*, 146:29–60, 1969.
22. J. R. Hindley and J. P. Seldin. *Introduction to Combinators and λ-Calculus*, volume 1. Cambridge University Press, 1988.
23. R. Holmes. Systems of combinatory logic related to Quine's 'New Foundations'. *Annals of Pure and Applied Logics*, 53, 1991.
24. G. P. Huet. A mechanization of type theory. In *3rd IJCAI*, pages 139–146, 1973.
25. G. P. Huet. A unification algorithm for typed λ-calculus. *TCS*, 1:27–57, 1975.
26. J.-J. Lévy. *Réductions correctes et optimales dans le lambda-calcul*. PhD thesis, Université Paris VII, France, 1978. Thèse d'État.
27. D. Miller and G. Nadathur. Higher-order logic programming. In *3rd ICLP*, 1986.
28. R. Milner. A theory of type polymorphism in programming. *J.Comp.Sys.Sci.*, 17:348–375, 1978.
29. G. Nelson and D. C. Oppen. Fast decision procedures based on congruence closure. *J.ACM*, 27(2):356–364, 1980.
30. T. Nipkow and Z. Qian. Modular higher-order E-unification. In *4th RTA*, pages 200–214, 1991.
31. T. Pietrzykowski. A complete mechanization of second order logic. *J.ACM*, 20(2), 1973.
32. T. Pietrzykowski and D. Jensen. A complete mechanization of ω-order type theory. *ACM Nat.Conf.*, 1:82–92, 1972.
33. D. Prawitz. An improved proof procedure. *Theoria*, 26:102–139, 1960.
34. W. Snyder. Higher-order E-unification. In *10th CADE*, LNAI 449, pages 573–587. Springer, 1990.
35. R. Statman. The typed λ-calculus is not elementary recursive. *TCS*, 9:73–81, 1979.

Program Extraction in a Logical Framework Setting

Penny Anderson

INRIA, Unité de Recherche de Sophia-Antipolis
2004 Route des Lucioles, BP 93,
06902 Sophia-Antipolis CEDEX, France
tel. 93.65.78.16
anderson@sophia.inria.fr

Abstract. This paper demonstrates a method of extracting programs from formal deductions represented in the Edinburgh Logical Framework, using the Elf programming language. Deductive systems are given for the extraction of simple types from formulas of first-order arithmetic and of λ-calculus terms from natural deduction proofs. These systems are easily encoded in Elf, yielding an implementation of extraction that corresponds to modified realizability. Because extraction is itself implemented as a set of formal deductive systems, some of its correctness properties can be partially represented and mechanically checked in the Elf language.

1 Introduction

Research in the development of verified programs through theorem proving has traditionally relied on systems based on a fixed logic or type theory (e.g., [3], [5], [12]). Given the current interest in variations on logics and programming languages for proofs-as-programs (e.g. [14], [15], [21]), a more flexible approach may be useful. As argued in [2], the use of a type theory as a logical framework contributes to the implementation of metaprograms for logic in a flexible, declarative and verifiable way. This is the approach to program extraction examined in this paper. Combined with existing work on the implementation of theorem proving [6] and the syntax and semantics of programming languages [13], this approach lays the groundwork for complete support for programming by theorem proving in a logical framework setting. The declarative style of encodings in a logical framework affords flexibility in the choice of logic, programming language, and notions of extraction, as well as ease of programming and some mechanical support for verification of metaprograms.

The Edinburgh Logical Framework (LF) [10] is a dependent type theory designed to support the specification of a variety of formal deductive systems. An LF type represents a judgment, and objects of that type represent deductions; given a proper encoding, the well-typedness of such an object is equivalent to the validity of the deduction it represents. The decidability of LF's type system provides a proof checker for deductions represented in this way. LF has been given an operational interpretation by the Elf language [18], which supports a logic programming style for the specification of proof search. This paper investigates the use of Elf to implement the extraction of programs from proofs and to partially verify this implementation.

The approach we take is to view each element of the problem, from the specification of syntax to program extraction, as a deductive system that can be easily transcribed into an Elf signature. We represent a logical language, its proof system, and the syntax of a typed λ-calculus by static Elf signatures, i.e., collections of clauses that define a syntax but are not used for search by the Elf interpreter. The semantics of the programming language, and type and program extraction are represented as dynamic Elf signatures, i.e., programs used for search, yielding an executable type checker, interpreter, and extractor. Because extraction is implemented as a set of formal deductive systems, some of its correctness properties can be partially represented and mechanically checked in the Elf language. This approach allows a single framework to support the study of a variety of logics, programming languages, and notions of extraction, within the limitations of the kinds of deductive systems that can be faithfully represented in LF.

The paper is organized as follows. In Sect. 2 we describe the Elf implementation of extraction. This requires as a preliminary the definition of a logic and a typed λ-calculus. In Sect. 3 we discuss some correctness properties of the extraction and how their proofs can be partially represented in Elf. Sect. 4 provides a summary and discussion.

2 Program extraction as a deductive system

Logic. We sketch an encoding in the style of Harper et al. [10] of natural-deduction style proofs for intuitionistic first-order arithmetic. For reasons of space we give details here only for implication and existential quantification. A full treatment is given in [1]. Here is a fragment of the abstract syntax for the logic with its encoding in Elf:

$$\begin{array}{lll} \text{Individuals} & t ::= x & \mid 0 \mid Sn \\ \text{Formulas} & F ::= \top & \mid \bot \mid t_1 = t_2 \mid F_1 \supset F_2 \mid \exists x \,.\, F \end{array}$$

```
i : type.                   true : o.
o : type.                   false : o.
zero : i.                   eq :  i -> i -> o.
succ : i -> i.              => : o -> o -> o.
                            exists : (i -> o) -> o.
```

We will consider extraction from the following set of natural deduction rules, together with axioms for arithmetic:

$$\frac{}{\top}\,\top I \qquad \frac{\bot}{C}\,\bot E \qquad \frac{[t/x]A}{\exists x\,.\,A}\,\exists I$$

$$\frac{\begin{array}{c}\overline{A}^{\,p}\\ \vdots \\ B\end{array}}{A \supset B}\,\supset I^{p} \qquad \frac{A \supset B \quad A}{B}\,\supset E \qquad \frac{\exists x\,.\,A \quad \begin{array}{c}\overline{A}^{\,p}\\ \vdots \\ C\end{array}}{C}\,\exists E^{p}\,*$$

We represent the discharge of an assumption A by placing an annotated bar over it. The use of letters rather than numbers for annotations is useful for specifying extraction: we regard an annotation p as a *proof variable*, and write $p : \vdash A$ to express the association of p with A.

The rules are encoded in Elf as:

```
|- : o -> type.
truei : |- true.
falsee : {C:o} |- false -> |- C.
impliesi : (|- A -> |- B) -> |- (A => B).
impliese : |- (A => B) -> |- A -> |- B.
existsi : {A:i -> o} {T:i} |- (A T) -> |- (exists A).
existse : ({x:i} |- (A x) -> |- C) -> |- (exists A) -> |- C.
```

The use of LF's dependent types ensures that proof checking is LF type checking. The Elf syntax `{x:A} B` represents the LF dependent type construction $\Pi x : A\,.\,B$. The code omits many Π-quantifiers since Elf takes free variables in clauses to be implicitly Π-quantified, and types for them can often be inferred automatically[17]. Higher-order abstract syntax supports the representation of the introduction and discharge of assumptions, as well as the side conditions (indicated by the asterisk attached to the $\exists$-elimination rule) restricting the free occurrences of variables.

Programming language. We define a simply typed λ-calculus for representing extracted programs. Syntax, evaluation and type inference have been implemented [1] in the style of Michaylov and Pfenning [13], which extends the higher-order representations developed in λProlog by Hannan and Miller in [8], [7]. In this paper we consider only syntax and type inference, as background for the metatheory of the next section.

We use a Nuprl-like syntax [3] for programs in order to emphasize the close relation to the logic. Here is the portion of the language definition necessary for extraction from the fragment of logic we consider:

$$
\begin{array}{llr}
e ::= x \mid 0 \mid \mathbf{s}(e) \mid & & \textit{Natural numbers} \\
\quad \langle e_1, e_2 \rangle \mid \mathbf{spread}(e_1;\ x, y \,.\, e_2) \mid & & \textit{Pairs} \\
\quad \mathbf{lam}\, x \,.\, e \mid \mathbf{app}(e_1, e_2) \mid & & \textit{Functions} \\
\quad () \mid \mathbf{error}(e) & & \textit{Unit, error}
\end{array}
$$

This is straightforward to translate into Elf:

```
term : type.

0 : term.
s : term -> term.
pair : term -> term -> term.
spread : term -> (term -> term -> term) -> term.
lam : (term -> term) -> term.
app : term -> term -> term.
unity : term.
error : term -> term.
```

A natural operational semantics for the language is given in [1]. Most constructs are self-explanatory. The destructor for pairs may require some explanation: in $\mathbf{spread}(e_1;\ x, y \,.\, e_2)$, x and y are bound in e_2 to the components of a pair obtained by evaluating e_1. The construct $\mathbf{error}(e)$ signals an error and is extracted from proof by the intuitionistic absurdity rule $\bot$E.

Typing rules for this language can be formulated and implemented in Elf using the techniques of [13]. Types have the following syntax:

$$\tau ::= \mathsf{nat} \mid \tau_1 \times \tau_2 \mid \tau_1 \Rightarrow \tau_2 \mid \mathsf{unit}$$

with Elf encoding:

```
tp : type.                        ==> : tp -> tp -> tp.
nat : tp.                         unit : tp.
* : tp -> tp -> tp.
```

The typing judgment is of the form $\Gamma \vdash e \in \tau$, where Γ is a context of typing assumptions, and $\Gamma, x : \tau$ is the result of extending a given context Γ with the assumption that the variable x has type τ. We show only the fragment dealing with λ-abstraction and application:

$$\frac{\Gamma, x : \tau_1 \vdash e \in \tau_2}{\Gamma \vdash \mathbf{lam}\, x \,.\, e \in \tau_1 \Rightarrow \tau_2}\,\mathsf{tp\text{-}lam} \qquad \frac{\Gamma \vdash e_1 \in \tau_1 \Rightarrow \tau_2 \qquad \Gamma \vdash e_2 \in \tau_1}{\Gamma \vdash \mathbf{app}(e_1, e_2) \in \tau_2}\,\mathsf{tp\text{-}app}$$

Here is an Elf signature that implements the system:

```
of : term -> tp -> type.

tp_0 : of 0 nat.
tp_s : of (s M) nat <- of M nat.
tp_pair : of (pair M N) (A * B) <- of M A <- of N B.
tp_spread : of (spread Mpr N) C
            <- of Mpr (A * B)
            <- {x} of x A -> {y} of y B -> of (N x y) C.
tp_lam : of (lam M) (A ==> B)
         <- {x:term} of x A -> of (M x) B.
tp_app : of (app M N) B <- of M (A ==> B) <- of N A.
tp_unity : of unity unit.
tp_any : {A} of (error M) A <- of M B.
```

defined over higher-order syntax representations, the typing context is represented by Elf meta-level assumptions introduced during the search process (e.g., in the rule **tp_lam**).

Extraction. The encodings of proofs and functional programs as LF objects facilitate the treatment of type and program extraction as deductive systems. In [1] we give naive formulations of these systems, which extract types that mimic closely the structure of propositions and programs that mimic closely the structure of proofs. This naive extraction results in a program containing many subterms that carry no computationally useful information. Intuitively speaking, this is because the only formulas whose proofs involve choice are existential quantifications (and disjunction in the full logic). We call formulas free of positive occurrences of $\exists$ *uninformative*. By extension we call their proofs, the object types extracted from them, and the programs extracted from the proofs uninformative as well. We define extraction procedures for types and programs that simplify the extracted terms to remove uninformative subterms, while retaining computationally useful information. The extracted programs are well-typed and the extracted types can be inferred for them.

This notion of extraction is an adaptation to the Elf setting of the basic ideas of *modified realizability* developed for the Calculus of Constructions by Paulin-Mohring [16] which in turn takes from the PX system [11] the idea of syntactically defining a class of content-free terms. Sasaki [22] develops these ideas for Nuprl. The negative formulas of Schwichtenberg [23], [24] are used in a similar way to decrease the complexity of realizing terms.

The uninformative formulas are the *Rasiowa-Harrop*[25] formulas:

$$U ::= \top \mid t_1 = t_2 \mid \bot \mid A \supset U$$

where A is any formula. From proofs of these formulas we extract the unit element ().

Extraction is defined by the following judgments:

1. Uninf A (A is an uninformative formula)
2. Inf A (A is an informative formula)
3. $A \Downarrow^t \tau$ (the type τ is extracted from the formula A)
4. $t \Downarrow^i e$ (the program e is extracted from the individual term t)
5. $\mathcal{P} \Downarrow e$ (the program e is extracted from the proof $\mathcal{P}$)

The first two are simple syntactic properties of formulas: (1) is a straightforward deductive formulation of the grammar of uninformative formulas given above, and (2) is the complement of (1). The main judgments are the extraction of types and programs, guided by the syntactic analysis given by the auxiliary judgments.

The following rules define type extraction:

$$\frac{\text{Uninf}\, A}{A \Downarrow^t \mathsf{unit}}\,\mathsf{xst\text{-}uninf} \qquad \frac{\text{Inf}\, A \quad A \Downarrow^t \tau_1 \quad \text{Inf}\, B \quad B \Downarrow^t \tau_2}{A \supset B \Downarrow^t \tau_1 \Rightarrow \tau_2}\,\mathsf{xst}\supset$$

$$\frac{\text{Uninf}\, A \quad \text{Inf}\, B \quad B \Downarrow^t \tau}{A \supset B \Downarrow^t \tau}\,\mathsf{xst}\supset\mathsf{R} \qquad \frac{\text{Inf}\, A \qquad A \Downarrow^t \tau}{\exists x\, .\, A \Downarrow^t \mathsf{nat} \times \tau}\,\mathsf{xst}\exists. \qquad \frac{\text{Uninf}\, A}{\exists x\, .\, A \Downarrow^t \mathsf{nat}}\,\mathsf{xst}\exists\mathsf{L}$$

It is straightforward to transcribe them into Elf:

```
extract_tp : o -> tp -> type.

exts_u: extract_tp A unit <- uninf A.
exts_imp : extract_tp (A => B) (T1 ==> T2)
           <- inf A <- extract_tp A T1
           <- inf B <- extract_tp B T2.
exts_impr : extract_tp (A => B) T
            <- uninf A
            <- inf B <- extract_tp B T.
exts_ex : extract_tp (exists A) (nat * T)
          <- ({x:i} inf (A x))
          <- ({x:i} extract_tp (A x) T).
exts_exl : extract_tp (exists A) nat <- ({x:i} uninf (A x)).
```

Extraction from individual terms is trivial, mapping the natural numbers of the logic to the numerals of the programming language:

```
extract_tm : i -> term -> type.

ex_zero : extract_tm zero 0.
ex_succ : extract_tm (succ X) (s M) <- extract_tm X M.
```

Program extraction requires the use of a context of extraction assumptions. For an informative proof $\mathcal{P}$ the deduction of $\mathcal{P} \Downarrow e$ imitates the structure of $\mathcal{P}$ itself. In particular, wherever $\mathcal{P}$ introduces an assumption A with annotation p, the extraction deduction introduces an assumption $p \Downarrow p'$ for some fresh program variable p'. Similarly, wherever $\mathcal{P}$ introduces a parameter x, the extraction deduction introduces an assumption $x \Downarrow^i x'$ for a fresh program variable x'. Thus the extraction judgment is defined relative to a context of extraction assumptions Γ. All variables in a given context may be assumed to be distinct. We write $\Gamma, x \Downarrow^i x'$ for the result of extending Γ with the individual term extraction assumption $x \Downarrow^i x'$, and $\Gamma, p \Downarrow p'$ for the result of extending Γ with the proof extraction assumption $p \Downarrow p'$. The full form of the extraction judgment is thus $\Gamma \vdash \mathcal{P} \Downarrow e$.

The definition of program extraction is straightforward; the only complications that arise are due to the elimination rules of the logic. Extraction from proofs of uninformative formulas is trivial: we simply extract the unit term () without analysing the structure of the proof. From a proof by the intuitionistic absurdity rule ⊥E we extract a value **error**(e) where e is extracted from the proof of the premise; this is of course the unit value () since $\bot$ is uninformative. We show the fragment of the deductive system that treats implication and existential quantification:

$$\frac{\mathrm{Inf}\,A \quad \mathrm{Inf}\,B \quad \Gamma, p \Downarrow p' \vdash \mathcal{P} \Downarrow e}{\Gamma \vdash \boxed{\begin{array}{c} \overline{A}^{\,p} \\ \mathcal{P} \\ B \\ \hline A \supset B \end{array}\ {\supset}\mathrm{I}^p} \Downarrow \mathbf{lam}\, p' \,.\, e}\ \mathrm{XS{\supset}I} \qquad \frac{\mathrm{Uninf}\,A \quad \mathrm{Inf}\,B \quad \Gamma \vdash \mathcal{P} \Downarrow e}{\Gamma \vdash \boxed{\begin{array}{c} \overline{A}^{\,p} \\ \mathcal{P} \\ B \\ \hline A \supset B \end{array}\ {\supset}\mathrm{I}^p} \Downarrow e}\ \mathrm{XS{\supset}IR}$$

$$\frac{\mathrm{Inf}\,A \quad \mathrm{Inf}\,B \quad \Gamma \vdash \mathcal{P}_1 \Downarrow e_1 \quad \Gamma \vdash \mathcal{P}_2 \Downarrow e_2}{\Gamma \vdash \boxed{\begin{array}{cc} \mathcal{P}_1 & \mathcal{P}_2 \\ A \supset B & A \\ \hline \multicolumn{2}{c}{B} \end{array}\ {\supset}\mathrm{E}} \Downarrow \mathbf{app}(e_1, e_2)}\ \mathrm{XS{\supset}E} \qquad \frac{\mathrm{Uninf}\,A \quad \mathrm{Inf}\,B \quad \Gamma \vdash \mathcal{P}_1 \Downarrow e}{\Gamma \vdash \boxed{\begin{array}{cc} \mathcal{P}_1 & \mathcal{P}_2 \\ A \supset B & A \\ \hline \multicolumn{2}{c}{B} \end{array}\ {\supset}\mathrm{E}} \Downarrow e}\ \mathrm{XS{\supset}ER}$$

$$\frac{\Gamma \vdash t \Downarrow^i e_1 \quad \mathrm{Inf}\,A \quad \Gamma \vdash \mathcal{P} \Downarrow e_2}{\Gamma \vdash \boxed{\begin{array}{c} \mathcal{P} \\ [t/x]A \\ \hline \exists x \,.\, A \end{array}\ \exists\mathrm{I}} \Downarrow \langle\, e_1, e_2 \,\rangle}\ \mathrm{XS\exists I} \qquad \frac{\mathrm{Uninf}\,A \quad \Gamma \vdash t \Downarrow^i e}{\Gamma \vdash \boxed{\begin{array}{c} \mathcal{P} \\ [t/x]A \\ \hline \exists x \,.\, A \end{array}\ \exists\mathrm{I}} \Downarrow e}\ \mathrm{XS\exists IL}$$

$$\frac{\mathrm{Inf}\,A \qquad \Gamma \vdash \mathcal{P} \Downarrow e_1 \qquad \Gamma, x \Downarrow^{\iota} x', p \Downarrow p' \vdash \mathcal{Q} \Downarrow e_2}{\Gamma \vdash \boxed{\dfrac{\begin{array}{cc} & \overline{}^{\,p} \\ & A \\ \mathcal{P} & \mathcal{Q} \\ \exists x\,.\,A & C \end{array}}{C}\,\exists\mathrm{E}^{p}} \Downarrow \mathbf{spread}(e_1;\ x', p'\,.\,e_2)}\ \mathrm{XS}\exists\mathrm{E}$$

$$\frac{\mathrm{Uninf}\,A \qquad \Gamma \vdash \mathcal{P} \Downarrow e_1 \qquad \Gamma, x \Downarrow^{\iota} x' \vdash \mathcal{Q} \Downarrow e_2}{\Gamma \vdash \boxed{\dfrac{\begin{array}{cc} & \overline{}^{\,p} \\ & A \\ \mathcal{P} & \mathcal{Q} \\ \exists x\,.\,A & C \end{array}}{C}\,\exists\mathrm{E}^{p}} \Downarrow \mathbf{app}((\mathbf{lam}\,x'\,.\,e_2), e_1)}\ \mathrm{XS}\exists\mathrm{EL}$$

The rule XS∃EL has the interesting feature that extraction is performed on subproofs containing proof variables for which no extraction assumption is introduced in the context. The deduction can succeed only if $\Gamma \vdash \mathcal{Q} \Downarrow e$ can be deduced with the proof variable p occurring free in $\mathcal{Q}$. At first glance it might seem that extraction could fail without an assignment for p. But for uninformative formulas modified extraction does not need to examine the proof.

Again it is straightforward to translate this system into Elf; we show a fragment of the implementation:

```
uninf : o -> type.
inf : o -> type.

exs_un : extract (P: |- A) unity <- uninf A.
exs_falsee : extract (falsee C P) (error M)
            <- extract P M.

exs_impli2 : extract (impliesi (P: |- A -> |- B)) (lam M)
            <- inf A <- inf B
            <- {p: |- A} {p':term}
                (extract p p' -> extract (P p) (M p')).

exs_impli1 : extract (impliesi (P: |- A -> |- B)) M
            <- uninf A <- inf B
            <- {p: |- A} extract (P p) M.

exs_imple2 : extract (impliese (P1: |- (A => B)) P2) (app M1 M2)
            <- inf A <- inf B
            <- extract P1 M1 <- extract P2 M2.

exs_imple1 : extract (impliese (P1: |- (A => B)) P2) M
```

```
              <- uninf A <- inf B <- extract P1 M.

exs_existsi2 : extract (existsi A T P) (pair M N)
               <- ({x:i} inf (A x))
               <- extract_tm T M <- extract P N.

exs_existsi1 : extract (existsi A T _) M
               <- ({x:i} uninf (A x)) <- extract_tm T M.

exs_existse2 : extract (existse Q P) (spread N M)
               <- ({x:i} inf (A x))
               <- ({x:i} {x':term} extract_tm x x'
                   -> {p:|- (A X)} {p':term} extract p p'
                   -> extract (Q x p) (M x' p'))
               <- extract P N.

exs_existse1 : extract (existse Q (P: |- (exists A))) (app (lam M) N)
               <- ({X:i} uninf (A X))
               <- ({X:i} {x:term} extract_tm X x
                   -> {p: |- (A X)} extract (Q X p) (M x))
               <- extract P N.
```

There is one feature of this program that has not appeared before: some dependently-typed terms are annotated with their types. For example in the rule **exs_existse1** the major premise of the existential elimination must be $\exists x . A$ where A is uninformative. We annotate P with its type in order to express this premise.

3 Correctness properties of extraction

Some correctness properties of extraction can be partially verified in Elf by formulating deduction transformations along the lines described in [19], [9]. The verification technique is essentially that of [4], but the dependent types of **LF** eliminate the need for explicit reasoning about the validity of the objects involved, and the term and type reconstruction of Elf mechanize the management of many details.

We consider in some detail the property of *type soundness*:

Proposition 1. (Type soundness of extraction) *For any* $\mathcal{P} : \vdash A$, *e, and* τ, *if* $\vdash \mathcal{P} \Downarrow e$ *and* $\vdash A \Downarrow^t \tau$ *then* $\vdash e \in \tau$.

This property can be proved by induction over the structure of extraction deductions. The proof constructs formal deductions of typing judgments from given deductions of extraction judgments. The dual nature of Elf signatures – which can be viewed as either logic programs or language definitions – supports the direct expression of the constructive parts of the proofs. Each case of the induction is expressed as an Elf clause that matches a deduction of a particular shape.

When discussing the proof, we will need to name the formal deductions of extraction and typing. To say that some judgment J is derivable, we often write simply "J"; we write $\mathcal{D} :: J$ when $\mathcal{D}$ is a deduction of the judgment J.

Since extraction deductions in general depend on a context of extraction assumptions, we generalize Proposition 1 accordingly. We define a function from contexts of extraction assumptions to typing contexts:

Definition 2. Given a context of extraction assumptions $\Gamma = \langle\ \Gamma_1, \ldots, \Gamma_n\ \rangle$ with domain $x_1 \ldots, x_n$, define

1. $\lceil \Gamma_i \rceil = x_i' \in \mathsf{nat}$, if Γ_i is $x_i \Downarrow^i x_i'$
2. $\lceil \Gamma_i \rceil = p_i' \in \tau_i$, if Γ_i is $p_i \Downarrow p_i'$, $p_i : \vdash A_i$, and $A_i \Downarrow^t \tau_i$.
3. $\lceil \Gamma \rceil = \langle\ \lceil \Gamma_1 \rceil, \ldots, \lceil \Gamma_n \rceil\ \rangle$

Now we can generalize Proposition 1 to the following:

Lemma 3. (Type soundness of extraction in arbitrary contexts)
Given a proof $\mathcal{P}$ of a formula A, if $\Gamma \vdash \mathcal{P} \Downarrow e$ and $\vdash A \Downarrow^t \tau$ then $\lceil \Gamma \rceil \vdash e \in \tau$.

Since the extraction judgment depends on the judgment $t \Downarrow^i e$ (extraction from individual terms) a type soundness property for individual term extraction is also needed:

Lemma 4. (Type soundness for individual extraction) *If $\Gamma \vdash t \Downarrow^i e$ then $\lceil \Gamma \rceil \vdash e \in \mathsf{nat}$.*

The proof is trivial since the only terms in the object logic are natural numbers. Its representation in Elf is a very simple example of our partial verification technique. Here is the Elf signature that represents the proof of Lemma 4:

```
tsetm : extract_tm T M -> of M nat -> type.

tsetm_zero : tsetm ex_zero tp_0.
tsetm_succ : tsetm (ex_succ E) (tp_s D) <- tsetm E D.
```

The clause `tsetm_zero` corresponds to the base case of the proof, which constructs the depth-one typing derivation for the program expression 0. The clause `tsetm_succ` contains a subgoal that represents an appeal to the induction hypothesis.

The encoding of the proof of Lemma 3 in Elf (Fig. 1) follows the same basic principles. The declaration of the judgment `tse` expresses a relation between a program extraction deduction, a type extraction deduction, and a typing assignment deduction. Proving Lemma 3 amounts to giving a total function from the first two deductions to the third. The encoding of the proof is partial in the following sense: we can code this function as an Elf signature, and the well-typedness of each declaration in the signature guarantees that the construction

```
tse : extract (P: |- A) M -> extract_tp A T -> of M T -> type.

tse_un : tse (exs_un H) (exts_u H) tp_unity.

tse_falsee : tse (exs_falsee E) Et (tp_any _ D)
            <- tse E exts_false D.

tse_impliesi2 : tse (exs_impli2 E Ib Ia) (exts_imp Etb Ib Eta Ia) (tp_lam D)
               <- ({p} {p'} {e: extract p p'} {d} tse e Eta d
                   -> tse (E p p' e) Etb (D p' d)).
tse_impliesi1 : tse (exs_impli1 E Ib Ua) (exts_impr Etb Ib Ua) D
               <- ({p} tse (E p) Etb D).

tse_impliese2 : tse (exs_imple2 Ea Eab Ib Ia) Et (tp_app D2 D1)
               <- tse Eab (exts_imp Etb Ib Eta Ia) D1
               <- tse Ea Eta D2.
tse_impliese1 : tse (exs_imple1 Eab Ib Ua) Et D
               <- tse Eab (exts_impr Et Ib Ua) D.

tse_existsi2 : tse (exs_existsi2 E (Etm:extract_tm T M) Ia)
                   (exts_ex Et Ia) (tp_pair D2 D1)
              <- tsetm Etm D1
              <- tse E (Et T) D2.
tse_existsi1 : tse (exs_existsi1 (Etm:extract_tm T M) Ua) (exts_exl Ua) D
              <- tsetm Etm D.

tse_existse2 : tse (exs_existse2 Ee Ec I) Et (tp_spread D2 D1)
              <- tse Ee (exts_ex Et' I) D1
              <- ({x} {x'} {etm:extract_tm x x'} {p} {p'}
                  {e:extract_simp p p'} {d1} {d2}
                  tsetm etm d1 -> tse e (Et' x) d2 ->
                  tse (Ec x x' etm p p' e) Et (D2 x' d1 p' d2)).
tse_existse1 : tse (exs_existse1 Ee Ec U) Et
                   (tp_app D1 (tp_lam D2))
              <- tse Ee (exts_exl U) D1
              <- ({x} {x'} {etm:extract_tm x x'}
                  {d} tsetm etm d ->
                  {p} tse (Ec x x' etm p) Et (D2 x' d)).
```

Fig. 1. Elf representation of type soundness

carried out is correct. But there is no internal guarantee that the signature determines a total function (and clearly we cannot code the construction directly as an Elf function since it is not schematic). This guarantee could probably be obtained by applying the *schema checking* of [19]. We have partially schema-checked the proof by hand.

A simple lemma needed throughout the proof is:

Lemma 5. (Inversion for type extraction) *Given $\mathcal{E} :: A \Downarrow^t \tau$, the last inference rule of $\mathcal{E}$ is uniquely determined by the form of A.*

This is seen by inspection of the type extraction system.

The partial representation of the proof in Elf is shown in Fig. 1. We discuss the treatment of uninformative subproofs for extraction from the rules for existential quantification. If A is informative, to extract a program from a proof of $\exists x . A$ by $\exists$I we extract a pair $\langle e_1, e_2 \rangle$ representing a witness t and a proof of $[t/x]A$. But when A is uninformative, we extract just an expression e representing the witness t. In this case the extraction deduction must have the form:

$$\dfrac{\begin{matrix}\mathcal{U} & \mathcal{E}' \\ \mathrm{Uninf}\, A & \Gamma \vdash t \Downarrow^t e\end{matrix}}{\Gamma \vdash \boxed{\begin{matrix}\mathcal{P} \\ \dfrac{[t/x]A}{\exists x . A}\,\exists\mathrm{I}\end{matrix}} \Downarrow e}\;\mathrm{xs}\exists\mathrm{IL}$$

Because A is uninformative the type extracted from $\exists x . A$ must be nat. Then we can apply Lemma 4 (type soundness for term extraction) to $\mathcal{E}'$ to obtain a typing derivation $\mathcal{D} :: \lceil \Gamma \rceil \vdash e \in \mathsf{nat}$ as required. The clause **tse_existsil** of Fig. 1 represents this case.

Next we consider the case of xs$\exists$EL, where the object proof discharges an uninformative assumption A (clause **tse_existsel** of Fig. 1). The extraction deduction must have the form:

$$\dfrac{\begin{matrix}\mathcal{U} & \mathcal{E}_1 & \mathcal{E}_2 \\ \mathrm{Uninf}\, A & \Gamma \vdash \mathcal{P} \Downarrow e_1 & \Gamma, x \Downarrow^t x' \vdash \mathcal{Q} \Downarrow e_2\end{matrix}}{\Gamma \vdash \boxed{\dfrac{\begin{matrix} & \overline{A}^{\,p} \\ \mathcal{P} & \mathcal{Q} \\ \exists x . A & C\end{matrix}}{C}\,\exists\mathrm{E}^p} \Downarrow \mathbf{app}((\mathbf{lam}\, x' . e_2), e_1)}\;\mathrm{xs}\exists\mathrm{EL}$$

Assume $\mathcal{T}_2 :: \vdash C \Downarrow^t \tau$. Since A is uninformative we may construct the type extraction derivation $\mathcal{T}_1 =$

$$\dfrac{\begin{matrix}\mathcal{U} \\ \mathrm{Uninf}\, A\end{matrix}}{\exists x . A \Downarrow^t \mathsf{nat}}\;\mathrm{xst}\exists\mathrm{L}$$

By the induction hypothesis applied to $\mathcal{E}_1$ and $\mathcal{T}_1$, there is a typing deduction $\mathcal{D}_1 :: \lceil\Gamma\rceil \vdash e_1 \in \mathsf{nat}$; similarly by the induction hypothesis applied to $\mathcal{E}_2$ and $\mathcal{T}_2$, there is a deduction $\mathcal{D}_2 :: \lceil\Gamma, x \Downarrow^i x'\rceil \vdash e_2 \in \tau$. By definition $\lceil\Gamma, x \Downarrow^i x'\rceil = \lceil\Gamma\rceil, x' \in \mathsf{nat}$. Then construct the typing derivation

$$\dfrac{\dfrac{\begin{array}{c}\mathcal{D}_2\\ \lceil\Gamma\rceil, x' \in \mathsf{nat} \vdash e_2 \in \tau\end{array}}{\lceil\Gamma\rceil \vdash \mathbf{lam}\, x'.\, e_2 \in \mathsf{nat} \Rightarrow \tau}\,\textsf{tp-lam} \qquad \begin{array}{c}\mathcal{D}_1\\ \lceil\Gamma\rceil \vdash e_1 \in \mathsf{nat}\end{array}}{\lceil\Gamma\rceil \vdash \mathbf{app}(\mathbf{lam}\, x'.\, e_2, e_1) \in \tau}\,\textsf{tp-app}$$

The cases for implication are handled in essentially the same way, but without the need to treat individual parameters.

3.1 Discussion

In [1] we give a similar proof of an evaluation soundness property for a naive version of program extraction: given a proof $\mathcal{P}$ of a formula A, if $\vdash \mathcal{P} \Downarrow e$ and e evaluates to v then there is a proof $\mathcal{P}'$ of A such that $\vdash \mathcal{P}' \Downarrow v$. The proof of evaluation soundness for naive extraction is an induction on the structure of an evaluation deduction. Its partial representation in Elf constructs an object proof and its extraction deduction from the given extraction; since evaluation is closely related to proof reduction, this gives us a set of executable reductions for object proofs. Note that this is not a normalization theorem for the object logic, and because the programming language semantics does not evaluate under functional abstractions, the proof does not give even weak normal forms for object proofs in the sense of Prawitz [20].

An immediate consequence of type and evaluation soundness together is subject reduction for the set of programming language expressions that can be extracted from proofs.

The metatheory of the programming language can be encoded in the same way; see for example [19]. Type and evaluation soundness would then allow us to carry some metatheory over from the domain of programs to the domain of proofs; for instance, we could get a very weak normal form for natural deduction proofs from a proof that evaluation of an extracted program produces a "value", for some appropriate definition of value.

4 Conclusion

We have given a deductive formulation of program extraction and shown how this style leads directly to an implementation in Elf. The approach relies on defining the underlying logic and programming language by a hierarchy of deductive systems, with deductions of syntactic well-formedness at the base of the hierarchy and extraction deductions at the top. The decidability of LF's type system leads to implementations that are guaranteed to construct valid deductions.

Extending the hierarchy to transformations defined on extraction deductions is a natural step that allows us to partially represent in Elf some of the metatheory of extraction. The mechanical checking of the type-correctness of this representation is equivalent to the automatic partial verification of the metatheory.

The implementation approach is robust with regard to changes in the object logic and programming language, affording a good basis for experimentation with variations.

References

1. Penny Anderson. *Program Derivation by Proof Transformation.* PhD thesis, Department of Computer Science, Carnegie Mellon University, October 1993. Available as Technical Report CMU-CS-93-206.
2. David A. Basin and Robert L. Constable. Metalogical frameworks. In Gérard Huet and Gordon Plotkin, editors, *Logical Environments*, pages 1–29. Cambridge University Press, 1993. Also available as Max-Planck-Institüt für Informatik technical report MPI-I-92-205.
3. Robert L. Constable et al. *Implementing Mathematics with the Nuprl Proof Development System.* Prentice-Hall, Englewood Cliffs, New Jersey, 1986.
4. Joëlle Despeyroux. Proof of translation in natural semantics. In A. R. Meyer, editor, *Symposium on Logic in Computer Science*, pages 193–205, Cambridge, Massachusetts, June 1986. IEEE Computer Society Press.
5. Gilles Dowek, Amy Felty, Hugo Herbelin, Gérard Huet, Christine Paulin-Mohring, and Benjamin Werner. The Coq proof assistant user's guide. Rapport Techniques 134, INRIA, Rocquencourt, France, December 1991. Version 5.6.
6. Amy Felty. Implementing tactics and tacticals in a higher-order logic programming language. *Journal of Automated Reasoning*, 11:43–81, 1993.
7. John Hannan. *Investigating a Proof-Theoretic Meta-Language for Functional Programs.* PhD thesis, University of Pennsylvania, January 1991. Available as MS-CIS-91-09.
8. John Hannan and Dale Miller. A meta-logic for functional programming. In H. Abramson and M. Rogers, editors, *Meta-Programming in Logic Programming*, pages 453–476. MIT Press, 1989.
9. John Hannan and Frank Pfenning. Compiler verification in LF. In Andre Scedrov, editor, *Seventh Annual IEEE Symposium on Logic in Computer Science*, pages 407–418, Santa Cruz, California, June 1992. IEEE Computer Society Press.
10. Robert Harper, Furio Honsell, and Gordon Plotkin. A framework for defining logics. *Journal of the Association for Computing Machinery*, 40(1):143–184, January 1993.
11. Susumu Hayashi. An introduction to PX. In Gerard Huet, editor, *Logical Foundations of Functional Programming.* Addison-Wesley, 1990.
12. Lena Magnusson. The new implementation of ALF. In B. Nordström, K. Petersson, and G. Plotkin, editors, *Proceedings of the 1992 Workshop on Types for Proofs and Programs*, pages 265–282, Båstad, Sweden, June 1992. University of Göteborg.

13. Spiro Michaylov and Frank Pfenning. Natural semantics and some of its metatheory in Elf. In L.-H. Eriksson, L. Hallnäs, and P. Schroeder-Heister, editors, *Proceedings of the Second International Workshop on Extensions of Logic Programming*, pages 299–344, Stockholm, Sweden, January 1991. Springer-Verlag LNAI 596.
14. Chetan Murthy. *Extracting Constructive Content from Classical Proofs*. PhD thesis, Cornell University, August 1990.
15. Christine Paulin and Benjamin Werner. Extracting and executing programs developed in the inductive constructions system: a progress report. In G. Huet and G. Plotkin, editors, *Proceedings of the First Workshop on Logical Frameworks*, pages 377–390. Preliminary Version, May 1990.
16. Christine Paulin-Mohring. Extracting F_ω programs from proofs in the calculus of constructions. In *Sixteenth Annual Symposium on Principles of Programming Languages*, pages 89–104. ACM Press, January 1989.
17. Frank Pfenning. On the undecidability of partial polymorphic type reconstruction. *Fundamenta Informaticae*, 199? To appear. Preliminary version available as Technical Report CMU-CS-92-105, School of Computer Science, Carnegie Mellon University, Pittsburgh, Pennsylvania, January 1992.
18. Frank Pfenning. Logic programming in the LF logical framework. In Gérard Huet and Gordon Plotkin, editors, *Logical Frameworks*, pages 149–181. Cambridge University Press, 1991.
19. Frank Pfenning and Ekkehard Rohwedder. Implementing the meta-theory of deductive systems. In D. Kapur, editor, *Proceedings of the 11th International Conference on Automated Deduction*, pages 537–551, Saratoga Springs, New York, June 1992. Springer-Verlag LNAI 607.
20. Dag Prawitz. Ideas and results in proof theory. In J. E. Fenstad, editor, *Proceedings of the Second Scandinavian Logic Symposium*, pages 235–307, Amsterdam, London, 1971. North-Holland Publishing Co.
21. Christophe Raffalli. Machine deduction. To appear in the Proceedings of the Workshop on Types for Proofs and Programs, Nijmegen, The Netherlands, May 1993.
22. James T. Sasaki. *Extracting Efficient Code from Constructive Proofs*. PhD thesis, Cornell University, May 1986. Available as Technical Report TR 86-757.
23. Helmut Schwichtenberg. On Martin-Löf's theory of types. In *Atti Degli Incontri di Logica Mathematica*, pages 299–325. Dipartimento di Matematica, Università di Siena, 1982.
24. Helmut Schwichtenberg. A normal form for natural deductions in a type theory with realizing terms. In Ettore Casari et al., editors, *Atti del Congresso Logica e Filosfia della Scienza, oggi. San Gimignano, December 7–11, 1983*, pages 95–138, Bologna, Italy, 1985. CLUEB.
25. A. S. Troelstra and D. van Dalen. *Constructivism in Mathematics*, volume 121 of *Studies in Logic and the Foundations of Mathematics*. North-Holland, Amsterdam, 1988.

Higher-Order Abstract Syntax with Induction in Coq

Joëlle Despeyroux[1] and André Hirschowitz[2]

[1] INRIA – Sophia-Antipolis, 2004 Route des Lucioles, B.P. 93
F-06902 Sophia-Antipolis Cedex, France
joelle.despeyroux@sophia.inria.fr
[2] CNRS URA 168, University of Nice, F-06108 Nice Cedex 2, France
andre.hirschowitz@sophia.inria.fr

Abstract. Three important properties of Higher-Order Abstract Syntax are the (higher-order) induction principle, which allows proofs by induction, the (higher-order) injection principle, which asserts that equal terms have equal heads and equal sons, and the extensionality principle, which asserts that functional terms which are pointwise equal are equal. Higher-order abstract syntax is implemented for instance in the Edinburgh Logical Framework and the above principles are satisfied by this implementation. But although they can be proved at the meta level, they cannot be proved at the object level and furthermore, it is not so easy to know how to formulate them in a simple way at the object level. We explain here how Second-Order Abstract Syntax can be implemented in a more powerful type system (Coq) in such a way as to make available or provable (at the object level) the corresponding induction, injection and extensionality principles.

1 Introduction

The original motivation of our work is to investigate how to use a powerful theorem prover to perform proofs in Natural Semantics [11] written in the LF [9] style. We have chosen the system Coq [3] rather than other systems, like Elf [16] or Isabelle [15] for example, because Coq is equipped with a notion of inductive definitions [14] which provides induction and a recursion operator (called Match) both on expressions and on proofs.

The problem of the implementation of second-order syntax together with induction in Coq is not trivial because declarations like the following one are not legal:

'Inductive Set' $L_0 = Lam_0 : (L_0 \rightarrow L_0) \rightarrow L_0 \mid App_0 : L_0 \rightarrow L_0 \rightarrow L_0$.

Indeed, in the definition of the constructor $Lam_0 : (L_0 \rightarrow L_0) \rightarrow L_0$, the first occurrence of L_0 is *negative* and this is not allowed in an inductive definition.

Let us explain, on the above example, the main features of our solution.

In order to avoid negative positions, we use the following trick. We use a set *var* for variables, introduced by the following declaration:

Variable var : Set.

together with an axiom providing var with two distinct values. This assumption is much weaker than the usual one concerning variables. This reflects the fact that our treatment of variables is genuinely higher-order. Our lam-constructor has for its argument a function from var to L instead of from L to L. In order to complete the picture, we also need a constructor from var to L. This yields the following *inductive* declaration:

Inductive Set $L = Var : var \rightarrow L \mid Lam : (var \rightarrow L) \rightarrow L \mid App : L \rightarrow L \rightarrow L.$

For instance, the term $\lambda x.(x\ x)$ is encoded as

$(Lam\ (\lambda x : var.\ (App\ (Var\ x)\ (Var\ x))))$,

using the meta-level operator λ. Terms of L form our *provisional* syntax. Now we want to implement altogether closed and open terms. We see open terms as higher-order terms, in other words as functions of an arbitrary number of variables. We know of at least three approaches for implementing such functions:

- through implicit lists, by glueing in a single dependent type the sequence L_n of types: L, $L \rightarrow L$, $L \rightarrow L \rightarrow L$, ... Such a definition is not possible in the current Coq system, since the rule $Nodep_{Set,Type_{Set}}$ is not yet available;
- through a term *list* of type $nat \rightarrow Set \rightarrow Set$, where the intended meaning of $(list\ n\ A)$ is the type of lists of length n of elements of A;
- through infinite lists via the term $list = \lambda A : Set.nat \rightarrow A$.

Here below we explore the latter solution, which appeared to be the simplest one. Our infinite lists are easily equipped with the usual terms *cons*, *car* and *cdr*. Thus our final syntax is made of terms of type $(list\ L) \rightarrow L$. Not all such terms are convenient and we have to rule out exotic terms through a predicate $Valid$ of type $nat \rightarrow ((list\ L) \rightarrow L) \rightarrow Prop$. Finally, we have to identify $Valid$ terms which are *extensionally* equal in some natural sense; this is because Coq's object equality (more precisely the polymorphic equality on Sets provided in Coq) is not extensional.

The desired induction principle is generated by the inductive definition of $Valid$. The extensionality principle is given for free by our ad-hoc equality. As for the injection principle, we are able to prove it at the object level.

Our implementation of second-order syntax would be meaningless from our point of view if it did not allow convincing formulations and proofs in semantics. We wish to address this problem systematically in the future. In this paper, we present briefly a significant example, namely an implementation of a translation from a first-order (de Bruijn) version of our simply typed λ-calculus to our second-order description of the same calculus, together with the formulation and proof (at the object level) of the correctness of this translation. This proof illustrates nicely the use of the induction and injection principles on both sides.

The rest of the paper is organized as follows. In section 2, we explain our implementation of the above example of a simply-typed λ-calculus. In subsection 2.1, we review a first-order implementation of our λ-calculus in Coq. In subsection 2.2, we introduce our provisional syntax and discuss its properties. In subsection 2.3, we present our final syntax. In order to build a complete proof of the injection principle, we were led to introduce ad-hoc extensional notions of equality, which are studied here. In subsection 2.4, we present our object-level proof of translation. The statements proved in this subsection 2.4 are not the natural ones, since they involve our notion of equality, instead of Coq's object equality. This makes them more cumbersome. In subsection 2.5, we discuss alternative approaches through extensionality axioms needed for proofs of the original statements (those involving Coq's object equality). In section 3, we explain how to implement similarly a large class of second-order syntaxes. Related works are discussed in section 4, while future works are presented in the conclusion.

Note: Throughout the paper, Coq terms are pretty-printed using λ, $\forall$ and $\exists$ in place of [_], (_) and exists([_]_). We also omit the type information in the Match ((< T > $Match$ _)) and in Coq's object equality on Sets (< T > _ = _).

2 An example

We explain in this section our implementation of the example of the simply-typed λ-calculus considered in the above introduction.

2.1 First-order setting

First, let us review first-order syntax as it can be implemented in a theorem prover such as Coq. For a first-order implementation of a λ-calculus without variables, the de Bruijn approach is simple and efficient: in Coq, we may declare, following Huet [10]:

Inductive Set $fol = \ ref : nat \rightarrow fol \mid lam : fol \rightarrow fol \mid app : fol \rightarrow fol \rightarrow fol.$

Induction and Match. This declaration generates, for terms of type fol, both a Match operator and the following induction principle, available for object proofs:

$\forall P : fol \rightarrow Prop.$
$(\forall n : nat.\ (P\ (ref\ n)))$
$\rightarrow\ (\forall e : fol.\ (P\ e) \rightarrow (P\ (lam\ e)))$
$\rightarrow\ (\forall a : fol.\ (P\ a) \rightarrow \forall b : fol.\ (P\ b) \rightarrow (P\ (app\ a\ b)))$
$\rightarrow\ \forall e : fol.\ (P\ e).$

Injection principle. These two tools make it possible to prove at the object level the following injection principle, made of six theorems (we only give two of them here):

Theorem $lam\_app : \forall e : fol.\forall a, b : fol.\ \neg((lam\ e) = (app\ a\ b)).$
Theorem $lam\_lam : \forall a, b : fol.\ ((lam\ a) = (lam\ b)) \rightarrow a = b.$

Extensionality. In this setting already, the extensionality principle does not hold. We can easily produce two terms of type $fol \rightarrow fol$ which are extensionally equal but not equal. For instance, the identity function on fol can naturally be written as $\lambda x : fol.x$ or using the Match operator, which is a combination of a recursor operator and a case operator ((*_*) denotes comments in Coq):

$\lambda x : fol.$ $(Match\ x\ with$
$(*\ (ref\ n)\ *)\ \lambda n : nat.(ref\ n)$
$(*\ (lam\ y)\ *)\ \lambda y : fol.\lambda h_y : fol.(lam\ y)$
$(*\ (app\ y\ z)\ *)\ \lambda y : fol.\lambda h_y : fol.\lambda z : fol.\lambda h_z : fol.(app\ y\ z))$.

This is not such a drawback since, in this setting, we do not plan to manipulate higher-order terms.

Inversion. This is an important tool in Coq. As induction is not allowed on partially instanciated terms, a standard way to simulate a double induction on two predicates is to use induction on the first predicate, followed by the use of the inversion rules of the second predicate. We give here as an example, the inversion rules for the following predicate *valid*, which makes it possible to characterize closed terms (through the predicate $(valid\ 0)$).

Inductive Definition $valid : nat \rightarrow fol \rightarrow Prop$
$= valid\_ref : \forall n, m : nat.\ (m < n) \rightarrow (valid\ n\ (ref\ m))$
$\mid valid\_lam : \forall n : nat.\forall e : fol.\ (valid\ (S\ n)\ e) \rightarrow (valid\ n\ (lam\ e))$
$\mid valid\_app : \forall n : nat.\forall a, b : fol.\ (valid\ n\ a) \rightarrow (valid\ n\ b) \rightarrow (valid\ n\ (app\ a\ b))$.

Since the conclusions of the different rules do not unify, the inversion package simply reads as the following one:

$valid\_inv\_ref : \forall n, m : nat.(valid\ n\ (ref\ m)) \rightarrow (\ m < n)$
$valid\_inv\_lam : \forall n : nat.\forall e : fol.(valid\ n\ (lam\ e)) \rightarrow (valid\ (S\ n)\ e)$
$valid\_inv\_app : \forall n : nat.\forall a, b : fol.(valid\ n\ (app\ a\ b)) \rightarrow (valid\ n\ a) \wedge (valid\ n\ b)$.

The proof of this package, which is more or less standard (cf. eg. [3]), uses the injection principle (here on fol) in an essential way.

2.2 Provisional setting

In this section, we explain our *provisional* syntax. At first, we introduce a type var for variables.

Variable var : Set.

The keyword Variable makes var universally quantified for the rest of the session. Next we make sure that var is inhabited by at least two distinct values:

Axiom $var_2 : \exists x, y : var.\ (x \neq y)$.

Now our provisional syntax L is as follows:

Inductive Set $L = Var : var \rightarrow L \mid Lam : (var \rightarrow L) \rightarrow L \mid App : L \rightarrow L \rightarrow L$.

This definition generates some exotic terms: indeed, we want the type var to be used only for (bound) meta-variables; those terms using (ground) values of type var have to be ruled out. Also, for var an inductive type, we could have irreducible terms of type $var \rightarrow L$ different from Var, and, through Lam, these would again generate exotic terms. And it seems quite hard to formulate an assumption on var which makes it possible to prove that the terms of type $var \rightarrow L$ are the expected ones only. Here below (higher-order setting), we shall show how to rule out exotic terms.

Induction and Match. The previous declaration generates, for terms of type L, both a Match operator and the following induction principle, available for object proofs:

$\forall P : L \to Prop.$
$(\forall x : var.\ (P\ (Var\ x)))$
$\to\ (\forall e : (var \to L).\ (\forall x : var.\ (P\ (e\ x))) \to (P\ (Lam\ e)))$
$\to\ (\forall a : L.\ (P\ a) \to \forall b : L.\ (P\ b) \to (P\ (App\ a\ b)))$
$\to\ \forall e : L.\ (P\ e).$

First injection principle. The two previous tools make it possible to prove the injection principle for the type L, which is a package of six theorems:

Theorem $Lam\_app : \forall e : (var \to L).\forall a, b : L.\ \neg((Lam\ e) = (App\ a\ b)).$
Theorem $Lam\_lam : \forall a, b : (var \to L).\ ((Lam\ a) = (Lam\ b)) \to (a = b).\ \ldots$

Extensionality. As in the first-order case, the Match operator will generate for instance a term of type $L \to L$ which is extensionally equal but not equal to the identity on L. Even after having ruled out exotic terms and gone to the higher-order setting, it seems quite hard, and maybe impossible, to prove the desired extensionality principle. That is why we introduce the ad-hoc notions of equality, which give the desired extensionality principle for free.

Inductive Definition $eq_L : L \to L \to Prop$
$= eq_L\_var : \forall x : var.(eq_L\ (Var\ x)\ (Var\ x))$
$\mid eq_L\_lam : \forall a, b : (var \to L).(\forall x : var.(eq_L\ (a\ x)\ (a'\ x)))$
$\to (eq_L\ (Lam\ a)\ (Lam\ a'))$
$\mid eq_L\_app : \forall a, a', b, b' : L.\ (eq_L\ a\ a') \to (eq_L\ b\ b') \to (eq_L\ (App\ a\ b)\ (App\ a'\ b')).$

As in the first-order case, where we have given the inversion rules for the *valid* predicate, the previous first injection principle for L makes it possible to prove the rules for inversion of eq_L.

Second injection principle. We now have to suit our injection principle to this new equality. We get a package of six theorems, the proofs of which mainly use the inversion of eq_L.

Theorem $Lam\_app\_eq : \forall e : (var \to L).\forall a, b : L.\ \neg(eq_L\ (Lam\ e)\ (App\ a\ b)).$
Theorem $Lam\_lam\_eq : \forall e, e' : (var \to L).(eq_L\ (Lam\ e)\ (Lam\ e'))$
$\to \forall x : var.(eq_L\ (e\ x)\ (e'\ x)).\ \ldots$

2.3 Higher-order setting

As mentioned in the introduction, it is not yet possible to implement the list of types L_n as a dependent type in Coq. However, by curryfication, we may identify L_n with a type $(list\ n\ L) \to L$. This is how lists enter the picture. Now it turns out to be very uncomfortable to work with such a dependant type, because the type $(list\ n\ L)$ is not equal to the type $(list\ m\ L)$, even when n and m are dynamically equal. This is the reason why we chose infinite lists.

Lists. We simply define lists through: Definition $list = \lambda A : Set.nat \rightarrow A$.

Lists are defined together with the usual terms *cons* , *car*, *cdr* and *map*. An additional basic definition is provided: $proj_p$, that gives the p-th element of a list. A *cst* function builds a list from a given element. A bunch of theorems has been proved on these lists. A typical one is the following:

Theorem $cons\_car\_cdr_{ext} : \forall A : Set.\forall l : (list\ A).$
$\forall n : nat.\ (l\ n) = (cons\ A\ (car\ A\ l)\ (cdr\ A\ l\ )\ n).$

which states that a list is essentially the *cons* of its *car* and its *cdr*. We do not state it as follows:

'Theorem' $cons\_car\_cdr : \forall A : Set.\forall l : (list\ A).\ l = (cons\ A\ (car\ A\ l)\ (cdr\ A\ l\ )).$

because the proof of the latter statement needs some extensionality axiom, like the following one:

Axiom $ext_l : \forall A : Set.\forall f, g : (list\ A).\ (\forall x : nat.(f\ x) = (g\ x)) \rightarrow f = g.$

Actually, this problem of extensionality is recurrent all over our work.

Higher-order constructors. We shall implement our higher-order syntax within the type $(list\ L) \rightarrow L$, which will be denoted as LL. Exotic terms will be ruled out easily, and we shall be able to define a suitable equality. We introduce what we call the higher-order constructors, which will make apparent the tree structure of our higher-order terms.

Definition $\mathcal{R}ef = \lambda i : nat.\lambda x : (list\ L).\ (x\ i).$
Definition $\mathcal{L}am = \lambda e : LL.\lambda x : (list\ L).\ (Lam\ (\lambda y : var.\ (e\ (cons\ L\ (Var\ y)\ x)))).$
Definition $\mathcal{A}pp = \lambda a,\ b : LL.\lambda x : (list\ L).\ (App\ (a\ x)\ (b\ x)).$

These higher-order constructors are the exact counterpart of the constructors of fol. Indeed, we may define naturally the translation relating fol and LL:

Inductive Definition $trans : fol \rightarrow LL \rightarrow Prop$
$= trans\_ref : \forall n : nat.(trans\ (ref\ n)\ (\mathcal{R}ef\ n))$
$|\ trans\_lam : \forall e : fol.\forall e' : LL.(trans\ e\ e') \rightarrow (trans\ (lam\ e)\ (\mathcal{L}am\ e'))$
$|\ trans\_app : \forall a : fol.\forall a' : LL.(trans\ a\ a') \rightarrow$
$\forall b : fol.\ \forall b' : LL.(trans\ b\ b') \rightarrow (trans\ (app\ a\ b)\ (\mathcal{A}pp\ a'\ b')).$

In fact, as for the injection principle given at the end of the previous section, we have to use a modified version of the translation given above, involving our ad hoc equality eq_{LL} given below, instead of Coq's object equality. For example, the first rule of *trans* has to be read as:

$trans\_ref : \forall n : nat.\forall e : LL.(eq_{LL}\ e\ (\mathcal{R}ef\ n)) \rightarrow (trans\ (ref\ n)\ e).$

In the rest of this section, for each definition we shall give (more exactly for wf and $Valid$), we shall only give the simplest version, for clarity.

Coarse equality. In order to prove the desired extensionality principle, we shall define two notions of equality which we shall prove to coincide on well-formed terms. We start with the coarser one: two terms are made equal by this definition if they associate equal (in the sense of eq_L) values to any list of variables:

Definition $eq_{LLv} = \lambda a, b : LL.\forall x : (list\ var).$
$(eq_L\ (a\ (map\ var\ L\ Var\ x))(b\ (map\ var\ L\ Var\ x))).$

Extensional equality. We now turn to our final notion of equality. Two terms are equal by this definition if they associate equal (in the sense of eq_L) values to any list of terms. This notion is finer than the previous one.

Definition $eq_{LL} = \lambda a, b : LL.\forall x : (list\ L).(eq_L\ (a\ x)\ (b\ x))$.
Theorem $eq_{LL}\_eq_{LLv} : \forall a, b : LL.\ (eq_{LL}\ a\ b) \rightarrow (eq_{LLv}\ a\ b)$.

Ruling out exotic terms and the induction principle. It is easy now, using the higher-order constructors, to define inductively the *well-formed* terms of type LL:

Inductive Definition $wf :\ LL \rightarrow$ Prop
$= wf\_ref : \forall n : nat.(wf\ (\mathcal{R}ef\ n))$
$\mid wf\_lam :\ \forall e : LL.\ (wf\ e) \rightarrow (wf\ (\mathcal{L}am\ e))$
$\mid wf\_app : \forall a, b : LL.\ (wf\ a) \rightarrow (wf\ b) \rightarrow (wf\ (\mathcal{A}pp\ a\ b))$.

From this definition, Coq generates the following induction principle (more exactly an equivalent version of it):

$\forall P : LL \rightarrow Prop.$
$(\forall n : nat.(P\ (\mathcal{R}ef\ n)))$
$\rightarrow\ (\forall e : LL.\ (P\ e) \rightarrow (P\ (\mathcal{L}am\ e)))$
$\rightarrow\ (\forall a : LL.\ (P\ a) \rightarrow \forall b : LL.\ (P\ b) \rightarrow (P\ (\mathcal{A}pp\ a\ b)))$
$\rightarrow\ \forall e : LL.(wf\ e) \rightarrow (P\ e)$.

This induction principle is the exact counterpart of the induction principle generated by the definition of fol. We shall also need the counterpart of the induction principle generated by the definition of *valid*. For that, we just have to define the counterpart of *valid*:

Inductive Definition $Valid : \forall n : nat.\ LL \rightarrow$ Prop
$= Valid\_ref : \forall n, i : nat.(i < n) \rightarrow (Valid\ n\ (\mathcal{R}ef\ i))$
$\mid Valid\_lam : \forall n : nat.\ \forall e : LL.\ (Valid\ (S\ n)\ e) \rightarrow (Valid\ n\ (\mathcal{L}am\ e))$
$\mid Valid\_app : \forall n : nat.\forall a, b : LL.(Valid\ n\ a) \rightarrow (Valid\ n\ b) \rightarrow (Valid\ n(\mathcal{A}pp\ a\ b))$

Coarse injection principle. The injection principle corresponding to our coarse equality is composed as usual of six theorems. Only one of them need a wf assumption:

Theorem $Lam\_app\_var : \forall e : LL.\forall a, b : LL.\ \neg(eq_{LLv}\ (\mathcal{L}am\ e)\ (\mathcal{A}pp\ a\ b))$.
Theorem $Lam\_lam\_var : \forall a, b : LL.(wf\ a) \rightarrow (wf\ b) \rightarrow$
$(eq_{LLv}\ (\mathcal{L}am\ a)\ (\mathcal{L}am\ b)) \rightarrow (eq_{LLv}\ a\ b)$. ...

The proofs of these theorems mainly use the inversion of eq_L and the second injection principle given above. In addition to that the proof of theorem *Lam_lam_var* uses the following lemma (whose proof is straightforward):

Theorem $wf\_ext\_eq_L = \forall e : LL.(wf\ e) \rightarrow \forall x, y : (list\ L).(\forall n : nat.(x\ n) = (y\ n))$
$\rightarrow (eq_L\ (e\ x)\ (e\ y))$.

Thanks to the coarse injection principle, we can prove that our two notions of equality coincide on *well-formed* terms:

Theorem $eq_{LLv}\_eq_{LL} : \forall a : LL.(wf\ a) \rightarrow \forall b : LL.(wf\ b) \rightarrow$
$(eq_{LLv}\ a\ b) \rightarrow (eq_{LL}\ a\ b)$.

Final injection principle. The second and coarse injection principles make it possible to prove our final injection principle. The theorem $eq_{LLv}\_eq_{LL}$ given in the previous paragraph is a decisive tool in the proof of the theorems $\mathcal{L}am\_lam$ and $\mathcal{A}pp\_app$, which are the only ones who need a *well-formed* assumption:

Theorem $\mathcal{L}am\_app : \forall e : LL.\forall a, b : LL.\ \neg(eq_{LL}\ (\mathcal{L}am\ e)\ (\mathcal{A}pp\ a\ b))$.
Theorem $\mathcal{L}am\_lam : \forall a : LL.(wf\ a) \rightarrow \forall b : LL.(wf\ b)$
$\rightarrow (eq_{LL}\ (\mathcal{L}am\ a)\ (\mathcal{L}am\ b)) \rightarrow (eq_{LL}\ a\ b)$. ...

2.4 Proof of translation

In this section we shall describe a proof of correctness of our translation from the first-order syntax fol into the higher-order syntax L. Remember that we consider the variant of the translation given in 2.3 suited to our notion of equality. This example of proof illustrates two of our goals. Firstly, it is an example of a proof of adequacy of syntaxes. Secondly, it is an example of a proof in semantics, that makes intensive use of the tools that we have developed in the previous sections.

The correctness of our translation consists in four theorems, stating that the *trans* relation is a surjective function in both directions:

Theorem $trans\_sur\_l : \forall e : fol.\forall n : nat.(valid\ n\ e)$
$\rightarrow \exists e' : LL.(Valid\ n\ e') \wedge (trans\ e\ e')$.
Theorem $trans\_sur\_r : \forall e' : LL.\forall n : nat.(Valid\ n\ e')$
$\rightarrow \exists e : fol.(valid\ n\ e) \wedge (trans\ e\ e')$.
Theorem $trans\_lr : \forall n : nat.\forall e : fol.(valid\ n\ e) \rightarrow \forall a : LL.(Valid\ n\ a)$
$\rightarrow (trans\ e\ a) \rightarrow \forall b : LL.(Valid\ n\ b) \rightarrow (trans\ e\ b) \rightarrow (eq_{LL}\ a\ b)$.
Theorem $trans\_rl : \forall n : nat.\forall e : fol.(valid\ n\ e) \rightarrow \forall e' : LL.(Valid\ n\ e')$
$\rightarrow (trans\ e\ e') \rightarrow \forall f : fol.(valid\ n\ f) \rightarrow (trans\ f\ e') \rightarrow (e = f)$.

These four theorems are easily reduced to corresponding lemmas which do not involve the *valid* or *Valid* conditions. The proofs of the first two lemmas, stating surjectivity, are straightforward. The proofs of the last two lemmas proceed by a double induction on trans, (more exactly induction on *trans* followed by an inversion of *trans*). These proofs use all the injection principles given in the previous subsections.

2.5 Alternative approaches

The reason why we had to introduce ad-hoc equalities could be concentrated in the following statement:

Axiom $ext_l : \forall A : Set.\forall f, g : (list\ A).\ (\forall x : nat.(f\ x) = (g\ x)) \rightarrow f = g$.

This axiom is certainly not provable, since it modifies Coq's object equality by identifying for example the identity function on *nat* and the following term of type $nat \rightarrow nat$, which are extensionally equal:

$\lambda x : nat.\ (Match\ x\ with\ \ (*\ 0\ *)\ 0\ \ (*\ (S\ x)\ *)\ \lambda x, h_x : nat.(S\ x))$.

If we assume this ext_l axiom, we are able to implement our language and to prove the higher-order injection principle in a simpler way, without introducing ad-hoc equalities. Thus we wonder if this very natural axiom could be assumed without making the whole system inconsistent.

A less controversial -and still sufficient- axiom is the following one (where wf is defined using $=$ instead of eq_{LL}):

Axiom $ext_{wf} = \forall e : LL.(wf\ e) \rightarrow \forall x, y : (list\ L).$
$(\forall n : nat.(x\ n) = (y\ n)) \rightarrow (e\ x) = (e\ y).$

It seems quite difficult to prove this axiom at the object-level. However, it is possible to prove it at the meta-level.

3 Generalization

In this section, we explain how the ideas described above make it possible to implement in Coq, any second-order abstract syntax in the sense of [2], together with the corresponding induction, injection and extensionality principles.

3.1 The data

We consider here an arbitrary second-order abstract syntax, given for instance by a LF signature as follows:

$L_1, \ldots, L_n : Type;$
$c_1 : T_1; \ \cdots \ ; c_m : T_m;$

where the L_i's (denoting types) and the c_i's (denoting constructors of these types) are identifiers, while the T_i's belong to the grammar T defined as follows:

$L = L_1 \mid \ldots \mid L_n;$
$A = L \mid L \rightarrow A;$
$T = L \mid A \rightarrow T;$

To the previous sequence of grammars, we associate the following one, which is suited for replacing, in terms of T, negative occurrences of L's by the corresponding V's:

$L = L_1 \mid \ldots \mid L_n;$
$V = V_1 \mid \ldots \mid V_n;$
$A^v = L \mid V \rightarrow A^v;$
$T^v = L \mid A^v \rightarrow T^v;$

Since there is a natural bijection between the terms in L and the terms in V, there is also a natural bijection between the terms in A and the terms in A^v, and also between the terms in T and the terms in T^v. We denote by X^v the term associated with the term X by this bijection. We write $T_i = m_{i,1} \rightarrow \ldots \rightarrow m_{i,a_i} \rightarrow L_{p_i}$ and $m_{i,j} = L_{q_{i,j,1}} \rightarrow \ldots \rightarrow L_{q_{i,j,b_{i,j}}} \rightarrow L_{q_{i,j,0}}$.

Thus c_i has type:

$(L_{q_{i,1,1}} \rightarrow \ldots \rightarrow L_{q_{i,1,b_{i,1}}} \rightarrow L_{q_{i,1,0}}) \rightarrow \ldots$
$\rightarrow (L_{q_{i,j,1}} \rightarrow \ldots \rightarrow L_{q_{i,j,b_{i,j}}} \rightarrow L_{q_{i,j,0}}) \rightarrow \ldots$
$\rightarrow (L_{q_{i,a_i,1}} \rightarrow \ldots \rightarrow L_{q_{i,a_i,b_{i,a_i}}} \rightarrow L_{q_{i,a_i,0}})$
$\rightarrow L_{p_i}.$

The p, q, a, b's are, together with n and m, the integers encoding the syntax (its arity in the terminology of [2]). Observe that a and b are families of arbitrary integers (depending on one and two integers respectively) and that p and q are in $1 \ldots n$ (depending on one and three integers respectively). We fix the natural convention that if $(a_i = 0)$ then $c_i = L_{p_i}$ and if $(b_{i,j} = 0)$ then $m_{i,j} = L_{q_{i,j,0}}$.

3.2 Preliminary declarations

Now we describe a list of Coq declarations which are necessary for our implementation of this syntax. For this we introduce some further notations.

At first, because there is no mutual inductive definitions in Coq, we have to define our types L_i as a single dependent type. There is a standard way[3] to do this. First we define the type for parameters as an inductive type with n elements:

Inductive Set $Param = P_1 : Param \mid \ldots \mid P_n : Param.$

Then we use as above a type var, inhabited by at least two distinct values:

Variable var : Set. Axiom $var_2 : \exists x, y : var.\ (x \neq y).$

We build typed variables by multiplying the type var and the type $Param$:

Inductive Type $pvar : Param \rightarrow Set = Pvar : \forall p : Param.var \rightarrow (pvar\ p).$

3.3 Provisional syntax

Now we can introduce the provisional syntax as follows:

Inductive Type $L : Param \rightarrow Set$

$= Var : \forall i : Param.(pvar\ i) \rightarrow (L\ i) \mid C_1 : T_1^w \mid \ldots \mid C_m : T_m^w.$

where T_i^w is the term built from T_i^v by substituting $(L\ j)$ for occurrences of L_j, and $(pvar\ j)$ for occurrences of V_j (for all values of j).

Thus C_i has type T_i^w. We write $T_i^w = t_{i,1} \rightarrow \ldots \rightarrow t_{i,a_i} \rightarrow L_{p_i}$ where $t_{i,j} = (pvar\ q_{i,j,1}) \rightarrow\ \ldots\ \rightarrow (pvar\ q_{i,j,b_{i,j}}) \rightarrow (L\ q_{i,j,0})$.

The injection principle for the type L consists of four series of theorems. The first series contains only the following:

Theorem $Var\_Var : \forall p : Param.\forall x, y : (pvar\ p).$
$((Var\ p\ x) = (Var\ p\ y)) \rightarrow (x = y).$

Then for each $i \in 1 \ldots m$ we have:

Theorem $C_i\_C_i : \forall x_1, y_1 : t_{i,1}.\ldots\forall x_{a_i}, y_{a_i} : t_{i,a_i}.$
$((C_i\ x_1 \ldots x_{a_i}) = (C_i\ y_1 \ldots y_{a_i})) \rightarrow (x_1 = y_1) \wedge \ldots \wedge (x_{a_i} = y_{a_i}).$

For each $j \in 1 \ldots m$ we also have:

Theorem $Var\_C_j : \forall x : (pvar\ p_j).\forall y_1 : t_{j,1}.\ldots\forall y_{a_j} : t_{j,a_j}.$
$\neg((Var\ p_j\ x) = (C_j\ y_1 \ldots y_{a_j})).$

And for any couple $i < j$ in $1 \ldots m$ satisfying $p_i = p_j$, we have:

Theorem $C_i\_C_j : \forall x_1 : t_{i,1}.\ldots\forall x_{a_i} : t_{i,a_i}.\forall y_1 : t_{j,1}.\ldots\forall y_{a_j} : t_{j,a_j}.$
$\neg((C_i\ x_1 \ldots x_{a_i}) = (C_j\ y_1 \ldots y_{a_j})).$

The ad-hoc equality is introduced by the following definition:

Inductive Definition $eq_L : \forall i : Param.(L\ i) \rightarrow (L\ i) \rightarrow Prop$

$= eq_L\_var : \forall i : Param.\forall x : (pvar\ i).(eq_L\ i\ (Var\ i\ x)\ (Var\ i\ x))$

$\mid eq_L\_C_1 : \ldots$

$\mid \ldots$

$\mid eq_L\_C_i : \forall x_1, y_1 : t_{i,1}.(\forall z_1 : (pvar\ q_{i,1,1}).\ldots\forall z_{b_{i,1}} : (pvar\ q_{i,1,b_{i,1}}).$
$(eqL\ q_{i,1,0}\ (x_1\ z_1\ \ldots\ z_{b_{i,1}})\ (y_1\ z_1\ \ldots\ z_{b_{i,1}})))$

$\rightarrow \ldots$

$\rightarrow \forall x_{a_i}, y_{a_i} : t_{i,a_i}.(\forall z_1 : (pvar\ q_{i,a_i,1}).\ldots\forall z_{b_{i,a_i}} : (pvar\ q_{i,a_i,b_{i,a_i}}).$
$(eqL\ q_{i,a_i,0}\ (x_{a_i}\ z_1 \ldots z_{b_{i,a_i}})(y_{a_i}\ z_1 \ldots z_{b_{i,a_i}})))$

$\rightarrow (eq_L\ p_i\ (C_i\ x_1 \ldots x_{a_i})\ (C_i\ y_1 \ldots y_{a_i}))$

$\mid \ldots$

$\mid eq_L\_C_m : \ldots$

The second ground injection principle is again a package of four series of theorems. We only give one of them here. The others are a simple modification of the injection principle given above, where Coq's object equality on L is replaced by our eq_L equality. For each $i \in 1 \cdots m$ we have:

Theorem $C_i\_C_i\_eq : \forall x_1, y_1 : t_{i,1}. \cdots \forall x_{a_i}, y_{a_i} : t_{i,a_i}.$
$(eq_L\ p_i\ (C_i\ x_1 \cdots x_{a_i})\ (C_i\ y_1 \cdots y_{a_i}))$
$\rightarrow (\forall z_1 : (pvar\ q_{i,1,1}). \cdots \forall z_{b_{i,1}} : (pvar\ q_{i,1,b_{i,1}}).$
$(eqL\ q_{i,1,0}\ (x_1\ z_1\ \cdots\ z_{b_{i,1}})\ (y_1\ z_1\ \cdots\ z_{b_{i,1}})))$
$\wedge \cdots$
$\wedge(\forall z_1 : (pvar\ q_{i,a_i,1}). \cdots \forall z_{b_{i,a_i}} : (pvar\ q_{i,a_i,b_{i,a_i}}).$
$(eq_L\ q_{i,a_i,0}\ (x_{a_i}\ z_1\ \cdots\ z_{b_{i,a_i}})\ (y_{a_i}\ z_1\ \cdots\ z_{b_{i,a_i}}))).$

3.4 Higher-order setting

Next, our final type is the type of functions with values in $(L\ p)$ depending on n lists of arguments (one for each type):

Definition $mlist = \lambda L : (Param \rightarrow Set).\forall p : Param.nat \rightarrow (L\ p).$
Definition $LL = \lambda p : Param.(mlist\ L) \rightarrow (L\ p).$

Next, we define the higher-order constructors $\mathcal{C}_i$.

We define in general $\mathcal{C}$ for each term C of a type T of the form:

$T = ((pvar\ q_{1,1}) \rightarrow \cdots \rightarrow (pvar\ q_{1,b_1}) \rightarrow (L\ q_{1,0})) \rightarrow \cdots$
$\rightarrow ((pvar\ q_{a,1}) \rightarrow \cdots \rightarrow (pvar\ q_{a,b_a}) \rightarrow (L\ q_{a,0})) \rightarrow (L\ p).$

The term $\mathcal{C}$ is the following Coq term of type $(LL\ q_{1,0}) \rightarrow \cdots \rightarrow (LL\ q_{a,0}) \rightarrow (LL\ p)$:

$\mathcal{C} = \lambda z_1 : (LL\ q_{1,0}). \cdots \lambda z_a : (LL\ q_{a,0}).\lambda z : (mlist\ L).$
$(C\ \lambda x_1 : (pvar\ q_{1,1}). \cdots \lambda x_{b_1} : (pvar\ q_{1,b_1}).$
$(z_1\ (append\ ((Var\ q_{1,1}\ x_1) \cdots (Var\ q_{1,b_1}\ x_{b_1}))\ z))\ \ldots$
$\lambda x_1 : (pvar\ q_{a,1}). \cdots \lambda x_{b_a} : (pvar\ q_{a,b_a}).$
$(z_a\ (append\ ((Var\ q_{a,1}\ x_1) \cdots (Var\ q_{a,b_a}\ x_{b_a}))\ z))).$

Where $(append\ (s_1\ \cdots s_p)\ z)$ denotes the Coq term z in case $p = 0$, and the Coq term $(append\ (s_1\ \cdots s_{p-1})\ (mcons\ s_p\ z))$ otherwise; where again, for s of type $(L\ P_i)$, $(mcons\ s\ z)$ denotes the Coq term

$\lambda p : Param.\ (Match\ p\ with$
$(*\ p_1\ *)\ (z\ p_1)\ \cdots\ (*\ p_i\ *)\ (cons\ (L\ p_i)\ s\ (z\ p_i))\ \cdots\ (*\ p_n\ *)\ (z\ p_n)).$

The projections $\mathcal{R}ef : \forall i : Param.\forall n : nat.(mlist\ L) \rightarrow (L\ i)$ are defined by:
$\mathcal{R}ef = \lambda i : Param.\lambda n : nat.\lambda z : (mlist\ L).(z\ i\ n).$

In the following definition of our coarse equality, the term $mmap$, standing for 'multi-map', is the evident one:

Definition $eq_{LLv} = \lambda p : Param.\lambda E, E' : (LL\ p).\forall x : (mlist\ pvar).$
$(eq_L\ p\ (E\ (mmap\ var\ L\ Var\ x))\ (E'\ (mmap\ var\ L\ Var\ x))).$

Here is now our final notion of equality, which is finer than the previous one:

Definition $eq_{LL} = \lambda p : Param.\lambda e, e' : (LL\ p).\forall x : (mlist\ L).(eq_L\ p\ (e\ x)\ (e'\ x)).$
Theorem $eq_{LL}\_eq_{LLv} : \forall p : Param.\forall e, e' : (LL\ p).(eq_{LL}\ p\ e\ e') \rightarrow (eq_{LLv}\ p\ e\ e').$

Next we define the *well-formed* terms of type LL. This definition generates the desired induction principle.

Inductive Definition $wf: \forall p: Param.(LL\ p) \rightarrow$ Prop
$= wf\_ref : \forall p : Param.\forall n : nat.\forall E : (LL\ p).(eq_{LL}\ p\ E\ (\mathcal{R}ef\ p\ n)) \rightarrow (wf\ p\ E)$
$\mid wf\_C_1 : \forall E : (LL\ p_1).\forall E_1 : (LL\ q_{1,1,0}).\cdots\forall E_{a_1} : (LL\ q_{1,a_1,0}).$
$(eq_{LL}\ p_1\ E\ (\mathcal{C}_1\ E_1\ \cdots E_{a_1})) \rightarrow (wf\ q_{1,1,0}\ E_1) \rightarrow \cdots \rightarrow (wf\ q_{1,a_1,0}\ E_{a_1})$
$\rightarrow (wf\ p_1\ E)$
$\mid \cdots$
$\mid wf\_C_m : \forall E : (LL\ p_m).\forall E_1 : (LL\ q_{m,1,0}).\cdots\forall E_{a_m} : (LL\ q_{m,a_m,0}).$
$(eq_{LL}\ p_m\ E\ (\mathcal{C}_m\ E_1\ \cdots E_{a_m})) \rightarrow (wf\ q_{m,1,0}\ E_1) \rightarrow \cdots \rightarrow (wf\ q_{m,a_m,0}\ E_{a_m})$
$\rightarrow (wf\ p_m\ E).$

For the definition of $Valid$ we need the numbers $\delta_{i,j,p}$ of arguments of type L_p of terms of type $m_{i,j}$. In the following definition, for a meta-level integer d and an object-level integer v, we denote by $v + d$ the object-level integer which is defined as v if $d = 0$ and as $(S\ v + (d-1))$ otherwise.

Inductive Definition $Valid: \forall v_1, \cdots, v_n : nat.\forall p : Param.(LL\ p) \rightarrow$ Prop
$= Valid\_ref\_1 : \ldots$
$\mid Valid\_ref\_i : \forall E : (LL\ P_i).\forall v_1, \cdots, v_n : nat.\forall k : nat.\ (k < v_i)$
$\rightarrow (eq_{LL}\ P_i\ E\ (\mathcal{R}ef\ P_i\ k)) \rightarrow (Valid\ v_1 \cdots v_n\ P_i\ E)$
$\mid \cdots$
$\mid Valid\_C_i : \forall E : (LL\ p_i).\forall E_1 : (LL\ q_{i,1,0}).\cdots\ \forall E_{a_i} : (LL\ q_{i,a_i,0}).$
$(eq_{LL}\ p_i\ E\ (\mathcal{C}_i\ E_1\ \cdots E_{a_i})) \rightarrow$
$(Valid\ (v_1 + \delta_{i,1,1}) \cdots (v_n + \delta_{i,1,n})\ q_{i,1,0}\ E_1) \rightarrow \cdots \rightarrow$
$(Valid\ (v_1 + \delta_{i,a_i,1}) \cdots (v_n + \delta_{i,a_i,n})\ q_{i,a_i,0}\ E_{a_i}) \rightarrow (Valid\ v_1 \cdots v_n\ p_i\ E).$
$\mid \cdots$
$\mid Valid\_C_m : \ldots$

The first part of the injection principle corresponding to our coarse equality, namely the theorems
Var_Var_var, $Var\_C_j\_var$ and $C_i\_C_j\_var$ do not contain any wf-assumption. We expand the last series $C_i\_C_i\_var$ which do contain these assumptions.

Theorem $C_i\_C_i\_var : \forall x_1, y_1 : (LL\ q_{i,1,0}).\cdots\forall x_{a_i}, y_{a_i} : (LL\ q_{i,a_i,0}).$
$(wf\ q_{i,1,0}\ x_1) \rightarrow (wf\ q_{i,1,0}\ y_1) \rightarrow \cdots (wf\ q_{i,a_i,0}\ x_{a_i}) \rightarrow (wf\ q_{i,a_i,0}\ y_{a_i})$
$\rightarrow (eq_{LLv}\ p_i\ (\mathcal{C}_i\ x_1 \cdots x_{a_i})\ (\mathcal{C}_i\ y_1 \cdots y_{a_i}))$
$\rightarrow (eq_{LLv}\ q_{i,1,0}\ x_1\ y_1) \wedge \cdots \wedge (eq_{LLv}\ q_{i,a_i,0}\ x_{a_i}\ y_{a_i}).$

The proof of the above theorem uses the following lemma:

Theorem $wf\_ext\_eq_L = \forall p : Param.\forall E : (LL\ p).(wf\ p\ E) \rightarrow \forall x, y : (mlist\ L).$
$(\forall q : Param.\forall n : nat.(x\ q\ n) = (y\ q\ n)) \rightarrow (eq_L\ p\ (E\ x)\ (E\ y)).$

Thanks to the coarse injection principle, we can state that our two notions of equality coincide on *well-formed* terms:

Theorem $eq_{LLv}\_eq_{LL} : \forall p : Param.\forall a : (LL\ p).(wf\ p\ a) \rightarrow \forall b : (LL\ p).(wf\ p\ b)$
$\rightarrow (eq_{LLv}\ p\ a\ b) \rightarrow (eq_{LL}\ p\ a\ b).$

As before, the first part of the injection principle corresponding to eq_{LL}, namely the theorems $\mathcal{R}ef\_ref$, $\mathcal{R}ef\_\mathcal{C}_j$ and $\mathcal{C}_i\_\mathcal{C}_j$ do not contain any wf-assumption. We expand the last series $\mathcal{C}_i\_\mathcal{C}_i$ which do contain such an assumption.

Theorem $C_i\_C_i : \forall x_1 : (LL\ q_{i,1,0}).(wf\ q_{i,1,0}\ x_1) \rightarrow \forall y_1 : (LL\ q_{i,1,0}).(wf\ q_{i,1,0}\ y_1)$
$\rightarrow \cdots \rightarrow \forall x_{a_i} : (LL\ q_{i,a_i,0}).(wf\ q_{i,a_i,0}\ x_{a_i}) \rightarrow \forall y_{a_i} : (LL\ q_{i,a_i,0}).(wf\ q_{i,a_i,0}\ y_{a_i})$
$\rightarrow (eq_{LL}\ p_i\ (C_i\ x_1 \cdots x_{a_i})\ (C_i\ y_1 \cdots y_{a_i}))$
$\rightarrow (eq_{LL}\ q_{i,1,0}\ x_1\ y_1) \wedge \cdots \wedge (eq_{LL}\ q_{i,a_i,0}\ x_{a_i}\ y_{a_i}).$

3.5 Adequacy

In this subsection, we discuss correctness and adequacy of the generalization proposed in the previous subsections. The proofs of the two theorems stated in this subsection are straightforward, although tedious. We do not state them here because of space limitation.

The correctness is expressed by the following (meta) theorem:

Theorem 1. *Consider a second-order abstract syntax (given for instance through its arity, namely the package of integers n, m, a, b, p, q as above). Then:*

(i) The corresponding sequence of definitions (inductive or not) listed in this section is a correct sequence of Coq definitions.
(ii) The types of the corresponding sequence of theorems listed above are correct Coq types.
(iii) All these theorems have object proofs.
(iv) The meta-form of all these theorems is true.

In order to state adequacy, we have to build some category [2]. Let S be a second-order abstract syntax given as in the previous statement, with the integers n, m, a, b, p, q. The corresponding sequence of definitions listed above generates Coq types $(L\ P_i)$'s and $(LL\ P_j)$'s, the predicate $Valid$ and equalities eq_L and eq_{LL} from which we build a Cartesian category S_{Coq} as follows.

The objects of S_{Coq} are (indexed by) sequences of n natural integers, and product of objects corresponds to addition of sequences. We denote by L^I the object indexed by the sequence $I = (i_1, \ldots, i_n)$. In order to describe morphisms in S_{Coq}, since it is Cartesian, it is sufficient to describe $Hom(L^I, X)$ for indecomposable X's. The indecomposable objects are those indexed by the indecomposable indices, namely $I_1 := (1, 0, \ldots, 0), \ldots, I_n := (0, \ldots, 0, 1)$. We take for $Hom(L^I, L^{I_j})$ the set of Coq terms t of type $(LL\ P_j)$ satisfying $(Valid\ i_1 \cdots i_n\ t)$, modulo the equivalence relation $(eq_{LL}\ P_j)$ (we hope the category structure is sufficiently apparent; to settle it, one should use the properties of eq_{LL} listed above). Now, we can state the adequacy statement.

Theorem 2. *Let S be a second-order abstract syntax given as in the previous statement. Then the cartesian category S_{Coq} is naturally isomorphic with the first-order part of S.*

Thus, for a second-order abstract syntax given by a LF signature as in 3.1, we have implemented first order terms (i.e. terms whose type has shape $L_{i_1} \rightarrow \cdots \rightarrow L_{i_n} \rightarrow L_{i_0}$) as classes (with respect to some object-level equivalence relation, here eq_{LL}) of (tuples of) terms of some object-level type (here, roughly speaking, LL) satisfying some object-level predicate (here $Valid$).

Note that, in contrast with the natural LF implementation, we only implement first-order terms. This is sufficient for semantics purposes.

4 Related Work

The general notion of Higher-Order Abstract Syntax has been introduced in [4] and is currently being revisited in [2]. Higher-order abstract syntax is now commonly used, at least by people who use either the λ-Prolog language [13],or the Elf language [16] -an implementation of the LF Logical Framework [1][8][9], both for writing semantics of languages [5][7] and for developing proofs in those semantics [6][12][17]. Proofs in Elf [6][12][17] use induction. All these proofs rely on the introduction of an adequate induction principle.

On the other hand, using systematically Coq's inductive types, Gerard Huet developed in Coq a theory of simply-typed λ-calculus with complete proofs in the first-order setting.

To our knowledge, the method described in the present paper is the first one which allows writing semantics on higher-order abstract syntax in a system which provides inductive types.

5 Conclusions and Future Work

We have explained how to implement in Coq any second-order abstract syntax together with the corresponding induction, injection and extensionality principles. In performing this task, our main trouble came from the fact that Coq's object equality is not extensional. We have also produced samples of proofs using extensively these principles. Our work would not be relevant if our implementation of second-order syntax did not allow smooth formulation and object proofs for semantics. Although not presented here, we have already gathered a lot of positive experience about this and our next task is to present them in a systematic treatment. Just to satisfy the curiosity of the reader, we give here a rule for β-reduction:

$red_\beta : \forall e : LL.\forall v : LL.(red\ (App\ (\mathcal{L}am\ e)\ v)\ \lambda x : (list\ L).\ (e\ (cons\ (v\ x)\ x)))$.

Another task is to design and implement a top-level over Coq providing user-friendly support for implementing in our way object second-order syntaxes and performing object proofs on them. On the other hand, before tightening definitely our project to Coq, it seems reasonable to explore other theorem provers equipped with induction, in particular HOL and Isabelle, in order to verify that the difficulties we have encountered could not be overcome there in an easier way.

Acknowledgements Thanks go to Frank Pfenning for useful comments on an earlier draft version of the paper. We would like to thank Amy Felty and Christine Paulin-Mohring for many fruitful discussions, and more generally the Coq team for their quick and helpful e-mail answers. Finally we thank Yves Bertot for his very comfortable interface for the Coq system.

References

1. A. Avron, F. Honsell, and A. Mason. Using typed λ-calculus to implement formal systems on a machine. Technical Report ECS-LFCS-87-31, Edinburgh University, July 1987.
2. Th. Despeyroux and A. Hirschowitz. A categorical approach to higher-order abstract syntax. forthcoming paper, 1994.

3. G. Dowek, A. Felty, H. Herbelin, G. Huet, C. Murthy, C. Parent, Ch. Paulin-Mohring, and B. Werner. The coq proof assistant user's guide, version 5.8. Technical Report 154, Inria, Rocquencourt, France, May 1993.
4. C. Elliot and F. Pfenning. Higher-order abstract syntax. In *Proceedings of the ACM SIGPLAN' 88 International Conference on Programming Language Design and Implementation, Atlanta, Georgia, USA*, June 22-24, 1988.
5. J. Hannan and D. Miller. Enriching a meta-language with higher-order features. In *Proceedings of the Workshop on Meta-Programming in Logic Programming, Bristol*, June 1988.
6. J. Hannan and F. Pfenning. Compiler verification in LF. In IEEE, editor, *Proceedings of the LICS International Conference on Logic In Computer Sciences, Santa Cruz, California*, June 1992.
7. R. Harper. Systems of polymorphic type assignment in LF. Technical Report CMU-CS-90-144, Carnegie Mellon University, Pittsburgh, Pennsylvania, June 1990.
8. R. Harper, F. Honsell, and G. Plotkin. A framework for defining logics. In IEEE, editor, *Proceedings of the second LICS International Conference on Logic In Computer Sciences, Cornell, USA*, pages 194–204, 1987.
9. R. Harper, F. Honsell, and G. Plotkin. A framework for defining logics. Technical Report ECS-LFCS-91-162, Edinburgh University, June 1991.
10. G. Huet. Constructive computation theory. part I. Lecture notes. October 1992.
11. G. Kahn. Natural semantics. In *Proceedings of the Symp. on Theorical Aspects of Computer Science, Passau, Germany*, 1987. also available as a Research Report RR-601, Inria, Sophia-Antipolis, February 1987.
12. S. Michaylov and F. Pfenning. Natural semantics and some of its meta-theory in elf. In Lars Halln"as, editor, *Proceedings of the Second Workshop on Extentions of Logic Programing*, Springer-Verlag LNCS, 1991. also available as a Technical Report MPI-I-91-211, Max-Planck-Institute for Computer Science,Saarbrucken, Germany, August 1991.
13. D. Miller and G. Nadathur. An overview of λ-prolog. In MIT Press, editor, *Proceedings of the International Logic Programming Conference, Seattle, Washington*, pages 910–827, August 1988.
14. Ch. Paulin-Mohring. Inductive definitions in the system coq. rules and properties. In J.F. Groote M. Bezem, editor, *Proceedings of the International Conference on Typed Lambda Calculi and Applications, TLCA'93*, Springer-Verlag LNCS 664, pages 328–345, 1992. also available as a Research Report RR-92-49, Dec. 1992, ENS Lyon, France.
15. L. C. Paulson. The foundation of a generic theorem prover. *Journal of Automated Reasoning*, 5:363–397, 1989.
16. F. Pfenning. Elf: A language for logic definition and verified metaprogramming. In *Proceedings of the fourth ACM-IEEE Symp. on Logic In Computer Science, Asilomar, California, USA*, June 1989.
17. F. Pfenning and E. Rohwedder. Implementing the meta-theory of deductive systems. In *Proceedings of the CADE-11 Conference*, 1991.

Towards Efficient Calculi for Resource-Oriented Deductive Planning*

Stefan Brüning

FG Intellektik, FB Informatik, Technische Hochschule Darmstadt
Alexanderstraße 10, D-64283 Darmstadt (Germany)
E-mail: stebr@intellektik.informatik.th-darmstadt.de

Abstract. An important advantage of deductive approaches for solving planning problems is the possibility to exploit powerful proof methods and techniques to reduce the search space developed in the field of automated deduction. The aim of this paper is to adapt such techniques to build efficient resource-oriented planning systems.

1 Introduction

Recently, three new deductive approaches for solving planning problems were proposed. They are based on the linear connection method [2], an equational Horn logic [15], and on a fragment of linear logic [18]. One of the tempting features of these approaches is that they do not require to state frame axioms explicitly. In [13, 8] it was shown that the approaches are essentially equivalent. They are all built on the key idea that facts describing situations are resources which can be consumed and produced. More precisely, as pointed out in [13], a situation can be seen as a multiset of facts. The facts are consumed when the conditions of actions are to be satisfied and are produced as the effects of an action. Thus, planning in these approaches is closely related to planning in STRIPS [10, 17] except that multisets are used instead of sets. As argued in [14] multisets represent resources more adequately than sets and, moreover, it is more efficient to compute with multisets instead of sets. Furthermore, planning is performed in a purely deductive system. This allows the integration of arbitrary additional theories as well as the exploitation of powerful search procedures and heuristics developed in the fields of Automated Deduction and Logic Programming.

The aim of this paper is to provide techniques to build efficient resource-oriented planning systems. We concentrate on the approach based on the linear connection method. In the first part of the paper we therefore give an introduction to the linear connection method and develop a novel calculus which is similar to the extension calculus [3] whose concrete implementations (eg. see [16]) are highly successful.

In the second part of the paper we show that techniques avoiding redundancies, which are useful for first-order theorem proving, can also be incorporated into specialized calculi developed for solving planning problems. This will be

* The author is supported by the Deutsche Forschungsgemeinschaft (DFG) within project KONNEKTIONSBEWEISER under grant no. Bi 228/6-2.

exemplified using the calculus presented in the first part. We focus our attention on the following three aspects.

Firstly, we adapt techniques to avoid useless derivation steps which originally were developed in the field of Logic Programming [5]. Secondly, we present a technique to use lemmata throughout linear connection proofs. By generating lemmata it is possible to use subproofs, which have been generated once, several times (for instance see [11, 1]). Furthermore, it is quite often the case that some sequences of derivation steps which do not constitute a subproof have to be performed repeatedly. We therefore propose a technique to keep such sequences, called macros, instead of generating them again and again.

Formulating our techniques we had to pay special attention to the concept of resources. The aforementioned equivalence results allow to adapt the techniques to systems based on the equational Horn logic approach or on linear logic.

The paper is organized as follows: In Section 2 we introduce definitions and notations. In Section 3 disjunctive planning problems and their solutions are formally introduced. The linear connection method is discussed in Section 4. Based on the method a sound and complete calculus is introduced. This calculus can be augmented by techniques presented in Section 5 to Section 7. In Section 5 a loop check is presented, the use of lemmata is proposed in Section 6, and a possibility to store macros is given in Section 7. In Section 8 we conclude.

Due to lack of space proofs are omitted. They can be found in [7].

2 Preliminaries

We assume the reader to be familiar with the concepts of first-order logic. We use the following conventions throughout this paper: Relations, functions, and constants are denoted by lower case letters whereas variables are denoted by upper case letters. $\{E_1 \backslash E_2\}$ is the notation for a substitution replacing an expression — i.e. a term or a formula — E_1 by an expression E_2. The negation of a literal L is either denoted by $\neg L$ or by $\overline{L}$.

The connection method [3, 4] is usually presented as an affirmative method for proving the validity of a formula. Dealing with connection calculi we represent formulas in a two dimensional way, so called *matrices*: A matrix is a disjunction of clauses while a clause is a conjunction of matrices[2]. Conjunctive formula parts are listed vertically and disjunctive ones horizontally omitting the connectives $\wedge$ and $\vee$. Therefore, we assume formulas to be given in AND/OR form that allows no propositional connectives other than $\wedge$ and $\vee$, and restricts the negation sign to occur in literals only[3]. For instance, the formula $[p \wedge (q \vee r)] \vee s \vee l$ is represented by the following matrix:

$$\begin{array}{|cccc|} & p & s & l \\ q & r & & \end{array}$$

[2] Throughout this paper clauses are restricted to be conjunctions of disjunctions of literals.

[3] It is not allowed to generate a disjunctive normal form since the involved operations are not compatible with the concept of resources.

A *path* in a matrix is a sequence consisting of one element from each clause. For instance, the sequence $(B \vee C, D, E)$ is a path through the above matrix. A *connection* in a matrix is an unordered pair of literals with the same predicate symbol and different signs. It is *complementary* if the literals are identical except for the sign. An *indexed form* of a matrix M is a Matrix M' consisting of a set of copies of the clauses of M. To prove the validity of a matrix M we have to check the existence of an indexed form M' of M and a substitution σ that such that each path through $M'\sigma$ contains two literals which constitute a complementary connection (see [3]).

3 Disjunctive Planning Problems

A *disjunctive planning problem* (dpp) $\langle \mathcal{I}, \mathcal{A}, \mathcal{G} \rangle$ consists of a set of initial situations $\mathcal{I} = \{I_1, \ldots, I_n\}$, a set of goal situations $\mathcal{G} = \{G_1, \ldots, G_m\}$, and a set of actions $\mathcal{A}$ (see also [8]). Roughly speaking, the solution to a dpp provides sequences of actions such that for each initial situation there exists such a sequence leading to a goal situation.

A *situation* is represented by a multiset of atoms. An action α is of the form $C \leadsto \{E_1, \ldots, E_k\}$ where the multiset of atoms C denotes the *condition* of α and each multiset of atoms E_i a possible *effect* of α. The resources represented by the atoms in C are consumed by applying α whereas the resources represented by the atoms in E_i are produced if the application of α results in its i-th effect. We assume that all variables occurring in the effects of an action also occur in its precondition. As an action α containing n alternatives as condition can be expanded to an equivalent set of actions $\alpha_1, \ldots, \alpha_n$ where the condition of α_i corresponds to the i-th alternative of α, we assume that the condition of an action consists of only a single multiset.

Disjunctive planning problems are useful to formulate examples where actions can have different alternative effects. A plan including such actions naturally has to take each of these alternatives into account. In contrast to dpp's, *conjunctive planning problems* contain only one initial situation and an action is allowed to have at most one effect.

Example 1. Suppose a person named Bert is in a hurry and enters a bus without knowing exactly whether its the F-bus or the H-bus. Besides the bus ticket (ti) needed to drive with the bus, Bert has some flowers (fl) and wants to meet his girl friend who is waiting at the bus stop A (bsA). If Bert entered the F-bus, the bus will drive directly to this bus stop whereas in the other case the bus stops at station B (bsB) from where Bert has to walk 400 meters.

This scenario can be described as a dpp. The set of initial situations is $\{\dot{\{}fl, ti\dot{\}}\}$[4] representing Bert having the flowers and the bus ticket. The set of goal situations is $\{\dot{\{}bsA, fl\dot{\}}\}$ expressing that Bert is at bus station A to give the flowers to his girl friend. The elements of $\mathcal{A}$ are:

$dr: \dot{\{}ti\dot{\}} \leadsto \{\dot{\{}bsA\dot{\}}, \dot{\{}bsB\dot{\}}\}$ for driving with the bus
$wa: \dot{\{}bsB\dot{\}} \leadsto \{\dot{\{}bsA\dot{\}}\}$ for walking from station B to station A

[4] Multisets are denoted by the brackets $\dot{\{}$ and $\dot{\}}$ whereas sets are denoted as usual by $\{$ and $\}$. The operations $\dot{\subseteq}$, $\dot{\cup}$, and $\dot{-}$ denote the multiset extensions of the usual set operations $\subseteq$, $\cup$, and $-$.

Definition 1. An action $\alpha: C \rightsquigarrow \{E_1, \ldots, E_n\}$ is *applicable* to a situation S iff there is a substitution θ such that $C\theta \subseteq S$ holds. If α is applicable to S then the application of α to S yields the set of situations $\{(S \dot{-} C\theta) \dot{\cup} E_j\theta \mid 1 \leq j \leq n\}$.

Thus applying an action α containing n alternatives to a situation S results in n Situations $S_1, \ldots, S_n$. S_i does not contain the resources needed to apply α, viz the elements of C, but contains the resources produced by α in the i-th effect, viz the elements contained in E_i. For example, action *dr* can be applied to $\{\{ti, fl\}\}$ yielding the set $\{\{fl, bsA\}, \{fl, bsB\}\}$. The application of θ is required in case the atoms representing the involved resources contain variables.

If the application of an action to a situation S results in a set of situations $S_1, \ldots, S_k$, each subproblem is solved separately (that also happens to the set of initial situations). For example, if we split $\{\{fl, bsA\}, \{fl, bsB\}\}$ into $\{\{fl, bsA\}\}$ and $\{\{fl, bsB\}\}$ Bert's problem is already solved in the first alternative whereas we have to apply action *wa* to the second one.

Intuitively, a sequence of actions including the ability of splitting alternatives forms a plan. To define plans we first have to define so called *1-plans*. A 1-plan is a plan considering only sets of initial situations containing a sole element.

Definition 2. *1-plans* are inductively defined as follows.

1. The empty list [] is a 1-plan called the *empty plan*.
2. If p is a 1-plan and α is an action containing exactly one effect then $[\alpha, p]$ is a 1-plan.
3. If $p_1, \ldots, p_k$ are 1-plans and α is an action containing exactly k alternative effects $E_1, \ldots, E_k$ then $[\alpha, cond(E_1, p_1, \ldots, E_k, p_k)]$ is a 1-plan.
4. Nothing else is a 1-plan.

Definition 3. A *plan* is either a 1-plan or has the form $[cond(S_1, p_1, \ldots, S_k, p_k)]$ where $S_1, \ldots, S_k$ are situations and $p_1, \ldots, p_k$ are 1-plans.

The property of a plan p to solve a given dpp $\langle \mathcal{I}, \mathcal{A}, \mathcal{G} \rangle$ with a substitution σ is defined inductively as follows:

Definition 4.

1. The plan [] solves $\langle \mathcal{I}, \mathcal{A}, \mathcal{G} \rangle$ with σ iff for all $I \in \mathcal{I}$ there is a $G \in \mathcal{G}$ such that $I\sigma \dot{\supseteq} G\sigma$.
2. The plan $[cond(S_1, p_1, \ldots, S_k, p_k)]$ solves $\langle \{S_1, \ldots, S_k\}, \mathcal{A}, \mathcal{G} \rangle$ with σ iff plan p_i solves $\langle S_i, \mathcal{A}, \mathcal{G} \rangle$ with σ for $1 \leq i \leq n$.
3. The plan $[\alpha, p]$ solves $\langle \{S\}, \mathcal{A}, \mathcal{G} \rangle$ with σ iff $\alpha \in \mathcal{A}$ contains a sole effect, α is applicable in $S\sigma$, the application of α yields the situation R, and plan p solves $\langle \{R\}, \mathcal{A}, \mathcal{G} \rangle$ with σ.
4. The plan $[\alpha, cond(E_1\theta, p_1, \ldots, E_k\theta, p_k)]$ solves $\langle \{S\}, \mathcal{A}, \mathcal{G} \rangle$ with σ iff $\alpha \in \mathcal{A}$ is applicable in $S\sigma$ and the application of α yields the set of situations $\{R_1, \ldots, R_k\}$ such that plan p_i solves $\langle \{R_i\}, \mathcal{A}, \mathcal{G} \rangle$ with σ for $1 \leq i \leq n$.

For instance, the plan $[dr, cond(\{bsA\}, [], \{bsB\}, [wa, []])]$ solves the planning problem given in Example 1 (with the empty substitution).

4 Linear Connection Method

We know from [2] that connection proofs (see Section 2) solve conjunctive planning problems if, roughly speaking, each literal is engaged in at most one connection. This so-called linearity criterion which "implements" the concept of resources was modified in [8] in order to handle dpp's. Following this approach, a set of initial situations $\mathcal{I} = \{I_1, \ldots, I_n\}$ is encoded by the formula[5]

$$st([cond(I_1, P_1, \ldots, I_n, P_n)]) \rightarrow [i_1 \wedge st(P_1)] \vee \ldots \vee [i_n \wedge st(P_n)]. \quad (1)$$

The situation I_j[6] is represented by the conjunction of its atoms which is denoted by i_j[7]. Literals of the form $st(\ldots)$ are so-called *state literals*, whose only purpose is to record the actions taken in order to achieve a goal. For each conjunct $i_j \wedge st(P_j)$ the variable P_j records the plan needed to transform I_j into a goal situation. If $\mathcal{I}$ contains only one element, the antecedent of the implication is simplified to $st(P_1)$. For our example we get

$$st(P_1) \rightarrow ti \wedge fl \wedge st(P_1) \quad (2)$$

as representation of $\mathcal{I}$. A set $\mathcal{G}$ of goal situations is encoded as a finite disjunction of the form

$$g_1 \wedge st([]) \vee \ldots \vee g_m \wedge st([]), \quad (3)$$

where $[]$ denotes the empty plan and g_i is a conjunction representing the i-th element of $\mathcal{G}$. For our example, the set of goal situations is encoded by the formula

$$fl \wedge bsA \wedge st([]). \quad (4)$$

Since we want to model actions including several possible effects — in contrast to [2] — an action $\alpha : C \leadsto \{E_1, \ldots, E_k\}$ is encoded by a formula

$$st([\alpha, cond(E_1, P_1, \ldots, E_k, P_k)]) \wedge co \rightarrow [e_1 \wedge st(P_1)] \vee \ldots \vee [e_k \wedge st(P_k)], \quad (5)$$

where co and $e_1, \ldots, e_k$ are conjunctions of atoms representing the condition and the effects, respectively. Like in (1) plan P_i should be used if the agent observes that the application of the action results in the effect E_i. If an action has only one possible effect ($k = 1$) the antecedent of the above implication is simplified to $st([\alpha, P_1]) \wedge co$. For our example, we obtain the following formulas:

$$st([dr, cond(\{bsA\}, P_1, \{bsB\}, P_2)]) \wedge ti \rightarrow [bsA \wedge st(P_1)] \vee [bsB \wedge st(P_2)] \quad (6)$$

$$st([wa, Y]) \wedge bsB \rightarrow bsA \wedge st(Y) \quad (7)$$

Corresponding to [8], a globally linear connection proof of

$$\exists P : st(P) \wedge (2) \wedge (6) \wedge (7) \rightarrow (4) \quad (8)$$

[5] We assume all variables to be universally quantified.

[6] Clearly, multisets are no elements of first-order predicate logic; they may be alternatively represented as lists without any problems.

[7] Note, that factoring cannot be applied since that would contradict the concept of resources. Thus, the multiset $\{q, q\}$ is represented by $q \wedge q$ and not just q.

should provide a plan solving our exemplary planning problem as instantiation of the variable P. The corresponding matrix is shown in Figure 1. There, each dashed box surrounds a clause. The second clause represents (2), the third and fifth clause represent the formulas (6) and (7), respectively, whereas the fourth and last one represent (4).[8]

The definition of global linearity is based on the concept of linearity [2] and the concept of submatrices.

Definition 5. Let M be an indexed form of a matrix representing a conjunctive planning problem. A connection proof of a matrix M is called *linear* iff each occurrence of a literal is connected at most once. We require that only one instance i of the clause representing the initial situation can be used. Furthermore, the literal $\neg st(P)$ in (8) has to be connected with the positive state literal contained in i.[9]

Definition 6. Let M be an indexed form of a matrix representing a dpp. A *submatrix* of M emerges by deleting (1) all but one disjunction representing an initial situations in the corresponding clause instance, and (2) all but one disjunction representing an alternative effect of each clause instance which represents an action.[10]

Example 2. Consider the matrix M depicted in Figure 1. It has two submatrices. The first one emerges from M by deleting the disjunction $\neg bsA \vee \neg st(P_1)$ whereas the second one emerges from M by deleting the disjunction $\neg bsB \vee \neg st(P_2)$.

Linearity was introduced in [2] in order to generate plans for conjunctive planning problems. It guarantees that a resource can only be consumed (connected) once during a sequence of actions. Considering dpp's it suffices to demand linearity on subproofs, i.e. those parts of a proof generating sequences of actions leading from one initial situation to one goal situation. Since these sequences (subplans) are independent from each other[11], it should be possible to use a resource in several subplans, e.g. the flowers are used twice.

Definition 7. A connection proof of a matrix constituted by a set of connections C is *globally linear* iff for each submatrix M' of M there exists a subset of C constituting a linear proof of M'. Furthermore, each connection of C is contained in at least one such subset.

Example 3. Reconsider Example 2. The solid connections constitute a linear connection proof of the second submatrix. Each literal is engaged in at most one connection. The dashed connections together with the connections starting in

[8] Generally, each clause corresponds either to an element of the set of goal situations, an action, or the set of initial situations.

[9] This condition ensures that the generation of a plan always starts in the initial situation.

[10] Note, that a submatrix represents a conjunctive planning problem.

[11] We interpret alternatives as exclusive possibilities, i.e. when executing the generated plan we just have to execute just one subplan at each stage.

the first and second clause including the literals $\neg st(P)$, $st(P')$, $\neg ti$, and $\neg st(P')$ constitute a linear connection proof of the first submatrix. Thus, the proof of each submatrix is linear and therefore the whole proof is globally linear.

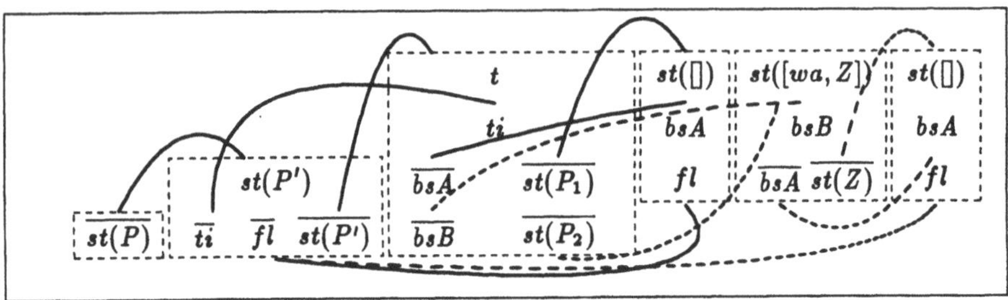

Fig. 1. A globally linear connection proof to Bert's problem (where $t = st([dr, cond(\{bsA\}, P_1, \{bsB\}, P_2)])$.

Theorem 8. *Let M be a matrix representing a dpp $\langle \mathcal{I}, \mathcal{A}, \mathcal{G} \rangle$. There is a plan p solving $\langle \mathcal{I}, \mathcal{A}, \mathcal{G} \rangle$ with a substitution σ iff p is generated by a globally linear connection proof of M.*[12]

In the remainder of this section we present a novel calculus to generate globally linear connection proofs. It is closely related to connection calculi for first-order theorem proving as presented in [3, 4] whose concrete implementations are highly successful (eg. see [16]). Let M be a matrix representing a dpp $\langle \mathcal{I}, \mathcal{A}, \mathcal{G} \rangle$. At each instant of time we have:

- a finite sequence $(c_1, \ldots, c_{k+1})$ of instances of chosen clauses from M. We always have $c_1 = \neg st(P)$ and c_2 is the clause representing the set of initial situations. The sequence of clauses $c_3, \ldots, c_{k+1}$ represents a sequence of actions $\alpha_3, \ldots, \alpha_{k+1}$.
- a finite sequence $(d_1, \ldots, d_{k+1})$; called the *sequence of unsolved goals*, where $d_j \dot{\subset} c_j$ holds.[13] The elements of d_2 represent initial situations which have not been addressed so far. Correspondingly, the elements of d_i for $i \geq 3$ represent the effects of α_i which have not been considered so far.
- a finite sequence $p = (l_1, \ldots, l_k)$, called the *active path*, where $l_j \in c_j \dot{-} d_j$ for $1 \leq j \leq k$ holds. l_2 represents the initial situation for which a plan is currently developed. Correspondingly, l_i for $i \geq 3$ represents the alternative of α_i for which a plan is currently generated.

[12] Note, that σ can be easily extracted from the connection proof as the substitution instantiating the variables occurring in the clauses encoding initial and goal situations.

[13] We can represent a clause either as a conjunction of disjunctions (without allowing factoring) or, alternatively, as multisets of disjunctions. In the same way a disjunction may be represented alternatively as a multiset of literals.

A *proof state* Δ is a tuple (M, p, D, E, σ) where M is a matrix, p is the active path, D is the sequence of unsolved goals, E is a set of connections, and σ is the current substitution. By $literals(p)$ we denote the multiset of non-state literals included in p. Thus, $literals(p)$ represents the (multiset of) resources contained in p. Δ is called *initial state* if $p = ()$, $D = (\{\neg st(P)\})$, $E = \emptyset$, and $\sigma = \epsilon$. It is called *final state* if $D = ()$ holds.

Definition 9. Let c be the clause representing the set of initial situations. A proof state Δ' is obtained from an initial state Δ by an *initialization step* ($\Delta \vdash_{init} \Delta'$) in case $\Delta = (M, (), (\{\neg st(P)\}), \emptyset, \epsilon)$ and $\Delta' = (M, (\neg st(P)), (d), \emptyset, \{P \backslash t\})$ holds, where d is the multiset containing the disjunctions of c which represent the initial situations, and $st(t)$ is the positive state literal in c.

Thus, an initialization step merely connects the literal $\neg st(P)$ contained in the initial state and the positive state literal $st(t)$ contained in the clause representing the set of initial situations. Afterwards, the elements in the sequence of unsolved goals represent the elements of the set of initial situations.

Definition 10. A proof state Δ' is obtained from a proof state Δ by a *planning step* ($\Delta \vdash_{plan} \Delta'$) in case we have:

- $\Delta = (M, (l_1, \ldots, l_k), (d_1, \ldots, d_{k+1}), E, \sigma)$, $k > 0$
- $\Delta' = (M, (l_1, \ldots, l_{k+1}), (d_1, \ldots, d_{k+1} \dot{-} \{l_{k+1}\}, \{e_1, \ldots, e_m\}), E', \sigma')$
- Let c be a new instance of a clause in M representing an action or a goal situation. Let $co_1, \ldots, co_n$ denote the literals in c representing the condition and $e_1, \ldots, e_m$ the disjunctions in c representing the alternative effects (m $= 0$ holds if c represents a goal situation).
- The negative state literal of l_{k+1} constitutes a complementary connection together with the positive state literal of c via a substitution δ.
- τ makes the connections $(co_1, d_1), \ldots, (co_n, d_n)$ complementary, where $\{d_1, \ldots, d_n\} \dot{\subseteq} literals((l_1, \ldots, l_{k+1}))$ holds, and (the explicit occurrence)[14] d_i is not contained in any connection of E $(1 \leq i \leq n)$.
- $E' = E \cup \{(co_1, d_1), \ldots, (co_n, d_n)\}$
- $\sigma' = \delta \circ \tau \circ \sigma$

This definition needs explanation. Roughly speaking, a planning step either represents the application of an action or checks whether a goal situation is reached. In terms of connection calculi, a planning step encodes one extension step and several reduction steps in one proof step. Let l_{k+1} be the selected goal of d_{k+1}. l_{k+1} is of the form $\neg st(X) \vee h_1 \vee \ldots \vee h_m$. Recall that l_{k+1} represents an effect of an action or an initial situation. The current situation — viz the available resources — is then described by the unconnected non-state literals included in the active path and l_{k+1}.

At first, the state literal included in l_{k+1} is connected via the substitution $\delta = \{X \backslash t\}$ with the state literal $st(t)$ of a new instance c of a clause representing an action or a goal situation. This corresponds to an extension step.

[14] For simplicity we omit a further indexing of atoms which is needed to distinguish several occurrences of the same atom.

We say c is *introduced* by the planning step. To guarantee that an action is applicable or a goal situation is reached we must ensure that the corresponding condition holds in the actual situation. Thus we check that there exists a multiset $\{d_1, \ldots, d_n\} \dot\subseteq literals(l_1, \ldots, l_{k+1})$ such that (co_i, d_i) is a complementary connection via a substitution τ, and d_i has not been connected before $(1 \leq i \leq n)$. This corresponds to n reduction steps using the connections $(co_1, d_1), \ldots, (co_n, d_n)$[15]. To ensure global linearity these connections are added to E.

Example 4. Consider the matrix depicted in Figure 1 *without* the connections. Assume that the initialization step was already performed connecting the leftmost literal $\neg st(P)$ with the literal $st(P')$ of the second clause. Thus the actual proof state is $(M, (\neg st(P)), (\emptyset, \{\neg ti \vee \neg fl \vee \neg st(P')\}), \emptyset, \{P \backslash P'\})$.

We get $l_{k+1} = \neg ti \vee \neg fl \vee \neg st(P')$ $(k = 1)$. The actual situation is represented by the multiset of unconnected non-state literals in the active path $(\neg st(P))$ and l_{k+1}. We select the third clause of the matrix representing the action dr to perform a planning step. We connect the literals $\neg st(P')$ and $st([dr, cond(\{bsA\}, P_1, \{bsB\}, P_2)])$. The action has a sole condition, viz the literal pa. Thus we have $co_1 = ti$ and $d_1 = \neg ti$. Since d_1 is included in l_{k+1} and, because $E = \emptyset$, it is not contained in any connection of E, the action is applicable yielding the proof state (M, p', D', E', σ') with

- $p' = (\neg st(P), \neg ti \vee \neg fl \vee \neg st(P'))$,
- $D' = (\emptyset, \emptyset, \{\neg bsA \vee \neg st(P_1), \neg bsB \vee \neg st(P_2)\})$,
- $E' = \{(\neg ti, ti)\}$, and
- $\sigma' = \{P \backslash st([dr, cond(\{bsA\}, P_1, \{bsB\}, P_2)]),$
  $P' \backslash st([dr, cond(\{bsA\}, P_1, \{bsB\}, P_2)])\}$.

Definition 11. A proof state $\Delta' = (M, p', D', E', \sigma)$ is obtained from a proof state $\Delta = (M, p, D, E, \sigma)$ by a *truncation step* $(\Delta \vdash_{tru} \Delta')$ in case the following conditions hold:

- $p = (l_1, \ldots, l_k)$
- $D = (d_1, \ldots, d_k, \emptyset)$
- $p' = (l_1, \ldots, l_{k-1})$
- $D' = (d_1, \ldots, d_k)$
- $E' = \{(r, s) \in E \mid r \text{ and } s \text{ do not occur in } c_k\}$[15]

In other words, truncation means retracting the active path from its last element if there is no unsolved goal in its clause instance. The connections including a literal of the clause containing this element can be removed from E.

If $\Delta \vdash_{init} \Delta'$, or $\Delta \vdash_{plan} \Delta'$, or $\Delta \vdash_{tru} \Delta'$ holds, we may simply write $\Delta \vdash \Delta'$.

Theorem 12. *(Correctness and completeness) Let M be a matrix representing a dpp $\langle \mathcal{I}, \mathcal{A}, \mathcal{G} \rangle$. Let $\Delta = (\Delta_1, \ldots, \Delta_n)$ be a sequence of proof states such that Δ_1 is an initial state and $\Delta_i \vdash \Delta_{i+1}$ for $1 \leq i < n$ holds. We require that only one instance of the clause representing $\mathcal{I}$ can be used.*

Δ_n is a final state iff the set of connections used throughout the derivation constitutes a globally linear proof of an indexed form of M.

---

[15] Note that, in order to distinguish several occurrences of the same atom, an additional indexing — which we omitted for simplicity — has to be performed.

5 Loop Checking

In the field of logic programming, various techniques for providing logic programming interpreters with a capability to preclude some infinite loops at run time were examined. Many of them (eg. see [5]) are based on tests comparing some goal with its subgoals. In [6] it was shown how such loop checks can be modified to augment connection calculi for first-order predicate logic. The idea to prevent useless looping is to discard a subgoal of a goal if the former is an equally or more difficult instance of the latter. The notion of difficulty is furnished by subsumption and the preconditions available to prove goals.

The aim of this section is to take over this approach to prevent that the calculus presented in the last section performs unnecessary loops. An unnecessary loop is a sequence of planning steps that does not change or increase the multiset of available resources — i.e. path literals which can be used by reduction steps of further planning steps. Such sequences cannot contribute to a solution[16].

Taking into account that a planning step consists of one extension and several reduction steps, loop checks developed for first-order connection calculi can be adapted easily — taking the concept of resources into account — to the calculus presented in the previous section. Furthermore, the definition of planning steps implies that a derivation only depends on the available resources. Thus, a loop check works as follows: Let $\Delta_1, \ldots, \Delta_n$ be a sequence of proof states where $\Delta_i \vdash_{plan} \Delta_{i+1}$ holds. If each reduction step included in a planning step to prove a goal of Δ_n can be performed while proving the selected goal of Δ_1 — i.e. the available resources of Δ_1 are a superset of those of Δ_n — at least the step $\Delta_{n-1} \vdash_{plan} \Delta_n$ is redundant.

Theorem 13. *Let $\Delta_1, \ldots, \Delta_n$ be a sequence of proof states such that $\Delta_i \vdash_{plan} \Delta_{i+1}$ for $1 \leq i < n$ holds. Let $\Delta_1 = (M, (l_1, \ldots, l_r), (d_1, \ldots, d_{r+1}), E, \sigma)$ and let l_{r+1} be the element of d_{r+1} selected to perform a planning step. Let R be the multiset of non-state literals in $l_1, \ldots, l_{r+1}$ which are not included in any connection of E.*

On the other hand, let $\Delta_n = (M, (l_1, \ldots, l_k), (d_1, \ldots, d_{k+1}), E', \sigma')$ and let l_{k+1} be the element of d_{k+1} selected to perform an planning step. Let R' be the multiset of non-state literals in $l_1, \ldots, l_{k+1}$ which are not included in any connection of E'.

The calculus remains sound and complete if backtracking[17] is performed if $R\sigma \dot{\supseteq} R'\sigma'$ holds.

Example 5. Suppose Bert has a dollar note and one quarter and needs two quarters to use a vending machine. Therefore he has to change his dollar into four quarters using a changing machine. This (somewhat strange) machine can also change *five* quarters into a dollar. Thus, we get two actions, namely $cd : \{d\} \rightsquigarrow \{\{q, q, q, q\}\}$ for changing dollars, and $cq : \{q, q, q, q, q\} \rightsquigarrow \{\{d\}\}$ for changing quarters which are represented by the following formulas:

[16] This aproach to detect unnecessary loops differs from other ones in planning like the one presented in [9]. There, loops are prevented by eliminating goal repetitions in a restricted way whereas our criterion is based on available resources.

[17] Ie. the last derivation step yielding Δ_n is undone.

$$st([cd, P_3]) \wedge d \rightarrow q \wedge q \wedge q \wedge q \wedge st(P_3) \tag{9}$$

$$st([cq, P_4]) \wedge q \wedge q \wedge q \wedge q \wedge q \rightarrow d \wedge st(P_4) \tag{10}$$

A corresponding connection proof may start as shown in the following matrix[18]: After changing the dollar into four quarters, the (five) quarters are changed back yielding one dollar. Obviously, the last application of action cq is redundant because after performing it the remaining resource is the dollar note whereas at the beginning Bert had a dollar and a quarter. Using the notion of Theorem 13 we get $R = \{\neg d, \neg q\}$ and $R' = \{\neg d\}$.

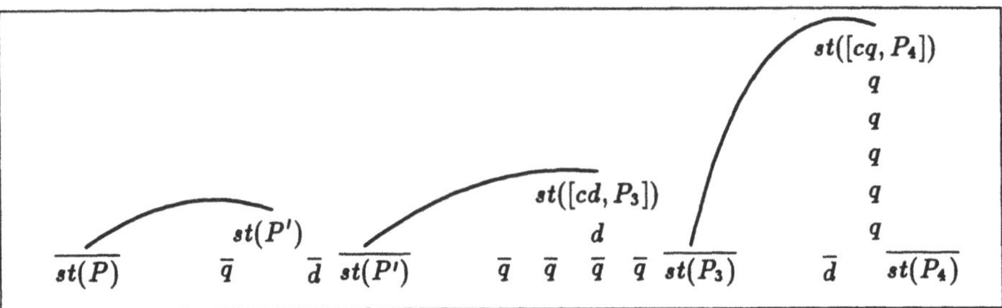

For the special case of conjunctive planning problems the pruning technique can be refined allowing an additional substitution τ on the path literals: The calculus remains sound and complete if backtracking is performed in case there exists a substitution τ such that $R\sigma\tau \dot{\supseteq} R'\sigma'$ holds. Since such a substitution influences the derivations of other open goals this is not possible for dpp's.

6 Lemmata

Mathematicians are using lemmas in order to prove complicated theorems. Whenever several applications of one lemma are necessary this approach corresponds to copying parts of a proof. This useful technique is known as lemmaizing in automated theorem proving (for instance cf. [11, 1]).

The use of lemmata becomes important during the generation of disjunctive plans. Considering conjunctive planning problems, a linear connection proof consists of only one derivation chain. Thus, no lemma can be generated throughout a derivation. Generating disjunctive plans this is different because the structure of a proof corresponds to a tree. Each subproof corresponding to one of its subtrees might be stored as a lemma[19]. The idea to reuse plans can also be found in [19] in a non-deductive environment.

[18] Here, and in the following matrices the connections between literals representing conditions and resources are omitted for simplicity.

[19] In a resolution based systems (for example see [12]) the memorization of lemmata (and macros, see Section 7) is implicit since a once generated resolvent is not removed. However, without employing some kind of set-of-support strategy a vast amount of lemmata or macros may be generated that are totally useless for the respective planning problem. Using the calculus presented in Section 4 this is different since the subproof represented by a lemma is used at least once.

Example 6. Suppose Bert has a dollar note and wants to buy a coke from a vending machine. To use the vending machine he needs a dime. A changing machine changes dollar notes either into four quarters or into two quarters and five dimes, depending on the supply of coins resting in the machine. Furthermore, the machine is able to change two quarters into five dimes. We get two actions, namely $cd : \{d\} \rightsquigarrow \{\{q, q, di, di, di, di, di\}, \{q, q, q, q\}\}$ for changing a dollar, and $cq : \{q, q\} \rightsquigarrow \{\{di, di, di, di, di\}\}$ for changing the quarters. These are represented by the following formulas:

$$st([cd, cond(\{q, q, di, di, di, di, di\}, P_3, \{q, q, q, q\}, P_4)]) \land d \rightarrow \qquad (11)$$
$$[q \land q \land di \land di \land di \land di \land di \land st(P_3)] \lor [q \land q \land q \land q \land st(P_4)]$$

$$st([cq, P_5]) \land q \land q \rightarrow di \land di \land di \land di \land di \land st(P_5) \qquad (12)$$

A connection proof generating the desired plan should start using a clause instance representing action *cd*. For each of the alternative effects of this action a plan has to be generated. The first one can use as resources two quarters and five dimes whereas the second one can use four quarters. Suppose a connection proof of the first alternative yields the plan *p*. To cope with the second alternative — since Bert wants to use the vending machine — action *cq* has to be applied. Afterwards exactly the same resources are available as in the former case. Thus, the proof generating plan *p* for the first alternative can also be used for the second alternative.

Definition 14. Let $\Delta = (\Delta_1, \ldots, \Delta_m)$ be sequence of proof states such that $\Delta_i \vdash \Delta_{i+1}$ for $1 \leq i < m$ holds. By the *derivation* of Δ we mean the sequence $\Delta_1 \vdash \ldots \vdash \Delta_m$. If

- $\Delta_1 = (M, (l_1, \ldots, l_k), (d_1, \ldots, d_{k+1} \dot\cup \{l_{k+1}\}), E, \sigma)$ and
- $\Delta_m = (M, (l_1, \ldots, l_k), (d_1, \ldots, d_{k+1}), E', \sigma')$

holds, we call Δ a *partial proof.* The multiset of non-state literals contained in $(l_1, \ldots, l_k, l_{k+1})$ which are engaged in a connection used by a planning step $\Delta_i \vdash_{plan} \Delta_{i+1}$ is called the *precondition* of Δ.

Theorem 15. *Let $\Delta = (\Delta_1, \ldots, \Delta_m)$ be a partial proof and Pre the precondition of Δ. $(g_1, h_1), \ldots, (g_n, h_n)$ is the sequence of connections used in Δ such that $\{g_1, \ldots, g_n\} = Pre$ holds. Let τ be the composition of the substitutions needed to unify the connections whose literals occur in clause instances introduced by the derivation of Δ.*

It is correct to add $(h_1 \land \ldots \land h_n \land st(P))\tau$ as a further disjunct to the disjunction representing the set of goal situations.

Example 7. Recall Example 6. Considering the first alternative we assume that it is possible to yield a subproof generating the plan $[buy, []]$ which describes how to buy the coke from the vending machine. The sole resources needed to perform this subplan is a dime. Using the technique to generate lemmata according to Theorem 15 it is possible to generate the formula $di \land st([buy, []])$ as a lemma that can be applied to find a proof for the second alternative immediately after performing the action *cq*.

7 Generating Macros

As mentioned above, the linear connection method for conjunctive planning problems does not offer a possibility to use lemmata. The search for a proof simply consists of applying planning steps until a goal situation is reached. However, it is often the case that some sequences of planning steps have to be performed several times. Such a sequence might constitute a part of a plan which has, for instance, to be iterated. It would be advantageous to keep such sequences instead of generating them each time again. Especially the depth of a derivation might shrink considerably which is essential since one fundamental problem of existing theorem provers is that they are not able to explore search spaces deeply.

Example 8. Suppose Bert has two dollar notes and wants to buy two cokes. To get a coke he has to change a dollar into four quarters and insert three of them into a vending machine. Thus, the initial situation is $\{d, d\}$, the goal situation is $\{c, c\}$, and the actions are $cd : \{d\} \leadsto \{\{q, q, q, q\}\}$ for changing a dollar, and $uv : \{q, q, q\} \leadsto \{\{c\}\}$ for using the vending machine. A connection proof which solves the problem generating the plan $[cd, [uv, [cd, [uv, []]]]]$ looks like:

$$\begin{array}{ccccccc}
 & & & st([uv,P_2]) & & st([uv,P_4]) & st([]) \\
 & & & q & & q & c \\
 & & st([cd,P_1]) & q & st([cd,P_3]) & q & c \\
 & st(P') & d & q & d & q & \\
\overline{st(P)} & \overline{d}\ \overline{d}\ \overline{st(P')} & \overline{q}\ \overline{q}\ \overline{q}\ \overline{q}\ \overline{st(P_1)} & \overline{c}\ \overline{st(P_2)} & \overline{q}\ \overline{q}\ \overline{q}\ \overline{q}\ \overline{st(P_3)} & \overline{c}\ \overline{st(P_4)} &
\end{array}$$

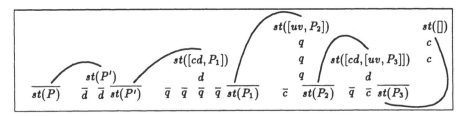

After performing the planning steps using the third and fourth clause representing the actions cd and uv, respectively, the partial plan $[cd, [uv, P_2]]$ is generated yielding a coke and a quarter from a dollar note. Thus, we are able to formulate the macro $cd, uv : \{d\} \leadsto \{\{c, q\}\}$ for getting a coke. Using this macro represented by the fifth clause in the following matrix, we obtain a shorter connection proof.

$$\begin{array}{cccccc}
 & & & st([uv,P_2]) & & st([]) \\
 & & & q & & c \\
 & & st([cd,P_1]) & q & st([cd,[uv,P_3]]) & c \\
 & st(P') & d & q & d & \\
\overline{st(P)} & \overline{d}\ \overline{d}\ \overline{st(P')} & \overline{q}\ \overline{q}\ \overline{q}\ \overline{q}\ \overline{st(P_1)} & \overline{c}\ \overline{st(P_2)} & \overline{q}\ \overline{c}\ \overline{st(P_3)} &
\end{array}$$

Definition 16. Let $\Delta = (\Delta_1, \ldots, \Delta_n)$ be a sequence of proof states such that $\Delta_i \vdash_{plan} \Delta_{i+1}$ for $1 \leq i < n$ holds. We assume that during the derivation of Δ no clause instance is employed representing an action including several effects. Let p_i be the active path of Δ_i and g_i be the selected goal of Δ_i. Furthermore, let R_i denote the multiset of unconnected negative non-state literals of p_i and g_i.

By $Pre(\Delta)$ we denote the multiset $R_1 \dot{-} (R_1 \dot{\cap} R_n)$[20] and by $Post(\Delta)$ we denote the multiset $R_n \dot{-} (R_1 \dot{\cap} R_n)$. $plan(\Delta)$ is the substitution of the plan variable contained in the state literal of g_1 caused by the derivation of Δ.

Thus, $Pre(\Delta)$ denotes the multiset of resources which must be available to perform the planning steps contained in Δ. $Post(\Delta)$ represents the multiset of resources which are generated throughout Δ.

Theorem 17. *Let $\Delta = (\Delta_1, \ldots, \Delta_n)$ be a sequence of proof states such that $\Delta_i \vdash_{plan} \Delta_{i+1}$ for $1 \leq i < n$ holds. Let $Pre(\Delta) = \{c_1, \ldots, c_r\}$, $Post(\Delta) = \{\neg k_1, \ldots, \neg k_l\}$, and $plan(\Delta) = [a_1, [\ldots, [a_m, P'] \ldots]$. Furthermore, let (c_1, h_1), $\ldots$, (c_r, h_r) be the sequence of connections used throughout the derivation of Δ connecting the literals included in $Pre(\Delta)$.*

It is correct to add a variant of

$$(h_1 \wedge \ldots \wedge h_r \wedge st([a_1, [\ldots, [a_m, P] \ldots]) \rightarrow k_1 \wedge \ldots \wedge k_l \wedge st(P))\tau \quad (13)$$

to the formulas representing actions, where τ is the composition of the substitutions needed to unify the connections whose literals occur in clause instances introduced by the derivation of Δ.

The technique to generate macros to some extent solves a lack of connection calculi in comparison to resolution based calculi. In resolution based calculi a resolvent, once generated, may be used again throughout the whole derivation. This feature, which is not present in ordinary connection calculi, can be simulated by generating new actions corresponding to Theorem 17. In particular, this may lead (in the best case) to exponentially shorter proofs.

The possibility to find proofs of much smaller size emphasizes, that the usage of lemmata and macros may become important. The remaining problem is to determine whether a certain lemma or macro should be introduced or not. There is no obvious way to do this — as there is no obvious way to find out which resolvents have to be generated in resolution calculi; however, it seems to be manageable since generating plans it should be possible to value a sequence of actions wrt. consumed and produced resources. Furthermore, heuristics (taking purely syntactical criterions such as the size of a lemma into account) which are successfully used in [1] can also be employed for our purposes.

8 Conclusion

In this paper we elaborated deductive planning based on the (extended) linear connection method. We were able to take advantage from the fact that the connection method for first-order logic and corresponding connection calculi are well understood. We proposed a new calculus which is closely related to successful calculi for general theorem proving. We further showed that techniques which are used in conventional connection calculi to reduce the search space can also be used to augment specialized calculi for solving planning problems.

[20] Again we have to ensure that several occurrences of the same atom are distinguished using an additional indexing.

Since the three planning approaches based on the connection method, equational Horn logic, and linear logic are essentially equivalent, our results concerning redundancy elimination can be adapted to calculi based on the two latter approaches.

References

1. O. L. Astrachan and M. E. Stickel. Caching and Lemmaizing in Model Elimination Theorem Provers. In *Proceedings of the Conference on Automated Deduction*, pages 224–238. Springer, 1992.
2. W. Bibel. A deductive solution for plan generation. *New Generation Computing*, 4:115–132, 1986.
3. W. Bibel. *Automated Theorem Proving*. Vieweg Verlag, Braunschweig, 1987.
4. W. Bibel. *Deduction: Automated Logic*. Academic Press, London, 1993.
5. R. N. Bol, K. R. Apt, and J. W. Klop. An analysis of loop checking mechanisms for logic programming. *Theoretical Computer Science*, 86:35–79, 1991.
6. S. Brüning. On Loop Detection in Connection Calculi. In *Proceedings of the Kurt Gödel Colloquium*, pages 144–151. Springer Verlag, 1993.
7. S. Brüning. Towards Efficient Calculi for Resource-Oriented Linear Deductive Planning. Technical report, FG Intellektik, FB Informatik, TH Darmstadt, 1993.
8. S. Brüning, G. Große, S. Hölldobler, J. Schneeberger, U. Sigmund, and M. Thielscher. Disjunction in plan generation by equational logic programming. In *Beiträge zum 7. Workshop Planen und Konfigurieren*, pages 18–26. Arbeitspapiere der GMD 723, January 1993.
9. R. Feldman and P. Morris. Admissible Criteria For Loop Control In Planning. In *Proceedings of the Eigth National Conference on Artificial Intelligence*, pages 151–157, 1990.
10. R. E. Fikes and N. J. Nilsson. STRIPS: A new approach to the application of theorem proving to problem solving. *Artificial Intelligence*, 5(2):189–208, 1971.
11. B. Fronhöfer and R. Caferra. Memorization of literals: An enhancement of the connection method. Technical report, Institut für Informatik, TU München, 1988.
12. C. Green. Application of theorem proving to problem solving. In *Proceedings of IJCAI 1969*, pages 741–747, 1969.
13. G. Große, S. Hölldobler, and J. Schneeberger. On linear deductive planning. Technical Report AIDA–92–08, FG Intellektik, FB Informatik, TH Darmstadt, 1992.
14. Gerd Große, Steffen Hölldobler, Josef Schneeberger, Ute Sigmund, and Michael Thielscher. Equational Logic Programming, Actions, and Change. In *Proc. Joint International Conference and Symposium on Logic Programming JICSLP'92*, 1992.
15. S. Hölldobler and J. Schneeberger. A new deductive approach to planning. *New Generation Computing*, 8:225–244, 1990.
16. R. Letz, J. Schumann, S. Bayerl, and W. Bibel. SETHEO — A High-Performance Theorem Prover for First-Order Logic. *JAR*, 8:183–212, 1992.
17. V. Lifschitz. On the semantics of STRIPS. In *Proc. of the Workshop on Reasoning about Actions and Plans*, pages 1–8, Los Altos, 1986. Morgan Kaufmann.
18. M. Masseron, C. Tollu, and J. Vauzielles. Generating plans in linear logic. In *Foundations of Software Technology and Theoretical Computer Science*, pages 63–75. Springer, LNCS *472*, 1990.
19. S. Thiébaux and J. Hertzberg. A semi-reactive planner based on a possible models action formalization. In *Artificial Intelligence Planning Systems: Proceedings of the First International Conference (AIPS92)*, San Mateo, CA, 1992. Morgan Kaufmann.

A Logic Programming Framework for the Abductive Inference of Intentions in Cooperative Dialogues

Paulo Quaresma* and José Gabriel Lopes

{pq,gpl}@fct.unl.pt,
Artificial Intelligence Center, UNINOVA
2825 Monte da Caparica, Portugal
April 18, 1994

Abstract. In this paper we propose a general logic programming framework allowing the recognition of plans and intentions behind speech acts through abductive reasoning. These inferences enables each agent to have an active participation in dialogues, namely in cooperative information-seeking dialogues. In our framework the possible actions, events, states and world knowledge are represented by extended logic programs (LP with explicit negation) and the abductive inference process is modeled by a framework wich is based on the Well Founded Semantics augmented with explicit negation (WFSX) and contradiction removal semantics (CRSX) ([PAA92]). It will be shown how this framework supports abductive reasoning with Event Calculus ([Esh88]) and some classical examples in the domain of information-seeking dialogues will be shown ([Lit85, Pol86]). Finally, some open problems will be pointed out.

1 Introduction

A natural language understanding system needs to infer the beliefs, the intentions and the plans of its interlocutors in order to intelligently participate in dialogues. One possible approach follows the classical planning scheme developed in the STRIPS ([FN71]) and NOAH ([Sac77]) model. In this model each plan is defined as a sequence of actions and each action is composed by a head, pre-conditions, constraints, effects and sub-actions. The inference of plans is done through the use of a library of plans and actions, some heuristic rules and the user possible goals. This approach has been used by Litman and Allen ([Lit85, LA87]) in order to infer plans behind speech acts in dialogues. Another approach has been followed by [AP92] and uses weighted abductive reasoning taking interpretation as an abductive process ([HSME88]).

We also take interpretation as abduction but, in contrast to the weighted abduction approach, we propose a general extended logic programming framework which supports the abduction of intentions behind speech acts delimiting the set of abducible predicates. We have used the event calculus to represent

* Owns a scholarship from JNICT, reference n^o BD/1766/IA

events, time and actions and a logic programming framework - Well Founded Semantics of eXtended Logic Programs (WFSX) augmented with Contradiction Removal Semantics (CRSX) - from the work of Pereira et al. ([PAA92]). This framework, has a well defined semantics and extends logic programming allowing to model several kinds of non-monotonic reasoning, namely default, abductive and hypothetical reasoning.

In section 2 a description of the extended logic programming framework showing how non-monotonic reasoning is dealt with is given. In section 3 the process of abductive reasoning with event calculus is described. Section 4 describes the language that was used to represent actions (from Gelfond and Lifschitz [GL92]). Section 5 describes the epistemic operators used to model the different attitudes. In section 6 the speech acts necessary to handle dialogues are described. In section 7 some examples are presented. Namely, it is shown how this framework enables a system to handle a dialogue where its interlocutor has built an incorrect plan and how it handles dialogues where there are misunderstandings. Finally in section 8 some open problems and future work will be pointed out.

2 Extended Logic Programming Framework

Non-monotonic reasoning capability is a requirement of any natural language processing system. In our approach this kind of reasoning is modeled by an extended logic programming framework which models actions, events, states and the world knowledge by extended logic programs. These programs are sets of normal and integrity rules having the form:

$$H \leftarrow B_1, \ldots, B_n, not\ C_1, \ldots, not\ C_m (m \geq 0, n \geq 0)$$

where H, B_1, ..., B_n, C_1, C_m are classical literals. A classical literal is either an atom A or its explicit negation $\neg A$. *not* stands for the negation by failure (NAF). In integrity rules H is the symbol $\perp$ (contradiction).

Programs with integrity constraints and explicit negation may be contradictory. The contradiction can be removed by adding to the original program the complements of some revisables ([PAA92]).

The framework described allows to model different types of non-monotonic reasoning, namely default, hyphotetical, and abductive reasoning.

- Default reasoning can be modeled adding to the program rules of the form:

Normally birds fly.

which can be written as:

1. fly(X) ← bird(X), not ab(X)

which states that if it is not possible to prove the abnormality of the bird X then it should fly.

– With a slight change it is possible to handle hypothetical reasoning:

Quakers might (or not) be pacifists

which can be written as:

1. pacifist(X) ← quaker(X), hypqp(X)
2. hypqp(X) ← not ¬ hypqp(X)
3. ¬ hypqp(X) ← not hypqp(X)

which states that quakers are pacifists if it is not possible to prove (by NAF) explicitly that they are not (and vice-versa).

– Abductive reasoning can be modeled with the rules:

F might be true (or not)

which can be written as:

1. $F \leftarrow not\ \neg F$
2. $\neg F \leftarrow not\ F$

which state that if it is not possible to prove $\neg F$ then F should hold (and vice-versa). This is the way how Pereira et al. ([PAA92]) relate explicit negation and negation by failure.

Using this approach it is possible to create an abductive program from an abductive theory (P, Ab) by adding to the program P for all literals L in the abducible list Ab two rules of the form:

1. $L \leftarrow not\ \neg L$
2. $\neg L \leftarrow not\ L$

In the domain of dialogues, we will allow the abduction of a limited set of predicates (see next section). This process is done through the use of this framework and the Event Calculus.

3 Abductive Planning with Event Calculus

In order to represent and reason about actions and events a modified version of the event calculus proposed by Eshgi ([Esh88]) and Missiaen ([Mis91]) was used.

In this formalism, events are action instances. They can be represented by the time at which they ocurred. Time is linear and time points are ordered by the precedence relationship $<$. Events are referents which are related to actions by the predicate $act(E, A)$. $happens(E)$ states that the event E occurs. $initiates(E, P)$ means that the event E initiates the property P, and $terminates(E, P)$ states that property P is terminated by the event E.

succeeds(E) means that the event E can occur, i.e., its preconditions are satisfied (this predicate is different from *happens* which means that the event did really happened). *holds_at*(P,T) means that property P holds at time T.

A plan consists of the set of facts defined using the predicates <, *happens*, and *act*. This set can represent a plan because it defines the events that may happen, the actions that are associated with those events, and the time ordering between the events.

The following logic program is proposed by Missiaen in order to describe what properties hold at a given time:

$$\begin{aligned} holds\_at(P,T) &\leftarrow happens(E), initiates(E,P), & (1)\\ &\quad\ succeeds(E), E < T, persists(E,P,T). \\ persists(E,P,T) &\leftarrow notclipped(E,P,T). & (2)\\ clipped(E,P,T) &\leftarrow happens(C), terminates(C,P), & (3)\\ &\quad\ succeeds(C), notout(C,E,T). \\ out(C,E,T) &\leftarrow (T = C; T < C; C < E). & (4) \end{aligned}$$

which states that the property P holds at time T if there was an event that happened before T, if that event initiates P and if P persists until T. A property P persists until T if it is not possible to prove (by NAF) the existence of an event that terminates the property P before T. However it is still an open problem to prove that this approach is correct, complete and/or sound wrt. the well founded semantics framework described in the previous section.

In this approach planning can be seen as an abductive process in which the set of abducible predicates is composed by:

Ab = {happens/1, act/2, </2}

Note that the predicate *succeeds/1* is not abducible. This feature implies that only the actions that are possible in a given time can be abduced.

4 Representing actions

In order to represent actions we have used a language which extends the proposal of Gelfond and Lifschitz ([GL92]). In this language actions can be represented by the following propositions:

1. A causes F if $P_1, \ldots, P_n$
2. F if $P_1, \ldots, P_n$
3. F after $A_1, \ldots, A_n$

The first rule means that action A causes the effect F if the pre-conditions P_1, ..., P_n hold; the second rule means that the fluent F holds if $P_1, \ldots, P_n$ hold; the last rule means that the fluent F holds after the sequence of actions $A_1, \ldots, A_n$.

We have defined a translation mechanism from this language into the event calculus language introduced earlier. For each action described by the first statement the following two rules are obtained:

$$succeeds(E) \leftarrow act(E, A), holds\_at(P_1, E), \ldots, holds\_at(P_n, E).$$
$$initiates(E, F) \leftarrow act(E, A), holds\_at(P_1, E), \ldots, holds\_at(P_n, E).$$

This scheme states that an event E associated with an action A at a time T succeeds if the pre-conditions hold at that time and as a consequence of this event the property F will hold in the future. As *act/2* is an abducible predicate, if it is necessary to prove *succeeds(E)* then *act(E,A)* might be abduced (if the pre-conditions hold at time E).

The second rule is translated into the following logical rule:

$$holds\_at(F, E) \leftarrow holds\_at(P_1, E), \ldots, holds\_at(P_n, E).$$

This rule states that the property F holds if the conditions $P_1, \ldots, P_n$ hold.

The last rule is translated into the following logical rule:

$$\begin{aligned} initiates(E_n, F) \leftarrow\ & happens(E_1), act(E_1, A_1), \\ & happens(E_2), act(E_2, A_2), E_1 < E_2, \\ & \ldots, \\ & happens(E_n), act(E_n, A_n), E_{n-1} < E_n. \end{aligned}$$

which states that the property F is initiated by the sequence of actions A_1, ..., A_n.

In order to apply the described framework to a specific domain we have to define the domain specific rules using these meta rules and then translate them into logical rules.

On the other hand, it is important to point out that we have not proved that the proposed transformations into the abductive event calculus are correct and complete.

5 Epistemic Operators

The epistemic operators needed for describing the agents' mental state are the following ([AP92, CL90]):

- int(a, α): agent a intends to do α
- bel(a, p): agent a believes that p is true
- ach(a, p):agent a believes p will become true as a consequence of its actions
- exp(a, p) $\leftarrow$ bel(a, p) or ach(a, p): agent a expects that p is true
- know(a, p): agent a knows property p

- knowif(a, p): agent a knows if property p is true
- knowref(a, t, p): agent a knows the term t of property p

More complex actions can be constructed from the operators *to* e *by*:

- to(α, p): the plan of performing α in order to make p true
- by(α, β, p): the plan of making β by doing α, while some fluent p holds

It's also necessary to define some rules that connect these epistemic operators:

int(A, α) *if* int(A, to(α, P)).
ach(A, P) *if* int(A, to(α, P)).

This rule means that if, at a given time, an agent A intends to do α in order to make P true, then he intends to do α and he wants P to become true. There is also the corresponding rule for the relation *by*:

int(A, α) *if* int(A, by(α, β, P))).
int(A, β) *if* int(A, by(α, β, P)))
exp(A, P) *if* int(A, by(α, β, P)))

This rule means that if, at a given time, an agent A intends to do α in order to have β done while P is true then he intends to do α and β and he expects P to be true.

We have also defined a different rule that connect the epistemic operators *bel* and *int* with the other actions:

bel(s, ach(a, E)) *if* bel(s, int(a, Act)) & (Act *causes* E)

This rule means that if s believes that a intends to do an *Act* then s believes a wants to achieve the state where the effects of that *Act* hold.

6 Speech Acts

Using the language described in the previous section we have defined expressions for some speech acts (from [AP80, CL90]). We will elaborate on the expressions for the speech acts needed in the examples of section 7.

1. inform(speaker, hearer, proposition)
2. informref(speaker, hearer, term, proposition)
3. informif(speaker, hearer, proposition)
4. request(speaker, hearer, action)

The first action is described by:

inform(S, H, P) *causes*
know(H, P) & know(H, know(S, P)) *if*
know(S, P) & int(S, inform(S, H, P)).

If a speaker S knows a specific proposition and intends to inform the hearer H about it and actually informs the hearer about it then the hearer will learn the proposition and he will know that the speaker knows it.

The second speech act is described by:

informref(S, H, T, P) *causes* knowref(H, T, P) *if*
knowref(S, T, P) & int(S, informref(S, H, T, P)).

If a speaker S knows about some aspect T of a proposition P and intends to inform the hearer H about it and actually acts in order to inform the hearer about it then the hearer will learn that fact.

The third speech act is defined by:

informif(S, H, P) *causes* knowif(H, P) *if*
knowif(S, P) & int(S, informif(S, H, P)).

This expression means that if the speaker S knows that a given property P is true and s/he informs the hearer H about that status then the hearer will learn about that fact.

The last speech act can be defined by:

request(S, H, A) *causes* int(H, A) & know(H, int(S, A)) *if*
int(S, A) & bel(S, cando(H, A)) & ¬ bel(S, cando(S, A)).

If a speaker S intends an action A to be done, and he believes he can't do action A, then he may request the hearer to do the action. This action causes the hearer H to want to perform the action (we are assuming a cooperative dialogue) and to know that the speaker wants the action to be done.

7 Examples

7.1 Incorrect User Plan

In the following example (adapted from [Pol86]) the user plan is detected to be incorrect if the user wants to achieve the stated goal.

- Q: I want to talk to Kathy. Do you know her phone number at the hospital?
- A: She has already been discharged. Her home number is 555-8321.

It is necessary to define a basic rule that elaborates on common sense reasoning:

bel(s, by(call(s, p), talk(s, h), at(h, p))) *if*
int(s, talk(s, h)) & bel(s, at(h, p)) & knowref(s, n, phone_number(n, p)).

This rule means that if a speaker intends to talk to a hearer, he believes the hearer is at place p, and he knows the phone number of p, then he believes that by calling to p he will talk to the hearer.

Using this rule and the Event Calculus as described in the previous sections it is possible to reason about the example presented. In this example the user question might create the following facts:

$happens(e1).$
$act(e1, inform(user, sys, int(user, talk(user, kathy)))).$
$happens(e0), e1 < e0$
$act(e0, request(user, sys, informref(sys, user, N, phone\_number(hospital, N)))).$

With action e1, and the $inform$ rule we'll have:

$$holds\_at(bel(sys, int(user, talk(user, kathy))), e0)$$

Using the rule for the request action $e0$ it is possible to abduce that the user wants to be informed about the hospital number.

$$holds\_at(int(user, informref(sys, user, N, phone\_number(hospital, N))), e0).$$

Using the rule for *informref* the system may infer that the user wants to be informed about the hospital phone number in order to know that number:

$$holds\_at(int(user, knowref(user, N, phone\_number(hospital, N))), e0).$$

With the first rule described in this section and these facts it is possible to infer:

$$holds\_at(bel(user, by(call(user, hospital), talk(user, kathy), at(hospital, kathy))), e0)$$

Meaning that the user believes that by calling to the hospital he will talk to Kathy. In order to do this inference it was necessary to abduce an action that initiated the fluent *bel(user, at(hospital, kathy))*.

On the other hand, suppose that the system knows that Kathy is at home:

$$initiates(e, bel(system, at(home, kathy))), e < e0.$$

It is possible to generate by the system an answer similar to the one given in the example showing the incorrectness of the user plan (from the system's point of view) and pointing out a possible solution.

7.2 Misunderstanding Dialogue

In this example (adapted from [Sch92, MH93]) there is a misunderstanding of the real intentions of the first speaker. In fact, after the second utterance, the second agent needs to revise the beliefs about the other agent intentions:

1. A: Do you know who's going to that meeting?
2. B: Yes.
3. A: Who?
4. B: Oh. Probably Mrs. McOwen and probably Mrs. Cadry and some of the teachers.

Using the speech acts and the epistemic operators previously defined it is possible to handle this kind of dialogue. The first utterance creates the following facts:

$$happens(e1),$$
$$act(e1, request(a, b, informif(b, a, knowref(b, T, going(T, meeting))))).$$

From these facts, using the rule for *request*, and abducing the pre-condition of that act it is possible to infer that:

$$holds\_at(int(a, informif(b, a, knowref(b, T, going(T, meeting)))), e1).$$

This property means that A wants to be informed if B knows who is going to the meeting.

Using the rule for *informif*, and inferring the effects of that act it is possible to deduce:

$$holds\_at(int(a, knowif(a, knowref(b, T, going(T, meeting)))), e1).$$

This inference means that the agent A has the intention to know if B really knows who is going to the meeting.

Consider that there was a previous event $e0$ stating that B knows that property:

$$e0 < e1,$$
$$initiates(knowref(b, people, going(people, meeting)), e0).$$

Then it is possible to B to generate the second utterance (using the rule for *informif*).

With the third utterance, the agent A creates a new set of facts:

$$happens(e2), e1 < e2,$$
$$act(e2, request(a, b, informref(b, a, T, going(T, meeting)))).$$

Using the same inference process it is possible to infer the following facts (using the rule for *informref*):

$$holds\_at(int(a, informref(b, a, T, going(T, meeting)))), e2).$$

And inferring the effects of the speech act *informref*:

$$holds\_at(int(a, knowref(a, T, going(T, meeting)))), e1).$$

This inference process allows the agent B to generate the fourth utterance.

Note that our framework handles this dialogue but is also able to support a more intelligent dialogur where the second utterence is replaced by the fourth, i. e. agent B understands that the first utterence is an indirect question.

8 Conclusions and Future Work

We have presented in this paper a logic programming framework that supports the abductive inference of actions and events through the use of extended logic programs, the event calculus, speech acts, and epistemic operators. The integration of these features allows us to model and to handle a large class of cooperative information-seeking dialogues in a very general approach. In fact, the results obtained show that this framework is able to handle some of the classical problems that arise in dialogues (non-specified goals, clarification sub-dialogues, error situations, wrong user plans, misunderstandings).

As it was pointed out this work has some connections with the work of Appelt and Pollack ([AP92]) using weighted abduction for plan ascription. In our work we have the abductive reasoning process integrated in a general non-monotonic logic programming framework using Event Calculus and based on epistemic operators and a speech acts theory.

As future work we will try to show how this framework can also model other kinds of dialogues, namely missleading and non-cooperative ones. In order to handle this larger class of problems, the framework should be incorporated in a more general natural language processing system such as the one described by Lopes and Quaresma ([Lop91, QL92]) where a multi-headed architecture coordinates several independent modules with the shared objective of supporting a robust natural language interaction.

References

[AP80] J. F. Allen and C. R. Perrault. Analyzing intention in utterances. *Artificial Intelligence*, (15):143–178, 1980.

[AP92] Douglas E. Appelt and Martha E. Pollack. Weighted abduction for plan ascription. *User Modeling and User-Adapted Interaction*, 2(1), 1992.

[CL90] P. Cohen and H. Levesque. Intention is choice with commitment. *Artificial Intelligence*, 42(3), 1990.

[Esh88] Kave Eshghi. Abductive planning with event calculus. In *ICLP*, 1988.

[FN71] R. E. Fikes and Nils J. Nilsson. Strips: A new approach to the application of theorem proving to problem solving. *Artificial Intellligence*, (2):189–208, 1971.

[GL92] M. Gelfond and V. Lifshitz. Representing actions in extended logic programs. In *Proceedings IJCSLP 92*, 1992.

[HSME88] J. Hobbs, M. Stickel, P. Martin, and D. Edwards. Interpretation as abduction. In *Proceedings of the 26th Annual Meeting of ACL*, 1988.

[LA87] D. Litman and J. Allen. A plan recognition model for subdialogues in conversations. *Cognitive Science*, (11):163–200, 1987.

[Lit85] Diane J. Litman. *Plan Recognition and Discourse Analysis: An Integrated Approach for Understanding Dialogues.* PhD thesis, Dep. of Computer Science, University of Rochester, 1985.

[Lop91] J. G. Lopes. Architecture for intentional participation of natural language interfaces in conversations. In C. Brown and G. Koch, editors, *Natural Language Understanding and Logic Programming III.* North Holland, 1991.

[MH93] Susan McRoy and Graeme Hirst. Abductive explanation of dialogue misunderstandings. In *EACL'93*, 1993.

[Mis91] Lode Missiaen. *Localized Abductive Planning with the Event Calculus.* PhD thesis, Univ. Leuven, 1991.

[PAA92] L. M. Pereira, J. J. Alferes, and J. N. Aparício. Contradiction removal semantics with explicit negation. In *Proc. Applied Logic Conf.*, 1992.

[Pol86] Martha E. Pollack. *Inferring Domain Plans in Question-Answering.* PhD thesis, Dep. of Computer and Information Science, University of Pennsylvania, 1986.

[QL92] P. Quaresma and J. G. Lopes. A two-headed architecture for intelligent multimedia man-machine interaction. In *B. de Boulay and V. Sgurev (eds). Artificial Intelligence V - methodology, systems, applications.* North Holland, 1992.

[Sac77] Earl D. Sacerdoti. *A Structure for Plans and Behavior.* American Elsevier, New York, 1977.

[Sch92] Emanuel Schegloff. Repair after next turn: The last structurally provided defense of intersubjectivity in conversation. *American Journal of Sociology*, 5(97):1295:1345, 1992.

Constraint Logic Programming in the Sequent Calculus

John Darlington and Yike Guo

Dept. of Computing
Imperial College
180 Queen's Gate
London SW7 2BZ

Abstract. In this paper, we are developing a new logical semantics of CLP. It is shown that CLP is based on an amalgamated logic embedding the entailment relation of constraints into a fragment of intuitionistic logic. Constrained SLD resolution corresponds to a complete proof search in the amalgamated logic. The framework provides not only the logical account on the definitional semantics towards CLP but also a general way to integrate constraints into various logic programming systems.

1 Introduction

Constraint logic programming has recently attracted much active research. Intuitively, constraint logic programming languages are designed by replacing unification with constraint solving over a computational domain. Therefore, logic programming can be pursued over any intended domain of discourse. Many CLP languages has been designed [JL87, Col87] and implemented [JL87, Col87]. Their computational domains include linear arithmetic[JL87], boolean algebra [KS89] and finite sets [MHS88]. Since the fundamental linguistic features of CLP can be separated from the details specific to any particular computational domain, it is natural to parameterise the semantics of CLP systems with the computational domains as parameters. In [JL87], Jaffer and Lassez proposed a CLP scheme as a general framework which may be instantiated with various intended domains.

In the CLP scheme, the meaning of a CLP program follows the logic programming perspective as a Horn logic theory. A domain of discourse, D, has to be axiomatised by a Horn logic (with equality) theory T_D which is a consistent theory containing only symbols from D. Such a domain theory satisfies the following *satisfaction completeness* condition: for every allowed D-constraint, c, either $T_D \models \exists(c)$ or $T_D \models \neg c$ where $\exists(c)$ denotes the existential closure of c. With this condition, all the models of T_D (D is obviously a model of T_D) behave similarly with respect to constraint satisfaction since, for any model A of T_D, if A does not satisfy $\exists(c)$ then $\neg c$ must be the logical consequence of T_D (so A satisfies $\neg c$). Thus, we can use any model of T_D to interpret the constraints. A domain theory which meets the satisfaction completeness condition is therefore called a *complete theory* in the literature. By axiomatising the intended computational domain D with its complete domain theory T_D, constraints become logical formulae. The logical semantics of a CLP program Γ is a first order theory $\Gamma \cup T_D$. Given a goal G which is a conjunction of constraints and atomic formulae, computation is proving that the existential closure of the goal $\exists(G)$ is a logical consequence of the theory, i.e. $\Gamma \cup T_D \models \exists(G)$.

Instantiating the CLP scheme with a set of constraints and a corresponding domain theory results in a CLP language. For example, the CLP(R) language [JL87] results from the choice of linear arithmetic constraints over real numbers. RCF is taken as a complete theory for the real number domain. Prolog can be viewed as a special CLP language where the allowed constraints are equations over finite labeled terms (Herbrand terms) and the domain theory is Clark's axiomatisation of equality of finite Herbrand terms [Cla78].

The CLP scheme provides a logical view on embedding constraint systems into Horn clause logic languages. However, this approach suffers the following main drawbacks:

- The semantics of a CLP language assume a complete first order axiomatisation of the underlying constraint system. To achieve such a complete axiomatisation, restrictions have to be imposed on the permissible constraint system.
- The role of logic and constraints are mixed so that constraints can not be used naturally to reason about and analyse CLP programs.
- Interpreting constraints as logical formulae complicates the modelling of some important constraint programming features such as constraint propagation.

It seems to be more natural to develop an alternative semantic perspective towards CLP based on the framework of definitional constraint programming [Guo93]. That is, the essence of constraint logic programming becomes programming a constraint system using Horn clause logic rather than embedding a constraint system into a logical theory. Recently, there have been CLP semantic models proposed that are consistent with this *definitional approach*. In [Smo89], Smolka proposed a scheme for CLP by regarding a CLP program as a set of definitions of *relational constraints*. That is, relations defined by a CLP program become new constraints extending the underlying constraint system. Constrained SLD resolution, formed by replacing the unification mechanism with a complete solver of the underlying constraint system, constitutes a complete solver for this extended constraint system. This understanding of constraint logic programming is more flexible and general than Jaffer and Lassaz's CLP scheme in the sense that no restriction is imposed on the underlying constraint system. A program is then not intended to be considered as a logical theory rather as a set of definitions of relational constraints. The semantics are closely related to the algebraic semantics of Jaffer and Lassaz's CLP scheme. In [MG91], Gabrielli and Levi proposed a semantic model of CLP, called π-interpretation, which generalises the algebraic semantics of CLP by interpreting programs directly in terms of constraints. In this model, each predicate in a CLP program denotes a set of constraints. The semantics aims to achieve the equivalence between the operational and the declarative semantics of CLP programs. The model is closely related to Colmerauer's view of his Prolog systems and CLP languages [Col82]. All these semantic models are based on the algebraic semantics of CLP by regarding clauses as recursive definitions of new relational constraints. The logical structure of such a definitional approach towards CLP has not been explored.

In this paper, we are developing a new semantics of CLP based on the sequent calculus to provide a logical model for the definitional approach towards CLP. It is shown that CLP can be based on an amalgamated logic embedding the entailment relation of constraints into a fragment of intuitionistic logic. Constrained SLD resolution corresponds to a complete proof search strategy in the amalgamated logic. The framework provides not only the logical account on the definitional semantics towards CLP but also a general way to integrate constraints into various logic programming systems.

2 Constraint Systems

As suggested in [SL92], by regarding constraints as formulae representing partial information, a constraint system can be defined by asserting an entailment relation between constraints. A constraint store is then viewed as an implicit representation of all the constraints it entails (i.e. its consequences). This view suggests a deductive perspective towards constraint systems which takes a more abstract account of constraints by hiding their internal structure. Following this deductive formalism, what is essential to a constraint is its deducible consequences. Constraint solvers are viewed as mechanisms to compute the entailment relation.

First of all, we take a general account of terms and substitutions by introducing the notion of a *term system* as presented in [J.C91]. Instead of defining substitution with respect to a concrete term structure, a term system provides an algebraic axiomatisation of substitution as a binary operator without committing to any concrete term representation.

Definition 2.1 (Term System) *A term system U is a triple $\langle T, S, V\rangle$ where T is a set of $U-$terms (terms for short), V is a countable set of $U-$variables (variables for short) and S is a set of V-indexed binary operators on T and V such that for all $x, y \in V$ and $t, t' \in T$, the following conditions are satisfied:*

$$
\begin{array}{lll}
s_x(t,x) & = t & \\
s_x(t,y) & = y & x \neq y \\
s_x(t, s_x(y,t')) & = s_x(y,t') & x \neq y \\
s_x(t', s_y(t'',t)) & = s_y(t'', s_x(t',t)) & \text{if } x \neq y, x \notin dep(t'') \text{ and } y \notin dep(t')
\end{array}
$$

where a term t is dependent on the variable x if $\exists t' \in T$ and $s_x \in S$ such that $s_x(t',t) \neq t$. x is then called a dependent variable. The set $dep(t)$ denotes all the dependent variables of t. When $x \notin dep(t)$, we say that the term t is independent of x.

Intuitively, $s_x(t,t')$ denotes the operation "substitute t for every occurrence of the variable x in t' ". We can denote $s_x(t,t')$ as $t'[t/x]$ following the conventional notation for writing substitutions. This notation can be then extended to substitutions on multiple variables by writing $s_{x1}(t_1, s_{x2}(t_2, \ldots, s_{xk}(t_k, t)\ldots)$ as $t[t_1/x_1, \ldots, t_k/x_k]$ under the assumption that $x_i \notin dep(t_j)$ for any $i \neq j$. Term systems provide an abstract view of substitution where the concrete structure of terms becomes nonessential. For any term in a term system $U : \langle T, S, V\rangle$, we denote the fact that $t \in T$ as $t \in U$.

Definition 2.2 **($(U,\mathcal{P})$-formulae)** *Let U be a term system and $\mathcal{P}$ be a set of predicate symbols over U-terms. A $(U,\mathcal{P})$-atomic formula is of the form $p(t_1,\ldots,t_n)$ where $p \in \mathcal{P}$ is a n-ary predicate and $t_i \in U$. A $(U,\mathcal{P})$-formula is formed by applying first order logic connectives and quantifiers to $(U,\mathcal{P})$-atomic formulae.*

As a convention, we always identify formulae that are different from each other only in their bound variables which can be renamed consistently. Substitutions on U-terms can be extended to be applicable to atomic formulae as usual by defining $p(t_1,\ldots,t_n)[t/x]$ as $p(t_1[t/x],\ldots,t_n[t/x])$. Substitutions on an arbitrary formula are defined as usual as substituting the variables in its component atomic formulae. For any set of $(U,\mathcal{P})$-formulae W and η, a set of logical operators, we use the notation W^η to denote the smallest set containing W and closed under the logical operators in the set η. The set of all variables in a syntactic entity (term, formula or a set of formulae) e is denoted as $\vartheta(e)$.

Given a term system U and a set of predicates $\mathcal{P}$, a constraint system can be defined by introducing basic logic structures over $(U,\mathcal{P})$-formulae to represent the notion of constraint stores. By adopting atomic $(U,\mathcal{P})$-formulae as the minimum syntactical construction of basic constraints, the sequent calculus can be used to specify the deductive properties of the entailment relation with respect to the basic operators of constraints. A $(U,\mathcal{P})$-constraint system with respect to a term system U can be defined as follows :

Definition 2.3 **(Constraint System)** *Given a term system U and a set $\mathcal{P}$ of predicates. Let D be a set of $(U,\mathcal{P})$-formulae. The set $\mathcal{P}_{fin}(D)$ denotes the set of all finite subsets of D. A $(U,\mathcal{P})$-constraint system is a structure $\langle Con, \vdash_c\rangle$ satisfying the following conditions:*

Constraint Stores: *$Con \subseteq D$ and $Con = Con^{\wedge,\exists}$. Each element of Con is called a constraint store.*

Entailment Relation: *The entailment relation $\vdash_c \subseteq \mathcal{P}_{fin}(Con) \times Con$ satisfies the following properties:*

$$\{d\} \vdash_c d \qquad \textit{(Reflexivity)}$$

$$\frac{S_2 \vdash_c d}{S_1, S_2 \vdash_c d} \qquad \textit{(Monotonicity)}$$

$$\frac{S_1 \vdash_c d \qquad S_2, d \vdash_c e}{S_1, S_2 \vdash_c e} \qquad \textit{(Transitivity (Cut))}$$

$$\frac{S, d, e \vdash_c u}{S, d \wedge e \vdash_c u}\,(\wedge\vdash_c) \qquad \frac{S \vdash_c d \qquad S \vdash_c e}{S \vdash_c d \wedge e}\,(\vdash_c\wedge)$$

$$\frac{S, d \vdash_c e}{S, \exists x.d \vdash_c e}\,(\exists\vdash_c) \qquad \frac{S \vdash_c d[t/x]}{S \vdash_c \exists x.d}\,(\vdash_c\exists)$$

In $(\exists\vdash_c)$, $x \notin \vartheta(S) \cup \vartheta(e)$.

Generic Condition: $\vdash_c$ *is* generic*: that is* $S[t/x] \vdash_c d[t/x]$ *whenever* $S \vdash_c d$, *for any term* $t \in U$.

Following the definition, a constraint system is defined by providing a set of possible constraint stores representing partial information and asserting an entailment relation between constraint stores. A valid constraint d can be asserted as $\vdash_c d$. On the other hand, a constraint store S is inconsistent iff $\forall d \in Con, S \vdash_c d$. We use $\perp$ to denote all inconsistent stores. The three structural rules (reflexivity, monotonicity and transitivity) indicate that the relation $\vdash_c$ is an entailment relation [Mes89] over constraints. The last four rules present the deductive meaning of two basic store constructors, conjunction and existential quantification. The generic condition of $\vdash_c$ states that all free variables in stores are implicitly universally quantified. Thus, the logical structure of a constraint system is given as the $(\exists, \wedge)$–fragment of intuitionistic logic to reflect the deductive feature of constraint stores. The deduction rules in the definition of constraint systems should be regarded as the properties of the entailment relation $\vdash_c$ rather than the inference rules. That is, a constraint system has a "built-in" entailment relation which satisfies all the deduction rules in the definition. Such an entailment relation is realised by the underlying solver of the system. In the following, we simply call a $(U, \mathcal{P})$-constraint system a constraint system whenever the underlying term structure is not important. The notion of a constraint system reflects the understanding of the fundamental features of constraint-based computation: processing constraint-represented partial information by incrementally refining a consistent constraint store. A constraint solver in a constraint system should be powerful enough to realise the "built-in" entailment relation.

3 Constraint Logic Languages

In order to simplify the presentation, the syntax of a CLP language can be redefined as follows to distinguish the formulae for programs and for goals.

Definition 3.1 *Let A range over atomic, first order, formulae, and let c range over basic constraints. The syntax of goals is defined by the following clause:*

$$G \triangleq c \mid A \mid G_1 \wedge G_2 \mid G_1 \vee G_2 \mid \exists X.G$$

The syntax of program clauses is defined by the following clause:

$$P \triangleq A \mid G \Rightarrow A \mid P_1 \wedge P_2 \mid \forall X.P$$

The correspondence between the clauses with this syntax and Horn clauses is clear. Any positive Horn clause is identified with a closed program clause as defined above and every closed program clause can be rewritten to be the conjunction of positive Horn clauses by applying prenixing and de Morgan's rules. The correspondence between goals and negative Horn clauses is also straightforward. In this section, we denote a CLP program by a tuple $\langle \Gamma, Q \rangle$ where Γ is a set of closed clauses and Q is a goal.

4 Constructing an Amalgamated Logic

We adopt the $(\exists, \forall, \wedge, \vee, \Rightarrow)$- fragment of intuitionistic logic as the underlying logic for the CLP languages. There are several different sequent calculi for intuitionistic logic [Kle67]. The system adopted here, defined by the deduction rules on sequents, is similar to the LJ system in [Kle67]. The deduction rules of the logic are summerised in Fig. 1.

As Gentzen proved, for any LJ proof, there is always a cut-free proof [Gal86]. In any cut-free deduction, the proof is only based on the subformulae appearing in the root of the proof tree. This *subformula property* can be stated as the following corollary:

Corollary 1. *If A is a subformula of any formula of a sequent in a cut-free deduction of $\Gamma \vdash_{LJ} \Delta$, then A is also a subformula of some formulae in Γ, Δ.*

The corollary allows us to use a proper fragment of the intuitionistic logic as the programming logic of CLP systems. The logic we adopt, called the Horn fragment of intuitionistic logic, HL, is essentially an LJ system with the $\neg \vdash$ and $\vdash \neg$ rules removed since negation is not used in a CLP language. A proof in the logic HL is still a LJ proof. Therefore, for any proof of the logic HL, there is a cut-free LJ proof. Moreover, by the above corollary, in such a cut-free LJ proof, $\neg \vdash$ and $\vdash \neg$ rules in LJ will never be used since we did not adopt negation in the logic. Therefore, such a cut-free LJ proof is actually a cut-free HL proof. Thus, we have the following cut-elimination theorem for HL.

Structure Rules :

$$\text{(Id)} \quad \frac{}{\Gamma, A \vdash A} \qquad \text{(Exchange)} \quad \frac{\Gamma, A, B \vdash \Delta}{\Gamma, B, A \vdash \Delta}$$

$$\text{(Contraction)} \quad \frac{\Gamma, A, A \vdash \Delta}{\Gamma, A \vdash \Delta} \qquad \text{(Weakening)} \quad \frac{\Gamma \vdash \Delta}{\Gamma, A \vdash \Delta}$$

Cut :

$$\frac{\Gamma_1, \vdash G \qquad \Gamma_2, G \vdash \Delta}{\Gamma_1, \Gamma_2 \vdash \Delta}$$

Deduction Rules:

$$(\wedge \vdash) \quad \frac{\Gamma, A, B \vdash \Delta}{\Gamma, A \wedge B \vdash \Delta} \qquad (\vdash \wedge) \quad \frac{\Gamma \vdash A \qquad \Gamma \vdash B}{\Gamma \vdash A \wedge B}$$

$$(\vee \vdash) \quad \frac{\Gamma, A \vdash \Delta \qquad \Gamma, B \vdash \Delta}{\Gamma, A \vee B \vdash \Delta} \qquad (\vdash \vee) \quad \frac{\Gamma \vdash A}{\Gamma \vdash A \vee B}, \frac{\Gamma \vdash B}{\Gamma \vdash A \vee B}$$

$$(\Rightarrow \vdash) \quad \frac{\Gamma, A \Rightarrow B \vdash A \qquad \Gamma, B \vdash \Delta}{\Gamma, A \Rightarrow B \vdash \Delta} 1 \qquad (\vdash \Rightarrow) \quad \frac{\Gamma, A \vdash B}{\Gamma \vdash A \Rightarrow B}$$

$$(\forall \vdash) \quad \frac{\Gamma, A[t/x] \vdash \Delta}{\Gamma, \forall x. A \vdash \Delta} \qquad (\vdash \forall) \quad \frac{\Gamma \vdash A}{\Gamma \vdash \forall x. A} \text{ where } x \notin \vartheta(\Gamma)$$

$$(\exists \vdash) \quad \frac{\Gamma, A \vdash \Delta}{\Gamma, \exists x. A \vdash \Delta} \text{ where } x \notin \vartheta(\Gamma) \cup \vartheta(\Delta) \qquad (\vdash \exists) \quad \frac{\Gamma \vdash A[t/x]}{\Gamma \vdash \exists x. A}$$

Fig. 1. Horn Fragment of Intuitionistic Logic

Theorem 4.1 *For any formulae Γ, Δ in HL, $\Gamma \vdash_{hl} \Delta$ iff the sequent $\Gamma \vdash \Delta$ has a cut-free proof.*

The deduction system of HL can easily amalgamate with a constraint system by taking constraints as special atomic formulae. Given a constraint system $(Con, \vdash_c)$, the deduction system of HL can be extended to embed the entailment relation of the constraints $\vdash_c$ by adopting ***constraint axioms*** of the form $S \vdash c$ where $S \subseteq_f Con$ is a finite set of constraints and c is a constraint such that $S \vdash_c c$. Since a constraint system has a "built-in" cut rule, the constraint axioms are deductive closed. That is , if $c_1, \ldots, c_k \vdash c$ and $c, d_1, \ldots, d_n \vdash d$ are axioms, then $c_1, \ldots, c_k, d_1, \ldots, d_n \vdash d$ is an axiom.

The deduction system determines an entailment relation $\vdash_{hc}$ for the amalgamated logic HC. The entailment relation of HL and the entailment relation between constraints are the subentailment relations of $\vdash_{hc}$. Moreover, $\vdash_{hc}$ preserves the structures of the two subentailment systems. That is, the following two equivalences hold:

1. $\Gamma \vdash_{hc} A \iff \Gamma \vdash_{hl} A$
   where Γ is a finite set of HL-formulae and A is a HL-formula.
2. $S \vdash_{hc} c \iff S \vdash_c c$
   where $S \in \mathcal{P}_{fin}(Con), c \in Con$

The following theorem states that the cut-elimination property still holds for any HC proof.

Theorem 4.2 *For any formulas Γ, Δ in HC, $\Gamma \vdash_{hc} \Delta$ iff the sequent $\Gamma \vdash \Delta$ has a cut-free proof.*

Proof. This theorem is proved by modifying the cut-elimination procedure for the LJ proof [Gal86]. First of all, we can define atomic constraints as principle formulae of constraint axioms. Since atomic constraints are not the principle formulae for any other deduction rules, we only need to eliminate the applications of the cut rule to two constraint axioms. By the deductive closed property of the constraint system, such an elimination is always possible.

A CLP program verifies the relation $\Gamma \vdash_{hc} \exists X.Q$ where $Q \in G$ by constructing constraints c_i constraining the parameter variables X such that for all c_i, we have $\vartheta(c_i) = X$ and $\Gamma \vdash_{hc} \forall X.c_i \Rightarrow Q$. The constraint c_i is called an ***answer constraint***.

5 A Complete Proof Strategy

Given a program $\langle \Gamma, Q \rangle$, computing an answer constraint c corresponds to searching for a proof for $\Gamma \vdash_{hc} \forall X.c \Rightarrow Q$ in HC. In the following, we will show that constrained SLD resolution forms a complete proof strategy for computing answer constraints for any CLP program. This result follows Miller's work on developing a general logic programming framework based on a proof strategy called *uniform proof* [NM+89].

Definition 5.1 (Uniform Proof) *A cut-free proof is uniform iff the succedent of each sequent is a single formula and every sequent whose succedent is a non-atomic formula is the lower sequent of a deduction step that introduces its top-level connective.*

First we will prove that the uniform proof is complete with respect to computing the entailment $\Gamma \vdash_{hc} \forall X.c \Rightarrow Q$ for any CLP program $\langle \Gamma, Q \rangle$ and constraint c such that $\vartheta(Q) = \vartheta(c) = X$. The following lemma shows that uniform proof is complete for CLP programs with respect to the logic HC.

Definition 5.2 (Non-uniform Occurrence) *A non-uniform occurrence in a non-uniform proof is an instance of a left rule which has an non-atomic succedent.*

Lemma 5.1 (Completeness of the Uniform Proofs) *Let $\langle \Gamma, Q \rangle$ be a CLP program and c be a constraint such that $\vartheta(Q) = \vartheta(c) = X$. Then $\Gamma \vdash_{hc} \forall X.c \Rightarrow Q$ iff the sequent $\Gamma, c \vdash Q$ has a uniform proof.*

Proof. The "if" part is obvious. On the other hand, since $\Gamma \vdash_{hc} \forall X.c \Rightarrow Q$ and $\forall X.c \Rightarrow Q$ is a universal closure, there is a cut-free proof in HC for the sequent $\Gamma, c \vdash Q$. We define the rank of a non-uniform occurrence as the height of the subproof of the right-hand premise when the applied rule is $\Rightarrow\vdash$, or the height of the subproof of the sole premise for any other left rules. According to the syntax of Γ and Q, it is clear that the only deduction rules used in the proof are $\wedge\vdash$, $\Rightarrow\vdash, \forall\vdash, \vdash\wedge, \vdash\exists$ and $\vdash\vee$. If the proof is not a uniform proof, then the following procedure can be used to transform a non-uniform proof into a uniform proof.

1. Select a non-uniform occurrence with the property that the sub-proofs of the premises of the rule are uniform. Let E be the non-atomic succedent in the conclusion of the application.
2. Since all sub-proofs of the premises of the rule are uniform, one premise of the application will be the conclusion of a right-rule that introduces the top connective of E. Following the subformula property, the left rules involved in a HC proof are only $(\wedge\vdash, \Rightarrow\vdash, \forall\vdash)$. By enumerating all combinations of the left-rules $(\wedge\vdash, \Rightarrow\vdash, \forall\vdash)$ below the right rules $(\vdash\exists, \vdash\vee, \vdash\wedge)$ in a proof, it can be checked that the left rule can be permuted up over the right rule. We illustrate the following permutation as a demonstration where the non-uniformity is the application of the $\Rightarrow\vdash$ rule which occurs below an instance of the $\vdash\vee$ rule. The non-uniform proof :

$$\dfrac{\begin{matrix}\Pi_1\\ \vdots \\ \Gamma, A \Rightarrow B \vdash A\end{matrix} \quad \dfrac{\begin{matrix}\Pi_2\\ \vdots\\ \Gamma, B, A \Rightarrow B \vdash G_1\end{matrix}}{\Gamma, B, A \Rightarrow B \vdash G_1 \vee G_2}(\vdash\vee)}{\Gamma, A \Rightarrow B \vdash G_1 \vee G_2}(\Rightarrow\vdash)$$

can be transformed into the following proof by permuting down the applied left rule $\Rightarrow\vdash$.

$$\dfrac{\dfrac{\begin{array}{cc}\Pi_1 & \Pi_2 \\ \vdots & \vdots \\ \Gamma, A \Rightarrow B \vdash A & \Gamma, B, A \Rightarrow B \vdash G_1\end{array}}{\Gamma, A \Rightarrow B \vdash G_1}(\Rightarrow\vdash)}{\Gamma, A \Rightarrow B \vdash G_1 \vee G_2}(\vdash \vee)$$

The procedure should be recursively applied to all the sub-proofs of the premises of the new final rule to permute newly introduced non-uniform occurrences. The recursion will terminate since the new non-uniform rule occurrences will always have smaller ranks.

Thus, by applying this procedure repeatedly, the non-uniform proof will finally be transformed into a uniform proof since there are only finite numbers of non-uniform occurrences of left rules in the proof.

The completeness of uniform proofs for CLP programs provides a goal-directed search procedure. Note that in the context of uniform proof, the left rule $\Rightarrow\vdash$ is only applied when the succedent of the proving sequent has already become atomic. Moreover, each open implication $B \Rightarrow A$ in the left-hand side of a sequent in a proof is a variation of a program clause which is generated by applying the $\forall \vdash$ rule. These facts indicate that the left rules in a uniform proof are used for backchaining. We formalise this claim by defining the following procedure for marking certain antecedent formulae in a unform proof. First of all we assume the program Γ is canonically represented as a set of closed Horn clauses of the form $\forall X.G \Rightarrow p(X)$. Thus, the $\wedge \vdash$ rule, which is used for extracting a program rule, will not be used in the proof. Only the applications of $\forall \vdash$ and $\Rightarrow\vdash$ need be considered.

1. For each identity inference,

$$\frac{}{\Gamma, A \vdash A}(Id \vdash)$$

   the formula A in the antecedent is marked.
2. If the formula $P[t/x]$ that occurs in the premise of $\forall \vdash$ is marked, then mark the occurrence of $\forall x.P$ in the conclusion.
3. If the formula A that occurs in the right-hand premise of $\Rightarrow\vdash$ is marked, the occurrence $G \Rightarrow A$ in the conclusion is marked.

Definition 5.3 (Simple Uniform Proof) *An application of a left-rule is simple if the occurrence of the formula containing the introduced connective is marked. A uniform proof is simple if all the applications of left rules are simple.*

Theorem 5.1 (Completeness of Simple Uniform Proofs) *Let $\langle \Gamma, Q \rangle$ be a CLP program and c be a constraint such that $\vartheta(Q) = \vartheta(c) = X$. Then $\Gamma \vdash_{hc} \forall X.c \Rightarrow Q$ iff the sequent $\Gamma, c \vdash Q$ has a simple uniform proof.*

Proof. The "if" part is obvious. Following the lemma 5.1, we know that each cut-free proof of the sequent $\Gamma, c \vdash Q$ can be converted into a uniform proof. Suppose the sequent $\Gamma, c \vdash Q$ is proved by a non-simple uniform proof Π. We show that Π can be permuted into a simple uniform proof. This permutation is similar to that in the proof of lemma 5.1. Select a non-simple occurrence of a left rule for which the subproofs of its premises are simple uniform proofs. One of the premises of this occurrence must also be formed by an application of a left rule. These two left rule applications can be permuted. For example, consider the following proof:

$$\dfrac{\dfrac{\begin{array}{cc}\Pi_1 & \Pi_2 \\ \vdots & \vdots \\ \Gamma \vdash G & \Gamma, P[t/X], B \vdash A\end{array}}{\Gamma, P[t/X], G \Rightarrow B \vdash A}(\Rightarrow\vdash)}{\Gamma, \forall X.P, G \Rightarrow B \vdash A}(\forall\vdash)$$

where Π_1 and Π_2 are simple uniform proofs. This proof can be converted into the following structure by permuting the two left rule applications.

$$\dfrac{\begin{array}{c}\Pi_1 \\ \vdots \\ \Gamma \vdash G\end{array} \quad \dfrac{\begin{array}{c}\Pi_2 \\ \vdots \\ \Gamma, P[t/X], B \vdash A\end{array}}{\Gamma, \forall X.P, B \vdash A}(\forall\vdash)}{\Gamma, \forall X.P, G \Rightarrow B \vdash A}(\Rightarrow\vdash)$$

This permutation procedure may continue since the converted proof may introduce new non-simple occurrence of left rules. That is, in this case, the subproof of the sequent:

$$\Gamma, \forall X.P, B \vdash A$$

may not be simple. This procedure always terminates. This fact can be justified by defining the rank of a non-simple occurrence similar to that for non-uniform occurrences and showing that the new introduced non-simple occurrences always have smaller ranks. Since there are finite non-simple occurrences of left rules, a non-simple uniform proof can be converted into a simple uniform proof.

The simple uniform proof strategy characterises a goal-directed backchaining deduction model. In fact, a chain of marked left rule occurrences has the following structure:

$$\dfrac{\begin{array}{c}\Pi_1 \\ \vdots \\ \vdots\end{array} \quad \dfrac{\dfrac{\begin{array}{c}\Pi_3 \\ \vdots \\ \Gamma \vdash G[\bar{t}/X]\end{array} \quad \dfrac{}{P(\bar{t})^* \vdash P(\bar{t})}(Id\vdash)}{\Gamma, (G[\bar{t}/X] \Rightarrow P(\bar{t}))^* \vdash P(\bar{t})}(\Rightarrow\vdash)}{\Gamma, (\forall X.G \Rightarrow P(X))^* \vdash P(\bar{t})}(\forall\vdash)}{\Pi_2}\text{some right rule}$$

Such a chain of deductions can be collapsed into a single deduction step, called *backchaining*:

$$\text{Backchaining } (BC\vdash)\ \frac{\Gamma \vdash G[\bar{t}/X]}{\Gamma, \forall X.G \Rightarrow P(X) \vdash P(\bar{t})} \quad \text{where } \forall X.G \Rightarrow P(X) \in \Gamma$$

We can replace all these chains by the application of the backchaining rule in a simple uniform proof. Thus, a complete proof strategy for CLP programs can be achieved by using backchaining as the only left rule. Clearly, such a strategy characterises constrained SLD resolution. In the following, we show that, due to its close relationship with simple uniform proofs, constrained SLD resolution forms a complete model for computing answer constraints for any CLP program.

First of all, we give a "fine-grained" specification of the constrained SLD resolution model by the following transition system:

Definition 5.4 (Transition System for Constrained SLD Resolution) *Let Γ be a CLP program and c, S, A, Q be syntactic variables ranging over constraints, sets of constraints, goal formulae and sets of goal formulae. A configuration is of form $\langle S, Q\rangle$. The constrained SLD resolution model can be presented by the following transition system:*

$$\begin{array}{llll}
\textit{Imposition:} & \langle S, \{c\} \cup Q\rangle & \rightarrow & \langle S \cup \{c\}, Q\rangle \ \textit{if} S \cup \{c\} \not\vdash_c \bot \\
\textit{Backchaining:} & \langle S, \{p(\bar{t})\} \cup Q\rangle & \rightarrow & \langle S, \{G[\bar{t}/X]\} \cup Q\rangle \ \forall X.G \Rightarrow p(X) \in \Gamma \\
\textit{Decomposition:} & \langle S, \{A_1 \wedge A_2\} \cup Q\rangle & \rightarrow & \langle S, \{A_1, A_2\} \cup Q\rangle \\
\textit{Renaming:} & \langle S, \{\exists x.A\} \cup Q\rangle & \rightarrow & \langle S, \{A[y/x]\} \cup Q\rangle \ y \textit{ is not free in } S, Q \\
\textit{Forking:} & \langle S, \{A_1 \vee A_2\} \cup Q\rangle & \rightarrow & \langle S, \{A_1\} \cup Q\rangle \\
 & \langle S, \{A_1 \vee A_2\} \cup Q\rangle & \rightarrow & \langle S, \{A_2\} \cup Q\rangle
\end{array}$$

Lemma 5.2 (Soundness) *For any transition $\langle S_i, Q_i\rangle \rightarrow \langle S_{i+1}, Q_{i+1}\rangle$, we have $\Gamma, S_{i+1}, Q_{i+1} \vdash_{hc} [Q_i]$ where $[Q]$ denotes the conjunction of all formulae in Q.*

Proof. The lemma is proved by case analysis on the definition of the transition relation. Note that for any transition

$$\langle S, \{A\} \cup Q\rangle \rightarrow \langle S', Q' \cup Q\rangle$$

The following inference is straightforward:

$$\frac{\dfrac{\Gamma, S', Q' \vdash A}{\Gamma, S', Q', Q \vdash A}\text{Weakening} \qquad \Gamma, S', Q', Q \vdash [Q]}{\Gamma, S', Q', Q \vdash [Q] \wedge A}(\vdash \wedge)$$

Since it is easy to show that $\Gamma, S', Q', Q \vdash_{hc} [Q]$, we only need to establish the proof $\Gamma, S', Q' \vdash A$.

1. In the case of constraint imposition, the inference is trivial since $S' = S \cup \{c\}$ and $S \cup \{c\} \vdash_c c$.
2. In the case of backchaining, the inference can be deduced as follows:

$$\cfrac{\cfrac{\cfrac{\cfrac{}{\Gamma, S', G[\bar{t}/x] \vdash G[\bar{t}/x]}(Id\vdash) \quad \cfrac{}{\Gamma, S', p(\bar{t}) \vdash p(\bar{t})}(Id\vdash)}{\Gamma, S', G[\bar{t}/x] \Rightarrow p(\bar{t}), G[\bar{t}/x] \vdash p(\bar{t})}(\Rightarrow\vdash)}{\Gamma, S', \forall X.G \Rightarrow p(X), G[\bar{t}/x] \vdash p(\bar{t})}(\forall\vdash)}{\Gamma, S', G[\bar{t}/x] \vdash p(\bar{t})}\text{Contraction}$$

3. In the case of decomposition, the inference is :

$$\cfrac{\cfrac{}{\Gamma, S', A_1, A_2 \vdash A_1}(Id\vdash) \quad \cfrac{}{\Gamma, S', A_1, A_2 \vdash A_2}(Id\vdash)}{\Gamma, S', A_1, A_2 \vdash A_1 \wedge A_2}(\vdash\wedge)$$

4. In the case of renaming, the inference becomes:

$$\cfrac{\cfrac{}{\Gamma, S', A[y/x] \vdash A[y/x]}(Id\vdash)}{\Gamma, S', A[y/x] \vdash \exists x.A}(\vdash\exists)$$

5. In the case of forking, the inference becomes:

$$\cfrac{\cfrac{}{\Gamma, S', A_i \vdash A_i}(Id\vdash)}{\Gamma, S', A_1 \vdash A_1 \vee A_2}(\vdash\vee_i)$$

Proposition 5.1 *Let $\langle\Gamma, Q\rangle$ be a CLP program. If transition system transforms the initial configuration $\langle\{\}, Q\rangle$ into a final configuration $\langle S_n, \{\}\rangle$ then we have $\Gamma \vdash_{hc} \forall X.S_n \Rightarrow Q$ where $X = \vartheta(S_n)$.*

Proof. By lemma 5.2, for any transition $\langle S_i, Q_i\rangle \rightarrow \langle S_{i+1}, Q_{i+1}\rangle$, $\Gamma, S_{i+1}, Q_{i+1} \vdash_{hc} [Q_i]$. Thus, for a transition sequence, $\langle\Gamma, S_i, Q_i\rangle \rightarrow \langle\Gamma, S_{i+1}, Q_{i+1}\rangle \rightarrow \langle\Gamma, S_{i+2}, Q_{i+2}\rangle$, we have $\Gamma, S_{i+1}, Q_{i+1} \vdash_{hc} [Q_i]$ and $\Gamma, S_{i+2}, Q_{i+2} \vdash_{hc} [Q_{i+1}]$. Thus, $\Gamma, S_{i+2}, Q_{i+2} \vdash_{hc} q$ for all $q \in Q_{i+1}$. Following the transitivity of the entailment relation $\vdash_{hc}$, we have $\Gamma, S_{i+1}, S_{i+2}, Q_{i+2} \vdash_{hc} [Q_i]$. Since $S_{i+2} \vdash_c S_{i+1}$, we have $\Gamma, S_{i+2}, Q_{i+2} \vdash_{hc} [Q_i]$. Therefore, by induction on the length of the transition derivation, we can show that the $\Gamma, S_n \vdash_{hc} Q$. Following the transition system, we know that $\vartheta(Q) \subseteq \vartheta(S_n) = X$. Thus, $\Gamma \vdash_{hc} \forall X.S_n \Rightarrow Q$.

Thus, each final configuration $\langle S, \{\}\rangle$ of a terminating transition forms an answer constraint $\exists(S)_{\vartheta(Q)}$.

Lemma 5.3 (Completeness) *Let $\langle\Gamma, Q\rangle$ be a CLP program and c be a constraint such that $\vartheta(Q) = \vartheta(c) = X$. If $\Gamma \vdash_{hc} \forall X.c \Rightarrow Q$ and $\vdash_c \exists(c)$, then there is a transition from $\langle\{\}, Q\rangle$ to $\langle S_i, \{\}\rangle$ such that $c \vdash_c \exists(S_i)_X$.*

Proof. Since $\Gamma \vdash_{hc} \forall X.c \Rightarrow Q$ and $\forall X.c \Rightarrow Q$ is a universal closure, there is a cut-free proof in HC for the sequent $\Gamma, c \vdash Q$. Thus, by the completeness of simple uniform proofs, the sequent has a simple uniform proof. The lemma is proved by establishing the correspondence between simple uniform proofs and the constrained SLD transition. Such a correspondence can be specified by the following mapping of sequents in the frontier of a simple uniform proof to a configuration in a constrained SLD transition:

$$\Delta \vdash S, \Delta \vdash A_1, \ldots, \Delta \vdash A_n, \Rightarrow \langle S, \{A_1, A_2, \ldots, A_n\}\rangle$$

and the following mapping of deductions to transitions:

$$\frac{\Delta \vdash c \qquad \Delta \vdash A}{\Delta \vdash c \wedge A} \Rightarrow \langle S, \{c \wedge A\}\rangle \rightarrow \langle S \cup \{c\}, \{A\}\rangle$$

$$\frac{\Delta \vdash A_1 \qquad \Delta \vdash A_2}{\Delta \vdash A_1 \wedge A_2} \Rightarrow \langle S, \{A_1 \wedge A_2\}\rangle \rightarrow \langle S, \{A_1, A_2\}\rangle$$

$$\frac{\Delta \vdash A_1}{\Delta \vdash A_1 \vee A_2} \Rightarrow \langle S, \{A_1 \vee A_2\}\rangle \rightarrow \langle S, \{A_1\}\rangle$$

$$\frac{\Delta \vdash A_2}{\Delta \vdash A_1 \vee A_2} \Rightarrow \langle S, \{A_1 \vee A_2\}\rangle \rightarrow \langle S, \{A_2\}\rangle$$

$$\frac{\Delta \vdash G[\bar{t}/X]}{\Delta \vdash p(\bar{t})} \Rightarrow \langle S, \{p(\bar{t})\}\rangle \rightarrow \langle S, \{G[\bar{t}/X]\}\rangle \text{ where } \forall X.G \Rightarrow p(X) \in \Gamma$$

The application of the $\vdash \exists$-rule

$$\frac{\Delta \vdash A[t/x]}{\Delta \vdash \exists x.A}$$

can not be directly mapped into a transition since there is no explicit substitution in the constrained SLD resolution rather it will be done implicitly by imposing constrains. This effect can be modeled by replacing the deduction:

$$\frac{\Delta \vdash A[t/x]}{\Delta \vdash \exists x.A}$$

in the proof tree by:

$$\frac{\Delta \vdash A[y/x]}{\Delta \vdash \exists x.A}$$

where y is a new variable which has no free occurrence in any formula in the proof tree. All the occurrences of t in the subproof of $\Delta \vdash A[t/x]$ are also replaced by y. In particular, each application of constraint axioms at the leafs of the subproof: $\phi \vdash \phi'$ becomes $\phi \vdash \phi'[y/t]$. Since $\phi \vdash_c \phi'$ and $y \notin \vartheta(\phi)$, $\phi \vdash_c \exists y.\phi'[y/t]$. In the new constructed tree, the application of the $\vdash \exists$-rule:

$$\frac{\Delta \vdash A[y/x]}{\Delta \vdash \exists x.A}$$

can be mapped to a transition:

$$\langle S, \{\exists x.A\}\rangle \rightarrow \langle S, \{A[y/x]\}\rangle$$

Thus, the whole tree can be mapped into a finite constrained SLD transition derivation. By applying this procedure, such a tree is generated from the simple uniform proof of $\Gamma, c \vdash Q$ to introduce a finite constrained SLD resolution derivation from $\langle\{\}, Q\rangle$ to $\langle S_i, \{\}\rangle$ following the defined mappings. Since all the constraints in S_i generated in this derivation correspond to the constraints at the leafs of the tree, $\forall c_i \in S_i \Rightarrow c \vdash_c \exists(c_i)_X$. Thus, $c \vdash_c \exists(S_i)_X$.

By this completeness lemma, constrained SLD resolution computes a set of most general answers to a goal constraint. In particular, we can define the set of *constraint denotations* for each predicate in a CLP program.

Definition 5.5 (Constraint Denotation Sets of Predicates) *Let p be a predicate defined in a CLP program . The constraint denotation set of p, $\mathcal{M}[\![p(X)]\!]$, is defined as: $\mathcal{M}[\![p(X)]\!] \triangleq \{\exists(S_i)_X \mid \langle\{\}, \{p(X)\}\rangle \rightarrow \langle S_i, \{\}\rangle\}$.*

By the completeness theorem, we can conclude that the constraint denotation set of a predicate contains the most general information about the predicate. That is, for any constraint c such that $\vartheta(c) = X$ and p is a predicate defined by a CLP program Γ, if $\Gamma \vdash_{hc} \forall X.c \Rightarrow p(X)$ then $\exists S \in \mathcal{M}[\![p(X)]\!]$ such that $\Gamma \vdash_{hc} \forall X.S \Rightarrow p(X)$ and $c \vdash_c S$.

The notion of constraint denotation provides a logical account of Gabbrielli and Levi's π-interpretations of constraint logic programs [MG91] where definite clauses in a CLP program are interpreted directly on the base of constraints, rather than on the set of ground atoms. A predicate p in a CLP program is interpreted as a set of *constrained atoms* of the form $\langle p(X), c\rangle$ where the constraint c represents the set of admissible solutions. Within this semantic framework, the intended model of a program denotes each predicate by the set of its computed constraints with respect to the program. That is, the denotation of a predicate p is the set: $D(p) = \{\langle p(X), \exists(S_i)_X\rangle \mid \langle\{\}, \{p(X)\}\rangle \rightarrow \langle S_i, \{\}\rangle\}$. Obviously, the set $D(p)$ coincides with the constraint denotation of p. Therefore, the collection of all the constraint denotations of the predicates in a CLP program forms the intended π-model of the program. This correspondence provides the logical meaning to the computed constraints of predicates. Thus, the π-interpretation is fully captured by the logical semantics proposed in the paper.

6 Conclusion

In this paper, we present a new logical semantics towards CLP by regarding CLP computation as a complete proof search procedure in an amalgamated logic formed by integrating the entailment relations of constraints into the Horn fragment of intuitionistic logic. The Gentzen-style sequent calculus is adopted to define the deductive structure of the logic. Logical formulas (goals) in a CLP program are "deducible constraints". Logical operators (connectives) are programming combinators behavioring as operators for controlling deduction. CLP computation becomes a complete proof search procedure computing the most general answers to a goal. This proof theoretic semantics provides a logical structure for the definitional approach towards CLP. It is shown that the logical meaning of the Gabbrielli and Levi's π-interpretations of constraint logic programs has been fully captured by the semantics. Moreover, this approach also provides a systematic route towards integrating a wider class of constraints into various logic programming systems. It is quite promising to develop a general *backchaining constraint programming language* framework by extending the framework to a class of logic programming languages characterised by Miller [NM+89] as adopting the uniform proof strategy.

References

[Cla78] Keith Clark. Negation as failure. In *Logic and Data Bases*, pages 293–322. Plenum Press, 1978.

[Col82] A. Colmerauer. Prolog and infinite trees. In K.L. Clark and S.A. Tarnlund, editors, *Logic Programming.* Academic Press, New Yok, 1982.

[Col87] A. Colmerauer. Opening the Prolog III universe. *Byte, July*, 1987.

[Gal86] Jean H. Gallier. *Logic for Computer Science.* John Wiley & Sons, 1986.

[Guo93] Yike Guo. *Definitional Constraint Programming.* PhD thesis, Dept. of Computing, Imperial College, 1993. Forthcoming.

[J.C91] J.Cirulis. An algebraization of first order logic with terms. In *Colloquia Mathematica Sociatatis Janos Boolyai, 54.* 1991.

[JL87] Joxan Jaffar and Jean-Louis Lassez. Constraint logic programming. In *Prod. of POPL 87*, pages 111–119, 1987.

[Kle67] S. Kleene. *Mathematical Logic.* New York: Wiley Interscience, 1967.

[KS89] Akira Aiba Ko Sakai. CAL: A Theoretical Background of Constraint Logic Programming and its Applications. *Journal of Symbolic Computation*, Aug. 1989.

[Mes89] Jose Meseguer. General logics. Technical Report SRI-CSL-89-5, SRI International, March 1989.

[MG91] Giorgio Levi Maurizio Gabbrielli. Modeling answer constraints in constraint logic programs. In *Prof. Eighth International Conference on Logic Programming.* The MIT Press, 1991.

[MHS88] M.Dincbas, P.Van Hentenryck, and H. Simonis. The Constraint Logic Programming Language CHIP. In *Procedings of the Internatioal Conference on Fifth Generation Computer System*, Tokyo,Japan, Nov. 1988.

[NM+89] Gopalan Nadathur, Dale Miller, et al. Uniform proofs as a foundation for logic programming. Technical report, Computer and Information Science Department, Univ. of Pennsylvania, 1989.

[SL92] V.A. Saraswat and Patrick Lincoln. Linear concurrent constraint programming. Technical report, Xerox PARC, Feb 1992. Unpublished Draft.

[Smo89] Gert Smolka. *Logic Programming over Polymorphically Order-Sorted Types.* PhD thesis, Vom Fachbereich Informatik der Universitat Kaiserlautern, May 1989.

On conditional rewrite systems with extra variables and deterministic logic programs*

Jürgen Avenhaus · Carlos Loría-Sáenz
Fachbereich Informatik, Universität Kaiserslautern
67653 Kaiserslautern (Germany)
E-mail: avenhaus@informatik.uni-kl.de

Abstract

We study deterministic conditional rewrite systems, i.e. conditional rewrite systems where the extra variables are not totally free but 'input bounded'. If such a system R is quasi-reductive then $\rightarrow_R$ is decidable and terminating. We develop a critical pair criterion to prove confluence if R is quasi-reductive and strongly deterministic. We apply our results to prove Horn clause programs to be uniquely terminating.

1 Introduction

Conditional rewrite systems are widely used as a high-level language to write functional programs. This may cause non-deterministic computations. So one wants to prove that such a system R is canonical, i.e. terminating and confluent. This guarantees that for any input all possible computations stop and give the same result. There are well-known methods to prove termination and confluence if no extra variables are allowed. (A variable in a rule ρ is called an extra variable if it does not appear in the left-hand side of ρ.) See [DO90] for a survey.

Functional programming naturally demands for the *where*-construct and this construct can be incorporated into the rewrite system approach nicely by allowing extra variables. But extra variables should be allowed only in a very restricted form since it is not clear how to instantiate them when only the variables in the left-hand side of a rule are instantiated for rewriting. So in this paper we restrict to deterministic rewrite rules (see [Ga91] and [BG89] for this notion): We require that the extra variables are 'input bounded'. In [Ga91] it is proved that $\rightarrow_R$ is computable and terminating if R is quasi-reductive. We prove that $\rightarrow_R$ is confluent if R is in addition strongly deterministic and all proper critical

*This research was supported by the Deutsche Forschungsgemeinschaft, SFB 314, Project D4

pairs are joinable. Note that no paramodulation pairs (overlapping into the conditions) and no resolution pairs (factoring of a condition) need to be computed. These pairs may be harmful for arbitrary conditional rewrite systems with extra variables [Ga91], [De91]. As far as critical pairs are concerned, we neither need to consider variable overlappings nor overlappings of a rule with itself on top level. (Both are needed if R is not strongly deterministic.).

For many strongly deterministic rewrite systems R encountered in practice it can be proved that all proper critical pairs are either unfeasible or context-joinable. Then R will be confluent, provided it is quasi-reductive.

The class of strongly deterministic rewrite systems seems to be interesting for two reasons. First, interesting problems can be specified rather naturally. And second, well-moded Horn clause programs can be translated into this class of rewrite systems (see [GW92]). We show how to prove that a well-moded program is uniquely terminating, i.e., any derivation starting with a well-moded query stops and all refutations give the same answer substitution. Our interest in studying deterministic rewrite systems stems from problems arising in the field of program synthesis [LS92]. Here conditional rewrite systems with extra variables naturally appear.

The paper is organized as follows: In section 2 we give the basic notations. We discuss the condition 'quasi-reductive' in section 3 and confluence in section 4. We prove logic programs to be uniquely terminating in section 5.

The results of section 3 are basically contained in [BG89]. We present them here to make the paper self-contained. Beyond that we present a simple but powerful method to prove quasi-reductivity.

The results presented in section 4 are related to those in [BG89]. The main differences are: (1) We do not want to start a completion algorithm but we want a simple test on confluence for a given deterministic quasi-reductive rewrite system. We believe that many 'natural specifications' occurring in practice are really confluent (or at least ground confluent). But this has to be verified. (2) We do not want to use the concept of a non-operational equation. (3) To test confluence we prove that critical pairs resulting from overlapping a rule by itself on top-level need not be considered.

To study unique termination of well-moded logic programs we follow [HA85] and [GW92]. In [GW92] only termination of derivations in well-moded logic programs is studied. We use the translation of well-moded logic programs into deterministic rewrite systems from that paper to extend results from [HA85].

2 Basic notations

We assume the reader to be familiar with basic rewriting techniques and notations. For survey papers we refer to [AM90] and [DJ90] and especially for conditional rewriting to [DO90].

A *signature* is a triple $sig = (S, \mathcal{F}, \tau)$. Here S is a set of sorts, $\mathcal{F}$ a set of operators and τ a function τ: $\mathcal{F} \to S^+$ denoting the arity of the operators. $\mathcal{T}(\mathcal{F}, \mathcal{V})$ is the set of terms over $\mathcal{F}$ and a set $\mathcal{V}$ of variables. A term is *ground* if it contains no variable. For a term t we denote by $O(t)$ the set of positions p in t such that t/p is not a variable. We denote by $t[s]_p$ the term that results from t by replacing t/p by s. We write $\equiv$ for the syntactic identity of terms. $Var(o)$ is the set of variables occurring in an object (term, equation, ...) o.

A partial ordering $\succ$ on $\mathcal{T}(\mathcal{F}, \mathcal{V})$ is *well-founded* if there is no infinite sequence $t_0 \succ t_1 \succ t_2 \succ \cdots$. It is *compatible with substitutions* (the term structure), if $s \succ s'$ implies $\sigma(s) \succ \sigma(s')$ for any substitution σ (respectively, $t[s]_p \succ t[s']_p$ for any term t and position p in t). A *reduction ordering* is a partial ordering that is well-founded, compatible with substitutions and compatible with the term structure. We denote by $\rhd$ the proper subterm relation and by $\succ_{st} = (\succ \cup \rhd)^+$ the smallest ordering that contains $\succ$ and $\rhd$. It is well-founded if $\succ$ is a reduction ordering. There are well-known methods to construct reduction orderings, we mention the recursive path ordering RPO and the lexicographic path ordering LPO. For these orderings we have $\succ = \succ_{st}$. For a survey paper on orderings see [De87].

We study conditional rewrite systems with extra variables. In this case it is convenient to consider oriented conditions. An *unconditional oriented equation* is a pair of terms, written $u \to v$. An *oriented condition* C is a finite sequence of unconditional oriented equations $C \equiv u_1 \to v_1, \ldots, u_n \to v_n$. It is called *operational* for a set V_0 of variables if

$$Var(u_i) \subseteq V_0 \cup Var(u_1 \to v_1) \cup \ldots \cup Var(u_{i-1} \to v_{i-1})$$

for $i = 1, \ldots, n$. (This implies $Var(u_1) \subseteq V_0$). Let R be a rewrite system such that $\to_R$ is already defined. A substitution σ is a *solution* of $C \equiv u_1 \to v_1, \ldots, u_n \to v_n$ wrt. R if

$$\sigma(u_i) \xrightarrow{*}_R \sigma(v_i) \quad \text{for all} \quad 1 \leq i \leq n$$

σ is *irreducible* if $\sigma(x)$ is irreducible for all $x \in V$. σ *extends* τ with $Dom(\tau) = V_0$ if $\sigma(x) \equiv \tau(x)$ for all $x \in V_0$. If C is empty then every σ is a solution of C wrt. R and V_0.

Note that the problem to compute all solutions of C that extend τ reduces to rewriting and matching. So, if $\to_R$ is computable, terminating and locally finite (i.e., $\Delta_R(t) = \{s \mid t \to_R s\}$ is finite) then the set of solutions of C wrt. to R that extend τ is finite and computable.

Definition 2.1 *A* deterministic rule *is a formula* $C \Longrightarrow l \to r$ *such that* $C \equiv u_1 \to v_1, \ldots, u_n \to v_n$ *is operational for* $Var(l)$ *and* $Var(r) \subseteq Var(l) \cup Var(C)$ *and* l *is not a variable. The set of* extra variables *of this rule is* $\mathcal{E}Var(C \Longrightarrow l \to r) = Var(C) - Var(l)$.

A deterministic term rewrite system *(a DTRS, for short) is a finite set R of deterministic rules.*

We simply write $l \to r$ instead of $C \Longrightarrow l \to r$ if C is empty. We next define the rewrite relation $\to_R$ for a DTRS R.

Definition 2.2 *Let R be a DTRS. The rewrite relation $\to_R$ is the smallest relation $\to$ satisfying $t[\sigma(l)]_p \to t[\sigma(r)]_p$ whenever $C \Longrightarrow l \to r$ is a rule in R and σ is a solution of C wrt. R and $Var(l)$.*

Example 2.1

a) The following R computes from a given non-empty list l the pair $\langle z, l_1\rangle$ where z is the last element of l and l_1 is l with z deleted.

$$\begin{array}{lcl} R: & & f(x.nil) \to pair(x, nil) \\ f(y.l) \to pair(z, l_1) & \Longrightarrow & f(x.y.l) \to pair(z, x.l_1) \end{array}$$

b) The following R computes the Fibonacci-numbers

$$\begin{array}{lcl} & & 0 + y \to y \\ & & s(x) + y \to s(x+y) \\ & & fib(0) \to pair(s(0), 0) \\ fib(x) \to pair(z_1, z_2), z_1 + z_2 \to z_3 & \Longrightarrow & fib(s(x)) \to pair(z_3, z_1) \end{array}$$

We have defined a DTRS with oriented conditions. Such a system without extra variables and all right hand sides in a condition being irreducible ground terms is called a normal conditional rewrite system in [DO90]. There are some other ways to evaluate the conditions. If a condition $u = v$ is to be evaluated by a joinability test then we write $u \downarrow v$. A system with a joinability test for the conditions is called a standard conditional rewrite system in [DO90]. For functional programming it is reasonable to allow both sorts of conditions, one for testing and the other one for computing. So a rule would be of the form

$$u_1 \to v_1, \ldots, u_n \to v_n, s_1 \downarrow t_1, \ldots, s_m \downarrow t_m \Longrightarrow l \to r$$

The conditions $s_i \downarrow t_i$ can easily be transformed into oriented conditions $s_i \to x_i, t_i \to x_i$ using new extra variables x_i. For this reason we only allow oriented conditions. In the next section we will consider quasi-reductive rules only in order to have $\to_R$ computable and terminating. For standard conditional rewriting the conditions 'reductive' and 'decreasing' are needed for the same purpose. It will be easy to see that, given a decreasing standard rule $s_1 \downarrow t_1, \ldots, s_m \downarrow t_m \Longrightarrow l \to r$ with no extra variables, then the transformed rule $s_1 \to x_1, t_1 \to x_1, \ldots, s_m \to x_m, t_m \to x_m \Longrightarrow l \to r$ is deterministic and quasi-reductive. So our approach is a generalization of standard conditional rewriting. See [DOS88] for proving confluence of different kinds of conditional rewrite systems without extra variables.

3 Quasi-reductive DTRSs

Now we impose a condition on DTRSs R so that $\rightarrow_R$ is computable and terminating [GW92].

Definition 3.1 *Let $\succ$ be a reduction ordering on $\mathcal{T}(\mathcal{F},\mathcal{V})$. A DTRS R is* quasi-reductive *wrt. $\succ$ if for every substitution σ and every rule $u_1 \rightarrow v_1, \ldots, u_n \rightarrow v_n \Longrightarrow l \rightarrow r$ in R*

(i) $\sigma(u_j) \succeq \sigma(v_j)$ for $1 \leq j \leq i$ implies $\sigma(l) \succ_{st} \sigma(u_{i+1})$

(ii) $\sigma(u_j) \succeq \sigma(v_j)$ for $1 \leq j \leq n$ implies $\sigma(l) \succ \sigma(r)$

A DTRS R is called quasi-reductive *if there is a reduction ordering $\succ$ such that R is quasi-reductive wrt. $\succ$.*

Now we prove that a quasi-reductive DTRS can be used for effective computations. We make this precise in Theorem 3.1 (see [GW92]). Let $\Delta^\star_R(t) = \{s \mid t \xrightarrow{\star}_R s\}$ denote the set of R-successors of t.

Theorem 3.1 *Let R be a DTRS that is quasi-reductive wrt. $\succ$. Then for every term t the set $\Delta^\star_R(t)$ is finite and effectively computable. We have $\rightarrow_R \subseteq \succ$, so R is terminating.*

Proof: Let R be quasi-reductive wrt. $\succ$. We prove the statement of the Theorem by induction on $\succ_{st}$. We have $t \rightarrow_R s$ if there is a position p in t, a rule $C \Longrightarrow l \rightarrow r$ in R and a substitution σ such that $\sigma(l) \equiv t/p$ and σ is a solution of C wrt. R and $Var(l)$. Since R is finite it is enough to prove that for each rule $C \Longrightarrow l \rightarrow r$ there are only finitely many such solutions and one can compute them all.

Let $C \equiv u_1 \rightarrow v_1, \ldots, u_n \rightarrow v_n$ and τ be given such that $\tau(l) \equiv t/p$ and $Dom(\tau) = Var(l)$. We need to compute all solutions σ of C that extend τ. Let $\sigma_0 = \tau$. Since R is quasi-reductive we have $Var(u_1) \subseteq Var(l)$ and $\sigma_0(l) \succ_{st} \sigma_0(u_1)$. By induction hypothesis $\Delta^\star_R(\sigma_0(u_1))$ is finite and computable. So we can compute all matches $\sigma'(v_1) \equiv w, w \in \Delta^\star_R(\sigma_0(u_1))$, σ' extends σ_0. Let σ_1 be such a match, then σ_1 is a solution of $u_1 \rightarrow v_1$ and $\sigma_1(u_1) \succeq \sigma_1(v_1)$ and so $\sigma_1(l) \equiv \tau(l) \succ_{st} \sigma_1(u_2)$. In this way one can compute all solutions σ_i of $u_1 \rightarrow v_1, \ldots, u_i \rightarrow v_i$ extending τ, and we have $\sigma_i(u_j) \succeq \sigma_i(v_j)$ for $j = 1, \ldots, i$, so $\sigma_i(l) \succ_{st} \sigma_i(u_{i+1})$. For $i = n$ we also have $\tau(l) \equiv \sigma_n(l) \succ \sigma_n(r)$.

This proves that the set $\{s \mid t \rightarrow_R s\}$ is finite and computable and that $\rightarrow_R \subseteq \succ$ holds. So $\Delta^\star_R(t)$ is finite and computable, too. □

As a by-product of this proof we get

Corollary 3.1 *Let R be a DTRS that is quasi-reductive wrt. $\succ$. If $\sigma(l) \rightarrow_R \sigma(r)$ by $\rho \equiv u_1 \rightarrow v_1, \ldots, u_n \rightarrow v_n \Longrightarrow l \rightarrow r$ in R then $\sigma(l) \succ_{st} \sigma(u_i) \succeq \sigma(v_i)$ for all $1 \leq i \leq n$.*

We now discuss how to prove that a DTRS is quasi-reductive. A simple approach is to eliminate in a deterministic rule $\rho \equiv u_1 \rightarrow v_1, \ldots, u_n \rightarrow v_n \Longrightarrow l \rightarrow r$ the extra variables by backward substitution and then to apply a test for reductivity on the resulting rule. To do so we define the transformed rule $\overline{\rho}$ of ρ as follows: For $x \in \mathcal{E}Var(\rho)$ let $\alpha(x)$ be the smallest i such that $x \in Var(v_i)$. We simultaneously define terms $\overline{u}_i$ and substitutions φ_i by

$$\begin{aligned} \varphi_1 &= id \\ \varphi_{i+1} &= \{x \leftarrow \overline{u}_{\alpha(x)} \mid x \in Var(v_1, \ldots, v_i) \cap \mathcal{E}Var(\rho)\} \\ \overline{u}_i &\equiv \varphi_i(u_i) \end{aligned}$$

Definition 3.2 *Let $\rho \equiv u_1 \rightarrow v_1, \ldots, u_n \rightarrow v_n \Longrightarrow l \rightarrow r$ be a deterministic rule. The backward substituted rule $\overline{\rho}$ is $\overline{u}_1 \rightarrow c, \ldots, \overline{u}_n \rightarrow c \Longrightarrow l \rightarrow \overline{r}$ where c is a new constant and $\overline{r} \equiv \varphi_{n+1}(r)$.*

Lemma 3.1 *Let $\succ$ be a reduction ordering. Let R be a DTRS such that for every rule ρ in R and its backward substituted form $\overline{\rho} \equiv \overline{u}_1 \rightarrow c, \ldots, \overline{u}_n \rightarrow c \Longrightarrow l \rightarrow \overline{r}$ we have*

$$l \succ_{st} \overline{u}_i \text{ for } 1 \leq i \leq n \text{ and } l \succ \overline{r}$$

then R is quasi-reductive wrt. $\succ$.

Example 3.1
$\rho \equiv f(x) \rightarrow pair(y_1, y_2),\ y_1 + y_2 \rightarrow y_3 \Longrightarrow f(s(x)) \rightarrow pair(y_3, y_1)$.
Backward substitution gives $\overline{\rho} \equiv f(x) \rightarrow c, f(x) + f(x) \rightarrow c \Longrightarrow f(s(x)) \rightarrow pair(f(x) + f(x), f(x))$. Let $\succ$ be the RPO with precedence $f > pair, +$. Then $\succ = \succ_{st}$ and

$$f(s(x)) \succ f(x),\ f(x) + f(x),\ pair(f(x) + f(x), f(x)).$$

Hence ρ is quasi-reductive wrt. $\succ$.

In [AL93] one can find a method to integrate a system $\{s_i \geq t_i \mid 1 \leq i \leq n\}$ of inequations into the construction of an RPO in order to prove R quasi-reductive. For another method to prove quasi-reductivity we refer to [GW92]. For a method to decide whether R is quasi-reductive wrt. to a given LPO we refer to [Co90].

4 Confluence of a DTRS

We study under which conditions a DTRS R is confluent. We assume that R is quasi-reductive. In this case $\rightarrow_R$ is terminating and so it is sufficient to prove local confluence. The criterion to be developed for proving local confluence is based on critical pairs. We start with examples to demonstrate the problems arising from extra variables.

Example 4.1

a) $R:$

$$\begin{array}{rl} & 0+y \to y \\ & s(x)+y \to x+s(y) \\ x+y \to z+z' \Longrightarrow & f(x,y) \to z \end{array}$$

We have $f(s(0),0) \to_R s(0)$ and $f(s(0),0) \to 0$, but not $s(0) \downarrow_R 0$. This example shows that a critical pair resulting from overlapping a rule with itself at top-level may be harmful. We call such a critical pair improper.

b) $R:$

$$\begin{array}{rlcl} & a & \to & c \\ & g(a) & \to & h(b) \\ & h(b) & \to & g(c) \\ g(x) \to h(z) \Longrightarrow & f(x) & \to & z \end{array}$$

We have $f(c)_R \leftarrow f(a) \to_R b$ but not $f(c) \downarrow_R b$. This example shows that variable overlappings may be harmful.

Notice that in both examples R is a quasi-reductive DTRS. Since we do not want to consider variable overlappings and improper critical pairs we have to look for additional conditions that make them harmless.

Definition 4.1 *Let R be a DTRS.*
a) A term v is strongly irreducible *wrt. R if $\sigma(v)$ is irreducible for every irreducible substitution σ.*
b) R is called strongly deterministic *(an SDTRS, for short) if for every rule $u_1 \to v_1, \ldots, u_n \to v_n \Longrightarrow l \to r$ in R each v_i is strongly irreducible wrt. R.*

Notice that both DTRSs in Example 4.1 are not strongly deterministic. The DTRs given in Example 2.1 are strongly deterministic.

Definition 4.2 *Let R be a DTRS and $C_1 \Longrightarrow l_1 \to r_1$ and $C_2 \Longrightarrow l_2 \to r_2$ be rules in R that have no variables in common. Let $p \in O(l_1)$ such that $\sigma = mgu(l_2, l_1/p)$ exists. Then*

$$\sigma(C_1), \sigma(C_2) \Longrightarrow \sigma(l_1[r_2]_p) = \sigma(r_1)$$

is a critical pair. *It is called* improper *if the rules differ only by a variable renaming and $l_1 \equiv l_1/p$, otherwise it is called* proper. *Let $CP(R)$ denote the set of proper critical pairs that can be built by pairs of rules in R. A critical pair $C \Longrightarrow s = t$ is* joinable *if $\tau(s) \downarrow_R \tau(t)$ for each solution τ of C wrt. R.*

Theorem 4.1 *Let R be an SDTRS that is quasi-reductive wrt. $\succ$. R is confluent iff all critical pairs in $CP(R)$ are joinable.*

Proof: Clearly, if R is confluent then all critical pairs in $CP(R)$ are joinable. So we now assume that all critical pairs in $CP(R)$ are joinable and prove by induction on $\succ_{st}$: If $t' \; {}_R\!\overset{*}{\longleftarrow} t \overset{*}{\longrightarrow}_R t''$ then $t' \downarrow_R t''$.
If $t' \equiv t$ or $t'' \equiv t$ then $t' \downarrow_R t''$ holds. So assume $t' \; {}_R\!\overset{*}{\longleftarrow} t_1 \; {}_R\!\longleftarrow t \longrightarrow_R t_2 \overset{*}{\longrightarrow}_R t''$. We will prove $t_1 \downarrow_R t_2$, then an inductive argument easily gives $t' \downarrow_R t''$.

Assume

$$\begin{array}{lll} t \rightarrow_R t_1 & \text{using} & C_1 \Longrightarrow l_1 \rightarrow r_1,\ \sigma_1,\ \text{position } q \text{ in } t \\ t \rightarrow_R t_2 & \text{using} & C_2 \Longrightarrow l_2 \rightarrow r_2,\ \sigma_2,\ \text{position } p \text{ in } t \end{array}$$

If t/p and t/q are disjoint subterms of t then $t_1 \downarrow_R t_2$ trivially holds. So we may assume that t/p is a subterm of t/q. If $t \rhd t/q$, then $t \succ_{st} t/q$ and we have $t_1 \downarrow_R t_2$ by induction hypothesis on t/q. So we assume $t \equiv t/q$. Then we have $t \equiv \sigma_1(l_1)$ and $t/p \equiv \sigma_2(l_2)$. There are two cases: (α) $p \in O(l_1)$ and (β) p is a position in l_1 with l_1/p a variable or p is not a position in l_1.

(α) : In this case there is a critical pair $C \Longrightarrow s_1 = s_2$ and a substitution τ such that $t_1 \equiv \tau(s_1)$ and $t_2 \equiv \tau(s_2)$ and τ is a solution of C wrt. R and $Var(l_1, l_2)$. If this critical pair is proper then it is in $CP(R)$ and hence joinable. This gives $t_1 \downarrow t_2$. So assume that this critical pair is improper. Then $t \equiv \sigma_1(l_1) \equiv \sigma_2(l_2)$ and we may assume that $C_1 \Longrightarrow l_1 \rightarrow r_1$ and $C_2 \Longrightarrow l_2 \rightarrow r_2$ are identical, i.e. $C_i \Longrightarrow l_i \rightarrow r_i \equiv C \Longrightarrow l \rightarrow r$ for $i = 1, 2$. We have $\sigma_1(x) \equiv \sigma_2(x)$ for all $x \in Var(l)$ and we will prove $\sigma_1(x) \downarrow_R \sigma_2(x)$ for all $x \in Var(C \Longrightarrow l \rightarrow r)$. Since $t_1 \equiv \sigma_1(r)$ and $t_2 \equiv \sigma_2(r)$ this will prove $t_1 \downarrow_R t_2$.

Let $C = u_1 \rightarrow v_1, \ldots, u_n \rightarrow v_n$ and let σ_1', σ_2' be irreducible substitutions such that $\sigma_i(x) \overset{*}{\longrightarrow}_R \sigma_i'(x)$ for $i = 1, 2$ and all $x \in \mathcal{E}Var(C \Longrightarrow l \rightarrow r)$. It is enough to prove that $\sigma_1'(x) \equiv \sigma_2'(x)$ for all $x \in \mathcal{E}Var(C \Longrightarrow l \rightarrow r)$. If $x \in Var(u_1 \rightarrow v_1)$ then $x \in Var(v_1)$ since $Var(u_1) \subseteq Var(l)$. We have $\sigma_1'(v_1) \; {}_R\!\overset{*}{\longleftarrow} \sigma_1(u_1) \equiv \sigma_2(u_1) \overset{*}{\longrightarrow} \sigma_2'(v_1)$ and $\sigma_i'(v_1)$ is irreducible since σ_i' is irreducible. (Here we need that R is strongly deterministic and hence the v_j are strongly irreducible.) Since $t \succ_{st} \sigma_i(u_1)$ we have $\sigma_1'(v_1) \downarrow_R \sigma_2'(v_1)$ by induction hypothesis on $\sigma_1(u_1)$. This gives $\sigma_1'(v_1) \equiv \sigma_2'(v_1)$ and hence $\sigma_1'(x) \equiv \sigma_2'(x)$.

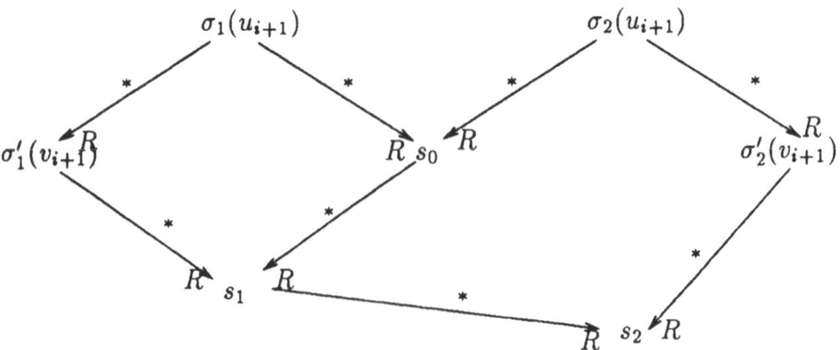

Now assume $\sigma_1'(x) \equiv \sigma_2'(x)$ for all $x \in Var(u_1 \to v_1, \ldots, u_i \to v_i) - Var(l)$, we have to prove $\sigma_1'(x) \equiv \sigma_2'(x)$ for $x \in Var(u_{i+1} \to v_{i+1}) - Var(l)$. If $x \in Var(u_{i+1})$ then this is trivial since $C \Longrightarrow l \to r$ is deterministic. So let $x \in Var(v_{i+1})$. We have s_0 in the preceding picture since $\sigma_1(y) \downarrow_R \sigma_2(y)$ for all $y \in Var(u_{i+1})$.

The term s_1 exists by induction hypothesis on $\sigma_1(u_{i+1})$ since $t \succ_{st} \sigma_1(u_{i+1})$, and s_2 exists by induction hypothesis on $\sigma_2(u_{i+1})$. This proves $\sigma'(v_{i+1}) \downarrow_R \sigma_2'(v_{i+1})$ and now $\sigma_1'(x) \equiv \sigma_2'(x)$ follows as above.

(β) : In this case there is a variable $x \in Var(l_1)$ such that $\sigma_2(x) \to_R t_0$ with $C_2 \Longrightarrow l_2 \to r_2$ and σ_2. Define τ to be the substitution $\tau(y) \equiv \sigma_1(y)$ if $y \not\equiv x$ and $\tau(x) \equiv t_0$. Let τ' be an irreducible substitution with $\tau(y) \xrightarrow{*}_R \tau'(y)$ for all y. Then we have

$$\begin{aligned} t &\equiv \sigma_1(l_1) \to_R t_1 \equiv \sigma_1(r_1) \xrightarrow{*}_R \tau(r_1) \xrightarrow{*}_R \tau'(r_1) \\ t &\equiv \sigma_1(l_1) \to_R t_2 \equiv t[\sigma_2(r_2)]_p \xrightarrow{*}_R \tau(l_1) \xrightarrow{*}_R \tau'(l_1) \end{aligned}$$

(Here we assume that t and $C_1 \Longrightarrow l_1 \to r_1$ have no variables in common). We prove that τ' is a solution of C_1 wrt. R and $Var(l_1)$. Then we have $\tau'(l_1) \to_R \tau'(r_1)$ and so $t_1 \downarrow_R t_2$.

Let $C_1 = u_1 \to v_1, \ldots, u_n \to v_n$. We know that $\sigma_1(u_i) \xrightarrow{*}_R \sigma_1(v_i)$ and have to prove $\tau'(u_i) \xrightarrow{*}_R \tau'(v_i)$. We have $\tau'(u_i)\ {}_R\!\xleftarrow{*} \tau(u_i)\ {}_R\!\xleftarrow{*} \sigma_1(u_i) \xrightarrow{*}_R \sigma_1(v_i) \xrightarrow{*}_R \tau'(v_i)$. By induction hypothesis on $\sigma_1(u_i)$ – notice that $t \succ_{st} \sigma_1(u_i)$ holds by Corollary 3.3 – we have $\tau'(u_i) \downarrow \tau'(v_i)$ and hence $\tau'(u_i) \xrightarrow{*}_R \tau'(v_i)$ since $\tau'(v_1)$ is irreducible. So τ' is indeed a solution of C_1 wrt. R and $Var(l_1)$. □

Note that there are two problems related to this result: (i) Given a term v, is it strongly irreducible ? (ii) Given a conditional equation $C \Longrightarrow s = t$, is it joinable ? Unfortunately, both of these problems are undecidable for a deterministic and quasi-reductive R. (One can reduce Post's Correspondence Problem to both of these problems. See [AL93].) But we will develop tools to prove that v is strongly irreducible and $C \Longrightarrow s = t$ is joinable wrt. R.

Definition 4.3 *Let R be a DTRS*
a) A term v is absolutely irreducible wrt. R if for all $p \in O(v)$ and each rule $C \Longrightarrow l \to r$ in R v/p and l are not unifyable.
b) R is absolutely deterministic if for every rule $u_1 \to v_1, \ldots, u_n \to v_n \Longrightarrow l \to r$ in R each v_i is absolutely irreducible wrt. R.

It is easy to test whether a DTRS is absolutely deterministic and absolutely deterministic DTRSs frequently appear in practise: In many applications a DTRS is used to define functions over 'free constructors'. If R is such a system and all right-hand sides of conditions in R are constructor terms then R is absolutely deterministic. Also, the rewrite systems called 'normal' in [DO90] are absolutely deterministic.

Lemma 4.1 *Let R be a DTRS.*
a) If v is absolutely irreducible wrt. R then v is strongly irreducible wrt. R.
b) If R is absolutely deterministic then R is strongly deterministic.
c) It is undecidable whether a quasi-reductive DTRS is strongly deterministic.

We now develop a sufficient criterion for confluence of a quasi-reductive SDTRS. It is based on contextual rewriting. We use here a more restrictive version of contextual rewriting than that used in [BG89]. It is easier to implement and results in easier proofs.

Let $C = \{u_1 \rightarrow v_1, \ldots, u_n \rightarrow v_n\}$ be a set of oriented equations, called here a *context*. We denote by $\overline{C}$ its skolemized form, i.e., $\overline{C}$ results from C by replacing each variable x by a new constant $\overline{x}$. If t is a term, then $\overline{t}$ results from t by replacing each $x \in Var(C)$ by the constant $\overline{x}$. We write $s \rightarrow_{R,C} t$ if $\overline{s} \rightarrow_{R \cup \overline{C}} \overline{t}$. Obviously, we have

Lemma 4.2 *If $s \xrightarrow{*}_{R,C} t$ then $\sigma(s) \xrightarrow{*}_R \sigma(t)$ for every solution σ of C.*

Definition 4.4 *Let R be a DTRS that is quasi-reductive wrt. $\succ$ and let $C \Longrightarrow s = t$ be a critical pair resulting from $C_i \Longrightarrow l_i \rightarrow r_i$ for $i = 1, 2$ and $\sigma = mgu(l_1/p, l_2)$. We call $C \Longrightarrow s = t$* unfeasible *if there are terms t_0, t_1, t_2 such that $\sigma(l_1) \succ_{st} t_0$, $t_0 \xrightarrow{*}_{R,C} t_1$, $t_0 \xrightarrow{*}_{R,C} t_2$ and t_1, t_2 are not unifyable and strongly irreducible. We call $C \Longrightarrow s = t$* context-joinable *if there is some t_0 such that $s \xrightarrow{*}_{R,C} t_0$, $t \xrightarrow{*}_{R,C} t_0$.*

Note that in the definition of an unfeasible critical pair $C \Longrightarrow s = t$ we have $\sigma(l_1) \succ u$ if $u \rightarrow v$ in C and $Var(u) \subseteq Var(\sigma(l_1))$. So we may choose t_0 to be any such term u. In many cases a quasi-reductive SDTRS can be proved to be confluent by the following Theorem.

Theorem 4.2 *Let R be an SDTRS that is quasi-reductive wrt. $\succ$. If every critical pair in $CP(R)$ is either unfeasible or context-joinable then R is confluent.*

Proof: We repeat the proof of Theorem 4.1. The only point we have to consider is the first case in (α): Let $C \Longrightarrow s_1 = s_2$ be a proper critical pair resulting from $C_i \Longrightarrow l_i \rightarrow r_i, i = 1, 2$, and $\sigma = mgu(l_1/p, l_2)$. There is a solution τ of C such that $t \equiv \tau\sigma(l_1)$ and $t_1 \equiv \tau(s_1), t_2 \equiv \tau(s_2)$. By induction hypothesis on t we may assume: If $s' \,{}_R\!\xleftarrow{*} s \xrightarrow{*}_R s''$ and $\tau\sigma(l_1) \succ_{st} s$ then $s' \downarrow_R s''$. Then we have to prove $t_1 \downarrow_R t_2$.

$C \Longrightarrow s_1 = s_2$ is not unfeasible: Otherwise there are t_0, t'_0, t''_0 such that $\sigma(l_1) \succ_{st} t_0, t_0 \xrightarrow{*}_{R,C} t'_0, t_0 \xrightarrow{*}_R t''_0$ and t'_0, t''_0 are not unifyable and strongly irreducible. Since τ is a solution of C we have by Lemma 4.2 that $\tau\sigma(l_1) \succ_{st} \tau(t_0), \tau(t_0) \xrightarrow{*}_R \tau(t'_0)$ and $\tau(t_0) \xrightarrow{*}_R \tau(t''_0)$. Let μ be an irreducible substitution such that $\tau(x) \xrightarrow{*}_R \mu(x)$ for all x. Then $\tau(t_0) \xrightarrow{*}_R \mu(t'_0)$ and $\tau(t_0) \xrightarrow{*}_R \mu(t''_0)$ and

$\mu(t_0') \not\equiv \mu(t_0'')$. By induction hypothesis on $\tau(t_0)$ we have $\mu(t_0') \downarrow_R \mu(t_0'')$. But this is impossible since $\mu(t_0')$ and $\mu(t_0'')$ are irreducible.

So $C \Longrightarrow s_1 = s_2$ is context-joinable. Since τ is a solution of C we have $t_1 \equiv \tau(s_1) \downarrow_R \tau(s_2) \equiv t_2$ by Lemma 4.2 □

Let $C \Longrightarrow s = t$ be a critical pair of some R. If $s \equiv t$ then it is called *trivial*. A trivial critical pair is always context-joinable. If C contains $u \rightarrow a$ and $u \rightarrow b$, where a and b are distinct irreducible constants, then $C \Longrightarrow s = t$ is unfeasible. But there are less trivial examples where Theorem 4.2 is applicable.

Example 4.2 *(see [BG89])*
We specify the Quicksort-algorithm

$$
\begin{array}{lcl}
R: & & 0 \leq x \rightarrow true \\
 & & s(x) \leq 0 \rightarrow false \\
 & & s(x) \leq s(y) \rightarrow x \leq y \\
 & & app(nil, l_2) \rightarrow l_2 \\
 & & app(x.l_1, l_2) \rightarrow x.app(l_1, l_2) \\
 & & split(x, nil) \rightarrow pair(nil, nil) \\
x \leq y \rightarrow false, split(x, l) \rightarrow pair(l_1, l_2) & \Longrightarrow & split(x, y.l) \rightarrow pair(y.l_1, l_2) \\
x \leq y \rightarrow true, split(x, l) \rightarrow pair(l_1, l_2) & \Longrightarrow & split(x, y.l) \rightarrow pair(l_1, y.l_2) \\
 & & sort(nil) \rightarrow nil \\
split(x, l) \rightarrow pair(l_1, l_2) & \Longrightarrow & sort(x.l) \rightarrow \\
 & & \qquad app(sort(l_1), x.sort(l_2))
\end{array}
$$

There is only one proper critical pair, it is $C \Longrightarrow pair(y.l_1, l_2) = pair(l_1, y.l_2)$ *with* $C \equiv x \leq y \rightarrow true, split(x, l) \rightarrow pair(l_1, l_2), x \leq y \rightarrow false, split(x, l) \rightarrow pair(l_1', l_2')$ *and it results from rules (7) and (8). Since* C *contains* $x \leq y \rightarrow false$ *and* $x \leq y \rightarrow true$*, this critical pair is unfeasible.* R *is strongly deterministic and* R *is quasi-reductive wrt. to a semantic path ordering [St93], [Ge92]. So we have a simple proof that* R *is confluent.*

5 Uniquely terminating well-moded logic programs

We now apply the results of the previous sections to well-moded logic programs.

A logical program is a set of Horn-clauses. Normally such a program is used to describe a search in a search space. In this case no distinction is made between input and output positions for the predicate symbols. But it has turned out that logic programs are also widely used to write programs in a functional manner. In this case each predicate symbol is assigned a fixed 'mode' to distinguish between input and output positions. To compute with such a moded program one starts with a query such that its input positions are filled by ground terms. Then, doing logical operations the information sweeps into the output positions.

So the question arises whether a well-moded logic program is uniquely terminating, i.e., whether for each input all possible computations stop and give the same result. In this section we develop means to assure this property.

This problem has been studied earlier by the first author [HA85]. The results presented here go far about those presented there. For example, we do not restrict to hierarchical specifications of the logic program. Here we follow the approach of [GW92]. In that paper only termination of computations in logic programs is studied. Here we are also interested in guaranteeing uniqueness of the results.

We start with some notations and definitions but we assume that the reader has some knowledge on logic programming and SLD derivations.

A *signature* is a quadruplerup $sig_0 = (S, \mathcal{P}_0, \mathcal{F}_0, \tau_0)$ where S is a set of sorts, $\mathcal{F}_0$ is a set of function symbols, $\mathcal{P}_0$ is a set of predicate symbols and $\tau_0 : \mathcal{F}_0 \cup \mathcal{P}_0 \rightarrow S^+$ assigns to each function and predicate symbol its arity. If $P \in \mathcal{P}_0$ and $t_1, \ldots, t_n$ are terms then $P(t_1, \ldots, t_n)$ is an *atom*. A *Horn-clause* is a formula of the form $A \leftarrow B_1, \ldots, B_m$ where $m \geq 0$ and A, B_i are atoms. A *logic program* $\mathcal{P}$ is a set of Horn-clauses. A *query* is a formula of the form $\leftarrow B_1, \ldots, B_m$ where $m \geq 1$ and B_i are atoms.

A logic program $\mathcal{P}$ is *moded* if for every occurrence of an atom $A \equiv P(t_1, \ldots, t_n)$ there is a function $m_A : \{1, \ldots, n\} \rightarrow \{in, out\}$. If $m_A(i) = in$ ($m_A(i) = out$) then position i is called an *input position* (*output position*) of A. A variable x occurs in an input (output) position in A if $x \in Var(t_i)$ for some i with $m_A(i) = in$ ($m_A(i) = out$).

To evaluate a moded logic program $\mathcal{P}$ we only consider left-to-right SLD derivations. They always select the left-most literal of a query for the next resolution step. So we restrict to LR-well-moded programs as defined next.

Definition 5.1 *a) Let $C \equiv A \leftarrow B_1, \ldots, B_m$ be a clause and $x \in Var(C)$. The head A of C is called a* producer *(*consumer*) of x, if x occurs in an input (output) position of A. The body atom B_j is called a producer (consumer) of x, if x occurs in an output (input) position of B_j.*
b) The clause $B_0 \leftarrow B_1, \ldots, B_m$ is called LR-well-moded, *if every variable x in the clause has a producer B_i $(0 \leq i \leq n)$ such that for every consumer B_j of x we have $i < j$. A logic program $\mathcal{P}$ is* LR-well-moded *if every clause in $\mathcal{P}$ is LR-well-moded.*
c) A query $\leftarrow B_1, \ldots, B_m$ is LR-well-moded *if every variable x in the query has a producer B_i such that for every consumer B_j of x we have $i < j$.*

By this definition, if $\leftarrow B_1, \ldots, B_m$ is LR-well-moded and $B_1 \equiv P(t_1, \ldots, t_n)$ then t_i are ground terms for all input positions i of B_1. One easily proves [GW92]

Lemma 5.1 *Let $\mathcal{P}$ be an LR-well-moded logic program and $G_0, G_1, \ldots$ a left-to-right SLD-derivation starting with an LR-well-moded query G_0. Then all queries G_i are LR-well-moded, and the first atom of every non-empty G_i is ground on all its input positions.* □.

Now we associate to every logic program $\mathcal{P}$ over the signature $sig_0 = (S, \mathcal{P}_0, \mathcal{F}_0, \tau_0)$ a DTRS $R(\mathcal{P})$ over the signature $sig = (S, \mathcal{F}, \tau)$. Here $\mathcal{F}$ consists of the $f \in \mathcal{F}_0$ and for each atom $A \equiv P(t_1, \ldots, t_n)$ with input positions $i_1, \ldots, i_k$ and output positions $i_{k+1}, \ldots, i_n$ the two function symbols Pin and $Pout$. We associate to the atom $A \equiv P(t_1, \ldots, t_n)$ the rule $\rho(A) \equiv Pin(t_{i_1}, \ldots t_{i_k}) \rightarrow Pout(t_{i_{k+1}}, \ldots, t_{i_n})$. We associate to a clause $C \equiv A \leftarrow B_1, \ldots, B_m$ the rule

$$\rho(C) \equiv \rho(B_1), \ldots, \rho(B_n) \Longrightarrow \rho(A)$$

and to $\mathcal{P}$ the system $R(\mathcal{P}) = \{\rho(C) \mid C \text{ in } \mathcal{P}\rangle$.

Example 5.1

$$\begin{array}{llcl} \mathcal{P}: & APP(nil, l_2, l_2) & \leftarrow & \\ & APP(x.l_1, l_2, x.l_3) & \leftarrow & APP(l_1, l_2, l_3) \end{array}$$

a) If all atoms have mode $m(1) = m(2) = in, m(3) = out$ then

$$\begin{array}{lcl} R(\mathcal{P}) & & APPin(nil, l_2) \rightarrow APPout(l_2) \\ APPin(l_1, l_2) \rightarrow APPout(l_3) & \Longrightarrow & APPin(x.l_1, l_2) \rightarrow APPout(x.l_3) \end{array}$$

b) If all atoms have mode $m(1) = m(2) = out, m(3) = in$ then

$$\begin{array}{lcl} R(\mathcal{P}) & & APPin(l_2) \rightarrow APPout(nil, l_2) \\ APPin(l_3) \rightarrow APPout(l_1, l_2) & \Longrightarrow & APPin(x.l_3) \rightarrow APPout(x.l_1, l_2) \end{array}$$

In both cases $R(\mathcal{P})$ is strongly deterministic and quasi-reductive. In case a) $R(\mathcal{P})$ is confluent, but in case b) $R(\mathcal{P})$ is not confluent.

The following lemma states that $R(\mathcal{P})$ is always absolutely deterministic if $\mathcal{P}$ is LR-well-moded.

Lemma 5.2

a) If $C = A \leftarrow B_1, \ldots, B_n$ is LR-well-moded then $\rho(C)$ is deterministic.
b) If $\mathcal{P}$ is LR-well-moded then $R(\mathcal{P})$ is absolutely deterministic.
c) If $\leftarrow B_1, \ldots, B_m$ is an LR-well-moded query and $\rho(B_1) \equiv Pin(t_1, \ldots, t_n) \rightarrow Pout(s_1, \ldots, s_k)$ then all t_i are ground terms.

Proof: a) This follows directly from the definitions.
b) $R(\mathcal{P})$ is deterministic by a). If $u_1 \rightarrow v_1, \ldots, u_n \rightarrow v_n \Longrightarrow l \rightarrow r$ is a rule $R(\mathcal{P})$ then v_i is of the form $Pout(s_1, \ldots, s_k)$ and l is of the form $Pin(t_1, \ldots, t_n)$. So each v_i is absolutely irreducible wrt. $R(\mathcal{P})$. Hence $R(\mathcal{P})$ is absolutely deterministic.
c) This follows from Lemma 5.1. □

The following lemma relates computations in $\mathcal{P}$ to computations in $R(\mathcal{P})$. It is proved in [GW92].

Lemma 5.3 *Let $\mathcal{P}$ be an LR-well-moded logic program such that $R(\mathcal{P})$ is quasi-reductive and let $\leftarrow B$ be an LR-well-moded query. If there is a left-to-right SLD refutation of $\leftarrow B$ with computed answer substitution θ and $\rho(B) \equiv Pin(t_1,\ldots,t_m) \rightarrow Pout(s_1,\ldots,s_k)$ then $Pin(t_1,\ldots,t_m) \rightarrow_R Pout(\theta(s_1),\ldots,\theta(s_k))$* $\Box$.

We now come to the main result of this section.

Definition 5.2 *An LR-well-moded logic program $\mathcal{P}$ is* uniquely terminating *if for every LR-well-moded query $\leftarrow B$ every left-to-right SLD-derivation is terminating and every left-to-right SLD-refutation computes the same answer substitution θ.*

Theorem 5.1 *Let $\mathcal{P}$ be an LR-well-moded logic program such that $R(\mathcal{P})$ is quasi-reductive and every critical pair in $CP(R(\mathcal{P}))$ is either unfeasible or context-joinable. Then $\mathcal{P}$ is uniquely terminating.*

Proof: By Theorem 4.5 of [GW92] every left-to-right SLD-derivation starting with an LR-well-moded query $\leftarrow B$ terminates. Since $R(\mathcal{P})$ is strongly deterministic it is confluent by Theorem 4.2. Now the statement follows from Lemma 5.3. $\Box$

Example 5.2
The following logic program is intended to compute from a given list l the last element z of l and the list l' resulting from l by eliminating z (compare with Example 2.1).

$\mathcal{P}$: $P(x.nil, x, nil) \leftarrow$
$P(x.y.l, z, x.l') \leftarrow P(y.l, z, l')$

Translation of $\mathcal{P}$ into a rewrite system gives

$$R(\mathcal{P}): \quad \begin{array}{rl} & Pin(x.nil) \rightarrow Pout(x, nil) \\ Pin(y.l) \rightarrow Pout(z, l') \Longrightarrow & Pin(x.y.l) \rightarrow Pout(z, x.l') \end{array}$$

We prove that $R(\mathcal{P})$ is quasi-reductive by using the backward substitution technique: We have to prove that $Pin(x.y.l) \succ Pout(Pin(y.l), x.Pin(y.l))$. This holds true for the RPO based on the precedence $Pin > Pout, Pin > .$. We have $CP(R(\mathcal{P})) = \emptyset$, so $R(\mathcal{P})$ is confluent and $\mathcal{P}$ is uniquely terminating.

References

[AL93] Avenhaus, J., Loría-Sáenz, C.: Canonical conditional rewrite systems containing extra variables, SEKI-Report SR-93-03, Univ. Kaiserslautern (1993).

[AM90] Avenhaus, J., Madlener, K.: Term rewriting and equational reasoning, in: R.B. Banerji, ed., Formal Techniques in Artifical Intelligence, North Holland, Amsterdam (1990), pp. 1 - 43.

[BG89] Bertling, H., Ganzinger, H.: Completion-time optimization of rewrite-time goal solving, 3rd RTA (1989), LNCS 355, pp. 45 - 58.

[CO90] Comon, H.: Solving inequations in term algebras, 5th IEEE Symposium on Logic in Computer Science, LICS (1990), pp. 62 - 69.

[De87] Dershowitz, N.: Termination, 1st RTA (1985), LNCS 202, pp. 180 - 224 and J. Symbolic Comp. 3 (1987), pp. 69 - 116.

[De91] Dershowitz, N.: Ordering-based strategies for Horn-clauses, 12th IJCAI (1991), pp. 118 - 124.

[DJ90] Dershowitz, N., Jouannaud, J.P.: Rewriting systems, in J. van Leeuwen, ed., Handbook of Theoretical Computer Science, Vol. B, Elsevier, Amsterdam (1990), pp. 241 - 320.

[DO90] Dershowitz, N., Okada, M.: A rationale for conditional equational programming, TCS 75 (1990), pp. 111 - 138.

[DOS88] Dershowitz, N., Okada, M., Sivakumar, G.: Confluence of conditional rewrite systems, 1st CTRS (1988), LNCS 308, pp. 31 - 44.

[Ga91] Ganzinger, H.: Order-sorted completion: the many-sorted way, TCS 89 (1991), pp. 3 - 32.

[Ge92] Geser, A.: On a monotonic semantic path ordering, Ulmer Informatik-Berichte No. 92 - 13, Universität Ulm (1992).

[GW92] Ganzinger, H., Waldmann, U.: Termination proofs of well-moded logic programs via conditional rewrite systems, 3rd CTRS (1992), LNCS 656, pp. 430 - 437.

[HA85] Heck, N., Avenhaus, J.: On logic programs with data-driven computations, EUROCAL-85 (1985), LNCS 204, pp. 433 - 443.

[Hu80] Huet, G.: Confluent reductions: Abstract properties and applications to term rewriting systems, J. ACM 27 (1980), pp. 797 - 821.

[Ka87] Kaplan, S.: Simplifying conditional term rewriting systems: Unification, termination and confluence, JSC (1987), pp. 295 - 334.

[LS93] Loría-Sáenz, C.: A theoretical framework for reasoning about program construction based on extensions of rewrite systems, Dissetation, Univ. Kaiserslautern, 1993.

[St93] Steinbach, J.: Private communication.

A Bottom-up Reconstruction of the Well-founded Semantics for Disjunctive Logic Programs

Cristian Papp

Faculty of Informatics, University "Al. I. Cuza",
Iasi, R-6600, Romania

Abstract. In his paper [12] Ross extends the well-founded semantics for normal logic programs [16] to disjunctive logic programs. His definition is top-down and it is closer to a procedural semantics than to the elegant fixpoint definition of the well-founded semantics for normal logic programs. In the present paper, we propose a declarative, bottom-up fixpoint definition of the well-founded semantics for disjunctive logic programs. Our construction of the greatest unfounded set of extended literals is similar with the construction of the greatest unfounded set for normal programs. As a consequence, the connection between the well-founded semantics for normal programs and the well-founded semantics for disjunctive programs is made clearer.

1 Introduction

Disjunctive logic programs were defined in [6, 8] as a natural extension of definite logic programs, by allowing disjunctions of atoms in the heads of the clauses. The next step, taken in [7], is to allow negative literals in the bodies of the program clauses, and thus extending both the normal logic programs and the disjunctive logic programs. The new class was called in [7] *general disjunctive programs*. In this paper we shall use the name of disjunctive logic program to refer the class of general disjunctive logic programs.

There has been much recent work on extending the semantics of normal logic programs to the disjunctive case. The *stratified disjunctive logic programs* were defined and a corresponding iterated fixpoint semantics was proposed in [7]. This semantics extends the stratification semantics of Apt, Blair and Walker [1]. The *stable model semantics* of Gelfond and Lifschitz [3] was extended to the disjunctive case by Przymusinski [10].

The *well-founded semantics* has been introduced in [16]. It is a 3-valued semantics and it seems to be the most adequate extension of the *perfect model semantics* [1, 9, 15] from the class of *stratified programs* to the class of *all* the logic programs. Its key concept is that of *unfounded set* of atoms with respect to a given (partial) interpretation. The well-founded semantics for normal programs is constructed in a bottom-up manner, as the least fixpoint of a closure operator defined on the semi-lattice of partial interpretations.

There are two different proposals for extending the well-founded semantics to disjunctive logic programs. The first of them, defined by Ross in [12] is also called the well-founded semantics. As a matter fact, Ross has offered two alternatives for the mentioned extension which differ one from another by the way they interpret the disjunction. Since Minker had published his paper on the *generalized closed world assumption* [5], it is tradition to give an *exclusive* interpretation of the disjunction. In this line of tradition, Ross has defined the *strong well-founded semantics*. The other approach is to give an inclusive interpretation of the disjunction. One of the few papers which presents an *inclusive* treatment of disjunction is due to Ross and Topor [13]. A rule of inference, called the *disjunctive database rule* (DDR), is presented. In this spirit Ross has defined another possible extension of the well-founded semantics, extension which he has called the *weak well-founded semantics*. This latter semantics is also a generalization of the DDR. Ross has considered the possibility to mix the two proposed semantics into a single semantics which takes into account the particular intended meaning of each disjunction and treating it accordingly. He called this semantics the *optimal well-founded semantics*. None of Ross's semantics is the extension of the perfect model semantics [9].

The second proposal is due to Przymusinski and it is called the *stationary semantics* [11]. This semantics is both an extension of the well-founded semantics and of the perfect model semantics. The question of which semantics is the most adequate extension of the well-founded semantics is outside the scope of this paper. The interested reader may consult both [12] and [11] for pros and cons. In this paper we are concerned only with Ross's semantics.

Neither Ross well-founded semantics, nor Przymusinski stationary semantics is defined as a fixpoint of some operator or use the notion of unfounded set of disjunctions of atoms. Ross has defined the well-founded semantics for disjunctive logic programs in an operational, top-down manner. However, there are strong reasons to search for bottom-up definitions, based on the notion of unfounded set. Firstly, fixpoint semantics is more declarative. Secondly, database query processing is implemented bottom-up in most of the systems. Thirdly, it is desirable when extending results, that the definition of the more general concept to be a clear generalization of the simpler one.

The aim of this paper is to give fixpoint definitions of the well-founded semantics for disjunctive logic programs. The most difficult problem we encounter if we try to extend the well-founded semantics to disjunctive logic programs is the definition of the notion of unfounded set of disjunctions of atoms. We avoid this by giving directly a procedure which constructs the greatest unfounded set of a disjunctive program with respect to a given partial interpretation. As in the normal case, our procedure is not effective in general. Then, the well-founded semantics is defined similar with the normal case as the fixpoint of an operator on the semi-lattice of partial interpretations. We show that our fixpoint semantics coincide with the well-founded semantics for disjunctive logic programs as it was defined by Ross.

The plan of the paper is as follows. In section 2 we present the basic notions needed to understand the rest of the paper. The definition of the well-founded semantics for normal programs and its extension to disjunctive logic programs is presented in section 3. The new fixpoint definition and the proof of its equivalence with the definition given in [12] are presented in section 4. The conclusions are presented in section 5.

Due to the space limitations, some proofs are omitted or only sketched.

2 Basic Notions and Definitions

In this section we present the basic notions and definitions which are needed in the rest of the paper. We assume that the reader already knows basic notions of mathematical logic and logic programming. For more details the interested reader may consult [4].

An *extended atom* is a disjunction of atoms. An *extended literal* is an extended atom or the negation of an extended atom. An *extended positive literal* is an extended atom. An *extended negative literal* is the negation of an extended atom. The empty disjunction is interpreted as being *false*.
A *disjunctive clause* is a rule of the form

$$d \leftarrow l_1 \wedge l_2 \wedge \ldots \wedge l_k$$

where d is a disjunction containing at least one atom, $k \geq 0$ and each l_i is an extended literal, for $i = 1,\ldots,k$. All variables in the clause are assumed to be universally quantified at the front of the clause. A *disjunctive logic program* is a set of disjunctive clauses.

If S is a set of literals, we shall denote by $\neg \cdot S$ the set of literals formed by taking the complement of each of the literals in S. We say that S is *consistent* if it does not contain a pair of complementary literals (i.e. if $S \cap \neg\cdot S = \emptyset$).

Definition 2.1: A (3-valued) *interpretation* I for a normal program P is a consistent set of ground literals. For a given atom a, we interpret I as follows:

- If $a \in I$ then a is *true* with respect to I.
- If $\neg a \in I$ then a is *false* with respect to I.
- If neither $a \in I$ nor $\neg a \in I$ then a is *undefined* with respect to I.

The set of all 3-valued interpretations for a normal program forms a complete semi-lattice under set inclusion.

If S is a set of extended literals, the *closure* of S, written $cl(S)$, is the least set S' of extended literals containing S that satisfies the following two conditions:

- If the disjunction d is in S' then every disjunction containing d is in S'.
- For all disjunctions d_1 and d_2, $\neg d_1 \in S'$ and $\neg d_2 \in S'$ iff $\neg(d_1 \vee d_2) \in S'$.

We say that S is *consistent* if $cl(S)$ does not contain a pair of complementary extended literals.

The following is an obvious generalization of Definition 2.1:

Definition 2.2: A (3-valued) *extended interpretation* for a disjunctive program is a consistent set of ground extended literals. If d is a disjunction then

- If $d \in I$ then d is *true* with respect to I.
- If $\neg d \in I$ then d is *false* with respect to I.
- If neither $d \in I$ nor $\neg d \in I$ then d is *undefined* with respect to I.

If I is a set of extended literals, we shall denote by *pos(I)* the set of extended atoms which have a positive occurrence in I and by *neg(I)* the set of extended atoms which appear negated in I.

The *Herbrand universe of* a normal (disjunctive) logic program P,denoted *HU(P)*, is the set of ground terms which can be formed from the function symbols and constants which appear in P. The *Herbrand base* of P, denoted *HB(P)*, is the set of atomic formulas formed by predicate symbols in P whose arguments are in the Herbrand universe of P. The *extended Herbrand base* of P, denoted *EHB(P)*, is the set of disjunctions of atoms from *HB(P)*. If P is a normal (disjunctive) program and r a normal (disjunctive) clause in P. An *instantiated rule* is a normal (disjunctive) clause obtained from r by substituting terms from *HU(P)* for all the variables in r. The *Herbrand instantiation* of P, denoted *ground(P)*, is the set of all instatiated rules of P.

3 The Well-Founded Semantics

In this section we briefly present the definitions of the well-founded semantics for normal and disjunctive programs. For more details and examples, the interested reader may consult [16] and [12].

Definition 3.1: Let P be a normal program and *HB(P)* its Herbrand base. Let I be a given interpretation. We say that $A \subseteq HB(P)$ is an *unfounded set of P with respect to I* if each atom $p \in A$ satisfies the following condition: For each (Herbrand) instantiated rule r of P whose head is p, at least one of the following holds:

1. The complement of some literal in the body of r is in I.

2. Some positive literal in the body of r is in A.

It is immediate that the union of arbitrary unfounded sets is an unfounded set. Thus, we can define the *greatest unfounded set of P with respect to I*, denoted by $U_P(I)$, as the union of all sets that are unfounded with respect to I.

The transformations T_P, U_P and W_P are defined as follows:

- $p \in T_P(I)$ if and only if there is some (Herbrand) instantiated rule r of P such that r has head p and each literal in the body of r is in I.
- $U_P(I)$ is the greatest unfounded set of P with respect to I.
- $W_P(I) = T_P(I) \cup \neg \cdot U_P(I)$.

It is straightforward to show that W_P is monotonic, and so it has a least fixpoint. This least fixpoint is called the *well-founded model* of P.

Let us note that the definition of the greatest unfounded set is not constructive. We present below a constructive alternative definition taken from [16].

Definition 3.2: Let I be a 3-valued interpretation. Define $\varphi_{P,I} : 2^{HB(P)} \to 2^{HB(P)}$ such that: A ground atom p is in $\varphi_{P,I}(J)$ if and only if there is a ground instance of a rule in *ground(P)*, say

$$p \leftarrow b_1 \wedge \ldots \wedge b_n \wedge \neg c_1 \wedge \ldots \wedge \neg c_m ,$$

such that

- no subgoal is false in I.
- all b_k are in J.

Let $J_I^\gamma = \varphi_{P,I}^\gamma(\emptyset)$. Clearly, $\varphi_{P,I}$ is monotonic, and J_I^γ reaches a limit J_I^∞.

Lemma 3.1: $U_P(I) = (HB(P) - J_I^\infty)$.

The above lemma provide us an alternative constructive definition for U_P. It is this alternative definition we shall use to obtain a bottom-up definition for the well-founded semantics for disjunctive logic programs. We postpone this definition until Section 4. We present now the well-founded semantics for disjunctive logic programs as it was defined by Ross in [12].

The Well Founded Semantics for Disjunctive Programs

First, let us see which are the difficulties which are encountered in defining a suitable form of well-founded semantics for disjunctive logic programs.

Consider the following disjunctive logic program:

Example 3.1: Let P be the disjunctive program:

$$p \leftarrow t \land v$$
$$t \leftarrow \neg q$$
$$v \leftarrow \neg r$$
$$q \lor r$$

For this program, we would expect both q and r to be undefined, as we do not know which of q and r holds. For the same reason, each of t and v should be undefined. However, we may reasonably expect p to be false, since the rule for p requires *both t and v* to be true, which in turn requires both q and r to be false (if t and v are to be "supported"). The difficulty arise from the fact that we could have a conjunction of negative literals (or more generally extended literals) $\neg q \land \neg r$ which is false, while none of its constituent conjuncts is. This example shows that Definition 2.1 does not extend naturally to disjunctive programs. This have determined Ross to prefer top-down definitions for the well-founded semantics for disjunctive logic programs, which we present below.

Definition 3.3: Let Q be an extended interpretation. We say Q' is *strongly derived* from Q (written $Q \leftarrow Q'$) if Q contains a disjunction d and there is some instantiated rule r given by

$$h \leftarrow r_1 \land \ldots \land r_n \land \neg s_1 \land \ldots \land \neg s_m$$

such that either

(S1) $h \subseteq d$ and $Q' = (Q - \{d\}) \cup \{r_1 \lor d, \ldots, r_n \lor d, \neg s_1, \ldots, \neg s_m\}$ or

(S2) $h \not\subseteq d$, $h \cap d \neq \emptyset$ (say $c = h - d$) and

$Q' = (Q - \{d\}) \cup \{r_1, \ldots, r_n, \neg s_1, \ldots, \neg s_m, \neg c\}$.

The next definition makes possible to give an inclusive interpretation of the disjunction.

Definition 3.4: Let Q be an extended interpretation. We say that Q' is *weakly derived* from Q if Q contains a disjunction d and there is some instantiated rule r given by

$$h \leftarrow r_1 \land \ldots \land r_n \land \neg s_1 \land \ldots \land \neg s_m .$$

such that either

(W1) $h \subseteq d$ and $Q' = (Q - \{d\}) \cup \{r_1 \lor d, \ldots, r_n \lor d, \neg s_1, \ldots, \neg s_m\}$ or

(W2) $h \not\subseteq d$, $h \cap d \neq \emptyset$ and $Q = (Q - d) \cup \{r_1, \ldots, r_n, \neg s_1, \ldots, \neg s_m\}$.

Let d be a ground disjunction and let $Q_0 = \{d\}$. Suppose Q_1 is strongly (weakly) derived from Q_0, Q_2 is strongly (weakly) derived from Q_1 and so on. We call the sequence $Q_0, Q_1, \ldots$ a *strong (weak) derivation sequence* for d. A strong (weak) derivation sequence may be finite or infinite, and there may be more than one derivation sequence for a particular disjunction. An *active* strong (weak) derivation sequence for d is a finite derivation sequence for d whose last element is either empty or contains only negative extended literals.

An *ordinary basis* for a disjunction d is the last element of an active strong (weak) derivation sequence all of whose derivation steps use S1 (W1). A *strong (weak) basis* for a disjunction d is the last element of an active strong (weak) derivation sequence at least one of whose derivation steps uses S2 (W2).

Let $Q = \{ \neg l_1, \ldots, \neg l_n \}$ be an arbitrary set of ground negative extended literals. Then we let $\overline{Q}$ denote the disjunction $l_1 \vee \ldots \vee l_n$. Note that Q may be empty, denoting "true". In this case $\overline{Q}$ denotes "false".

The *strong (weak) global* tree Γ_d^S (Γ_d^W) for a given disjunction d is defined as follows:

- The root of Γ_d^S (Γ_d^W) is d.
- If the disjunction d' is any node of Γ_d^S (Γ_d^W) then its children are all disjunctions of the form $\overline{Q}$, where Q ranges over *all* (ordinary, strong, weak) bases for d'.

If Q is an ordinary (strong, weak) basis for d', then $\overline{Q}$ is called an ordinary (strong, weak) child of d. Truth assignments of ground disjunctions in Γ_d^S (Γ_d^W) are defined as follows:

- If *every* (ordinary, strong, weak) child of d' is true, then d' is false. (In particular, d' is false if it has no children).
- If some ordinary child of d' is false, then d' is true.
- Any node which is not true or false according to the above rules is undefined.

We may also define the *level* of a ground disjunction. A disjunction that is true in Γ_d^A has level one more that the minimum level of all its false children, and the level of a disjunction which is false is one more than the least upper bound of the level of its true children.

Definition 3.5: Let $M_{WF}^S(P)$ ($M_{WF}^W(P)$) denote the extended interpretation such that for all disjunctions d

- If d is true in Γ_d^S (Γ_d^W), then $d \in M_{WF}^S(P)$ ($d \in M_{WF}^W(P)$).
- If d is false in Γ_d^S (Γ_d^W), then $\neg d \in M_{WF}^S(P)$ ($\neg d \in M_{WF}^W(P)$).

- If d is undefined in Γ_d^S (Γ_d^W), then neither $d \in M_{WF}^S(P)$ $(d \in M_{WF}^W(P))$ nor $\neg d \in M_{WF}^S(P)$ $(\neg d \in M_{WF}^W(P))$.

We call $M_{WF}^S(P)$ $(M_{WF}^W(P))$ the *strong (weak) well-founded model of P.*

Theorem 3.1: ([12]) For normal programs, both the strong and weak well-founded semantics coincide with the standard well-founded semantics.

The difference between the strong and the weak well-founded semantics comes from the second rule in the definition of strong (weak) derivation of extended interpretation (i.e. S2 and W2 from Definition 3.4 and Definition 3.5). Neither S2 nor W2 will help us to derive a positive disjunction. The purpose of the second condition in each case is to help determine whether a negative disjunction should be inferred. For more comments and examples see [12].

4 Fixpoint Definition of the Well-Founded Semantics for Disjunctive Logic Programs

Fixpoint semantics is one of the most attractive features in logic programming. It provides us with a full declarative meaning of the program and it is convenient for theoretical proofs. Beside this, it may provide us with a natural bottom-up query evaluation procedure for logical databases. Bottom-up evaluation is highly preferred to top-down in the database community [14]. It should be also desirable that the definition of the strong (weak) well-founded semantics to be as much possible similar to the definition of the well-founded semantics for normal programs. This are in the opinion of the author of this paper strong reasons to pursue for a fixpoint reformulation of the well-founded semantics for disjunctive logic programs.

To proceed, we need generalizations of the operators T_P and U_P. There is no problem to give a suitable definition for the operator T_P and Minker had already provide such a definition [7]. We shall use in our paper a slightly modified definition for T_P. Nevertheless, this definition yield the same semantics which we should obtained if we have used Minker original definition. We have preferred the modified version for technical reasons.

Let P be a disjunctive logic program. The operator T_P is defined on the set of the 3-valued extended interpretations as follows. Let I be a 3-valued extended interpretation and d an extended ground atom. Then $d \in T_P(I)$ if and only if there is some instantiated rule r in *ground(P)* given by

$$h \leftarrow r_1 \wedge \ldots \wedge r_l \wedge \neg s_1 \wedge \ldots \wedge \neg s_k$$

such that $h \subseteq d$ and $\{r_1 \vee d, \ldots, r_l \vee d, \neg s_1, \ldots, \neg s_k\} \subseteq cl(I)$, where

$cl(I)$ denotes the closure of I.

As we have remarked, there is no simple generalization of Definition 2.1 to fit for disjunctive logic programs. We shall use instead a construction of $U_P(I)$ similar to that given by Lemma 3.3. As Example 3.1 suggest, we must keep track of the conjunction of negative extended literals on which an extended atom depends.

Definition 4.1: Let I be a set of ground extended literals. An *admissible negative support* with respect to I is a finite set of negative extended ground literals $\{\neg l_1, \ldots, \neg l_k\}$ such that $l_1 \vee \ldots \vee l_k \notin cl(I)$. A *negative supported extended atom* with respect to I is a pair d/Q, where d is a ground extended atom and Q is an admissible negative support with respect to I. We shall denote the set of all the negative supported extended atoms of a given disjunctive program P with respect to a set of ground extended literals I by $NS_P(I)$. If $J \subseteq NS_P(I)$ we shall denote by $\lambda(J)$ the set of extended atoms in J by forgetting their negative support. It is an easy observation that if $I_1 \subseteq I_2$ then $NS_P(I_2) \subseteq NS_P(I_1)$.

The intuition behind the notion of negative supported atom is that d might be true with respect to I if the conjunction of the negative extended literals in Q is not false with respect to I.

Our definition of negative supported literals might appear to be similar to Fages *justified atoms* [2]. However, the negative supported literals and the justified atoms differ in both their definition and their use.

While the justification of an atom is a set of *positive* literals of which truth *ensure* the truth of the justified atom, the negative support is a set of *negative* extended literals which have the meaning that if their conjunction is *not false* then the supported extended atom *might* be *not false*. Also, while the negative support is relative to some given interpretation the justification is independent of any interpretation. Another difference is that we shall use sets of negative supported extended atoms which may contain identical extended atoms which have different negative support. Fages uses in his paper [2] only sets of uniquely justified atoms.

We shall construct the greatest unfounded set with respect to a given extended interpretation using the following transformations. Let P be a disjunctive logic program and I a set of ground extended literals. Let us consider the following monotonic transformations on sets of negative supported extended atoms:

- $\varphi_{P,I} : 2^{NS_P(\emptyset)} \to 2^{NS_P(\emptyset)}$ is defined as follows. $d/Q \in \varphi_{P,I}(J)$ iff there is some instantiated rule $h \leftarrow r_1 \wedge \ldots \wedge r_n \wedge \neg q_1 \wedge \ldots \wedge \neg q_m$ such that the following condition holds true:

$h \subseteq d$, $r_k \vee d/Q_k \in J$ for $k = 1, \ldots, n$, $Q = \bigcup_{k=1}^{n} Q_k \cup \{\neg q_1, \ldots, \neg q_m\}$ and

$Q, Q_1, \ldots, Q_n$ are admissible with respect to I.

- $\psi^S_{P,I} : 2^{NS_P(\emptyset)} \to 2^{NS_P(\emptyset)}$ is defined as follows. $d/Q \in \psi^S_{P,I}(J)$ iff there is some instantiated rule $h \leftarrow r_1 \wedge \ldots \wedge r_n \wedge \neg q_1 \wedge \ldots \wedge \neg q_m$ such that the following condition holds true:

$h \not\subseteq d$, $h \cap d \neq \emptyset$, $c = h - d$, $r_k / Q_k \in J$ for $k = 1, \ldots, n$,

$Q = \bigcup_{k=1}^{n} Q_k \cup \{\neg q_1, \ldots, \neg q_m, \neg c\}$ and $Q, Q_1, \ldots, Q_n$ are admissible with respect to I.

- $\psi^W_{P,I} : 2^{NS_P(\emptyset)} \to 2^{NS_P(\emptyset)}$ is defined as follows. $d/Q \in \psi^W_{P,I}(J)$ iff there is some instantiated rule $h \leftarrow r_1 \wedge \ldots \wedge r_n \wedge \neg q_1 \wedge \ldots \wedge \neg q_m$ such that the following condition holds true:

$h \not\subseteq d$, $h \cap d \neq \emptyset$, $r_k / Q_k \in J$ for $k = 1, \ldots, n$,

$Q = \bigcup_{k=1}^{n} Q_k \cup \{\neg q_1, \ldots, \neg q_m\}$ and $Q, Q_1, \ldots, Q_n$ are admissible with respect to I.

- $\Psi^S_{P,I} : 2^{NS_P(\emptyset)} \to 2^{NS_P(\emptyset)}$ is defined by $\Psi^S_{P,I}(J) = \varphi_{P,I}(J) \cup \psi^S_{P,I}(J)$.
- $\Psi^W_{P,I} : 2^{NS_P(\emptyset)} \to 2^{NS_P(\emptyset)}$ is defined by $\Psi^W_{P,I}(J) = \varphi_{P,I}(J) \cup \psi^W_{P,I}(J)$.

We can now present the construction of $U_P(I)$. Since Ross have defined two extensions of the well-founded semantics, we shall define two corresponding notions of unfounded sets: the *greatest strong unfounded set* of *P* with respect to *I*, denoted by $U^S_P(I)$ and the *greatest weak unfounded set* of *P* with respect to *I*, denoted by $U^W_P(I)$.

Definition 4.4: Let *P* be a disjunctive logic program, and *I* an extended interpretation. The *greatest strong unfounded set* of *P* with respect to *I*, and the *greatest weak unfounded set* of *P* with respect to *I* are defined by the following equalities:

- $U^S_P(I) = (EHB(P) - \lambda(\Psi^{S\,\infty}_{P,I}))$.
- $U^W_P(I) = (EHB(P) - \lambda(\Psi^{W\,\infty}_{P,I}))$.

Analogically with the normal case, we define
$W^S_P(I) = T_P(I) \cup \neg\cdot U^S_P(I)$ and
$W^W_P(I) = T_P(I) \cup \neg\cdot U^W_P(I)$.
In the rest of the paper we shall use the subscript (superscript) *A* to replace

any of the subscripts (superscripts) S and W. The following definition is similar to Definition 3.4:

Definition 4.5: Let α ranges over all countable ordinals. The sets I_A^α and I_A^∞ are defined as follows:

- For limit ordinal, α, $I_A^\alpha = \bigcup_{\beta < \alpha} I_A^\beta$.
- For successor ordinal $\alpha = \gamma + 1$, $I_A^{\gamma+1} = W_P^A(I_A^\gamma)$.
- $I_A^\infty = \bigcup_\alpha I_A^\alpha$.

Lemma 4.1: For any ordinal δ, I_A^δ is a monotone and consistent set of extended literals.

Proof (sketch): The fact that I_A^δ is monotone results from the fact that $I_1 \subseteq I_2$ implies that $NS_P(I_2) \subseteq NS_P(I_1)$. The proof of the consistency is more complicated and it follows several steps. For technical reasons, let us define the following sequence of negative supported extended literals.

- For limit ordinal α, $J_A^\alpha = \bigcup_{\beta < \alpha} J_A^\beta$.
- For successor ordinal,
  $\alpha = \gamma + 1$, $J_A^{\gamma+1} = \{d/Q : d/Q \in \varphi_{P,I_A^\gamma}(J_A^\gamma),\ Q \subseteq I_A^\gamma\}$.

We shall prove the consistency by transfinite induction on δ. Suppose that I_A^α is consistent for all ordinals α, $\alpha < \delta$. First we prove by transfinite induction on α that $pos(I_A^\alpha) \subseteq \lambda(J_A^\alpha)$.

Next, let us fix an ordinal α, $\alpha < \delta$. It can be proved by induction on β that if $\beta < \alpha$, then $J_A^\beta \subseteq \varphi^\infty_{P,I_A^\alpha}$.

In the next step we prove by transfinite induction on α, $\alpha < \delta$ that $J_A^\alpha \subseteq \varphi^\infty_{P,I_A^\alpha}$.

Finally, we can prove that by transfinite induction on δ that I_A^δ is consistent. The case when δ is a limit ordinal is obvious. In the case that δ is a limit ordinal, $\delta = \alpha + 1$, we shall make use of the inclusions proved in the previous steps. □

Since I_A^α is monotone and consistent, we can take I_A^∞ to represent the semantics of the program.

The next two lemmas are needed in the proof of the main theorem of this paper. The proofs are by straightforward (transfinite) induction and are omitted.

Lemma 4.2: Let d be a ground disjunction and suppose that d has an active strong (weak) derivation of length k whose last element is Q. Then $d/Q \in \Psi^{Sk}_{P,\emptyset}$ $(d/Q \in \Psi^{Wk}_{P,\emptyset})$. Moreover, if Q is an ordinary base for d then $d/Q \in \varphi^{k}_{P,\emptyset}$.

Lemma 4.3: If $d/Q \in \Psi^{A\infty}_{P,\emptyset}$ then d has an active strong (weak) derivation whose last element is Q. Moreover, if $d/Q \in \varphi^{\infty}_{P,\emptyset}$ then Q is an ordinary base for d.

Before we prove the central result of this paper, let us consider again the program of example 3.1. $I^0_S = \emptyset$ and $T_P(I^0_S) = cl(\{q \vee r\})$. The negative supported extended atoms $t/\{\neg q\}$ and $v/\{\neg r\}$ are both in φ^{1}_{P,I^0_S} and $p/\{\neg q, \neg r\}$ is in $\varphi^{2}_{P,I^0_S} = \varphi^{\infty}_{P,I^0_S}$. $\lambda(\varphi^{\infty}_{P,I^0_S}) = EHB(P)$ and so, $U^S_P(I^0_S) = \emptyset$ and $I^1_S = cl(\{q \vee r\})$. In the next step T_P leaves I^1_S unchanged, $pos(I^2_S) = I^1_S$. It is still the case that $t/\{\neg q\}$ and $v/\{\neg r\}$ are in φ^{1}_{P,I^1_S}, but $p/\{\neg q, \neg r\} \notin \varphi^{2}_{P,I^1_S}$, because $\{\neg q, \neg r\}$ is not admissible with respect to I^1_S. $U^S_P(I^1_S) = \{p\}$ and $I^2_S = cl(\{q \vee r, \neg p\})$ is the least fixpoint of W^S_P. Note that the semantics given by I^2_S satisfies our intuition about the meaning of the program.

Theorem 4.1: Let P be a disjunctive logic program. Then $M^A_{WF}(P) = I^{\infty}_A$.

Proof: $(\subseteq)$: Let d be an extended atom such that d is true (false) with respect to $M^A_{WF}(P)$. We prove the result by transfinite induction on the level α of d in Γ^A_d.

- Suppose that α is a successor ordinal, $\alpha = \beta + 1$. Assume first that d is true in Γ^A_d. It follows that d has an active strong (weak) derivation whose last element is Q, such that Q is an ordinary base for d and $\overline{Q}$ fail at a level γ, $\gamma < \alpha$. Since $d/Q \in \varphi^{\infty}_{P,\emptyset}$ (Lemma 4.2) and $Q \subseteq I_A^{\infty}$ (inductive hypothesis) it follows that $d/Q \in \varphi^{\infty}_{P,I_A^{\infty}}$ and $Q \subseteq I_A^{\infty}$. By Lemma 4.1, it results that $d \in T_P(I_A^{\infty}) = pos(I_A^{\infty})$ which means that d is true in I_A^{∞}. Now assume that d is false in Γ_d^A. Then for all active strong (weak) derivations $d \leftarrow \ldots \leftarrow Q$, $\overline{Q}$ is successful at a level γ, $\gamma < \alpha$. Applying the inductive hypothesis, it follows that for any such Q, $\overline{Q} \in pos(I_A^{\infty})$. This means that if $d/Q \in \Psi^{A\,\infty}_{P,\emptyset}$, then $Q \notin NS_P(I_A^{\infty})$ and so $d \notin \lambda(\Psi^{A\,\infty}_{P,I_A^{\infty}})$. Then $d \in U_P(I_A^{\infty}) = neg(I_A^{\infty})$.

• Suppose that α is a limit ordinal. The case $\alpha = 0$ is trivial. By the construction of global trees, a ground disjunction can only be successful or failed at a level that is a successor ordinal.

($\supseteq$): suppose that d is a ground disjunction, $d \in pos(I_A^{\infty})$. Then there is an ordinal α such that $d \in pos(I_A^{\alpha})$. As usual, the proof will be by transfinite induction on α. The case when α is a limit ordinal comes trivial from the inductive hypothesis. Assume that α is a successor ordinal, $\alpha = \beta + 1$. Then $d \in T_P(I_A^{\beta})$ which means that there is an instantiated rule $h \leftarrow r_1 \wedge \ldots \wedge r_n \wedge \neg q_1 \wedge \ldots \wedge \neg q_m$ such that $r_k \vee d \in I_A^{\beta}$ and $\{\neg q_1, \ldots, \neg q_m\} \subseteq I_A^{\beta}$. From the inductive hypothesis and Lemma 4.5 it follows that for every $k = 1,\ldots,n$ there is an Q_k such that there is an active strong (weak) derivation $b_l \vee d \leftarrow \ldots \leftarrow Q_k$ such that $\overline{Q_k}$ is false with respect to $M_{WF}^A(P)$ and $q_1 \vee \ldots \vee q_m$ is false in $M_{WF}^A(P)$. It results that d has an active strong (weak) derivation such that $Q = \bigcup_{k=1}^{n} Q_k \cup \{\neg q_1, \ldots, \neg q_m\}$ is an ordinary base for d and $\overline{Q}$ is false with respect to $M_{WF}^A(P)$.

The case when d is false in I_A^{∞} is treated similarly. □

5 Conclusion

In this paper we have presented a bottom-up, fixpoint definition for the extensions of the well-founded semantics to disjunctive logic programs defined previously by Ross in a top-down, operational manner. In this setting Ross semantics can be viewed as a sound and complete procedure which implements the declarative semantics defined in the present paper.

Acknowledgement

I would like to thank the anonymous referees for helpful comments on earlier versions of the present paper.

References

1. K. R. Apt, H. Blair and A. Walker. Towards a Theory of Declarative Knowledge. In J. Minker, editor, *Foundations of Deductive Databases and Logic Programming,* pages 89-104, Los Altos, Ca, 1988. Morgan Kaufmann.

2. F. Fages. A New Fixpoint Semantics for General Logic Programs Compared with the Well-Founded and the Stable Model Semantics. In D. H. D. Warren and P. Szeredi, editors, *Seventh International Conference on Logic Programming, 1990,* pages 442-458.

3. M. Gelfond and V. Lifschitz. The Stable Semantics of Normal Logic. Programs. In K. Bowen and R. A. Kowalski editors, *Fifth International Conference on Logic Programming, 1988,* MIT Press.

4. J. W. Lloyd. Foundations of Logic Programming, second edition, Springer-Verlag, 1987.

5. J. Minker. On Indefinite Databases and the closed world assumption. In *Proc. Sixth Conference* on Automated Deduction, pages 292-308. Springer-Verlag, 1982.

6. J. Minker and A. Rajasekar. Disjunctive Logic Programming. In *Sixth International Conference on Logic Programming, 1989,* MIT Press.

7. J. Minker, A. Rajasekar. Stratification Semantics For Normal Disjunctive Logic Programs. In E. Lusk, R. A. Overbeek, editors, *Proceedings of the North American Conference on Logic Programming, 1989,* MIT Press.

8. J. Minker and A. Rajasekar. A Fixpoint Semantics for Disjunctive Logic Programs. *Journal of Logic Programming*, 9:45-74, 1990.

9. T. Przymusinski. On the Declarative Semantics of Deductive Databases and Logic Programs. In J. Minker, editor, *Foundations of Deductive Databases and Logic Programming,* pages 193-216, Los Altos, CA, 1988, Morgan Kaufmann.

10. T. Przymusinski. Three Value Stable Semantics For Disjunctive Logic Programs. In D. H. D. Warren and P. Szeredi, editors, *Seventh International Conference on Logic Programming, 1990,* pages 459-477, MIT Press.

11. T. Przymusinski. Stationary Semantics For Disjunctive Logic Programs. In S. Debray and M. Hermenegildo, editors, *Proceedings of the North American Conference on Logic Programming, 1990,* MIT Press.

12. K. A. Ross. The Well Founded Semantics for Disjunctive Logic Programs. In W. Kim, J.-M. Nicolas and S. Nishio, editors, *Deductive and Object-Oriented Databases,* pages 385-402, Elsevier Science Publishers B. V. (North-Holland), 1990.

13. K. A. Ross and R. Topor. Inferring Negative Information from Disjunctive Databases. *Journal of Automated Reasoning,* 4:397-424, 1988.

14. J. D. Ullman. Bottom-up Beats Top-down for Datalog. In *Proceedings of the 8th ACM Symposium on Principles of Database Systems* (1989), pages 140-149.

15. A. Van Gelder. The Alternating Fixpoint of Logic Programs with negation. In J. Minker, editor, *Foundations of Deductive Databases and Logic Programming,* Los Altos, CA, 1988, Morgan Kaufmann.

16. A. Van Gelder, K. A. Ross, and J. S. Schlipf. The Well-Founded Semantics for General Logic Programs, *JACM, 38, 3* (1991), pages 620-650.

An Efficient Computation of the Extended Generalized Closed World Assumption by Support–for–Negation Sets

Dietmar Seipel

University of Tübingen
Sand 13, D - 72076 Tübingen, Germany
seipel@informatik.uni-tuebingen.de

Abstract. Closed world assumptions are one of the major approaches for non–monotonic reasoning in artificial intelligence. In [16] this formalism is applied to disjunctive logic programs, i.e. logic programs with positive disjunctive rule heads and positive atoms in the rule bodies. The disjunctive closure operator $\mathcal{T}_P^S$ allows for the derivation of the set $\mathcal{MS}_P$ of all positive disjunctive clauses logically implied by the program P, the *minimal model state*. On the other hand, disjunctive clauses over negated atoms are derived in the *extended generalized closed world assumption* $\mathcal{EGCWA}_P$. Such a clause is the negation of a conjunction of positive atoms. $\mathcal{EGCWA}_P$ contains all conjunctions which are *false* in all minimal Herbrand models of the program.
We present efficient Δ–iteration techniques for computing the closed world assumption $\mathcal{EGCWA}_P$ based on an iterative computation of the set of all support–for–negation sets $SN(C)$ for conjunctions C, i.e. certain sets of clauses which characterize $\mathcal{EGCWA}_P$: $C \in \mathcal{EGCWA}_P$ iff $\mathcal{MS}_P \models SN(C)$. The support–for–negation sets $SN(A)$ for atoms A are easily derived from the minimal model state $\mathcal{MS}_P$. We will propose a *bottom–up* computation deriving the support–for–negation sets of longer conjunctions from shorter ones based on an algebraic formula given by [16]: $SN(C_1 \wedge C_2) = SN(C_1) \vee SN(C_2)$. We will present techniques for the efficient computation of these disjunctions of two clause sets and a Δ–iteration approach for computing the support–for–negation sets of a sequence of growing minimal model states.
For disjunctive normal logic programs, i.e. logic programs with positive disjunctive rule heads and – possibly – negated atoms in the rule bodies, these operators form a basis for computing the *generalized disjunctive well–founded semantics*.

1 Introduction

Deductive databases use logic programming and techniques from non–monotonic reasoning for building a powerful, declarative language for specifying data and queries in relational databases. There has been a great deal of research on the processing of definite Horn clauses with definite facts, cf. [3], [22], [4]. Recursive programs are evaluated iteratively in a set–oriented fashion based on the primitive operations of relational algebra, which can be executed efficiently on databases. The desired result is the least fixpoint of the definite consequence operator $\mathcal{T}_P$, which equals the minimal Herbrand model $\mathcal{M}_P$, cf. [15]. More advanced applications require the support of disjunctive rules and disjunctive facts: The deduction of independencies in probabilistic reasoning, cf. [17], [21], and the overlapping of rectangles in spatial databases, cf. [1], are examples falling into this category.

In general, a disjunctive normal logic rule has a head given by a disjunction of positive atoms and a body given by a conjunction of positive and negated atoms. Disjunctive logic programs are programs consisting of indefinite (disjunctive) rules without negated atoms in the body. They specify a set of logically implied disjunctive facts (i.e. positive ground clauses), the so-called *minimal model state* $\mathcal{MS}_P$, cf. [16]. Efficient techniques for computing $\mathcal{MS}_P$ iteratively as the least fixpoint of the disjunctive consequence operator $\mathcal{T}_P^S$ are currently investigated. Various semantics for indefinite rules with negation are given in literature: well-founded semantics [23], generalized well-founded semantics [2], generalized disjunctive well-founded semantics [16], stationary semantics [18] and stable model semantics [12], [11]. A classification of these semantics w.r.t. certain criteria is given by [8].

The *generalized disjunctive well-founded semantics* of [16] for disjunctive normal logic programs is based on four fundamental operators for deriving *true* ground disjunctions of only positive atoms or only negated atoms. It is three-valued, since not all disjunctions or conjunctions are assigned a truth value *true* or *false*. Some remain *unknown*.

Two of the operators, the positive and the negative consequence operator $\mathcal{T}_S^D$ and $\mathcal{F}_S^D$, respectively, operate on disjunctive normal logic programs and so-called state pairs $S = <T, F>$, where T and F is a set of disjunctions and conjunctions, respectively, of positive atoms, the disjunctive and the conjunctive Herbrand state. The disjunctions in T are considered *true*, the conjunctions in F are considered *false*. $\mathcal{T}_S^D$ derives some new *true* disjunctions form S and the program P, thus enlarging the disjunctive Herbrand state T. $\mathcal{F}_S^D$ derives new *false* atoms (atomic conjunctions) from S and P, thus enlarging the conjunctive Herbrand state F. In two separate iterations the fixpoints of $\mathcal{T}_S^D$ and $\mathcal{F}_S^D$ are computed, the so-called disjunctive well-founded semantics of P. It is three-valued as well and it generalizes the two-valued well-founded semantics for normal logic programs – with definite rule heads – to disjunctive normal logic programs. $\mathcal{T}_S^D$ and $\mathcal{F}_S^D$ will not be considered further in this paper.

Two other operators act on the disjunctive transformation $P = Dis(P', S)$ of a given disjunctive normal logic program P' w.r.t. an actual state pair S. The disjunctive consequence operator $\mathcal{T}_P^S$ allows for the derivation of the *minimal model state* $\mathcal{MS}_P$. $\mathcal{MS}_P$ can be characterized as the set of all ground disjunctions which are *true* in all Herbrand models of P, or equivalently as the set of all ground disjunctions logically implied by the program P. On the other hand, conjunctive clauses are derived by the *extended generalized closed world assumption*: $\mathcal{EGCWA}_P$ contains all conjunctions which are *false* in all minimal

Herbrand models of the program P. Equivalently, the corresponding disjunctions of negated atoms in the set $\neg\mathcal{EGCWA}_P$ are considered *true*. It is proven in [16], that $\neg\mathcal{EGCWA}_P$ is the maximal set of such disjunctions, which is consistent with the minimal model state $\mathcal{MS}_P$ of the program in the sense, that no new positive disjunctions can be derived from their union.

By theses operators, repeatedly minimal model states and extended generalized closed world assumptions are computed w.r.t. growing state pairs.

We present efficient Δ-iteration techniques for computing the closed world assumption $\mathcal{EGCWA}_P$ based on an iterative computation of the set of all support-for-negation sets $SN(C)$ for conjunctions C, which characterize $\mathcal{EGCWA}_P$: $C \in \mathcal{EGCWA}_P$ iff $\mathcal{MS}_P \models SN(C)$. The support-for-negation sets $SN(A)$ for atoms A are easily derived from the minimal model state $\mathcal{MS}_P$ by resolving all disjunctions with $\neg A$. Normally, if only a single support-for-negation set $SN(C)$ is required, it is faster to derive it by SLI-resolution, cf. [16]. Since we need all of them for deriving the whole $\mathcal{EGCWA}_P$, we use an algebraic approach based on the simple formula $SN(C_1 \wedge C_2) = SN(C_1) \vee SN(C_2)$ proven in [16]. It allows for the computation of support-for-negation sets of longer conjunctions from shorter ones in a *bottom-up* computation with the following advantages:

- A lot of *redundancy* is avoided, since the same operations can be shared between many different support derivations in bottom-up computation.
- *Database techniques* like massive joins can be adapted and used.

The rest of this paper is organized as follows: We will review some of the definitions and theoretical foundations for disjunctive logic programming and their fixpoint semantics given in [16]. Following, we will describe an efficient bottom-up Δ-iteration technique with subsumption for disjunctive logic programs that iteratively derives the disjunctive facts of $\mathcal{MS}_P$. Then we will turn to the more general disjunctive normal logic programs. We will describe the extended generalized closed world assumption $\mathcal{EGCWA}_P$ and again some bottom-up Δ-iteration techniques for its computation.

2 Foundations of Disjunctive Logic Programming

Syntactically, a *deductive database* $DDB = (DB, P)$ is given by a set DB of facts, which resemble a relational database, and a logic program P, which consists of a set of rules for deriving new facts from DB.

(i) Given some atoms $p_i(X_i)$ $(1 \leq i \leq m,\ m \in \mathbb{N}_+)$ and some literals $L_j(Y_j)$ $(1 \leq j \leq n,\ n \in \mathbb{N}_0)$. Then $p_1(X_1) \vee \ldots \vee p_m(X_m)$ is a disjunctive *fact* and

$$r:\quad p_1(X_1) \vee \ldots \vee p_m(X_m) \text{ :- } L_1(Y_1), \ldots, L_n(Y_n).$$

is a disjunctive normal *rule*, where the atoms $p_1(X_1), \ldots, p_m(X_m)$ form the rule's head and the literals $L_1(Y_1), \ldots, L_n(Y_n)$ form its body. r is disjunctive, iff all its body literals L_i are positive. r is normal, iff $m = 1$.
The disjunctive normal logic program containing all the *ground instances* of rules in P is denoted by $Ground(P)$.

The *semantics* of a deductive database $DDB = (DB, P)$ is defined according to the bottom–up or naive evaluation algorithms, cf. [16], as the least fixpoint of a consequence operator $\mathcal{T}_P^S$.

(ii) The *disjunctive Herbrand base* DHB_P of a disjunctive logic program P is given by the set of positive ground clauses

$$DHB_P \ = \ \{ \ A_1 \vee \ldots \vee A_k \mid k \geq 1, \ A_i \in HB_P, \ 1 \leq i \leq k \ \},$$

where HB_P denotes the Herbrand base of P. A *disjunctive Herbrand state* – or simply Herbrand state – D of P is a subset $D \subseteq DHB_P$. The *canonical form* and the *expansion* of D are

$$can(D) = \{ \ C \in D \mid \text{there is no proper subclause } C' \text{ of } C \text{ in } D \ \},$$
$$exp(D) = \{ \ C \in DHB_P \mid \text{there is a subclause } C' \text{ of } C \text{ in } D \ \},$$

respectively, i.e. $can(D) \subseteq D \subseteq exp(D)$. D is expanded, iff $exp(D) = D$.

(iii) The *set difference* with subsumption and the *set disjunction* of two Herbrand states D_1 and D_2 is given by

$$D_1 \setminus_s D_2 = \{ \ C \in D_1 \mid \text{there is no subclause } C' \text{ of } C \text{ in } D_2 \ \},$$
$$D_1 \vee D_2 = \{ \ C_1 \vee C_2 \mid C_1 \in D_1, \ C_2 \in D_2 \ \}.$$

(iv) The *disjunctive consequence operator* $\mathcal{T}_P^S : 2^{DHB_P} \rightarrow 2^{DHB_P}$ of a disjunctive logic program P maps Herbrand states to Herbrand states:

$$\mathcal{T}_P^S(D) \ = \ \{ C \in DHB_P \mid \ C' \text{ :- } B_1, \ldots, B_n \text{ is in } Ground(P),$$
$$B_i \vee C_i \in D, \ 1 \leq i \leq n, \ C \text{ is the smallest factor of } C' \vee C_1 \vee \ldots \vee C_n \}.$$

A *model state* D of P is an expanded Herbrand state of P such that every minimal Herbrand model of D is a Herbrand model of P.

Example 1. A very frequently used logic program P is the one that specifies the transitive closure of a graph given by an *arc*–relation:

$$P = \ \{ \ path(X,Y) \text{ :- } path(X,Z), path(Z,Y);$$
$$path(X,Y) \text{ :- } arc(X,Y) \ \}.$$

Although P is definite, when applied to a graph given by indefinite information for *arc*, it is necessary to use the more general disjunctive consequence operator $\mathcal{T}_P^S$ instead of the definite one for deriving all the disjunctive facts implied by P. From the Herbrand state $D_0 \ = \ \{ \ arc(a,b) \vee arc(a,c), arc(b,d), arc(c,d) \ \}$, the Herbrand states $D_{i+1} = \mathcal{T}_P^S(D_i)$ $(0 \leq i \leq 2)$ are derived:

$$D_1 = \{ \ arc(a,b) \vee path(a,c), path(a,b) \vee arc(a,c), path(b,d), path(c,d) \ \},$$
$$D_2 = \{ \ path(a,b) \vee path(a,c), path(a,d) \vee arc(a,c), path(a,d) \vee arc(a,b) \ \},$$
$$D_3 = \{ \ path(a,d) \vee path(a,c), path(a,d) \vee path(a,b) \ \}.$$

From the Herbrand state $D_3' \ = \ D_3 \cup \{ \ path(b,d), path(c,d) \ \}$ we get $\mathcal{T}_P^S(D_3') \ = \ \{ \ path(a,d) \ \}$. Thus, $\mathcal{T}_P^S$ can also derive definite facts from disjunctive facts.

For every *definite* logic program P the minimal Herbrand model $\mathcal{M}_P$ of P is equal to the following sets, cf. [15]: the logical consequences $A \in HB_P$ of P, the least fixpoint $lfp(\mathcal{T}_P)$ of the definite consequence operator $\mathcal{T}_P$, $\mathcal{T}_P \uparrow \omega$, and the logical consequences $A \in HB_P$ of $\mathcal{M}_P$.

In general a *disjunctive* logic program P does not have a unique minimal model, but a set $\mathcal{MM}_P$ of minimal models. For disjunctive logic programs, model states are the structure corresponding to models for logic programs. They can be characterized based on the disjunctive consequence operator: an expanded Herbrand state D of P is a model state of P, iff $\mathcal{T}_P^S(D) \subseteq D$. As for Herbrand models of definite logic programs, every intersection of model states again is a model state. Thus, there is a unique *minimal model state* $\mathcal{MS}_P$: the intersection $\cap_{i \in J} MS_i$ of the set $\{MS_i\}_{i \in J}$ of all model states of P. $\mathcal{MS}_P$ is expanded, since model states are expanded, and it is equivalent to the following Herbrand states, cf. [16]: the logical consequences $C \in DHB_P$ of P, the expanded least fixpoint $exp(lfp(\mathcal{T}_P^S))$, the expansion $exp(\mathcal{T}_P^S \uparrow \omega)$ of the ω-power $\mathcal{T}_P^S \uparrow \omega$, and the set of all clauses $C \in DHB_P$ implied by all minimal models $M \in \mathcal{MM}_P$ of P.

For a definite logic program P, the minimal Herbrand model $\mathcal{M}_P$ is equal to the canonization $can(\mathcal{MS}_P)$ of the minimal model state.

3 The Disjunctive Δ–Iteration Technique

Semi–naive or Δ–iteration was originally defined for definite logic programs. For extending it to the fixpoint computation of a disjunctive logic program P, we need the Δ–version of the disjunctive consequence operator $\mathcal{T}_P^S$.

Definition 1. The *disjunctive consequence operator* $\mathcal{T}_P^S : 2^{DHB_P} \times 2^{DHB_P} \rightarrow 2^{DHB_P}$ of a disjunctive logic program P is applied to Herbrand states $D, \Delta D$:

$$\begin{aligned}\mathcal{T}_P^S(D, \Delta D) \;=\; \{\, & C \in DHB_P \mid C' \text{ :- } B_1, \ldots, B_n \text{ is in } Ground(P),\ (\ n = 0 \ \ or \\ & (\ B_i \vee C_i \in D \cup \Delta D,\ 1 \leq i \leq n, \text{ and some } B_i \vee C_i \text{ is in } \Delta D\ )\ ), \\ & C \text{ is the smallest factor of } C' \vee C_1 \vee \ldots \vee C_n \,\}.\end{aligned}$$

The algorithm Δ–ITERATION of Fig. 1 formulates the disjunctive Δ–iteration based on the Δ–version of $\mathcal{T}_P^S$. When applied to the empty Herbrand state $D = \emptyset$, it yields the least fixpoint of $\mathcal{T}_P^S$. The basic operations of Δ–ITERATION are the following. From a computational point of view, $\mathcal{T}_P^S$ derives a multiset D_1 of disjunctive facts, which has to be pruned by removing duplicates. The time complexity of *pruning* is $n \log n$, where $n = |D_1|$ is the number of facts in D_1. *Δ–computation* w.r.t. subsumption of the set $D_2 \setminus_s D$ of all disjunctive facts in D_2 which are not subsumed by disjunctive facts in D takes time $n_1 \cdot n_2$, where $n_1 = |D|$, $n_2 = |D_2|$. *Canonization* is the computation of all disjunctive facts in a Herbrand state D_3 which are not properly subsumed by other – i.e. shorter – disjunctive facts in the same state. It takes time n^2, where $n = |D_3|$.

Lemma 2. *Given a disjunctive logic program P and Herbrand states $D, \Delta D$ of P:*

$$can(\ prune(\mathcal{T}_P^S(D, \Delta D)) \setminus_s D\ ) \;=\; can(\ prune(\mathcal{T}_P^S(D, \Delta D))\ ) \setminus_s D.$$

Algorithm Δ-ITERATION (P, D)

```
{ initialization }
ΔD := D;

{ iteration }
while ( |ΔD| > 0 )
    D1 := T_P^S(D, ΔD);
    D2 := prune(D1);
    D3 := D2 \s D;
    ΔD := can(D3);
    D  := can(D ∪ ΔD);
end
```

Fig. 1. Disjunctive Δ-ITERATION

Based on these considerations, we derive an efficient version of the disjunctive Δ-iteration by suitably arranging the basic operations, cf. [20]. Experiments with Δ-ITERATION, cf. Table 1, revealed that the comparatively cheap pruning operation reduces the multiset D_1 of derived facts to about 30% of its size. Then the applied Δ-computation yields a further reduction to about 1 % of the size of D_1 in time $O(|D_2| \cdot |D|)$, where normally D is much smaller than D_2. Finally, the most expensive operation *can* is delayed as far as possible. It is applied to the smallest Herbrand state D_3 and reduces it to about 0.5% of the size of D_1.

iteration	1	2	3	4	
$\mathcal{T}_P^S$	0.26	2.69	28.71	11.22	42.0%
prune	0.01	0.53	11.46	4.13	12.6%
$\setminus_s$	0.05	1.21	19.68	11.33	32.0%
can	0.27	2.45	1.13	0.01	3.5%
can	0.55	5.17	4.19	0.02	9.9%

iteration	1	2	3	4	
$\mathcal{T}_P^S$	100	2.209	33.406	12.667	100%
prune	50	891	8.612	5.235	31%
$\setminus_s$	44	208	151	0	0.9%
can	44	132	47	0	0.5%
can	0	3	30	0	14%

Table 1. Time in seconds and number of tuples after the different operators in tree-based Δ-ITERATION

Algorithm Δ–ITERATION can be efficiently supported by a data structure for disjunctive facts, the so-called *clause trees*, cf. [20]. Another data structure, the so-called *model tree*, was proposed by [16], [10] for representing the set of all minimal models of a Herbrand state instead of the clauses of the Herbrand state. Both types of trees are used for a fast hyperresolution of further disjunctive facts by $\mathcal{T}_P^S$ and for purposes of subsumption elimination. In this general setting, a clause tree is a set tree for a Herbrand state S and a model tree is a set tree for a set S of models.

Definition 3 (Set Tree). Given a set $S = \{S_1, \ldots, S_n\}$ of some finite sets S_i $(1 \leq i \leq n,\ n \in \mathbb{N}_0)$. A *set tree* $\mathcal{T} = (V, E)$ with a node labeling $l : V \rightarrow 2^{\mathcal{A}_S}$, where $\mathcal{A}_S = \cup_{i=1}^{n} S_i$, *represents* S, iff

(i) each node $v \in V$ represents a set $set(v)$ as follows: $set(v)$ is the union of the sets $l(v')$ which label the nodes v' on the path from the root to v,

(ii) the sets $set(v)$ of the leaves $v \in V$ are in S, and every set $S_i \in S$ is represented by exactly one leaf of the set tree.

Heuristics for constructing a set tree $\mathcal{T} = (V, E)$ representing a set S in a good way can be based on the graph–theoretic notion of minimal Steiner trees, cf. [20]. The goal is to minimize the sum $weight(\mathcal{T}) = \sum_{e \in E} length(e)$ of the edge lengths, where for an edge $e = (v_1, v_2) \in E$: $length(e) = \mid set(v_2) \setminus set(v_1) \mid$.

Tree–resolution with clause trees has been analyzed for the frequently occurring definite transitive closure rules with disjunctive facts, cf. Table 1. For general disjunctive logic programs involving disjunctive rules the method is applicable as well, and yields even more efficient evaluation.

4 The Extended Generalized Closed World Assumption

The generalized disjunctive well–founded semantics, cf. [16], assigns to a disjunctive normal logic program P a state pair $S = \langle T, F \rangle$ consisting of a disjunctive Herbrand state T and a conjunctive Herbrand state F, i.e. a set of ground conjunctions. The clauses in T (F) are considered *true* (*false*).

Definition 4. Given a disjunctive normal logic program P.

(i) The *conjunctive Herbrand base* CHB_P of P is

$$CHB_P \;=\; \{\ A_1 \wedge \ldots \wedge A_k \mid k \geq 1,\ A_i \in HB_P,\ 1 \leq i \leq k\ \}.$$

A *conjunctive Herbrand state* F of P is a subset $F \subseteq CHB_P$. The *canonical form* and the *expansion* of F are given by

$$can(F) = \{\ C \in F \mid \text{there is no proper subconjunction } C' \text{ of } C \text{ in } F\ \},$$
$$exp(F) = \{\ C \in CHB_P \mid \text{there is a subconjunction } C' \text{ of } C \text{ in } F\ \}.$$

respectively, i.e. $can(F) \subseteq F \subseteq exp(F)$. F is expanded, iff $exp(F) = F$.

(ii) A *state pair* $S = \langle T, F \rangle$ of P consists of a disjunctive Herbrand state T and a conjunctive Herbrand state F.

For a disjunctive logic program P, we already know that the minimal model state $\mathcal{MS}_P$ of P is the set of ground disjunctions which are *true* in all (minimal) Herbrand models of P. The *dual approach* is followed by the extended generalized closed world assumption: $\mathcal{EGCWA}_P$ will contain the set of ground conjunctions which are *false* in all minimal Herbrand models of P.

Definition 5. The *extended generalized closed world assumption* of a disjunctive logic program P is given by

$$\mathcal{EGCWA}_P = \{ C \in CHB_P \mid C \text{ is } \mathit{false} \text{ in all minimal Herbrand models of } P \}.$$

Example 2. The disjunctive logic program $P = \{ c :- a, \ \ a \vee b \}$ derives the minimal model state $\mathcal{MS}_P = \{a \vee b, b \vee c, a \vee b \vee c\}$ and has the set $\mathcal{MM}_P = \{\{a, c\}, \{b\}\}$ of minimal Herbrand models. Thus, the set of all ground conjunctions which are *false* in all $M \in \mathcal{MM}_P$ is given by $\mathcal{EGCWA}_P = \{a \wedge b, b \wedge c, a \wedge b \wedge c\}$.

The extended generalized closed world assumption is *maximal consistent* with the minimal model state $\mathcal{MS}_P$: i.e. it contains exactly the ground conjunctions $A_1 \wedge \ldots \wedge A_k$ which can be assumed to be *false* without making it possible to derive new positive ground disjuncts from $\mathcal{MS}_P$ and the disjunctions $\neg A_1 \vee \ldots \vee \neg A_k$.

The extended generalized closed world assumption will be applied to a certain disjunctive logic program $Dis(P, S)$ obtained from a disjunctive normal logic program P by a transformation w.r.t. a given state pair S. $Dis(P, S)$ is a ground disjunctive logic program which is produced if in the ground instances of the rules of P all negated body atoms are moved to the rule head – yielding positive atoms – and atoms which are *true* or *false* w.r.t. the state pair S are removed from the resulting rules. Finally, rules with *true* heads or *false* bodies, respectively, are removed. Note, that $Dis(P, S)$ is a possibly infinite disjunctive logic program.

Definition 6. Given a disjunctive normal logic program P and a state pair $S = <T, F>$.

(i) The *disjunctive transformation* $Dis(P) = \{ C' \vee B_{m+1} \vee \ldots \vee B_{m+n} :- B_1, \ldots, B_m \mid C' :- B_1, \ldots, B_m, \neg B_{m+1}, \ldots, \neg B_{m+n} \in P \}$ of P is a disjunctive logic program.

(ii) The *disjunctive transformation* $Dis(P, S)$ of P w.r.t. S is a ground disjunctive logic program derived by transforming $Ground(Dis(P))$ as follows. Given a disjunctive rule $r = A_1 \vee \ldots \vee A_k :- B_1, \ldots, B_n \in Ground(Dis(P))$:

1. Remove the rule r if $A_{i_1} \vee \ldots \vee A_{i_l} \in T$ for some subdisjunction of its head atoms – i.e. the head is *true* in S – or if $A_1, \ldots, A_k \in F$ – i.e. the head is *false* in S – or if $B_{i_1} \wedge \ldots \wedge B_{i_l} \in F$ for some subconjunction of its body atoms – i.e. the body is *false* in S.
2. Reduce the rule r by removing *true* atoms $B_i \in T$ form the body of r and *false* atoms $A_i \in F$ from the head of r.

(iii) The $\mathcal{S}^{\mathcal{E}}$*-derived state pair* is $\mathcal{S}^{\mathcal{E}}(S) = S \cup <\mathcal{MS}_{Dis(P,S)}, \mathcal{EGCWA}_{Dis(P,S) \cup T}>$, where $S_1 \cup S_2 = <T_1 \cup T_2, F_1 \cup F_2>$ for two state pairs $S_i = <T_i, F_i>$.

Remember that the extended generalized closed world assumption $\mathcal{EGCWA}_P$ of a disjunctive logic program P is maximal consistent with the minimal model state $\mathcal{MS}_P$. Applied to the disjunctive logic program $Dis(P,S) \cup T$, this means that no new positive ground disjunctions can be derived from the state pair $< \mathcal{MS}_{Dis(P,S) \cup T}, \mathcal{EGCWA}_{Dis(P,S) \cup T} >$ and thus from the weaker state pair $\mathcal{S}^{\mathcal{E}}(S)$.

Example 3. For the disjunctive normal logic program P_1 and the state pair $S = < \{a \vee b\}, \{e, f(a)\} >$ we get the disjunctive transformation $Dis(P_1)$:

$$P_1 = \{ \; c \;\text{:-}\; a, \neg e; \;\; a \vee b \vee e; \;\; e \vee f(X) \;\text{:-}\; c, d(X); \;\; a \vee c \;\text{:-}\; e, \neg d(a) \; \},$$
$$Dis(P_1) = \{ \; c \vee e \;\text{:-}\; a; \;\; a \vee b \vee e; \;\; e \vee f(X) \;\text{:-}\; c, d(X); \;\; a \vee c \vee d(a) \;\text{:-}\; e \; \}.$$

The disjunctive transformation of P_1 w.r.t. S is $Dis(P_1, S) = \{ \; c \;\text{:-}\; a \; \}$. Thus, $Dis(P_1, S) \cup T$ is the disjunctive logic program P from Example 2 and the $\mathcal{S}^{\mathcal{E}}$-derived state pair is given by $\mathcal{S}^{\mathcal{E}}(S) = < \emptyset, \{a \wedge b, b \wedge c, a \wedge b \wedge c\} >$.

5 Generalized Δ–Iteration Techniques

Computing the extended generalized closed world assumption of a disjunctive logic program can be speeded up by tree–based Δ–iteration techniques applied to certain *support–for–negation sets* for the conjunctive facts. These sets can be derived efficiently by an iteration from the minimal model state $\mathcal{MS}_P$, if $can(\mathcal{MS}_P)$ is finite.

During the various $\mathcal{S}^{\mathcal{E}}$–derivation steps in the computation of the generalized disjunctive well–founded semantics of a disjunctive normal logic program, there are repeated computations of the $\mathcal{EGCWA}$ and thus of support–for–negation sets w.r.t. monotonically growing model states. Instead of computing the support–for–negation sets of an enlarged minimal model state from the scratch, we use update formulas for deriving them from the support–for–negation sets w.r.t. the previous minimal model state.

The ground *disjunctive transformation* $Dis(P,S)$ of a disjunctive normal logic program P usually is infinite. Therefore, instead of $Dis(P,S)$ we use the finite, non–ground disjunctive transformation $Dis(P)$ with a special associated consequence operator $\mathcal{T}^S_{P,S}$ defined in terms of $Dis(P)$ and the state pair S. $\mathcal{T}^S_{P,S}$ can be evaluated based on the same Δ–iteration techniques as ordinary disjunctive consequence operators.

5.1 Efficient Computation of Support–for–Negation Sets

The extended generalized closed world assumption $\mathcal{EGCWA}_P$ of a disjunctive logic program P is derived based on an iterative computation of support–for–negation sets w.r.t. the minimal model state $\mathcal{MS}_P$.

Definition 7. Given a disjunctive logic program P. The *support–for–negation set* of a conjunction $A_1 \wedge \ldots \wedge A_k \in CHB_P$ w.r.t. $D \subseteq DHB_P$ is

$$SN(D, A_1 \wedge \ldots \wedge A_k) \; = \; \{ \; C_1 \vee \ldots \vee C_k \mid A_i \vee C_i \in D \text{ for } 1 \leq i \leq k \; \}.$$

Example 4. For the disjunctive logic program P of Example 2 with the minimal model state $\mathcal{MS}_P = \{a \vee b, b \vee c, a \vee b \vee c\}$ the support–for–negation sets are

$$SN(\mathcal{MS}_P, a) = \{b, b \vee c\},\ SN(\mathcal{MS}_P, c) = \{b, a \vee b\},\ SN(\mathcal{MS}_P, b) = \{a, c, a \vee c\},$$
$$SN(\mathcal{MS}_P, a \wedge b) = SN(\mathcal{MS}_P, b \wedge c) = SN(\mathcal{MS}_P, a \wedge b \wedge c)$$
$$= \{a \vee b, b \vee c, a \vee b \vee c\},\ SN(\mathcal{MS}_P, a \wedge c) = \{b, a \vee b, b \vee c, a \vee b \vee c\},$$

Theorem 8 (Characterization). *For a disjunctive logic program P it holds:*

$$\mathcal{EGCWA}_P = \{\ A_1 \wedge \ldots \wedge A_k \mid (\mathcal{MS}_P \models A_i \vee C_i \ \mathit{for}\ 1 \leq i \leq k)$$
$$\mathit{implies}\ (\mathcal{MS}_P \models C_1 \vee \ldots \vee C_k)\ \}$$
$$= \{\ C \in CHB_P \mid SN(\mathcal{MS}_P, C) \setminus_s \mathcal{MS}_P = \emptyset\ \}.$$

We will present a technique for computing $\mathcal{EGCWA}_P$ based on the support–for–negation sets $SN(\mathcal{MS}_P, C)$. In [16] these sets are denoted by $SN(C)$ without explicitly noting the context $\mathcal{MS}_P$. The computation can be expressed more easily with the notion of SN^r–sets, canonized subsets of the SN–sets where all disjunctions, which are subsumed by the Herbrand state D, are removed.

Definition 9. Given a disjunctive normal logic program P and $D \subseteq DHB_P$. The *reduced support-for-negation set* of $C \in CHB_P$ w.r.t. D is

$$SN^r(D, C) \ = \ can(\ SN(D, C) \setminus_s D\ ).$$

The following evaluation technique deals with SN^r–sets, which are subsets of the corresponding SN–sets and can be handled much more efficiently. The theorem of [16] relating the SN–sets to the $\mathcal{EGCWA}$ translates to SN^r–sets:

Theorem 10. *For a disjunctive logic program P it holds:*

$$\mathcal{EGCWA}_P = \{\ C \in CHB_P \mid SN^r(\mathcal{MS}_P, C) = \emptyset\ \}.$$

Example 5. The disjunctive logic program P of example 2 derives the reduced support–for–negation sets

$$SN^r(\mathcal{MS}_P, a) = \{b\},\ SN^r(\mathcal{MS}_P, c) = \{b\},\ SN^r(\mathcal{MS}_P, b) = \{a, c\},$$
$$SN^r(\mathcal{MS}_P, a \wedge b) = SN^r(\mathcal{MS}_P, b \wedge c) = SN^r(\mathcal{MS}_P, a \wedge b \wedge c) = \emptyset,$$
$$SN^r(\mathcal{MS}_P, a \wedge c) = \{b\},$$

and thus $\mathcal{EGCWA}_P = \{a \wedge b, b \wedge c, a \wedge b \wedge c\}$.

The support–for–negation sets $SN(D, A)$ for atoms A are easily derived from the Herbrand state D. The support–for–negation sets of longer conjunctions are derived from shorter ones based on an algebraic formula given by [16]. A similar formula also holds for the reduced support–for–negation sets.

Theorem 11 (Recursion Formulas). *Given $D \subseteq DHB_P$, $C_1, C_2 \in CHB_P$:*

$$SN(D, C_1 \wedge C_2) \ = \ SN(D, C_1) \vee SN(D, C_2).$$
$$SN^r(D, C_1 \wedge C_2) \ = \ can(\ (SN^r(D, C_1) \vee SN^r(D, C_2)) \setminus_s D\ ).$$

A *bottom-up computation* of all the reduced support-for-negation sets using Δ-iteration techniques will be proposed. The algorithm Δ-ITERATION-SN given in Fig. 2 computes the generalized closed world assumption $\mathcal{GCWA}_P = \mathcal{EGCWA}_P \cap HB_P$ and the canonization $\mathcal{EGCWA} = can(\mathcal{EGCWA}_P \setminus HB_P)$ for a disjunctive logic program P. It is based on the minimal model state $\mathcal{MS}_P$, which has to be computed before. $\mathcal{GCWA}_P$ can be determined easily as the set $HB_P \setminus \cup_{C \in \mathcal{MS}_P} C$ of atoms in HB_P which do not occur in any clause of $\mathcal{MS}_P$.

Algorithm Δ-ITERATION-SN($\mathcal{MS}_P, \mathcal{GCWA}_P, \mathcal{EGCWA}$)

{ initialization }

$\mathcal{MS} := can(\ \mathcal{MS}_P\ );$

$\mathcal{SN} := \{\ (A, SN(\mathcal{MS}, A)) \mid A \in HB_P \text{ and } SN(\mathcal{MS}, A) \neq \emptyset\ \};$

$\mathcal{GCWA}_P := \{\ A \in HB_P \mid SN(\mathcal{MS}, A) = \emptyset\ \};$

{ recursion }

SNR($\mathcal{SN}, \mathcal{MS}, \mathcal{SN}^r, \mathcal{EGCWA}$).

Fig. 2. Δ-ITERATION-SN

Procedure SNR, cf. Fig. 3, uses a *divide-and-conquer* approach for computing the support collection $\mathcal{SN}^r$ of all pairs $(C, SN^r(C))$ for conjunctions $C \in CHB_P$, where $SN^r(C) \neq \emptyset$ (non-trivial pairs). Each intermediate support collection $\mathcal{SN}^r$ contains the pairs for all conjunctions C over a certain $I \subseteq HB_P$. The initial set $I = \{A \in HB_P | SN^r(A) \neq \emptyset\}$ is recursively split into two arbitrary subsets $I = I_1 \cup I_2$. Correspondingly, $\mathcal{SN} = \{(A, SN^r(A)) | A \in I\}$ is split into subsets $\mathcal{SN}_i = \{(A_i, SN^r(A_i)) | A_i \in I_i\}$, $i = 1, 2$, from which the support collections $\mathcal{SN}_i^r = \{(C_i, SN^r(C_i)) | C_i \subseteq I_i, SN^r(C_i) \neq \emptyset\}$ over I_i are computed recursively.

Procedure SNR($\mathcal{SN}, \mathcal{MS}, \mathcal{SN}^r, \mathcal{E}$);

if $|\mathcal{SN}| > 1$

then { divide and conquer }

split $\mathcal{SN}$ into $\mathcal{SN}_1$ and $\mathcal{SN}_2$;

SNR($\mathcal{SN}_1, \mathcal{MS}, \mathcal{SN}_1^r, \mathcal{E}_1$); SNR($\mathcal{SN}_2, \mathcal{MS}, \mathcal{SN}_2^r, \mathcal{E}_2$);

MERGE($\mathcal{MS}, \mathcal{SN}_1^r, \mathcal{SN}_2^r, \mathcal{SN}^r, \mathcal{E}_1, \mathcal{E}_2, \mathcal{E}$);

else { base case }

$\mathcal{SN}$ contains exactly one pair $(A, SN(\mathcal{MS}, A))$;

$\mathcal{SN}^r := \{\ (A, SN(\mathcal{MS}, A))\ \};\ \ \mathcal{E} := \emptyset;$

Fig. 3. Divide-and-conquer method

The *merging*, cf. Fig. 4, of two derived support collections $\mathcal{SN}_i^r$ over I_i constructs the set disjunctions $SN^r(\mathcal{MS}, C_1) \vee SN^r(\mathcal{MS}, C_2)$ for all support pairs $(C_i, SN^r(\mathcal{MS}, C_i)) \in \mathcal{SN}_i^r$, $i = 1, 2$, removes duplicates (*prune*), and yields

$$SN^r(\mathcal{MS}, C_1 \wedge C_2) \;=\; can(\; prune(\; SN^r(\mathcal{MS}, C_1) \vee SN^r(\mathcal{MS}, C_2)\;) \setminus_s \mathcal{MS}\,).$$

The derived support collection $\mathcal{SN}^r$ contains the non–trivial pairs $(C, SN^r(C))$ for conjunctions C over $I = I_1 \cup I_2$. The minimal conjunctions $C_1 \wedge C_2$, where the derived set $SN^r(\mathcal{MS}, C_1 \wedge C_2)$ is empty, are returned.

Procedure MERGE($\mathcal{MS}, \mathcal{SN}_1^r, \mathcal{SN}_2^r, \mathcal{SN}^r, \mathcal{E}_1, \mathcal{E}_2, \mathcal{E}$);

{ set disjunctions }
for each $(C_1, SN^r(\mathcal{MS}, C_1)) \in \mathcal{SN}_1^r$ **and** $(C_2, SN^r(\mathcal{MS}, C_2)) \in \mathcal{SN}_2^r$
  $S_1 := SN^r(\mathcal{MS}, C_1) \vee SN^r(\mathcal{MS}, C_2)$;
  $S_2 := prune(S_1)$; $S_3 := S_2 \setminus_s \mathcal{MS}$;
  $SN^r(\mathcal{MS}, C_1 \wedge C_2) := can(S_3)$;

{ result assignments}
$\mathcal{SN}^r := \{\, (C_1 \wedge C_2, SN^r(\mathcal{MS}, C_1 \wedge C_2)) \mid SN^r(\mathcal{MS}, C_1 \wedge C_2) \neq \emptyset \,\}$;
$\mathcal{E}_3 := can(\; \{\, C_1 \wedge C_2 \mid SN^r(\mathcal{MS}, C_1 \wedge C_2) = \emptyset \,\}\;)$;
$\mathcal{E} := \mathcal{E}_1 \cup \mathcal{E}_2 \cup \mathcal{E}_3$

Fig. 4. Merging of SN^r–sets and $\mathcal{EGCWA}$–sets

An *optimized implementation* of MERGE uses the following techniques for the derivation of $SN^r(\mathcal{MS}, C_1 \wedge C_2)$ from $SN^r(\mathcal{MS}, C_i)$, $i = 1, 2$. Firstly, the *reduction* of $D \subseteq DHB_P$ w.r.t. $C \in CHB_P$ removes all C' which contain an atom of C: $reduce(D, C) \;=\; \{\, C' \in D \mid$ no atom of C occurs in $C'\,\}$. Applied to $S_1 = reduce(SN^r(\mathcal{MS}, C_1), C_2)$ and $S_2 = reduce(SN^r(\mathcal{MS}, C_2), C_1)$ we have

$$SN^r(\mathcal{MS}, C_1 \wedge C_2) \;=\; can(\; prune(\; S_1 \vee S_2\;) \setminus_s \mathcal{MS}\,).$$

Secondly, from $can(S_1 \vee S_2) = can(\; ((S_1 \setminus_s S) \vee (S_2 \setminus_s S)) \cup S\;)$, where $S = can(exp(S_1) \cap exp(S_2))$, and $can((S_1 \vee S_2) \setminus_s \mathcal{MS}) = can(S_1 \vee S_2) \setminus_s \mathcal{MS}$ we get

$$SN^r(\mathcal{MS}, C_1 \wedge C_2) \;=\; can(\; prune(\; ((S_1 \setminus_s S) \vee (S_2 \setminus_s S)) \cup S\;) \setminus_s \mathcal{MS}\,).$$

Experiments with Δ–ITERATION–SN, e.g. for the transitive closure program with minimal model states of about 150 disjunctive facts, cf. Table 2, have revealed, that the reduction operation (r) significantly reduces the average number of disjunctive clauses in the (initial) reduced support–for–negation sets and thus reduces the evaluation time. The canonization operation (c) also significantly reduces the average size of the reduced support–for–negation sets, but surprisingly increases the overall computation time. Thus, the version (r,–) using only the reduce operation is faster than the one (r,c) with reduce and can, which in

	reduce	∨	prune	$\setminus_s$	can	total
(r,–)	1.55	4.50	2.54	12.10	--	25.09
(r,c)	1.20	2.87	1.92	7.42	11.84	29.05
(–,–)	--	7.49	4.58	16.78	--	33.03

	initial	reduce	∨	prune	$\setminus_s$	can
(r,–)	57.10	33.53	33.11	24.53	16.39	16.39
(r,c)	29.00	16.99	16.68	15.32	9.69	4.62
(–,–)	57.10	57.10	56.66	42.37	16.39	16.39

Table 2. Time in seconds for Δ–ITERATION–SN and average number of clauses in reduced support–for–negation sets

turn is faster than the one (–,–) with none of them. Note that there is always some additional time (included in total) spend with scheduling operations.

We are also investigating the computation of $can(\mathcal{EGCWA}_P)$ from the set $\mathcal{MM}_P$ of all minimal models based on Definition 5. For the tested examples, however, this derivation technique for $\mathcal{EGCWA}_P$ was slower than Δ–ITERATION–SN, even when optimized with model trees.

5.2 Update Formulas for Support–for–Negation Sets

During the various derivation steps in the computation of the generalized disjunctive well–founded semantics of a disjunctive normal logic program a sequence of monotonically growing state pairs $S =< T, F >$ is generated by alternating applications of the introduced operator $\mathcal{S}^{\mathcal{E}}$ and another operator $\mathcal{S}^{\mathcal{D}}$ given in [16]. It can be shown, that for the disjunctive programs $P' = Dis(P, S) \cup T$ the minimal model states $\mathcal{MS}_{P'}$ are monotonically increasing. Thus, the $\mathcal{S}^{\mathcal{E}}$–steps require the repeated computation of the $\mathcal{EGCWA}_{P'}$ w.r.t. monotonically growing model states $\mathcal{MS}_{P'}$. Instead of computing the support–for–negation sets of an enlarged minimal model state from the scratch, we incrementally use the support–for–negation sets of the smaller minimal model state.

The following theorem gives update formulas for deriving the reduced support-for–negation sets of a the union of two disjunctive Herbrand states from the separate reduced support–for–negation sets of the two disjunctive Herbrand states.

Theorem 12. *Given a disjunctive logic program P, Herbrand states D and ΔD, an atom $A \in HB_P$ and conjunctions $C_1, C_2 \in CHB_P$. For $\Delta SN^r(D, \Delta D, C) = SN^r(D \cup \Delta D, C) \setminus_s SN^r(D, C)$ we get:*

$$\begin{aligned} SN^r(D \cup \Delta D, A) &= can(\ (SN^r(D, A) \cup SN^r(\Delta D, A)) \setminus_s (D \cup \Delta D)\ ), \\ SN^r(D \cup \Delta D, C_1 \wedge C_2) &= (\ can(\ \Delta SN^r(D, \Delta D, C_1) \vee \Delta SN^r(D, \Delta D, C_2)\ ) \\ &\qquad \cup SN^r(D, C_1 \wedge C_2)\ )\ \ \setminus_s (\ D \cup \Delta D\ ), \end{aligned}$$

5.3 The Disjunctive Transformation $Dis(P, S)$

The ground disjunctive transformation $Dis(P,S)$ of a disjunctive normal logic program P w.r.t. a state pair $S =<T, F>$ usually is a large – in the presence of variables and function symbols infinite – logic program, which is computationally intractable. Fortunately, we can replace the disjunctive consequence operator $\mathcal{T}^S_{Dis(P,S)}$ by the following, equivalent consequence operator $\mathcal{T}^S_{P,S}$ defined in terms of S and the smaller, non-ground disjunctive transformation $Dis(P)$.

Definition 13. Given a disjunctive normal logic program P and a state pair $S =<T, F>$. The *consequence operator* $\mathcal{T}^S_{P,S} : 2^{DHB_P} \to 2^{DHB_P}$ of P w.r.t. S maps Herbrand states to Herbrand states:

$$\begin{aligned}\mathcal{T}^S_{P,S}(D) = \{\, C \in DHB_P \mid\ & A_1 \vee \ldots \vee A_k \;\text{:-}\; B_1, \ldots, B_n \in Ground(Dis(P)),\\ & \{\, B_1 \vee C_1, \ldots, B_n \vee C_n \,\} \subseteq can(D \cup (T \cap HB_P)),\\ & A_1 \vee \ldots \vee A_k \notin exp(T),\ \ B_1 \wedge \ldots \wedge B_n \notin exp(F),\\ & \{\, A_1, \ldots, A_k \,\} \setminus F = \{\, A_{i_1}, \ldots, A_{i_l} \,\} \neq \emptyset,\\ & C \text{ is the smallest factor of } A_{i_1} \vee \ldots \vee A_{i_l} \vee C_1 \vee \ldots \vee C_n \,\}.\end{aligned}$$

Theorem 14. *Given a disjunctive normal logic program P and a state pair $S =<T, F>$. Then $\mathcal{T}^S_{Dis(P,S)} \uparrow \omega = \mathcal{T}^S_{P,S} \uparrow \omega$.*

6 Summary and Outlook

We have developed a system called DisLog for the efficient evaluation of disjunctive normal logic programs under the generalized disjunctive well-founded semantics. It is implemented as a meta-interpreter in Prolog.

One basic concept for computing the generalized disjunctive well-founded semantics of a disjunctive, normal logic programs P is the repeated application of the operator $\mathcal{S}^{\mathcal{E}}$ computing the minimal model state and the extended generalized closed world assumption w.r.t. certain disjunctive transformations of P. The basic operators for computing minimal model states are the disjunctive consequence operator $\mathcal{T}^S_P$, the Δ-operator $\setminus_s$ with subsumption and the canonization operator *can* for Herbrand states. Tree-based versions of these operators are applied in a Δ-iteration for computing the minimal model state $\mathcal{MS}_P$ and the extended generalized closed world assumption $\mathcal{EGCWA}_P$ of a disjunctive logic program P. The support-for-negation sets for conjunctive facts can be derived efficiently by an iteration from $\mathcal{MS}_P$.

The operator $\mathcal{S}^{\mathcal{D}}$ for state pairs given in [16], which is based on a positive and a negative consequence operator $\mathcal{T}^D_S$ and $\mathcal{F}^D_S$ is implemented efficiently in DisLog as well. The least fixpoint of the composite operator $\mathcal{S}^{\mathcal{ED}} = \mathcal{S}^{\mathcal{E}} \circ \mathcal{S}^{\mathcal{D}}$ for state pairs is the generalized disjunctive well-founded state pair.

Acknowledgment

The author would like to thank his colleague Helmut Thöne for the many useful comments he has provided.

References

[1] *A. Abdelmoty, M. Williams, N. Paton:* Deduction and Deductive Databases for Geographic Data Handling, Proc. Intl. Symposium on Advances in Spatial Databases 1993 (SSD'93), pp. 443-464.

[2] *C. Baral, J. Lobo, J. Minker:* Generalized Well-Founded Semantics for Logic Programs, Proc. Intl. Conf. on Automated Deduction 1989, pp. 102-116.

[3] *F. Bancilhon, R. Ramakrishnan:* An Amateur's Introduction to Recursive Query Processing Strategies, Proc. ACM SIGMOD 1986, pp. 16-52.

[4] *S. Ceri, G. Gottlob, L. Tanca:* Logic Programming and Databases, Springer, 1990.

[5] *W. Chen, D.S. Warren:* A Goal-Oriented Approach to Computing Well-Founded Semantics, Proc. Joint Intl. Conf. and Symp. on Logic Prog. 1992, pp. 589-603.

[6] *W. Chen, D.S. Warren:* Query Evaluation under the Well-Founded Semantics, Proc. ACM PODS 1993.

[7] *S.K. Das:* Deductive Databases and Logic Programming, Addison-Wesley, 1992.

[8] *J. Dix:* Classifying Semantics of Disjunctive Logic Programs, Proc. Joint. Intl. Conf. and Symp. on Logic Programming 1992, pp. 798-812.

[9] *U. Fuhrbach:* Computing Answers for Disjunctive Logic Programs, Proc. ILPS Workshop on Disjunctive Logic Programs 1991.

[10] *J.A. Fernández, J. Minker:* Theory and Algorithms for Disjunctive Deductive Databases, Programmirovanie J. 1993, Academy of Sciences of Russia.

[11] *M. Fitting:* The Family of Stable Models, Journal of Logic Programming, vol. 17(3,4), 1993, pp. 197-225.

[12] *M. Gelfond, V. Lifschitz:* The Stable Model Semantics for Logic Programming, Proc. Intl. Conf. and Symp. on Logic Programming 1988, pp. 1070-1080.

[13] *U. Güntzer, W. Kießling, R. Bayer:* On the Evaluation of Recursion in (Deductive) Database Systems by Efficient Differential Fixpoint Iteration, Proc. Intl. Conf. on Data Engineering 1987, pp. 120-129.

[14] *G. Köstler, W. Kießling, H. Thöne, U. Güntzer:* The Differential Fixpoint Operator with Subsumption, Proc. Intl. Conf. DOOD 1993, pp. 35-48.

[15] *J.W. Lloyd:* Foundations of Logic Programming, Springer, second edition, 1987.

[16] *J. Lobo, J. Minker, A. Rajasekar:* Foundations of Disjunctive Logic Programming, MIT Press, 1992.

[17] *J. Pearl:* Probabilistic Reasoning in Intelligent Systems: Networks of Plausible Inference, Morgan Kaufman, 1988.

[18] *T.C. Przymusinski:* Stationary Semantics for Disjunctive Logic Programs and Deductive Databases, Proc. North-American Conf. of Logic Prog. 1990, pp. 42-59.

[19] *D. Seipel, H. Argenton:* Evaluation Techniques for Disjunctive Logic Programs, Proc. Symposium on Operations Research 1993.

[20] *D. Seipel:* Tree-Based Fixpoint Iteration for Disjunctive Logic Programs, Proc. Workshop on Logic Prog. with Incomplete Inf., Intl. Symp. on Logic Prog. 1993.

[21] *D. Seipel, H. Thöne:* An Application of Disjunctive Logic Programming with Incomplete Information, Proc. Intl. Conf. on Expert Syst. for Development 1994.

[22] *J.D. Ullman:* Principles of Database and Knowledge-Base Systems, Volume I,II, Computer Science Press, 1988/89.

[23] *A. Van Gelder, K.A. Ross, J.S. Schlipf:* The Well-Founded Semantics for General Logic Programs, JACM, vol. 38(3), 1991, pp. 620-650.

Multi-SLD Resolution

Donald A. Smith[1] and Timothy J. Hickey[2]

[1] Department of Computer Science, University of Waikato, Hamilton, New Zealand
Email: dsmith@cs.waikato.ac.nz, *Fax:* (07) 838-4155
[2] Department of Computer Science, Brandeis University, Waltham, MA 02254,
Email: tim@cs.brandeis.edu, *Fax:* (617) 736-2741

Abstract. Multi-SLD resolution is a variant of SLD resolution based on a simple idea: *Let the allowed constraints be closed under disjunction, and provide a mechanism for collecting solutions to a goal and turning the solutions into a disjunctive constraint.* This idea leads to an operational model of logic programming, called *data or-parallelism,* in which multiple constraint environments partially replace backtracking as the operational embodiment of disjunction. The model has a natural implementation on data-parallel computers since each disjunct of a disjunctive constraint can be handled by a single (virtual) processor. In this paper, we

- formalize the notions of multi-SLD resolution, multi-derivation, multi-SLD tree, and environment tree;
- prove the soundness and completeness of multi-SLD resolution; and
- describe and justify several useful optimization techniques based on the form of constraints in a multi-derivation: the distinction between engine and multi variables, templates, and sharing of bindings in the environment tree.

Together these results provide the foundations for a new operational semantics of disjunction in logic programming.

1 Introduction

We describe a resolution rule, multi-SLD resolution, that has the novel property of yielding a natural, data parallel implementation of or-parallelism. We give a formal definition of multi-SLD resolution and the related concepts of multi-derivation and multi-SLD tree. We then go on to prove the soundness and completeness of multi-SLD and to examine some properties of the set of substitutions comprising the constraint component of the state of a multi-derivation. On this basis, we devise several useful optimizations.

Previous papers [23] [21] informally introduced multi-SLD resolution and the Prolog dialect MultiLog: described a machine architecture (the Multi-WAM) for executing MultiLog programs; and presented benchmark results for sequential and parallel implementations of the language. Even on a uniprocessor computer, multi-SLD was shown to be faster than SLD for many (most?) combinatorial search problems. For example, the Instant Insanity puzzle from [29] runs about 3 times faster on uniprocessor MultiLog than on uniprocessor Prolog, using comparable WAM technology. For a contrived program that checks bits strings for palindromicity, uniprocessor MultiLog is over 88 times faster than uniprocessor

Prolog. The reason for this speedup is explained briefly below and in more detail in a companion paper [24], where a predictive model is given that accounts for observed speedups to within a constant factor. A second companion paper, [25], presents and analyzes the complexity of several representation schemes for managing substitutions in MultiLog. The first author's dissertation, [27], discusses all of these issues in more detail.

Informally, multi-SLD resolution can be described as follows. The abstract machine state of a multi-SLD interpreter consists of two components: a list of goals, and a disjunction ((multi)set) of substitutions.[3] There are two sorts of multi-SLD resolution steps. In a normal multi-SLD resolution step, some atom is selected from the goal list and resolved against some clause in the program; since there are multiple substitutions in the constraint component, unification of the atom with the head of the clause occurs independently in the various substitutions. If any substitutions survive the resolution step, then the surviving substitutions, extended with the bindings resulting from head unification, become the constraint component of the next abstract machine state, whose goal list is found by replacing the selected atom with the body of the clause.

In a **disj** multi-SLD resolution step, a subcomputation is begun on the selected atom (which in practice is annotated by the unary control operator **disj**) and some *finite*, nonempty subset of the solutions to the selected atom is collected and installed as the new constraint component. The new goal component consists of the previous goal list minus the selected atom. If control backtracks into the **disj** goal, then another non-empty, finite subset of solutions is collected and installed, and so on.

The canonical example that illustrates multi-SLD resolution and the resulting data or-parallelism is the query[4]

```
| ?- generate(X),test(X).
```

To solve this query, standard Prolog enumerates the solutions to **generate/1** one by one via backtracking and tests each solution separately with **test/1**. A control or-parallel implementation [1] [8] starts up multiple Prolog search engines to explore subparts of the SLD tree in parallel. In contrast, if we prefix the goal **generate(X)** with the operator **disj**, then an implementation based on multi-SLD resolution collects subsets of the solutions to **generate/1** and creates a set of binding environments which are tested en mass (in parallel) by **test/1**. As a result, **test/1** is executed once per subset rather than once per solution, and fewer instructions are executed overall.

Moreover, powerful optimizations are available for data or-parallel Prolog that are not available for control or-parallel Prolog due to the latter's multiple threads of control. With multi-SLD resolution, the various substitutions in the constraint component of the abstract machine state share much structure, and the unifications in the various substitutions are not, after all, independent. The

[3] More generally and from the viewpoint of CLP, the second component consists of a disjunction of allowed constraints.

[4] In general, multiple variables can get bound by a **disj** goal.

shared, common component of computation (in `test/1`) can 'factored out' so that computations are performed (and structures are built on the heap) only once per subset of solutions.

The plan of the present paper is as follows. Section 2 formally defines multi-SLD resolution and the related concepts of multi-derivation and multi-SLD tree. Section 3 introduces the notion of environment tree, which describes the shared structure of substitutions resulting from multi-derivations; it then uncovers an additional type of sharing among substitutions. Section 4 proves the soundness and completeness of multi-SLD resolution and compares the relative completeness of depth-first SLD and multi-SLD interpreters. Section 5 presents a formal justification of two implementation techniques: the distinction between engine (sequential) and multi (parallel) variables, and templates. The last section considers related and future work.

2 Multi-SLD Resolution

In this section we make precise the operational semantics of MultiLog by formalizing the notions of multi-SLD resolution, multi-derivation, and multi-SLD tree. The reader interested mainly in the optimizations may wish to skip to Section 3. We assume the standard definitions and notations of (constraint) logic programming [13] [9].

In an abstract operational model of a CLP language, the state of a derivation is a pair $G \diamond C$, where G (the goal component) is a list of user atoms, C (the constraint component) is an allowed constraint and $\diamond$ is a synonym for $\wedge$. Starting from an initial state whose goal component is the query and whose constraint component is the empty constraint *true*, the resolution rule tells how to progress non-deterministically to the next state. In standard CLP languages this rule is just resolution, and a sequence of states progressing according to the resolution rule is called a (unary) derivation.

In Multi-SLD the constraint component is a disjunction. This fact by itself is not foreign to the CLP framework, in which the allowed constraints can be any logical formula. What is new, though, is the mechanism for creating disjunctive constraints, as well as the implementation techniques available and the style of programming that results. We describe multi-SLD resolution for the special case where the Herbrand Universe is the domain of computation; the extension to other constraint domains is straightforward.

In order for a derivation to continue from a state $G \diamond C$ it is necessary for C to be solvable. That is, the existential closure of C must evaluate to *true* in the theory of the constraint domain. Logically, when C is a disjunction, it is sufficient for just one disjunct to be solvable, and we have investigated [27] the effects of lazily evaluating the disjunctive constraints. But here we assume that unsolvable disjuncts are deleted from the constraint component, so that at each step the constraint component consists of a disjunction of solvable formulas. To this end, let S be a function which, applied to a constraint C, reduces C to a simplified form. In MultiLog, S is Herbrand's solved form algorithm (unification) applied to each disjunct, with *false* disjuncts deleted (subsumed disjuncts could also be removed). The result is a DNF formula: a disjunction of solved form sets of equations.

Let $\Box$ be the empty goal. Assume some fixed computation rule for selecting atoms to participate in resolution steps. Define a *multi-derivation* from query G_0 and program P to be a (finite or infinite) sequence of states $S_0, S_1, \ldots$, where $S_0 \equiv (G_0 \diamond true)$ and for $i > 0$, S_{i-1} derives S_i, written $S_{i-1} \Longrightarrow S_i$, by the multi-resolution rule of Figure 1. Let $\Longrightarrow^*$ be the reflexive transitive closure of $\Longrightarrow$. If a multi-derivation is finite and ends in a state with an empty goal component and with a non-*false* constraint C, then we write $S_0 \Longrightarrow^* (\Box \diamond C)$.

The multi-resolution rule is divided into two cases, depending on whether the selected atom is a *normal* user atom (e.g., `p(f(X))`), or a `disj` goal (e.g., `disj q(Y,g(X,Y))`). In practice, the interpreter or compiler could decide which goals should be labeled with `disj` operators. In this sense, the choice between the two multi-resolution rules is arbitrary, and each time an atom is selected a new decision could be made which rule to use.

---

1. (normal multi-resolution rule) Suppose the current state is $A_1, \ldots, A_n \diamond (E_1 \vee \ldots \vee E_m)$; the selected atom, A_i, is a normal user atom; $H \leftarrow B_1, \ldots, B_k$ is a new renaming of a clause in P; and

$$C \equiv \bigvee_{1 \leq j \leq m} (E_j \wedge (A_i = H))$$

with $S(C) \not\equiv false$. Then

$$A_1, \ldots, A_n \diamond (E_1 \vee \ldots \vee E_m)$$
$$\Longrightarrow$$
$$A_1, \ldots, A_{i-1}, B_1, \ldots, B_k, A_{i+1}, \ldots, A_n \diamond S(C)\ .$$

This rule is just the standard resolution rule for CLP languages explicitly specialized to the case where the constraint component is a disjunction and where the domain of computation is the Herbrand Universe.

2. (`disj` multi-resolution rule) Suppose the current state is $A_1, \ldots, A_n \diamond C$; the selected atom A_i is a disjunctive goal (`disj` A); $F \subseteq_{finite} \{C^{Sol} | (A \diamond C) \Longrightarrow^* (\Box \diamond C^{Sol})\}$; and $F \neq \emptyset$. Then

$$A_1, \ldots, A_n \diamond C$$
$$\Longrightarrow$$
$$A_1, \ldots, A_{i-1}, A_{i+1}, \ldots, A_n \diamond \bigvee_{C^{Sol} \in F} C^{Sol}\ .$$

In words, a nonempty, finite subset F of the solutions to $A \diamond C$ is obtained. The new state has a goal component consisting of the remaining goals and a constraint component equal to the disjunction of constraints in F.

Fig. 1. Multi-SLD Resolution

The nondeterminism in the choice of clauses and in the choice of solutions for `disj` goals is essential: breadth-first search (or some equivalent search strategy such as iterative deepening) is in general necessary to guarantee completeness. For a goal `disj` A, breadth-first search requires concurrent consideration of subsets of solutions to A.

By *answer* we mean a constraint (disjunction of substitutions) returned by a successful multi-derivation. By *solution* we mean a substitution returned as a disjunct in some answer. For 8 queens, MultiLog and Prolog both return 92 solutions. But Prolog returns 92 answers (via backtracking), while MultiLog returns just one answer (assuming all solutions are returned at once to each `disj` goal).

2.1 Multi-SLD Tree

An SLD tree describes the search space of an SLD interpreter with a given selection function for a program P and query Q [13]. For Multi-SLD resolution the corresponding structure is the *multi-SLD tree.*

Multi-SLD trees are parameterized by a selection function on atoms in a goal list and by a partition function Φ on the solutions to `disj` goals. Each node is labeled by a pair consisting of a goal list and a set of substitutions. In addition, `disj` nodes (defined below) are labeled, recursively, with multi-SLD trees. The root is labeled by the query goal and a set consisting of an empty substitution. Each arc is labeled, in a manner to made precise below, by a set of substitutions representing the bindings resulting from that multi-SLD resolution step. The set of substitutions labeling each node is obtained by composition of substitutions on arcs along the path from the root.

There are two kinds of nodes corresponding to the two multi-resolution cases above. For *normal nodes*, the selected atom is not annotated with `disj`; normal nodes have one child for each multi-resolvent of the selected user atom. For `disj` nodes, the selected atom is annotated with `disj`; `disj` nodes have a finite or infinite number of child nodes, depending on whether the argument goal has a finite number of solutions or an infinite number of solutions, respectively. Each leaf is marked either as a *success node* (labeled by the empty goal together with an answer), as a *failure node* (if the node is a normal node with no resolving clauses, or the node is a `disj` node with no solutions and no infinite multi-derivations), or as a *loop node* (in which case it is a `disj` node for a goal that has no solution and that has infinite multi-derivations).

A branch in a multi-SLD tree can be identified with a multi-derivation.

Suppose normal node n is labeled with goal list $A_1, \ldots, A_{i-1}, A_i, A_{i+1}, \ldots, A_n$ and set of substitutions $\theta_1, \ldots, \theta_k$; A_i is the selected atom; and $H \leftarrow B_1, \ldots, B_m$ is a (new renaming of a) clause in P such that H can be unified with $A\theta_j$ for some j. Then there is a child node c of n labeled with $A_1, \ldots, A_{i-1}, B_1, \ldots, B_m, A_{i+1}, \ldots, A_n$ and the set of all substitutions θ' such that for some $j \in \{1, \ldots, k\}$ $A_i\theta_j = H$ has mgu σ_j and $\theta' = \theta_j\sigma_j$. The arc from n to c is labeled with the set of mgus σ_j. Notice that there are as many child nodes as there are clauses that multi-resolve with the selected atom given the input substitutions $\theta_1, \ldots, \theta_k$.

Suppose **disj** node n is labeled with goal list G and nonempty set of substitutions $S' = \{\theta_1, \ldots, \theta_k\}$; and **disj** A is the selected atom. Let T be a multi-SLD tree with root node labeled with goal list A and substitutions S'; and let S be the possibly infinite, possibly empty set of solutions appearing at success nodes of T. Finally, let $S_1, S_2, \ldots$ be some partition of S, dependent on the given partition function Φ, such that each S_i is non-empty and finite. Then n is labeled with the multi-SLD tree T, and n has child nodes $c_1, \ldots$, each labeled with goal $G-$(**disj** A) and sets of substitutions $S_1, S_2, \ldots$, respectively. The arc from n to child node c_i is labeled with $\{\sigma | \exists \phi \in S_i \exists j \in \{1, \ldots, k\} \,.\, \phi = \theta_j \sigma\}$. That is, the arc is labeled with the differential substitutions σ that represent the bindings resulting from goal A, one substitution for each solution in the set S_i at c_i.

3 Two Types of Sharing

In this section we uncover some facts about the logical form of environments in a multi-derivation. We expose two types of sharing among environments, corresponding to the two multi-resolution rules. These facts will be used both in proving soundness and completeness and in devising efficient implementations of multi-SLD resolution.

3.1 Sharing from disj Multi-resolution Steps: Environment Trees

After a multi-resolution step, each of the substitutions in the constraint component extends some unique input substitution from before the step. Moreover, for **disj** multi-resolution steps, any given input substitution can have multiple output substitutions extending it; if the argument goal succeeds m times then each input substitution can have up to m child substitutions.

As multiple **disj** goals are encountered, execution results in an implicit tree of substitutions, organized according to the parent-child relationship. Each surviving disjunct in the constraint component extends some *ancestor* disjunct in each previous constraint component of the multi-derivation. These ideas are formalized in the notion of *environment tree*, which we present with an example. (See [27] for the precise, straightforward definition.) Figure 2 shows the tree of environments resulting from execution of the following program and query. We assume all solutions are obtained for each **disj** goal. (The atoms **disj p(X)**, etc. on the right are for documentation only and are not part of the environment tree.)

```
| ?-  disj p(X),disj q(X,Y),r(Y),disj s(Z).
p(a). p(b). p(c).        q(a,1). q(a,2).  q(c,4). q(c,6).
r(Y):- Y<6.              s(a). s(b).
```

The structure of the environment tree motivates the implementation technique in which environments are represented in the form of a tree with shared ancestor bindings. The alternative representation in which each environment is a vector, requires copying input environments during the collection of solutions to **disj** goals.In [24] [27] we analyze the time and space complexity of these two representation schemes under various assumptions. In summary, the

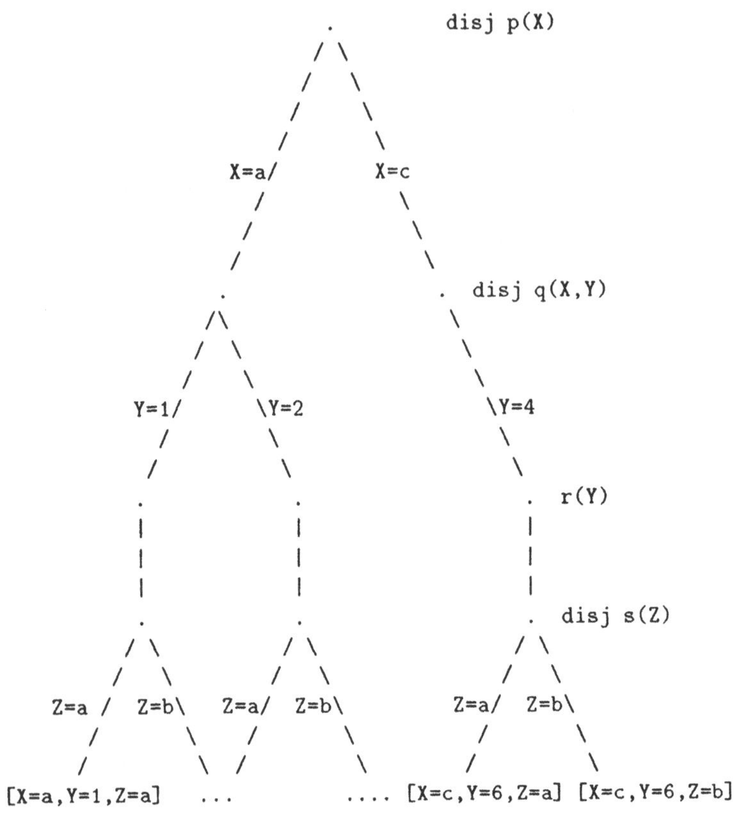

Fig. 2. Environment Tree

analyses suggest that the environment tree model should be competitive with the copy-vector model on both sequential and parallel computers, despite the non-constant cost of dereferencing. This surprising result depends on the use of *top-down dereferencing* in the environment tree, whereby bindings are passed down from the root to the leaf processors. Since a (balanced) tree with n leaves has $O(n)$ nodes, total dereferencing time will be $O(n)$, versus $O(n \log n)$ using bottom-up dereferencing. Furthermore, unification can often fail or succeed at once in whole subtrees. However, the performance of the environment tree model will be highly dependent on the data, the 'constants' will higher, and the implementation will likely be more complex.

3.2 Sharing from Normal Multi-resolution Steps

Consider that a multi-SLD derivation consists of a sequence of normal multi-resolution steps interspersed with (occasional) `disj` multi-resolution steps. Each surviving disjunct after a normal step is consistent with the head unification associated with the step. And each disjunct contains, where appropriate, bindings resulting from the head unification associated with the step. If the head of the clause contains `[H|T]` in some argument position, then all disjuncts with `[]` in that position fail the unification. And any disjuncts with a variable in the argument position are extended with a binding of that variable to `[H|T]`.

Consequently, at any step of a multi-derivation, the various disjuncts of the constraint component share equations resulting from normal multi-resolution steps appearing in the multi-derivation up to that point. That is, after a normal multi-resolution step involving unification $A_i = H$, for each subsequent constraint component $E_1 \vee \ldots\ldots \vee E_n$, it holds that for each j, $E_j \rightarrow (A_i = H)$.

The significance of this fact is that disjuncts appearing together in a constraint component share many of the same bindings; only bindings dependent on **disj** goals can differ between substitutions appearing together in the constraint component. This fact is the basis for the distinction between 'engine' (sequential) and 'multi' (parallel) variables of Section 5.1.

4 Soundness and Completeness

Logically, the **disj** operator is a no-op and its only effect is as a control annotation that selects constraint processing (the **disj** multi-resolution steps of Section 2) rather than backtracking (the normal multi-resolution step) for solving the argument goal. Our task here is to show that the operational semantics of MultiLog respects the logical semantics: that the same solutions are returned by a (fair) MultiLog interpreter as by a (fair) Prolog interpreter. We claim:

Theorem 1. *Multi-SLD resolution determines the same set of solutions as SLD resolution.*

And hence the former retains the soundness and completeness of the latter [13].

The proof, which seems almost unnecessary relies on showing that for any solution returned as a disjunct in some multi-derivation using program P and query Q, there is an identical solution returned by a unary-derivation using P' and Q', and vice versa, where P' (Q') is P (Q) with all **disj** operators removed.

Consider a multi-derivation $(G_0 \diamond C_0), (G_1 \diamond C_1), \ldots, (\Box \diamond C_n)$, where C^{Sol} appears as a disjunct in C_n. We convert the multi-derivation of answer C_n using program P and query Q into a unary derivation of C^{sol} using program P' and query Q'. Perform the following two steps in order.

1. **Expand**. If the derivation contains a **disj** transition, choose the topmost such transition

   $$A_1, \ldots, A_{i-1}, \texttt{disj}\ A, A_{i+1}, \ldots, A_n \diamond C \Longrightarrow A_1, \ldots, A_{i-1}, A_{i+1}, \ldots, A_n \diamond C'$$

   Observe that C' was obtained by disjoining some finite subset of the answers to $A \diamond C$. Each such answer was the constraint component (itself a disjunction) at the end of some successful multi-derivation from $A \diamond C$. Also observe that there is a unique constraint component C^{ans} in C' which

is an ancestor[5] of C^{sol}. Insert between the two states of the derivation the unique multi-derivation that derived C^{ans} (adding the unresolved goals $A_1, \ldots, A_{i-1}, A_{i+1}, \ldots, A_n$ to each goal component). Finally, delete the **disj** operator before A.
Repeat this step until the derivation contains no disj transition.

2. **Delete.** In each C_i, delete any disjunct which is not an ancestor of C^{Sol}.

New disjunctive transitions may be inserted in the expansion step but because the original multi-derivation for G_i was finite, the step cannot be repeated infinitely often. Each constraint component consists of a single disjunct, the derivation contains no disj operators, and each transition is a normal resolution step. So, the derivation is unary from program P' and query Q'. This yields the proof of soundness.

To prove completeness, we need to show that given any successful SLD derivation using a Prolog program P' and query Q' there is a corresponding successful multi-SLD derivation for MultiLog program P and and Q where arbitrary goals are prefixed by disj. Note that in the definition for multi-SLD resolution we require that *some* finite subset of the solutions to a disj goal be collected, but which finite subset is non-deterministic. Clearly, by letting the finite subset be the singleton solution used in the unary derivation, we can construct a corresponding multi-derivation.

Q.E.D.

The completeness result makes essential use of non-determinism and hence a complete implementation requires some sort of breadth-first search. But in fact, the use of multiple environments amounts to a partial breadth-first exploration of the search tree, and as a result it can lead to increased completeness of depth-first interpreters. For a simple example of increased completeness, consider:

```
q(0). q(1). r. r:- loop. loop:- loop.
| ?- disj q(X),r.
```

Prolog would return just X=0 and then loop. But, assuming that both solutions to q/1 are collected, MultiLog returns the disjunctive answer X=0 or X=1 and then loops. However, for the following similar example, the tables are turned: MultiLog loops without returning any answers (since the first clause of r/1 succeeds on the disjunct X=1). But Prolog returns X=0 and then loops.

```
q(0). q(1). r(1):- loop. r(0). loop:- loop.
| ?- disj q(X),r(X).
```

5 Justification of Two Optimization Techniques

At each step of a multi-SLD derivation, the constraint component consists of a disjunction (set) of substitutions. A naive implementation of multi-SLD resolution would store and manipulate these substitutions totally independently, as suggested by the abstract definitions. Yet in general, the various substitutions

[5] See Section 3.1 for the notion of ancestor. Here we assume that each disjunct is its own ancestor.

share much structure. Section 3.1 has already introduced an optimization based on the sharing that results from `disj` goals when multiple output substitutions extend a given input substitution. In this section we justify two additional optimization techniques that are based on the form of the constraints resulting from multi-SLD resolution. The optimizations are available when a variable is bound to (nearly) the same term in all substitutions of the constraint component; there are several nonobvious but common cases in which such shared bindings occur.

5.1 The Distinction Between Engine and Multi Variables

It is common for a variable to be bound to the same value in each substitution of the constraint component. For efficiency's sake, it is beneficial to store the bindings of such variables once, independently of the bindings of those variables whose values vary among substitutions.

Accordingly, our implementation represents the abstract constraint component C in the concrete form $\alpha \wedge \beta$, where α is a conjunction (a substitution) representing the shared, common bindings, and β is a disjunction representing the bindings that differ among substitutions. Variables bound in α are called *engine* (sequential) variables; variables bound in β are called *multi* (parallel) variables [23], [27]. Unifications involving engine variables are faster than unifications involving multi variables, since the disjuncts in β need not play a role.

There are two fundamental ways in which a variable can come to be bound to the same term in each environment. The two ways correspond to the two multi-resolution rules: normal and `disj`. To understand this, we first introduce the concepts of `disj`-dependent and `disj`-independent variables.

At any given step of a multi-derivation, some variables — called the **`disj`-dependent variables** — have been *bound or created* during unifications associated with previous `disj` multi-resolution steps. The remaining variables — the **`disj`-independent variables** — have been created[6] and possibly bound during unifications associated with normal steps (outside any `disj` goals). A `disj`-independent variable becomes a `disj`-dependent variable if it gets bound during a `disj` multi-resolution step; this happens if the variable is passed in as part of an argument to the `disj` goal and if the variable then gets bound during execution of the goal.

The most obvious way for a variable to be bound to the same term in different substitutions is for it to be a `disj`-dependent variable that has the same value in different solutions to a `disj` goal. Thus, with the following program and query

```
p(a,1). p(a,2).
| ?- disj p(X,Y).
```

[6] Variables appearing in the query start out as `disj`-independent variables. It is possible for unbound variables to take up no storage at all — for example, if substitutions are represented by association lists. But in the common case when variables are represented by cells in memory, `disj`-independent variables are associated with cells in α, rather than in β.

disj-dependent variable X gets bound to a in both solutions to the disj goal. In the optimization called *constraint lifting* [26], bindings common to the solutions to a disj goal can be 'lifted' into α. Since in general there can be many solutions to a disj goal, the cost of constraint lifting can be quite high. Constraint lifting (during indexing) is optional in our current implementation, and disj-dependent variables are by default multi variables, which are stored in β.

The second way in which a variable can come to be bound to the same term in all substitutions of the constraint component is perhaps less obvious but was suggested in Section 3.2. A disj-independent variable that gets bound outside any disj goals is, by necessity, bound to the same term in different substitutions. This is so even if the term contains embedded disj-dependent variables. Indeed, each disjunct of the constraint component after a normal multi-resolution step is the conjunction ($E_j \wedge A_i = H$) of some disjunct E_j from before that step with a new constraint, $A_i = H$. Since the equation $A_i = H$ appears in *every* disjunct of the DNF formula, there is advantage in storing resulting bindings of disj-independent variables once, globally, instead of once per disjunct. Accordingly, disj-independent variables are always engine variables stored in α.

Consider, for example, the following program and query, which binds L to lists of binary digits.

```
bit(0). bit(1).
bits([]).  bits([H|T]):- disj bit(H),bit(T).
| ?- bits(L).
Yes  L = [].  More? y
Yes  L = [A], (A=0 or A=1).  More? y
Yes  L = [A,B], (A=0,B=0 or A=0,B=1 or A=1,B=0 or A=1,B=1).  More? y
....
```

The disj-independent variable L and each cdr of L (the variable T in the body of the second clause for bit/1) get bound either to [] or to a cons cell. ($A_i = H$ corresponds to bits(L)=bits([]) or to bits(L)=bits([H|T]).) It is reasonable to store the bindings of L and T once, globally. This representation is reflected in the format of the output in the example query above.

The unification of A_i and H in a normal multi-resolution step is performed in two stages, with input $\alpha \wedge \beta$ and output $\alpha' \wedge \beta'$ (or failure). First, the unification $A_i\alpha = H\alpha$ is performed; if this results in the unification of an engine variable with a term not containing that engine variable, then the engine variable gets bound to that term. (This is so even if the engine variable gets unified with a multi-variable: the former gets bound to the latter.) The resulting binding appear in the output α'. Second, if the above unification $A_i\alpha = H\alpha$ requires the unification of a multi-variable with anything other than an engine variable, then that unification is performed in each disjunct of β, with output in β'.

When constraint lifting is not being used, the engine variables are precisely the disj-independent variables, and the multi variables are precisely the disj-dependent variables. In that case, α is a conjunction of equations representing the shared, common bindings that are independent of disj goals, and β is a disjunction representing the bindings dependent on disj goals.

In MultiLog, a unification involving engine variables is done once per *set* of solutions to previous generators. Without the `disj` operator or without the distinction between engine and multi variables, the unification would be repeated once per each solution to the generators. Thus, the engine/multi distinction saves time (repeated unifications) and space (multiple allocations of variable and heap cells) and thereby further leverages the benefits of data or-parallelism. See [27] for details on the mechanism used to maintain the distinction.

5.2 Same Shape Substitutions and the 'Templates' Optimization

Let $\{\theta_1, \ldots, \theta_m\}$ be the solutions collected for a `disj` goal and let $\{v_1, \ldots, v_n\}$ be the variables bound by any solutions in $\{\theta_1, \ldots, \theta_m\}$. For each i such that $1 \leq i \leq n$ consider the set of terms $\{v_i\theta_1, \ldots, v_i\theta_m\}$, regarding each term as a finite tree. Then we say that all solutions *have the same shape*, iff for each variable v_i the set of trees are isomorphic modulo the leaves. That is, solutions differ only by binding different constants to leaves of the trees, and all internal nodes are the same.

More formally, say that a substitution is a *finite domain substitution* if it is of the form $[w_1 \leftarrow t_1, \ldots, w_m \leftarrow t_m]$, where $w_1, \ldots, w_m$ are variables and $t_1, \ldots, t_m$ are either constants or variables. Let $S = \{\theta_1, \ldots, \theta_n\}$ be the set of solutions to some goal G. All solutions are *of the same shape* iff there exists a substitution θ such that for $i = 1, \ldots, n$, $\theta_i = \theta\eta_i$ for some finite domain substitution η_i. The substitution θ is then called the *shape* of the solutions; $G\theta$ represents the most specific instance of G that is more general than each term in $G\theta_1, \ldots, G\theta_n$.

When all solutions to a `disj` goal have the same shape, it is likely that the operations involved in performing subsequent unifications will be the same in all environments and will be easily carried out in a data parallel fashion. (For example, one processor of a SIMD computer can handle unification in one environment [23].) But if the generated environments have different shapes, then unification will likely involve different operations in different environments; furthermore, different subsets of environments will likely be consistent with different clauses of subsequent goals, so that much backtracking and much trailing of environments [23] will occur.

For many combinatorial search problems, all solutions to the generators have the same shape in the above sense. Yet there is an even stronger condition that increases the efficiency of data parallelism. The point is that even if a variable is bound to a term of the same shape in each environment, the variable might be bound to a *different* such tree in each environment. To increase the efficiency of data parallelism, it is desirable for such a variable to be bound globally, as an engine variable, to a term of the given shape, with multi-variables at the leaves; only these multi-variables should vary among the environments.

So if θ is the shape of all solutions to a goal `disj` G, it is useful to *prebind* the variables in G according to the bindings in θ. Each term $v\theta$, where v is one of the variables bound by θ, is called a *template*. Clearly, this optimization preserves correctness, since by assumption, all solutions have the given shape and new (multi-) variables are used at the leaves.

This optimization technique has proved crucial to the performance of MultiLog. Space is saved since the term representing the shape is created but once. Multi-unification is simplified since each environment can be a finite domain substitution. In the common case where the multi-unification processors are slower than the engine processor, time is saved as well. See [27] for further information on how the optimization is performed.

6 Discussion

In this paper we defined multi-SLD resolution and proved its soundness and completeness. We introduced the notions of environment tree, multi-derivation, and multi-SLD tree. We described and justified several optimization techniques that enhance the benefits of data or-parallelism: the distinction between engine and multi variables, templates, and the sharing of ancestor bindings.

The basic ideas behind multi-resolution and data or-parallelism were presented in [21] and [23], where (indirectly) related work was considered: control-or parallelism [35], [1], [8]; finite domain logic programming [33] [7]; DAP Prolog [10]; top-down set-at-a-time query languages (LPS [12], LDL [4]); Reform [3] [16] and Parallel Bounded Quantifiers [2] (these two correspond to data and-parallelism); and Constructive Negation [5], [6], [28], [18].

Since the publication of [21] and [23] a more closely related work has emerged. Firebird [30] is a concurrent, committed-choice constraint logic programming language [17] whose execution model involves two components: an and-parallel inference engine (the front-end) and a massively parallel constraint solver (the back-end). "In a non-deterministic derivation step, if there is any unbound domain variable X in the system with domain $\{a_1, \ldots, a_n\}$, Firebird will create n or-parallel branches, each of which executes with an additional constraint $X = a_i$, $1 \leq i \leq n$." In principle these n partitions are independent computations, but in practice data parallelism is achieved by restricting computation so that "the same goal is evaluated in all partitions, but with different sets of arguments", represented by a vector. Since Firebird is a committed-choice language, backtracking is not available, and completeness would, it seems, be lost.

Several researchers have investigated program transformation techniques for turning or-parallelism into (committed choice) and-parallelism [32] [31] [19] [15]. The basic idea is to rewrite a given logic program into a continuation passing style in which the various solutions to an OR goal are collected into a list by AND goals.[7] The question presents itself: can we likewise turn and-parallelism into (data) or-parallelism? We think so. Suppose the goal `process(In,Out)` has to be applied to all items `In` in some input relation `gen/1`, and the outputs `Out` have to be combined into a list `OutList`. We suggest turning this and-parallel query into the following data or-parallel query:

```
| ?- disj gen(In),process(In,Out),combine(Out,OutList).
```

[7] The "solution sharing" of [15] seems to be related to the benefits engendered by the engine/multi distinction; but MultiLog goes further by sharing or-parallel computations in both P and Q in P,Q, and not just in P. This topic warrants further investigation.

The idea is to make multiple environments in which **In** is bound to the various items in **gen/1**; then the call to **process(In,Out)** will compute concurrently on the items in the list. Finally, the goal **combine(Out,OutList)** will merge the various solutions into a single output; **combine** could use **findall** or a data parallel combining operation such as **max**, **sum**, or **reduce**.

In this paper we have concentrated on constraints over the Herbrand universe where only (disjunctions of) equations are allowed as constraints. Allowing more general sorts of disjunctive constraints opens the door to 'multi-CLP', as well as to implementations of constructive negation [5], [6], [28], [18]. In the case of the Herbrand domain, when there are an infinite number of function symbols, each finite equality formula is known to be equivalent, by quantifier elimination [11] [14] [22], to a disjunction of conjunctions of existentially quantified equations and negations of existentially quantified equations. Negations of existentially quantified equations have an efficient implementation in terms of delayed evaluation (**freeze**) and **dif** [20] [22]. (For example, $\neg\exists Y$ s.t. $X = f(Y,Y)$ translates into **freeze(X,(X isnot f/2 ; X=f(A,B),dif(A,B)))**, where **isnot/2** can be defined as:

X isnot F/N:- functor(X,F2,N2),dif(f(F,N),f(F2,N2)).)

By allowing disjunctive constraints over quantified equations and disequations, one obtains a language that directly generalizes MultiLog and that is capable of expressing any finite equality formula.

Acknowledgements

The first author thanks Jacques Cohen for valuable help with his writing.

References

1. K. Ali and R. Karlsson. The Muse Or-Parallel Prolog model and its performance. In *NACLP*, pages 757–776, 1990.
2. H. Arro, J. Barklund, and J. Bevemyr. Parallel bounded quantifiers: Preliminary results. In *Proceedings of the JICSLP'92 Post-Conference Joint Workshop on Distributed and Parallel Logic Programming Systems*, 1992.
3. J. Barklund. *Parallel Unification*. PhD thesis, Uppsala University, 1990.
4. C. Beeri, S. Naqvi, R. Ramakirishhan, O. Shmueli, and S. Tsur. Sets and negation in a logic database langauge (LDL1). In *PODS*. ACM Press, 1987.
5. D. Chan. Constructive negation based on the completed database. In *ICLP88*. MIT Press, 1988.
6. D. Chan. An extension of constructive negation and its application in coroutining. In *NACLP89*. MIT Press, 1989.
7. M. Dincbas, P. Van Hentenryck, H. Simonis, and A. Aggoun. The constraint logic programming language CHIP. In *2nd FGCS*, 1988.
8. E. Lusk et. al. The Aurora or-parallel prolog system. *New Generation Computing*, 7:243–271, 1990.
9. J. Jaffar and J.-L. Lassez. Constraint logic programming. In *Proceedings 14th POPL*, 1987.
10. Péter Kacsuk. *Execution Models of Prolog for Parallel Computers*. MIT, 1990.
11. K. Kunen. Answer sets and negation as failure. In *ICLP87*, 1987.

12. G. Kuper. Logic programming with sets. In *PODS*. ACM Press, 1987.
13. J.W. Lloyd. *Foundations of Logic Programming*. Springer-Verlag, 2nd edition, 1987.
14. M. J. Maher. Complete axiomatizations of the algebra of finite, rational, and infinite trees. In *Third LICS*, 1988.
15. André Mariën and Bart Demoen. Findall without Findall/3. In Warren [34], pages 408–423.
16. H. Milroth. *Reforming Compilation of Logic Programs*. PhD thesis, Uppsala University, 1990.
17. Vijay A. Saraswat. *Concurrent Constraint Programming*. MIT, 1990.
18. T. Sato and F. Motoyoshi. A complete top-down interpreter for first order programs. In *ILPS91*. MIT Press, 1991.
19. T. Sato and H. Tamaki. Existential continuation. 6, 1989.
20. D. A. Smith. Constraint operations for CLP(FT). In *ICLP91*. MIT Press, 1991.
21. D. A. Smith. Multilog: Data or-parallel logic programming. In *JICSLP '92 Workshop on Parallel Implementations of Logic Programming Systems*, 1992.
22. D. A. Smith. Simpler quantifier elimination for equality formulas. Technical Report CS-92-167, Brandeis University, 1992.
23. D. A. Smith. Multilog: Data or-parallel logic programming. In Warren [34].
24. D. A. Smith. Why multi-sld beats sld (even on a uniprocessor). Technical report, University of Waikato, (submitted to ALP) 1994.
25. D. A. Smith. Analysis of environment representation schemes for multilog. Technical report, University of Waikato, (submitted to PLILP) 1994.
26. D. A. Smith and T. Hickey. Partial evaluation of a CLP language. In *Proceedings of NACLP90*. MIT Press, 1990.
27. D.A. Smith. *MultiLog: Data Or-Parallel Logic Programming*. PhD thesis, Brandeis University, 1993.
28. P. Stuckey. Constructive negation for constraint logic programming. In *LICS*, 1991.
29. E. Tick. *Parallel Logic Programming*. MIT, 1991.
30. Bo-Ming Tong and Ho-Fung Leung. Concurrent constraint logic programming on massively parallel simd computers. In *International Logic Programming Symposium*, 1993.
31. K. Ueda. Making exhaustive search programs deterministic : Part II. In *ICLP*, pages 356–375, 1987.
32. Kazunori Ueda. Making exhaustive search programs deterministic. In *ICLP*, pages 270–282, 1986.
33. P. VanHentenryck. *Constraint Satisfaction in Logic Programming*. MIT Press, 1989.
34. David S. Warren, editor. *Proceedings of the Tenth International Conference on Logic Programming*, Budapest, Hungary, 1993. The MIT Press.
35. D.H.D. Warren. Or-parallel execution models of prolog. In *TAPSOFT*, 1987.

On Anti-Links [†]

Bernhard Beckert[‡], *Reiner Hähnle*[‡], *Anavai Ramesh*[*], *and Neil V. Murray*[*]

[‡] Institute for Logic, Complexity and Deduction Systems, Universität Karlsruhe, Karlsruhe, Germany. (email: beckert / haehnle@ira.uka.de)

[*] Institute for Programming & Logics, Department of Computer Science, University at Albany, Albany, NY 12222. (email: rameshag / nvm @cs.albany.edu)

Abstract.

The concept of *anti-link* is defined, and useful equivalence-preserving operations on propositional formulas based on anti-links are introduced. These operations eliminate a potentially large number of subsumed paths in a negation normal form formula. The operations have linear time complexity in the size of that part of the formula containing the anti-link.

These operations are useful for prime implicant/implicate algorithms because most of the computational effort in such algorithms is spent on subsumption checks.

1. Introduction

Many algorithms have been proposed to compute the prime implicates of propositional boolean formula. Most algorithms [1,2,3,4,14] assume that the input is either in conjunctive normal form (CNF) or in disjunctive normal form (DNF). Other algorithms [10] require the input to be a conjunction of DNF formulas. In [12], a set of techniques for finding the prime implicates of formulas in negation normal form (NNF) is proposed. Those techniques are based on *dissolution*, an inference rule introduced in [8], and on an algorithm called PI. Classes of formulas have been discovered for which these techniques are polynomial but for which any CNF/DNF-based technique must be exponential in the size of the input. Ngair has also introduced similar examples; however, our method is more general than Ngair's which is based on order theory [10].

In [12] the PI algorithm is described; there, PI is used to enumerate all the prime implicates of a *full dissolvent*, an NNF formula that has no conjunctive links (defined later). PI repeatedly does subsumption checks to keep intermediate results as small as possible. However these checks are expensive. Most result in failure, and they have to be done on sets which can be exponentially large. The time required for these operations can be reduced by using a more compact representation of the intermediate results [1], but avoiding as many such checks as possible is the focus of this paper.

We show that the full dissolvent can be restructured before applying PI such that many non-prime implicates are removed without doing subsumption checks at

[†] This research was supported in part by National Science Foundation Grant CCR-9101208 (Ramesh and Murray) and by Deutsche Forschungsgemeinschaft within the Schwerpunktprogramm Deduktion (Hähnle and Beckert).

all. We define *disjunctive* and *conjunctive anti-links*[1] in NNF formulas, and we identify operations to remove such anti-links and their associated subsumed paths. This leaves fewer subsumption checks for the PI algorithm.

In the next section we describe our path semantics viewpoint and our graphical representation of formulas in classical logic. In Section 3 we introduce *anti-links* and develop useful equivalence-preserving operations based on them.

2. Foundations: Facts on Formulas in Negation Normal Form

We assume the reader to be familiar with the notions of *atom, literal*, and *formula* from classical logic. We consider only formulas in *negation normal form* (NNF): The only connectives used are conjunction and disjunction, and all negations are at the atomic level. This restriction is reasonable, since formulas that contain implications and negations at any level can be converted to NNF in polynomial time. We deal only with propositional logic in this paper, although some of the following results like the Path Dissolution Rule are completely general.

In this section, we introduce a number of technical terms and definitions that are treated in detail in [9]. They are required for the development of the anti-link operations defined in Section 3, and they make the paper self-contained even for readers not familiar with dissolution.

2.1. Semantic Graphs

A *semantic graph G* is a triple *(N,C,D) of nodes, c-arcs*, and *d-arcs*, respectively, where a node is a literal occurrence, a c-arc is a conjunction of two semantic graphs, and a d-arc is a disjunction of two semantic graphs. Any of N,C,D may be empty. If N is empty, G is either *true* (empty conjunction) or *false* (empty disjunction). Each semantic graph used in the construction of a semantic graph is called an *explicit subgraph*, and each proper explicit subgraph is contained in exactly one arc. Note that when a graph contains occurrences of *true* and *false*, the obvious truth-functional reductions apply. Unless otherwise stated, we will assume that semantic graphs are automatically so reduced and that empty graphs are *false*. We will typically use *G* to refer to both the graph and to the corresponding node set when the meaning is evident from context.

We use the notation $(X, Y)_c$ for the c-arc from X to Y and similarly use $(X, Y)_d$ for a d-arc; the subscript may be omitted when no confusion is possible. Arbitrary subformulas are denoted by upper case italic letters; plain upper case letters are used for single nodes.

In Figure 1, the formula on the left is displayed graphically on the right. Note that c-arcs and d-arcs are indicated by the usual symbols for conjunction and disjunction. Essentially, the only difference between a semantic graph and a formula in NNF is the point of view, and we will use either term depending upon the desired emphasis. For a more detailed exposition, see [9].

If A and B are nodes in a graph, and if $\mathbf{a} = (X, Y)_\alpha$ is an arc (α=c or α=d) with A in X and B in Y, we say that **a** is the arc *connecting* A and B, and that A and B are *α-connected.* In Figure 1, C is c-connected to each of B, A, $\bar{C}$, D, and E and

[1] Anti-links and some associated operators were first proposed by Beckert and Hähnle – personal communication. The first motivation for studying anti-links arose in connection with regular clausal tableau calculi (Letz, p. 114 [6]). The anti-link rule as it will be defined later can be viewed as an implementation of the regularity condition in [6] for the propositional non-clausal case (Letz considered the first-order clausal case). There, refinements of general inference rules are considered, whereas the anti-link rule allows implementation as a preprocessing step.

$$((\neg C \wedge A) \vee D \vee E) \wedge (\neg A \vee (B \wedge C)) \quad \equiv \quad \begin{array}{ccccc} \bar{C} & & & & \\ \wedge & \vee & D & \vee & E \\ A & & & & \\ & \wedge & & & \\ & & B & & \\ \bar{A} & \vee & \wedge & & \\ & & C & & \end{array}$$

Figure 1.

is d-connected to $\bar{A}$.

Let *G* be a semantic graph. A *partial c-path through G* is a set of nodes such that any two are c-connected, and a *c-path* through *G* is a partial c-path that is not properly contained in any partial c-path. The c-paths of the graph in Figure 1 above are: {C, A, A}, {C, A, B, C}, {D, A}, {D, B, C}, {E, A}, {E, B, C}. We similarly define d-path using d-arcs instead of c-arcs. The following lemma is obvious.

Lemma 1. Let *G* be a semantic graph. Then an interpretation I satisfies (falsifies) *G* iff I satisfies (falsifies) every literal on some c-path (d-path) through *G*.

2.1.1. Subgraphs

We will frequently find it useful to consider subgraphs that are not explicit; that is, given any set of nodes, we would like to examine that part of the graph consisting of exactly that set of nodes. The previous example is shown below on the left; the subgraph relative to the set {A, D, $\bar{A}$,} is the graph on the right.

$$\begin{array}{ccccc} \bar{C} & & & & \\ \wedge & \vee & \mathbf{D} & \vee & E \\ \mathbf{A} & & & & \\ & \wedge & & & \\ & & B & & \\ \bar{\mathbf{A}} & \vee & \wedge & & \\ & & C & & \end{array} \qquad\qquad \begin{array}{ccc} \mathbf{A} & \vee & \mathbf{D} \\ & \wedge & \\ & \bar{\mathbf{A}} & \end{array}$$

For a precise definition of subgraph, see [9].

2.1.2. Blocks

The most important subgraphs are the *blocks*. A *c-block H* is a subgraph of a semantic graph with the property that any c-path p that includes at least one node from *H must pass through H*; that is, the subset of p consisting of the nodes that are in *H* must be a c-path through *H*. A *d-block* is similarly defined with d-paths. In Figure 1, the subgraph relative to the node set {A,D,E,A,C} is a c-block. However, it is not a d-block since the d-path {A,B} restricted to the subgraph is {A}, which is a proper sub-path of {A,C} in the subgraph.

A *full block* is a subgraph that is both a c-block and a d-block. One way to envision a full block is to consider conjunction and disjunction as n-ary connectives. Then a full block is a subset of the arguments of one connective, i.e., of one explicit subformula. For example, in Figure 1, {C,A,E} is a full block. Full blocks may be treated as essentially explicit subgraphs, and the Isomorphism Theorem from [7] assures us that they are the only structures that may be so treated. For example, $\{\bar{C}, A, E\}$ can be written as $\begin{array}{c} C \\ \wedge \\ A \end{array} \vee E$ or as $(\{\bar{C}, A\}, E)_d$.

Let H be a full block; H is a conjunction or a disjunction of fundamental subgraphs of some explicit subgraph M. If the final arc (main connective) of M is a conjunction, then we define the *c-extension* of H to be M and the *d-extension* of H to be H itself. The situation is reversed if the final arc (main connective) of M is a d-arc. We will use the notation CE(H) and DE(H) for the c- and d-extensions, respectively, of H. In Figure 1, CE($\bar{A}$) = $\bar{A}$ and DE($\bar{A}$) = $\bar{A} \vee \overset{B}{\underset{C}{\wedge}}$.

In this paper, we compute c- and d-extensions of single nodes only. Single nodes are always full blocks and so testing for this property will be unnecessary. If we assume that formulas are represented as n-ary trees, computing these extensions can be done in constant time; we merely determine whether the given node's parent is a conjunction or a disjunction, and the appropriate extension is then either the node itself or the parent.

2.2. Path Dissolution

A *c-link* is defined to be a complementary pair of c-connected nodes; d-connected complementary nodes form a d-link. Unless stated otherwise, we use the term link to refer to a c-link. Path dissolution is in general applicable to collections of links; here we restrict attention to single links. Suppose then that we have literal occurrences A and $\bar{A}$ residing in conjoined subgraphs X and Y, respectively. Consider, for example, the link $\{A, \bar{A}\}$ in Figure 1. Then the entire graph $G = (X \wedge Y)$ is the smallest full block containing the link, where

$$X = \overset{\bar{C}}{\underset{A}{\wedge}} \vee D \vee E \quad \text{and} \quad Y = \bar{A} \vee \overset{B}{\underset{C}{\wedge}} .$$

The *c-path complement* of an arbitrary subgraph H with respect to X, written CC(H, X), is defined to be the subgraph of X consisting of all literals in X that lie on paths that do not contain nodes from H; the *c-path extension* of H with respect to X, written CPE(H, X), is the subgraph containing all literals in X that lie on paths that *pass through H*.

In Figure 1, CC(A, X) = (D $\vee$ E); CPE(A, X) = ($\bar{C} \wedge$ A). (Note that CPE has two arguments whereas CE has but one; intuitively, CE has an implicit second argument that is always the entire graph in which the explicit argument occurs. For instance, CPE(A, G) = ($\bar{C} \wedge A \wedge Y$) and CE(A) = CPE(A,$X$) = ($\bar{C} \wedge$ A).)

It is intuitively clear that the paths through ($X \wedge Y$) that do not contain the link are those through (CPE(A, X) $\wedge$ CC(A, Y)) plus those through (CC(A, X) $\wedge$ CPE(A,Y)) plus those through (CC(A, X) $\wedge$ CC(A, Y)). The reader is referred to [9] for the formal definitions of CC and of CPE and for the proofs of the lemmas below. (The CC and CPE definitions are also presented in Section 3.3).

Lemma 2. Let H be an arbitrary subgraph of G. The c-paths of CPE(H, G) are precisely the c-paths of G that pass through H.

Corollary. CPE(H, G) is exactly the subgraph of G relative to the set of nodes that lie on c-paths that pass through H.

Lemma 3. Let H be an arbitrary subgraph of G. The c-paths of CC(H, G) are precisely the c-paths of G that do not pass through H.

Corollary. CC(H, G) is exactly the subgraph of G relative to the set of nodes that lie on c-paths that do not pass through H.

Lemma 4. If H is a c-block, then CC(H, G) $\cup$ CPE(H, G) = G.

In the development of anti-link operations, we will require the dual operations of CC and CPE. We use DC for the *d-path complement* and DPE for the *d-path extension* operators. Their definitions and properties are straightforward by duality, and the above lemmas and corollaries about CC and CPE all hold in dual form for DC and DPE. The above informal treatment of these operators is adequate for an intuitive description of dissolution. However, precise definitions are given in Section 3, where they will be required in proving the correctness of the anti-link operations introduced there.

Let $H = \{A, \overline{A}\}$ be a link, and let $M = (X, Y)_c$ be the smallest full block containing *H*. The only way that *H* can be a single c-block is if *H* is a full block (it is trivially a d-block). In that case, $H = M$, and A and $\overline{A}$ must be (up to commutations and reassociations) arguments of the same conjunction.

In general we define DV(*H, M*), the *dissolvent of H in M*, as follows: If *H* is a single c-block, then DV(*H, M*) = CC(A, *M*) = CC($\overline{A}$, *M*) = *false*. Otherwise (i.e., if *H* consists of two c-blocks),

$$\mathrm{DV}(H, M) \;=\; \begin{matrix}\mathrm{CPE}(A, X)\\ \wedge\\ \mathrm{CC}(\overline{A}, Y)\end{matrix} \;\vee\; \begin{matrix}\mathrm{CC}(A, X)\\ \wedge\\ \mathrm{CPE}(\overline{A}, Y)\end{matrix} \;\vee\; \begin{matrix}\mathrm{CC}(A, X)\\ \wedge\\ \mathrm{CC}(\overline{A}, Y)\end{matrix}$$

It follows from the corollaries and Lemma 4 that either of the two graphs shown below may also be used for DV(*H, M*).

$$\begin{matrix}X\\ \wedge\\ \mathrm{CC}(\overline{A}, Y)\end{matrix} \;\vee\; \begin{matrix}\mathrm{CC}(A, X)\\ \wedge\\ \mathrm{CPE}(\overline{A}, Y)\end{matrix} \qquad \text{or} \qquad \begin{matrix}\mathrm{CC}(A, X)\\ \wedge\\ Y\end{matrix} \;\vee\; \begin{matrix}\mathrm{CPE}(A, X)\\ \wedge\\ \mathrm{CC}(\overline{A}, Y)\end{matrix}$$

The three versions of DV(*H, M*) are not identical as graphs, but all three do have the identical c-paths: all those of the original full block *M* except those of CPE(A, *X*) ∧ CPE($\overline{A}$, *Y*), i.e., except those through the link.

Theorem 1. Let *H* be a link in a semantic graph *G*, and let M be the smallest full block containing *H*. Then *M* and DV(*H, M*) are logically equivalent.

A proof of Theorem 1 (in its full generality, where *H* is an arbitrary dissolution chain) can be found in [9].

We may therefore select an arbitrary link *H* in *G* and replace the smallest full block containing *H* by its dissolvent, producing (in the ground case) an equivalent graph. We call the resulting graph the *dissolvent of G with respect to H* and denote it Diss(*G,H*). Since the paths of the new graph are all that appeared in *G* except those that contained the link, this graph has strictly fewer c-paths than the old one. As a result, finitely many dissolutions (bounded above by the number of c-paths in the original graph) will yield a linkless equivalent graph. This proves

Theorem 2. At the ground level, path dissolution is a strongly complete rule of inference.

2.3. Prime Implicates/Implicants

We briefly summarize basic definitions regarding implicates. The treatment for implicants is completely dual and is indicated by appropriate dual expressions in parentheses.

A disjunction (conjunction) P of literals is an implicate (implicant) of a formula *G*, iff $G \models P$ ($P \models G$).

A disjunction (conjunction) D subsumes another D′ iff D $\models$ D′ (D′ $\models$ D).

If a disjunction (conjunction) D′ is not equivalent to *true* (*false*) then D subsumes D′ iff D $\subseteq$ D′. *True* (*false*) is subsumed by all disjunctions (conjunctions). A *true* disjunction (*false* conjunction) can subsume another *true* disjunction (*false* conjunction) only.

A disjunction (conjunction) D is a prime implicate (implicant) of a formula *G* iff

1) D is not *true* (*false*).
2) D is an implicate (implicant) of *G*.
3) For all literals l_i in D, $G \not\models (D - \{l_i\})$ $((D - \{l_i\}) \not\models G)$.

2.4. Fully Dissolved Formulas

If we dissolve in a semantic graph *G* until it is linkless, we call the resulting graph the *full dissolvent of G* and denote it by FD(*G*). Observe that FD(*G*) is dependent on the order in which links are activated. However, the set of c-paths in FD(*G*) is unique: It is exactly the set of satisfiable c-paths in *G*. Because FD(*G*) is link-free, the consequences, i.e., implicates, of *G* are represented in the d-paths of FD(*G*). In a dual manner, we may define dissolution for disjunctive links; in that case, FD(*G*) has no disjunctive links, and the implicants of *G* are represented in the c-paths of FD(*G*). These relationships are made precise by Theorem 3 below.

In the discussion that follows, we will often refer to subsumption of d- and c-paths rather than of disjuncts and conjuncts. Paths are defined as sets of literal occurrences, but with regard to subsumption, we consider the *literal sets* of paths. We denote by l(p) the literal set of path p. In this way, no change in the standard definitions is necessary. The theorem below was proved in [12].

Theorem 3. In any non-empty formula in which no c-path (d-path) contains a link, every implicate (implicant) of the formula is subsumed by some d-path (c-path) in the formula.

Corollary: Every prime implicate (implicant) of a reduced DNF (CNF) formula, i.e., one with no *false* conjuncts (*true* disjuncts), is subsumed by some d-path (c-path) in the formula.

This follows directly from Theorem 3 because such a DNF (CNF) formula has no c-paths (d-paths) with links.

In [12], the prime implicates of *G* are computed by first obtaining FD(*G*); then, knowing that all implicates are present in the d-paths of FD(*G*), the PI algorithm computes the set of prime implicants ψ(FD(*G*)), where

$$\begin{aligned}\psi(\mathcal{F}) \;=\; & \{P \mid (P \text{ is a d-path through } \mathcal{F}) \wedge \\ & (P \neq \mathit{true}) \wedge (\forall \text{ d-paths } Q \text{ through } \mathcal{F},\ l(Q) \not\subset l(P))\}\ .\end{aligned}$$

When used in this way, PI extracts all unsubsumed (non-tautological) d-paths from an NNF formula without c-links. In general, PI computes $\psi(\mathcal{F})$ for an arbitrary NNF formula $\mathcal{F}$.

3. Subsumed Paths and Anti-Links

Our goal in this section is to first identify as many subsumed paths as possible in an efficient manner and then eliminate them. The presence of anti-links (both disjunctive and conjunctive) in a graph may indicate that subsumed d-paths are present in the graph. We now define anti-links and then discuss ways to identify and remove subsumed paths due to anti-links.

Let $M=(X,Y)_d$ be a d-arc in a semantic graph G and let A_X and A_Y be occurrences of the literal A in X and in Y respectively. Then we call $\{A_X,A_Y\}$ a *disjunctive anti-link.* Note that M is the smallest full block containing the anti-link. If $M=(X,Y)_c$ is a c-arc in a semantic graph G and if A_X and A_Y are nodes in X and in Y respectively, then we call $\{A_X,A_Y\}$ a *conjunctive anti-link.*

3.1. Redundant Anti-links

We now identify those disjunctive anti-links which do imply the presence of subsumed paths. We say a disjunctive anti-link $\{A_X,A_Y\}$ with respect to the graph G is *redundant* if either $CE(A_X) \neq A$ or $CE(A_Y) \neq A$.

Let $\{A_X,A_Y\}$ be a disjunctive anti-link in graph G, where $M=(X,Y)_d$ is the smallest full block containing the anti-link. We define $\mathcal{DP}_{A_X,A_Y,G}$ to be the set of all d-paths of M which pass through both $CE(A_X)-\{A_X\}$ and A_Y or through both $CE(A_Y)-\{A_Y\}$ and A_X. Consider the following example:

$$\begin{array}{ccc} A \vee C & & A \\ \wedge & \vee & \wedge \\ B & & E \vee C \end{array}$$

The two occurrences of A form a disjunctive anti-link; M is the entire graph, and X and Y are the left and right arguments of the main disjunction, respectively. Because $CE(A_Y)-\{A\}=Y-\{A\}=(E \vee C)$ and $DPE(A_X, X)=A \vee C$, $\mathcal{DP}_{A_X,A_Y,G}$ contains the d-path $p=\{A_X, C, E, C\}$. But since $CE(A_X)=A_X$, there are no paths through $CE(A_X)-\{A_X\}$; p is the only member of $\mathcal{DP}_{A_X,A_Y,G}$. Nevertheless, the anti-link is redundant, and p is subsumed by $p'=\{A_X, C, A_Y\}$ (with literal set {A,C}). Notice that had M been embedded in a larger graph G', every d-path q containing p in G' is subsumed by a corresponding d-path q' that differs from q only in that q' contains p' instead of p.

In general, one or both of the literals in a redundant anti-link $\{L_X, L_Y\}$ is an argument of a conjunction, and $\mathcal{DP}_{L_X,L_Y,G} \neq \emptyset$. In the above example, the two occurrences of C are both arguments of disjunctions, and thus comprise a non-redundant anti-link for which $\mathcal{DP}_{C_X,C_Y,G}=\emptyset$.

Although only redundant disjunctive anti-links contribute directly to subsumed d-paths, non-redundant anti-links do not prohibit the existence of subsumed paths. However, such non-redundant anti-links do not themselves provide any evidence that such paths are in fact present.

Theorem 5. Let $\{A_X,A_Y\}$ be a redundant disjunctive anti-link in semantic graph G. Then each d-path in $\mathcal{DP}_{A_X,A_Y,G}$ is properly subsumed by a d-path in G that contains the anti-link.

Proof: Recall that a d-path (c-path) in a graph G is said to *pass through* a subgraph X of G if the path when restricted to the set of nodes in X, forms a d-path (c-path) in X. Let $p \in \mathcal{DP}_{A_X,A_Y,G}$, and assume without loss of generality that p passes through both $CE(A_X)-\{A_X\}$ and A_Y. Note that $CE(A_X)-\{A_X\}$ is non-empty and that $M=(X \vee Y)$ is the largest full block containing the anti-link. We may write $CE(A_X)$ as $(A_X \wedge C_1 \wedge \cdots \wedge C_n)$, where $n \geq 1$.

Let $p=p_X p_Y p_o$ where p_X and p_Y are p restricted to X and to Y, respectively, and p_o is p restricted to nodes outside of both X and Y. By construction, $A_X \notin p_X$ and thus p_X passes through some C_i, $1 \leq i \leq n$. So $p_X=p_X' p_{C_i}$, where p_{C_i} is p_X restricted to C_i, and hence $p=p_X' p_{C_i} p_Y p_o$. The d-path $p_X' \cup \{A\}$ clearly passes through X, and since $A_Y \in p_Y$, $p'=p_X' A_X p_Y p_o$ subsumes p. □

3.2. An Anti-Link Operator

The identification of redundant disjunctive anti-links can be done easily by checking to see if either $CE(A_X) \neq A_X$ or $CE(A_Y) \neq A_Y$. After identifying a redundant anti-link, it is possible to remove it using the *disjunctive anti-link dissolvent* (DADV) operator; in the process, all d-paths in $\mathcal{DP}_{A_X,A_Y,G}$ are eliminated, and the two occurrences of the anti-link literal are collapsed into one. Let $\{A_X,A_Y\}$ be a disjunctive anti-link and let $M = (X, Y)_d$ be the smallest full block containing the anti-link. Then

$$
\mathrm{DADV}(\{A_X, A_Y\}, M) \quad = \quad
\begin{array}{rcl}
\mathrm{DC}(A_X,X) & \vee & \mathrm{DC}(A_Y,Y) \\
 & \wedge & \\
\mathrm{DC}(\mathrm{CE}(A_X),X) & \vee & \mathrm{DPE}(A_Y,Y) \\
 & \wedge & \\
\mathrm{DPE}(A_X,X) & \vee & \mathrm{CC}(A_Y,Y)\ .
\end{array}
$$

Consider again the example from Section 3.1:

$$
\begin{array}{ccccc}
A \vee C & & & & A \\
\wedge & & \vee & & \wedge \\
B & & & & E \vee C
\end{array}
$$

We have $\mathrm{DC}(A_X, X) = B$ and $\mathrm{DC}(A_Y, Y) = (E \vee C)$, so the upper conjunct in DADV is $(B \vee E \vee C)$. For the middle conjunct, $\mathrm{CE}(A_X) = A_X$, $\mathrm{DC}(\mathrm{CE}(A_X), X) = B$, and $\mathrm{DPE}(A_Y, Y) = A_Y$; this conjunct is $(B \vee A)$. Finally in the lower conjunct, $\mathrm{DPE}(A_X, X) = (A \vee C)$ and $\mathrm{CC}(A_Y, Y) = \varnothing$ (*false*), so this reduces to $(A \vee C)$. The result is:

$$
\mathrm{DADV}(\{A_X, A_Y\}, M) \quad = \quad
\begin{array}{ccl}
B & \vee & E \vee C \\
 & \wedge & \\
B & \vee & A \\
 & \wedge & \\
A & \vee & C
\end{array}
$$

We point out that although DADV produces a CNF formula in this simple example, in general it does not. In particular, the above graph can be simplified as the consequence of easily recognizable conditions, and the resulting graph is not in CNF. For the details, see Case 1 of Section 3.5.

3.3. Extension and Path Complement Operators

A number of more primitive operators are used in the definition of DADV; they are described in [9] and have been presented informally in Section 2. We present the formal definitions here in order to prove Lemma 5 below, and, in the next subsection, to verify that DADV has the desired properties.

Let H be an arbitrary subgraph of G. Then

$$\mathrm{CPE}(\varnothing, G) \;=\; \varnothing \;(\textit{false}) \qquad \text{and} \qquad \mathrm{CPE}(G,G) \;=\; G$$

$$\mathrm{CPE}(H, G) \;=\; \bigvee_{i=1}^{n} \mathrm{CPE}(H_{F_i},F_i) \qquad \text{if the final arc of } G \text{ is a d-arc}$$

$$\mathrm{CPE}(H, G) \;=\; \bigwedge_{i=1}^{k} \mathrm{CPE}(H_{F_i},F_i) \;\wedge \bigwedge_{j=k+1}^{n} F_j \qquad \text{if the final arc of } G \text{ is a c-arc}$$

where $F_1, \cdots, F_k$ are the fundamental subgraphs of G that meet H, and $F_{k+1}, \cdots, F_n$ are those that do not.

$$\mathrm{DPE}(\varnothing, G) = \varnothing\ (\mathit{true}) \quad \text{and} \quad \mathrm{DPE}(G, G) = G$$

$$\mathrm{DPE}(H, G) = \bigwedge_{i=1}^{n} \mathrm{DPE}(H_{F_i}, F_i) \quad \text{if the final arc of } G \text{ is a c-arc}$$

$$\mathrm{DPE}(H, G) = \bigvee_{i=1}^{k} \mathrm{DPE}(H_{F_i}, F_i) \ \vee \bigvee_{j=k+1}^{n} F_j \quad \text{if the final arc of } G \text{ is a d-arc}$$

where $F_1, \cdots, F_k$ are the fundamental subgraphs of G that meet H, and $F_{k+1}, \cdots, F_n$ are those that do not.

Using the same notation we define the c- and d-path complements of H in G as follows:

$$\mathrm{CC}(\varnothing, G) = G \quad \text{and} \quad \mathrm{CC}(G, G) = \varnothing\ (\mathit{false})$$

$$\mathrm{CC}(H, G) = \bigvee_{i=1}^{n} \mathrm{CC}(H_{F_i}, F_i) \quad \text{if the final arc of } G \text{ is a d-arc}$$

$$\mathrm{CC}(H, G) = \bigwedge_{i=1}^{k} \mathrm{CC}(H_{F_i}, F_i) \ \wedge \bigwedge_{j=k+1}^{n} F_j \quad \text{if the final arc of } G \text{ is a c-arc}$$

where $F_1, \cdots, F_k$ are the fundamental subgraphs of G that meet H, and $F_{k+1}, \cdots, F_n$ are those that do not.

$$\mathrm{DC}(\varnothing, G) = G \quad \text{and} \quad \mathrm{DC}(G, G) = \varnothing\ (\mathit{true})$$

$$\mathrm{DC}(H, G) = \bigwedge_{i=1}^{n} \mathrm{DC}(H_{F_i}, F_i) \quad \text{if the final arc of } G \text{ is a c-arc}$$

$$\mathrm{DC}(H, G) = \bigvee_{i=1}^{k} \mathrm{DC}(H_{F_i}, F_i) \ \vee \bigvee_{j=k+1}^{n} F_j \quad \text{if the final arc of } G \text{ is a d-arc}$$

where $F_1, \cdots, F_k$ are the fundamental subgraphs of G that meet H, and $F_{k+1}, \cdots, F_n$ are those that do not.

Lemma 5. If G is a graph and A is a literal occurrence in G, then

$$\mathrm{CC}(\mathrm{A}, G) = (\mathrm{DPE}(\mathrm{A}, G) - \{\mathrm{A}\}) \wedge \mathrm{DC}(\mathrm{CE}(\mathrm{A}), G) .$$

Proof: We prove the lemma by showing that the formula on the left and the formula on the right possess exactly the same set of d-paths. The proof is done via induction on the syntactic structure of G.

If G is a literal, then $G = \mathrm{A}$ and both CC(A, G) and ((DPE(A, G) − {A}) ∧ DC(CE(A), G)) are empty. (DC(CE(A), G) = DC(A, A) = *true*, but (DPE(A, G) − {A}) = {A} − {A} = *false* = CC(A, A) .)

If G = (X ∨ Y), then without loss of generality assume A belongs to X. Hence CC(A, G) = CC(A, X) ∨ Y. By the induction hypothesis, the d-paths of CC(A, X) are just those of (DPE(A, X) − {A}) ∧ DC(CE(A), X)). So CC(A, G) = (DPE(A, X) − {A}) ∧ DC(CE(A), X)) ∨ Y.

Now consider the right hand side of the equation. Since A is in X, DPE(A, G) = DPE(A, X) ∨ Y. Therefore, DPE(A, G) − {A} = DPE(A, X) − {A} ∨ Y. Also, CE(A) will be disjoint from Y, and thus DC(CE(A), G) = DC(CE(A), X) ∨ Y. Therefore we can write the right hand side of the equation as (DPE(A, X) − {A} ∨ Y) ∧ (DC(CE(A), X) ∨ Y). By factoring out the subgraph Y we get an equivalent subgraph ((DPE(A, X) − {A}) ∧ DC(CE(A), X)) ∨ Y having the same d-paths. But this is just the graph to which the left hand side reduced via the induction hypothesis.

Finally suppose G = (X ∧ Y); again assume that A is in X. Now there are two subcases to consider.

a) If CC(A, G) is the empty graph , then A in X is not d-connected to any other subgraph in X. Hence X is of the form $\mathrm{A} \wedge C_1 \wedge \cdots \wedge C_n$ (where $n \geq 0$). But then $G = \mathrm{A} \wedge C_1 \wedge \cdots \wedge C_n \wedge Y$, CE(A) = G, and DPE(A, G) = DPE(A, X) = A. As a result, DC(CE(A), G) and DPE(A, G) − {A} are both the empty subgraph.

b) If CC(A, G) is not empty, then CC(A, G) = CC(A, X) ∧ Y, and CC(A, X) cannot be the empty graph. Therefore, by the induction hypothesis, CC(A, G) = (DPE(A, X) − {A}) ∧ DC(CE(A), X) ∧ Y. Focusing now on the right hand side of the equation, DPE(A, G) = DPE(A, X) by definition. The c-extension of A can only include nodes from X (otherwise, CC(A, G) would be empty, contrary to the subcase b) condition). Therefore, DC(CE(A), G) = DC(CE(A), X) ∧ Y. Therefore the right hand side of the equation is (DPE(A, X) − {A}) ∧ (DC(CE(A), X) ∧ Y). This is just the result obtained for the left hand side in this subcase. □

3.4. Correctness of DADV

In Theorem 6 below we show that DADV({A_X,A_Y},G) is logically equivalent to G and does not contain those d-paths in $\mathcal{DP}_{\mathrm{A}_X,\mathrm{A}_Y,G}$.

Theorem 6. Let $M = (X \vee Y)$ be the smallest full block containing {A_X,A_Y}, a disjunctive anti-link in semantic graph G. Then DADV({A_X, A_Y}, M) is equivalent to M and differs in d-paths from M as follows: Those d-paths in $\mathcal{DP}_{\mathrm{A}_X,\mathrm{A}_Y,M}$ are not present, and any d-path of M containing the anti-link is replaced by a path with the same literal set having only one occurrence of the anti-link literal.

Proof: Note that A_X and A_Y are literal occurrences (and hence d-blocks) in X and in Y respectively. By the duals of Lemmas 2, 3, and 4, X is equivalent to DC(A_X,X) ∧ *DPE*(A_X,X), and from the distributive law,

$$M \quad = \quad \begin{array}{c} \mathrm{DC}(\mathrm{A}_X, X) \ \vee \ Y \\ \wedge \\ \mathrm{DPE}(\mathrm{A}_X, X) \ \vee \ Y \end{array}$$

Similarly, Y is equivalent to DC(A_Y,Y) ∧ *DPE*(A_Y,Y), and we expand the upper occurrence of Y and distribute.

$$M \quad = \quad \begin{array}{c} \mathrm{DC}(\mathrm{A}_X, X) \vee \mathrm{DC}(\mathrm{A}_Y, Y) \\ \wedge \\ \mathrm{DC}(\mathrm{A}_X, X) \vee \mathrm{DPE}(\mathrm{A}_Y, Y) \\ \wedge \\ \mathrm{DPE}(\mathrm{A}_X, X) \vee Y \end{array}$$

By the duals of Lemmas 2 and 3, not only have we rewritten M equivalently, but the d-paths of M have been preserved. We will continue to rewrite M; our goal is to eventually put it in an equivalent form in which the paths of $\mathcal{DP}_{\mathrm{A}_X,\mathrm{A}_Y,M}$ have been omitted.

Consider the d-paths of $\mathrm{DC}(\mathrm{A}_X, X)$ – the d-paths in X that miss A_X. They either miss $\mathrm{CE}(\mathrm{A}_X)$, the c-extension of A_X, or pass through $\mathrm{CE}(\mathrm{A}_X) - \{\mathrm{A}_X\}$. Hence we have $\mathrm{DC}(\mathrm{A}_X, X) = \mathrm{DPE}(\,(\mathrm{CE}(\mathrm{A}_X) - \{\mathrm{A}_X\}\,), X) \wedge \mathrm{DC}(\mathrm{CE}(\mathrm{A}_X), X)$, and d-paths are preserved. By replacing the lower occurrence of $\mathrm{DC}(\mathrm{A}_X, X)$ in the previous graph, we get the following graph M′ which is equivalent to M and has the same d-paths as M.

$$M' \quad = \quad \begin{array}{ccc} & & \mathrm{DC}(\mathrm{A}_X, X) \vee \mathrm{DC}(\mathrm{A}_Y, Y) \\ & & \wedge \\ \begin{array}{c} \mathrm{DPE}(\,(\mathrm{CE}(\mathrm{A}_X) - \{\mathrm{A}_X\}\,), X) \\ \wedge \\ \mathrm{DC}(\mathrm{CE}(\mathrm{A}_X), X) \end{array} & & \vee \; \mathrm{DPE}(\mathrm{A}_Y, Y) \\ & & \wedge \\ & & \mathrm{DPE}(\mathrm{A}_X, X) \vee Y \end{array}$$

Every d-path in the subgraph $\mathrm{DPE}(\,(\mathrm{CE}(A_X) - \{\mathrm{A}_X\}\,), X) \vee \mathrm{DPE}(\mathrm{A}_Y, Y)$ is in $\mathcal{DP}_{\mathrm{A}_X,\mathrm{A}_Y,M}$. By Theorem 5, all these paths are subsumed by other d-paths. Therefore, we can remove the subgraph $\mathrm{DPE}(\,(\mathrm{CE}(A_X) - \{\mathrm{A}_X\}\,), X)$ from M' while preserving equivalence to get the graph M″ shown below.

$$M'' \quad = \quad \begin{array}{c} \mathrm{DC}(\mathrm{A}_X, X) \vee \mathrm{DC}(\mathrm{A}_Y, Y) \\ \wedge \\ \mathrm{DC}(\mathrm{CE}(\mathrm{A}_X), X) \vee \mathrm{DPE}(\mathrm{A}_Y, Y) \\ \wedge \\ \mathrm{DPE}(\mathrm{A}_X, X) \vee Y \end{array}$$

Again by using arguments dual to the one given earlier for X , we have

$$Y \quad = \quad \begin{array}{c} \mathrm{DPE}(\mathrm{A}_Y, Y) \\ \wedge \\ \mathrm{DPE}(\,(\mathrm{CE}(\mathrm{A}_Y) - \{\mathrm{A}_Y\}\,), Y) \\ \wedge \\ \mathrm{DC}(\mathrm{CE}(\mathrm{A}_Y), Y) \end{array}$$

In particular, the d-paths of the two are identical.

Replacing Y in M″ we find that every d-path in the subgraph $\mathrm{DPE}(\mathrm{A}_X, X) \vee \mathrm{DPE}(\,(\mathrm{CE}(A_Y) - \{\mathrm{A}_Y\}\,), Y)$ is in $\mathcal{DP}_{\mathrm{A}_X,\mathrm{A}_Y,M}$. Again by Theorem 5, these paths are also subsumed by other d-paths. Therefore we can remove the subgraph $\mathrm{DPE}(\,(\mathrm{CE}(A_Y) - \{\mathrm{A}_Y\}\,), Y)$ and preserve equivalence; M''' results.

$$M''' = \begin{array}{c} DC(A_X, X) \vee DC(A_Y, Y) \\ \wedge \\ DC(CE(A_X), X) \vee DPE(A_Y, Y) \\ \wedge \\ DPE(A_X, X) \vee \begin{array}{c} DPE(A_Y, Y) \\ \wedge \\ DC(CE(A_Y), Y) \end{array} \end{array}$$

The d-paths in M''' are those d-paths of M excluding the d-paths in $\mathcal{DP}_{A_X,A_Y,M}$. Consider now the d-paths of $DPE(A_X, X) \vee DPE(A_Y, Y)$ in M'''. They are exactly those of M (and of M''') that contain the anti-link: They each contain two occurrences of the literal A. Hence we can remove the node A_Y from $DPE(A_Y, Y)$ to get M''''.

$$M'''' = \begin{array}{c} DC(A_X, X) \vee DC(A_Y, Y) \\ \wedge \\ DC(CE(A_X), X) \vee DPE(A_Y, Y) \\ \wedge \\ DPE(A_X, X) \vee \begin{array}{c} DPE(A_Y, Y) - \{A_Y\} \\ \wedge \\ DC(CE(A_Y), Y) \end{array} \end{array}$$

Applying Lemma 5 to M'''' we get the following graph which is $DADV(\{A_X, A_Y\}, M)$.

$$DADV(\{A_X, A_Y\}, M) = \begin{array}{c} DC(A_X, X) \vee DC(A_Y, Y) \\ \wedge \\ DC(CE(A_X), X) \vee DPE(A_Y, Y) \\ \wedge \\ DPE(A_X, X) \vee CC(A_Y, Y) \end{array}$$

In constructing $DADV(\{A_X, A_Y\}, M)$, we have removed only subsumed d-paths and altered only d-paths that contain the anti-link by collapsing the double occurrence of the anti-link literal. Hence $DADV(\{A_X, A_Y\}, M)$ is equivalent to M, does not contain the anti-link, and does not contain any d-path of $\mathcal{DP}_{A_X,A_Y,M}$. □

Theorem 6 gives us a method to remove disjunctive anti-links and some subsumed d-paths: Simply identify a redundant anti-link $H = \{A_X, A_Y\}$ and the smallest full block M containing it, and then replace M by $DADV(H, M)$. The cost of this operation is proportional to the size of the graph replacing M. Also, c-connected literals in M do not become d-connected in $DADV(H, M)$. Thus truly new disjunctive anti-links are not introduced. However, parts of the graph may be duplicated, and this may give rise to additional copies of anti-links not yet removed. Nevertheless, persistent removal of redundant disjunctive anti-links (in which case $\mathcal{DP}_{A_X,A_Y,M} \neq \emptyset$) is a terminating process, because the number of d-paths is strictly reduced at each step. This proves

Theorem 7. Finitely many applications of the DADV operation on redundant anti-links will result in a graph without redundant disjunctive anti-links, and termination of this process is independent of the choice of anti-link at each step. □

Although we can remove all the redundant disjunctive anti-links in the graph, this process can introduce new conjunctive anti-links. Such anti-links may indicate the presence of subsumed d-paths, but the situation is not as favorable as with disjunctive anti-links – see Section 3.7.

3.5. Simplifications

Obviously, DADV($\{A_X, A_Y\}$, M) can be syntactically larger than M. Under certain conditions we may use simplified alternative definitions for DADV. These definitions result in formulas which are syntactically smaller than those that result from the general definition. The following is a list of possible simplifications.

1. If $CE(A_X) = A_X$ (and $CE(A_X) \neq X$), then $DC(CE(A_X), X) = DC(A_X, X)$. Therefore by (possibly non atomic) factoring on $DC(A_X, X)$ and observing that $(DC(A_Y, Y) \wedge DPE(A_Y, Y)) = Y$, DADV($\{A_X, A_Y\}$, M) becomes

$$\begin{array}{ccc} DC(A_X,X) & \vee & Y \\ & \wedge & \\ DPE(A_X,X) & \vee & CC(A_Y,Y) \end{array}$$

It turns out that this rule applies to the example used in Sections 3.1 and 3.2, and shown below.

$$\begin{array}{ccc} \begin{array}{c} A \vee C \\ \wedge \\ B \end{array} & \vee & \begin{array}{c} A \\ \wedge \\ E \vee C \end{array} \end{array}$$

Since $CE(A_X) = A_X$, the simplified rule for this case results in the following graph.

$$\begin{array}{ccc} B & \vee & \begin{array}{c} E \vee C \\ \wedge \\ A \end{array} \\ & \wedge & \\ A & \vee & C \end{array}$$

2. If $CE(A_X) = X$, then $DC(CE(A_X), X) = \varnothing$ (*true*). Hence $DPE(A_X, X) = A_X$ and $DC(A_X, X) = X - \{A_X\}$. DADV($\{A_X, A_Y\}$, M) becomes

$$\begin{array}{ccc} X - \{A_X\} & \vee & DC(A_Y,Y) \\ & \wedge & \\ A_X & \vee & CC(A_Y, Y) \end{array}$$

3. If both Case 1 and Case 2 apply, then $CE(A_X) = X = A_X$, and the above formula simplifies to

$$A_X \vee CC(A_Y, Y)$$

Note that in all the above versions of DADV, the roles of X and Y can be interchanged.

3.6. Disjunctive Anti-Links and Factoring

It is interesting to note that the DADV operation contains factoring (i.e., the ordinary application of the distributive law to a pair of conjunctions containing a common argument) as a special case. This is just the condition for Case 2 above except that both $\mathrm{CE}(\mathrm{A}_X) = X$ and $\mathrm{CE}(\mathrm{A}_Y) = Y$ hold. Under these conditions, $\mathrm{DADV}(\{\mathrm{A}_X, \mathrm{A}_Y\}, M)$ becomes

$$\begin{array}{c} X - \{\mathrm{A}_X\} \ \vee \ Y - \{\mathrm{A}_Y\} \\ \wedge \\ \mathrm{A} \end{array}$$

This is the graph obtained by disjunctive factoring [9].

The DADV operator also captures the absorption law (or merging). If A_X and A_Y are both arguments of the same disjunction, then $X = \mathrm{A}_X$, $Y = \mathrm{A}_Y$, and $\mathrm{DADV}(\{\mathrm{A}_X, \mathrm{A}_Y\}, M) = \mathrm{A}_X$. Note, however, that the anti-link is not redundant in this case.

3.7. Conjunctive Anti-Links

There are conjunctive anti-links that always indicate the presence of d-paths that are subsumed by others, and they are easy to detect. However, the conditions to be met are much more restrictive than those for redundant disjunctive anti-links. Consider a conjunctive anti-link $\{\mathrm{A}_X, \mathrm{A}_Y\}$, where the smallest full block M containing the anti-link is $(\mathrm{A}_X \wedge Y)$. Every d-path in Y which passes through A_Y will be subsumed by the d-path consisting of the single literal A_X. Hence we can replace Y by $\mathrm{DC}(\mathrm{A}_Y, Y)$.

This is a kind of dual to Case 3 of the simplified versions of DADV discussed earlier. There, the anti-link $\{\mathrm{A}_X, \mathrm{A}_Y\}$ is disjunctive and $M = (\mathrm{A}_X \vee Y)$. The simplified DADV operation just replaces Y by $\mathrm{CC}(\mathrm{A}_Y, Y)$. Note that the conjunctive anti-link operation above removes subsumed d-paths, whereas the Case 3 disjunctive anti-link operation can either remove paths or merely remove the second occurrence of the anti-link literal on paths that contain the anti-link. Both operations involve d-paths, and both have strictly dual operations that would affect c-paths instead.

4. Conclusion and Future Work

We have introduced anti-links and defined useful equivalence-preserving operations on them. These operations can be employed so as to strictly reduce the number of d-paths in an NNF formula. Unlike path dissolution, which removes unsatisfiable (or tautological, in the dual case) paths, anti-link operations remove subsumed paths without any direct checks for subsumption. This is significant for prime implicate computations, since such computations tend to be dominated by subsumption checks.

Some experimental results on a dissolution- and PI-based prime implicate system are reported in [12]. That system should be extended to include anti-link operations, so as to test their effectiveness in practice. The applicability of our techniques to Ngair's examples [10] is also worthy of study, because for many of his examples the full dissolvent contains useful anti-links. Also, his method requires a normal form that is somewhat more general than CNF or than DNF, whereas our techniques require only NNF and are thus more general.

References

1. de Kleer, J. An improved incremental algorithm for computing prime implicants. *Proceedings* of *AAAI-92*, 780-785.
2. Jackson, P., and Pais, J. Computing prime implicants. *Proceedings* of *CADE-10*, Kaiserslautern, W. Germany, July, 1990. In *LNAI*, Springer-Verlag, Vol. 449, 543-557.
3. Jackson, P. Computing prime implicants incrementally. *Proceedings* of *CADE-11*, Saratoga Springs, NY, June, 1992. In *LNAI*, Springer-Verlag, Vol. 607, 253-267.
4. Kean, A., and Tsiknis, G. An incremental method for generating prime implicants/implicates. *Journal of Symbolic Computation* **9** (1990), 185-206.
5. Kean, A., and Tsiknis, G. Assumption based reasoning and clause management systems. *Computational Intelligence* **8**,1 (Nov. 1992),1-24.
6. Letz, R. First-order calculi and proof procedures for automated deduction. Ph.D. thesis, TH Darmstadt, June 1993.
7. Murray, N.V., and Rosenthal, E. Inference with path resolution and semantic graphs. *J.ACM* 34,2 (April 1987), 225-254.
8. Murray, N.V., and Rosenthal, E. Path dissolution: A strongly complete rule of inference. *Proceedings* of *AAAI-87*, Seattle, WA, July 12-17, 1987, 161-166.
9. Murray, N.V., and Rosenthal, E. Dissolution: Making paths vanish. *J.ACM* **40**,3 (July 1993), 504-535.
10. Ngair,T. A new algorithm for incremental prime implicate generation. *Proceedings of IJCAI-93*, Chambery, France, August, 1993.
11. Przymusinski, T.C. An algorithm to compute circumscription. Artificial Intelligence **38** (1989), 49-73.
12. Ramesh, A., and Murray, N.V. Non-clausal deductive techniques for computing prime implicants and prime implicates. *Proceedings* of *LPAR-93*. St. Petersburg, Russia, July 13-20,1993. In *LNAI*, Springer-Verlag, Vol. 698, 277-288.
13. Reiter, R. and de Kleer, J. Foundations of assumption-based truth maintenance systems: preliminary report. *Proceedings of AAAI-87*, Seattle, WA, July 12-17, 1987, 183-188.
14. Slagle, J.R., Chang, C.L., and Lee, R.C.T. A new algorithm for generating prime implicants. *IEEE Transactions on Computers,* **C-19(4)** (1970), 304-310.
15. Strzemecki, T. Polynomial-time algorithms for generation of prime implicants. *Journal of Complexity* **8** (1992), 37-63.

A Generic Declarative Diagnoser for Normal Logic Programs

Lunjin Lu

The University of Birmingham, Birmingham B15 2TT, U.K.

Abstract. In this paper we develop a generic declarative diagnoser for normal logic programs that is based on tree search. The soundness and the completeness of the diagnoser are proved. The diagnoser is generic in that it can be used with different search strategies such as the bottom-up, top-down, top-down zooming and divide-and-query strategies in the literature. The user can specialise the diagnoser by choosing their own search strategy. The diagnoser also has a smaller search space than diagnosers reported in the literature. This is achieved by using the acquired part of the intended interpretation of the program to prune the search space before it is searched.

1 Introduction

An error that makes a program exhibit an unexpected behaviour is called a bug while the unexpected behaviour that a bug causes is called a bug symptom. After a bug symptom has been found, the programmer has to locate and identify the bug that causes the bug symptom and correct the bug in order to obtain the expected program behaviour. The process of locating and identifying the bug that causes a bug symptom is called program diagnosis. A software tool that supports such a process is called a diagnoser. Declarative program diagnosis is an interactive process whereby a declarative diagnoser obtains the intended interpretation of the program from an oracle, usually the programmer, and compares the intended interpretation with the actual interpretation of the program. There has been much research into declarative logic program diagnosis [4, 8, 11, 13, 18, 19, 22].

A buggy logic program may exhibit many kinds of bug symptom. It may produce a wrong answer, fail to produce a correct answer, fall into looping, call procedures with wrong types of arguments, or violate the safe rule of negation as failure, etc. This paper is concerned with the first two kinds of bug symptom.

We assume that readers are familiar with the terminology of logic programming [13]. Let ϵ be the identity substitution and P a logic program. We define the success set of P as

$$SS(P) = \{A \mid A \textit{ is an atom and } \epsilon \textit{ is a computed answer for } P \cup \{\leftarrow A\}\}$$

$SS(P)$ possibly contains non-ground atoms and describes the operational behaviour of logic programs more precisely than the success set defined in terms of ground atoms [21]. A model-theoretic counterpart of $SS(P)$ for definite programs is given in [7].

Definition 1 *Let P be a logic program and I an interpretation.*

(1) An atom A is an inconsistency symptom of P w.r.t. I if A is invalid in I and $A \in SS(P)$.
(2) An atom A is an insufficiency symptom of P w.r.t. I if A is satisfiable in I and P finitely fails on A.

Definition 2 *Let P be a logic program and I an interpretation.*

(1) A clause instance $A \leftarrow W$ is an inconsistent clause instance of P w.r.t. I if $A \leftarrow W$ is an instance of a clause of P and $A \leftarrow W$ is invalid in I.
(2) An atom A is an uncovered atom of P w.r.t. I if A is valid in I and, for every clause $A' \leftarrow W$ of P s.t. A and A' unify with m.g.u. θ, $W\theta$ is unsatisfiable in I. An atom A is an incompletely covered atom of P w.r.t. I if an instance of A is an uncovered atom of P w.r.t. I.

If there is an inconsistency or insufficiency symptom of P w.r.t. I then there is an inconsistent clause instance of P w.r.t. I or an incompletely covered atom of P w.r.t. I [8, 12, 13, 22]. Therefore, given an inconsistency or insufficiency symptom of P w.r.t. I, a declarative diagnoser for logic programs searches for an inconsistent clause instance of P w.r.t. I or an incompletely covered atom of P w.r.t. I. Many declarative diagnosers for logic programs have been developed. Shapiro [18, 19] developed the algorithmic debugging method[1] and exemplified the method through pure Prolog. Ferrand [8] adapted the algorithmic debugging method for definite logic programs. Lloyd [12, 13] presented a declarative diagnoser for arbitrary logic programs. The diagnoser is a meta-program which makes it easy to improve its performance by adding control information as meta-calls. Lloyd [12, 13] obtained a top-down diagnoser by adding control information. Yan [22] improved the top-down diagnoser by reorganising its control information.

Each of these declarative diagnosers for logic programs has an inconsistency diagnosis procedure and an insufficiency diagnosis procedure. The inconsistency diagnosis procedure is called with an inconsistency symptom of P w.r.t. I as its input and the insufficiency diagnosis procedure is called with an insufficiency symptom of P w.r.t. I as its input.

The main advantage of using a declarative diagnoser is that the oracle does not need to know anything about the operational aspect of the program. All that they need to know about is the intended interpretation of the program. The quantity of queries may be large and reducing the quantity of queries has been the main objective of much research into declarative diagnosis [3, 4, 6, 16, 17]. The quantity of queries is dependent on the size of the search space and the search strategy [13, 19].

In this paper we present a declarative diagnoser for normal programs. A normal program consists of a set of normal clauses of the form $A \leftarrow L_1, \cdots, L_m$

[1] We use the term diagnosis instead of debugging because debugging is a process which involves bug detection and bug correction as well as bug diagnosis.

where A is an atom and each literal L_i is either an atom or the negation of an atom. The SLDNF resolution procedure is used to implement normal programs. To ensure the soundness of the SLDNF resolution procedure, a safe computation rule or a weak safe computation rule must be used. A safe computation rule always selects a positive literal or a ground negative literal. A weak safe computation rule always selects a positive literal or a negative literal $\neg A_i$ s.t. A_i will not be instantiated if P succeeds on A_i. The diagnosis of unsafe uses of negation as failure is beyond of the scope of this paper. We assume that no unsafe use of negation as failure arises during the execution of an inconsistency or insufficiency symptom of P w.r.t. I.

Our diagnoser has a smaller search space than the diagnosers reported in the literature. The intended interpretation I of a logic program P consists of the set of atomic formulae that should be proved by P and the set of the atomic formulae that should be disproved by P. Whilst program P is being debugged, the oracle incrementally provides the debugging system with the intended interpretation I of P. Therefore, at some stage of debugging, the debugging system has already acquired part I' of I. Our declarative diagnoser uses I' to reduce the size of the search space.

Given an inconsistency symptom A of P w.r.t. I, our diagnoser first constructs a tree called an I-congruent partial proof tree (cpp) for P and A and then diagnoses P by searching this tree. An I-*cpp* for P and A is similar to a proof tree for P and A [1] except that a leaf of an I-*cpp* for P and A is an atom that is valid in I while a leaf of a proof tree for P and A is the atom *true*. Because I' is a part of I, an I'-*cpp* for P and A is also an I-*cpp* for P and A. Therefore, an I'-*cpp* for P and A can be used where an I-*cpp* for P and A is required. Whilst an I'-*cpp* tree for P and A is being constructed it is not necessary to query the oracle because I' has already been known to the debugging system. An I'-*cpp* for P and A is in size smaller than or equal to a proof tree for P and A because an I'-*cpp* for P and A may contain only one node for an atom that is valid in I' while a proof tree for P and A has a subtree for the same atom. When I' is empty, an I'-*cpp* for P and A is a proof tree for P and A. As I' increases during debugging, our diagnoser is able to construct a smaller and smaller I'-*cpp* for P and A.

Given an insufficiency symptom A of P w.r.t. I, our diagnoser first constructs a tree called an I-complete partial SLDNF tree (cps) for $P \cup \{\leftarrow A\}$ and then diagnoses by searching this tree. An I-*cps* for $P \cup \{\leftarrow A\}$ is similar to an SLDNF tree for $P \cup \{\leftarrow A\}$ [13] except that a node $\leftarrow W$ in an SLDNF tree for $P \cup \{\leftarrow A\}$ has a child node for each goal $\leftarrow W'$ that is derived from $\leftarrow W$ and P, while a node $\leftarrow W$ in an I-*cps* for $P \cup \{\leftarrow A\}$ only needs to have a child node for a goal $\leftarrow W'$ that is derived from $\leftarrow W$ and P s.t. W' is satisfiable in I. In other words, if W' is unsatisfiable in I then node $\leftarrow W'$ and the subtree rooted at $\leftarrow W'$ can be removed from an I-*cps* for $P \cup \{\leftarrow A\}$. Because I' is a part of I, an I'-*cps* for $P \cup \{\leftarrow A\}$ is also an I-*cps* for $P \cup \{\leftarrow A\}$. Hence, an I'-*cps* for $P \cup \{\leftarrow A\}$ can be used where an I-*cps* for $P \cup \{\leftarrow A\}$ is needed. The construction of an I'-*cps* for $P \cup \{\leftarrow A\}$ does not need to query the oracle because I' has already been known to the debugging system. An I'-*cps* for $P \cup \{\leftarrow A\}$ is smaller in size than an SLDNF tree for $P \cup \{\leftarrow A\}$ because a node $\leftarrow W$ in an SLDNF tree for $P \cup \{\leftarrow A\}$ usually has more child nodes than in an I'-*cps* for $P \cup \{\leftarrow A\}$. When I' is empty, an I'-*cps* for $P \cup \{\leftarrow A\}$ is an SLDNF tree for $P \cup \{\leftarrow A\}$. As I' increases during debugging, our diagnoser is able to construct a smaller and smaller I'-*cps* for $P \cup \{\leftarrow A\}$.

Our diagnoser is generic in that different tree search strategies can be used with the diagnoser and the user can specialise the diagnoser by specifying the search strategy to be used.

Section 2 formally introduces the concepts of I-*cpp* and I-*cps* and establishes that they are sufficient for the purpose of diagnosis, that is, an inconsistency symptom A of P w.r.t. I can be diagnosed by searching an I-*cpp* for P and A, and an insufficiency symptom A of P w.r.t. I can be diagnosed by searching an I-*cps* for $P \cup \{\leftarrow A\}$. Section 3 presents the diagnoser and proves its soundness and completeness. In section 4, we show the generality of our declarative diagnoser and compares the diagnoser with the declarative diagnosers in the literature with respect to the size of the search space. Section 5 concludes the paper and points to some further work on our declarative diagnoser.

2 Search Space

This section formally introduces the notions of I-*cpp* and I-*cps* and shows that an inconsistency symptom A of P w.r.t. I can be diagnosed by searching an I-*cpp* for P and A and an insufficiency symptom A of P w.r.t. I can be diagnosed by searching an I-*cps* for $P \cup \{\leftarrow A\}$.

Let T be a tree, r the root of T, and v a node of T. v is a branch node if v is neither the root of T nor a leaf of T. The height of T, written as $h(T)$, is the length of the longest path of T. $n(T)$ denotes the number of nodes of T. The level of v in T, denoted by $l(v,T)$, is the length of the path from r to v. T_v denotes the sub-tree of T that is rooted at v. Notice that $T = T_r$.

Definition 3 An ordered tree T is a literal-labelled tree if each node of T is a literal. Let L be a node of T and $L_1, L_2, \cdots, L_k$ the children of L in that order. We say that $L \leftarrow L_1, L_2, \cdots, L_k$ is the root implication of T_L and write it as $RI(T, L)$.

Definition 4 Let P be a normal program, I an interpretation and A an atom.

(1) A partial proof tree T for P and A is a literal-labelled tree satisfying the following two conditions. (i) The root of T is A. (ii) For each non-leaf node L' of T, either $RI(T, L')$ is an instance of a clause of P or $RI(T, L') = (\neg A' \leftarrow true)$ where A' is an atom on which P finitely fails.
(2) T is a proof tree for P and A if T is a partial proof tree for P and A, and every leaf node of T is *true*.
(3) A partial proof tree T for P and A is an I-*cpp* for P and A if every leaf node of T is a literal that is valid in I.

A proof tree for P and A is an *I-cpp* for P and A because *true* is valid in I. This definition of a proof tree is similar to that of [1]. The leaves of a proof tree defined in [1] are instances of unit clauses of P while they are *true* according to the above definition that treats a unit clause as having body *true*.

Example 1 Let P be the following buggy quick sort program. P has a bug that is indicated by a comment.

```
qs([X|L],L0):- pt(L,X,L1,L2),qs(L1,L3),qs(L2,L4),ap([X|L3],L4,L0).
                                                %ap(L3,[X|L4],L0)
qs([],[]).

pt([X|L],Y,L1,[X|L2]):- Y=<X,pt(L,Y,L1,L2).
pt([X|L],Y,[X|L1],L2):- Y>X, pt(L,Y,L1,L2).
pt([],X,[],[]).

ap([X|L1],L2,[X|L3]):- ap(L1,L2,L3).
ap([],L,L).
```

Let the intended interpretation I be as usual. $qs([2,3,1],[2,1,3])$ is an inconsistency symptom of P w.r.t. I. Suppose that the acquired part I' of I consists of the knowledge of built-in predicates. Then the following is an I'-*cpp* for P and $qs([2,3,1],[2,1,3])$ and hence an *I-cpp* for P and $qs([2,3,1],[2,1,3])$.

```
qs([2,3,1],[2,1,3])-----------------|                              (1)
|--pt([3,1],2,[1],[3])    (2)       |--qs([3],[3])                 (18)
|  |--2=<3                (3)       |  |--pt([],3,[],[])           (19)
|  |--pt([1],2,[1],[])    (4)       |  |  |--true                  (20)
|     |--2>1              (5)       |  |--qs([],[])                (21)
|     |--pt([],2,[],[])   (6)       |  |  |--true                  (22)
|        |--true          (7)       |  |--qs([],[])                (23)
|--qs([1],[1])            (8)       |  |  |--true                  (24)
   |--pt([],1,[],[])      (9)       |  |--ap([3],[],[3])           (25)
   |  |--true             (10)      |     |--ap([],[],[])          (26)
   |--qs([],[])           (11)      |        |--true               (27)
   |  |--true             (12)      |--ap([2,1],[3],[2,1,3])       (28)
   |--qs([],[])           (13)         |--ap([1],[3],[1,3])        (29)
   |  |--true             (14)            |--ap([],[3],[3])        (30)
   |--ap([1],[],[1])      (15)               |--true               (31)
      |--ap([],[],[])     (16)
         |--true          (17)
```

The above tree is smaller than a proof tree for P and $qs([2,3,1],[2,1,3])$ because in a proof tree for P and $qs([2,3,1],[2,1,3])$ each of node (3) (labelled with $2 =< 3$) and node (5) (labelled with $2 > 1$) has a child labelled with *true*.

Example 2 Let P and I be the same as in example 1. Suppose that at some stage during debugging, the acquired part I' of I consists of the knowledge of built-in predicates and the knowledge that $qs([X],[X])$ is valid in I for all possible X. Then removing nodes 9-17 and 19-27 from the tree in example 1 will result in an I'-*cpp* for P and $qs([2,3,1],[2,1,3])$ and hence an I-*cpp* for P and $qs([2,3,1],[2,1,3])$. This tree and the tree in example 1 are both I-*cpp* for P and $qs([2,3,1],[2,1,3])$. But the former is much smaller than the latter. This example shows that, given the same inconsistency symptom A of P w.r.t. I, our diagnoser is able to construct a smaller and smaller I-*cpp* for P and A as I' increases during debugging.

Lemma 1 *Let P be a normal program, I an interpretation, A an atom that is invalid in I, and T an I-*cpp *for P and A. Then there is a node L' of T s.t. $RI(T,L')$ is invalid I. Furthermore, either $RI(T,L')$ is an inconsistent clause instance of P w.r.t. I, or $RI(T,L') = (\neg A' \leftarrow \text{true})$ and A' is an insufficiency symptom of P w.r.t. I.* ∎

Lemma 1 states that an inconsistency symptom A of P w.r.t. I can be diagnosed by searching an I-*cpp* T for P and A to find a node L' of T s.t. $C = RI(T,L')$ is invalid in I. Either C is an inconsistent clause instance of P w.r.t. I, or $C = (\neg A' \leftarrow true)$ s.t. A' is an insufficiency symptom of P w.r.t. I.

Definition 5 An ordered tree T is a goal-labelled tree if each node of T is a goal.

Definition 6 Let P be a normal program, R a computation rule, G and G' normal goals, and I an interpretation.

(1) We say that G' is derived from G and P via R and write $G \xrightarrow{P,R} G'$ if $G = \leftarrow L_1,\cdots,L_i,\cdots,L_m$, L_i is the selected literal of G by R, and either (i) L_i is positive, there is a clause $A \leftarrow W$ of P s.t. L_i and A unify with a m.g.u. θ, and $G' = \leftarrow (L_1,\cdots,L_{i-1},W,L_{i+1},\cdots,L_m)\theta$, or (ii) L_i is negative with $L_i = \neg A_i$, P finitely fails on A_i, and $G' = \leftarrow (L_1,\cdots,L_{i-1},L_{i+1},\cdots,L_m)$.
(2) $\mathcal{C}(G,P,R)$ is the set of all the goals that are derived from G and P via R, that is, $\mathcal{C}(G,P,R) = \{G' | G \xrightarrow{P,R} G'\}$.
(3) $\mathcal{E}(G,P,R,I)$ is the subset of $\mathcal{C}(G,P,R)$ s.t. for each goal $G' = \leftarrow W'$ in $\mathcal{E}(G,P,R,I)$, W' is satisfiable in I.

$$\mathcal{E}(G,P,R,I) = \{\leftarrow W' \mid (\leftarrow W' \in \mathcal{C}(G,P,R)) \textit{ and } W' \textit{ is satisfiable in } I\}$$

Definition 7 Let P be a normal program, R a computation rule, G a normal goal, T a goal-labelled tree s.t. the root of T is G, and I an interpretation.

(1) T is a partial SLDNF tree for $P \cup \{G\}$ via R if any two nodes G^1 and G^2 of T s.t. G^2 is a child of G^1 satisfy $G^2 \in \mathcal{C}(G^1,P,R)$.
(2) T is an SLDNF tree for $P \cup \{G\}$ via R if T is a partial SLDNF tree for $P \cup \{G\}$ via R s.t. if G^1 is a node of T, then each G^2 in $\mathcal{C}(G^1,P,R)$ is also a node of T and G^2 is a child of G^1.

(3) T is an *I-cps* for $P \cup \{G\}$ via R if T is a partial SLDNF tree for $P \cup \{G\}$ via R s.t. if G^1 is a node of T, then each G^2 in $\mathcal{E}(G^1, P, R, I)$ is also a node of T and G^2 is a child of G^1.

The definition of an SLDNF tree is equivalent to that given in the literature such as [13]. The notion of an *I-cps* T for $P \cup \{G\}$ via R captures the idea that if P is correct w.r.t. I, then any successful derivation of $P \cup \{G\}$ via R corresponds to a path from the root of T to a leaf of T which is $\Box$. It follows from definition 7 that an SLDNF tree for $P \cup \{G\}$ via R is an *I-cps* for $P \cup \{G\}$ via R for any I. If A is an insufficiency symptom of P w.r.t. I, then an I-cps for $P \cup \{\leftarrow A\}$ via a fair computation rule R is a finite tree, and none of its leaves is $\Box$ because any derivation of $P \cup \{\leftarrow A\}$ terminated with $\Box$ corresponds to a proof tree for P and $A\theta$ for some θ.

Example 3 Let P be the following buggy program. The intended interpretation for d(X,Ys,Zs) is that either X is in list Ys but not in list Zs or X is in list Zs but not in list Ys. The intended interpretation for m(X,L) is that X is in list L.

```
d(X,Ys,Zs):- m(X,Ys),\+ m(X,Zs).        m(X,[X|Xs]).
d(X,Ys,Zs):- m(X,Zs),\+ m(X,Zs).        m(X,[Y|Ys]):- m(X,Ys).
                          % \+ m(X,Ys)
```

$d(3, [1, 2, 4], [2, 3])$ is an insufficiency symptom of P w.r.t. I. Suppose that the acquired part I' of I is empty. Then the following is an *I-cps* for $P \cup \{\leftarrow d(3, [1, 2, 4], [2, 3])\}$ via the left-to-right computation rule. $\leftarrow$ is written as '?'. This tree is also an SLDNF tree for $P \cup \{\leftarrow d(3, [1, 2, 4], [2, 3])\}$ via the left-to-right computation rule.

```
?d(3,[1,2,4],[2,3]----------------|                                  (1)
|-?m(3,[1,2,4]),\+m(3,[2,3])  (2)  |-?m(3,[2,3]),\+m(3,[2,3])  (6)
  |-?m(3,[2,4]),\+m(3,[2,3])  (3)    |-?m(3,[3]),\+m(3,[2,3])  (7)
    |-?m(3,[4]),\+m(3,[2,3])  (4)      |-?\+m(3,[2,3])         (8)
      |-?m(3,[]),\+m(3,[2,3]) (5)      |-?m(3,[]),\+m(3,[2,3]) (9)
```

Example 4 Let P and I be the same as in example 3. $Q \wedge \neg Q$ is unsatisfiable in I' for any Q and any consistent I'. So, removing nodes 6-9 from the tree in example 3 will result in an *I'-cps* for $P \cup \{\leftarrow d(3, [1, 2, 4], [2, 3])\}$ via the left-to-right computation rule. This tree and the tree in example 3 are both *I-cps* for $P \cup \{\leftarrow d(3, [1, 2, 4], [2, 3])\}$ via the left-to-right computation rule. But the former is much smaller than the latter. This example shows that, given the same insufficiency symptom A of P w.r.t. I, our diagnoser is able to constructs a smaller and smaller *I-cps* for $P \cup \{\leftarrow A\}$ via a fixed computation rule as I' increases during debugging.

Definition 8 Let I be an interpretation, T a goal-labelled tree and $\leftarrow W$ a node of T. We say $\leftarrow W$ is a critical node of T w.r.t. I if either W is satisfiable in I and $\leftarrow W$ is a leaf of T, or W is satisfiable in I and for each child $\leftarrow W'$ of $\leftarrow W$, W' is unsatisfiable in I.

Lemma 2 *Let P be a normal program, G^1 a normal goal, R a computation rule, I an interpretation, T an I-cps for $P \cup \{G^1\}$ via R, then there is a critical node G of T w.r.t. I. Furthermore, if $G = \leftarrow W = \leftarrow L_1, \cdots, L_{i-1}, L_i, L_{i+1}, \cdots, L_m$ with L_i being the selected literal of G by R then either (1) L_i is a positive literal and L_i is an incompletely covered atom of P w.r.t. I or (2) $L_i = \neg A_i$ where A_i is an atom and A_i is an inconsistency symptom of P w.r.t. I.* ∎

Lemma 2 states that an insufficiency symptom A of P w.r.t. I can be diagnosed by searching an *I-cps* T for $P \cup \{\leftarrow A\}$ via a fair computation rule R to find a critical node G of T w.r.t. I. $G \neq \square$ since P finitely fails on A. Let L be the selected literal L of G by R. Either L is an incompletely covered atom of P w.r.t. I, or $L = \neg A'$ and A' is an inconsistency symptom of P w.r.t. I.

3 A generic diagnoser

This section presents our declarative diagnoser for normal programs and proves its soundness and completeness. This declarative diagnoser will be referred to as π and in presented in Edinburgh Prolog [9].

Let T be a tree and v a node in T. We use $T - T_v$ to denote the tree resulting from deleting T_v, the sub-tree rooted at v, from T and $T \backslash T_v$ to denote the tree resulting from replacing T_v of T with a node v.

The inconsistency diagnosis procedure of π is *inconsistency*$(+A, -D)$. When called with an inconsistency symptom A of P w.r.t. I, *inconsistency*/2 succeeds with D being either an inconsistent clause instance of P w.r.t. I or an incompletely covered atom of P w.r.t. I. *inconsistency*/2 first calls *cpp*/2 to construct an *I-cpp* T for P and A. Then *inconsistency*/2 calls *invalid_impl*/2 to find a node L' of T s.t. $C = RI(T, L')$ is invalid. If C is an instance of a clause of P, *inconsistency*/2 returns with C as its output. Otherwise $C = (\neg A' \leftarrow true)$ with A' being an insufficiency symptom of P w.r.t. I. In this case, *inconsistency*/2 calls *insufficiency*/2 to diagnose the insufficiency symptom A' of P w.r.t. I. The specification for *cpp*$(+A, -T)$ is that T is an *I-cpp* for P and A.

```
inconsistency(A,D) :-
  cpp(A,T),
  !,
  invalid_impl(T,C),
  (
     C=(\+A1:-true)
  -> insufficiency(A1,D)
  ;  D = C
  ).
```

```
invalid_impl(T,C) :-
  height(T,1),
  root_impl(T,C).
invalid_impl(T,C) :-
  branch_node(T,L),
  !,
  (
     valid(L)
  -> '\'(T,L,T1)
  ;  '%'(T,L,T1)
  ),
  invalid_impl(T1,C).
```

invalid_impl$(+T, -C)$ succeeds with $C = RI(T, L')$ being invalid in I for some node L' of T if T is a literal-labelled tree whose root is invalid in I and each of whose leaves is valid in I. height$(+T, -H)$ succeeds with $h(T) = H$. branch_node$(+T, -L)$ succeeds with L being a branch node of T. *root_impl*$(+T, -C)$ succeeds with C being the root implication of T. valid$(+L)$ succeeds iff L is valid in I. '%'$(+T, +L, -T1)$ succeeds with $T1 = T_L$ if L is a node of T. '\'$(+T, +L, -T1)$ succeeds with $T1 = T \backslash T_L$ if L is a node of T.

The insufficiency diagnosis procedure of π is *insufficiency*$(+A, -D)$. When called with an insufficiency symptom A P w.r.t. I, *insufficiency*/2 succeeds with D being either an inconsistent clause instance of P w.r.t. I or an incompletely covered atom of P w.r.t. I. *insufficiency*/2 first calls *cps*/2 to construct an *I-cps* T for $P \cup \{\leftarrow A\}$. Then *insufficiency*/2 calls *critical*/2 to find a G node of T s.t. G is a critical node of T w.r.t. I. Let L be the selected literal of G by R. If L is positive, *insufficiency*/2 returns with L as its output. Otherwise, $L = \neg A'$ with A' being an inconsistency symptom of P w.r.t. I. In this case *insufficiency*/2 calls *inconsistency*/2 to diagnose inconsistency symptom A' of P w.r.t. I. *cps*$(+G, -T)$ succeeds with T being an *I-cps* for $P \cup \{G\}$ via a fixed fair computation rule R. *selected*$(+G, -L)$ succeeds with L is the selected literal of G by R.

```
insufficiency(A,D) :-            |    critical(T,G) :-
  cps('?'(A),T),                 |      height(T,0),
  !,                             |      root(T,G).
  critical(T,G),                 |    critical(T,G) :-
  selected(G,L),                 |      \+ height(T,0),
  (                              |      non_root(T,'?'(W)),
     L=\+A1                      |      !,
  -> inconsistency(A1,D)         |      (
  ;  D = L                       |         satisfiable(W)
  ).                             |      -> '%'(T,'?'(W),T1)
                                 |      ;  '-'(T,'?'(W),T1)
                                 |      ),
                                 |      critical(T1,G).
```

critical$(+T, -G)$ succeeds with G being a critical node of T w.r.t. I if T is a goal-labelled tree s.t. W is satisfiable in I where $\leftarrow W$ is the root of T. *root*$(+T, -G)$ succeeds with G being the root of T. *non_root*$(+T, -G)$ succeeds with G being a node of T other than the root of T. '-'$(+T, +G, -T1)$ succeeds with $T1 = T - T_G$ if G is a node T. *satisfiable*$(+W)$ succeeds iff W is satisfiable in I.

At a certain stage of diagnosis, I' embodies the knowledge about the intended interpretation I that have been acquired by the diagnoser. When the diagnoser constructs an *I-cpp* (or an *I-cps*), it uses I' to decide if a literal L is *known* to be valid in I (or if a conjunction W of literals is *known* to be unsatisfiable in I). These judgements are made by a set of rules based on I' and other knowledge that the diagnoser have acquired. One example rule is that A is valid in I if A is an instance of another atom that is valid in I.

It is possible that the validity of a literal L in I or the unsatisfiability of a conjunction W of literals in I may not be detected by the set of rules at a certain stage either becuase I' does not have enough information or because the set of rules are not complete. This does not affect the soundness and the completeness of π that are given later.

Example 5 We now show a session of using diagnoser π. The program is a buggy quick sort program. When a query is imposed on the oracle by *satisfiable*/1 or *valid*/1, variables in the atom concerned are replaced with generated mnemonic names that should be understood to be local to the query. The top-down zooming strategy [14] is used to search both *I-cpp* and *I-cps* . Before the diagnosis session begins, the acquired part I' of the intended interpretation I contains the following.

- calls to *ap*/3 or built-in procedures do not result in any bug symptom.
- $qs([X],[X])$ is valid in I.

The definitions for *qs*/2 and *ap*/3 are the same as those in example 1 and *pt*/4 is defined as follows.

```
pt([X|L],Y,L1,[X|L2]):- | pt([X|L],Y,[X|L1],L2):- | pt([],X,[],[]).
                %Y<X,   |  Y=<X,          %Y>=X,  |
  pt(L,Y,L1,L2).        |  pt(L,Y,L1,L2).         |
```

```
| ?- qs([2,1],L).
L = [2,1]
yes
| ?- inconsistency(qs([2,1],[2,1]),D).
Is qs([],[]) valid? y.          Is pt([1],2,[],[1]) valid? n.
Is pt([],2,[],[]) valid? y.
D = (pt([1],2,[],[1]) :- pt([],2,[],[]))
yes
| ?- % the user corrects the bug in the 1st clause for pt/4
| ?- qs([2,1],L).
no
| ?- insufficiency(qs([2,1],L),D).
Is pt([1],2,A,B) satisfiable? y.       A = ? [1].       B = ? [].
D = pt([1],2,_12938,_12939)
yes
| ?- % the user corrects the bug in the 2nd clause for pt/4
| ?- qs([2,1],L).
L = [2,1]
yes
| ?- inconsistency(qs([2,1],[2,1]),D).
D = (qs([2,1],[2,1]) :-
     pt([1],2,[1],[]),qs([1],[1]),qs([],[]),ap([2,1],[],[2,1]))
yes
```

```
| ?- % the user corrects the bug in the 1st clause for qs/2.
| ?- qs([2,1],L).
L = [1,2]
yes
| ?-
```

The following theorems establish the soundness and the completeness of π.

Theorem 1 (Soundness of π) *Let P be a normal program, A an atom and I an interpretation.*

(1) If A is an inconsistency symptom of P w.r.t. I and $inconsistency(A, D) \in SS(\pi)$, then D is either an inconsistent clause instance of P w.r.t. I, or an incompletely covered atom of P w.r.t. I.
(2) If A is an insufficiency symptom of P w.r.t. I and $insufficiency(A, D) \in SS(\pi)$, then D is either an inconsistent clause instance of P w.r.t. I, or an incompletely covered atom of P w.r.t. I. ∎

Theorem 2 (Completeness of π) *Let P be a normal program, A an atom and I an interpretation.*

(1) If A is an inconsistency symptom of P w.r.t. I, then there is some D s.t. D is either an inconsistent clause instance of P w.r.t. I, or an incompletely covered atom D of P w.r.t. I and $inconsistency(A, D) \in SS(\pi)$.
(2) If A is an insufficiency symptom of P w.r.t. I, then there is some D s.t. D is either an inconsistent clause instance of P w.r.t. I, or an incompletely covered atom D of P w.r.t. I and $insufficiency(A, D) \in SS(\pi)$. ∎

4 Related work

This section compares our diagnoser with the diagnosers reported in the literature w.r.t. the search strategy and the search space, two major factors that affect the quantity of queries.

4.1 Generality of π

Since procedure *invalid_impl*/2 uses only the first branch node of a literal-labelled tree enumerated by *branch_node*/2, we can implement *branch_node*/2 as the following without compromising the soundness and the completeness of π.

```
branch_node(T,N):- branch_node_1(T,N).
```

where the specification for *branch_node_1*/2 is that *branch_node_1*(T, N) succeeds once and only once with N being a branch node of T. The different implementations of *branch_node_1*/2 will result in different performances of the inconsistency diagnosis procedure *inconsistency*/2 in terms of the quantity of queries.

A top-down inconsistency diagnosis procedure based on tree search [4, 14, 20] can be obtained by using an implementation of *branch_node_1/2* s.t. *branch_node_1(T, N)* succeeds with N being a child of the root of T. A bottom-up inconsistency diagnosis procedure based on tree search [20] can be obtained by using an implementation of *branch_node_1/2* s.t. *branch_node_1(T, N)* succeeds with N being the parent node of a leaf node of T. The divide-and-query inconsistency diagnosis procedure [18, 19] can be obtained through an implementation of *branch_node_1/2* s.t. *branch_node_1(T, N)* succeeds with N being a node of T s.t. $|n(T_N) - n(T)/2| \leq |n(T_{N'}) - n(T)/2|$ for any other node N' of T. The top-down zooming inconsistency diagnosis procedure [14] can be obtained by using an implementation of *branch_node_1/2* s.t. *branch_node_1(T, N)* succeeds with N being a node of T satisfying either (1) N is a node of T other than the root of T, and (2) N and the root of T have the same predicate name, and (3) N is not subordinate to any node of T that satisfies (1) and (2), or N is a child of the root of T when no node of T satisfies (1) and (2).

Similarly, we can implement *non_root/2* as the following without affecting the soundness and the completeness of π.

```
non_root(T,N):- non_root_1(T,N).
```

where the specification for *non_root_1/2* is that *non_root_1(T, N)* succeeds once and only once s.t. N is a node of T other than the root node of T. The different implementations of *non_root_1/2* will result in different performances of the insufficiency diagnosis procedure *insufficiency/2* in terms of the quantity of queries.

A top-down insufficiency diagnosis procedure can be obtained by using an implementation of *non_root_1/2* s.t. *non_root_1(T, N)* succeeds with N being a child of the root of T. A bottom-up insufficiency diagnosis procedure can be obtained by using an implementation of *non_root_1/2* s.t. *non_root_1(T, N)* succeeds with N being a leaf node of T.

insufficiency/2 can be specialised resulting in a divide-and-query insufficiency diagnosis procedure through an implementation of *non_root_1/2* s.t. *non_root_1(T, N)* succeeds with N being a node of T s.t. $|n(T_N) - n(T)/2| \leq |n(T_{N'}) - n(T)/2|$ for any other node N' of T.

The formulation of π not only enables standard tree search strategies such as top-down, bottom-up and divide-and-query to be used, but also allows more flexible strategies to be used as long as these strategies conform to the specifications for *branch_node_1/2* and *non_root_1(T, N)*. This provides us with a platform for evaluating various strategies as well as tailoring the declarative diagnoser to a user who prefers a particular search strategy.

4.2 Search space

The search space of a declarative diagnoser is one of the major factors that affect the quantity of queries. We briefly compare the search space of our declarative diagnoser π with the search spaces of the declarative diagnosers in the literature.

Suppose that A is the inconsistency symptom of P w.r.t. I to be diagnosed. An inconsistency diagnosis procedure based on tree search [4, 14, 18, 19, 20], including the divide-and-query diagnoser [18, 19], is a specialised version of *inconsistency/2*. These inconsistency diagnosis procedures search for an inconsistent clause instance of P w.r.t. I in the set of all the clause instances that are used in one successful derivation of $P \cup \{\leftarrow A\}$, that is, the clause instances that are used in one proof tree for P and A. The search space of *inconsistency/2* is the set of all the clause instances that are used in one *I-cpp* for P and A. Because an *I-cpp* for P and A is smaller than a proof tree for P and A, *inconsistency/2* has a smaller search space.

There are inconsistency diagnosis procedures that are not based on tree search [8, 12, 13, 18, 19, 22]. Such inconsistency diagnosis procedures search a larger space than *inconsistency/2*. We exemplify this through the single stepping inconsistency diagnosis procedure [18, 19]. The single stepping inconsistency diagnosis procedure simulates Prolog's execution of A. Whenever a call A' has been executed successfully with a computed answer θ, the oracle is asked if $A'\theta$ is valid in I. If $A'\theta$ is valid in I, the single stepping inconsistency diagnosis procedure continues to simulate Prolog's execution of the remaining calls. Otherwise, $A'\theta$ is invalid in I. Let $C = H' \leftarrow L'_1, L'_2, \cdots, L'_m$ be the clause instance used to solve A'. $(L'_1, L'_2, \cdots, L'_m)\theta$ is already known to be valid in I. Therefore, $C\theta$ is an inconsistent clause instance of P w.r.t. I. Let R' be the left-to-right computation rule. The single stepping inconsistency diagnosis procedure searches for an inconsistent clause instance of P w.r.t. I in the set of all the clause instances used in the first successful SLDNF derivation of $P \cup \{\leftarrow A\}$ via R' and all the clause instances used in all the unsuccessful SLDNF derivations of $P \cup \{\leftarrow A\}$ via R' that are previous to the successful SLDNF derivation of $P \cup \{\leftarrow A\}$. The other inconsistency diagnosis procedures that are not based on tree search can be shown to have larger spaces than *inconsistency/2* as well.

Suppose that A is the insufficiency symptom of P w.r.t. I to be diagnosed. *insufficiency/2* searches for an incompletely covered atom of P w.r.t. I in the set of all the selected atoms of all the nodes of an *I-cps* for $P \cup \{\leftarrow A\}$ via a fixed computation rule R. The search space of the insufficiency diagnosis procedures presented in [4, 14, 16, 17] is the set of all the selected atoms of all the nodes of a SLDNF tree for $P \cup \{\leftarrow A\}$. Because an *I-cps* for $P \cup \{\leftarrow A\}$ is smaller than a SLDNF tree for $P \cup \{\leftarrow A\}$, *insufficiency/2* has a smaller search space than these insufficiency diagnosis procedures.

The insufficiency diagnosis procedures presented in [8, 12, 13, 22] have larger search spaces than *insufficiency/2* because, given an insufficiency symptom A of P w.r.t. I, their search spaces are larger than the set of all the selected atoms of all the nodes of a SLDNF tree for $P \cup \{\leftarrow A\}$. See [15] for a detailed analysis of the search spaces of the insufficiency diagnosis procedures in the literature.

4.3 Search space pruning versus oracle automation

The objective of reducing the quantity of queries has also been pursued by fully or partly automating the oracle. Diagnosers in [2, 6] use a full specification. A full specification makes it possible to completely avoid querying the user because any query about the intended interpretation I can be answered by using the specification. Diagnosers in [3, 4, 10] use assertions about the intended interpretation I to answer queries. Whenever a query is necessary, these diagnosers will try to answer the query by using only the assertions. Those queries that cannot be answered this way are imposed on the oracle. The assertions are descriptions of the acquired part I' of the intended interpretation I.

Given an inconsistency symptom A of P w.r.t. I, our diagnoser constructs an *I-cpp* for P and A using I'. The effect is equivalent to pruning a proof tree for P and A before it is searched. Similarly, given an insufficiency symptom A of P w.r.t. I, our diagnoser constructs an I-cps for $P \cup \{\leftarrow A\}$ using I'. The effect is equivalent to pruning a SLDNF tree for $P \cup \{\leftarrow A\}$ before it is searched.

Using I' to prune the search space before it is searched rather than to answer queries makes sense. Firstly, a smaller search space means a smaller upper bound for the quantity of queries. See [13] for a detailed analysis for inconsistency diagnosis procedures. Secondly, given an inconsistency symptom A of P w.r.t. I, if a proof tree for P and A is searched, then a search strategy may select a node L and query the oracle about the validity of L if the validity of L cannot be decided by using I'. If L is subordinate to another node L' in the proof tree s.t. L' is valid in I', then an *I-cpp* for P and A that is constructed using I' will not contain node L because L' is valid in I'. Therefore, this query can be spared. A similar argument applies to insufficiency diagnosis. This does not apply to the top-down search strategy. However, the top-down strategy may not be either the optimal strategy for the diagnosis problem at hand or the strategy preferred by the user. We share with [5] the opinion that the user should be allowed to choose their own strategy.

5 Conclusion

We have presented the generic declarative diagnoser π for normal logic programs and established its soundness and its completeness. π is generic in the sense that it can be used with various tree search strategies. π has a smaller search space than the declarative diagnosers in the literature when diagnosing an inconsistency or insufficiency symptom of P w.r.t. I.

References

1. P. Deransart. Proofs of Declarative Properties of Logic Programs. In J.Diaz and F.Orejas, editors, *Proceedings of International Joint Conference on TAPSOFT'89*, pages 207–226, Barcelona, Spain, March 1989.
2. N. Dershowitz and Y.-J. Lee. Deductive Debugging. In *Proceedings of 1987 Symposium of Logic Programming*, pages 298–306. The IEEE Computer Society Press, 1987.
3. W. Drabent, S. Nadjm-Tehrani, and J. Maluszynski. The Use of Assertions in Algorithmic Debugging. In ICOT, editor, *The Proceedings of the International Conference on Fifth Generation Computer Systems.* ICOT, 1988.

4. W. Drabent, S. Nadjm-Tehrani, and J. Maluszynski. Algorithmic Debugging with Assertions. In Harvey Abramson and M.H. Rogers, editors, *Meta-Programming in Logic Programming*, pages 502–521. The MIT Press, 1989.
5. M. Ducassé. Opium$^+$, a Meta-Debugger for Prolog. In Y. Kodratoff, editor, *Proceedings of the eighth ECAI*, pages 272–277, Münich, August 1-5 1988. Pitman.
6. A. Edman and S.-Å. Tärnlund. Mechanization of an Oracle in a Debugging System. In *Proceedings of the Eighth International Joint Conference on Artificial Intelligence*, volume 2, pages 553–555, Karlsruhe, West Germany, August 1983.
7. M. Falaschi, G. Levi, and C. Palamidessi. Declarative Modelling of the Operational Behavior of Logic Programs. *Theoretical Computer Science*, 69:289–318, 1989.
8. G. Ferrand. Error Diagnosis in Logic Programming, an Adaptation of E.Y. Shapiro's method. *The Journal of Logic Programming*, 4(3):177–198, 1987.
9. A.M.J. Hutching, D.L. Bowen, L. Byrd, P.W.H. Chung, F.C.N. Pereira, L.M. Pereira, R.Rae, and D.H.D. Warren. Edinburgh Prolog (the new implementation) user's manual. AI Applications Institute, University of Edinburgh, 8 October 1986.
10. T. Kanamori, T. Kawamura, M. Maeji, and K.Horiuchi. Logical Program Diagnosis from Specifications. ICOT Technical Report TR-447, March 1989.
11. Y. Lichtenstein and E. Shapiro. Abstract Algorithm Debugging. In R.A. Kowalski and K.A. Bowen, editors, *Proceedings of the fifth International Conference and Symposium on Logic Programming*, pages 512–531. The MIT Press, 1988.
12. J.W. Lloyd. Declarative Error Diagnosis. *New Generation Computing*, 5(2):133–154, 1987.
13. J.W. Lloyd. *Foundations of Logic Programming*. Springer-Verlag, 1987.
14. M. Maeji and T. Kanamori. Top-Down Zooming Diagnosis of Logic Programs. ICOT Technical Report TR-290, August 1987.
15. L. Naish. Declarative Diagnosis of Missing Answers. Technical Report 88/9 (Revised May 1991), Department of computer science, The University of Melbourne, May 1991.
16. L.M. Pereira. Rational Debugging in Logic Programming. In E. Shapiro, editor, *Proceedings of the 3rd International Logic Programming Conference*, pages 203–210. Springer Verlag, 1986. Lecture Notes in Computer Science no. 225.
17. L.M. Pereira and M. Calejo. A Framework for Prolog Debugging. In R.A. Kowalski and K.A. Bowen, editors, *Proceedings of the fifth International Conference and Symposium on Logic Programming*, pages 481–495. The MIT Press, 1988.
18. E. Shapiro. Algorithmic Program Diagnosis. In *ACM Conference Record of the ninth annual ACM Symposium on Principles of Programming Languages*, pages 299–308, Albuquerque, New Mexico, Jan. 25-27 1982.
19. E. Shapiro. *Algorithmic Debugging*. The MIT Press, 1983.
20. L. Sterling and E. Shapiro. *The Art of Prolog*. The MIT Press, 1986.
21. M.H. van Emden and R.A. Kowalski. The Semantics of Predicate Logic as a Programming Language. *Artificial Intelligence*, 23(10):733–742, 1976.
22. S.Y. Yan. Foundations of Declarative Debugging in Arbitrary Logic Programming. *International Journal of Man Machine Studies*, 32:215–232, 1990.

Goal Dependent vs. Goal Independent Analysis of Logic Programs

M. Codish[1] M. García de la Banda[2]
M. Bruynooghe[3] M. Hermenegildo[2]

[1] Dept. of Math. and Comp. Sci., Ben-Gurion Univ., Israel. codish@bengus.bgu.ac.il
[2] Facultad de Informática, Universidad Politécnica de Madrid, Spain. {maria,herme}@fi.upm.es
[3] Dept. of Comp. Sci., Katholieke Universiteit Leuven, Belgium. maurice@cs.kuleuven.ac.be

Abstract. Goal independent analysis of logic programs is commonly discussed in the context of the bottom-up approach. However, while the literature is rich in descriptions of top-down analysers and their application, practical experience with bottom-up analysis is still in a preliminary stage. Moreover, the practical use of existing top-down frameworks for goal independent analysis has not been addressed in a practical system. We illustrate the efficient use of existing goal dependent, top-down frameworks for abstract interpretation in performing goal independent analyses of logic programs much the same as those usually derived from bottom-up frameworks. We present several optimizations for this flavour of top-down analysis. The approach is fully implemented within an existing top-down framework. Several implementation tradeoffs are discussed as well as the influence of domain characteristics. An experimental evaluation including a comparison with a bottom-up analysis for the domain *Prop* is presented. We conclude that the technique can offer advantages with respect to standard goal dependent analyses.

1 Introduction

The framework of abstract interpretation [7] provides the basis for a semantic approach to data-flow analysis. A program analysis is viewed as a non-standard semantics defined over a domain of data descriptions where the syntactic constructs in the program are given corresponding non-standard interpretations. For a given language, different choices of a semantic basis for abstract interpretation may lead to different approaches to analysis of programs in that language. For logic programs we distinguish between two main approaches: "bottom-up analysis" and "top-down analysis". The first is based on a bottom-up semantics such as the classic T_P semantics, the latter on a top-down semantics such as the SLD semantics. In addition, we distinguish between "goal dependent" and "goal independent" analyses. A goal dependent analysis provides information about the possible behaviors of a specified (set of) initial goal(s) and a given logic program. This type of analysis can hence be viewed as mapping a program and an initial goal description to a description of the corresponding behaviours. In contrast, a goal independent analysis considers only the program itself. In principle the result of such an analysis can be viewed as a mapping from initial goal descriptions to corresponding descriptions of goal behaviours. Consequently a goal independent analysis typically consists of two stages. The first, in which a goal independent mapping is derived from the program; and the second in which this mapping is applied to derive specific information for various different initial goal descriptions.

Traditionally, the standard meaning of a logic program P is given as the set of ground atoms in P's vocabulary which are implied by P. The development of top-down analysis frameworks was originally driven by the need to abstract not only the declarative meaning of programs, but also their behavior. To this end it is straightforward to enrich the operational SLD semantics into a collecting semantics which captures call patterns (i.e. how particular predicates are activated while searching for refutations), and success patterns (i.e. how call patterns are instantiated by the refutation of the involved predicate). Consequently, it is quite natural to apply a top-down approach to derive goal dependent analyses.

Falaschi *et al.* [9] introduce a bottom-up semantics which also captures operational aspects of a program's meaning. This semantics basically consists of a non-ground version of the T_P operator. The meaning of a program is a set of possibly non-ground atoms which can be applied to determine the answers for arbitrary initial goals. This semantics is the basis for a number of frameworks for the bottom-up analysis of logic programs [1, 3]. An analysis based on the abstraction of this semantics is naturally viewed as goal independent.

It is the above described state of affairs which has led to the "folk belief" that top-down analyses of logic programs are goal dependent while bottom-up analyses are goal independent. In fact, bottom-up computations have also been used for query evaluation in the context of deductive databases where "magic sets" and related transformation techniques are applied to make the evaluation process goal dependent. These same techniques have also been applied to enable bottom-up frameworks of abstract interpretation to support goal dependent analysis (see [3] for a list of references). This work breaches the folk belief and suggests that bottom-up frameworks have a wider applicability. In contrast, the practical application of top-down frameworks for goal independent analysis has received little attention. The purpose of this paper is to fill this gap. Moreover, we observe that there are currently a number of fine tuned generic top-down frameworks which are widely available. In contrast, implementation efforts for bottom-up frameworks are still in a preliminary stage. Hence, an immediate benefit of our study is to make goal independent analyses readily available using existing top-down frameworks.

We conclude that the real issue is not top-down vs. bottom-up but rather goal dependent vs. goal independent. As already pointed out by Jacobs and Langen [12], goal dependent analysis can be sped up by using the results of a goal independent analysis, and whether this results in a loss in precision has to do with the characteristics of the abstract domain.

Sections 2, 3 and 4 recall the relevant background and describe some simple transformations enhancing the efficiency of top-down goal independent analysis. Sections 5 and 6 present the main contribution of the paper: an evaluation of the appropriateness of a generic top-down framework (PLAI) for goal independent analysis and the value of a goal independent analysis as a means to speed up a subsequent goal dependent analysis. Sections 7 and 8 discuss the results and conclude.

2 Goal independent analysis in a top-down framework

It is relatively straightforward to apply a top-down framework to provide goal independent analyses much the same as those provided by bottom-up frameworks. To see this consider that, as argued in [9], the non-ground success set obtained by the Falaschi *et al.* semantics is equivalent to the set $\{\, p(\bar{x})\theta \,|\, p/n \in P \text{ and } \theta \text{ is an answer substitution for } p(\bar{x}) \,\}$. This provides the basis for a naive but straightforward goal independent, top-down analysis. An approximation of the non-ground success set of a program is obtained by performing the top-down analysis for the set of "flat" initial goal descriptions $\langle p(\bar{x}); \kappa_\epsilon \rangle$ where p/n is a predicate in P and κ_ϵ is the (most precise) description of the empty substitution. The same result can be obtained with a single application of the top-down framework by adding to a program P the set of clauses $\{\, analyze \leftarrow p(\bar{x}) \,|\, p/n \in pred(P) \,\}$ where $analyze/0 \notin pred(P)$. Given the initial call pattern $(analyze; \kappa)$ (with κ any abstract substitution), there is a call pattern $(p(\bar{x}); \kappa_\epsilon)$ for every $p/n \in pred(P)$. We will refer to this transformation as the *naive* transformation and the corresponding analysis as the *naive* analysis.

In this paper we use the top-down framework described in [16] (PLAI). The framework is based on a collecting semantics which captures both success and call patterns. For sharing analyses, the information is represented as lists of lists which appear as comments within the text of the program. The information describes properties of possible substitutions when execution reaches different points in the clause. The information given after the head describes properties of all clause variables after performing head unification. The information given after each subgoal describes properties of all clause variables after executing the clause up to and including the subgoal.

Example 1. Consider the following simple program **P**:

```
mylength(Y,N):- mylength(Y,0,N).
mylength([ ],N,N).
mylength([X|Xs],N1,N):- N2 is N1+1, mylength(Xs,N2,N).
```

The naive transformation adds the following clauses to **P**:

```
analyze:- mylength(X,Y).
analyze:- mylength(X,Y,Z).
```

A goal independent analysis using the *Sharing* domain [11, 15] gives the following:

```
(1)  analyze :-                      %[[X],[Y]]
             mylength(X,Y).          %[[X]]
(2)  analyze :-                      %[[X],[Y],[Z]]
             mylength(X,Y,Z).        %[[X],[Y,Z]]
```

```
(3)  mylength(Y,N) :-               %[[Y],[N]]
             mylength(Y,0,N).       %[[Y]]
(4)  mylength([ ],N,N).             %[[N]]
(5)  mylength([X|Xs],N1,N) :-       %[[N1],[N],[X],[X,Xs],[Xs],[N2]]
             N2 is N1+1,            %[[N],[X],[X,Xs],[Xs]]
             mylength(Xs,N2,N).     %[[X],[X,Xs],[Xs]]
```

In the *Sharing* domain [11, 15] an abstract substitution is a set of sets of program variables (represented as a list of lists). Intuitively, each set $\{v_1, \ldots, v_n\}$ specifies that there may be a substitution where the terms bound to the clause variables contain a variable occurring in the terms bound to $v_1, \ldots, v_n$ and occurring in none of the other terms. If a variable v does not occur in any set, then there is no variable that may occur in the terms to which v is bound and thus those terms are definitely ground. If a variable v appears only in a singleton set, then the terms to which it is bound may contain only variables which do not appear in any other term. For example, after executing the recursive call in clause (5) the variables N, N1 and N2 are ground while X and Xs are possibly non-ground. Moreover, if they are non ground, they may possibly share. The analysis provides also the following information indicating the set of call and success patterns:

Atom	Call Pattern	Success Pattern
analyze	[ ]	[ ]
mylength(A,B,C)	[[A],[B],[C]]	[[A],[B,C]]
mylength(A,B)	[[A],[B]]	[[A]]
mylength(A,0,B)	[[A],[B]]	[[A]]
mylength(A,B,C)	[[A],[C]]	[[A]]

Note that while the first three rows give the goal independent information, the other two represent the answers inferred for two specific call patterns which were needed for the abstract computation. □

Observe that the analysis described in Example 1 is inefficient in that it provides information concerning call patterns which are not required in a goal independent analysis. A more efficient analysis is obtained by transforming the program so that all calls in the body of a clause are "flat" and involve only fresh variables. As a consequence, any call encountered in the top-down analysis is in its most general form and corresponds to the call patterns required by a goal independent analysis. This transformation is referred to as the *efficient* transformation and involves replacing each call of the form $q(\bar{t})$ in a clause body by $q(\bar{x}), \bar{x} = \bar{t}$[1] where $\bar{x}$ are fresh variables. The corresponding analysis is called the *efficient* analysis.

Example 2. Applying the efficient transformation to the program in Example 1 gives:

[1] Note, however, that in Prolog this transformation can result in a program which produces different answers, especially due to the presence of "impure calls" such as *is*/2. Such calls require special care in the goal independent analysis, see discussion at end of section 4.

```
analyze:- mylength(X,Y).           mylength([ ],N,N).
analyze:- mylength(X,Y,Z).         mylength([X|Xs],N1,N) :-
                                           N2 is N1+1,
mylength(Y,N) :-                           mylength(Xsa,N2a,Na),
        mylength(Ya,Ma,Na),                <Xsa,N2a,Na> = <Xs,N2,N>.
        <Y,0,N> = <Ya,Ma,Na>.
```

A goal independent analysis of this program eliminates the last two rows in the table of Example 1. □

As indicated by our experiments (described in the following sections) the "efficient" transformation provides a practical speed-up of up to 2 orders of magnitude (for the domain *Prop*) over the naive approach. As suggested also by Jacobs and Langen [12], we conjecture that the efficient top-down analysis is in fact equivalent to the corresponding bottom-up analysis. In particular, potential loss of precision with respect to a goal dependent analysis is determined by the characteristic properties of the domain.

3 Reusing goal independent information

In this section we illustrate how the results of a goal independent analysis can be (re-)used to derive goal dependent information. For answer substitutions there is no problem as it is well known that the non-ground success set of a program determines the answers for any initial goal. In fact, the same techniques applied in bottom-up analyses can be applied also for top-down goal independent analyses. Moreover, since the call $p(\bar{t})$ is transformed to $p(\bar{x}), \bar{x} = \bar{t}$, the (abstract) unification $\bar{x} = \bar{t}$ with the success pattern for the call $p(\bar{x})$ obtained in the goal independent analysis yields a safe approximation of the success pattern for the original query $p(\bar{t})$. This fact is well known in bottom-up analysis. However our aim is to use the results of the goal independent analysis to derive a safe approximation of all call patterns activated by a given initial call.

Several solutions to this problem are discussed in the literature. These include the magic-set transformation mentioned above as well as the characterization of calls described in [1] and formalized in [10]. Both of these approaches are based on the same recursive specification of calls. Namely: (1) if $a_1, \ldots, a_i, \ldots, a_m$ is an initial goal then $a_i\theta$ is a call if θ is an answer for $a_1, \ldots, a_{i-1}$ (in particular a_1 is a call); and (2) if $h \leftarrow b_1, \ldots, b_i, \ldots, b_n$ is a (renamed) program clause, a is a call, $mgu(a, h) = \theta$ and φ is an answer of $(b_1, \ldots, b_{i-1})\theta$ then $b_i\theta\varphi$ is a call.

Our approach is to perform a second pass of top-down analysis to derive the goal dependent information, but using the goal independent information available in order to simplify the process. The idea is to perform the goal dependent analysis in the standard way of the PLAI framework, except for the case of recursive predicates. This framework passes over an and/or graph when analysing a program [2]. In recursive cases, the framework performs several iterations over certain parts of the graph until reaching a fixpoint: when encountering a call $p(\bar{t})$ which is equivalent to an ancestor call, the framework does not analyse the clauses defining

$p(\bar{t})$ but instead uses a first approximation (based on results obtained for the ancestor call from the nonrecursive clauses). This initiates an iterative process over a subgraph which terminates when it is verified that a safe approximation is obtained. However, as the results of the goal independent analysis are available, these iterations can be avoided when performing the second pass proposed herein, which can be thus completed in a single traversal of the graph. Note that due to the efficient transformation $p(\bar{t})$ is replaced by $p(\bar{x})$, $\bar{x} = \bar{t}$. Then, since the success state of the call $p(\bar{x})$ is available from the goal independent analysis, the (abstract) unification $\bar{x} = \bar{t}$ yields a safe approximation of the success state of the call $p(\bar{t})$ and iteration is avoided.

Our approach is similar to that suggested by Jacobs and Langen [11, 12]. The main difference is that they reuse the goal independent information without entering the definition of predicates. In the terminology of [12], the goal independent information is viewed as a "condensed" version of the called predicate and replaces its definition. In contrast, our approach traverses the entire abstract and/or graph constructed in the goal independent phase, even when a more simple 'look-up' could be performed. However, iteration (or fixed point computation) is avoided. Moreover, we obtain information at all program points and for all call patterns encountered in a computation of the initial goal. It is interesting to note that from an implementation point of view, all phases are performed using the same top-down interpreter. We illustrate our approach with an example:

Example 3. Consider a *Sharing* analysis of the following simple Prolog program. The result of the goal independent analysis is indicated next to the program:

```
p([ ],[ ]).
p([X|Xs],[Y|Ys]):- X>Y,q(Xs,Ys).
q([ ],[ ]).
q([X|Xs],[Y|Ys]):- p(Xs,Ys).
```

Atom	Call Pat.	Success Pat.
p(X,Y)	[[X],[Y]]	[[X],[Y]]
q(X,Y)	[[X],[Y]]	[[X],[Y]]

Consider an initial query pattern of the form $\langle p(X, Y); [[Y]]\rangle$ which specifies that X is ground. We illustrate the difference between the standard top-down analysis and the analysis which reuses the results in the above table.

Both analyzers first compute information for the non-recursive clause of $p/2$ obtaining $[\,]$ as the first approximation of the answer. They then consider the second clause obtaining the abstract substitution $[[Y], [Y, Ys], [Ys]]$ (both X and Xs are ground), analyze the built-in $X > Y$ obtaining $[[Ys]]$, and call $q(Xs, Ys)$ with the call pattern $[[Ys]]$. A similar process applies to q with this call pattern: first, the information for the non-recursive clause of q is computed obtaining $[\,]$ as the first approximation of the answer, then the second clause is considered, obtaining the abstract substitution $[[Y], [Y, Ys], [Ys]]$ (both X and Xs are ground), $p(Xs, Ys)$ is called with call pattern $[[Ys]]$.

At this point, the call pattern is the same as the initial call, hence the ***modified*** top-down framework analyses $p(A, B), \langle A, B\rangle = \langle Xs, Ys\rangle$ under the abstract substitution $[[A], [B], [Ys]]$. It uses the precomputed table to look up the answer for $p(A, B)$ obtaining $[[A], [B], [Ys]]$ as result of the call. Abstract unification of $\langle A, B\rangle = \langle Xs, Ys\rangle$ gives the abstract substitution $[[Ys, B]]$. Projection on $\{Xs, Ys\}$ gives $[[Ys]]$. The least upper bound of the answers for the two clauses of $q/2$ gives the final result $[[Ys]]$ for $q(Xs, Ys)$. The least upper bound for the two clauses of $p/2$ results in $[[Ys]]$. Note that no fixed point computation is needed.

In contrast, the standard top-down framework takes the current approximation $[\,]$ of the answer for $p(Xs, Ys)$, computes $[[Y]]$ as the approximated answer substitution for the second clause of $q/2$ and takes the least upper bound of this answer and the one obtained for the first clause. This results in $[[Ys]]$ as the approximated answer for the call $q(Xs, Ys)$. The least upper bound for two clauses of $p/2$ gives $[[Ys]]$. Now, a new iteration is started for $p(X, Y)$ since the answer changed during the execution (from $[\,]$ which was the first approximation obtained from the non-recursive clauses, to $[[Y]]$) and there is a recursive subgoal $q(Xs, Ys)$ with call pattern $[Ys]$ which depends on $p(X, Y)$ with call $[[Y]]$; nothing changes during this new iteration and the fixpoint is reached. □

Note that it is still possible that several copies of a same clause are activated, namely when the clause is called with different patterns. The different versions will all be analyzed in the same iteration through the and/or graph whereas the usual top-down framework can iterate several times over (parts of) the and/or graph.

4 Domain dependent issues

There are some domain-dependent issues which can significantly affect the precision of the results obtained. The following example illustrates how, for some domains, a naive top-down analysis can provide a more precise analysis for some programs.

Example 4. Consider a simple (goal independent) type analysis of the following program:

```
rev(Xs, Ys) :- rev(Xs, [ ], Ys).
rev([ ], Ys, Ys).
rev([X|Xs], R, Ys) :- rev(Xs, [X|R], Ys).
```

A reasonable (top-down or bottom-up) goal independent analysis for rev/3 will infer that the first argument is of type 'list' while the second and third arguments are of type 'any'. A naive top-down analysis can infer that both arguments of rev/2 are of type 'list' because the initial call to rev/3 has a second argument of type list, while a bottom-up analysis, as well as an efficient top-down analysis, will infer that the first argument is of type 'list' and the second of type 'any'. □

The above example illustrates that the precision of an analysis is highly dependent on the ability of the underlying abstract domain to capture information (such as sharing) which enables a good propagation of the property being analyzed.

Jacobs and Langen [12] prove that top-down and bottom-up analyses are guaranteed to be equally precise when they involve an abstract unification function which is *idempotent*, *commutative* and *additive*. Idempotence implies that repeating abstract unification does not change the result. Commutativity allows abstract unification to be performed in any order. Finally, additivity guarantees that precision is not lost when performing least upper bounds. Clearly these conditions impose a restriction on the abstract domain — as a weak domain cannot support an abstract unification algorithm which satisfies these properties. It is interesting to note that while idempotence is satisfied for most of the domains proposed in the literature, the other two properties are not. Consequently, the answer to the question ***should we prefer (top-down or bottom-up) goal independent analyses*** remains an issue for practical experimentation.

In the remainder of the paper we describe an experimental investigation involving three well known abstract domains, namely, ***Prop*** [13], ***Sharing*** [11, 15] and ***ASub*** [17]. We note that ***Prop*** satisfies all three of the above mentioned conditions (there is an abstract unification algorithm for ***Prop*** which satisfies these conditions). For ***Sharing***, the first two conditions are satisfied, while ***ASub*** satisfies only idempotence.

It is interesting to note that additivity in the abstract domain becomes more relevant when performing goal independent analyses. This is because, due to the lack of propagation of information from an initial call, abstract substitutions in an abstract computation tend to contain less information than in the goal-dependent case. Moreover, the accuracy lost when performing least upper bounds becomes more acute as we handle abstract substitutions containing less information. The same holds for commutativity. When more groundness information is available during the abstract computation (due to propagation of information from an initial goal) the inability of the domain to remember dependencies between variables has less effect on accuracy. In fact we observe in [5] that the groundness information obtained with *ASub* is essentially the same as obtained with *Sharing* (for a rich set of benchmarks). We reason that most real Prolog programs tend to propagate groundness in a top-down manner. We expect that (lack of) commutativity will become more relevant in goal-independent analyses although, less important in a naive top-down analyses than in bottom-up or efficient top-down analysis.

Another important issue concerns the behavior of "impure goals". Consider for example an abstract domain which captures definite freeness information. In a standard top-down analysis if we know that the clause `p(X,Y) :- ground(X), Y=a` is called with X a free variable then we may assume that the clause fails. In contrast, in a top-down goal independent analysis, the initial goal call pattern is always $\{\epsilon\}$ and we must assume downwards closure of all descriptions. Likewise, a goal dependent sharing analysis involving the clause `p(X,Y) :- X==Y` with call pattern $[[X],[Y]]$ may assume that `X==Y` implies that X and Y are ground due to the lack of sharing between X and Y. Such reasoning is not valid in a goal independent analysis.

5 Objectives, experiments and results

Our objective is to illustrate the relative impact of the issues discussed in the previous sections on efficiency and accuracy of goal independent analyses. Our study focuses on a top-down framework, due to its availability. We compare the standard top-down, goal dependent framework with the alternative two phase analysis which first infers goal independent information and then reuses it to obtain goal dependent information for given initial goals.

For goal independent analyses we compare the *naive* and *efficient* approaches described in Section 2. The efficient approach is implemented not as a program transformation but instead by modifying the top-down framework itself which is also modified to keep and reuse goal independent information.

Given the expected dependence of the results on the characteristics of the domains, we have implemented three analyzers, using the domains *ASub*, *Sharing*, and *Prop*. For *Prop* we use the same implementation strategy as described in [4] and provide a comparison with the bottom-up analyses described in [4]. The implementation is based on a technique called "abstract compilation" [8, 18] in which a program is analyzed by applying the *concrete* semantics to an abstraction of the program itself. We note that the bottom-up analysis for *Prop* is based on a highly optimised analyzer which is specific for this type of domain. In contrast, the top-down analysis is performed within the general purpose PLAI framework. Hence, the efficiency results are naturally in favour of the bottom-up analysis. The accuracy results are, as expected, identical.

It should be noted that in our experiments we are using only "strong" domains, i.e. domains that are relatively complex and quite precise. This is done first because they are more likely to represent those used in practice, and also because using goal independent analysis on weak domains is clearly bound to give low precision results.

Tables 1, 2 and 3 respectively present the results of the experiments performed with the *Prop*, *Sharing* and *Asub* domains. The benchmark programs are the same as those used in [4] and in [6] for evaluating the efficiency of their bottom-up approach. All analyses are obtained using SICStus 2.1 (native code) on a SPARC10. All times are in seconds. The columns in the respective tables describe the following information:

Name: the benchmark program and the arguments of the top-level predicate.
GI: the results for the goal independent analyses

- **BU**: time for the bottom-up analyzer described in [4].
  Available only for Prop – Table 1.
- $\mathbf{GI}^{ef}$: time for the efficient top-down goal independent analysis.
- $\mathbf{GI}^{n}$: time for the naive top-down goal independent analysis.
- $\mathbf{Size}^{n}$: A measure of the average and maximal (between parenthesis) sizes of the results given by the naive top-down goal independent analyses.
  For *Prop* (Table 1), the number of disjuncts in the resulting disjunctive normal forms and for *Sharing* and *ASub* (Tables 2 and 3), the number of variables in the resulting abstract substitutions.
- Δ: the percentage of *predicates* for which the analysis using $\mathbf{GI}^{ef}$ is less accurate than that obtained by $\mathbf{GI}^{n}$.
  Only in Tables 2 and 3 (for Prop both techniques give identical results).

$\mathbf{GD}^{reuse}$: the results for the goal dependent analyses which reuse the (efficient) goal independent information:

- **Query**: some example call patterns (for *Prop*, a propositional formula on the variables of the top-level predicate).
- **Tm**: the time.
- **RP**: number of look-ups (in the results of the goal independent phase)
- **Size**: The same measure of the size as above, but this time it only takes into account the answers obtained in the goal independent phase which have been looked-up. This information is included to give a rough idea of the complexity of the abstract unification operations involved.

GD^{standard}: results for the standard top-down, goal dependent analyses in computing the goal dependent information for the indicated query.

- **Tm**: the time.
- **> 1**: number of fixed point computations that take more than one iteration. These are the non-trivial computations.
- **> 2**: number of fixed point computations which take more than two iterations. Note that the last iteration usually takes much less time than the others. So these computations are bound to be more costly than those which involve only two iterations.

Δ: the % of program *points* at which the information inferred by the **GD**^{reuse} is less accurate than that obtained by the standard **GD**^{standard} approach. Only in Tables 2 and 3 (for Prop both techniques give identical results).

6 Discussion of the results

We first compare the two approaches proposed for gathering goal independent information using a top-down framework. The results for *Prop* and *Asub* show that GI^{ef} is consistently considerably better than GI^{n}. This is because the abstract unification functions for those domains are relatively simple, and thus the overhead due to the additional operations introduced by the *efficient* transformation is always smaller than the call computation overhead in GI^{n}. On the other hand, in the results for *Sharing* although GI^{ef} is considerably faster in most cases, there are others where this difference is not as large, and a few in which GI^{ef} in fact performs slightly worse than GI^{n}. This is explained by the complexity of the abstract unification function for *Sharing*.

From the precision point of view, of course, for *Prop* there is no loss of precision. Relatively high precision is maintained in *Sharing*, while some more important loss appears for *Asub*. This reflects the fact that *Asub* is a weaker domain than *Sharing* w.r.t. the three basic properties. Thus, GI^{ef} appears to present a good precision / cost compromise.

We now compare GD^{reuse} (the goal dependent phase with goal independent information available), with a standard goal dependent computation. GD^{reuse} is almost consistently faster (or equal) to GD^{standard}, and the difference in speed is proportional to the number of fixed points avoided with respect to GD^{standard} and the complexity of these, as can be observed from the "> 1" and "> 2" columns. This last column seems to be the one that best predicts the differences

Name	GI				GD^{reuse}				GD^{standard}		
	BU	GI^{ef}	GI^{n}	Size	Query	Tm	RP	Size	Tm	> 1	> 2
reverse (A,B)	0.01	0.04	0.28	2.0 (2)	A	0.04	3	2.0 (2)	0.04	0	0
					true	0.26	17	2.0 (2)	0.49	10	5
qsort (A,B)	0.01	0.04	0.39	1.7 (2)	A	0.33	19	1.4 (2)	0.33	0	0
					true	0.74	31	1.3 (2)	0.74	0	0
queens (A,B)	0.03	0.11	0.70	2.0 (3)	A	0.18	10	2.5 (3)	0.18	0	0
					true	0.78	40	2.6 (3)	1.07	6	2
pg (A,B)	0.04	0.39	2.47	1.3 (2)	A	0.41	17	1.5 (2)	0.42	0	0
					true	0.41	17	1.5 (2)	0.42	0	0
plan (A,B)	0.04	0.21	1.40	1.9 (5)	A	0.47	9	2.5 (4)	0.47	0	0
					true	0.46	9	2.5 (4)	0.47	0	0
gabriel (A,B)	0.08	0.45	4.38	1.9 (4)	A	3.05	162	3.1 (4)	6.04	57	17
					true	3.06	162	3.1 (4)	6.05	57	17
cs (A)	0.40	2.49	16.09	2.2 (6)	A	1.25	31	2.9 (4)	1.37	3	1
					true	1.72	32	2.9 (4)	1.82	3	1
press (A,B)	0.40	3.24	30.50	2.3 (8)	A	20.62	966	2.6 (4)	35.85	124	35
					true	20.65	966	2.6 (4)	37.85	115	32
read (A,B)	0.32	2.71	33.27	1.9 (9)	A	20.15	355	2.2 (9)	56.96	214	100
					true	20.17	355	2.2 (9)	57.05	214	100
peep (A,B,C)	0.47	4.10	37.07	2.6 (10)	A	7.65	82	2.2 (4)	9.94	37	7
					true	29.66	370	2.7 (4)	70.99	181	81

Table 1. *Prop* results

in performance: any time this number is high the differences are significant. This result would be expected since this column indicates the number of "heavy" fixed point computations in the GD^{standard} approach.

The exception is in the *Asub* analysis. There, for some programs, the analysis is less precise in more than 50% of the program points. A consequence of this is that domain elements are a lot larger (imprecision increases the number of pairs) and that their processing is more time consuming. In some cases the difference is substantial enough to undo the effect of saved fixed point iterations.

On the other hand, while GD^{reuse} is almost consistently faster than GD^{standard}, the difference is not as big as one might expect. This is due to the fact that a very efficient fixed point is being used in GD^{standard}, which, by keeping track of data dependencies and incorporating several other optimizations, performs very few fixed point iterations – often none.

From the point of view of the precision of the information obtained the results are identical for *Prop*, and slightly different for the slightly weaker *Sharing* domain. This precision is quite surprising and implies that not much information is lost in least upper bound operations, despite the weakness of *Sharing* in performing them. This seems to imply that the information being "LUBed" is highly consistent (i.e. all clauses give similar information - while one can easily write artificial predicates not having this property, it is not unexpected that such predicates are rare in real

Name	GI				GD^{reuse}				GD^{standard}			Δ
	GI^{ef}	GI^{n}	Size^{n}	Δ	Query	Tm	RP	Size	Tm	> 1	> 2	%
init_susbt (X,Y,Z,W)	0.9	173.5	3.1 (5)	0	[[Z],[W]]	0.2	9	4.2 (5)	0.2	0	0	0
					[[Y],[Z],[W]]	0.7	15	4.1 (5)	0.9	6	1	0
					[[X],[Y],[Z],[W]]	98.1	21	4.7 (5)	193.7	21	4	0
serialize (X,Y)	0.7	3.0	2.3 (4)	0	[[Y]]	2.8	14	3.4 (4)	3.0	8	0	0
					[[X],[Y]]	2.9	14	3.4 (4)	3.1	8	0	0
					[[X],[X,Y],[Y]]	2.9	14	3.4 (4)	3.1	8	0	0
map-color (X,Y,Z,W)	1.4	1.9	2.1 (3)	0	[[Y],[Z],[W]]	1.5	5	2.6 (3)	3.1	8	0	0
grammar (X,Y)	0.1	0.1	1.9 (3)	0	[[X],[Y]]	0.1	0	0 (0)	0.1	0	0	0
					[[X],[X,Y],[Y]]	0.1	0	0 (0)	0.1	0	0	0
browse (X,Y)	3.9	14.0	2.3 (5)	0	[ ]	13.6	18	2.5 (5)	16.4	9	0	0
					[[X],[Y]]	0.2	10	2.1 (3)	0.4	8	0	0
					[[X],[X,Y],[Y]]	0.2	9	2.1 (3)	0.3	6	0	0
bid (X,Y,Z)	0.5	1.4	1.5 (3)	0	[ ]	0.3	7	2.9 (3)	0.3	0	0	0
deriv (X,Y,Z)	0.8	1.9	2.5 (3)	0	[[Z]]	0.9	35	2.7 (3)	0.9	0	0	0
					[[Y],[Z]]	0.9	35	2.7 (3)	0.9	0	0	0
rdtok (X,Y)	0.7	1.5	2.0 (5)	0	[[X],[Y]]	1.2	47	2.0 (3)	2.0	25	13	0
					[[X],[X,Y],[Y]]	1.2	47	2.0 (3)	2.0	25	13	0
read (X,Y)	10.6	206.0	2.4 (11)	4	[[Y]]	1.5	22	4.5 (6)	1.5	18	11	0
					[[X],[Y]]	66.4	73	4.6 (6)	257.9	270	115	0
boyer (X)	3.7	7.5	2.3 (5)	0	[ ]	1.7	15	2.5 (3)	4.0	45	19	0
					[[X]]	1.7	13	2.6 (3)	4.0	44	18	0
peephole (X,Y)	33.4	19.4	3.3 (6)	0	[[Y]]	4.1	60	2.1 (3)	7.3	28	7	0
					[[X],[Y]]	11.1	63	2.1 (3)	19.8	36	10	0
ann (X,Y)	418.1	381.8	3.3 (12)	6	[[X],[Y]]	22.2	69	2.9 (6)	27.8	40	11	2.4
					[[X],[X,Y],[Y]]	22.1	69	2.9 (6)	27.7	39	10	2.4

Table 2. *Sharing* results

programs). The case of the *read* benchmark in the *Sharing* analyzer would appear surprising in the sense that although some information is lost by GI^{ef} there is no loss of information after the GD^{reuse} pass w.r.t. GD^{standard}. This is due to the fact that the predicate that changes is not used in the goal dependent computation for the query patterns analyzed. Less surprising is the fact that the weaker *Asub* domain presents more differences in the information obtained.

In order to perform a completely fair comparison of the goal independent and goal dependent approaches one should really compare the GD^{standard} time with the sum of the GI^{ef} (or GI^{n}) time and the GD^{reuse} time, since to obtain information with GD^{reuse} it is necessary to perform the GI^{ef} analysis first. In this case the results are mixed in the sense that there is still a net gain in performance for benchmarks and call patterns which require several complex fixed point iterations from GD^{standard}, but there is also a net loss in other cases. This is surprising and shows again that GD^{standard} is quite good at avoiding fixed point iterations.

	GI				GD^{reuse}				$GD^{standard}$			Δ
Name	GI^{ef}	GI^{n}	$Size^{n}$	%	Query	Tm	RP	Size	Tm	> 1	> 2	%
init_susbt (X,Y,Z,W)	0.2	0.4	3.14 (5)	0	([X,Y],[])	0.3	9	4.2 (5)	0.4	5	0	0
					([X],[])	0.3	12	3.8 (5)	0.5	8	0	0
					([],[])	0.3	9	4.4 (5)	0.4	6	0	0
serialize (X,Y)	0.2	0.2	2.3 (4)	0	([X],[])	0.1	8	2.8 (4)	0.2	5	1	12.5
					([],[])	0.1	8	2.8 (4)	0.2	5	1	12.5
					([],[[X,Y]])	0.4	9	2.8 (4)	0.4	6	1	12.5
map-color (X,Y,Z,W)	0.2	0.3	2.6 (4)	0	([X],[])	0.3	6	2.5 (3)	0.3	2	0	0
grammar (X,Y)	0.0	0.0		0	([],[])	0.0	0	0 (0)	0.0	0	0	0
					([],[[X,Y]])	0.1	0	0 (0)	0.1	0	0	0
browse (X,Y)	0.3	1.1	2.0 (4)	11.8	([],[])	0.6	18	2.4 (4)	0.5	7	0	71.4
					([],[])	0.1	9	1.6 (3)	0.2	6	0	0
					([],[[X,Y]])	0.6	13	1.5 (3)	0.7	9	0	0
bid (X,Y,Z)	0.3	1.0	1.8 (4)	5	([],[])	0.5	8	2.6 (3)	0.3	0	0	76.2
deriv (X,Y,Z)	0.6	2.1	2.5 (3)	0	([X,Y],[])	3.1	72	2.3 (3)	0.8	0	0	91.1
					([X],[])	3.1	72	2.2 (3)	0.8	0	0	91.1
rdtok (X,Y)	0.7	1.0	2.6 (4)	33.3	([],[])	1.0	43	2.9 (4)	1.4	23	12	17.9
					([],[[X,Y]])	1.0	43	2.9 (4)	1.4	23	12	17.9
read (X,Y)	2.1	9.3	2.5 (10)	4	([X],[])	4.8	61	3.2 (4)	1.8	18	11	74.5
					([],[])	3.7	46	3.3 (4)	10.4	121	50	0
boyer (X)	0.7	1.1	2.3 (5)	0	([X],[])	0.8	15	2.1 (3)	1.4	45	19	0
					([],[])	0.8	15	2.2 (3)	1.4	45	19	0
peephole (X,Y)	1.8	2.9	3.6 (6)	0	([X],[])	1.7	58	2.2 (4)	2.5	21	3	0
					([],[])	1.9	58	2.2 (4)	3.0	25	6	0
ann (X,Y)	2.9	11.5	3.0 (10)	3	([],[])	3.9	79	2.8 (6)	5.1	37	9	6.5
					([],[[X,Y]])	5.4	94	2.8 (6)	6.6	40	10	6.5

Table 3. *Asub* results

The GI^{ef}+GD^{reuse} approach is interesting in that it arguably provides more predictable execution times (although still highly dependent on the query pattern), sometimes avoiding cases in which $GD^{standard}$ incurs larger overheads due to complex fixed point calculations. The combined GI^{ef}+GD^{reuse} analysis seems to be of advantage in the special case of programs that reuse their predicates in many ways and with different call patterns. However, our results show that this is not often the case, at least for our benchmarks. Thus, $GD^{standard}$ seems to end up probably winning when analyzing normal isolated programs. A further advantage for $GD^{standard}$ is that it is quite general in that it does not require any special strengths from the domains to keep the precision that one would expect from them.

The overall conclusion seems to be that the combined GI^{ef}+GD^{reuse} analysis is specially suited for situations where the results obtained in the goal independent phase have the potential of being reused many times. A typical example of this is library modules. They may be preanalyzed to obtain goal independent information which is stored with the module. Then only the GD^{reuse} pass is needed to specialize that information for the particular goal pattern corresponding to the use of the library performed by the program that calls it.

7 Conclusions

Our experiments with the *Prop* domain indicate that the efficient version of our goal independent analysis making use of the generic top-down framework is a viable alternative to a goal independent analysis using a bottom-up implementation as its speed is within a factor of 10 of a highly tuned ad hoc implementation of a bottom-up analysis for prop.

A goal dependent analysis which can use the results of a goal independent analysis is, for programs where the difference in precision is insignificant, consistently faster than a goal dependent analysis which starts from scratch. Also the analysis time is more closely related to the program size and becomes more predictable. This is due to the fact that the goal dependent analysis starting from scratch can require an unpredictable amount of iterations before reaching a fixpoint for its recursive predicates. While the precision is the same when abstract unification is idempotent, commutative and additive, the loss of precision is quite small for the *Sharing* domain which is not additive. The reason seems to be that the different clauses of real program predicates usually return very similar abstract states, such that the lub operator in practice rarely introduces a loss of precision. On the other hand, the loss of precision can be substantial in the *Asub* domain which also violates the commutativity condition.

Finally, the *Sharing* domain illustrates a case where, for some programs, the goal independent analysis can take an unexpected long time. This is caused by the peculiarities of the sharing domain. The size of an abstract state is in the worst case exponential in the number of program variables, this worst case typically shows up in absence of (groundness) information, and is much more likely to occur in a goal independent analysis than in a goal dependent analysis. Indeed, in the latter case, the information coming from the typical queries curtails the size of the abstract states.

Acknowledgements

We acknowledge support by CEC DGXIII ESPRIT Project "PRINCE" and CICYT project TIC91-0106-CE. M. Bruynooghe is supported in part by the Belgium National Fund for Scientific Research. María José García de la Banda is supported in part by a Spanish Ministry of Education Grant. We thank John Gallagher specially for many useful discussions and Marc Corsini and Badouin Le Charlier for providing us with some of the benchmarks used.

References

1. R. Barbuti, R. Giacobazzi, and G. Levi. A general framework for semantics-based bottom-up abstract interpretation of logic programs. *ACM Transactions on Programming Languages and Systems*, 15:133–181, 1993.

2. M. Bruynooghe. A Practical Framework for the Abstract Interpretation of Logic Programs. *Journal of Logic Programming*, 10:91–124, 1991.
3. M. Codish, D. Dams, and E. Yardeni. Bottom-up abstract interpretation of logic programs. *Journal of Theoretical Computer Science*, 124:93–125, 1994.
4. M. Codish, B. Demoen. Analysing Logic Programs using "Prop"-ositional Logic Programs and a Magic Wand. In *Proceedings International Logic Programming Symposium*. Vancouver, October 1993. MIT Press.
5. M. Codish, A. Mulkers, M. Bruynooghe, M. de la Banda, and M. Hermenegildo. Improving Abstract Interpretations by Combining Domains. In *Proc. ACM SIGPLAN Symposium on Partial Evaluation and Semantics Based Program Manipulation*. ACM, 1993.
6. M. Corsini, K. Musumbu,A. Rauzy,B. Le Charlier. Efficient bottom-up abstract interpretation of Prolog by means of constraint solving over symbolic finite domains. *Proc. of the Fifth International Symposium on Programming Language Implementation and Logic Programming.* Tallinn, August 1993, LNCS 714, Springer Verlag.
7. P. Cousot and R. Cousot. Abstract Interpretation: A Unified Lattice Model for Static Analysis of Programs by Construction or Approximation of Fixpoints. In *Conf. Rec. 4th Acm Symp. on Prin. of Programming Languages*, pages 238–252, 1977.
8. S. K. Debray and D. S. Warren. Automatic Mode Inference for Prolog Programs. *Journal of Logic Programming*, 5(3):207–229, September 1988.
9. M. Falaschi, G. Levi, M. Martelli, and C. Palamidessi. Declarative Modelling of the Operational Behaviour of Logic Programs. *Theoretical Computer Science*, 69:289–318, 1989.
10. J. Gallagher, M. Codish, E. Shapiro. Specialisation of Prolog and FCP Programs Using Abstract Interpretation. *New Generation Computing*, 6 (1988) 159-186.
11. D. Jacobs and A. Langen. Accurate and Efficient Approximation of Variable Aliasing in Logic Programs. In *1989 North American Conference on Logic Programming*. MIT Press, October 1989.
12. D. Jacobs and A. Langen. Static Analysis of Logic Programs for Independent And-Parallelism. *Journal of Logic Programming*, 13(2 and 3):291–314, July 1992.
13. K. Marriott and H. Søndergaard. Semantics-based dataflow analysis of logic programs. *Information Processing*, pages 601–606, April 1989.
14. K. Marriott, H. Sondergaard, and P. Dart. A Characterization of Non-Floundering Logic Programs. In *Proc. of the 1990 North American Conference on Logic Programming*. MIT Press, 1990.
15. K. Muthukumar and M. Hermenegildo. Determination of Variable Dependence Information at Compile-Time Through Abstract Interpretation. In *1989 North American Conference on Logic Programming*. MIT Press, October 1989.
16. K. Muthukumar and M. Hermenegildo. Compile-time Derivation of Variable Dependency Using Abstract Interpretation. *Journal of Logic Programming*, 13(2 and 3):315–347, July 1992.
17. H. Sondergaard. An application of abstract interpretation of logic programs: occur check reduction. In *European Symposium on Programming, LNCS 123*, pages 327–338. Springer-Verlag, 1986.
18. R. Warren, M. Hermenegildo, and S. Debray. On the Practicality of Global Flow Analysis of Logic Programs. In *Fifth International Conference and Symposium on Logic Programming*, pages 684–699, Seattle,Washington, August 1988. MIT Press.

A Kind of Achievement by Parts Method

Ph. Mathieu and J.P. Delahaye

Laboratoire d'Informatique Fondamentale de Lille
U.A. 369 du C.N.R.S., Université de Lille I,
59655 Villeneuve d'Ascq Cedex. FRANCE.
e-mail : mathieu@lifl.fr

Topics: Logic of Knowledge - Deduction - Complete computation

Abstract. How to add new rules to a knowledge base Kb_1 to obtain a new knowledge base Kb_2 for which forward chaining on Kb_2 with any extensional knowledge base Ekb gives all the two-valued consequence literals of $Kb_1 \cup Ekb$. We have shown in a previous paper that there exists such a method that we call Achievement.

$$\text{if } (Kb_1 \cup Ekb) \models L \text{ then } L \in FwCh(Kb_2 \cup Ekb) \text{ with } Kb_2 = Ach(Kb_1)$$

Unfortunately these achievement methods have a great complexity in time and space which depends on the size of the initial knowledge base. Thus we try to achieve knowledge bases by parts to have a weaker complexity.

$$Kb = Kb_1 \cup \ldots \cup Kb_n, \quad Ach(Kb) = Ach(Kb_1) \cup \ldots \cup Ach(Kb_n)$$

The aim of this paper is to give several methods to split knowledge bases in order to apply achievement by parts methods.

1 Introduction.

Definition 1. A **rule** is a formula of the form $l_1, \ldots, l_k \rightarrow l_0$ with l_i literals (we allow negation in rule conclusion). The set of literals used before the arrow of a rule r is noted $prem(r)$ and the literal used after the arrow is noted $conc(r)$. A **knowledge base** is a set of rules. We call **variants** of a rule r the set of rules denoted $Var(r)$ which contains all the rules which have the same clausal form than r (a rule which contains n literals has n variants). For example $Var(a \wedge b \rightarrow c) = \{a \wedge b \rightarrow c\ , a \wedge \neg c \rightarrow \neg b\ , \neg c \wedge b \rightarrow \neg a\}$. We note Ato_i the set of atoms used in a knowledge base Kb_i and we define $Her_i = Ato_i \cup \neg Ato_i$ and $Her = \cup Her_i$
An **interpretation** m is a set of atoms. If an atom $a \in m$ we write also $m(a) = T$ (and we say that a is true) and if $a \notin m$ we write $m(a) = F$ (and we say that a is false). A **model** for a set of formulas is an interpretation which satisfies all the formulas of the given set. A literal c is a **logical consequence** of a knowledge base Kb (and we note $Kb \models c$) if it is true in every model of this set [1].
A set of rules Kb is said to be saturated iff for each rule $r \in Kb$ for which $prem(r) \in Kb$ then $conc(r) \in Kb$. For a knowledge base Kb we denote $FwCh(Kb)$ the minimal saturated set of rules which contains Kb. It is in fact the set obtained after saturation with a **forward chaining**. We consider that we compute $FwCh(Kb)$ in the following

way: While there exists a rule r of Kb with $prem(r) \in Kb$ and $conc(r) \notin Kb$, add $conc(r)$ to Kb. If the opposite form of $conc(r)$ is already present in Kb, stop the algorithm with a message "contradiction detected".

The forward chaining algorithm which is usually used in many expert systems is not complete with respect to the usual two-valued logic when negation is used. For example $\neg a$ cannot be deduced from $a \rightarrow b$ and $\neg b$, whereas $\neg a$ is a logical consequence. Other examples are more complex : $c \rightarrow d,\ \neg a \wedge \neg b \rightarrow \neg d,\ a \rightarrow e,\ b \rightarrow e$. In this example e is a logical consequence of the knowledge base with c as extensional knowledge base, which is not deduced by forward chaining.
To avoid these drawbacks several methods are possible.

- writing only knowledge bases for which forward chaining is complete with any extensional knowledge base added (without negation for example) [7].
- using a complete algorithm like Davis–Putnam [4] or SL–resolution. Of course, in an expert system framework you must run these methods as soon as the extensional knowledge base changes, thus very often, and as we know that these algorithms have a great complexity in time (NP-complete problem [2]) there is no longer any hope to obtain efficient methods for the general case.
- adding rules to the knowledge base Kb we are interesting in, to obtain a new knowledge base Kb' for which literals computed by forward chaining are the consequence literals of Kb and that, for every extensional knowledge base added after. We call **achievement** such methods. It defines what we have called a **logical compilation** for knowledge bases [6][8].

For example the precedent knowledge base $\{c \rightarrow d,\ \neg a \wedge \neg b \rightarrow \neg d,\ a \rightarrow e,\ b \rightarrow e\}$ can be achieved by adding the rules $\{\neg d \rightarrow \neg c,\ d \wedge \neg b \rightarrow a,\ d \wedge \neg a \rightarrow b,\ \neg e \rightarrow \neg a,\ \neg e \rightarrow \neg b,\ d \rightarrow e\}$. You can easily verify that a forward chaining is able to compute all the consequence literals of the first knowledge base with any extensional knowledge base added.

Definition 2. We call a **full achievement operation** [6] [8] a method which transforms an initial knowledge base Kb into a knowledge base denoted $Ach(Kb)$ for which all the consequence literals of $Kb \cup Ekb$ with Ekb a set of literals (also called extensional knowledge base), can be obtained by a forward chaining saturation on $Ach(Kb) \cup Ekb$, and which allows to detect inconsistencies on Kb or on $Kb \cup Ekb$.

To prove that an operation Ach is a full achievement operation, we must then show that if $Kb \cup Ekb \models c$ then $c \in FwCh(Ach(Kb) \cup Ekb)$, and if $Kb \cup Ekb$ is not consistent this can be detected during the compilation. All the proofs of this paper are based on constructions and manipulations of models. Of course, by definition, if Ach is a full achievement operation, m a model for $Kb \cup Ekb$ and $m(c) = T$ then $c \in FwCh(Ach(Kb) \cup Ekb)$.
Achievement methods are not the aim of this paper (for some of them see [8]). We suppose here that such methods exist (noted $Ach(Kb)$) and we propose several methods to split knowledge bases in order to apply achievement by parts.

$$Kb = Kb_1 \cup \ldots \cup Kb_n,\quad Ach(Kb) = Ach(Kb_1) \cup \ldots \cup Ach(Kb_n)$$

2 A trivial case.

Definition 3 Scheme 0. Kb is a knowledge base of the form $\bigcup_{i=1}^{k} Kb_i$ where $Ato_i \cap Ato_j = \emptyset$, $\forall i, j \in \{1, \ldots, k\}$, $i \neq j$

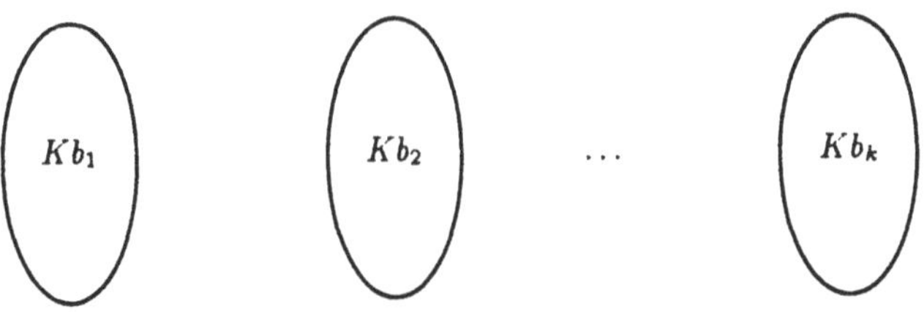

Fig. 1. Scheme 0

Theorem 4. *If Kb is a knowledge base according to Scheme 0 then*

$$Kb \rightarrow \left[\bigcup_{i=1}^{k} Ach(Kb_i)\right]$$

is a full achievement operation.

Proof. Let c be a literal with $c \in Her_i$, S a set of literals with $S \subset Her$ for which $Kb \cup S$ is consistent. If $Kb \cup S \models c$ then $Kb_i \cup (S \cap Her_i) \models c$ (if m_i is a model for $Kb_i \cup (S \cap Her_i)$ we can complete it to construct a model m for $Kb \cup S$). From hypothesis $m(c) = T$, thus $m_i(c) = T$) thus $c \in FwCh(Ach(Kb_i) \cup (S \cap Her_i))$ □

3 A single rule to link knowledge bases.

Definition 5 Scheme 1. $Kb = Kb_1 \cup Kb_2 \cup \{a_2 \rightarrow a_1\}$ with $a1, a2$ two literals, $Ato_1 \cap Ato_2 = \emptyset$ and $a_1 \in Ato_1$, $a_2 \in Ato_2$.

Theorem 6. *Let Kb be a knowledge base according to Scheme 1, c a literal with* $c \in Her$, *S a set of literals with* $S \subset Her$, *Ach a full achievement operation and* $* : Kb \rightarrow [Ach(Kb_1) \cup Ach(Kb_2) \cup \{a_2 \rightarrow a_1\} \cup \{\neg a_1 \rightarrow \neg a_2\}]$.
If $Kb \cup S \models c$ *and* $Kb \cup S$ *is consistent then FwCh(*(Kb)) gives c .*

Proof. We note $S_1 = S \cap Her_1$ and $S_2 = S \cap Her_2$

1. $c \in Her_1$

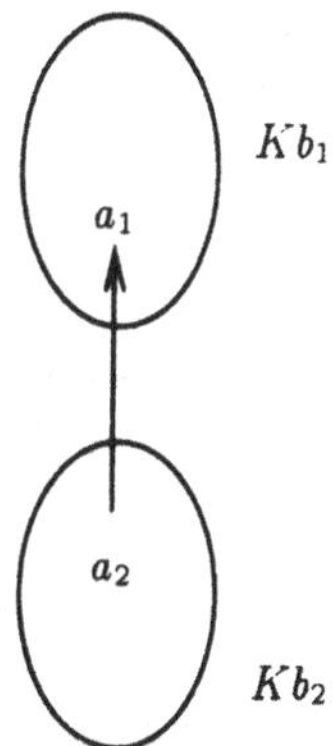

Fig. 2. Scheme 1

(a) $Kb_1 \cup S_1 \models a_1$
Let m_1 be a model for $Kb_1 \cup S_1$. We have $m_1(a_1) = T$. Let m be a model for $Kb \cup S$. $m' = m_1 \cup (m \cap Ato_2)$ is a model for $Kb \cup S$ (we have $m'(a_2 \rightarrow a_1) = T$ since $m'(a_1) = m_1(a_1) = T$). Thus $m'(c) = T$ (we use the fact that $Kb \cup S \models c$). Thus $m_1(c) = T$. This proves that $Kb_1 \cup S_1 \models c$, thus $c \in FwCh(Ach(Kb_1) \cup S_1)$ and thus $c \in FwCh(*(Kb) \cup S)$.

(b) $Kb_1 \cup S_1 \not\models a_1$ and $Kb_2 \cup S_2 \not\models a_2$
Let m_1 be a model for $Kb_1 \cup S_1$ and m_2 a model for $Kb_2 \cup S_2$ for which $m_2(a_2) = F$ (This model exists because of $Kb_2 \cup S_2 \not\models a_2$. $m = m_1 \cup m_2$ is a model for $Kb \cup S$ (we have $m(a_2 \rightarrow a_1) = T$ since $m(a_2) = m_2(a_2) = F$). Thus $m(c) = T$ (we use the fact that $Kb \cup S \models c$). Thus $m_1(c) = T$. This proves that $Kb_1 \cup S_1 \models c$, thus $c \in FwCh(Ach(Kb_1) \cup S_1)$ and then $c \in FwCh(*(Kb) \cup S)$.

(c) $Kb_1 \cup S_1 \not\models a_1$ and $Kb_2 \cup S_2 \models a_2$
$FwCh$ gives a_2 because of the second part of the hypothesis, thus $FwCh$ gives a_1.
We just have to show that $Kb_1 \cup S_1 \cup \{a_1\} \models c$.
Let m_1 be a model for $Kb_1 \cup S_1 \cup \{a_1\}$ and m_2 a model for $Kb_2 \cup S_2$ $m = m_1 \cup m_2$ is a model for $Kb \cup S$ (we have $m(a_2 \rightarrow a_1) = T$ since $m(a_2) = m_2(a_2) = T$ and $m(a_1) = m_1(a_1) = T$). Thus $m(c) = T$ thus $m_1(c) = T$. This proves that $Kb_1 \cup S_1 \cup \{a_1\} \models c$ and then $c \in FwCh(*(Kb) \cup S)$

2. $c \in Her_2$. This case is symetric to the first one. □

Remark. This demonstration shows that we can apply successively:

1. $FwCh$ on $Ach(Kb_1)$.
2. $FwCh$ on $\{\neg a_1 \rightarrow \neg a_2\}$.
3. $FwCh$ on $Ach(Kb_2)$.
4. $FwCh$ on $\{a_1 \rightarrow a_2\}$.
5. $FwCh$ on $Ach(Kb_1)$.

Proposition 7. *If Kb is according to Scheme 1, and if $Kb \cup S$ is inconsistent then $FwCh(*(Kb) \cup S)$ gives an inconsistency.*

Proof.

1. $Kb_1 \cup S_1 \models \neg a_1$ and $Kb_2 \cup S_2 \models a_2$.
   $FwCh(*(Kb) \cup S)$ gives $\neg a_1, a_2$. $FwCh(*(Kb) \cup S)$ gives also a_1 (because of $a_2 \rightarrow a_1$). $FwCh(*(Kb) \cup S)$ gives then an inconsistency.
2. $Kb_1 \cup S_1 \not\models \neg a_1$
   We suppose that $FwCh(*(Kb) \cup S)$ does not find an inconsistency. Then $FwCh(Ach(Kb_1) \cup S_1)$ does not find the inconsistency. Thus $Kb_1 \cup S_1$ is consistent. Let m_1 be a model for $Kb_1 \cup S_1$ for which $m_1(a_1) = T$ (This is possible because of $Kb_1 \cup S_1 \not\models \neg a_1$). $FwCh(Ach(Kb_2) \cup S_2)$ does not find an inconsistency, thus $Kb_2 \cup S_2$ is consistent. Let m_2 be a model for $Kb_2 \cup S_2$. $m_1 \cup m_2$ is a model for $Kb \cup S$ (we have $m_1 \cup m_2(a_2 \rightarrow a_1) = T$ since $m(a_1) = m_1(a_1) = T$). This is in contradiction with the hypothesis that $Kb \cup S$ is inconsistent. Thus $FwCh(*(Kb) \cup S)$ gives an inconsistency.
3. $Kb_2 \cup S_2 \not\models a_2$
   This case is symetric to the case 2. □

Proposition 8. *If Kb is according to Scheme 1, and Kb is inconsistent then $Ach(Kb_1)$ gives the empty clause or $Ach(Kb_2)$ gives the empty clause or $FwCh(*(Kb))$ gives an inconsistency.*

Proof. We just apply the proposition 6 with $S = \emptyset$. □

Note 9 Practical use of propositions 6 and 7.

1. When we want to use the theorem 6 to make an achievement by parts, the inconsistency of Kb can be undetected, but when we will use $FwCh$ on $Ach(Kb_1) \cup Ach(Kb_2) \cup \{a_2 \rightarrow a_1\} \cup \{\neg a_1 \rightarrow \neg a_2\}$ we obtain this detection.
2. If Kb is consistent, the proposition 6 shows that $FwCh$ will detect inconsistencies on $Kb \cup S$. We can then delete the hypothesis which says that $Kb \cup S$ must be consistent.

To summarize : If Kb is a knowledge base according to Scheme 1 we can say that $*(Kb)$ followed by $FwCh(*(Kb))$ is a full achievement method.

Note 10 Theorem 6 generalized.
Let $Kb = Kb_1 \cup \ldots \cup Kb_k \cup G$ where G is a set of rules of the form $a_i \rightarrow a_j$ with $a_i \in Kb_i$.
We assume that $\{(i,j) | a_i \rightarrow a_j \in G\}$ is the graph of a tree (the direction is not significant). $i \neq j \Rightarrow Ato_i \cap Ato_j = \emptyset$.
Let $c \in Her$, $S \subset Her$ for which $Kb \cup S$ is consistent. If $Kb \cup S \models c$ then $FwCh\left(\bigcup_{i=1}^{k} Ach(Kb_i) \cup S \cup G \cup \{\neg a_j \rightarrow \neg a_i | a_i \rightarrow a_j \in G\}\right)$ gives c.

Proof. We just have to use repeatedly the theorem 6. □

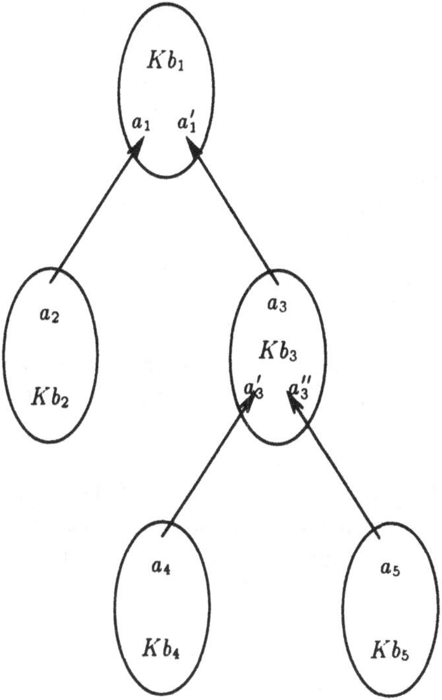

Fig. 3. Theorem 6 generalized

Note 11. When theorem 6 is generalized,

1. to detect the inconsistency of Kb, we just have to run $FwCh(B)$ where
   $B = \left(\bigcup_{i=1}^{k} Ach(Kb_i) \cup \{a_i \rightarrow a_j, \neg a_j \rightarrow \neg a_i | a_i \rightarrow a_j \in G\}\right)$.
2. If Kb is consistent, $FwCh(B \cup S)$ will detect inconsistencies of $Kb \cup S$

Counter-example 1 : Theorem 6 does not work if the link rule contains many premisses.

Proof. Consider a knowledge base built in the following way :
$Kb_1 = \{a \rightarrow a'\}, Kb_2 = \{\neg b_1 \rightarrow c, \neg b_2 \rightarrow c\}$
Kb_1 and Kb_2 are linked with the rule $b_1 \wedge b_2 \rightarrow c$

$Ach(Kb_1) = \{a \rightarrow a', \neg a' \rightarrow \neg a\}$
$Ach(Kb_2) = \{\neg b_1 \rightarrow c, \neg c \rightarrow b_1, \neg b_2 \rightarrow c, \neg c \rightarrow b_2\}$
$Var(b_1 \wedge b_2 \rightarrow c) = \{b_1 \wedge b_2 \rightarrow c, b_1 \wedge \neg c \rightarrow \neg b_2, \neg c \wedge b_2 \rightarrow \neg b_1\}$

$Kb \cup \{\neg a'\} \models c \; (\neg a' \rightarrow \neg a \rightarrow \neg b_1 \vee \neg b_2 \rightarrow c)$.
Unfortunately c is not given by $FwCh$ on the achievement by parts. □

Counter-example 2 : theorem 6 does not work if there are several link rules (each with one premise).

Proof. Consider a knowledge base built in the following way :
$Kb_1 = \{a_1 \wedge b_1 \rightarrow c_1\}$
$Kb_2 = \{c_2 \rightarrow a_2, c_2 \rightarrow b_2\}$
Kb_1 and Kb_2 are linked with the rules $\{a_2 \rightarrow a_1, b_2 \rightarrow b_1\}$

$Ach(Kb_1) = Var(a_1 \wedge b_1 \rightarrow c_1) = \{a_1 \wedge b_1 \rightarrow c_1, \neg c_1 \wedge b_1 \rightarrow \neg a_1, a_1 \wedge \neg c_1 \rightarrow \neg b_1\}$
$Ach(Kb_2) = \{c_2 \rightarrow a_2, \neg a_2 \rightarrow \neg c_2, c_2 \rightarrow b_2, \neg b_2 \rightarrow \neg c_2\}$

$Kb \cup \{\neg c_1\} \models \neg c_2$ (because $\neg c_1 \rightarrow \neg a_1 \vee \neg b_1 \rightarrow \neg a_2 \vee \neg b_2 \rightarrow \neg c_2$). Unfortunately $\neg c_2$ is not given by $FwCh$ on achievement by parts result with variants of link rules. □

Counter-example 3: Theorem 6 does not work if there are many link rules which contain only one premise either if these rules are used in the achievement of each part (it is the same example than the precedent one, but link rules have been added to Kb_1 and Kb_2).

Proof. Consider a knowledge base built in the following way :
$Kb_1 = \{a_1 \wedge b_1 \rightarrow c_1, a_2 \rightarrow a_1, b_2 \rightarrow b_1\}$
$Kb_2 = \{c_2 \rightarrow a_2, c_2 \rightarrow b_2, a_2 \rightarrow a_1, b_2 \rightarrow b_1\}$

$Ach(Kb_1) = Var(\{\neg a_1 \vee \neg b_1 \vee c_1,\ \neg a_2 \vee a_1,\ \neg b_2 \vee b_1,\ \neg a_2 \vee \neg b_1 \vee c_1,\ \neg a_2 \vee \neg b_2 \vee c_1,\ \neg a_1 \vee \neg b_2 \vee c_1\})$

$Ach(Kb_2) = Var(\{\neg c_2 \vee a_2,\ \neg c_2 \vee b_2,\ \neg c_2 \vee a_1,\ \neg a_2 \vee a_1,\ \neg b_2 \vee b_1,\ \neg c_2 \vee b_1\})$

You can see that $Kb \cup \{\neg c_1\} \models \neg c_2$. Unfortunately c_2 cannot be obtained by $FwCh$ on the achievement by parts. □

4 A full achievement by parts method with restrictions.

Definition 12 Scheme 2. $Kb = Kb_1 \cup \ldots \cup Kb_k \cup \{a_1 \wedge \ldots \wedge a_k \rightarrow b\}$ with $\forall i, j\ i \neq j \Rightarrow Ato_i \cap Ato_j = \emptyset$ and $\forall i\ b \notin Ato_i,\ \neg b \notin Ato_i,\ a_i \in Her_i$

Theorem 13. *Let Kb be a knowledge base according to Scheme 2, c a literal with $c \in Her$, S a set of literals with $S \subset Her$, Ach a full achievement operation and $* : Kb \rightarrow \left[\bigcup_{i=1}^{k} Ach(Kb_i) \cup \{a_1 \wedge \ldots \wedge a_k \rightarrow b\}\right]$.*
If $Kb \cup S \models c$ and $Kb \cup S$ is consistent and $b, \neg b \notin S$ then FwCh((Kb)) gives c .*

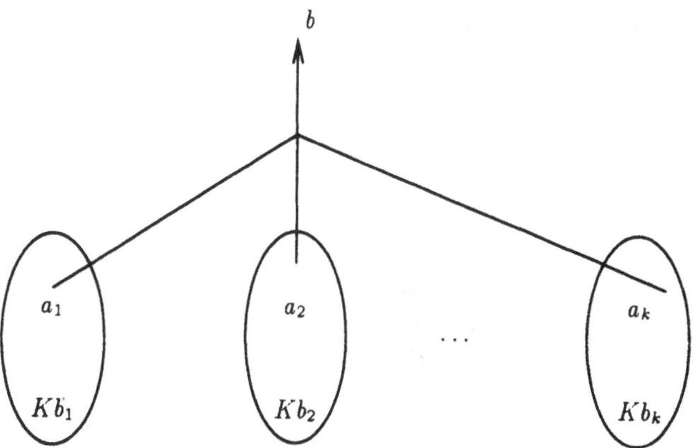

Fig. 4. Scheme 2

Proof.

1. $c = b$
   We suppose that $Kb_1 \cup S_1 \not\models a_1$. Let m_1 be a model for $Kb_1 \cup S_1$ for which $m_1(a_1) = F$. By the same way we note m_i a model for $Kb_i \cup S_i, i \geq 2$. $m = m_1 \cup \ldots \cup m_k$ is a model for $Kb \cup S$. It is also a model of $Kb_i \cup S_i, i \geq 1$. It is also a model for $a_1 \wedge \ldots \wedge a_k \rightarrow b$ because $m(a_1) = m_1(a_1) = F$. Unfortunately $m(b) = F$ and thus m is not according to the hypothesis $Kb \cup S \models c$. Thus $Kb_1 \cup S_1 \models a_1$, and by the same way for every i $Kb_i \cup S_i \models a_i$. Thus $FwCh$ gives $a_1, \ldots, a_k$ and then gives b.
2. $i \geq 1, c \in Her_i$
   Let m_{i_0} be a model for $Kb_{i_0} \cup S_{i_0}$. We will show that $m_{i_0}(c) = T$ which is sufficient to prove that $Kb_{i_0} \cup S_{i_0} \models c$ and thus that $FwCh(*(Kb))$ gives c. Let m_i be a model for $Kb_i \cup S_i$ for every $i \in \{1, \ldots, k\}$ $i \neq i_0$. We construct $m = m_1 \cup \ldots \cup m_k \cup \{b\}$. m is a model of $Kb \cup S$ (it is a model for $a_1 \wedge \ldots \wedge a_k \rightarrow b$ because of $m(b) = T$). Thus $m(c) = T$ (because of $Kb \cup S \models c$), thus $m_{i_0}(c) = T$.

□

Remark. This proof shows that we can use $FwCh$ successively on

$Ach(Kb_1), \ldots, Ach(Kb_k), a_1 \wedge \ldots \wedge a_k \rightarrow b$ without any risk to loose anything. We can also use all the $Ach(Kb_i)$ both and then use $a_1 \wedge \ldots \wedge a_k \rightarrow b$

Proposition 14. *If Kb is according to Scheme 2 and if $Kb \cup S$ is not consistent then there exists i for which $Kb_i \cup S_i$ is not consistent, and then $FwCh(*(Kb))$ can detect this inconsistency.*

Proof. If m_i is a model for $Kb_i \cup S_i$ then $m = m_1 \cup \ldots \cup m_k \cup \{b\}$ is a model for $Kb \cup S$. □

Proposition 15. *If Kb is according to Scheme 2 and if Kb is not consistent then there exists i for which Kb_i is not consistent, and thus when we compute $Ach(Kb_1) \cup \ldots \cup Ach(Kb_k)$ we will detect this inconsistency.*

Proof. We just have to use the proposition 14 with $S = \emptyset$. □

Note 16 Use of the propositions 13 and 14.
When we use the theorem 13 we don't have to think about consistency.

Note 17 Theorem 13 generalized.

1. We can allow several a_i in the same Kb_i
2. We can allow several rules of the form $a_1^i \wedge \ldots \wedge a_k^i \rightarrow b_i$, but $\{b_1, \ldots, b_k\}$ must be consistent (all the b_i are different).

Note 18 Theorems 6 and 13 generalized.
The theorems 6 and 13 allows us to achieve by parts complexe knowledge bases like the following one.

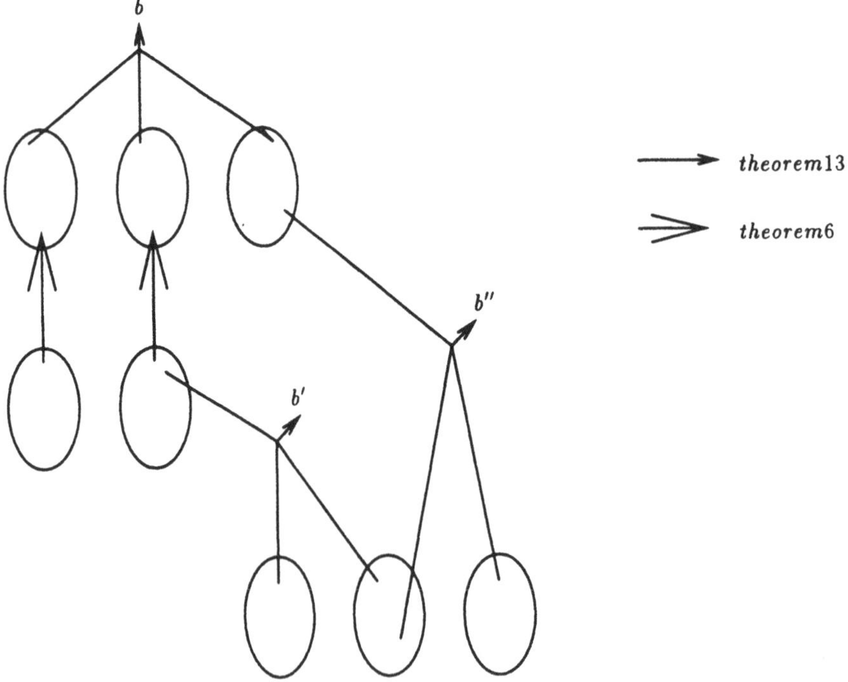

Fig. 5. Theorems 6 and 13 generalized.

5 The most useful one.

Definition 19 Scheme 3. $Kb = Kb_0 \cup Kb_1 \cup \ldots \cup Kb_k \cup \{a_1 \wedge \ldots \wedge a_k \rightarrow \neg a_0\}$ with $a_i \in Kb_i$ and $\forall i, j\ i \neq j \Rightarrow Ato_i \cap Ato_j = \emptyset$

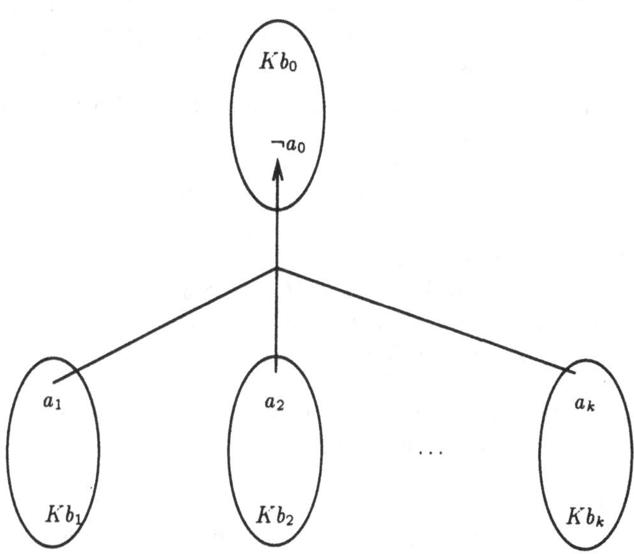

Fig. 6. Scheme 3

Theorem 20. *Let Kb be a knowledge base according to Scheme 3, c a literal with* $c \in Her$, *S a set of literals with* $S \subset Her$, *Ach a full achievement operation and* $* : Kb \rightarrow \left[\bigcup_{i=0}^{k} Ach(Kb_i) \cup Var(a_1 \wedge \ldots \wedge a_k \rightarrow \neg a_0)\right]$.
If $Kb \cup S \models c$ *and* $Kb \cup S$ *is consistent then FwCh(*(Kb)) gives c .*

Proof.

1. $c \in Her_0$
   (a) $Kb_0 \cup S_0 \models \neg a_0$
   Let m_0 be a model for $Kb_0 \cup S_0$. We have $m_0(a_0) = F$. Let m be a model for $Kb \cup S$, $m' = m_0 \cup (m \cap (Ato_1 \cup \ldots \cup Ato_k))$ is a model for $Kb \cup S$ (no problem for $Her_0, \ldots, Her_k$ and for $a_1 \wedge \ldots \wedge a_k \rightarrow \neg a_0$). m' gives V because $m'(\neg a_0) = m_0(\neg a_0) = T$, thus $m'(c) = T$, thus $Kb_0 \cup S_0 \models c$, thus $FwCh(*(Kb) \cup S)$ gives c.
   (b) $Kb_0 \cup S_0 \not\models \neg a_0$ and $\exists i_0 \in \{1, \ldots k\}\ Kb_{i_0} \cup S_{i_0} \not\models a_{i_0}$
   Let m_0 be a model for $Kb_0 \cup S_0$ and m_{i_0} a model for $Kb_{i_0} \cup S_{i_0}$ for which

$m_{i_0}(a_{i_0}) = F$. If $m' = m_0 \cup m_{i_0} \cup \left(m \cap \bigcup_{i=1,\ i\neq i_0}^{k} Ato_i\right)$ then m' is a model for $Kb \cup S$. There is no problem for all the $Kb_i \cup S_i$, and for $a_1 \wedge \ldots \wedge k \rightarrow \neg a_0$ it comes from $m'(a_{i_0}) = m_{i_0}(a_{i_0}) = F$, thus $m'(c) = T$, thus $m_0(c) = T$, thus we have $Kb_0 \cup S_0 \models c$, thus $FwCh(*(Kb) \cup S)$ gives c.

(c) $Kb_0 \cup S_0 \not\models \neg a_0$ and $\forall i \in \{1, \ldots k\}\ Kb_i \cup S_i \models a_i$
$FwCh$ gives $a_1, \ldots, a_k$ and then gives also $\neg a_0$. Thus we just have to show that $Kb_0 \cup S_0 \cup \{\neg a_0\} \models c$. Let m_0 be a model for $Kb_0 \cup S_0 \cup \neg a_0$ and m a model for $Kb \cup S$. $m' = m_0 \cup (m \cap (Ato_1 \cup \ldots \cup Ato_k))$ is a model for $Kb \cup S$. For $a_1 \wedge \ldots \wedge a_k \rightarrow \neg a_0$ it comes from $m'(\neg a_0) = m_0(\neg a_0) = T$, thus $m'(c) = T$, thus $m_0(c) = T$, thus it shows that $Kb_0 \cup S_0 \cup \{\neg a_0\} \models c$.

2. The other cases are symetric to this one (it is possible because we have added $Var(a_1 \wedge \ldots \wedge a_k \rightarrow \neg a_0)$). □

Remark. This proof shows that the use of $FwCh$ can be made in the following way :

1. run $FwCh$ separately on the $Kb_i \cup S_i$
2. try to use one the rules of $Var(a_1 \wedge \ldots \wedge k \rightarrow \neg a_0)$.
3. if one of the variants has been used in the second point, run $FwCh$ on the $Kb_i \cup S_i$ which correspond to the new fact added.

Proposition 21. *Let Kb according to Scheme 3, if $Kb \cup S$ is not consistent then $FwCh(*(Kb) \cup S)$ gives an inconsistency.*

Proposition 22. *Let Kb according to the Scheme 3, if Kb is not consistent then $Ach(Kb_0) = \emptyset$ or ... or $Ach(Kb_k) = \emptyset$ or $FwCh(*(Kb))$ gives an inconsistency.*

Note 23 Practical use of propositions 20 and 21.
If Kb is according to Scheme 3 then $*(Kb)$ followed by $FwCh(*(Kb))$ is a full achievement method.

Note 24 Propositions 20 and 21 generalized.

1. It is not possible to allow several a_i in the same Kb : Counter-example 1.
2. It is not possible to allow several rules to link the Kb_i : Counter-example 2.
3. But it is possible to use iteratively theorems 13 and 20 (theorem 6 with a notation change is a particular case of theorem 20)

6 Try them on examples.

$$i \in \{1, \ldots, n\} \begin{cases} a_1^i \wedge a_2^i \rightarrow b_i \\ \neg a_1^i \rightarrow c \\ \neg a_2^i \rightarrow c \\ b_1 \wedge \ldots \wedge b_n \rightarrow d \end{cases}$$

Use of theorem 13: Instead of achieving a knowledge base of $3n + 1$ rules, we just have to achieve a knowledge base of $3n$ rules and add the last rule.

$$i \in \{1,\ldots,n\} \begin{cases} a_1^i \wedge a_2^i \rightarrow b_i \\ \neg a_1^i \rightarrow c^i \\ \neg a_2^i \rightarrow c^i \\ b_1 \wedge \ldots \wedge b_n \rightarrow d \end{cases}$$

Use of theorem 13: Instead of achieving a knowledge base of $3n+1$ rules, we just have to achieve n knowledge bases of 3 rules and link them with 1 rule.

$$i \in \{1,\ldots,n\} \begin{cases} a_1^i \wedge a_2^i \rightarrow b^i \\ \neg a_1^i \rightarrow c^{i+1} \\ \neg a_2^i \rightarrow c^{i+1} \\ b^i \rightarrow \neg c^i \end{cases}$$

Use of theorem 6: Instead of achieving a knowledge base of $4n$ rules, we just have to achieve n knowledge bases of 3 rules.

$$i \in \{1,\ldots,n\} \begin{cases} a_{2i} \wedge a_{2i+1} \rightarrow d_i \\ \neg e_i \wedge \neg f_i \rightarrow \neg d_i \\ e_i \rightarrow a_i \\ f_i \rightarrow a_i \end{cases}$$

Use of theorem 20: Instead of achieving a knowledge base of $4n$ rules, we just have to achieve n knowledge bases of 3 rules.

7 Conclusion.

The forward chaining algorithm, often used in many deductive systems is not complete when negation is used. To avoid this drawback we have proposed in previous papers [6] [8] a method which is able to compute the missing rules of the knowledge base to make a complete compulation with Forward Chaining. We have called such methods "achievement methods". In this paper we have proposed several methods to split knowledge bases in order to apply achievement by parts methods. This will allow us to transform large knowledge bases more quickly. We have implemented these methods in Prolog and we actually translate this program in C to make tests on large knowledge bases.

References

1. C.L.Chang and R.C.T. Lee.- Symbolic Logic and Mechanical Theorem Proving. Academic Press, inc. 1973.
2. S. Cook.- The complexity of theorem-proving procedures. Proc. 3rd ann. ACM symp. on theory of computing. ACM New-York pp 151-158, 1971.
3. J.P. Delahaye.- Forward chaining and computation of two-valued and three-valued models. 7th Int. Conf. on Expert Systems and Applications, Avignon 87. p1341-1360.
4. M. Davis, H. Putnam.- A Computing Procedure for Quantification Theory. JACM 7, p201-215, 1960.

5. K. Kunen.- Negation in Logic Programming. Journal of Logic Programming, vol 4, 1987, p289-308.
6. P. Mathieu et J.P. Delahaye.- The logical Compilation of Knowledge Bases. Proceedings of JELIA 90, Amsterdam, Lecture Notes In AI, 478 , Springer Verlag, pp386-398.
7. P. Mathieu et J.P. Delahaye.- For which bases forward chaining is sufficient ? Proceedings of Cognitiva 90, Madrid, 1990, pp 699-702.
8. P. Mathieu.- La notion d'achèvement et ses applications aux interpreteurs de regles. Ph.D. Thesis, Univ. Lille1 ,1991.
9. P. Siegel.- Representation et utilisation de la connaissance en calcul propositionnel. These d'Etat- GIA Marseille Luminy, 1987.
10. J.C. Shepherdson.- Negation in logic programming. Foundations of deductive databases and logic programming (J.Minker ed), Morgan Kaufmann, 1988, p19-88.
11. R. Turner.- Logics for Artificial Intelligence. Ellis Horwood, 1984.

Projection in Temporal Logic Programming*

Zhenhua Duan**, Maciej Koutny and Chris Holt

Department of Computing Science
University of Newcastle upon Tyne
Newcastle upon Tyne NE1 7RU, U.K.

Abstract. We define a projection operator in the framework of the temporal logic programming. Its syntax and semantics are presented and illustrated with examples. We also discuss the implementation details of the projection construct.
Keywords: Temporal logic, programming, projection.

1 Introduction

Temporal Logic Programming [6, 7, 9] is a paradigm for the specification and verification of sequential and concurrent programs. Within a temporal logic programming language, such as Tempura [6], the next, always and chop are useful operators for sequential programs, while conjunction and parallel composition are basic operators for concurrent programming. An advantage of the conjunction construct is its simplicity. However, it seems appropriate for dealing with fine-grained parallel operations that proceed in lock-step. The parallel composition operator ($\|$, see Section 2), on the other hand, permits the combined processes to specify their own intervals. Thus it is better suited to the coarse-grained concurrency of a typical multiprocessor, where each process proceeds at its own speed. Moreover, processes combined through the parallel composition operator share all the states and may interfere with one another. Therefore, it is interesting and desirable to investigate other ways of handling parallel computations which would combine some features of both conjunction and parallel composition operators.

Projection, p *proj* q, was originally employed for the purpose of modelling hardware assuming different granularities of time [6] (see Section 3). It requires that process p be repeatedly executed over a sequence of successive subintervals. This can be inconvenient because it is not always desirable to execute the same process several times. Moreover, it requires both processes p and q to terminate at the same time. In general, it is not the case that processes are executed so regularly.

In this paper we introduce a new projection operator, $(p_1, \ldots, p_m)$ *prj* q, which can be thought of as a combination of the parallel and projection operators. Intuitively, it means that q is executed in parallel with $p_1; \ldots; p_m$ over an

* This research was partially supported by the SERC Grant 491105.
** Present address: Computer Science Department, University of Sheffield, Regent Court, 211 Portobello Street, Sheffield S1 4DP, U.K.

interval obtained by taking the endpoints (randezvous points) of the intervals over which $p_1, \ldots, p_m$ are executed. The projection construct permits the processes $p_1, \ldots, p_m, q$ to be autonomous, each process having the right to specify the interval over which it is executed. In particular, the sequence of processes $p_1, \ldots, p_m$ and process q may terminate at different time points. Although the communication between processes is still based on shared variables, the communication and synchronization only take place at the rendezvous points (global states), otherwise they are executed independently. The projection operator also enables the specification of program execution using different time scales.

The paper is organised as follows: The next section introduces the syntax and semantics of the temporal logic we use. In Section 3, the new projection operator is defined and some of its basic properties are shown. In Section 4, the implementation details of the new operator are discussed. Section 5 contains examples.

2 Logic Framework

Our underlying logic is the first order temporal logic [3, 5] with chop [1, 8], and is an extension of ITL [6].

2.1 Syntax

Let Π be a countable set of ***propositions***, and V be a countable set of typed static and dynamic ***variables***. The ***terms*** e of the logic and formulas p are given by the following grammar:[3]

$$e ::= x \mid \bigcirc e \mid \ominus e \mid f_0 \mid f_1(e) \mid f_2(e,e) \mid \ldots$$
$$p ::= \pi \mid e = e \mid P_1(e) \mid P_2(e,e) \mid \ldots \mid \neg p \mid p \wedge p \mid \exists x : p \mid \bigcirc p \mid \ominus p \mid p;p$$

In $f_i(e_1, \ldots, e_i)$ and $P_i(e_1, \ldots, e_i)$ it is assumed that the types of the terms are compatible with those of the arguments of f_i and P_i.
The derived connectives, $\vee$, $\rightarrow$ and $\leftrightarrow$, as well as the logic constants, $true$ and $false$, are defined as usual. We also use the following derived formulas:

$$empty = \neg \bigcirc true \qquad more = \neg empty$$

$$\Diamond p = true; p \qquad \Box p = \neg \Diamond \neg p$$

$$\odot p = \neg \bigcirc \neg p \qquad p \parallel q = (p \wedge (q; true)) \vee (q \wedge (p; true))$$

$$skip = len(1) \qquad len(n) = \begin{cases} empty & n = 0 \\ \bigcirc len(n-1) & n > 1 \end{cases}$$

The temporal operators are called ***previous*** ($\ominus$), ***next*** ($\bigcirc$), ***chop*** (;), ***always*** ($\Box$), ***sometimes*** ($\Diamond$), ***weak next*** ($\odot$) and ***parallel*** ($\parallel$).

[3] x is a variable, f_i is a function of arity i, π is a proposition and P_i is an atomic predicate (different from equality) of arity i. In particular, f_0 is a constant term.

2.2 Semantics

A *state* s is an assignment which for each variable $v \in V$ defines $s[v]$, and for each proposition $\pi \in \Pi$ defines $s[\pi]$. $s[v]$ is a value of the appropriate type or *nil* (undefined), whereas $s[\pi] \in \{true, false\}$.

An *interval* $\sigma = \langle s_0, s_1, \ldots \rangle$ is a non-empty (possibly infinite) sequence of states. The length of σ, denoted by $|\sigma|$, is defined as ω if σ is infinite; otherwise it is the number of states in σ minus 1. For $0 \leq i, j \leq |\sigma|$ we will use $\sigma_{(i..j)}$ to denote the subinterval $\langle s_i, s_{i+1}, \ldots, s_j \rangle$.[4] It is assumed that each static variable is assigned the same value in all the states in σ. The concatenation of a finite σ with another interval (or empty string) σ' is denoted by $\sigma \cdot \sigma'$.

An *interpretation* is a tuple $\mathcal{I} = (\sigma, i, k, j)$, where $\sigma = \langle s_0, s_1, \ldots \rangle$ is an interval, i and k are integers, and j is an integer or ω, such that $i \leq k \leq j \leq |\sigma|$. We use (σ, i, k, j) to mean that a formula or term is interpreted over a subinterval $\sigma_{(i..j)}$ with the current state being s_k.

For every term e, the evaluation of e relative to interpretation $\mathcal{I} = (\sigma, i, k, j)$ is defined in $\mathcal{I}[e]$ by induction on terms in the following way, where v is a variable and $e_1, \ldots, e_m$ are terms:

$$\mathcal{I}[v] = s_k[v]$$

$$\mathcal{I}[f(e_1, \ldots, e_m)] = \begin{cases} f(\mathcal{I}[e_1], \ldots, \mathcal{I}[e_m]) & \text{if } \mathcal{I}[e_h] \neq nil \text{ for all } h \\ nil & \text{otherwise} \end{cases}$$

$$\mathcal{I}[\bigcirc e] = \begin{cases} (\sigma, i, k+1, j)[e] & \text{if } k < j \\ nil & \text{otherwise} \end{cases}$$

$$\mathcal{I}[\circleddash e] = \begin{cases} (\sigma, i, k-1, j)[e] & \text{if } i < k \\ nil & \text{otherwise} \end{cases}$$

The satisfaction relation for formulas, $\models$, is defined as the least relation satisfying the inductive definitions on formulas in Table 1.
One can show that $\mathcal{I} \models p$ if and only if $(\sigma_{(i..j)}, 0, k-i, j-i) \models p$.[5] Moreover, if p is a formula which does not use the previous operator then $\mathcal{I} \models p$ if and only if $(\sigma_{(k..j)}, 0, 0, j-k) \models p$. If there is an interpretation $\mathcal{I}$ such that $\mathcal{I} \models p$ then p is *satisfiable*. If $\mathcal{I} \models p$, for all interpretations $\mathcal{I}$, then p is *valid*, denoted by $\Vdash p$. We also define the satisfaction relation for intervals. Given an interval σ, $\sigma \models p$ if $(\sigma, 0, 0, |\sigma|) \models p$. Moreover, $\models p$ if $\sigma \models p$, for all intervals σ.

---

[4] When $i > j$, $\sigma_{(i..j)}$ is the empty string.

[5] That is the relevant part of σ in $\mathcal{I} = (\sigma, i, k, j)$ is $\sigma_{(i..j)}$. In particular, the valuations of variables and predicates outside the bounds given by i and j do not matter.

Table 1. Definition of $\models$

$\mathcal{I} \models true$	
$\mathcal{I} \not\models false$	
$\mathcal{I} \models \pi$	if $s_k[\pi] = true$.
$\mathcal{I} \models P(e_1, \ldots, e_m)$	if, for all h, $1 \leq m \leq m$, $\mathcal{I}[e_h] \neq nil$ and $P(\mathcal{I}[e_1], \ldots, \mathcal{I}[e_m]) = true$.
$\mathcal{I} \models e = e'$	if $\mathcal{I}[e] = \mathcal{I}[e']$.
$\mathcal{I} \models \neg p$	if $\mathcal{I} \not\models p$.
$\mathcal{I} \models p \wedge q$	if $\mathcal{I} \models p$ and $\mathcal{I} \models q$.
$\mathcal{I} \models \bigcirc p$	if $k < j$ and $(\sigma, i, k+1, j) \models p$.
$\mathcal{I} \models \odot p$	if $i < k$ and $(\sigma, i, k-1, j) \models p$.
$\mathcal{I} \models p; q$	if there is an integer h, $k \leq h \leq j$, such that $(\sigma, i, k, h) \models p$ and $(\sigma, h, h, j) \models q$.
$\mathcal{I} \models \exists x : p$	if for some interval σ' which has the same length as σ, $(\sigma', i, k, j) \models p$ and the only difference between σ and σ' can be in the values assigned to variable x.

3 New Projection Operator

3.1 Syntax and Semantics

The new projection construct is defined as

$$(p_1, \ldots, p_m)\ prj\ q$$

where $p_1, \ldots, p_m$ and q are formulas ($m \geq 1$). To ensure smooth synchronization between $p_1, \ldots, p_m$ and q, in the implementation of the projection described in the next section, the previous operator is not allowed within q. However, it can be used in the p_l's. To define the semantics of the projection operator we need an auxiliary operator for intervals.

Let $\sigma = \langle s_0, s_1, \ldots \rangle$ be an interval and $r_1, \ldots, r_h$ be integers ($h \geq 1$) such that $0 \leq r_1 \leq r_2 \leq \ldots \leq r_k \leq |\sigma|$. The *projection* of σ onto $r_1, \ldots, r_h$ is the interval

$$\sigma \downarrow (r_1, \ldots, r_k) = \langle s_{t_1}, s_{t_2}, \ldots, s_{t_l} \rangle$$

where $t_1, \ldots, t_l$ is obtained from $r_1, \ldots, r_h$ by deleting all duplicates.[6] For example,

$$\langle s_0, s_1, s_2, s_3, s_4 \rangle \downarrow (0, 0, 2, 2, 2, 3) = \langle s_0, s_2, s_3 \rangle.$$

The semantics of the projection operator is defined, as before, relative to an interpretation $\mathcal{I} = (\sigma, i, k, j)$. Formally,

$$\mathcal{I} \models (p_1, \ldots, p_m)\ prj\ q$$

if $\sigma \downarrow (k) \models q$ and $\mathcal{I} \models p_1; \ldots; p_m$, or if there are integers $r_1, r_2, \ldots, r_h$ ($1 \leq h \leq m$) such that $k \leq r_1 \leq r_2 \leq \ldots \leq r_h \leq j$ and the following hold:

[6] $t_1, \ldots, t_l$ is the longest strictly increasing subsequence of $r_1, \ldots, r_h$.

- $(\sigma, i, k, r_1) \models p_1$ and for $1 < l \leq h$, $(\sigma, r_{l-1}, r_{l-1}, r_l) \models p_l$.
- If $h < m$ then $\sigma\downarrow(k, r_1, \ldots, r_h) \models q$ and $(\sigma, r_h, r_h, j) \models p_{h+1}; \ldots; p_m$.
- If $h = m$ then $\sigma\downarrow(k, r_1, \ldots, r_h)\cdot\sigma_{(r_h+1..j)} \models q$.

In programming language terms, the interpretation of $(p_1, \ldots, p_m)$ prj q is somewhat sophisticated as we need *two* sequences of clocks (states) running on different time scales: one is a local state sequence, over which $p_1, \ldots, p_m$ are executed, the other is a global state sequence over which q is executed. Process q is executed in a parallel manner with the sequence of processes $p_1, \ldots, p_m$. The execution proceeds as follows (see Execution 1): First, q and p_1 start at the first global state and p_1 is executed over a sequence of local states until its termination. Then (the remaining part of) q and p_2 are executed at the second global state. Subsequently, p_2 is continuously executed over a sequence of local states until its termination, and so on. Although q and p_1 start at the same time, $p_1, \ldots, p_m$ and q may terminate at different time points. If q terminates before some p_{h+1}, then, subsequently, $p_{h+1}, \ldots, p_m$ are executed sequentially. If $p_1, \ldots, p_m$ are finished before q, then the execution of q is continued until its termination.

```
t0        t2        t4        t6
|---------|---------|---------|
|<-----------q--------------->|
t0   t1   t2   t3   t4   t5   t6   t7   t8
|----|----|----|----|----|----|----|----|
|<---p1-->|<---p2-->|<---p3-->|<---p4-->|

(a): q terminates before p4

t0        t2        t4        t6        t8   t9   t10
|---------|---------|---------|---------|----|----|
|<-----------------q----------------------------->|
t0   t1   t2   t3   t4   t5   t6   t7   t8
|----|----|----|----|----|----|----|----|
|<---p1-->|<---p2-->|<---p3-->|<---p4-->|

(b): p4 terminates before q

t0        t2        t4        t6        t8
|---------|---------|---------|---------|
|<-----------------q------------------->|
t0   t1   t2   t3   t4   t5   t6   t7   t8
|----|----|----|----|----|----|----|----|
|<---p1-->|<---p2-->|<---p3-->|<---p4-->|

(c): q and p4 terminate at the same point

Execution 1: Possible executions of (p1,p2,p3,p4) prj q
```

Projection can be thought of as a special parallel computation which is executed on different time scales. Consider the following formulas:

$$p_1 \stackrel{def}{=} len(2) \ \wedge \ \Box(more \rightarrow (\bigcirc i = i + 2))$$

$$p_2 \stackrel{def}{=} len(4) \ \wedge \ \Box(more \rightarrow (\bigcirc i = i + 3))$$

$$p_3 \stackrel{def}{=} len(6) \ \wedge \ \Box(more \rightarrow (\bigcirc i = i + 4))$$

$$q \ \stackrel{def}{=} len(4) \ \wedge \ (i = 2) \ \wedge \ (j = 0) \ \wedge \ \Box(more \rightarrow (\bigcirc j = j + i)).$$

Then executing (p_1, p_2, p_3) *prj* q yields the following result:

```
  t0      t2              t6                      t12 t13
  |-------|---------------|-----------------------|---|
  |-----------------------q----------------------->|
  t0  t1  t2  t3  t4  t5  t6  t7  t8  t9  t10 t11 t12
  |---|---|---|---|---|---|---|---|---|---|---|---|
  |<--p1->|<-----p2------>|<--------- p3--------->|
i=2   4   6   9   12  15  18  22  26  30  34  38  42
j=0       2               8                       26  68
```

Execution 2: Projection computation

The original projection operator defined in [6], p *proj* q, and the new projection operator defined above are not directly comparable. In the former, the formula p is executed repeatedly over a series of consecutive subintervals whose endpoints form the interval over which q is executed. This may result in repeating the same global state in the execution of q several times if some of the copies of p are executed over subintervals of zero length (in contrast, our definition in Section 3 rules this out). Moreover, in p *proj* q, the series of p's and the q always terminate at the same state. We feel that although p *proj* q and $(p_1, \ldots, p_m)$ *prj* q do share some important properties, they still possess sufficiently distinct features to be treated independently as complementary constructs useful in the programming environment in which different time scales need to be considered.

3.2 Properties of Projection Operator

Projection enjoys a number of interesting properties. The theorem below is intended to formalize some of them. In what follows, a formula p is called *non-local* if for all σ, $\sigma \models p$ implies $|\sigma| \geq 1$.

Theorem 1. *Let $p, q, p_1, \ldots, p_m$ be formulas.*

1. $\models (empty\ prj\ q) \leftrightarrow q$.
2. $\models (q\ prj\ empty) \leftrightarrow q$.
3. $\models ((empty, p_1, \ldots, p_m)\ prj\ empty) \leftrightarrow (p_1; \ldots; p_m)$.
4. $\models (skip\ prj\ q) \leftrightarrow q$, *if q is non-local.*
5. $\models (q\ prj\ skip) \leftrightarrow q$, *if q is non-local.*
6. $\models ((p, q)\ prj\ skip) \leftrightarrow (p; q)$, *if p or q is non-local.*
7. $\Vdash p \parallel q$
   $\leftrightarrow p \wedge ((empty, q, true)\ prj\ empty) \vee q \wedge ((empty, p, true)\ prj\ empty)$.
8. $\Vdash (p_1, \ldots, (p_i \vee p_i'), \ldots, p_m)\ prj\ q$
   $\leftrightarrow (p_1, \ldots, p_i, \ldots, p_m)\ prj\ q \vee (p_1, \ldots, p_i', \ldots, p_m)\ prj\ q$.
9. $\Vdash (p_1, \ldots, p_m)\ prj\ (p \vee q)$
   $\leftrightarrow (p_1, \ldots p_m)\ prj\ p \vee (p_1, \ldots, p_m)\ prj\ q$.

Proof. **(1)** Suppose $\sigma \models empty\ prj\ q$. If $\sigma{\downarrow}(0) \models q$ and $\sigma \models empty$ then $|\sigma| = 0$ and hence $\sigma \models q$. Otherwise, there is r, $0 \leq r \leq |\sigma|$, such that $(\sigma, 0, 0, r) \models empty$ and $\sigma{\downarrow}(0, r)\cdot\sigma_{(r+1..|\sigma|)} \models q$. The former yields $r = 0$. Hence $\sigma \models q$.
Conversely, if $\sigma \models q$ then, by taking $r_1 = 0$, one can show that $\sigma \models empty\ prj\ q$.

(2) Suppose $\sigma \models q\ prj\ empty$. If $\sigma{\downarrow}(0) \models empty$ and $\sigma \models q$ then we are done. Otherwise, there is r, $0 \leq r \leq |\sigma|$, such that $(\sigma, 0, 0, r) \models q$ and $\sigma{\downarrow}(0, r)\cdot\sigma_{(r+1..|\sigma|)} \models empty$. The latter means that $r = |\sigma| = 0$. Hence $\sigma \models q$.
Conversely, if $\sigma \models q$ then, since $\sigma{\downarrow}(0) \models empty$, $\sigma \models q\ prj\ empty$.

(3) Suppose $\sigma \models (empty, p_1, \ldots, p_m)\ prj\ empty$. If $\sigma{\downarrow}(0) \models empty$ and $\sigma \models empty; p_1; \ldots; p_m$ then clearly $\sigma \models p_1; \ldots; p_m$. Otherwise, there are integers $r_1, \ldots, r_h$ $(1 \leq h \leq m+1)$ such that $0 \leq r_1 \leq \ldots \leq r_h \leq |\sigma|$ and the following hold:

- $(\sigma, 0, 0, r_1) \models empty$
- For $1 < l \leq h$, $(\sigma, r_{l-1}, r_{l-1}, r_l) \models p_{l-1}$
- If $h < m+1$ then $\sigma{\downarrow}(0, r_1, \ldots, r_h) \models empty$ and $(\sigma, r_h, r_h, |\sigma|) \models p_h; \ldots; p_m$.
- If $h = m+1$ then $\sigma{\downarrow}(0, r_1, \ldots, r_h)\cdot\sigma_{(r_h+1..|\sigma|)} \models empty$.

We first observe that $r_1 = 0$. Moreover, if $h < m+1$ then $r_1 = \cdots = r_h = 0$ and hence $\sigma \models p_1; \ldots; p_m$. If $h = m+1$ then $|\sigma| = r_1 = \cdots = r_h = 0$, yielding $\sigma \models p_1; \ldots; p_m$.
Conversely, if $\sigma \models p_1; \ldots; p_m$ then, by taking $h = 1$ and $r_1 = 0$, one can show that $\sigma \models (empty, p_1; \ldots; p_m)\ prj\ empty$.

(4) Suppose $\sigma \models skip\ prj\ q$. We first observe that $\sigma{\downarrow}(0) \models q$ and $\sigma \models skip$ is impossible since q is non-local. Hence there is r, $0 \leq r \leq |\sigma|$, such that $(\sigma, 0, 0, r) \models skip$ and $\sigma{\downarrow}(0, r)\cdot\sigma_{(r+1..|\sigma|)} \models q$. The former implies $r = 1$ and hence $\sigma \models q$.
Suppose $\sigma \models q$. Then, since q is non-local, $|\sigma| \geq 1$. Hence $\sigma \models skip\ prj\ q$ can be shown by taking $r_1 = 1$.

(5) Suppose $\sigma \models q\ prj\ skip$. We first observe that $\sigma{\downarrow}(0) \models skip$ and $\sigma \models q$ is impossible. Hence there is r, $0 \leq r \leq |\sigma|$, such that $(\sigma, 0, 0, r) \models q$ and $\sigma{\downarrow}(0, r)\cdot\sigma_{(r+1..|\sigma|)} \models skip$. The former implies $r \geq 1$ (since q is non-local). This

and the latter means that $r = |\sigma|$. Hence $\sigma \models q$.
Conversely, if $\sigma \models q$ then, by taking $r_1 = |\sigma|$ we obtain $(\sigma, 0, 0, r_1) \models q$ and $\sigma\downarrow(0, r_1) \models \textit{skip}$. Note that the latter follows from $r_1 \geq 1$ (q is non-local).

(6) Suppose $\sigma \models (p, q)\ \textit{prj skip}$. We first observe that $\sigma\downarrow(0) \models \textit{skip}$ and $\sigma \models p; q$ is impossible. Thus one of the following must hold:

- There is r, $0 \leq r \leq |\sigma|$, such that $(\sigma, 0, 0, r) \models p$, $\sigma\downarrow(0, r) \models \textit{skip}$ and $(\sigma, r, r, |\sigma|) \models q$. Hence $\sigma \models p; q$.
- There are integers r_1, r_2 such that $0 \leq r_1 \leq r_2 \leq |\sigma|$, $(\sigma, 0, 0, r_1) \models p$, $(\sigma, r_1, r_1, r_2) \models q$ and $\sigma\downarrow(0, r_1, r_2)\cdot\sigma_{(r_2+1..|\sigma|)} \models \textit{skip}$. Since at least one of p and q is non-local, we must have $r_1 \geq 1$ or $r_2 \geq r_1 + 1$. Thus, from $\sigma\downarrow(0, r_1, r_2)\cdot\sigma_{(r_2+1..|\sigma|)} \models \textit{skip}$ it follows that $|\sigma| = r_2$. Hence $\sigma \models p; q$.

Conversely, suppose $\sigma \models p; q$. Then there is l, $0 \leq l \leq |\sigma|$ such that $(\sigma, 0, 0, l) \models p$ and $(\sigma, l, l, |\sigma|) \models q$. Since at least one of p and q is non-local, either $l \geq 1$ or $|\sigma| > 0 = l$. If the former holds then, by taking $h = 1$ and $r_1 = l$, one can show that $\sigma \models (p, q)\ \textit{prj skip}$. If the latter holds then one can come to the same conclusion by taking $h = 2$, $r_1 = 0$ and $r_2 = |\sigma|$.

Finally, (7) follows from (3), and (8,9) follow directly from the definition of the semantics of the projection operator and

$$\Vdash q_1; \ldots; (q_j \vee q_j'); \ldots; q_s \leftrightarrow (q_1; \ldots; q_j; \ldots; q_s) \vee (q_1; \ldots; q_j'; \ldots; q_s).$$

4 Implementation of Projection Operator

The programming language we used is a subset of the underlying logic. It is an extension of the Tempura [6] augmented with framing, parallel, projection, and await operators [2]. In addition, the variables within a program are allowed to refer to their previous values. The negation of temporal formulas, being fundamentally non-deterministic, is not a primitive operator of the language. Instead, the conditional, *more* and *empty*, all defined in terms of negation, are taken as primitives. Programs can use several kinds of expressions, employing equality, conditional, assignment and iterative operators.

To implement the projection operator, we have developed a new interpreter using the SICSTUS Prolog.

4.1 Implementation strategy

The implementation is based on the tableau methods, i.e. to execute a formula is to transform it to a logically equivalent conjunction of two formulas, *Present* and *Remains*, where the former consists of immediate assignments to program variables, output of program variables, *true*, *false*, *more* and *empty*. The role of *more* and *empty* is to indicate whether or not the interval is terminated. The *Remains* is what is executed in the subsequent state (if any). It is in a *reduced form* if it only consists of conjuncts with a leading weak next operator. When preparing the execution of the next state, the procedure *next_w* is used to remove these weak next operators from the conjuncts and what is actually executed at the next state is the resulting formula, *Next*. Formally,

$$Present = \bigwedge_{i=1}^{m} present_i$$

$$Remains = \bigwedge_{i=1}^{n} \odot w_i$$

$$Next = \bigwedge_{i=1}^{n} w_i$$

where each w_i is a Tempura formula and

$$present_i ::= x = a \mid display(a) \mid true \mid more \mid empty.$$

4.2 Done flag

The interpreter employs several flags to manage the reductions. One of the important ones, *done* flag, indicates whether or not an interval is terminated. At the beginning of the execution of each state, *done* flag is set to *nil*, and then the interpreter sets its value to either *true* or *false*, depending on whether the *more* or *empty* conjunct has been encountered. If the program fails to specify properly the interval for the program, the interpreter cannot set the *done* flag; it remains equal to *nil*. Thus an error is detected and indicated.

4.3 Program structure

The execution of a Tempura program proceeds through a number of states. The execution at a state is composed of reductions in several passes. After the last pass, the executed formula is reduced to the $Present \wedge Remains$ form. In fact, *Present* is dissolved during the reduction. Its effect is reflected in updating and displaying the values of variables, setting the *done* flag, etc. What remains after the last pass of the reduction is *Remains* which is executed at the next state if the interval over which the formula is executed is not yet finished.

4.4 Reduction of projection

The projection construct $(p_1, \ldots, p_m)$ *prj* q is implemented as follows: It is processed by first allocating a *done* flag initialized to *nil* to serve as a *done* flag for projected interval on which the statement q is executed and transforming the statement to the internal construct IC,

$$IC = \begin{cases} project((p_2, \ldots, p_m), p_1, q, done(nil)) & \text{if } m > 1 \\ project(empty, p_1, q, done(nil)) & \text{if } m = 1 \end{cases}$$

which is immediately re-reduced. The construct $project(R, P, Q, done(D1))$ is executed by first saving the current doneflag to OLD and setting the doneflag to *done*($D1$). The statement Q is then reduced in the context to a new statement Q'. Afterwards, the current doneflag is saved to $D2$ and the old doneflag, *done*(OLD), is restored, and the statement P is then reduced in the context to a new statement P'. If P' or Q' is not fully reduced, the overall *project* statement is rewritten as $project(R, P', Q', done(D2))$. This is returned as the result of the reduction. On the other hand, if P' and Q' are both fully reduced then, with the notation

$$\begin{aligned} D &= next\_w(P') \\ E &= next\_w(Q') \\ choose(R1,(R2)) &= (R1; choose((R2))) \\ choose(R1) &= R1 \end{aligned}$$

the overall *project* statement is transformed as in Figure 1. This tests the done flag indexed by *done*($D2$). If it is true, the interval in which Q was reduced is finished and therefore the $next\_w(P')$ is executed followed by remaining formulas $(R1, (R2))$, chosen by the procedure *choose*, if they were not empty. On the other hand, if $done(D2) = done(false)$ the interval in which Q was executed is not yet finished. Therefore, the formula D is executed followed by the resumption of the projection statement.

```
if done(D2) = done(true)
then
    if R = (R1, (R2))
    then ○ (D; choose(R1, (R2)))
    else
        if R = R1
        then ○ (D; R1)
        else
            if R = empty
            then ○ D
else
    if done(D2) = done(false)
    then
        if R = (R1, (R2))
        then ○ (D; project((R2), R1, E, done(nil)))
        else
            if R = R1
            then ○ (D; project(empty, R1, E, done(nil)))
            else
                if R = empty
                then ○ (D; project(, empty, empty, E, done(nil)))
```

Fig. 1. Rewriting *project* statement

5 Examples

We now present two simple applications of the projection construct. The first is a pulse generator for variable x which can assume two values: 0 (low) and 1 (high). We first define two types of processes: The first one is $hold(i)$ ($i \geq 1$) which is executed over an interval of length i and ensures that the value of x remains constant in all but final state:

$$hold(i) \stackrel{def}{=} len(i) \wedge \Box(\bigcirc more \rightarrow (\bigcirc x = x)).$$

The other is $switch(j)$ which ensures that the value of x is first set to 0 and then changed at every subsequent state:

$$switch(j) \stackrel{def}{=} (x = 0) \wedge len(j) \wedge \Box(more \rightarrow (\bigcirc x = 1 - x)).$$

Having defined $hold(i)$ and $switch(j)$ we can define pulse generators with varying number and length of low and high intervals for x,

$$pulse(i_1, \ldots, i_k) \stackrel{def}{=} (hold(i_1), \ldots, hold(i_k))\ prj\ switch(k).$$

The second example is that of special parallel computation. Consider the formula $((len(i_1), len(i_2), \ldots, len(i_k))\ prj\ q) \wedge p$. This allows processes p and q to be executed in a special parallel manner in which p is executed over a series of subintervals, and q is executed at their endpoints:

```
t0      t2                 t6                 t10
|-------|------------------|------------------|
|------------------------q--------------->|
t0  t1  t2  t3  t4  t5  t6  t7  t8  t9 t10 t11 t12
|---|---|---|---|---|---|---|---|---|---|---|---|
|<-------------------- p--------------------->|
```

Execution 3: Special parallel computation

6 Conclusion

The projection operator $(p_1, \ldots, p_m)\ prj\ q$ presented in this paper is rather powerful. For example, it can be used to specify computations on different time scales. We feel it has a potential of being a useful operator in temporal logic programming. Another possible application area is that of the real time systems. In this case, we could treat $p_1, \ldots, p_m$ as formulas over a series of dense or real intervals and q as a formula over a projected discrete interval.

References

1. Barringer H., Kuiper R. and Pnueli A.: Now you may compose temporal logic specifications. Proceedings of 16th ACM Symposium on Theory of Computing, 51–63 (1984).
2. Duan Z., Holt C. and Moszkowski B.: An interpreter for an executable subset of extended interval temporal logic with framing and concurrent operators. BCTCS 8, Newcastle upon Tyne, March (1992).
3. Kröger F.: Temporal logic of programs. Springer-Verlag (1987).
4. Lamport L.: The temporal logic of actions. Digital, System Design Center, December (1991).
5. Manner Z. and Pnueli A.: The temporal logic of reactive and concurrent systems. Springer-Verlag (1992).
6. Moszkowski B.: Executing temporal logic programs. Cambridge University Press Cambridge (1986).
7. Ness L.: L.0: A parallel executable temporal logic language. Proceeding of the ACM SIGSOFT, International Workshop on Formal Methods in Software Development, Napa, California, May (1990).
8. Rosner R. and Pnueli A.: A choppy logic. First Annual IEEE Symposium on Logic In Computer Science, LNCS, Springer Verlag, 306–314 (1986).
9. Tang Z.: Toward a unified logic basis for programming languages. Proceedings of IFIP'83 Congress, Amsterdam, Elsevier Science Publishers B.V. (North-Holland), 425–429 (1983).

Author Index

Springer-Verlag and the Environment

We at Springer-Verlag firmly believe that an international science publisher has a special obligation to the environment, and our corporate policies consistently reflect this conviction.

We also expect our business partners – paper mills, printers, packaging manufacturers, etc. – to commit themselves to using environmentally friendly materials and production processes.

The paper in this book is made from low- or no-chlorine pulp and is acid free, in conformance with international standards for paper permanency.

Lecture Notes in Artificial Intelligence (LNAI)

Vol. 619: D. Pearce, H. Wansing (Eds.), Nonclassical Logics and Information Processing. Proceedings, 1990. VII, 171 pages. 1992.

Vol. 622: F. Schmalhofer, G. Strube, Th. Wetter (Eds.), Contemporary Knowledge Engineering and Cognition. Proceedings, 1991. XII, 258 pages. 1992.

Vol. 624: A. Voronkov (Ed.), Logic Programming and Automated Reasoning. Proceedings, 1992. XIV, 509 pages. 1992.

Vol. 627: J. Pustejovsky, S. Bergler (Eds.), Lexical Semantics and Knowledge Representation. Proceedings, 1991. XII, 381 pages. 1992.

Vol. 633: D. Pearce, G. Wagner (Eds.), Logics in AI. Proceedings. VIII, 410 pages. 1992.

Vol. 636: G. Comyn, N. E. Fuchs, M. J. Ratcliffe (Eds.), Logic Programming in Action. Proceedings, 1992. X, 324 pages. 1992.

Vol. 638: A. F. Rocha, Neural Nets. A Theory for Brains and Machines. XV, 393 pages. 1992.

Vol. 642: K. P. Jantke (Ed.), Analogical and Inductive Inference. Proceedings, 1992. VIII, 319 pages. 1992.

Vol. 659: G. Brewka, K. P. Jantke, P. H. Schmitt (Eds.), Nonmonotonic and Inductive Logic. Proceedings, 1991. VIII, 332 pages. 1993.

Vol. 660: E. Lamma, P. Mello (Eds.), Extensions of Logic Programming. Proceedings, 1992. VIII, 417 pages. 1993.

Vol. 667: P. B. Brazdil (Ed.), Machine Learning: ECML – 93. Proceedings, 1993. XII, 471 pages. 1993.

Vol. 671: H. J. Ohlbach (Ed.), GWAI-92: Advances in Artificial Intelligence. Proceedings, 1992. XI, 397 pages. 1993.

Vol. 679: C. Fermüller, A. Leitsch, T. Tammet, N. Zamov, Resolution Methods for the Decision Problem. VIII, 205 pages. 1993.

Vol. 681: H. Wansing, The Logic of Information Structures. IX, 163 pages. 1993.

Vol. 689: J. Komorowski, Z. W. Raś (Eds.), Methodologies for Intelligent Systems. Proceedings, 1993. XI, 653 pages. 1993.

Vol. 695: E. P. Klement, W. Slany (Eds.), Fuzzy Logic in Artificial Intelligence. Proceedings, 1993. VIII, 192 pages. 1993.

Vol. 698: A. Voronkov (Ed.), Logic Programming and Automated Reasoning. Proceedings, 1993. XIII, 386 pages. 1993.

Vol. 699: G.W. Mineau, B. Moulin, J.F. Sowa (Eds.), Conceptual Graphs for Knowledge Representation. Proceedings, 1993. IX, 451 pages. 1993.

Vol. 723: N. Aussenac, G. Boy, B. Gaines, M. Linster, J.-G. Ganascia, Y. Kodratoff (Eds.), Knowledge Acquisition for Knowledge-Based Systems. Proceedings, 1993. XIII, 446 pages. 1993.

Vol. 727: M. Filgueiras, L. Damas (Eds.), Progress in Artificial Intelligence. Proceedings, 1993. X, 362 pages. 1993.

Vol. 728: P. Torasso (Ed.), Advances in Artificial Intelligence. Proceedings, 1993. XI, 336 pages. 1993.

Vol. 743: S. Doshita, K. Furukawa, K. P. Jantke, T. Nishida (Eds.), Algorithmic Learning Theory. Proceedings, 1992. X, 260 pages. 1993.

Vol. 744: K. P. Jantke, T. Yokomori, S. Kobayashi, E. Tomita (Eds.), Algorithmic Learning Theory. Proceedings, 1993. XI, 423 pages. 1993.

Vol. 745: V. Roberto (Ed.), Intelligent Perceptual Systems. VIII, 378 pages. 1993.

Vol. 746: A. S. Tanguiane, Artificial Perception and Music Recognition. XV, 210 pages. 1993.

Vol. 754: H. D. Pfeiffer, T. E. Nagle (Eds.), Conceptual Structures: Theory and Implementation. Proceedings, 1992. IX, 327 pages. 1993.

Vol. 764: G. Wagner, Vivid Logic. XII, 148 pages. 1994.

Vol. 766: P. R. Van Loocke, The Dynamics of Concepts. XI, 340 pages. 1994.

Vol. 770: P. Haddawy, Representing Plans Under Uncertainty. X, 129 pages. 1994.

Vol. 784: F. Bergadano, L. De Raedt (Eds.), Machine Learning: ECML-94. Proceedings, 1994. XI, 439 pages. 1994.

Vol. 795: W. A. Hunt, Jr., FM8501: A Verified Microprocessor. XIII, 333 pages. 1994.

Vol. 798: R. Dyckhoff (Ed.), Extensions of Logic Programming. Proceedings, 1993. VIII, 360 pages. 1994.

Vol. 799: M. P. Singh, Multiagent Systems: Intentions, Know-How, and Communications. XXIII, 168 pages. 1994.

Vol. 804: D. Hernández, Qualitative Representation of Spatial Knowledge. IX, 202 pages. 1994.

Vol. 808: M. Masuch, L. Pólos (Eds.), Knowledge Representation and Reasoning Under Uncertainty. VII, 237 pages. 1994.

Vol. 810: G. Lakemeyer, B. Nebel (Eds.), Foundations of Knowledge Representation and Reasoning. VIII, 355 pages. 1994.

Vol. 814: A. Bundy (Ed.), Automated Deduction — CADE-12. Proceedings, 1994. XVI, 848 pages. 1994.

Vol. 822: F. Pfenning (Ed.), Logic Programming and Automated Reasoning. Proceedings, 1994. X, 345 pages. 1994.

Vol. 827: D. M. Gabbay, H. J. Ohlbach (Eds.), Temporal Logic. Proceedings, 1994. XI, 546 pages. 1994.

Lecture Notes in Computer Science